MEMOIRS

OF

JOHN QUINCY ADAMS.

From a Portrait by Leslie.   Engraved by Forbes & Co.

MRS. L. C. ADAMS.

MEMOIRS

OF

JOHN QUINCY ADAMS,

COMPRISING PORTIONS OF

HIS DIARY FROM 1795 TO 1848.

EDITED BY

CHARLES FRANCIS ADAMS.

VOL. III.

Select Bibliographies Reprint Series

BOOKS FOR LIBRARIES PRESS
FREEPORT, NEW YORK

First Published 1874-77
Reprinted 1969

STANDARD BOOK NUMBER:
8369-5021-6

LIBRARY OF CONGRESS CATALOG CARD NUMBER:
71-85454

PRINTED IN THE UNITED STATES OF AMERICA

TABLE OF CONTENTS.

iii

MEMOIRS

OF

JOHN QUINCY ADAMS.

VOL. III.—I

MEMOIRS OF JOHN QUINCY ADAMS.

CHAPTER IX. (*Continued.*)

THE NEGOTIATION FOR PEACE.

August 7th, 1814. The British Commissioners arrived last evening, and are lodged at the Hôtel du Lion d'Or. Mr. Baker, the Secretary to the Commission, called this morning, first upon Colonel Milligan, who lodges at the Hôtel des Pays-Bas, and where Mr. Baker supposed we were yet all lodged. He afterwards came and called on Mr. Bayard, and notified to him the arrival of the British Commissioners, with a proposal from them that we should meet them to-morrow at one o'clock, afternoon, at their lodgings, and exchange our full powers, and arrange the mode of proceeding between us for the future. Mr. Bayard received this notification, which he agreed to communicate to his colleagues, and promised that we would send an answer this evening.

We had a meeting at noon, and were all of opinion that this first step of the British Commissioners was advancing, on their part, an offensive pretension to superiority. I referred my colleagues to Martens, book vii. chap. iv. section 3, of his Summary, where the course now taken by the British Commissioners appears to be precisely that stated there to be the usage from Ambassadors to Ministers of an inferior order. I proposed that Mr. Hughes should call in the evening on Mr. Baker, and say that we should be happy to meet and confer with the Commissioners, and exchange full powers with them,

3

at any time which they would indicate, and at any place other than their own lodgings. Mr. Bayard and Mr. Clay made other propositions, and, after deliberating upon them about two hours, on Mr. Bayard's proposal we adjourned, to meet again at half-past three. At this meeting, Mr. Bayard produced the case in Ward's History of the Law of Nations, vol. ii. chap. xvi., of the Commissioners between Spain and England, at Boulogne, in 1600, which in almost every particular resembles the present, and at which the Spanish Commissioners made, and the English resisted, the pretension now advanced by the English. Mr. Bayard and Mr. Gallatin were reluctant at taking any notice of this matter; not that they felt it differently, or doubted that it was intended on the part of the British Commissioners, but from an aversion to clog the negotiation with any question of mere ceremony. We adjourned the meeting again to dine, and finally concluded to send Mr. Hughes with the message I had proposed, substituting, at Mr. Gallatin's suggestion, instead of the expression, " at any place other than their own lodgings," the milder terms, " at any place which may be mutually agreed upon," and authorizing Mr. Hughes to name the Hôtel des Pays-Bas.

Mr. Hughes performed his message, and about ten in the evening Mr. Baker came and informed Mr. Bayard, and afterwards all the mission, assembled in Mr. Clay's chamber, that the British Commissioners agreed to meet us at the appointed hour, and at the Hôtel des Pays-Bas.

Mr. Bayard, to sound and ascertain their feelings, had proposed to Mr. Baker that the meeting should be at our house, and offered to show him an excellent room for the purpose; but Baker declined even looking at the room.

8th. We had a meeting of the mission at noon, in which we had some deliberation concerning the manner in which it would be proper to proceed with the British Commissioners. At one o'clock we went, accompanied by Mr. Hughes, to the Hôtel des Pays-Bas, and found the British Commissioners already there. They are James, Lord Gambier, Henry Goulburn, Esquire, a member of Parliament and Under-Secretary of State, and William Adams, Esquire, a Doctor of Civil Laws.

The Secretary to the Commission is Anthony St. John Baker. Mr. Russell was absent, not having yet returned from Dunkirk. After the first ordinary civilities had passed, we produced, on both sides, the originals and copies of our full powers. The copies, attested by the Secretary of each Commission respectively, were exchanged. Lord Gambier then addressed us, with assurances on the part of the British Government of their sincere and earnest desire that this negotiation might terminate in a successful issue, and the ardent hope of the British Commissioners that we might all have the satisfaction of restoring the blessings of peace to our respective countries.

This I answered by making similar assurances on our part, expressing the high satisfaction with which we received theirs, and the promise for myself and my colleagues to bring to these discussions the disposition to meet every sentiment of candor and conciliation with the most cordial reciprocity, concurring, as we did, with the utmost earnestness and sincerity, in the hope that we might eventually have the happiness of reconciling two nations whose true interests could best be promoted by peace and amity with each other.

Mr. Goulburn, the second British Commissioner, then replied. He renewed the professions of the sincere desire of the British Government for peace, and added the most explicit declaration that nothing that had occurred since the first proposal for this negotiation would have the slightest effect on the disposition of Great Britain with regard to the terms upon which the pacification might be concluded. He proceeded to say that the British Government thought it would be most conducive to this end to discard all retrospective considerations with regard to anything that had taken place, and had instructed them in relation to certain points which they supposed would naturally arise for discussion upon this negotiation. These points he was charged by his colleagues to state; with a request to be informed whether they were such as by our instructions we were authorized to discuss, and that we would also on our part state any other points upon which we also might be instructed to propose for discussion. Those which he was directed to present were—1. The forcible seizure of mariners on board of

American merchant vessels, and, connected with that subject, the claim of the King of Great Britain to the allegiance of all the native-born subjects of Great Britain.   2. The including of the Indian allies of Great Britain; and, for the purpose of obtaining a permanent pacification, the drawing of a boundary line for the Indians; and it was necessary to observe that on both parts of this point Great Britain considered them as a *sine qua non* to the conclusion of a treaty.   3. The partial revision of the boundary line between the United States and the British possessions in North America—upon which, on a question asked by Mr. Bayard, he explained that in such revision Great Britain did not contemplate an acquisition of territory.   He then said that besides these three points it was thought proper in candor to state that in relation to the fisheries, although it was not intended to contest the right of the United States to them, yet so far as respected the concession to land and dry fish within the exclusive jurisdiction of the British, it was proposed not to renew that without an equivalent.

I said that I would confer with my colleagues, and at our next meeting would report our answer upon the points proposed by them, which I recapitulated, and also the statement of such further points as we should present for discussion. Mr. Goulburn urged an immediate answer upon the question whether we were instructed particularly upon the point which they were directed to make a *sine qua non;* but I declined answering on any point without first consulting with my colleagues. We agreed to meet again to-morrow at eleven o'clock.

I mentioned the offer made to us by the Mayor, and afterwards repeated by the Intendant, immediately after our first arrival here. They are now both absent at Brussels. It was preferred, however, both by the British Commissioners and ourselves, to have the meetings alternately at our own houses, and Lord Gambier said that as they were not now very well accommodated, if it was agreeable to us, the meeting to-morrow should be at our house; to which we readily agreed. We then returned home, and about an hour afterwards we went and paid them a visit at their lodgings.

On returning from thence, we met to consider of the answer to be given them, and the points to be proposed on our part. We sat until dinner-time, and again immediately after dinner. While we were sitting, we received the dispatches and letters from America brought by the French corvette and forwarded to us by Mr. Crawford. Mr. Gallatin, Mr. Hughes, and myself sat deciphering the dispatches from the Secretary of State until nearly one o'clock of the morning.

9th. We had agreed upon a meeting of the mission at half-past nine o'clock this morning, and we actually met in Mr. Bayard's chamber at ten. We agreed on the answer to be made on the points presented for discussion by the British Commissioners and on those to be presented by us.

The British Commissioners came at eleven; and, in the name of the mission, I stated that we were instructed upon the first and third points presented by them, and that on the second and fourth points we were not. I then proceeded to state the points proposed on our part. 1. A definition of blockade, and, as far as may be mutually agreed, of other neutral and belligerent rights. 2. Certain claims of indemnity to individuals for captures and seizures preceding and subsequent to the war. 3. I added that we were instructed upon a variety of other points which might with propriety be subjects for discussion, either upon a negotiation for peace or upon that of a treaty of commerce, which, in the event of a propitious termination of this negotiation, we were also authorized to conclude; that in order to simplify and facilitate as much as possible the great object of peace, we had discarded every point which did not more peculiarly belong to that and was not immediately relevant to it.

They replied that their powers extended only to the conclusion of a peace, but that they did not mean to say, or wish us to understand, that there would be any objection on the part of Great Britain to treating upon commercial objects in the event of a successful issue to this negotiation.

I said that it readily accounted for our not being instructed on the two points of the Indian boundary and the fisheries— that they had not been objects of controversy between the two

Governments heretofore; that they were points entirely new, and that it was a matter of course that our instructions should be confined to the subjects of difference in which the war originated, and to the topics of discussion known by the American Government to exist.

It was further remarked by Mr. Clay that the American Government could have anticipated no propositions of this nature from the letter of Lord Castlereagh proposing the negotiation; to which Mr. Goulburn replied that it could not be expected Lord Castlereagh would, in the proposal for the negotiation, enumerate the points which would become subjects of discussion in the course of it, as they would naturally depend upon events occurring after the proposal and until the commencement of the negotiation.

I said it was our wish to receive from the British Commissioners the views of their Government upon all the points, and that we were willing to discuss them all.

Mr. Goulburn asked whether, if they should enter into the discussion, we could give them an expectation that it would terminate in our agreeing to a provisional article, which we would sign, subject to the ratification of our Government.

I answered that, having no specific instructions upon the subject, whatever article we could agree to must of course be unauthorized, and we could not say previous to discussion whether an article could be formed to which we should feel ourselves under our discretionary powers justified in acceding. This related principally to the point of the Indian boundary, the British *sine qua non.*

Mr. Gallatin said that so far as respected the including of the Indians in the peace, the United States would have neither interest nor wish to continue the war with the Indians when that with Great Britain should be terminated; that Commissioners had already been appointed to treat of peace with the Indians, and very probably the peace might already be made. He said that the policy of the United States towards the Indians was the most liberal of that pursued by any nation; that our laws interdicted the purchase of lands from them by any individual, and that every precaution was used to prevent the frauds upon them which had heretofore been practised by others. He stated that this proposition to give them a distinct boundary, different from the boundary already existing, and by a treaty between the United States and Great Britain, was not only new, it was unexampled. No such treaty had been made by Great Britain, either before or since the American Revolution, and no such treaty had, to his knowledge, ever been made by any other European power.

Mr. Goulburn said that they were certainly treated as in some respects sovereigns, since treaties were made with them both by Great Britain and the United States.

Treaties with them Mr. Gallatin admitted, but treaties between European powers defining their boundaries there were, to his knowledge, none.

Mr. Bayard asked what was understood by Great Britain to be the effect and operation of the boundary line proposed. Was it to restrict the United States from making treaties with them hereafter as heretofore? from purchasing their lands, for instance? Was it to restrict the Indians from selling their lands? Was it to alter the condition of the Indians, such as it has hitherto existed?

Mr. Goulburn answered that it was intended as a barrier between the British possessions and the territories of the United States; that it was not to restrict the Indians from selling their lands, although it would restrict the United States from purchasing them.

Dr. Adams said that both Great Britain and the United States would be restricted from purchasing the lands, but the Indians would not be restricted from selling them to a third party. As to further discussion upon the point, Dr. Adams said that, however desirous they were of getting over the difficulty, they thought it would be an unprofitable discussion unless they could see some result to which it was likely to lead.

They proposed to adjourn for an hour, to give us time to consult together whether we could say that we might eventually agree to a provisional article; but we were not desirous of such consultation.

Mr. Gallatin said that the difficulty which we had suggested
was stated merely on a principle of candor; that it would
have been easy for us to say at once that there might be an
article formed on the subject to which we might agree, and
afterwards to break off upon the details of any such article;
but that the proceeding was more frank and explicit to avow
at once the full extent of our objection.

The British Commissioners then proposed to suspend the
conferences until they could consult their Government on this
state of things. They proposed to send off a messenger this
evening, and it was proposed by them that a protocol of the
two meetings should be drawn up by the two secretaries separately, and that we should compare them together and make a
final record from the two of the proceedings on these days. To
this we agreed.

As they went away, I told Lord Gambier that I hoped in
their communication to their Government they would express
how much we had been gratified at the candid and conciliatory
manner which the British Commissioners had adopted with us.
Mr. Clay added that upon this subject they could not express
themselves too strongly.

They answered that they should be altogether deficient in
their duty if they omitted to express their sentiments in these
respects. They agreed to meet again at our house to-morrow,
at twelve o'clock, noon. I was immediately charged by my
colleagues to make the rough draft of the protocol for Mr.
Hughes. I drew it up accordingly. It was corrected by
Messrs. Bayard, Gallatin, and Clay, and given to Mr. Hughes
to make out a fair copy of it for to-morrow morning.

10th. At twelve o'clock we met the British Commissioners,
and compared the two reports which had been drawn up on
their part and on ours, to make the protocol of the two former
conferences. There was no material difference between the
two on the proceedings of the first day. But the British Commissioners objected to various parts of our report of those of
the second day, particularly to those parts which stated the
explanation they had given of the point respecting the proposed
Indian boundary, and to the reasons assigned by us why our

Government had not provided us with instructions on that point, and the one concerning the fisheries. Their objection was that these things were argumentative, and that the protocol should contain a mere statement of facts.

Dr. Adams observed that if it contained our reasons for the omission of the two points from our instructions, it should also contain their reasons for supposing that our instructions might have provided for them. I admitted this, if in fact any such reasons had been assigned by them; but they had not. Mr. Goulburn stated that he thought this assignment of reasons, and the explanatory paragraphs, were more proper to be inserted in a dispatch to our Government than upon the protocol, which is a mere record of facts. He said, if matter of argument were admitted on one side it must also be admitted on the other, and must eventually contain everything said at the conferences, which, if we should have many, would swell it up to an excessive volume.

We replied that the explanatory paragraphs were material to unfold the full import of their proposals. Mr. Bayard put it pointedly to them that they had not disclosed their full meaning. He said their proposition respecting the Indian boundary, as put by themselves, was not intelligible to us. Did they mean to take a portion of our territory and assign it to the Indians? Did they mean, in a word, to alter the condition of the Indians in relation to the United States?

The British Commissioners manifested here a slight movement of impatience at these questions, and of regret at having answered so explicitly those that Mr. Bayard had put to them yesterday. They said they could not be expected to develop at this stage of the business, if at any time, the ultimate views and intentions of their Government in this proposal; but they assented to an alteration in their own statement of the point.

Dr. Adams said that it could not be said there was a territory *assigned* to people which was already in their possession.

Mr. Goulburn used the words Dominions and Territories of the Indians.

I remarked to them that they must be aware the terms Dominions, Territories, and Possessions, as applied to Indians, were of very different import from the same terms as applied to civilized nations; that this difference was well known and understood, and in the same manner hitherto, by all the European nations.

Mr. Goulburn said it was, however, necessary to use one or the other of those words, and finally preferred that of Territory.

Our draft had stated that the British Commissioners had *declined* entering further into the discussion unless we would say that an article might be drawn up on this point, to which we might accede provisionally and subject to the ratification of our Government; and that they had proposed to suspend the conferences until they could consult their Government on this state of things. They objected also to the insertion of this in the protocol.

We urged that this was not only a fact, but a fact so material to the statement of what had actually taken place, that without it the protocol itself must be imperfect.

Dr. Adams said he thought it was expressed rather too strongly, to say that they had *declined* entering into the discussion.

Mr. Clay reminded him of the express words used by himself, which he admitted, but said those were remarks which he had thrown out rather in the manner of friendly discussion than intimating a fixed purpose to decline it in future.

We readily agreed to omit the expression that they had *declined* further discussion, but pressed them, on the fact of their having suspended the conferences, to send a messenger to their Government.

They said they had mentioned their intention to us only from the perfect candor of their proceedings, and perhaps over-hastily; that if we should insist upon putting it on the protocol, the only effect of it would be to seal up their lips hereafter, and put them upon a reserve which they should be unwilling to assume.

Mr. Gallatin repeated the remark that the omission would

leave the protocol imperfect, as it would appear·from it that our request for further discussion had not been answered—when in fact it had.

They thought there was no necessity the answer should appear, but that it might stand, with the expression of the wish; and its result to be seen hereafter.

As we could not prevail upon them to express anything upon the record but what suited them, we finally agreed to omit everything to which they objected. We then left Mr. Hughes and Mr. Baker to make out, from the two dra⁀s, the protocol, to be the common record of both parties. Immediately after this conference (at which Mr. Russell was present) we had a meeting of the mission; at which I was charged to prepare the draft of a dispatch to the Secretary of State. This task I deferred to the morning, and was employed during all the leisure of this day in taking the minutes in this journal of our proceedings on the two former days. Shortly after the conference we had a visit from the British Commissioners.

11th. I made the first draft of a dispatch to the Secretary of State. We had a meeting at noon, at which I read it. We agreed that each of my colleagues should take it in turn and make any alterations and additions to it that he shall think proper, after which we are to meet again and put it into its final form to be sent. I gave it to Mr. Bayard, who returned it to me at dinner-time, having made his notes to be added to it.

12th. We had a meeting of the mission, at which we determined to request Captain Angus to be ready to sail on the 25th of this month, and to address a note to the British Commissioners, requesting that application be made to the Lords of the Admiralty for a cartel for the Chauncey to return to America. She came as a cartel, and is now at Gottenburg. Mr. Clay had mentioned it to the British Commissioners at our last meeting, and they answered, as I had anticipated they would, that they would transmit very readily any application from us to the Admiralty, but that they had no authority to give a cartel themselves, and that we must send them a written note for any such applications. We had also a question whether we could allow Mr. Connell to go as a passenger in the ship. The new passport omits the proviso forbidding a cargo and passengers, but expresses that she is to go in ballast, and with the persons named on it or charged with the conveyance of dispatches. The persons named are Mr. Smith and his family (as I had requested), Messrs. Dallas, Todd, Milligan, and Emlin. Mr. Clay proposed that Mr. Connell should be charged with dispatches; but Mr. Gallatin said he had promised Mr. Dallas he should have that office to perform. Mr. Clay and Mr. Russell thought that Connell might be made the bearer of dispatches until they arrived in America, with directions to deliver them over there to Mr. Dallas. I not only disapproved this, but inconsiderately said it would be a *trick* I should think highly improper. Mr. Russell, and more especially Mr. Clay, were hurt at my use of this expression; and it was understood by all my colleagues that the passport authorized us to send Mr. Connell; but it was concluded that it would be displeasing to Mr. Dallas to give Mr. Connell the dispatches, even with the injunction to deliver them to Mr. Dallas in America. I do not think it would have been an ingenuous proceeding, after having pledged ourselves that no person should go as a passenger without the express consent of the British Government. But the use of the word *trick* was harsh and unnecessary. The correct principle in this case is to do nothing that may not be boldly avowed. I should have said this, and no more.

13th. Lord Gambier and Dr. Adams, Mr. Baker and Mr. Gambier, Mr. Shaler and Mr. Meulemeester, dined with us. Mr. Goulburn sent an excuse this morning, he is unwell and confined to the house, having burst a blood-vessel, as they say, in the throat, and having yesterday lost his voice, so that he could not speak. We had no meeting this day, my draft of a dispatch being still in the hands of my colleagues. Mr. Gallatin had it all day yesterday, and gave it this morning to Mr. Clay; he kept it a short time, and then gave it to Mr. Bayard, who took it for the second time, and retained it until this evening, when he gave it to Mr. Russell.

After being employed great part of this day in writing, I was engaged two or three hours in looking over treaties for the articles respecting the Indians and the fisheries. Mr. Meulemeester spent the evening with us. I played a game of chess with Mr. Shaler.

Lord Gambier told me that he had been in Boston in the year 1770, with his uncle, who then had the naval command there; that he was then a boy of twelve years of age; that in 1778 he was at New York during our contest, and then commanded a frigate. He spoke to me of my father as having known him at that time, and also of the family of Mr. Bowdoin. He mentioned the English Bible Society, of which he said he had the happiness to be one of the vice-presidents, and of a correspondence they had with the Bible Society in Boston, of which I told him I was a member. He expressed great satisfaction at the liberality with which they had sent a sum of money to replace the loss of some Bibles which had been taken by a privateer as they were going to Halifax.

Mr. Bayard asked Lord Gambier, upon some remark that Jerome Bonaparte's son was born in England, how the doctrine of allegiance would apply to him. His Lordship laughed, and said, "We won't talk about that now." I asked Dr. Adams to what part of England his family belonged. He said that originally they came from Pembrokeshire, in Wales, but they had removed from thence four or five generations since, and of late had resided in Essex. Their arms were a plain red cross. They had heretofore been possessed of a considerable estate in Wales, no part of which, however, had descended to the present generation. I think we are not cousins.

Mr. Russell gave me this morning a folio sheet of amendments and corrections to my draft of a dispatch for the Secretary of State, and Mr. Bayard brought me an entire new draft. Mr. Russell's amendments were chiefly grammatical and verbal —the capital letters, the commas and points, and the caution to spell until with only one l. Several of them, under the idea of amending the style, made a different statement of facts from that which really occurred. The amendments to the narrative of a party who was present at the transactions related, made by a person who was not present, are not very likely to improve its accuracy; but Mr. Bayard's passion for amending went further.   He had drawn up a totally new statement, in his own language, not one sentence of which agreed with mine.   When we met, I proposed immediately that Mr. Bayard's draft should be substituted for mine to be the basis of the dispatch.   This was agreed to; but it then became necessary to settle the question upon a variety of things which he had omitted to notice and which had been contained in my draft.   We found it difficult upon these points to harmonize in all our impressions, and it was finally concluded that Mr. Gallatin should take Mr. Bayard's draft, make such alterations and amendments in it as we appeared to concur in, and then give it to Mr. Hughes to be copied.   There was no other way of getting a dispatch ready; for if Mr. Bayard's draft had been taken to be altered, corrected, and amended as mine was, at the end of another week we should have had twenty sheets of paper written, instead of seven, and still have to begin the dispatch.

16th. We postponed until to-morrow the meeting of the mission, Mr. Gallatin being not yet ready with his remarks upon Mr. Bayard's draft.

17th. I employed this morning in writing to the Secretary of State.   At noon we had a meeting of the mission, when Mr. Gallatin produced a third draft of a dispatch to the Secretary of State, upon which, after some amendments, we finally agreed. The Duke of Cambridge passed through the city this day; also Mr. Whitbread.   The Intendant called on me this afternoon and proposed to invite us to dine with him next Tuesday. He asked me whether we should have any objection to being invited with the British Commissioners.   I assured him we should not.

18th. We had a meeting of the mission at two o'clock, when we signed the dispatch to the Secretary of State, No. 2, containing the account of our first conferences with the British Commissioners.   I was charged also to make the draft of another dispatch, accounting for the detention of the John Adams, and to serve as a justification for Captain Angus.

19th. The Mayor called at noon, as he had appointed, and went with me to the Public Library.   Mr. Gallatin was unwell, and the other gentlemen did not incline to go.   I therefore went alone. The library is chiefly theological and juridical, and may consist of four or five thousand volumes. The Librarian, named Monsieur Valvyn, was polite to excess, and made me a speech. He showed me several manuscripts written before the invention of printing—some of them with paintings and vignettes, but not of the best execution. The most curious was a Latin translation of Plutarch's Lives, done by several hands. There was a small manuscript, said to be of the eighth century, a small Latin Bible, a Prayer Book, highly illuminated, and a compilation, upon something like the plan of an Encyclopædia. There were also several first impressions of the fifteenth century, one of which was printed at Ghent in 1485. Of modern rarities, he had Didot's folio editions of Virgil and Racine; a circular advertisement in the handwriting of Jean Jacques Rousseau, 1769, warning the public that all the editions of his works, and particularly those of Marc Michel Rey, were mutilated and falsified; a letter in the handwriting of Voltaire (not signed), 1737, in great want of money, and full of bad spelling. Rousseau's advertisement was in a gilt frame. The Librarian had an album, in which, at his request, I wrote my name, with a device. He invited me to come again, with my colleagues. The Mayor promised to come on Monday and go with us to see Mr. Schamp's collection of pictures.

On returning home, I met my colleagues at two o'clock. I had the draft of a dispatch accounting for the detention of the John Adams. Mr. Gallatin objected to a passage stating that the first cause of this was the transfer of the negotiation to this city, and was supported in the objection by Mr. Bayard and Mr. Russell. It was struck out.

Mr. Baker had been here from the British Commissioners, requesting a conference at their house at three o'clock. We went as requested. On taking their seats at the table, Mr. Goulburn had a dispatch from their Government before him, which, he informed us, was the answer to that which they had sent by their messenger. He proceeded to state its contents. The British Government expressed some surprise that we had not been instructed on the points of an Indian pacification, and boundary, as it might naturally have been expected that Great

Britain could not consent to make a peace and leave her allies at the mercy of a more powerful enemy. She might therefore justly have supposed that the American Government would have furnished us with instructions to agree to an article on this subject; but the least she can demand is, that the American Commissioners should sign a provisional article, subject to the ratification of their Government, so that if it should be ratified the treaty should take effect, and if not, that it should be null and void. And we were desired to understand that if unfortunately the conferences should be suspended by our refusal to agree to such an article, Great Britain would not consider herself bound, upon a renewal of the negotiations, to abide by the terms which she now offers. As we had requested to be explicitly informed of the views and intentions of Great Britain in proposing this article, we were to know that the Indian territories were to be interposed as a barrier between the British Dominions and the United States, to prevent them from being conterminous to each other, and that neither Great Britain nor the United States should acquire by purchase any of these Indian lands. For the line Great Britain was willing to take the Treaty of Greenville for the basis, with such modifications as might be agreed upon. With respect to the other boundary line, that of the British territories, Great Britain still adhered to the principle of asking for no conquests. But as Great Britain, on the side of Canada, was the weaker of the two nations, and had no designs of conquest there, and as it had been stated that the United States had, on their part, had the design of conquering Canada, it was required by Great Britain that the United States should stipulate to have no naval force upon the Lakes, from Ontario to Superior; and neither to build any forts in future, nor to preserve those already built upon their borders. It would also be necessary for Great Britain to obtain a communication between the provinces of New Brunswick and Canada, a mere road from Halifax to Quebec, which would take off a small corner of the province of Maine. These propositions must be considered as proofs of the moderation of Great Britain, since she might have demanded a cession of all the borders of the Lakes to herself. She would also require a continuance of the right of navigating the Mississippi, as secured to her by the former treaties.

Mr. Gallatin asked what was proposed to be done with the inhabitants, citizens of the United States, already settled beyond the line of the Treaty of Greenville—the Territories of Michigan, of Illinois, and part of the State of Ohio, amounting perhaps to one hundred thousand, many of whom had been settled there with their ancestors one hundred years.

Mr. Goulburn said that their case had not been considered by the British Government; that it might be a foundation for the United States to claim a particular modification of the line, and if that should not be agreed to they might remove.

Dr. Adams said that undoubtedly they must shift for themselves.

Mr. Bayard asked whether the proposition respecting the Indian pacification and boundary was still presented as a *sine qua non*; to which they answered that undoubtedly it was.

He asked whether that relating to the Lakes was of the same character.

Dr. Adams answered, "One *sine qua non* at a time is enough. It will be time enough to answer your question when you have disposed of that we have given you."

I observed that, for my own part, I should not wish for another conference before we should have received from the British Commissioners a written statement of their propositions.

This was agreed to on all sides, and they suggested that they should also expect our written answer to their note prior to the next conference.

I observed there might be in their note itself some things susceptible of verbal explanation, which we might desire before we should send the answer; in which case, I presumed, they would have no objection to our asking another conference.

To this they assented, though not without some objection from Dr. Adams, which he finally gave up. They promised to furnish us the written note as soon as possible. Lord Castlereagh himself arrived in this city last night, and proceeds in a day or two to Brussels. Our conference lasted about an hour.

After dinner we had a meeting of the mission, and determined to write another dispatch to the Secretary of State, but not to wait for the written note of the British Commissioners, nor to delay the departure of the John Adams an hour longer. Mr. Gallatin made minutes for this dispatch, and agreed to make the draft of it, to be ready to-morrow morning.

In my account of our conference with the British Commissioners this morning I omitted to state the following facts. Mr. Gallatin, adverting to the late account in the English newspapers of their having taken possession of Moose Island, in the Bay of Passamaquoddy, enquired whether the statement which had been published was correct, that they meant to keep it.

They said it was; that it was a part of the province of Nova Scotia; that they did not even consider it a subject for discussion.

Mr. Goulburn said he could demonstrate in the most unanswerable manner that it belonged to them, and Dr. Adams said we might as well contest their right to Northamptonshire.

Mr. Gallatin asked whether, in requiring us to keep no naval force on the Lakes and no forts on their shores, they intended to reserve the right of keeping them there themselves. They said they certainly did.

After the conference was finished, Mr. Bayard said to Mr. Goulburn, that if the conferences were suspended he supposed Goulburn would take a trip to England. Goulburn said, "Yes, and I suppose you will take a trip to America."

In general, their tone was more peremptory and their language more overbearing than at the former conferences. Their deportment this day was peculiarly offensive to Mr. Bayard. Mr. Clay has an inconceivable idea, that they will finish by receding from the ground they have taken.

20th. Mr. Gallatin's draft of another dispatch to the Secretary of State was considered, and, with some alterations, agreed to at a meeting of the mission before dinner. We received this day from the British Commissioners their official note, and sent a copy of it to the Secretary of State, but we would not detain the ship until we could send them a copy of our answer. It is probable that our answer, and the reply

which will be given to it, may close the negotiation. Lord
Castlereagh proceeded this day on his journey to Brussels.
In Mr. Bayard's draft of our long dispatch he had closed with
a paragraph complimentary to the personal deportment of the
British Commissioners. We now struck it out.

21st. I began the first draft of an answer to the note of the
British Commissioners, which gave me occupation for the day,
and which I did not finish. Mr. Clay had written something
on his part, and Mr. Gallatin, according to his custom of composition, had taken minutes of the subjects to be treated and
the ideas to be contained in it. All these were read at our
meeting at two o'clock this afternoon. I found, as usual, that
the draft was not satisfactory to my colleagues. On the general
view of the subject we are unanimous, but in my exposition
of it, one objects to the form and another to the substance of
almost every paragraph. Mr. Gallatin is for striking out every
expression that may be offensive to the feelings of the adverse
party. Mr. Clay is displeased with figurative language, which
he thinks improper for a state paper. Mr. Russell, agreeing in
the objections of the two other gentlemen, will be further for
amending the construction of every sentence; and Mr. Bayard,
even when agreeing to say precisely the same thing, chooses
to say it only in his own language. It was considered by all
the gentlemen that what I had written was too long, and with
too much argument about the Indians. It is, however, my
duty to make the draft of the dispatch, and they usually hold
me to it. We received invitations to dine next Saturday with
the British Commissioners: the chance is that before that time
the whole negotiation will be at an end.

22d. I finished this morning my draft of an answer to the
note of the British Commissioners, and gave it before breakfast
to Mr. Gallatin, who kept it for his amendments and additions
the whole day.

23d. We had this morning a meeting of the mission, when
my draft of an answer to the note of the British Commissioners,
with Mr. Gallatin's corrections and alterations, Mr. Clay's two or
three paragraphs, and an attempt at a totally new draft begun
and not finished by Mr. Bayard, were read and discussed;

and Mr. Hughes was directed to make out a new draft from the shreds and patches of them all. About one-half of my draft was agreed to be struck out; a half of the remainder was left for consideration. We all dined at the Intendant's. The British Commissioners were there, and Mrs. Goulburn, whom I had not before seen. The company was of twenty-five persons, among whom were the Mayor, the Intendant's two sons, and the wife of the eldest, and his daughter, Madame de la Poterie, and her husband. The ladies were very agreeable. The Intendant's eldest son was not in good humor with the allies, and expressed without hesitation his wish for a war, to restore this country to France.

24th. We had a short meeting of the mission in the morning, to consider the new draft of the answer to the British note; but Mr. Bayard was not present, and Mr. Russell wished to make a revision of the paper before it was finally discussed. The meeting was therefore adjourned until immediately after dinner, and we then sat until eleven at night, sifting, erasing, patching, and amending, until we were all wearied, though none of us was yet satiated with amendment. Of the part of my own draft which had been left for consideration, two-thirds were now struck out. The remnant left of mine certainly does not form a fifth part of the paper as finally settled, and it is patched with scraps from Mr. Gallatin, and scraps from Mr. Bayard, and scraps from Mr. Clay, all of whom are dissatisfied with the paper as finally constructed. Each of us takes a separate and distinct view of the subject-matter, and each naturally thinks his own view of it the most important. The peculiar difficulty with Mr. Bayard is, that his view is always exclusive. My draft contained a view of the law of nations as applied to the relations between settlements of European origin in America and the Indians. I thought it important, because the article proposed to us by the British Commissioners as a *sine qua non* would produce a total change of the public law in that respect, and because Lord Castlereagh had pledged the faith of his Government not to ask anything contrary to the established maxims of public law. Almost the whole of what I had written on this subject has been struck out; and when I stated that the right of civilized nations to settle upon lands where Indians had been was explicitly recognized by Vattel, Mr. Bayard called upon me to produce the passage, and was perfectly unaware that I could produce it much more strongly than I had stated it.

25th. We had a meeting this morning, when the answer to the note of the British Plenipotentiaries was finally agreed to and signed. It was carried to them by Mr. Hughes, and will bring the negotiation very shortly to a close.

26th. I had some conversation with Mr. Gallatin and Mr. Russell on the expediency of my returning to St. Petersburg by the way of Vienna. It was first proposed to me by Mr. Gallatin, and is advised both by him and Mr. Russell. There are considerations both for and against it, upon which it will be proper to deliberate. We had a short meeting of the mission this morning, but did nothing.

27th. We had a short meeting of the mission at two o'clock, but had no business to transact. There was some conversation upon the proposal suggested by Mr. Gallatin, that I should return to St. Petersburg by the way of Vienna. I declared my readiness to go, if the mission would authorize me to communicate to the Emperor of Russia the official documents of the negotiation. Mr. Gallatin and Mr. Russell were willing to give me this authority, but Mr. Clay thought it must be left to my discretion. Mr. Bayard was not present, but will certainly be of Mr. Clay's opinion. I wished for an immediate decision, that I might have an opportunity of writing to Mr. Crawford on the subject, and receiving his answer before we go ; but, as there is not only a diversity but an equal division of opinion upon the proposal, I could not press it any further. We all dined with the British Plenipotentiaries. There was no other company than their own family present. We came home about nine in the evening.

28th. We had a short meeting at two o'clock, and concluded upon leaving this house at the expiration of our month, the day after to-morrow. As we shall certainly not have occasion to stay here more than a week or ten days at the utmost, we had proposed to Lanmeier to remain, paying the rent not for the whole month, but in proportion to the time we shall stay. But, although his partner had yesterday agreed to this proposal, they sent us this morning a joint letter, stating that they paid their rent by the month, and had other contracts of the same kind, and making appeals to our generosity. We therefore determined not to enter upon the second month.

29th. Upon a further consultation with our landlord, Mr. Lanmeier Quetelet, we have concluded to remain here without removing until our departure from Ghent, and to pay him rent for half a month, at the rate of twelve hundred francs the month, as probably some of us will be at least ten days longer here.

31st. Mr. Baker, the Secretary of the British Plenipotentiaries, came this morning and enquired for Mr. Hughes, who not being here, he asked for Mr. Gallatin; he told him that in consideration of the great importance of their reply to our note, they had concluded to refer it to their Government for instructions. It would occasion only a delay of a few days. He did not say when they had sent it to England; but on Saturday Mr. Goulburn had told Mr. Bayard that they should reply without delay and without referring to their Government. Mr. Gallatin thinks they sent our note to Brussels, to Lord Castlereagh, and that he has chosen to refer it to England.

September 1st. This morning I paid a visit to the British Plenipotentiaries and to Mrs. Goulburn. I did not, however, see her, but only her husband. Lord Gambier and Dr. Adams, with Mr. Baker, went yesterday to Brussels, to return on Saturday. Mr. Goulburn told me that after having prepared their note in reply to ours, from the great importance of the subject, they had thought best to transmit it to their Government for approbation before they sent it in to us. He said he expected their messenger this evening; and I enquired whether he expected to receive by him the answer to their last reference. He said that would depend on the time which it took their dispatch to arrive in England, but he thought it more probable that the answer would come next Sunday—that their messengers came regularly twice a week, on Thursdays and Sundays. I told him I hoped his Government would reconsider some parts of their former propositions before they sent their final instructions. He did not think it probable, and I found the more I conversed with him the more the violence and bitterness of his passion against the United States disclosed itself. His great point in support of the Indian boundary was its necessity for the security of Canada. He said that the United States had manifested the intention and the determination of conquering Canada; that, "excepting us," he believed it was the astonishment of the whole world that Canada had not been conquered at the very outset of the war; that nothing had saved it but the excellent dispositions and military arrangements of the Governor who commanded there; that in order to guard against the same thing in future, it was necessary to make a barrier against our settlements, upon which neither party should encroach; that the Indians were but a secondary object, but that as being the allies of Great Britain she must include them, as she made peace with other powers, including Portugal as her ally; that the proposition that we should stipulate not to arm upon the Lakes was made with the same purpose—the security of Canada. He could not see that there was anything humiliating in it; that the United States could never be in any danger of invasion from Canada, the disproportion of force was too great. But Canada must always be in the most imminent danger of invasion from the United States, unless she was guarded by some such stipulation as they now demanded; that it could be nothing to the United States to agree not to arm upon the Lakes, since they never had actually done it before the present war. Why should they object to disarming there, where they had never before had a gun floating?

I answered that the conquest of Canada had never been an object of the war on the part of the United States; that Canada had been invaded by us in consequence of the war, as they themselves had invaded many parts of the United States—it was an effect, and not a cause, of the war; that the American Government never had declared the intention of conquering Canada.

He referred to Hull's proclamation.

I answered that the Government was not answerable for that,

any more than the British Government was answerable for Admiral Cochrane's proclamation, which had been disavowed. He said that the American Government had not disavowed Hull's proclamation, and that no proclamation of Admiral Cochrane's had been disavowed by the British Government.

I replied that the American Government had never been called upon either to avow or disavow Hull's proclamation, but that I had seen in a printed statement of the debates in the House of Commons, that Lord Castlereagh had been called upon to say whether Admiral Cochrane's proclamation had been authorized or not, and had answered that it was not.

He said that Lord Castlereagh had been asked whether a proclamation of Admiral Cochrane's, encouraging the negroes to revolt, had been authorized by the Government, and had answered in the negative—that is, that no proclamation encouraging the negroes to revolt had been authorized; but the proclamation of Admiral Cochrane, as referred to, gave no such encouragement; there was nothing about negroes in it. It merely offered employment, or a settlement in the British colonies, to such persons as might be disposed to leave the United States.

I referred him to the term free used in connection with that of settlements, and observed that it was true the word negroes was not used in it, but that no person in America could mistake its meaning; that it was unquestionably intended to apply to the negroes, and that the practice of many of their naval commanders corresponded with it; that it was known some of them, under such inducements, had taken away blacks, who had afterwards been sold in the West India Islands.

Upon this he manifested some apparent agitation, and said that he could undertake to deny it in the most unqualified terms; that the character of British naval officers was universally known, their generosity and humanity could not be contested; and, besides that, since the act of Parliament of 1811, the act of selling any man for a slave, unless real slaves, from one British island to another, was felony without benefit of clergy.

I replied that, without contesting the character of any class of people generally, it was certain there would be in all classes individuals capable of committing actions of which others would be ashamed; that, at a great distance from the eye and control of the Government, acts were often done with impunity which would be severely punished nearer home; that the facts I had stated to him were among the objects which we were instructed to present for consideration if the negotiation should proceed, and he might in that case find it more susceptible of proof than he was aware.

He thought it impossible, but that it was one of those charges against their officers, of which there were many, originating only in the spirit of hostility, and totally destitute of foundation.

With respect to the Indian allies, I remarked that there was no analogy between them and the case of Portugal; that the stipulation which might be necessary for the protection of Indians situated within the boundaries of the United States who had taken the British side in the war was rather in the nature of an amnesty than of a provision for allies. It resembled more the case of subjects who, in cases of invasion, sometimes took part with the enemy, as had sometimes occurred to Great Britain in Ireland.

He insisted that the Indians must be considered as independent nations, and that we ourselves made treaties with them and acknowledged boundaries of their territories.

I said that, wherever they would form settlements and cultivate lands, their possessions were undoubtedly to be respected, and always were respected, by the United States; that some of them had become civilized in a considerable degree—the Cherokees, for example, who had permanent habitations, and a state of property like our own. But the greater part of the Indians could never be prevailed upon to adopt this mode of life; their habits and attachments and prejudices were so averse to any settlement, that they could not reconcile themselves to any other condition than that of wandering hunters. It was impossible for such people ever to be said to have possessions. Their only right upon land was a right to use it as hunting-grounds, and when those lands where they hunted became necessary or convenient for the purposes of settlement, the system adopted by the United States was, by amicable arrangement with them, to compensate them for renouncing the right of hunting upon them, and for removing to remoter regions better suited to their purposes and mode of life. This system of the United States was an improvement upon the former practice of all European nations, including the British. The original settlers of New England had set the first example of this liberality towards the Indians, which was afterwards followed by the founder of Pennsylvania. Between it and taking the lands for nothing, or exterminating the Indians who had used them, there was no alternative. To condemn vast regions of territory to perpetual barrenness and solitude that a few hundred savages might find wild beasts to hunt upon it, was a species of game law that a nation descended from Britons would never endure. It was as incompatible with the moral as with the physical nature of things. If Great Britain meant to preclude forever the people of the United States from settling and cultivating those territories, she must not think of doing it by a treaty. She must formally undertake, and accomplish, their utter extermination. If the Government of the United States should ever submit to such a stipulation, which I hoped they would not, all its force, and that of Britain combined with it, would not suffice to carry it long into execution. It was opposing a feather to a torrent. The population of the United States in 1810 passed seven millions; at this hour it undoubtedly passed eight. As it continued to increase in such proportions, was it in human experience, or in human power, to check its progress by a bond of paper purporting to exclude posterity from the natural means of subsistence which they would derive from the cultivation of the soil? Such a treaty, instead of closing the old sources of discussion, would only open new ones. A war thus finished would immediately be followed by another, and Great Britain would ultimately find that she must substitute the project of exterminating the whole American people for that of opposing against them her barrier of savages.

"What!" said Mr. Goulburn, "is it, then, in the inevitable nature of things that the United States must conquer Canada?"

" No."

" But what security, then, can Great Britain have for her possession of it ?"

" If Great Britain does not think a liberal and amicable course of policy towards America would be the best security, as it certainly would, she must rely upon her general strength, upon the superiority of her power in other parts of her relations with America, upon the power which she has upon another element, to indemnify herself, by sudden impression upon American interests, more defenceless against her superiority, and in their amount far more valuable, than Canada ever was or ever will be."

He recurred again to our superior force, and to the necessity of providing against it. He said that in Canada they never took any of the Indian lands, and the Government (meaning the Provincial Government) was prohibited even from granting them ; that there were among the Indians very civilized people, and there was particularly one whom he knew, Norton, who commanded some of those engaged with them in this war, and who was a very intelligent and well-informed man ; that this removing of the Indians from their lands to others was the very thing they complained of; that it drove them over into their provinces, and made them encroach upon the Indians in their provinces.

This was a new idea to me. I told him I had never heard any complaint of this kind before, and I supposed a remedy for it would very easily be found.

He made no reply, and seemed as if, in the pressure for an argument, he had advanced more than he was inclined to maintain. It was the same with regard to the proposal that we should keep no armed force on or near the lakes of Canada. He did not admit that there was anything humiliating or unusual in it; but he evaded repeatedly the question how he, or the English nation, would feel, if the proposition were made to them of binding themselves by such a stipulation.

I finally said that if he did not feel that there was anything dishonorable to the party submitting to such terms, it was not a subject susceptible of argument. I could assure him that we and our nation would feel it to be such; that such stipulations were indeed often extorted from the weakness of a vanquished enemy, but they were always felt to be dishonorable, and had certainly occasioned more wars than they had ever prevented.

After changing the subject of the conversation to the pictures which we and they had drawn at the lottery, I took my leave and returned home. In reflecting upon it, I remark—1. The inflexible determination to adhere to the Indian boundary and barrier. 2. The avowal of Cochrane's proclamation to the negroes, and the explanation of Lord Castlereagh's disavowal. 3. The bitterness and rancor against the Americans, and the jealousy at their increasing strength and population. 4. The irritability at the statement of facts relative to the sale of the blacks enticed away, and at the comparison between their employing our Indians against us and Irish subjects aiding a French invader. Goulburn is personally the most inveterate of the three Plenipotentiaries, and the most in the confidence of his Government.

We had a large company of ladies and gentlemen to dinner— the Intendant of the Department of the Scheldt, Count d'Hane de Steenhuyse and his lady, Mr. D'Hane Dons, his son, and lady, Mr. Van Pottelsberghe de la Poterie and his lady, the Intendant's only daughter, Captain Constant d'Hane, another son, Mr. and Madame de Meulemeester Van Aken, Mr. and Madame Meulemeester Meulemeester, Mr. and Madame Greban, and Mr. and Madame Van Aken, the Comte de Lens, Mayor of the city, Mr. Goesin Verhaeghe, his first adjoint, Mr. Cornelissen, Mr. Canar, Mr. Charles Meulemeester, and Messieurs Shaler, Todd, and Irving. We sat down at table thirty persons. We had a band of music in the room adjoining our dining-hall, who performed at intervals during the dinner-time and all the evening. Our garden was illuminated with variegated colored lamps, and after dinner we walked in it half an hour with the ladies. The Intendant left us about eight in the evening, to go and examine his dispatches. All the rest of the company remained, and we spent the evening at cards. I played with the Intendant's lady, Madame Meulemeester, and Mr. Cornelissen. The party broke up about midnight, and, after they were

gone, Mr. Clay won from me at a game of all-fours the picture
of an old woman that I had drawn as a prize in the lottery of
pictures in which we had all taken tickets. He also won from
Mr. Todd the bunch of flowers which Mr. Russell had drawn,
and which Todd had won from Mr. Russell.

5th. I have been copying Mr. Clay's private journal of the conferences, which it may be useful hereafter to compare with my
own. This morning the British Commissioners sent their reply
to our last note, which was received by Mr. Gallatin and by
him brought in to me. We had shortly after a meeting of the
mission, when it was read and considered. Mr. Bayard pronounced it a very stupid production. Mr. Clay was for answering it by a note of half a page. I neither thought it stupid nor
proper to be answered in half a page. Each of the gentlemen
wanted it for some hours, and Mr. Gallatin proposed to make an
analysis of its contents, to minute what would deserve to be
noticed in our answer, to which we all agreed. After dinner
Mr. Meulemeester and Mr. Bentzon called upon us, and we
went with them to the private theatre at "La Rhétorique."
The performance was in Flemish, and before it was half over
I found myself falling asleep. I therefore came away, and
walked half an hour on the Place d'Armes. The house was
crowded again, and chiefly with women.

6th. We had our usual meeting of the mission, from two to
four o'clock. We concluded to send our note to the British
Commissioners, requesting a passport for the Herald to take
out our dispatches, and passports for a number of American
citizens to go as passengers in her. Mr. Hughes took my
draft of the note to copy and send.

Mr. Gallatin produced his analysis of the last note from the
British Commissioners, and his minutes of the points to be
noticed in answering it. We discussed them, and it was agreed
that Mr. Gallatin should draft an answer conformably to his
minutes, to be presented at our meeting to-morrow.

Mr. Bayard manifested symptoms of inclining to concessions
on the points proposed by the British Commissioners, and
which we have rejected. He proposed offering to the British
Commissioners for the Indians a "statu quo ante bellum," or

a declaration that we do not consider the Treaty of Greenville as abrogated.

Mr. Clay and myself were for admitting no stipulations about the Indians in a treaty with England.

Mr. Gallatin proposed to offer at least to refer to our Government a stipulation for disarming on both sides on the Lakes. I objected our positive instructions, and produced them. I proposed to take the grounds that the very employment of Indians by Great Britain was contrary to the laws of war, and that she had a sufficient pledge for the security of Canada from sudden invasion by the mass of our floating commerce, upon which, by her superiority at sea, she could always lay as suddenly her hand.

It was agreed to take this last point as I proposed, but not the other. Mr. Bayard was absent during great part of the meeting. Mr. Gallatin suggested the idea that after the rupture of the negotiation our Government might keep Ministers in Europe, always empowered to resume it whenever there might be an opportunity.

7th. We had our mission meeting at two o'clock. Mr. Gallatin produced his draft of a note. It was agreed that Mr. Bayard and Mr. Clay should take it together until this evening; that I should have it for to-morrow morning, and Mr. Russell after me; that we should meet to-morrow as soon as we should have finished our minutes of amendments and additions. I renewed and urged the proposal to introduce a paragraph complaining of the employment of savages as contrary to the laws of war, and it was agreed that I should prepare a paragraph to that effect for consideration. Just before going to bed I went into Mr. Clay's chamber, and received from him Mr. Gallatin's draft of a note with the amendments proposed by Mr. Bayard and Mr. Clay.

8th. III. 45. Just before rising, I heard Mr. Clay's company retiring from his chamber. I had left him with Mr. Russell, Mr. Bentzon, and Mr. Todd at cards. They parted as I was about to rise. I was up nearly half an hour before I had daylight to read or write. From that time until ten I was employed on the draft and minutes of Mr. Gallatin, Mr. Bayard, and Mr. Clay. I struck out the greatest part of my own previous draft, preferring that of Mr. Gallatin upon the same points. On the main question, relative to the Indian boundary, I made a new draft of several paragraphs, comprising the principal ideas of them all, and introducing an additional view of the subject of my own. I had also prepared a paragraph concerning the employment of savages. I was not a little gratified to find that Mr. Bayard in his draft had taken the true and strong ground respecting Indian rights, and had even quoted the very passage of Vattel which I had produced to him at our meeting on the 25th of last month, and at which he had then appeared to be a little nettled. I read my new draft to Mr. Gallatin in his chamber, and at eleven o'clock gave the papers to Mr. Russell.

At noon we met, and sat till dinner-time, preparing from all our sketches a final draft to be copied by Mr. Hughes. My new paragraph respecting Indian rights was adopted without much alteration. That against the employment of savages was fully adopted in substance, but with a multitude of amendments. I retired from the dinner-table and made a second fair draft of it, to be copied by Mr. Hughes. The concluding paragraph, and one or two others, were left to be finally settled to-morrow morning.

9th. In the pressure of my occupations, I find it difficult to keep my journal along without arrears. This morning I brought up the last two days, and then was busied in drawing projects of paragraphs for our note, and consulting about them with Mr. Russell and Mr. Gallatin till eleven o'clock. We had then a meeting of the mission, and found, upon reading over Mr. Hughes's copy of our draft, that it would be necessary to make out still another copy to be sent. Mr. Clay, Mr. Russell, and Mr. Hughes each took a separate sheet, and the copy was made out between three and four in the afternoon. Mr. Hughes took it to the British Plenipotentiaries.

10th. The Prince of Orange, sovereign of the Netherlands, arrived here this morning, accompanied only by two officers. The troops were under arms, and the bells were ringing almost the whole day. He stopped at the Intendant's, and all the civil and military authorities of the place were presented to him.

We sent at two o'clock Mr. Hughes to enquire when it would be agreeable to him to receive us. He was then gone out to visit the Penitentiary, the Botanical Garden, and a manufactory. He did not return till nearly six o'clock, and then sent us word that he would receive us immediately. We were all prepared, and had just dined. He received us in a chamber, where he was alone. He conversed principally with Mr. Gallatin and myself, and spoke a few words to Mr. Bayard. With Mr. Gallatin he talked altogether about Switzerland and Geneva, which, as Mr. Bayard noticed, he called "votre pays." He immediately recognized me, and observed it was a long time since he had seen me; talked of the Hague, of Berlin, of Russia, of his own father, and mine; of his mother, of his wife, and of mine; of the Emperor of Russia, and the Congress of Vienna; the weather, the roads, and the journey he was going upon to the island of Zeeland. Our conference with him did not exceed a quarter of an hour. We all went in the evening to the theatre, where the performances were the "Caliph of Bagdad," wretchedly performed, and "Ambroise, ou Voilà ma Journée." The house was thin, and of the auditory five-sixths were foreigners —mostly English officers and soldiers. The Prince came in between the two operas. The orchestra played immediately the national Dutch air, and God save the King. The Prince was cheered, as the English call it, but, excepting by the scarlet uniforms, the shouting was very laborious. I sat part of the evening in Mr. Meulemeester's box with his lady. On our return home we found the city was illuminated.

14th. We had the mission meeting at two P.M. A letter was received from the Hereditary Prince of Orange, dated Headquarters at Brussels, stating that he had been informed that the quartermaster of the second regiment of Hollandish chasseurs, who had deserted and absconded, and was charged with having carried off public moneys in his charge, had taken the direction towards Ghent, to apply to us for a passport to go to America; and, as it was necessary to secure such a dangerous man, we were required, if he should make such an application to us, to have him arrested, and to give the Prince information of it. The Prince is Commander-in-chief of all the English troops, and troops in English pay, in the Netherlands. It became a question what should be done with this letter. Mr. Gallatin doubted whether we should answer it at all. Mr. Bayard was for answering that we would comply with the requisition. I was for answering, but not for complying with the requisition, nor for promising that we would. The requisition itself appeared to me an infringement of our immunities as public Ministers. We can certainly be amenable to no military requisition, and most especially to none of an English general officer. Mr. Bayard finally drafted a short answer, acknowledging the receipt of the Prince's letter, and saying that we grant no passports to foreigners to go to America. We took it for consideration.

Mr. Clay mentioned to us the uneasiness of Mr. Shaler, who thinks himself neglected by the mission and had written us a letter proposing to withdraw from it. The principal cause of offence is, that he was not presented with the rest of the mission last week to the Prince of Orange. Mr. Clay prevailed upon him not to send his letter.

15th. Began the copying of the papers relative to the transactions between us and the British Plenipotentiaries. This forenoon our joint landlord, Mr. Ducobie, came and informed us that the Baron Van der Capellen, the Minister Secretary of State to the Sovereign Prince of the Netherlands, had arrived in the city; that he was at the Intendant's, and that Lanmeier had been ordered to prepare a dinner for him. On consulting with Mr. Gallatin, we determined to send an invitation for the Baron and his suite to dine with us, for which purpose Mr. Gallatin addressed a note to the Intendant. The Baron accepted the invitation, with excuses for appearing in a travelling dress. It was about five when our company was all assembled—the Baron Van der Capellen, his lady, and Mr. Valck, the Prince of Orange's Secretary for Holland; Lord Gambier, Mr. and Mrs. Goulburn, and Mr. Edward Goulburn, his brother; Dr. Adams, Mr. Baker, and Mr. Gambier; the Intendant and his lady; his son D'Hane Dons, and his wife; his daughter, Madame de la Poterie, and her husband; his two sons Louis and Constant; the Count de Lens, Mayor of the city; Mr.

and Mrs. Meulemeester, and Mr. Charles Meulemeester; and Messrs. Shaler, Hughes, and Todd. We were thirty-one at table.

Before dinner, Lord Gambier asked me if I should return immediately to St. Petersburg. I said, " Yes; that is, if you send us away." . . . He replied with assurances how deeply he lamented it, and with a hope that we should one day be friends again—which I assured him I wished with equal ardor. I sat between Mrs. Goulburn and Madame Van der Capellen, both of whom I found very agreeable. The Baron, his lady, and Mr. Valck left us immediately after dinner, about eight o'clock : they were obliged to go this night to Brussels. The Intendant went shortly after, to read his dispatches, and the English party went away about nine. The rest of the company spent the evening with us, and retired about midnight. We had the band of music, and the garden was illuminated in the evening. I passed it at cards, with the Intendant's lady, Mrs. Meulemeester, and Mr. Russell.

Mr. Goulburn told Mr. Clay that they had dispatched our last note to England on the same day they had received it, and expected the answer next Monday or Tuesday. He had no doubt it would terminate our business, and said we must fight it out.

We had a short meeting of the mission at two o'clock, and had letters from Mr. Bourne on the subject of the protest of Captain Angus's bills by the house of Glennie and Son, at London. I proposed an addition to Mr. Bayard's draft of an answer to the Hereditary Prince of Orange, but it was determined to suspend the subject till to-morrow.

16th. We had a short meeting of the mission at two o'clock, and wrote to Messrs. Baring, giving Captain Jones a credit for one thousand pounds sterling. It was concluded to leave the letter from the Hereditary Prince of Orange unanswered.

20th. I was closing my copy of four pages, when the third note from the British Plenipotentiaries was brought to me, together with some late English newspapers that they had sent us. After reading the note, and the two proclamations of General Hull and General Smyth, enclosed with it, I took them immediately in to Mr. Gallatin. They were shortly after read by our other colleagues, and we had, at one o'clock, a meeting of the mission. The British note is overbearing and insulting in its tone, like the two former ones; but it abandons a great part of the *sine qua non*, adhering at the same time inflexibly to the remainder. The effect of these notes upon us when they first come is to deject us all. We so fondly cling to the vain hope of peace, that every new proof of its impossibility operates upon us as a disappointment. We had a desultory and general conversation upon this note, in which I thought both Mr. Gallatin and Mr. Bayard showed symptoms of despondency. In discussing with them I cannot always restrain the irritability of my temper. Mr. Bayard meets it with more of accommodation than heretofore, and sometimes with more compliance than I expect. Mr. Gallatin, having more pliability of character and more playfulness of disposition, throws off my heat with a joke. Mr. Clay and Mr. Russell are perfectly firm themselves, but sometimes partake of the staggers of the two other gentlemen.

Mr. Gallatin said this day that the *sine qua non* now presented—that the Indians should be positively included in the peace, and placed in the state they were in before the war— would undoubtedly be rejected by our Government if it was now presented to them, but that it was a bad point for us to break off the negotiation upon; that the difficulty of carrying on the war might compel us to admit the principle at last, for now the British had so committed themselves with regard to the Indians that it was impossible for them further to retreat.

Mr. Bayard was of the same opinion, and recurred to the fundamental idea of breaking off upon some point which shall unite our own people in the support of the war.

In this sentiment we all concur. But, as its tendency is to produce compliance with the British claims, it is necessary to guard against its leading us in that career too far. I said it was not more clear to me that the British would not finally abandon their present *sine qua non*, than it had been that they would adhere to their first; that if the point of the Indians was a bad point to break upon, I was very sure we should never find a good one. If that would not unite our people, it was a hopeless pursuit.

Mr. Gallatin repeated, with a very earnest look, that it was a bad point to break upon.

"Then," said I, with a movement of impatience and an angry tone, "it is a good point to admit the British as the sovereigns and protectors of our Indians."

Gallatin's countenance brightened, and he said, in a tone of perfect good humor, "That's a non-sequitur." This turned the edge of the argument into mere jocularity. I laughed, and insisted that it was a sequitur, and the conversation easily changed to another point.

The gentlemen agreed to make out between them (Mr. Clay and Mr. Hughes) a copy of the note, from which a second press-copy should be taken; that Mr. Gallatin should then have the original, to make the analysis of it for to-morrow's meeting. The passion for making our answer short was again avowed, and again opposed by me. I urged Mr. Gallatin to spare neither his paper nor the time of our adversaries, and to be careful to leave nothing important unanswered. I have at the same time offered to subscribe any·answer which any one of the gentlemen would draw up in half a page and would himself sign as our answer. My principle has been, that if we do enter upon argument it ought to be at full length. I also made the proposal of offering to the British an article including the Indians, in the nature of an amnesty; for which I thought we should be warranted by our instruction to endeavor to obtain an amnesty for the Canadians who have taken part with us. I had already several times suggested this idea, which had not been admitted or rejected. It was not now agreed to, but left for consideration.

21st. IV. 30. Wrote about half an hour by candle-light this morning. This being the day of the autumnal equinox, I must henceforth, for half a year, rise by the light of the morning stars. I wrote again four pages of copying, and we had our mission meeting.

Mr. Gallatin produced his analysis of the last British note, and his minutes of the proposed answer, which he is to draft.

The original of the British note was delivered to me.   I found both Mr. Gallatin and Mr. Bayard this day as firm on the points we had yesterday discussed as any of us.

In the evening we all attended a tea- and card-party at Mr. Meulemeester de Meulemeester's, where I played whist with him, Madame Canighem, and another lady, name unknown.   As we came home, Mr. Clay mentioned to me his satisfaction at finding that Mr. Bayard was now so strong in sentiment with us. Of Mr. Gallatin he had always been sure.   There was another card-party in Mr. Clay's chamber last night, and I heard Mr. Bentzon retiring from it after I had risen this morning.

22d. Although I am released from the duty of drafting the answers to the British notes by my colleagues, and this part of our duty has been assumed by Mr. Gallatin with their and my consent, I think it still incumbent upon me to make a draft of an answer, as if the whole business rested upon myself.   I have thus the advantage of presenting for consideration whatever appears important to myself, and I oblige myself to give all possible attention to the subjects in controversy, and to the grounds of our adversaries.   I began, therefore, this morning, a draft of an answer to their last note, and wrote upon it, almost without intermission, until dinner-time.   Mr. Gallatin was engaged at the same time upon his draft, but did not finish it.   I gave him the first sheet of my draft, to make what use of it he pleased.   He sent the first sheet of his to Messrs. Bayard and Clay, for their consideration.

23d. I finished just before noon my draft of an answer to the last note from the British Plenipotentiaries, and gave the second sheet to Mr. Gallatin.   He had not finished his draft, but at two o'clock we had our meeting of the mission, and he produced his draft as finished.   It was read, together with parts of mine, and the whole was then given to Mr. Gallatin to mark off what was to be retained of both, to be then sent round and revised by us all, preparatory to the second presentation of it, as a draft to be decided upon by a joint deliberation.   The two original drafts were about of the same length, but the views taken of the contested points were materially different.   Mr. Gallatin's chiefly consisted of two arguments—one concerning the boundary of

the district of Maine, and the other concerning the condition of
the Indians.   My arguments on these topics were very short,
but I had replied at large to the accusatory matter of the British
note, had retorted pointedly upon the Britons their own charges,
and insisted on the moral and religious duty of the American
nation to cultivate their territory, though to the necessary
extinction of all the rights of savage tribes, by fair and amicable
means.   I had also the proposal for the article of amnesty to
include the Indians.   It was agreed to adopt this article, though
with objections to almost every word in which I had drawn it
up.   This is a severity with which I alone am treated in our
discussions by all my colleagues.   Almost everything written
by any of the rest is rejected or agreed to with very little
criticism, verbal or substantial.   But every line that I write
passes a gauntlet of objections by every one of my colleagues,
which finally issues, for the most part, in the rejection of it all.
I write and propose a great deal more than all the rest together,
Mr. Gallatin excepted.   I have in the end, I believe, not more
than my fifth part in the papers, as we dispatch them.   This must
be, in a great measure, the fault of my composition, and I ought
to endeavor to correct the general fault from which it proceeds.

24th. The miscellaneous draft was this morning sent by Mr.
Gallatin to Messrs. Bayard and Clay, then to Mr. Russell, and,
between one and two o'clock, to me. Our meeting was to have
been at three, but I found it impossible to get through the
revision of the papers by that time.

25th. I found it impossible to make a suitable revision of the
papers for the draft of our note without attempting to make a
new draft of great part of it, which I accordingly attempted.
Before I had finished it, Mr. Gallatin came into my chamber,
and showed some impatience for a meeting. I was prepared
about noon.   Mr. Russell was gone out to breakfast.   We
found in Mr. Clay's chamber some English newspapers, among
which was the Times of the 21st, containing the British Lieutenant-General Drummond's official account of the battle of
25th July, the first of our defeats, of which a long and heavy
series is before us.   There was a Mr. Mifflin, last from Hamburg, and lately from England, in Mr. Clay's chamber.

We met at one o'clock, and sat until past five, debating the new draft of our answer to the British note. I had proposed to leave out a large part of Mr. Gallatin's draft, but he insisted upon retaining most of what he had written, and it was retained. In this debate I had continued evidence of two things. One, that if any one member objects to anything I have written, all the rest support him in it, and I never can get it through. The other, that if I object to anything written by Mr. Gallatin, unless he voluntarily abandons it every other member supports him, and my objection is utterly unavailing. They supported him thus this day in a paragraph respecting Florida, directly in the face of our instructions, which I produced and read. I was reduced to the necessity of declaring that I would not sign the paper with the paragraph as he had drawn it. He objected to mine because it said that the proceedings of the American Government could be completely justified with regard to Florida. Gallatin said he did not think they could ; that he had opposed for a whole year what had been done, before he could succeed in stopping the course they had taken. Mr. Bayard said that he was very much committed on the subject of Florida, too; and Mr. Clay, though he thought the Government perfectly justifiable, did not perceive any necessity for saying so. Mr. Russell was of the same opinion. I had no alternative but to say I would not sign the paper with the paragraph as Mr. Gallatin had written it ; for that pointedly said that we would not discuss the subject of Florida with the British Plenipotentiaries, though our instructions had expressly authorized us to bring it before them. Mr. Gallatin finally consented himself to take my paragraph with an alteration.

On the other hand, in repelling an insolent charge of the British Plenipotentiaries against the Government of the United States, of a system of perpetual encroachment upon the Indians under the pretence of purchases, I had taken the ground of the moral and religious duty of a nation to settle, cultivate, and improve their territory—a principle perfectly recognized by the laws of nations, and, in my own opinion, the only solid and unanswerable defence against the charge in the British note. Gallatin saw and admitted the weight of the argument,

but was afraid of ridicule.   Bayard, too, since he has been
reading Vattel, agreed in the argument, and was willing to
say it was a duty.   But the terms God, and Providence, and
Heaven, Mr. Clay thought were canting, and Russell laughed
at them.   I was obliged to give them up, and with them what
I thought the best argument we had.   My proposal of the
amnesty passed more smoothly, and almost without alteration.
There were, indeed, marks for erasure, which would have demolished it entirely, but which had been made before the gentlemen had recurred to the printed precedents of former treaties.
Fortunately, all the most perilous words of my draft were
found used in the precedents, and the objections against them
vanished.   Among the parts of Mr. Gallatin's note which I
had proposed to strike out was a pointed question to the British
Plenipotentiaries, to which I objected, because I thought it
admitted of a solid answer, and because, so far as it was not
answerable, it had been substantially put in both our former
notes.   He adhered to it, and my objection was overruled.   He
had one passage saying that the sovereignty of the territory in
question was transferred by the treaty of peace of 1783 from
the King of Great Britain to the United States, which I told
him was a tremendous concession.   He contended at first even
for that, but was soon convinced it could not be maintained,
and gave it up without debate.   We postponed our dinner until
between five and six, and agreed at last to the draft as it was
to be copied—Mr. Gallatin taking his paragraphs which I had
proposed to strike out, but which are to be retained, to alter
them as he thinks proper; as he found some alteration of them
would be necessary.

26th. We had a meeting at two o'clock.   Mr. Hughes attended
with the note prepared, which we signed, and which he immediately took to the house of the British Plenipotentiaries.

27th. Mr. Goulburn and Mr. Baker paid us visits, but I did
not see them.   They excused themselves and all the British
mission from coming to our proposed tea- and card-party on
Thursday evening.   They said they intended taking the present
opportunity to pay a visit to Antwerp.   Mr. Goulburn's brother
went off this morning for England, and took our note with him,

so that we shall not have the answer to it until Tuesday or Wednesday of next week.

29th. As I was sitting at my writing-table this morning, before eight o'clock, one of the servants of the house opened my door, and my brother-in-law, Mr. George Boyd, of Washington City, came in quite unexpectedly. He comes as a messenger with dispatches from the Department of State to the mission, and from the Treasury Department to Mr. Crawford, Mr. Gallatin, and myself. He left Washington the 12th of last month, at twelve hours' notice, and sailed on the 16th, from New York, in the Transit, a fast-sailing Baltimore schooner. He arrived at Bordeaux the 17th of this month, at Paris the 23d, and here this morning at six o'clock, having travelled from Paris day and night. His dispatches and newspapers are to the 12th of August. Those from the Treasury are in the first instance for Mr. Gallatin, with powers to negotiate a loan in Holland of six millions of dollars. They are to me only in the case of Mr. Gallatin's absence, and to Mr. Crawford in case the loan should not be obtainable at Amsterdam. Boyd was obliged to come without a cartel, Admiral Cockburn, by orders from Admiral Cochrane, having refused to grant one after that of the Chauncey until the American Government should have received dispatches from us. It is remarkable that the British Commissioners in their last note to us brought it as a sort of charge against the American Government, that they had not furnished us with instructions since they had been informed of the pacification in Europe. Mr. Clay had a letter from his wife, mentioning his being elected again to the next Congress. From the time of Mr. Boyd's arrival until dinner we were all employed in deciphering the dispatches and reading the newspapers. In the National Intelligencers of the 6th and 9th of August there were unofficial articles purporting that the United States had made a treaty at Greenville, 16th July, with almost all the Indians who have been such a stumbling-block in the way of our negotiation. Mr. Clay proposed sending a note to the British Plenipotentiaries communicating these extracts from the newspapers. In the evening we had our large tea- and card-party, which became a ball. Invitations had been sent to about one hundred and fifty persons, and there were about one hundred and thirty who came. None of the British Legation. All the principal noblesse and merchants of the city were here. The company began to assemble between seven and eight o'clock. At eleven we had a supper; after which the dancing recommenced, and the party broke up just before three in the morning. I played whist with the Intendant's lady, Madame Borlut de Lens, the Mayor's sister, and Prince d'Aremberg, the Commander-in-Chief of all the Belgian troops. I danced part of a Boulangère. Our garden was illuminated with the variegated colored lamps, and there was an inscription of eight poor French verses over the central gate, between the garden and back yard. Mr. Cornelissen asked me to lend him some American newspapers to make extracts from them for publication. He promised to call for them to-morrow morning.

30th. Mr. Cornelissen came this morning between eight and nine o'clock, and I gave him two of the National Intelligencers, to make extracts from them for publication. But he had not had them more than an hour, before Mr. Clay came into my chamber, with a note ready drawn, to send to the British Plenipotentiaries, about the treaty with the Indians at Greenville, and complaining of the refusal by Admiral Cochrane to grant a passport for a vessel to bring us dispatches. Mr. Gallatin and myself both doubted the propriety of sending mere newspaper authority for the Indian treaty, of which not a word is said to us in our dispatches of later date from the Secretary of State. But Mr. Clay thought it so important, and was so urgent, that we consented to make the communication. We had a meeting at half-past twelve o'clock, and agreed to the draft of a note, as altered by Mr. Gallatin; and again, in Mr. Clay's chamber, at two, when we signed the note. It was enclosed with the extracts from the papers, a copy of Cockburn's letter to Mr. Monroe, refusing a passport for a vessel to take dispatches, and of a note from Mr. Monroe to Lord Castlereagh; and they are all to be sent to-morrow, by Mr. Todd, to the British Commissioners, who have not yet returned from Antwerp. Two messages were sent for the newspapers to Mr. Cornelissen, who finally returned them. Mr. Russell removed his effects back to the Hôtel des

Pays-Bas. He and Mr. Clay and Mr. Hughes went upon a party of pleasure to Brussels, to return next Monday. Mr. Shaler called on me this morning and brought the London Statesman of the 24th, with accounts from America to 28th August. There is the letter from General Gaines, announcing the repulse of the British attack on Fort Erie on the 15th of August, and the arrival of Admiral Cochrane in the Chesapeake on the 16th. The next news will be of the taking of Washington or Baltimore.

October 1st. When I returned home, Mr. Gallatin had just heard of the taking of Washington City, and the destruction of the navy-yard and public buildings there, by the British, on the 25th August. An American arrived from Ostend had seen the Gazette account of it, and Mr. Lewis, returned from Paris, brings the same intelligence, as brought by the Ajax, the Dutch vessel which took out Mr. Changuion, the Dutch Minister, and which has arrived at Havre de Grace, having left Boston the 1st of September.

2d. I had a sleepless night, but could not rise within an hour of my usual time, owing to the coldness of the weather. It was almost impossible to write. After breakfast I went out with Mr. and Mrs. Meulemeester, Mr. Charles Meulemeester, Madame Greban, Mr. Bayard, Mr. Gallatin, and his son, to a village called Wetteren, about eight miles from the city, to the country-seat of a widow lady named Vilain, whose house and garden are very elegant. She has a valuable library, and collections of pictures, prints, medals, coins, minerals, marbles, and curiosities of all kinds. She received us with much politeness, and entertained us with a collation. She has a son about eighteen, who was lately in England with Mr. Charles Meulemeester. We returned, and took a family dinner with the Meulemeesters at their house. In the evening we went to the theatre, and saw " Azemia, ou les Sauvages," only the last act, and " Richard Cœur de Lion." I was too drowsy and cold and distressed to be amused. When I came home, Mr. Gallatin had Mr. Shaler's Statesman, containing an official account, published by the British Government, of the taking and destruction of Washington.

5th. By lighting my fire in the morning I find it again possible to write, and was engaged all the morning in copying papers. Mr. Connell called upon me, and mentioned an article in the Journal des Débats, on the destruction of Washington by the English, which he afterwards sent us to read. We had a meeting of the mission at two o'clock; Mr. Russell mentioned a letter he had received from Mr. Petry, in the office of Foreign Affairs at Paris. Mr. Clay proposed that a communication should be made of the state of the negotiation to the Emperor of Russia, and to the French Government—upon which there was some desultory conversation, but no final determination. Mr. Gallatin asked me to make a draft of such a paper for the Emperor of Russia.

6th. I was engaged all the morning in drafting a letter to Count Nesselrode, containing a narrative of the progress and present state of the negotiation, to be laid before the Emperor of Russia, at Vienna. I showed it to Mr. Gallatin, and observed to him, that if the mission should approve of it, I would propose to Mr. Smith to carry it as a special messenger; a measure which had been some days since suggested to me by Mr. Gallatin. I told him that my object would be to secure another advantage by this step, that of obtaining information which might be useful to us respecting the state of affairs at Vienna; the proceedings of the Congress, and the chances favorable to our cause, which might there turn up. I thought it possible he might have an opportunity to obtain valuable information by his acquaintance with the Duke of Serra Capriola, the Sicilian Minister, who is there, and probably with views which would make him friendly to ours. Of all this Mr. Gallatin expressed his approbation.

The meeting of the mission at two o'clock was in my chamber, where most of my colleagues had already met to read the papers. At the meeting I read a translation of my draft for a letter to Count Nesselrode, upon which no remarks were made, it being considered as belonging to my particular Russian mission. Mr. Clay said that a narrative thus particular was very proper to be communicated to the Emperor of Russia, but for a similar communication to Mr. Crawford, to be made to the

French Government, twenty lines would be enough.   Mr. Gallatin asked him to draw up a letter for the purpose, to be presented at the meeting to-morrow, to which he agreed.

7th. While Shaler was with me, Mr. Clay came in with his draft of a letter to Mr. Crawford, and, observing that Shaler was one of us, read it aloud.   Afterwards, at two o'clock, we had the meeting of the mission.   Mr. Clay read his draft of the letter to Mr. Crawford, upon which some slight remarks were made by our other colleagues, and some alterations suggested, which he adopted.   Mr. Russell asked me how I proposed to transmit the letter to Count Nesselrode.   I said, if the mission approved of it, by Mr. Smith, and I gave the reasons upon which I had thought of adopting that course.   Mr. Russell said Mr. Shaler had been to him and informed him of his expectation of being employed to carry this communication to Mr. Crawford.   Mr. Clay said that Mr. Shaler might be sent to Mr. Crawford, and at the same time Mr. Smith might be sent directly to Vienna.   I observed that, not being perfectly satisfied of the propriety of the measure at all, I should send to Vienna only according to the advice the mission should give me.   Mr. Clay said he certainly should give no advice as to the person to be sent.   I said that when I received the letter from the mission advising me to send to Vienna, I should take my measures accordingly; that if they gave me no advice, I should communicate the progress and result of the negotiation to the Russian Government in the regular form, and after my return to St. Petersburg.   The communication to Vienna was no measure of mine.   It might prove useful, or otherwise, according to circumstances.   I doubted still more of the expediency of the communication, at present, to France.   If France had any motive of her own to seek for the information, she would be quick enough in seeking it, without our hurrying to give it to her; that as to any interest of our own to be promoted by the communication, I could not readily perceive it.   I believed both France and Russia knew as well as we did that England did not intend to make peace with us in this negotiation.   The Emperor of Russia, at least, had been aware of it when Mr. Gallatin saw him at London in June, and Harris's last letters to me from St. Petersburg showed that the Government there still expected the same. I thought it deserved also to be considered, if the Crown Prince of Sweden, or a Swedish Minister, should be at Vienna, whether the communication ought not to be made to that Government at the same time as to France and Russia. All my colleagues were of opinion that it should not, though I urged that our instructions from home applied to that Government as well as to the others; that the communication, if made at the same time, would be taken as a friendly act, and if withheld, might be considered otherwise. The mission thought it was altogether at our discretion either to make or to withhold the communication, and that it would be best to withhold it, considering the Crown Prince's dependence upon England. Mr. Gallatin thought Mr. Crawford should be advised to make the communication to the French Government verbally, rather than in writing. Mr. Clay was for leaving the manner at his own discretion, and Mr. Russell, for having it recommended to him by a private letter to make it verbally. Mr. Gallatin, at the request of Mr. Russell, promised to draw up a letter of advice to me to send to Vienna—to be submitted for consideration to-morrow.

8th. At two, we had the meeting of the mission. Mr. Gallatin's draft of a letter from the mission to me was produced. It requested me to send a special messenger to Vienna to communicate to the Emperor of Russia the state of our negotiation, and to give us any information which he could collect there and which it might be useful to the public service for us to possess. I then requested that they would fix upon the person who should be charged with this mission, and also direct me in what manner the expense of it is to be defrayed—whether to be charged to the joint mission or to the Legation to Russia. Mr. Clay and Mr. Russell insisted that the selection of the messenger fell particularly within my province, as Minister to the Emperor of Russia. I said that Mr. Smith, being the Secretary of the Legation to Russia, known as such to the Emperor and to Count Nesselrode, was, in my opinion, the most proper person to be charged with the letter. But there were other duties which concerned the joint mission, and which they proposed should be enjoined upon the same messenger. Mr. Smith had particular advantages for the discharge of this duty, which I had yesterday stated, and he was to me the most confidential person that I could employ. But motives of delicacy, well known to them, would induce me to decline sending him unless with their approbation.

Mr. Clay and Mr. Russell said that if I insisted upon their recommending a person to me, it would be Mr. Shaler, for he had been attached to the joint mission for that particular purpose (of which, however, there is no written evidence).

Mr. Gallatin said he did not think Mr. Shaler the proper person. To deliver the letter to Count Nesselrode, there could be no person so proper as the Secretary to the Legation to Russia. For the other part of the business, it required a person of address and of habits in society, not possessed by Mr. Shaler, though he was a man perfectly confidential and of very good understanding.

Mr. Gallatin asked me whether he should strike out that part of his draft recommending the employment of a special messenger, and leaving it at my discretion how to send the letter.

I said I should then send it by the post. Mr. Gallatin said that would not do. I said I should then ask them to indicate to me the mode by which I should send the letter; I was ready to say to them in writing what I then said verbally. Mr. Clay and Mr. Russell waxed loud, and Mr. Clay very warm. They said they had nothing to do with the appointment of the messenger, that it was my business exclusively, and if I wanted their opinion, they had given it. I said, with too much warmth, that they might be assured I was as determined as they were. Each of us must act upon his own responsibility. The proposed measure itself was theirs, and not mine. Its usefulness was, in my own opinion, problematical, but I was ready to acquiesce in their judgment and to execute their charge. I only asked them to name to me the person whom I should send as the messenger, and whoever they named should certainly be sent.

Mr. Clay said, with great heat and anger, that he would give his opinion in writing; that he should be ashamed not to take such a responsibility upon himself; and he added, with a scorn-

ful sneer, that he supposed Mr. Crawford would send to ask us
how he should perform our request. "A soft answer turneth
away wrath;" but I have not always a soft answer at my own
command; the next best expedient to check contention is to
suppress all angry reply, and I am not always sufficiently master
of myself to do that. I was so to-day. I was silent. The
answer was perfectly obvious, that Mr. Crawford had no special
messenger to send; that he had no share in the responsibility
of the measure itself; that he was to be requested to perform
one of the ordinary duties of his office, and that if in the execution of the act recommended by us to him there were any
circumstances of a delicate nature connected with the mode of
performing it, he would be fully justified in asking our advice
and direction in relation to it. But I did not say this. I
restrained my feelings, and made no reply.

We adjourned, and I took a short walk before dinner. While
we were sitting at the dinner-table, the fourth note of the British
Plenipotentiaries was brought to us. It enclosed a proposed
article, which is offered as an ultimatum on the subject of the
Indian pacification. We agreed to meet and consider of it to-
morrow at the usual hour.

9th. V. From which time until our meeting at two in the
afternoon I was engaged in copying the note yesterday received
from the British Plenipotentiaries. At the meeting we had
some desultory conversation on the subject of the answer to
be given to the British note. We came to no determination,
but agreed to meet at eleven to-morrow morning. Mr. Bayard
suggested the propriety of asking for a conference before we
should answer the note. He thought we could not break off
on the refusal to accept the article proposed, but that we might
demand, before we accepted it, their whole project of a treaty.
Yet if they should eventually refuse to give their project until
we should formally have admitted their article, he was still not
for breaking off. Mr. Clay was for rejecting any proposition
to disarm upon the Lakes, if we admitted the present article;
because he considered that the two articles together would deliver the whole western country up to the mercy of the Indians.
The inconvenience and danger of admitting any preliminary

article thus dictated was distinctly perceived by us, but none of us were prepared to break off upon it.

10th. We had our meeting of the mission at twelve, and had much further conversation concerning the answer to the last British note. Mr. Clay and Mr. Gallatin were very desirous it should be short—not more than four pages. I was of opinion it ought to be long—at least as long as the note itself. It was agreed, however, that Mr. Gallatin should prepare a draft, to be offered to the meeting to-morrow.

11th. Mr. Gallatin was not prepared with his draft of the answer to the last note from the British Plenipotentiaries, so that the mission barely met and adjourned. I hear nothing more of the projected missions to Mr. Crawford and to Vienna; I believe them to be of very little consequence.

12th. I made a draft of an answer to the last note from the British Plenipotentiaries, but had not finished it when the time of our meeting came. At the meeting, Mr. Gallatin produced his draft, and I read parts of mine. They differed much in the tone of the composition. The tone of all the British notes is arrogant, overbearing, and offensive. The tone of ours is neither so bold nor so spirited as I think it should be. It is too much on the defensive, and too excessive in the caution to say nothing irritating. I have seldom been able to prevail upon my colleagues to insert anything in the style of retort upon the harsh and reproachful matter which we receive. And they are now so resolved to make the present note short, that they appeared to reject everything I had written, and even much of Mr. Gallatin's draft. We agree to accept the article offered to us as an ultimatum. Mr. Gallatin's idea is to adopt it, as perfectly conformable to the views we ourselves had previously taken of the subject. Mine is to consider and represent it as a very great concession, made for the sake of securing the peace. But in this opinion I am alone. I also strongly urged the expediency of avowing as the sentiment of our Government that the cession of Canada would be for the interest of Great Britain as well as the United States. I had drawn up a paragraph upon the subject conformable to our instructions. My colleagues would not adopt it. My own concern is, that when our instructions come to be published, as they must and will be, they will be compared with the arguments pointedly urged in all our notes, and will countenance a charge of duplicity against us and our Government. I have believed from the time of the second British note that they possess copies of our instructions; but if they do not, our own Government must eventually publish them; and although there is nothing in our note really inconsistent with them, there are many things which may be so represented. We have now the opportunity to avow the object of our Government, and at the same time to execute our instructions and to guard against the appearance hereafter of their having been detected. I was for availing ourselves of it, but cannot obtain the concurrence of my colleagues.

Mr. Clay took the two drafts, to shorten that of Mr. Gallatin and to adopt from mine anything that he might think proper to be taken. Mr. Bayard and myself sat after dinner until past ten o'clock, conversing upon subjects of American politics and of our present negotiation. He was extremely friendly and confidential in his manner, and spoke with an open-heartedness which I very cordially returned. He appears very anxious for the acceptance of the article offered us by the British Plenipotentiaries, and dwells with the greatest earnestness on the project of accomplishing the peace, or of uniting our whole country in support of the war against our eternal and irreconcilable foe.

13th. We had a meeting of the mission at two. Mr. Clay had a new draft of an answer to the last note of the British Plenipotentiaries. I disliked it very much in all its parts, but could obtain only that small parts of it should be struck out. It was finally settled as it is to be sent, and given to Mr. Hughes, to be prepared for our signatures at eleven o'clock to-morrow morning.

14th. The British Ministers sent us the Times of the 10th and 11th, containing the official accounts of the taking of Machias and other towns in Passamaquoddy Bay, and the destruction of the frigate Adams by the expedition from Halifax, under Sir T. C. Sherbrooke, together with the failure of our attempt to take Michillimackinac, and the taking of Plattsburg by the British Canadian Army.   At noon we met in Mr. Clay's chamber and signed our answer to the fourth note from the British Plenipotentiaries, which Mr. Hughes immediately took to them.   Mr. Clay, who was determined to foresee no public misfortune in our affairs, bears them with less temper, now they have come, than any other of us.   He rails at commerce and the people of Massachusetts, and tells what wonders the people of Kentucky would do if they should be attacked.

15th. At two o'clock we had the meeting of the mission. The instructions from the Secretary of State to Mr. Shaler were produced, and they direct him to go to the place wherever a Congress might be held for a general peace, and communicate any useful information that he could obtain there to the joint mission and to the Government.   I had never seen nor heard of these instructions before.   Mr. Russell had told me that was the object of Shaler's appointment, and Mr. Clay and Mr. Russell had given him a power at Gottenburg, which I had seen. But I knew nothing of his instructions.   I immediately said I was ready to agree to anything which my colleagues should think advisable in the case.   Mr. Clay proposed that Mr. Shaler should be dispatched to Vienna, to give us, and the Government, and Mr. Crawford, information concerning the proceedings of the Congress.   He added that though he still thought a communication to the Emperor of Russia might be proper, yet since the last note we received from the British Plenipotentiaries and our answer, it might as well be postponed, or at least must be somewhat altered.   Mr. Gallatin advised that if Shaler went, he should first go to Paris, and there get a passport from Mr. Crawford, which would be less likely to excite suspicion or remark than if he should go directly from this place.   Thus the matter rests for the present.

16th. Mr. Bayard had yesterday a visit from Lord Gambier, who told him they had sent our note, on the same evening they had received it, for England.   It will of course be ten days from that time before we receive the reply.   Mr. Gallatin, with his son, Mr. Bayard, and Mr. Hughes, intend taking this interval of leisure for an excursion to Antwerp, and perhaps to Brussels.

18th. Wrote to my wife, and a short letter to Mr. Crawford.

The copying was of course suspended, and from breakfast-time the day was engrossed by a multitude of objects. The papers for Mr. Boyd were not finished, and he could not go this day. Mr. Eli was going with him in his chaise to Paris. Mr. Shaler rather roughly prevailed on Mr. Eli to resign his seat to him, much to the dissatisfaction of Mr. Boyd, and, after all, we this day decided in meeting that Shaler should not go, at least for the present. It became clear at last that if he went we must give him a written authority, or at least an approbation to go, and that we must furnish him with money or a credit. He asked for a thousand dollars. I told him that if I had seen his instructions I should have proposed to send him to Vienna a month ago. He said that on our first arrival here he had given Mr. Russell his instructions, requesting him to show them to me ; that Mr. Russell, some time afterwards, had returned them to him and told him that he had shown them to me. This was a mistake ; I never saw them until last Saturday. I repeated to Mr. Russell, at our meeting this day, Shaler's statement. Mr. Russell said Shaler had told him the same thing ; that he had no recollection of having shown me Shaler's instructions, but Shaler had reminded him that on returning them to him, and being asked by him whether I had made any remarks upon them, he told Shaler I had made some question how far his appointment was constitutional. I told Mr. Russell that I believed I had made this remark, but it was on seeing the letter from the Secretary of State to the joint mission, attaching Shaler to it as a *contingency ;* and not upon his instructions, which I never saw. At length Mr. Russell expressed some doubts as to the expediency of Shaler's going to Vienna, and said he had lately remarked certain indiscretions of vanity in him which showed he was not well qualified for such a mission, and might do more harm than good in it. For example, he had yesterday said to him, in the hearing of Stillwell, Jacob Barker's agent for the Chauncey, that he thought our last note to the British Plenipotentiaries was a *sneaking* note ; and sitting at dinner, Stillwell, Bates, and Connell being present, Shaler had taken from his pocket his instructions from the Secretary of State, and handed them over to Mr. Russell, putting his finger on a certain part of the paper, and saying, " There is the instruction that you must give me."

Mr. Bayard immediately said that the day before yesterday Shaler spoke to him, in the hearing of Stillwell, about the contents of the last note from the British Plenipotentiaries to us, as freely as if Stillwell had been a member of the mission; had told him what an able note it was, and said, when he had read it, he trembled for fear we should not be able to answer it.

Mr. Clay thought but little of all this. He said Stillwell was such a stupid fellow, Shaler might say much more in his hearing without hazarding anything. And Shaler had first told him of the young Americans who were here upon a stipend from English commercial houses to discover and report news from the negotiation. Mr. Clay required that the vote should be taken whether Shaler should, or should not, go to Vienna.

I asked him for his vote first. He said it was for Mr. Bayard to answer first. I asked Bayard, who answered, *No.* Mr. Russell and Mr. Gallatin answered the same. Mr. Clay then declined answering at all, but said he had not changed his opinion. I can now comprehend why the responsibility of sending Shaler to Vienna was to have been put upon me alone, and why Shaler was to have been fastened upon me as the man, without any one of my colleagues appearing to have recommended him to me. Shaler came in just as the vote had been taken, and all my colleagues, in a few minutes, successively left the room. I was left to inform him of the change of our views, and that the mission to Vienna was at least to be postponed. He had been sent by Mr. Hughes to receive our directions, but did not appear dissatisfied at the alteration of our purpose. He said he himself thought it was too late, and had yesterday said so to Mr. Russell. Stillwell sent us a letter, stating that he placed the Chauncey at our disposal, though it was contrary to his instructions from his owner to send her home

As we were sitting at the dinner-table this evening, an Italian, named Ginnasi, an acquaintance of Mr. Gallatin's, an antiquarian and virtuoso, who has a project of settling a State of Italians in America, came to visit him. Mr. Gallatin, a few minutes after, left the room; the other gentlemen did the same; and I was left to keep company with Mr. Ginnasi, who detained me more than an hour. In the mean time, Mr. Clay gave me a letter to the mission just received from Mr. Crawford, partly in cipher. On deciphering it, I found it contained a proposition upon which he requested us to deliberate and give him our opinion. I was very desirous to answer the letter by Mr. Boyd. I took it first to Mr. Gallatin, and afterwards to Mr. Russell at his lodgings; the other gentlemen could not be found. I sent word to them, and agreed with Messrs. Russell and Gallatin that we should have a meeting at my chamber at nine o'clock to-morrow morning. I had some conversation with Mr. Russell, who read me a letter he was writing to Mr. Crawford, and who now told me he was much dissatisfied with our last note to the British Plenipotentiaries. I reminded him that I had not only declared myself dissatisfied with it, but had offered another draft, and of a totally different character. I asked him why he had not supported me. He said he had expected Mr. Clay would have been the most stubborn of us all upon the point relative to the Indians, and, finding him give way, and being himself the youngest member of the mission, and being from a State that cared nothing about Indian affairs, he had not thought it was his business to be more stiff about it than others. I told him of the long conversation I had with Bayard, and how powerfully Bayard had operated upon me in it. I added that he had previously had a similar conversation with Clay, and I believed had worked still more forcibly upon him. Russell said that Bayard always talked about keeping a high tone, but when it came to the point he was always on the conceding side.

19th. At nine this morning we had the meeting of the mission, to deliberate upon Mr. Crawford's proposition. It was important, and there was a diversity of opinion relating to it. But Mr. Gallatin, and his son, and Mr. Bayard, with Mr. Hughes, were going upon an excursion to Antwerp, and perhaps to Bergen op Zoom, and to Brussels; they could not delay their journey, and we had not time to discuss the subject. I barely prevailed upon them to agree to a short and indecisive answer to Mr. Crawford, to be sent by Mr. Boyd, promising a more positive answer hereafter.

22d. We received this day the fifth note from the British Plenipotentiaries. It has the same dilatory and insidious character as their preceding notes, but is shorter.

23d. We had a meeting of the mission at two o'clock, to consider the note yesterday received from the British Plenipotentiaries. Mr. Bayard was not present. Mr. Gallatin had made a draft of a note in reply, upon which some remarks were made and some alterations suggested. Mr. Clay and Mr. Russell proposed to send Mr. Shaler to Paris with a second answer to the proposal upon which Mr. Crawford consulted us, and which we answered by Mr. Boyd. I asked Mr. Gallatin what necessity there could be for sending Shaler to Paris; he said he supposed it was to get rid of him.

24th. We had a meeting of the mission this morning in my chamber, at which Mr. Gallatin's draft of the answer to the last note from the British Plenipotentiaries was considered, with some alterations proposed by Mr. Bayard and Mr. Clay. It was finally agreed to as altered, then copied fair by Mr. Hughes, signed by us, and taken by him to the British Commissioners. It was determined to dispatch Mr. Shaler to Paris with copies of the last British note and of our answer, and a letter to Mr. Crawford, confirming the advice we gave him last week. I proposed to wait until we should receive the passport for the Transit, when there will be a real occasion to dispatch a special messenger to Paris; and I objected to incurring the expense of sending Shaler now. My opinion was overruled, and I was charged to draft a letter to Mr. Crawford, and also a dispatch to the Secretary of State, to enclose copies of the notes which have passed between the British Plenipotentiaries and us. Mr. Hughes returned with the Times newspapers to the 21st, containing numerous articles of American news—Armstrong's assignment of reasons for retiring from the War Department, the President's Proclamation of 1st September on the taking of Washington, the capitulation of Alexandria, and the incendiary declaration of Admiral Cochrane. We had them all read while at dinner.

26th. Shaler went off for Paris yesterday, and Mr. Russell takes his lodgings. We met merely to compare and sign papers. I drafted two more short letters to the Secretary of State, and a passport for Connell. Took them to all the members of the mission—to Mr. Clay and Mr. Russell at their lodgings, and to Mr. Hughes at his, to be copied. We all dined with the British Plenipotentiaries. No other company there than ourselves and Mr. Van Aken. It was a dull dinner. Lord Gambier complained of the incendiaries who were constantly employed in the English newspapers, blowing the flames of war. He spoke also of the sort of warfare now carried on between some of the London and Paris papers. He asked me if we had made any acquaintances here. I said we had. He replied that they knew nobody but the Intendant's family. We came away almost immediately after dinner, to attend the meeting of the Society of Fine Arts and of Letters. Mr. Gallatin, Mr. Bayard, and myself had been made honorary members of this Society. Mr. Clay, Mr. Russell, and Mr. Hughes had received the same compliment from the Society of Agriculture and Botany. The two Societies had drawn our names by lots, three and three. But this, as St. Luke's day, was the celebration only of the first Society, and the invitations were only to Mr. Gallatin, Mr. Bayard, and me. Mr. Meulemeester, by mistake, had told Mr. Gallatin that they were generally for us all. Mr. Russell would not go. Mr. Clay attended, and was mortified on discovering the mistake. Almost all the other Americans in the city were there by invitations. The assembly consisted of about one hundred persons, principally artists. When we went in, Mr. Cornelissen, the Secretary, was reading a discourse on the fine arts, especially painting. A discourse was afterwards read by Mr. Van Huffel, the President—a painter —on the installation of the portraits of the Intendant and Mayor, both of whom were present. Mr. Gallatin, Mr. Bayard, and myself inscribed our names in the registers of the Society. Several pieces of music were performed by a band consisting of members of the Society. About ten o'clock we sat down to supper, about one hundred persons. I was seated between the Intendant and his cousin, the Count De la Faille. There were many toasts drunk, and, among others, one of " Success to the pacific labors of the American negotiators." I gave, in return, " Prosperity to the City of Ghent, and to the Society of Fine Arts and of Letters within its walls. May its artists always worthily support the glory of the country of Rubens !"

27th. Our mission meeting was merely to sign and make up the remaining papers and dispatches. But Mr. Clay entered a formal complaint about his having been misled in attending the meeting of the Society last evening, and about the non-communication of invitations to all the mission, when addressed to one. Mr. Gallatin had received a note from the Intendant for us all to dine with him to-day, but had forgotten to mention it to Mr. Russell. Mr. Gallatin explained that Mr. Clay's awkward situation last evening was owing to Mr. Meulemeester's mistake in telling him that the invitation to the meeting and supper of the Society was for all. Clay had some reason to be mortified, particularly as Mr. Cornelissen at the supper-table, last evening, had made a speech to explain how it came that Messrs. Clay, Russell, and Hughes had been made honorary members, not of that Society, but of the other. But Russell appeared to think his dignity most offended. He refused to go to-day to the Intendant's dinner, because there had not been a special invitation addressed by name to himself, and he seems to have been nettled at his aggregation with the Secretary, Hughes, to the Agricultural and Botanical Society, instead of that of the Fine Arts and of Letters. He said if the people of Ghent meant to show us civility they should treat us equally ; that he assumed for his part no superiority, and would not admit of any. Mr. Bayard, by way of disclaiming any assumption of superiority, said that any such pretension would be ridiculous, to which Russell rather sulkily replied, " Yes, it would be very ridiculous." Mr. Gallatin came off from this *bourrasque* coolly and without loss of temper. Fortunately, it had no bearing upon me, and I suffered it to pass by. While we harmonize upon essential objects, it would be a pity to dissent upon trifles. We all dined at the Intendant's, except Mr. Russell, and Todd, who was engaged in packing up for Mr. Connell. Prince d'Aremberg and some other general officers were there. We stayed the evening, when there was an additional party of ladies. Mr. Clay and myself played whist with the Intendant's lady and Madame de Crombrugge. The play was too low for Mr. Clay, who soon grew weary and impatient.

29th. At two o'clock we had a meeting of the mission. Mr. Russell was not present. We had some further desultory conversation concerning the drawing up a project of a treaty. Mr. Gallatin had made some minutes, upon which we had much loose conversation. I urged the propriety of making out at once the project in the form of a treaty, both for the sake of saving time and of being fully prepared to deliver it immediately to the British Plenipotentiaries whenever they shall consent to the exchange of projects. This was at last agreed to. Mr. Gallatin undertook to draw up the articles respecting the boundaries and Indians, and I promised to prepare those respecting impressment, blockade, and indemnities.

30th. I began making a draft for the project of a treaty. Mr. Gallatin was employed in the same manner. At two o'clock we had a meeting of the mission, but Mr. Clay was not present until the meeting was over, and Mr. Russell not at all. We looked over the articles drawn by Mr. Gallatin and myself, which being unfinished, we agreed to meet every day, at two o'clock, until the whole project shall be prepared. Mr. Gallatin proposes to renew the two articles of the Treaty of Peace of 1783, the stipulation for our right to fish, and dry and cure fish, within the waters of the British jurisdiction, and the right of the British to navigate the Mississippi. To this last article, however, Mr. Clay makes strong objections. He is willing to leave the matter of the fisheries as a nest-egg for another war, but to make the peace without saying anything about it; which, after the notice the British have given us, will be in fact an abandonment of our right. Mr. Clay considers this fishery as an object of trifling amount; and that a renewal of the right of the British to navigate the Mississippi would be giving them a privilege far more important than that we should secure in return. And as he finds, as yet, no member of the mission but himself taking this ground, he grows earnest in defence of it. He now recurs to our instructions forbidding us to permit our right to the fisheries to be brought into discussion. But I observed to him that those instructions were drawn without a knowledge of the question as it now stands. This is a point upon which Mr. Clay will evidently have great reluctance in assenting to what will, I believe, be found necessary.

31st. All the morning I was preparing the draft of an article for the project of a treaty, on the subject of indemnities. I was much embarrassed by not being able to find one of the papers referred to in our instructions. I, however, finally got the article ready. At two o'clock we had the meeting of the mission. We had much conversation upon the delays of the British Government in furnishing us passports for dispatch-vessels. Mr. Clay was for making a strong remonstrance on the subject, and for breaking off the negotiation upon that point if they did not give us satisfaction. As I was beginning to read my draft of articles for the project of a treaty, a packet was brought to us from the British Plenipotentiaries, together with the Times newspapers to the 28th inclusive. The dispatch contained their sixth note, dilatory and evasive as heretofore, and also a short unsigned note, with an Admiralty passport for the Transit. It was agreed to send immediately Mr. Todd with a copy of this note to Ostend, to reach Mr. Connell before the sailing of the Chauncey. He went away immediately after dinner. We had little deliberation, and came to no result upon the contents of the sixth note, for we all fell to reading the newspapers until dinner-time. Mr. Clay is losing his temper and growing peevish and fractious. I, too, must not forget to keep a constant guard upon my temper, for the time is evidently approaching when it will be wanted.

Day. My usual rising hour is between five and six in the morning, but I find myself inclining too much to relax from these hours of industry, and to run later into the evening than I have been accustomed these three years. The morning hour very generally corresponds with the evening hour, and the time before breakfast is invariably that upon which I can most depend. I light my candle and my fire immediately on rising, and now read and write about an hour by candle-light every morning. On Tuesdays and Fridays I write to my wife, which employs me until breakfast-time, nine o'clock, and commonly an hour or two afterwards. Our usual hour for the meeting of the mission is two P.M. We have occasional extraordinary meetings at other hours. The ordinary meeting almost always lasts till four, when we dine. If finished sooner, I now take a short walk in the interval. We dine at four, and usually sit at table until six or seven. About once a week I go to the theatre, which finishes between ten and eleven. Sometimes we pass the evening in company, and at others I walk on the Place d'Armes and call to see Mrs. Smith. I seldom read or write after dark, and am in bed sometimes before ten, and almost always by eleven. I am hitherto not at all embarrassed with the length of the evenings, and seldom close them so soon as I would choose. My chief fault now is a great relaxation of my customary exercise. This must be corrected.

November 1st. I copied the note yesterday received from the British Plenipotentiaries. Mr. Gallatin brought me a copy of the paper referred to in our instructions, and which I had been yesterday unable to find. At two o'clock we had the meeting of the mission, and further considered the note yesterday received. Mr. Clay and Mr. Russell were for replying that we would proceed no further unless the British Plenipotentiaries would explicitly agree to our proposed basis of a mutual restoration of territory taken during the war. It was, however, determined to give in reply a statement of all our points. A second question then arose, whether the statement should be at large in a note, or in the formal draft of a treaty. We finally concluded upon the latter, and the articles drawn by Mr. Gallatin and myself were taken by Mr. Russell to be examined by him, and successively by the other gentlemen. There was some further conversation upon the subject of the fisheries, and navigation of the Mississippi.

Mr. Clay renewed his objections against any article allowing the latter to the British. He made it a question whether we could agree to such an article, on the principle that, since Louisiana had become a State, it was a part of her sovereignty which the United States could not grant, and that in the law of Congress authorizing Louisiana to form a Constitution, he had thought it necessary, on the same principle, to introduce a section reserving the right of the people of Kentucky to navigate the river.

Mr. Gallatin answered that the formation of Louisiana into a State was subject to this privilege of the British, which had been stipulated in the Treaties of 1783 and 1794.

Mr. Clay replied that if they had been released from it by the war, he saw no reason for renewing it upon them by treaty now. He considered it as a privilege much too important to be conceded for the mere liberty of drying fish upon a desert. We were possessed of no facts to show us the value of this—he did not know what it was worth; but the Mississippi was destined to form a most important part of the interests of the American Union. Every day was developing more and more its importance. The British could have no more right to the navigation of it than to that of any other river exclusively within our jurisdiction—not so much as we have to navigate the St. Lawrence. I have hitherto taken no part in this discussion, and wish to postpone it as long as possible.

3d. We examined the drafts of articles by Mr. Gallatin and myself, as amended by the other gentlemen, and agreed to meet again at eleven o'clock to-morrow morning.

4th. We had the meeting of the mission at eleven, and discussed all the articles as drafted. Many alterations and amendments were agreed to. Mr. Clay, of all the members, had alone been urgent to present an article stipulating the abolition of the practice of impressment. I had proposed the article offered by our instructions of June 25th, which is, to refer the whole question to Commissioners after the peace. Mr. Clay was so urgent to present previously an article to settle the contest, that I acquiesced in his wishes. Mr. Bayard and Mr. Gallatin were against proposing it. Mr. Russell declined voting, until I declared myself with Mr. Clay, in favor of proposing Mr. Clay's article, and then Mr. Russell decided to propose it. But the great difficulty was with regard to the fisheries. Mr. Gallatin's draft proposed the renewal of the right of fishing, and drying fish, within the British jurisdiction, together with the right of the British to navigate the Mississippi, both taken from the Peace of 1783. I was in favor of this. Mr. Clay has an insuperable objection to the renewal of the right to the British of navigating the Mississippi. I then declared myself prepared either to propose Mr. Gallatin's article, or to take the ground that the whole right to the fisheries was recognized as a part of our national independence, that it could not be abrogated by the war, and needed no stipulation for its renewal. Mr. Gallatin argued that, on the same principle, the British right to navigate the Mississippi would also be established, without needing to be renewed. Mr. Clay was averse to either of the courses proposed, and said that, after all, if the British Plenipotentiaries should insist upon this point, we should all finally sign the treaty, without the provision respecting the fishery. Mr. Russell expressed some doubt whether he would sign without it, and I explicitly declared that I would not, without further instructions; I could not say that I would, with them.

5th. We had a meeting of the mission at eleven. Discussed further, and agreed upon, the draft of the articles to be proposed for the treaty. Mr. Clay's article respecting impressments was adopted. That concerning the fisheries and the navigation of the Mississippi, as drawn by Mr. Gallatin, was further debated, and the vote taken upon it. Mr. Clay and Mr: Russell voted against it; Mr. Bayard, Mr. Gallatin, and myself, for proposing it. After the vote was taken, Mr. Clay said that he should not sign the communication by which the proposal would be made.

7th. We had the meeting of the mission between eleven and twelve o'clock at my chamber. Mr. Clay proposed a paragraph for the note to be sent to the British Plenipotentiaries, as a substitute instead of the article respecting the fisheries and the navigation of the Mississippi which had passed by vote on Saturday. Mr. Clay said that in declaring at that time that he should not sign the note accompanying the project if it included Mr. Gallatin's article, he had not intended that it should in any manner affect the minds of any of us. If the article should be proposed and accepted, and a treaty otherwise not objectionable should be obtainable, he might perhaps ultimately accede to it; but the object was in his view so important that he could not reconcile it to himself to agree in making the proposal.

I had drawn the sketch of an article placing both the points precisely in their condition at the commencement of the war; to which Mr. Gallatin objected that it offered the British more than his draft, because it entitled them to the provision in the Treaty of 1794.

Mr. Clay preferred it to Mr. Gallatin's draft, because it would leave in all its force all the operation of our acquisition of Louisiana, as far as it impairs the British right of navigating the Mississippi, but he still would not agree to it. His proposed paragraph took the ground which I had originally suggested, that all the fishery rights formed a part of the recognition of our independence, and as such were by our instructions excluded from discussion.

I felt I should have preferred the proposal of Mr. Gallatin's article, as placing the subject out of controversy, but that, as we could not be unanimous for that, I was willing to take Mr. Clay's paragraph, by which we should reserve all our rights, and at the same time execute our instructions.

Mr. Gallatin apprehended that the British Plenipotentiaries might on that point not reply to us at all, and then if the peace should be made without an article renewing the fishing rights now contested by them, that the British Government would consider us as notified that the rights are at an end, and forcibly deprive our people of them.

I was very confident that the British Plenipotentiaries would reply to us, and not leave the subject at this stage without further notice; and if they persevered in contending that the rights were abrogated, we might ultimately refuse to sign the treaty on that ground.

Mr. Gallatin said his difficulty was, that he thought the British had in this case the argument with them, and that the treaty liberty of fishing and drying fish within their jurisdiction was abrogated by the war.

Mr. Bayard said that rather than differ among ourselves he would agree to substitute Mr. Clay's paragraph instead of the proposed article; and this was ultimately assented to by us all.

We then read over the articles as hitherto drawn up and corrected, and amended·them. Mr. Gallatin and myself are to
prepare for to-morrow the observations on the several articles
to be presented with the draft of the treaty.

8th. Employed the residue of the morning in making the
sketch of observations upon the articles of the treaty. We had
the meeting of the mission at two o'clock, but Mr. Bayard did
not come in till after three. Mr. Gallatin's draft of remarks
on the proposed articles, and mine, were both read. His were
upon all the articles; mine were confined to those that I had
originally drawn up. They were taken to be examined by the
other gentlemen before the meeting of to-morrow.

9th. At two we had the mission meeting. The two drafts of
a note had been examined by Mr. Bayard and Mr. Clay; they
had been sent to Mr. Russell at his lodgings, but he had been
absent, and did not receive them. It was agreed to have
another meeting after the theatre this evening, and Mr. Gallatin and myself compared the articles of the projet which Mr.
Hughes had ready. We gave him also the others to be copied.
About ten at night the play was over, and I attended the meeting of the mission; but Mr. Russell was not present, and we
adjourned to meet at eleven to-morrow morning. The sketches
for the note, with the amendments of Messieurs Bayard, Clay,
and Russell, were given to me, to be further revised by me and
by Mr. Gallatin to-morrow before the meeting.

10th. VI. 30. A second day belated. On examining the drafts
for the note with the amendments of Messrs. Clay, Bayard,
and Russell, I found more than three-fourths of what I had
written erased. There was only one paragraph to which I
attached importance, but that was struck out with the rest. It
was the proposal to conclude the peace on the footing of the
state before the war, applied to all the subjects of dispute between the two countries, leaving all the rest for future and
pacific negotiation. I abandoned everything else that was
objected to in my draft, but wrote over that paragraph again, to
propose its insertion in the note. I had gone through my
examination of the papers at breakfast-time, and Mr. Gallatin
took them. At eleven o'clock we had the meeting of the mis-

sion. Everything in the note, as amended, was agreed to without difficulty, excepting my proposed paragraph. Mr. Clay objected strongly against it, because we are forbidden by our instructions from renewing the article of the Treaty of 1794, allowing the British to trade with our Indians. Mr. Gallatin, who strenuously supported my proposition, thought it did not necessarily include the renewal of that article of the Treaty of 1794, because it only offers the state before the war with regard to the objects in dispute. The Indian trade never had been in dispute. He admitted, however, that if the British Government should accept the principle and propose the renewal of the treaties, we could not after this offer refuse it.

I stated in candor that I considered my proposal as going that full length; that I was aware it would be a departure from our instructions as prepared in April, 1813. But the Government, for the purpose of obtaining peace, had revoked our instructions of that date upon a point much more important in its estimation, the very object of the war; and I have no doubt would have revoked them on the other point, had it occurred to them that they would prove an obstacle to the conclusion of peace. I felt so sure that they would now gladly take the state before the war as the general basis of the peace, that I was prepared to take on me the responsibility of trespassing upon their instructions thus far. Not only so, but I would at this moment cheerfully give my life for a peace on this basis. If peace was possible, it would be on no other. I had, indeed, no hope that the proposal would be accepted. But on the rupture, it would make the strongest case possible in our favor, for the world both in Europe and America. It would put the continuance of the war entirely at the door of England, and force out her objects in continuing it.

Mr. Clay then said, if the proposal was to be made at all, now was not the time for making it. If our projet should be rejected, and we should hereafter find peace unattainable upon other terms, we might offer it as a last resource; but that it was not proper at present. As to the Indians, he had gone as far in concession upon that subject as was possible; he would concede no more; and if we wanted peace, Great Britain wanted it quite as much.   He saw no reason to believe that she would continue the war merely for the Indian trade.

I said it was for the British Government, not for me, to consider how far peace might be necessary for them. I believed they were not sufficiently convinced of its necessity. If my proposal was to be made at all, now was precisely the best time for making it, because it would take off whatever there might appear to be of exorbitancy in our demands, and would not, as it might hereafter, have the appearance of shrinking from our own grounds.   Mr. Gallatin dwelt upon the same argument, and urged that several of our articles very much needed some such softener.

Mr. Bayard thought now the most favorable time for making the proposal, as the state of the war is now much more favorable to us than we have reason to expect it will be in one or two months.

Mr. Russell wavered; he asked how the proposal offered more than the projet itself.

I told him that the projet offered all the knots of the negotiation for solution now; and the proposal was to make peace first, and leave them to be solved hereafter.

Mr. Clay finally said that he would agree to the insertion of my proposal in the note, but reserving to himself the right of refusing to sign the treaty if the offer should be accepted and the principle extended beyond his approbation.

The draft was then taken by Mr. Hughes to be copied out fair, and Mr. Gallatin, Mr. Russell, and myself remained to compare the residue of the articles as they were prepared.   A concluding article, providing for the ratifications and their exchange, was prepared by Mr. Gallatin and me; after which I went out and walked about an hour.   Mr. Hughes was prepared with the note at his rooms, at the back of our house.   I took the projet to him, and he copied on it the concluding article.   They were then brought back to our dining-room, and we signed the note—Mr. Clay still manifesting signs of reluctance. He objected to the formal concluding article, and thought it ridiculous, and he recurred again to the paragraph proposing the state before the war as the general basis of the treaty.   He said the British Plenipotentiaries would laugh at us for it. They would say, Ay, ay! pretty fellows you, to think of getting out of the war as well as you got into it!

I think it very probable this commentary will be made on our proposal; but what would be the commentary on our refusing peace on those terms? Mr. Russell dined with us about five o'clock, and immediately after dinner Mr. Hughes took our note and projet to the British Plenipotentiaries.

24th. At eight in the evening we went to the first redoute at the Hôtel de Ville. The company was not very numerous. We met there the British Plenipotentiaries. I told Lord Gambier of the publication by our Government of our dispatches and instructions. He expressed some astonishment that they should have been published before the negotiation was ended.

I told him that the nature of our Government and the character of the war had made it absolutely necessary, and that the American Government, from the nature of the propositions made in the first British note to us, had every reason to suppose the negotiation was ended. We had, at the time when that note was sent to us, been fully convinced that it would have been ended in a very few days. His Lordship would recollect that his own impressions, and those of his colleagues, had been the same. I had entertained then not the least expectation of being yet here on the first of September, but I hoped we were now much nearer to terms upon which we could agree.

He said there was but one article upon which he thought there would be difficulty, and that was the question as to the cession of territory. I told him I hoped we should not hear a word more of that.

He said they had received no reply from England to our last note, which they had immediately forwarded, but they expected a messenger to-morrow.

While we were at the redoute, Mr. Gallatin told me that our landlord, Mr. Ducobie, had sent him word that Mr. Shaler had arrived from Paris with dispatches for us. At ten o'clock we came home, and sent immediately to Mr. Shaler for the dispatches. Mr. Clay and Mr. Russell had walked there from the redoute, and opened them. They were sent to us by Mr. Gallatin's black servant, Peter, and were open. Mr. Shaler sent us word that he would call upon us to-morrow morning. There were three dispatches from the Secretary of State, one from the new Secretary of the Treasury, Mr. Dallas, and letters from Mr. Crawford. The last dispatch from the Secretary of State is dated 19th October, after the receipt of ours by the John Adams. It declares the President's entire approbation of our determination to reject the first proposals of the British Government, and it expressly authorizes us, if the negotiation should not be broken off, to conclude the peace on the basis of the status ante bellum—precisely the offer which we have made in our last note, and of which I found it so difficult to obtain the insertion.

27th. About eleven in the morning, Mr. Gallatin came into my chamber, with a note received from the British Plenipotentiaries. They have sent us back with this note the projet of a treaty which we had sent them, with marginal notes and alterations proposed by them. They have rejected all the articles we had proposed on impressment, blockade, indemnities, amnesty, and Indians. They have definitively abandoned the Indian boundary, the exclusive military possession of the Lakes, and the uti possidetis; but with a protestation that they will not be bound to adhere to these terms hereafter, if the peace should not be made now. Within an hour after receiving these papers we had a meeting of the mission at my chamber, when the note and the alterations to our projet proposed by the British Plenipotentiaries were read, and we had some desultory conversation upon the subject. All the difficulties to the conclusion of a peace appear to be now so nearly removed, that my colleagues all considered it as certain. I think it myself probable. But unless we take it precisely as it is now offered, to which I strongly incline, I distrust so much the intentions of the British Government, that I still consider the conclusion as doubtful and precarious.

It was agreed that we should meet at eleven o'clock to-morrow morning, and in the mean time that the note and projet should be taken successively by each of us, to make minutes for the reply to it. Mr. Gallatin suggested the propriety of asking a conference, to which I expressed some objection, but without insisting upon it. Mr. Bayard and Mr. Clay took the note and projet, and returned it to me with their minutes just before dinner. Mr. Gallatin took it this evening, with the promise to send it to me at six o'clock to-morrow morning.

28th. Mr. Gallatin's servant, Peter, brought me this morning, as the clock struck six, the British note and projet, with Mr. Gallatin's minutes upon them. I kept them until nine, made my own minutes upon them, and then sent all the papers, excepting my own minutes, which were of no importance, to Mr. Russell. As Mr. Gallatin understands the British projet, there are still some things in it so objectionable that they ought on no consideration to be admitted. At eleven o'clock we met, and continued in session until past four, when we adjourned to meet again at eleven to-morrow morning. Our principal discussion was on an article proposed by the British Government as a substitute for the eighth of our projet. And they have added a clause securing to them the navigation of the Mississippi, and access to it with their goods and merchandise through our territories.

To this part of the article Mr. Clay positively objected. Mr. Gallatin proposed to agree to it, proposing an article to secure our right of fishing and curing fish within the British jurisdiction. Mr. Clay lost his temper, as he generally does whenever this right of the British to navigate the Mississippi is discussed. He was utterly averse to admitting it as an equivalent for a stipulation securing the contested part of the fisheries. He said the more he heard of this the more convinced he was that it was of little or no value. He should be glad to get it if he could, but he was sure the British would not ultimately grant it. That the navigation of the Mississippi, on the other hand, was an object of immense importance, and he could see no sort of reason for granting it as an equivalent for the fisheries. Mr. Gallatin said that the fisheries were of great importance in the sentiment of the eastern section of the Union; that if we should sign a peace without securing them to the full extent in which they were enjoyed before the war, and especially if we should abandon any part of the territory, it would give a handle to the party there, now pushing for a separation from the Union and for a New England Confederacy, to say that the interests of New England were sacrificed, and to pretend that by a separate confederacy they could obtain what is refused to us.

Mr. Clay said that there was no use in attempting to conciliate people who never would be conciliated; that it was too much the practice of our Government to sacrifice the interests of its best friends for those of its bitterest enemies; that there might be a party for separation at some future day in the Western States, too.

I observed to him that he was now speaking under the impulse of passion, and that on such occasions I would wish not to answer anything; that assuredly the Government would be reproached, and the greatest advantage would be taken by the party opposed to it, if any of the rights of the Eastern States should be sacrificed by the peace; that the loss of any part of the fisheries would be a subject of triumph and exultation, both to the enemy and to those among us who had been opposed to the war; that if I should consent to give up even Moose Island, where there was a town which had been for many years regularly represented in the Legislature of the State of Massachusetts, I should be ashamed to show my face among my countrymen; that as to the British right of navigating the Mississippi, I considered it as nothing, considered as a grant from us. It was secured to them by the Peace of 1783, they had enjoyed it at the commencement of the war, it had never been injurious in the slightest degree to our own people, and it appeared to me that the British claim to it was just and equitable. The boundary fixed by the Peace of 1783 was a line due west from the Lake of the Woods to the Mississippi, and the navigation of the river was stipulated for both nations. It has been since that time discovered that a line due west from the Lake of the Woods will not touch the Mississippi, but goes north of it. The boundary, therefore, is annulled by the fact. Two things were contemplated by both parties in that compact—one, that the line should run west from the Lake of the Woods; the other, that it should touch the Mississippi. In attempting now to supply the defect, we ask for the line due west, and the British ask for the shortest line to the Mississippi. Both demands stand upon the same grounds—the intention of both parties at the Peace of 1783. If we grant the British demand, they touch the river and have a clear right to its navigation. If they grant our demand, they do not touch the river; but in conceding the territory they have a fair and substantial motive for reserving the right of navigating the river. I was not aware of any solid answer to this argument. I believed the right to this navigation to be a very useless thing to the British, especially after they have abandoned all pretence to any territorial possessions upon the river. But the national pride and honor were interested in it. The Government could not make a peace which would abandon it. They had the same reasons for insisting upon it that we had for insisting on the fisheries and the entire restoration of territory.

Mr. Clay said that by the British article now proposed they demanded not only the navigation of the river, but access to it through our territories generally, from any part of their dominions and by any road, and without any guard, even for the collection of our duties; that this might be an advantage to the people of Kentucky, for it was the shortest way to them for all imported merchandise. Goods could in that manner be sent by the St. Lawrence River from Europe to his house with a land carriage of not more than fourteen miles. But it would give the British access to our country in a dangerous and pernicious manner. It would give them the trade with the Indians in its full extent, and enable them to use all the influence over those savages which had already done us so much harm.

I observed that with regard to the trade with the Indians, I had no doubt the British Government meant and understood that to be already conceded in the article to which we had agreed; that I understood it so myself; that by restoring to the Indians all the rights they had in 1811, we had restored to them the right of trading with the British, and of having the British traders go among them for the purposes of trade; that if there could at any time have been a doubt that such would be its operation, the explanatory article after Mr. Jay's treaty and the Greenville Indian Treaty would remove it. How could we possibly be said to restore to the Indians the right of trade, if we debarred those who carried it on from trading with them? As to the duties, undoubtedly provision must be made for collecting them, and no doubt that would be agreed to.

Mr. Gallatin declared himself of the same opinion with me, as to the grant of the mere right of the navigation of the Mississippi; but he asked me why I had then hesitated so much about offering it as an equivalent for the fisheries.

Mr. Clay, on the other hand, thought there would be a gross inconsistency in asking a specific stipulation for the fisheries, after the ground we had taken, that no article was necessary to secure us in the enjoyment of them.

I said that my reluctance at granting the navigation of the Mississippi arose merely from the extreme interest that Mr. Clay and the Western people attached to it; that as to the ground we had taken upon the fisheries, I believed it firm and solid. I had put my name to it, and considered myself as responsible for it. But when some of my colleagues, who had also put their names to it, told me, in this chamber, among ourselves, that they thought the ground untenable, and that there was nothing in our principle, I found it necessary to mistrust my own judgment, particularly after the enemy had given us notice that they meant to deprive us of the fisheries in part, unless a new stipulation should secure them. If our principle was good for the fisheries on our part, it was good to the British for the navigation of the Mississippi. The Plenipotentiaries had made no reply to our remarks concerning the fisheries. That silence might be taken for acquiescence, and if there was nothing more I would rest it upon that. But they asked for a new stipulation of their right to navigate the Mississippi. This implied their opinion that they had lost the right as agreed to in the Treaty of 1783. It became necessary, therefore, for us to ask a similar stipulation for the fisheries within their jurisdiction; but I would not accept it even for the rights of fishing on the banks. I would not sign a treaty containing such a stipulation; for it would be a sort of admission that the right would be liable to forfeiture by every war we might have with Great Britain. I would not take, therefore, a stipulation for anything recognized in the Treaty of Peace as a right.

No more (said Mr. Gallatin) than an article acknowledging again our independence.

I said, Certainly.

Mr. Bayard thought there was a material difference between the rights secured by the Peace of 1783 to us, and the British right of navigating the Mississippi, in the same treaty. The rights recognized as belonging to us were certainly permanent, and not to be forfeited by a subsequent war. But we had nothing to grant. We recognized no new rights to the British. The Mississippi was not then ours to grant; it was held by Spain, and the aspect of the subject was entirely changed by our subsequent acquisition of Louisiana. Our argument for the fisheries might therefore be sound, and yet not apply to the British for the navigation of the Mississippi.

It became necessary to determine by a vote whether Mr. Gallatin's proposal to offer an article making the navigation an equivalent for the fisheries should be adopted, and it was determined that it should. At the meeting to-morrow he is to produce it, and the draft of a note to the British Plenipotentiaries.

29th. I had barely time to finish my letter to my wife, to go by this day's post, when the meeting of the mission began. Mr. Gallatin had prepared his draft of a note to the British Plenipotentiaries, closing with the request for a conference, and his proposed article offering the navigation of the Mississippi as an equivalent for the fisheries within the British jurisdiction. This renewed our discussion of the whole subject, but it was now on all sides good-humored. I had some doubt whether it would be perfectly safe to ask a conference, while we were so far from being agreed among ourselves. Mr. Clay said he could put the subject of the Mississippi navigation upon principles to which it was impossible we should not all agree. I said that nothing like that had been apparent from our discussion hitherto; that he certainly would not be willing that I should be the spokesman of his sentiments, and I did not think it likely that he would very accurately express mine.

He said he did not think there was so irreconcilable a differ-

ence in the structure of our minds ; and that it was remarkable
there was so exact a coincidence of views on this point between
persons at a great distance from each other as there was between Mr. Crawford and him.   Mr. Russell had received a
letter from Mr. Crawford, in which he had urged in very strong
terms objections against granting the navigation of the Mississippi as an equivalent for the fisheries, and had used the
same arguments against it as those he had adduced.

Mr. Gallatin brought us all to unison again by a joke.   He
said he perceived that Mr. Adams cared nothing at all about
the navigation of the Mississippi, and thought of nothing but
the fisheries.   Mr. Clay cared nothing at all about the fisheries,
and thought of nothing but the Mississippi.   The East was
perfectly willing to sacrifice the West, and the West was
equally ready to sacrifice the East.   Now, he was a Western
man, and would give the navigation of the river for the fisheries.
Mr. Russell was an Eastern man, and was ready to do the same.

I then told Mr. Clay that I would make a coalition with him
of the East and West.   If the British would not give us the
fisheries, I would join him in refusing to grant them the navigation of the river.

He said that the consequence of our making the offer would
be that we should lose both.

Upon the rest of Mr. Gallatin's draft there was no difference
of opinion, and little discussion.   It was admitted that if the
navigation of the river was granted, and access to it through
our territories, provision must be made for collecting the duties,
and their access must be limited to particular points of departure and a mere road.   Or if general access, like that which
they demand, should be granted, they ought to grant in return
to our people access through their territories to the St. Lawrence, and the navigation of that river.   I then suggested that
I wished to make an addition of one or two paragraphs to Mr.
Gallatin's draft of a note, the object of which would be to show
our sense of the importance of the concessions we had made,
and intimating our determination to make no cession of territory, and to sacrifice none of the rights or liberties which we
enjoyed at the commencement of the war.   There was an ad-

journment from two to three o'clock, for me to make the draft
of the additional paragraphs that I proposed. I had them
ready at the adjourned meeting. They were read and discussed
until past four, our dinner-time. It was finally concluded to
meet again to-morrow morning, at eleven, and in the mean time
that all my colleagues should successively revise my draft.

30th. I have insensibly run several days in arrears with this
journal, at a time when it has become important to keep close
to the current of time. I began therefore this morning to retrieve it. But at eleven o'clock came again the time for the
meeting of the mission, which was in my chamber. Mr. Gallatin had very much shortened, and very materially altered, my
paragraphs. Mr. Clay had brought a draft of his own. My
draft, as originally written, and as amended, and his, were all
read. Mr. Bayard was for omitting the whole. I objected to
Mr. Clay's, as having altogether departed from what I had
wished to say. Mr. Gallatin's amendments had very much
altered the character of my draft, but I acquiesced in them,
and it was concluded to admit them, and adopt my draft thus
amended as part of the note.

In waiving our claims of indemnities for losses subsequent to
the war, Mr. Gallatin thought there was one description of them
for which another effort ought to be made. It was for vessels
and property which were in English ports on the commencement of the war, and were seized without allowing them the
usual six months to depart. We had allowed the six months
for English vessels and property in our ports at the time of the
declaration; and it was agreed to send the British Plenipotentiaries a copy of that part of the statute, and ask a discussion of
the subject. I proposed also to send them a copy of the deposition we have respecting the sale by their officers in the West
Indies of negroes seduced from their masters in our Southern
States by promises of liberty. The part of our instructions
which asserts this fact has been noticed in both houses of Parliament in England. The Ministers have pledged themselves
to make strict enquiry into it, and I thought the communication of the proof furnished us by the Secretary of State might
be useful, as it would certainly become thereby public, and by

drawing the public attention to the practice might prevent its
repetition hereafter. It would probably cease when the officers
should no longer have the motive for stealing the negroes, in
the opportunity to sell them. But all my colleagues objected
against sending this paper. They said its tendency would only
be to irritate, when we should make our note as conciliatory
as possible; that the proof was weak, being only a single
deposition; that the charge as made in Mr. Monroe's instructions to us had more weight without this proof than it would
have with it.

I replied that the fact was stated to be of public notoriety;
that the deposition which we have is circumstantial upon one
particular instance, with names and dates, and that it testifies
also to the general practice; that no proof could be stronger,
so far as one witness could afford proof. It was, however,
determined not to send it. We adjourned from one o'clock
until three, while Mr. Hughes prepared the note thus agreed
to. At three we had a second meeting, and signed the note,
which Mr. Hughes immediately took to the British Plenipotentiaries. Some of the gentlemen went to the theatre and
returned. As we came home, Mr. Gallatin told me that an
answer had been received from the British Plenipotentiaries,
appointing to-morrow noon for the conference, at the Chartreux,
their own house.

Day. I rise usually between five and six, but not so regularly
as heretofore, my hour for retiring at night being more irregular. I begin the day with reading five chapters in the Bible,
and have this day finished in course the Old Testament. I
then write until nine o'clock, when I breakfast alone in my
chamber. Write again after breakfast, until we have the meeting of the mission, and when there is none, until three, afternoon. Walk an hour. We dine at four, and sit at table
usually till six. In the evening, I attend the theatre, redoute,
or concert, or pass an hour or two at Mr. and Mrs. Smith's
lodgings. Between ten and eleven I return to my chamber,
and betake myself immediately to the night's repose. There
are several particulars in my present mode of life in which there
is too much relaxation of self-discipline. I have this month

frequented too much the theatre and other public amusements; indulged too much conviviality, and taken too little exercise. The consequence is that I am growing uncomfortably corpulent, and that industry becomes irksome to me. May I be cautious not to fall into any habit of indolence or dissipation!

December 1st. At half-past ten this morning we had our meeting, previous to proceeding to the conference with the British Plenipotentiaries. Mr. Gallatin had prepared a minute of the alterations and amendments which we wish to obtain to the British projet, and an article for restoring the British rights to navigate the Mississippi, and our right to the fisheries within the British jurisdiction. This minute and article were to be left with the British Plenipotentiaries. We agreed upon the mode in which we should proceed in the conference, and at twelve o'clock went to their house. As soon as we were seated at the table, Lord Gambier said he was happy that we had now met again, and that it was with much fairer prospects of success than when we had met last; that as we had left to them the option of the place of meeting, they had proposed their own house, supposing it equally agreeable to us. We had really thought it no mark of civility in them to name their own house, nor was it even conformable to our agreement at the commencement of the negotiation, which was, that we should meet alternately at the houses of each other. Our last conference had been at their house, and, regularly, this should have been at ours. Of this, however, we took no notice, and I declared our hearty concurrence in the sentiment of satisfaction expressed by Lord Gambier at the improvement in the prospects of a successful termination to the negotiation since our last meeting. I then observed, that in our note of yesterday we had stated the motives upon which we had requested the present conference; that we had agreed to many of the alterations proposed by them to the projet of a treaty which we had sent to them; that we had consented to waive the articles to which they had objected, with the exception of part of one of them, which we still wished to discuss, and with respect to which we had enclosed to them a provision made by an act of Congress at the commencement of the war. There were some of the alterations proposed by them, however, to which we could not agree. We wished to obtain explanations concerning some others, and also to fill the blanks of times and places in several of the articles. The mode of proceeding which we had thought it would be proper to adopt was, to take the projet and refer in regular order to the passages to which we objected, stating successively the ground of our objections.

This was accordingly done. The first objection we made was to an alteration in the first article, respecting the restoration of territory, places, and possessions taken during the war; our projet had made it universal without exception. The British proposed alteration was, to limit the restoration to territories *belonging* to one party and taken by the other. I stated that our objection to the alteration was, that it made one party the judge whether any territory taken by it did or did not belong to the other. It would enable either party to refuse giving up at its option any portion of the possessions of the other taken by it, merely by saying, This does not belong to you. It was contrary to the tenor of the articles by which a provision was made for settling all the questions of disputed boundary, and contrary to the general basis which had been agreed to of the state before the war, substituting instead of it present possession, upon which we had declined to treat, and which they had explicitly abandoned.

Mr. Goulburn and Dr. Adams insisted upon retaining the alteration. Goulburn said that he did not know of any part of the territory taken by either party which it could hold as not belonging to the other, except the islands in the Bay of Fundy, which, as we had written to our Government, one of them had said they considered as belonging to Great Britain as clearly as Northamptonshire; that there could be no reason for restoring that which must ultimately be adjudged to them, and if it should finally prove otherwise, the possession could not be long retained, as in the next article the final decision of the disputed question was provided for.

Mr. Gallatin said that our objection was, that the alteration instead of settling disputes only laid the foundation for a new one. Suppose the treaty concluded. Each party will immediately demand the delivery of possession of the places taken from it. The other refuses to deliver this or that place, and says, This does not belong to you. A new dispute is thus started upon the very execution of the treaty. Nor did it apply merely to the case of Moose Island. There were several islands in the river and Lakes in the same predicament.

Mr. Goulburn said he did not know that any of the islands in the river or Lakes had been taken by either party from the other during the war.

I observed that as to the question of right, our opinions and theirs would of course not be the same, and in ours, the island of Grand Menan, in the Bay of Fundy, a larger and more valuable island than any of those they so confidently claimed, was as much ours as the city of New York.

Mr. Goulburn said that the mass of evidence they had upon the subject was immensely voluminous; that he had been prepared at one time to enter upon the discussion of the question, but there could be no use now in battling it upon points for which another mode of settlement was agreed upon.

Dr. Adams said that the objection to the alteration was one which might be applied to every stipulation of every treaty. It was not to be presumed that a Government agreeing to a stipulation would not carry it into effect with good faith; that he did not see that the retaining possession of what belonged to them came at all within the principle of uti possidetis; that the status ante bellum could mean only the state as of right, and that the restoration of possession to be required could only be of rightful possession.

I said that possession was in its nature matter of fact, and not of right; that when therefore the restoration of possession was to be stipulated, the state before the war was mere matter of fact. The right of course would remain the same as before the war, without stipulation; and if possession taken during the war was retained, it could only be on the principle of uti possidetis, and not on that of status ante bellum.

Mr. Bayard said it was not necessary to suppose bad faith or a disposition to elude the execution of the treaty on either side. The alteration would give rise to a new dispute, with the

utmost fidelity and sincerity on both sides.   One party claims
the delivery of territory taken from it, and which it sincerely
and honestly believes to belong to it.   The other refuses to
deliver it, believing with equal sincerity and confidence that it
belongs to itself. Here is immediately a new dispute. Suppose
the case that the place belongs to neither of the parties.   Suppose the case that it belongs to both.   On either of these sup-
positions you have immediately a new dispute.   The restoration
to the state existing before the war is a plain and simple principle, a matter of fact, about which no dispute can arise.

No reply was made to these remarks, which Mr. Bayard
afterwards told me he made with particular reference to the
settlement on Columbia River.   But, as the British Plenipotentiaries manifested no signs of yielding, I proposed to pass
on to the next article.

This related to the periods fixed for the cessation of hostilities
and the restoration of prizes taken at sea.   We had in our
original projet followed in form the precedents of the Treaty
of Peace in 1782, but had assumed the signature of the treaty
as the date from which the terms for the cessation of hostilities
in the different latitudes were to commence.   They had substituted the exchange of the ratifications as the date, and we
had agreed to this alteration.   We had agreed in our own meetings to propose to shorten the periods for the cessation of hostilities.

I observed that I hoped we should finally agree upon a treaty,
of the ratification of which there would be no doubt, so that it
might be considered as a mere formality.   The peace would
then be made six weeks or two months before it could be ratified.
We wished that no time might be lost, and we had therefore
shortened all the terms—that of the Channel and the North Seas
particularly, within a period even shorter than might be necessary for the exchange of the ratifications to be known.   The
conclusion of the treaty would, however, be known, and we
supposed it might be more for the advantage of Great Britain
than for that of the United States that the period of hostilities
should be abridged in this quarter.

They said that wherever the advantage might be, the orders

to the commanders of ships and other officers could not be issued until the exchange of the ratifications was known. The ratification of the treaty would indeed be in England a mere formality, for they had authority to bind their Government; their full power promising to ratify what they should do. They hoped there would be no doubt of an immediate ratification in America, but our full power did not positively promise it.

Mr. Gallatin said it could not, because the ratification of treaties was by our Constitution reserved to the President and the Senate, and required the consent of two-thirds of the latter.

We finally took the article which they had drawn up on this subject, my colleagues observing that we should perhaps on examination find it preferable to our own.

The next articles were those stipulating the appointment of commissioners to ascertain and settle the boundary lines. We had proposed the appointment of three sets of three commissioners, following exactly the precedent of those for ascertaining the St. Croix River in Mr. Jay's treaty. The British projet proposes only two commissioners, and if they, one being appointed by each Government, should not agree, then to leave the decision to a friendly sovereign. We agreed to this alteration. They had, however, drawn an entire new article in lieu of our third, and they had begun with a quotation from the Treaty of Peace of 1783. The quotation was incomplete, and presented no distinct sense. Mr. Goulburn observed that there had been an omission of one line in the copy sent us, and Lord Gambier said he had observed it in making out his copy of the projet. I had also observed it, and we were prepared to supply the omission ; which was done. But the British projet had included in the description of the disputed boundary only certain islands in the Bay of Fundy, which Mr. Gallatin thought was intended to exclude from the judgment of the commissioners Moose Island, that being not in the Bay of Fundy, but in the Bay of Passamaquoddy ; and connected with the determination to restore only the territory belonging to us, he supposed was meant not only to keep possession of Moose Island, but to place it without the powers of the commissioners to decide upon the title to it. The British Plenipo-

tentiaries, however, immediately agreed to the alteration pro-
posed by Mr. Gallatin, including the islands in the Bay of
Passamaquoddy, and that of Grand Menan, in the Bay of Fundy.
This removed one of the great remaining obstacles to the peace.

Then came the question about filling the blanks of the places
where the commissioners were to meet in the first instance.
Mr. Goulburn said they had thought of filling two of the blanks
with places in the British Dominions, and two within the United
States. They mentioned St. Johns for the third article, and
Montreal for the fourth. Mr. Gallatin proposed St. Andrews,
in the Province of New Brunswick, for both, as being the spot
nearest and most convenient to the scene of operations. It was
agreed to be inserted; Lord Gambier remarking that Mr. Gallatin, by his local knowledge of that country, knew best what
was the fittest place; and Dr. Adams asking whether St. Andrews was a considerable place. The blank in the fifth article
was filled with Albany. The eighth article was that on which
there will be the greatest obstacles in coming to an ultimate
agreement. It is the boundary west from the Lake of the
Woods. In the course of the correspondence, the British Plenipotentiaries had proposed the line of Mr. King's unratified
convention of 1803, the shortest line from the lake to the
Mississippi. We had proposed a line agreed to in the proposed
convention of 1807, between Messrs. Monroe and Pinkney and
Lords Auckland and Holland. The British Government now
propose a line due west, in the 49th parallel of latitude, with an
additional clause, that the British shall have the free navigation
of the Mississippi, and free access to it through our territories
generally, with their goods, wares, and merchandise. I observed
that we proposed to strike out this clause; that it consisted of
two parts: first, the navigation of the river for his Britannic
Majesty's subjects, and secondly, the access to it for them
through our territories. With regard to the first, the right was
stipulated for British subjects by the Treaty of Peace of 1783.
We had stated in our note, sent with our projet, that we considered that Treaty of 1783 as bearing a peculiar character, and
that it was not liable, like ordinary treaties, to be abrogated by
a subsequent war; that the American Government had con-

sidered the rights and liberties secured by it to the people of
the United States as requiring no new and additional stipulation, and had therefore not authorized us to bring them into
discussion. To this part of our note the British Plenipotentiaries had made no reply. We knew not whether their silence
was owing to the acquiescence of their Government in the
principle we had advanced, or to some other cause.

Lord Gambier said, No, no.

But, continued I, the British right to navigate the Mississippi stands on the same foundation—the Peace of 1783. We
admit that if our principle is good to us for the fisheries within
the British jurisdiction, it is good for the British right to navigate the Mississippi within our jurisdiction. If the British
Government so considers them, there is no need of a new
stipulation in either case. But by asking a new one for the
Mississippi, it was to be inferred that Great Britain considered
the rights on both sides to be forfeited by the war, and she now
asked a new right to navigate the Mississippi without offering
for it any equivalent. If a new engagement was necessary for
one of the privileges, it was necessary for the other, and we
had prepared an article which we would leave with them to
restore both. As to their access to the Mississippi through
our territories, if the right to navigate the river was granted,
access to it by one road must be allowed; but it would be
obviously necessary to guard it by a provision for the collection
of duties; and if a general access, without limitation of place,
was to be granted, we thought a reciprocal right would be
necessary for the people of the United States through the
British territories to the St. Lawrence, and the free navigation
of the river.

This observation, that they were asking for a new right, without offering an equivalent, appeared to take the British Plenipotentiaries altogether by surprise.

Mr. Gallatin told them that if they considered the remainder
of the article, the 49th parallel of latitude, an equivalent, he
wished them to understand that we attached no importance to
it at all. It would, indeed, be a convenience to have the boundary settled, but the lands there were of so little value, and the

period when they might be settled was so remote, that we were perfectly willing that the boundary there should remain as it is now, and without any further arrangement. If it was agreeable to them, we had no sort of objection to striking out the whole of the eighth article.

Mr. Goulburn said that as by agreeing to the west line, in the latitude 49, they gave up all claim to any possessions on the Mississippi, it was necessary to stipulate for the right of navigation on the river, and for access to it through our territories. It was of no use to them at present, but it might eventually be of some advantage to them. It was a provision for futurity rather than for the present time.

I said that whatever it might be, it was a privilege to which their Government appeared to attach considerable importance, and they could not expect it would be granted by the United States without an equivalent.

Goulburn said they had no authority to agree to our article, and they must refer it to their Government. The whole treaty must be taken together, and the equivalent must be found in the concessions of Great Britain in the other articles. Dr. Adams expressed the same idea, and Lord Gambier said, Yes, yes, yes.

Mr. Gallatin told them that there was no concession of Great Britain in any of the other articles. We had insisted upon the mutual restoration of territory, and had invariably declined treating on any other basis. We should by that only get back our own, and we should restore to Great Britain what was hers. As to all the articles for the settlement of boundary, they might be mutually useful, but we had no particular interest in them. We had accepted the mode of settlement proposed by Great Britain instead of our own, and we were quite willing, if she desired it, to strike out every one of those articles, but we could not admit this unexpected claim without some equivalent.

Mr. Goulburn said they had informed us in their first note that the claim would be made.

Mr. Gallatin replied they had; but that in their note of 21st September, to which we had since been expressly referred by them, as containing the *whole* of their demands, it was not mentioned.

We now passed to the article concerning indemnities.

I remarked that we had consented to waive all claims for them that have arisen subsequent to the commencement of the war, excepting for vessels which had been in British ports when the war commenced and had been there seized. We had sent them a copy of a section of an act of Congress, passed immediately after the declaration of war, allowing British vessels then in the ports of the United States six months to depart; and our instructions authorized us to say that the permission had been extended, in the execution of the law, even beyond the time limited by its letter.

Dr. Adams and Mr. Goulburn have but a feeble control of their temper. Adams began by an argument, as if he had been in Doctors' Commons. He said that he had examined the section of the law we had sent, and it appeared to him not to *make out a case* for a claim near so strong as our note had stated it; that it only gave authority to the President to give passports to British vessels to depart. Why, this was no more than what the King had power to do in England at all times; that America had declared war against England, and of course all American vessels in the English ports had been seized. At first they had only laid the hand upon them, and kept them sequestered until it was seen what was the result of the proposals made for peace by Admiral Warren. Afterwards they were all condemned, and a claim for indemnities for them was not only without foundation, but utterly unprecedented among nations.

I replied that it was not merely the law, but the execution of the law, and the extension of the indulgence granted by it, even beyond the time expressed in it, which we considered as warranting a claim to a similar liberality on the part of Great Britain; that so far from its being unprecedented, we considered it as the common custom of nations. I had not at hand any of the writers on the Law of Nations, but I felt the utmost confidence that the principle was sanctioned by them; that there was scarcely a treaty between commercial nations in modern times that did not contain it as a stipulation, and it was generally viewed as a stipulation merely in affirmance of the acknowledged principle; that with regard to the manner of carrying on a war, neither the law nor the usages of nations recognized any distinction of right founded on the declaration of war, whether made by the one party or by the other.

Dr. Adams insisted that there was a material difference in the consideration which party declared the war; and renewed the assertion, that a demand for indemnity on such a ground was utterly unprecedented; that when war was declared by one party, its ships in the ports of the other were of course seized. They were sometimes kept, until it was seen whether peace would be restored, and if not, they were condemned; and if the other party did otherwise, it mattered not, whether from liberality or any other motive, it gave no claim whatsoever either for indemnity or for restoration.

Mr. Goulburn said that he remembered having received at the time a letter from one of his friends in Liverpool, informing him that he had seized an American vessel there.

Mr. Gallatin asked what was done with such vessels when they were condemned; whether they were considered as droits of the Admiralty, or given to the seizors.

Goulburn and Adams said a portion of them was given to the seizor. Both of them appeared to be nettled at the question. Goulburn said that it would be humiliating and disgraceful in Great Britain to allow any such claim for indemnity; that it was requiring her to pay a shameful *tribute* for peace; that it had been demanded by France in the war of 1756, and refused.

Mr. Gallatin said that was for vessels taken at sea before the war was declared.

Goulburn said it was demanded by France in the last war, and had been the pretext upon which the English prisoners in France, when the war commenced, had been detained as prisoners.

Mr. Gallatin said, looking earnestly at Goulburn, " Has it not been considered throughout Europe that this measure of Bonaparte's was not only extremely harsh in its character, but unquestionably in violation of the law of nations?"

Goulburn hesitatingly said, " Yes; but it was done on the pretence of retaliation for our detention of French property."

" Thus," said I, " our claim in the present instance is at least not unprecedented."

" Ay," said Goulburn, with a coarse and insulting tone; " but we do not admit Bonaparte's construction of the law of nations."

Mr. Gallatin afterwards told me that his object in asking the last question was to obtain an admission from them that the detention of the British in France was in violation of the law of nations, because the principle applied to their own conduct in detaining as prisoners the American seamen they had impressed before the war.

We had now gone through the topics on which we had asked the conference, and recurred to the points upon which we had not agreed. Mr. Gallatin mentioned the Mississippi and the fisheries, and gave Mr. Goulburn the article he had prepared for restoring them.

Mr. Bayard said there was also the restoration of—— Dr. Adams, thinking that he meant the restoration of the ships, or *property afloat*, which they had said was liable to immediate seizure on the breaking out of the war, while they admitted that by the usage of nations in modern times all other property was respected, did not give Mr. Bayard time to finish his sentence. " No; as to that," said he, " we shall not refer it to our Government—we reject it at once." Mr. Bayard said he had meant the restoration of territory. "Oh! . . . ay! . . . ah!" said Adams; " yes, we can refer that."

" We may as well refer it," said Goulburn, " as we must refer the other; but, gentlemen, we cannot say that our Government will not require something else. We had hoped we could have concluded without referring again to our Government. We mean to say, that we were now authorized to sign the treaty as we sent it to you."

" We made no question," said Mr. Clay, " that you would sign the treaty, if we agreed to it in your own terms."

" Yes," said Goulburn, very awkwardly; " but we only regret the *delay*, and should have wished to have concluded now. We wish the delay may not be imputed to us."

As we rose to take leave, Dr. Adams expressed a wish that

what had passed between us might be kept at present entirely secret, and that if we should sign a treaty, it should be not mentioned or disclosed to any person for at least twenty-four hours, that their messenger might have a start of that time, to carry the first news to the Government. He said there was so much commercial speculation upon our transactions, that it was very desirable nothing should be said by any of us to give advantages to any person. " Because, you know," said he, " one does not know to whom it might be attributed." We assented to these observations; but Mr. Bayard afterwards said he thought they were very indelicate. Perhaps they were; but, after Milligan's expedition to England in August, and the circumstances attending it, I thought them quite excusable.

2d. When we received, last Sunday, the note from the British Plenipotentiaries, with their proposals and alterations of our projet, it became probable that we should ultimately sign a treaty of peace. Mr. Russell then proposed that we should henceforth keep the state of the negotiation exclusively to ourselves, and communicate the papers to no person whatsoever, excepting our Secretary, Mr. Hughes. This was agreed to by us all. Nevertheless, Mr. Bentzon went off the next morning for London, and Mr. Howland for Havre. Bentzon called upon me about eight o'clock of the morning of his departure, and was as inquisitive about the state of the negotiation as he could indirectly be. With Mr. Gallatin he was more direct in his enquiries. Bentzon's father-in-law, John Jacob Astor, of New York, had before the war made a settlement at the mouth of Columbia River, on the Pacific Ocean. A British ship-of-war, the Raccoon, has, during the war, broken it up. Bentzon stated to Mr. Gallatin that Astor had a ship at Canton, in China; that if peace should be made, the instant it is signed Astor intends to dispatch an order from England, without waiting for the ratification in America, to the ship at Canton to proceed immediately to Columbia River and renew the settlement there before the British will have time to anticipate him. Bentzon supposed that there was a public interest connected with this project, important enough to induce us to communicate to him the state of the negotiation and the prospects of peace. Mr. Gallatin observed to him that he must in that case communicate his proposals in writing, and we would deliberate upon them. Bentzon drew up a paper, and gave it to Mr. Gallatin, with liberty to show it to me, and perhaps to Messrs. Bayard and Clay, but not to Mr. Russell. Of course we could neither deliberate upon it nor give Mr. Bentzon the information he desired. He told me that morning that he must go to London, where he expected the frigate would be ready to sail for the West Indies on the first of December. He is one of the Danish Commissioners appointed to receive delivery of the Danish islands from the British. He said he had yesterday received information from Paris that his colleague had already left that city for London, which made it necessary for him to hasten his departure; but if he should not find the frigate there, we should have him back here again. I gave him a packet of letters for Mr. Beasley.

Howland went off very suddenly, and we know that he was here with views of speculation. Shaler became so inquisitive to Mr. Russell upon the state of the negotiation, that Russell at last told him we had laid ourselves under an injunction of secrecy concerning it. Shaler took offence at this, as a manifestation that he had lost our confidence, and the next day informed Mr. Russell and Mr. Clay that he wished to return immediately to Paris and to the United States in the Transit. He complained much about the loss of our confidence, and asked Mr. Russell who it was that had proposed the injunction of secrecy. Russell told him that was a part of the secret. We have agreed, however, to ask that Shaler's passport from the British Admiralty to go by the Neptune may be transferred for the Transit. He did not choose to go by the Herald, and was unwilling to lose his opportunity of going by the Neptune. This morning Shaler came and took leave of me.

3d. The arrears of this journal, though of few days, have become important. The transactions of the present week, from our receipt of the British note and projet of a treaty last Sunday, have been such as made it desirable to commit them as soon as possible to writing. They have at the same time left me so little leisure that I have not been able to keep my record even with the current of time. In the minutes I am here making, as well of our mission meetings as of the conferences with the British Plenipotentiaries, I can only note the most important particulars which occur, and I have frequent occasion to remark that the impression, and even the understanding, of what is said, differs very much among different persons.

7th. Received from the British Plenipotentiaries two notes: one in answer to the application for a passport for Shaler to go by the Transit—that they have sent it to their Government; the other asking for proof of the assertion by the American Secretary of State that negroes taken by the British from the Southern States had been sold in the West Indies.

8th. I made this morning a draft of an answer to propose to my colleagues to be sent to the British Plenipotentiaries to the note received yesterday from them respecting the seduction and sale of negroes taken from our Southern States by British officers. The note gives us an express assurance that any officer found guilty of such practices shall be punished in an exemplary manner. But it confounds together the two acts of seducing the slaves and afterwards selling them, and promises only to punish the whole. It is the seduction of the slaves that constitutes the offence against us. As to the sale of them afterwards, the British Government have no right to ask of us, and we have no sufficient motive to give them, proofs of the fact, unless they will disavow and pledge themselves also to punish the other.

I therefore in my draft offered to produce the proof if they would engage to indemnify the owners of the negroes for the loss of them; and for the proof of seduction, referred to Admiral Cochrane's proclamation of 2d April last, of which we have sent a copy with one of our former notes.

I requested a meeting of the mission at my chamber at noon. It was accordingly held; I read the draft I had made, but there appeared much diversity of opinion as to the proper mode of proceeding in this case. Mr. Bayard is afraid of irritating the British Government. Mr. Gallatin thinks our proof weak, and seems to have a doubt, though he does not exactly avow it, whether the fact can be proved. We have only one affidavit, but that is as strong both to the general practice and to a particular instance in the knowledge of the deponent as any proof could be. Hughes remarked to me, however, that the deponent's Christian name was Patrick, which he did not like. I asked him, why? He answered, Irish. Mr. Gallatin was averse to requiring of the British Government to disavow and punish the seduction, because, he said, they would not only refuse to do it, but that all the opponents of the slave-trade would approve and justify the act. Mr. Russell said he had taken much the same view of the subject as that in my draft; but it was finally proposed and agreed to postpone the answer until we shall hear further from the British Plenipotentiaries on the main subject of the treaty.

9th. Mr. Clay came into my chamber this morning and read to me the draft which he had been making of an answer to the negro note from the British Plenipotentiaries. It differed not much in substance from mine of yesterday, and was in a milder form, asking for explanation. I told him I was well satisfied with it, and only wished an addition noticing Cochrane's proclamation. Mr. Baker called upon us from the British Plenipotentiaries, to request a conference at such time and place as we should choose. We named to-morrow noon, at our house. Mr. Bayard, Mr. Gallatin, and myself only saw Mr. Baker. We asked him if there was anything new from England. He said their usual messenger had arrived with papers two or three days later than those previously received, but he did not know whether any news was in them, and he intimated a doubt whether the Liffey frigate had arrived in so short a passage from Quebec as had been stated. Mr. Bayard spoke to me again about the negro note. He is for answering, that the indemnity for the loss of the negroes having been refused, we are not authorized to furnish our proofs, but will refer the note to our Government. He had not seen Mr. Clay's draft of an answer. I told him the substance of it, but he said he did not admire that course; he thought it calculated merely to produce irritation upon a collateral subject, which might tend to defeat the negotiation itself.

10th. We had a meeting of the mission this morning, and at

twelve had a conference with the British Plenipotentiaries at our house. Lord Gambier opened it by observing that the first thing to be done was to settle the protocol of the first meeting, which Mr. Baker had drawn up, and which he then read. We admitted it with some alterations, which we suggested, and to which the British Plenipotentiaries agreed. Mr. Hughes is to have a copy of it.

Lord Gambier then proceeded to state the determination of the British Government upon the points referred to them after the last conference. They insisted upon retaining the words "belonging to" as applied to the territory to be restored, but were willing to modify the expressions in such manner as to avoid the objection that it gave each party the right to judge in the first instance of what did or did not belong to the other. This modification might be by confining the exception to the general restoration, to the islands in Passamaquoddy Bay. As to them, the British Government considered their title so clear that it was a great concession in them to allow the right to them to be brought into discussion, and that they should be included in the objects to be settled by commissioners.

I said that we could not reply to this, or any other proposal from the British Government, until we should have an opportunity of consulting together.

Lord Gambier then passed to the eighth article. He stated that the British Government had considered the 49th parallel of latitude agreed to as our boundary from the Lake of the Woods, as no more than an equivalent for the right of the British to navigate the Mississippi, claimed by the part of the article to which we had objected.

His Lordship was corrected by his two colleagues, who reminded him that their Government meant it was no less than an equivalent; that is, a full equivalent.

" Did not I say so?" said his Lordship.

His colleagues told him he had not. Well, he had meant so, because the 49th parallel of latitude had given to the United States an increase of territory.

I said that it was no increase of territory, but rather a diminution of territory to the United States. The line prescribed

by the Treaty of 1783 was from the northwest corner of the
Lake of the Woods to the Mississippi, due west. But this line
was a nullity; it was not in rerum naturâ. A line due west
from the Lake of the Woods, it had been found, did not touch
the Mississippi. But by the terms of the treaty we were entitled to a line due west from the northwest corner of the lake,
and that was north of 49; by accepting that parallel we really
gave up some of our territory, perhaps half a degree of
latitude.

Dr. Adams said that, as to that, the views of the two Governments might be matter of controversy, but the British Government were willing to leave that part of the article as it stood.
They did not assent to either of the alternatives—to leave out
the whole article, or to strike out simply the last paragraph, or
to strike it out and substitute the provision we had proposed,
confirming their rights to navigate the Mississippi, and our
rights to the fisheries within their jurisdiction. But they
would agree to strike it out, offering a substitute of their own.
This was, that Great Britain agreed to negotiate with the United
States for granting the fisheries within the British jurisdiction
for an equivalent to be granted by the United States; and
that the United States agreed to negotiate with Great Britain
for granting to British subjects the right to navigate the Mississippi for an equivalent to be granted by Great Britain.

Mr. Baker read this article, and it was left with us for consideration.

Mr. Gallatin hinted a wish again to amend the first part of
the article, to guard against the possibility that the 49th parallel
of latitude should not touch the Lake of the Woods. He said
the proof that it did consisted of a single observation, taken by
a Mr. Thomson in MacKenzie's journey. This was, however,
not pressed. We had Arrowsmith's last map (1811) of North
America, and Mr. Clay said he had no doubt the 49th degree
would touch the lake. In accepting the article proposed by
the British Plenipotentiaries for the periods of the cessation of
hostilities, Mr. Gallatin proposed some alterations, both of the
latitudes and of the terms. The most material one was, to
shorten, from the term of forty-five to thirty days from the

exchange of ratifications, the period for the two channels, particularly to include the port of Liverpool. The proposed alterations, were taken by the British Plenipotentiaries for consideration. . We had some desultory conversation with regard to the method of securing the transmission of the treaty as speedily as possible, that it might arrive in America before the 4th of March. I proposed that we should sign three copies of the treaties, all as originals, to guard against the accidents to which a single vessel will be liable. Lord Gambier said he had intended to propose the same thing. But Dr. Adams thought that the great seal of England could be affixed only to one ratification.

Mr. Bayard observed that however general a rule that might be, an exception might be considered proper for the peculiarity of a treaty with a power beyond the ocean. Mr. Goulburn promised that they would propose it to their Government; and I proposed, if the difficulty of putting the great seal to duplicates was insuperable, that the periods for ceasing hostilities should be dated not from the exchange of the ratifications, but from the time of the ratification in America; because our Government could ratify upon an authentic copy, but the exchange could only be for the ratification under the great seal.

Dr. Adams made some difficulties still about shortening the terms. He said there must be time for giving notice to the cruisers, for those people, when they had taken prizes, were very unwilling to give them up. I had said that the worst that could happen would be, if a few prizes should be taken without notice, that they must be restored—an evil not to be compared to that of keeping the general commercial intercourse unnecessarily closed. I observed it was impossible to expect the American ratification could be received in England earlier than March, and at that season a difference of fifteen days would be important to the spring exportations from the British ports to the United States.

This consideration appeared to make some impression upon all the British Plenipotentiaries.

They offered two new articles, one stipulating a concurrence of measures for abolishing the slave-trade, and the other, that the Courts of justice should be open in each of the two countries to the subjects and citizens of the other. Dr. Adams observed of the first that it was nothing at all, a matter of no consequence, binding to no particular act, and only sanctioning legislative acts which both had adopted. Mr. Gallatin said the Courts in England had actually proceeded to condemn American vessels for violations of the laws of the United States against the slave-trade; but that there would be a difficulty in the Courts of the United States to give a similar judgment against British vessels for the violation of the English statutes on the same subject; that it could be done only by a treaty in which the offence should be assimilated to piracy and it should be agreed to punish the offenders as pirates.

Mr. Bayard said that no such treaty could be made; that piracy was an offence against all nations, and punishable by every nation; that a nation might, if it pleased, make any other act of its own subjects punishable as piracy by its own Courts, but no nation, and no two nations, could make that piracy which is not recognized as such by other nations.

Mr. Gallatin said he was aware of that, but they might assimilate it to piracy, and make it punishable in the same manner. Mr. Bayard denied that they could.

Dr. Adams said that the judgment in England had been only in one case—he had been concerned in it, and named the vessel. The Lords of the Council had long hesitated, and there had been a great diversity of opinion among them upon it; they finally decided upon a communication of the law of the United States by Mr. Pinkney, and his urgent solicitation. As to the opening of the Courts of justice, the Doctor said, laughing, that was an article that all lawyers should support.

Mr. Clay intimated that such an article might have been necessary at the Peace of 1783, but it would be unnecessary now. Mr. Goulburn said it could only be for further security, and to quiet the apprehensions of persons who might think it would be otherwise.

A remark was made to us that it would be proper to alter the title of Lord Gambier, who at the time of his appointment to this mission was a Vice-Admiral of the white squadron, but has since been promoted, and is now a Vice-Admiral of the red squadron. To this alteration we of course agreed.

After a conference of about two hours, they left us, and we continued another hour in session. We considered generally the subject of their proposals, and each of us made his remarks upon them. Mr. Gallatin was much in favor of the slave-trade article, and had originally drawn one up to be proposed on our part. I had some objections to it, as tending to give dissatisfaction to France, Spain, and Portugal, with whom Britain is now negotiating on the same subject, and who are very unwilling to yield to the British views upon it. The article for opening the Courts we considered as unnecessary and objectionable. But the two great points of difficulty remaining are the restoration of the islands in Passamaquoddy Bay and the article about the Mississippi and the fisheries. We agreed still to persist in our objection to the words "belonging to," and to their modifications, excepting those islands -from the general restoration. We also determined to object to the modification of the eighth article, as altogether unnecessary, stipulating only what the parties may at any time agree to without stipulation, and admitting on our part a principle contrary to that which we have stated to have been prescribed by our Government. But my colleagues were only for making an experiment of resistance, and I am for making it positive and determinate.

Mr. Gallatin said that the only object they could have in offering their present proposal relative to the Mississippi and the fisheries was to beat us off from our own ground. The stipulation that the parties will negotiate hereafter amounts to nothing, but it admits that both the rights secured by the Peace of 1783 are forfeited.

Mr. Bayard said they had precisely inverted our proposition. We had offered the navigation of the Mississippi as the equivalent for the fisheries in their jurisdiction; they offer to abandon the navigation if we will abandon that part of the fisheries.

Mr. Gallatin said that we should certainly lose that part of the fisheries; that our ground for claiming them was untenable, and we never could support it; that he was very sorry it had ever been stipulated in the Peace of 1783, and he would not have accepted it as an offer.

I told him that my name was to an official paper assuming the ground which he now pronounced untenable, and so was his.

He said that we had only assumed it as the principle upon which our Government had instructed us not to bring the fisheries into discussion; that he did not consider himself as pledged to it at all as his own opinion.

I told him that I was pledged to it as mine; and believed the ground to be perfectly tenable and solid. I was confident it could be supported, too, for our people would exercise it, and could not be prevented from exercising it, without the constant maintenance of an armed force to drive them from it far more expensive than the object would be worth, and more than Great Britain would maintain. I added that the present British proposition proved most clearly to me two things: one, that *they* did not consider our ground in regard to the fisheries as weak or untenable, since they offered to abandon all pretensions to the right of navigating the Mississippi if we would give up our claim to that part of the fisheries, such as it is; the other, that *they* considered that part of our fishing rights as more than an equivalent for the navigation of the Mississippi, since we had offered to continue both, the one for the other, which they declined, and proposed to us in its stead to abandon both, the one for the other.

Mr. Gallatin admitted the correctness of my first inference, but Mr. Clay disputed the second. He said the offer of the British to abandon both rights did not prove that they thought ours worth more than theirs, but that they could obtain more for conceding it.

We adjourned to meet again at eleven to-morrow morning.

11th. The meeting was in my chamber, and it was near noon before we were all assembled. The questions were resumed, What should be done with the present British proposals, and in what manner; whether by another conference or by a written note?

Mr. Russell was averse to the conference. He thought it

much safer for us that the discussions should be in writing rather than verbal. It is evident that the British Plenipotentiaries can do nothing of themselves. They have no discretionary powers. They must refer everything we propose to their Government. When we write, they refer our propositions in our own words and supported by our own reasoning. When we merely confer, we leave the statement of our arguments entirely to them. They give them their own coloring, and naturally make their case as favorable to themselves as they can.

I was of the same opinion, with the additional motive of hastening to a conclusion of our business. We have not advanced a step in our conferences, nor shall we advance a step until we come to writing.

Mr. Gallatin said the British Government was now evidently desirous of peace, and of concluding as soon as possible. The two new articles were proofs of that, for they were merely to make the peace palatable to their nation.

I said I entertained still great doubts of their intentions; that my anxiety was much greater than it had been at any period of the negotiation, infinitely greater than when their demands had been so extravagant that we were sure of being supported by our country in rejecting them. When I saw them abandoning everything of any value in their demands, and stubbornly adhering to hairs, merely, as it seemed to me, to keep the negotiation open, I could not but deeply distrust their intentions. They clung to atoms involving principles which they had abandoned as applied to everything important.

Mr. Gallatin said that was the course of all negotiations; that Bonaparte had broken off with Austria at Prague merely upon a question whether he should keep or give up Hamburg and Trieste; that he had made war with England merely for Malta. But I said in those cases there was the determination of war on both sides, and if they had not broken on one point they would on another.

Mr. Gallatin said Bonaparte had, on the contrary, been very unwilling at that time to go to war with England, but England did intend the war.

1814.] *THE NEGOTIATION FOR PEACE.*

That is precisely what I apprehend now, and that she keeps these points open merely to gain time to break off at last, and then to have the pretence that the blame of breaking off upon a trifle was on our side.

Mr. Gallatin said it was an extraordinary thing that the question of peace or war now depended solely upon two points, in which the people of the State of Massachusetts alone were interested—Moose Island, and the fisheries within British jurisdiction.

I said that was the very perfidious character of the British propositions. They wished to give us the appearance of having sacrificed the interests of the Eastern section of the Union to those of the Western, to enable the disaffected in Massachusetts to say, the Government of the United States has given up *our* territory and *our* fisheries merely to deprive the British of their right to navigate the Mississippi.

Mr. Russell said it was peculiarly unfortunate that the interests thus contested were those of a disaffected part of the country.

Mr. Clay said that he would do nothing to satisfy disaffection and treason ; he would not yield anything for the sake of them.

" But," said I, " you would not give disaffection and treason the right to say to the people that their interests had been sacrificed ? "

He said, No. But he was for a war three years longer. He had no doubt but three years more of war would make us a warlike people, and that then we should come out of the war with honor. Whereas at present, even upon the best terms we could possibly obtain, we shall have only a half-formed army, and half retrieve our military reputation. He was for playing *brag* with the British Plenipotentiaries ; they had been playing *brag* with us throughout the whole negotiation ; he thought it was time for us to begin to play *brag* with them. He asked me if I knew how to play *brag*. I had forgotten how. He said the art of it was to beat your adversary by holding your hand, with a solemn and confident phiz, and outbragging him. He appealed to Mr. Bayard if it was not.

" Ay," said Bayard ; " but you may lose the game by bragging until the adversary sees the weakness of your hand." And Bayard added to me, " Mr. Clay is for bragging a million against a cent."

I said the principle was the great thing which we could not concede; it was directly in the face of our instructions. We could not agree to it, and I was for saying so, positively, at once. Mr. Bayard said that there was *nothing* left in dispute but the principle. I did not think so.

" Mr. Clay," said I, " supposing Moose Island belonged to Kentucky and had been for many years represented as a district in your Legislature, would you give it up as nothing? Mr. Bayard, if it belonged to Delaware, would you?" Bayard laughed, and said Delaware could not afford to give up territory.

Mr. Gallatin said it made no difference to what State it belonged, it was to be defended precisely in the same manner, whether to one or to another.

It was agreed positively to object to the British proposals on both points—the first, as inconsistent with the admitted basis of the status ante bellum; and the second, as unnecessary, contrary to our instructions, and a new demand, since we had been told that they had brought forward *all* their demands. We also determined to ask one more conference before we resorted to writing; at Mr. Bayard's suggestion, and because it would be expected by the British Plenipotentiaries that they should have notice of our wish to recur to writing.

It was asked by Mr. Gallatin whether we should at this conference, in rejecting the British proposals, offer the general status ante bellum, by which the renewal of the Treaties of 1783 and 1794 would both be included. He was for making it, because he thought it would be for our advantage. I was for repeating it, and dwelling upon it, because it was that from which alone I think we can obtain peace, and because I consider it as already made by us. Mr. Gallatin makes a distinction, that we only offered the status ante bellum upon all the subjects of *difference* between the parties, and not upon subjects about which there was no difference. I have uniformly disclaimed this distinction, though it was upon it alone that Mr. Clay was prevailed upon to sign the note containing the offer.

Mr. Clay now said that he would not propose the general status ante bellum; and we were not authorized to do so by our instructions.

Mr. Russell thought the authority in our instructions limited to the restoration of territory.

Mr. Gallatin answered that we had needed no new instruction for that; we had always had that authority.

I produced the instruction of 19th October. It is unlimited.

Mr. Clay said that the instruction was drawn without knowledge of the Indian article to which we had agreed; that in assenting to that article he had declared that was the utmost extent of the sacrifice in that quarter to which he would consent, and with that article he would never sign a treaty on the general status ante bellum, including the British right to trade with the Indians, so help him God to keep him steady to his purpose.

He said this in the harsh, angry, and overbearing tone which I, perhaps more than others, ought to excuse, as the involuntary effusion of a too positive temper. It always offends me in him; but I took no notice of it this day.

Mr. Gallatin and Mr. Bayard said that every one of us must act according to his own sentiments, but Clay stalked to and fro across the chamber, repeating five or six times, " I will never sign a treaty upon the status ante bellum with the Indian article, so help me God!" Mr. Russell declared himself against proposing it to-morrow, and I again urged to propose it. Mr. Clay then said he should object to the conference altogether. We came to no express decision, but Mr. Bayard and Mr. Gallatin did not support me in the resolution to make the proposal, so that Mr. Clay actually beat again a majority by outbragging us. We sent Mr. Hughes to ask a conference with the British Plenipotentiaries at their house to-morrow.

I told Mr. Clay it was rather late for him to come out with his violent opposition to the Indian article, when I had at the time offered him to break upon it, and neither he nor Mr. Russell would support me, though both of them had since been so much against it.

He said I had been the first to say we must admit it, and

that it was even advantageous to us, by securing peace with
the Indians. I denied ever having said we must admit it. I
had said I considered it advantageous to us *in that respect,* as
it secured to us peace with the Indians; and I still continue of
that opinion. But I thought it otherwise so objectionable that
I appealed to his recollection, and to that of all my other colleagues, if I had not offered to reject the article, though at the
hazard of breaking off the negotiation.

Mr. Clay said that I had on the first day, when the article was
received, said so much in favor of admitting the article, that he
had reflected and made up his mind to admit it, declaring that
he would make no further sacrifice in that quarter. "But, however," said he, with a laugh, "you will not deny that you *signed*
the note first, and so you must be responsible for the article."

Bayard said, "Ay! but, Mr. Clay, there was no majority for it
till you had signed; you made the majority, and so you must
alone be responsible for the article."

Clay said, and I agreed with him, that at any rate the peace
would be bad enough. As for him, he believed it would break
him down entirely, and we should all be subject to much
reproach for it.

Bayard thought, on the contrary, it would be highly creditable to us. It would relieve the country from such an immense
pressure—twenty-one millions of taxes, commerce restored,
and substantially nothing given up.

I told him that when the people were secure in the enjoyment of all we should obtain, they would count it for nothing,
and only look at what we had yielded; and the very people
now the most clamorous against the war would then be equally
clamorous against the concessions made by us for peace.

Mr. Gallatin said that almost all treaties were unpopular, and
ours, if we made one, would share the common fate.

12th. At noon we went to the house of the British Plenipotentiaries, and held a conference with them until three.

After we were seated, I stated that we had deliberated upon
the last proposals presented by them—the differences yet to be
adjusted were only two, both of so small amount in point of
interest that they could hardly be subjects worthy of two such

nations as the United States and Great Britain to contend about. The first was reduced to a question about the temporary possession of the islands in Passamaquoddy Bay. We could not consent to cede the possession, permanent or temporary, of any part of the State of Massachusetts. We could not even have authority from the Government of the United States to make such a cession without the consent of the State; that, whatever might be the opinion of Great Britain with regard to her right to those islands, our conviction was entire that they belonged to the State of Massachusetts as much as any portion of its territory. It had been said by one of the British Plenipotentiaries that this exception would be no deviation from the principle of the status ante bellum. But it was an exception to it in the very purport of the phrase. It was a military possession taken during the war, which the British Government now insisted upon retaining. The possession in the United States had been undisturbed during the peace, and we only asked to be replaced in this, as in all the other cases, in the same state which existed at the commencement of the war.

Mr. Goulburn and Dr. Adams immediately took fire, and Goulburn lost all control of his temper. He has always in such cases a sort of convulsive agitation about him, and the tone in which he speaks is more insulting than the language that he uses. He said that if there could be no cession of territory without the consent of the State, there could be no safety for Great Britain in treating with the United States at all; for that if any parts of the disputed territory should be finally adjudged to Great Britain in the manner provided by the treaty, the delivery of it might be refused on the same pretence, that the State had not consented to it; that the possession by the United States of these islands had not been undisturbed—that they had always been known to be within the Government of Nova Scotia; that jurors had been drawn from them to attend the Courts in the province of New Brunswick; that when the Government of Massachusetts had first attempted to exercise jurisdiction there, strong remonstrances had been made against it by Governor Carleton; that Great Britain, merely from forbearance and to avoid hostilities, had avoided sending a military force to take possession; and that surely her forbearance ought not now to be urged against her as an obligation of right to restore the possession of what belongs to her.

Dr. Adams repeated with less virulence the same arguments, and both of them hinted not only that they must refer the subject back to their Government, but that they were extremely apprehensive, if we did not give up the point, their Government would break off the negotiation upon it. Dr. Adams said that as to the value of the interest, that was no consideration whatever; that the honor of the British nation was concerned in it, and what the islands were worth was entirely out of the question.

Mr. Gallatin replied that from the assertion by me, that the territory of a State could not be ceded by the Government of the United States without its consent, no inference could be drawn that where the right to the territory was in dispute, the Government of the United States was not fully competent to the adjustment of the dispute. If in this case the final decision of the referees should be in favor of Great Britain, it will be that the territory never belonged to Massachusetts, and no consent of hers to its cession can be necessary. No cession will be made. Of this principle Great Britain has already had proof by the decision of the commissioners concerning the river St. Croix, under the Treaty of 1794. By that decision, a portion of territory which had been in the possession of Massachusetts, and claimed by her, was found to belong to Great Britain, and the possession was delivered accordingly. But our objection was, that Great Britain, by now retaining a possession taken by force during the war, prejudged the question of right, which, by the article agreeing to the reference, she admitted to exist. Our acquiescence in her retaining that possession would be an admission of a better title on her part, and would affect the validity of our claim. With regard to the point of honor suggested by Dr. Adams, we could not enter into argument, as undoubtedly every nation must be its own judge of what concerned its own honor. But he trusted they would perceive that the argument applied as forcibly to us as to them. Our opinion of our right was as strong as theirs could possibly be of theirs. Our possession had been pacific, theirs was mere military occupation. Our possession had even preceded the Peace of 1783, though he knew we had never had a garrison there until 1808. It was now for the first time that he heard that Great Britain had ever exercised jurisdiction there since the Peace of 1783.

Mr. Goulburn said they had done so until 1798.

Mr. Bayard repeated in substance the distinction already taken by Mr. Gallatin between the authority of the United States to cede territory and that to settle a question of disputed title, and he added that by delivering possession to Great Britain, if the decision should finally be in favor of the United States, we should then have ceded a temporary possession of territory belonging to us.

I observed that my two colleagues had so fully explained the distinction upon which I had first stated our incompetency to cede, by virtue of authority from the United States, territory belonging to a State, without affecting our competency to provide for the adjustment of a dispute concerning the title to territory, that they had left me nothing further to say. We had undoubtedly authority to refer a dispute, and the possession would of course follow the decision. But until that decision we were bound to consider the territory as ours, and could have no authority to cede the possession of it.

Mr. Clay said that however that might be, and waiving the consideration of it, our objection to the alteration of the article was that it would make it inconsistent both with the general and the special principle of the whole treaty. The general principle was the restoration of all territory to the state before the war. The special principle was the reference to commissioners, and, if necessary, subsequently to a friendly sovereign, of all the disputes respecting territory. This would be an express departure from both.

Adams and Goulburn insisted that it was not in consequence of the occupation during the war of those islands that they wished to retain the possession, but because they considered them as their own.

I observed that Great Britain herself had more than ten years ago admitted in a formal convention that they were ours.

"That makes against you," said Goulburn, "for our Government refused a partial ratification of the Convention."

Mr. Bayard, with a view to cite the principle heretofore insisted upon by Great Britain in a similar case, asked how was the case of the Falkland Islands?

"Why," (in a transport of rage,) said Goulburn, "in that case we sent a fleet and troops and drove the fellows off; and that is what we ought to have done in this case."

I said I believed the gentleman's recollection of the case was not exact; that, as I remembered it, the Spaniards in that case had driven the British off, and Great Britain had insisted upon being restored to the possession, though she immediately afterwards abandoned it, and the claim to the islands themselves.

"Well," said Goulburn, "we fitted out a fleet and troops, and Spain knew that we would have taken them, and so she chose to give them up."

Lord Gambier, seeing the condition in which his colleague had placed himself, said the discussion was taking such a turn that he thought it would be advisable to pass on to something else.

Dr. Adams, however, in a moderated tone, said "that the case of the Falkland Islands did not at all apply in principle to this: that was an act of deliberate hostility committed by Spain in the midst of profound peace; this was a lawful occupation in the midst of war."

We then passed on to the substitute offered for the last paragraph of the eighth article. It is a stipulation to negotiate hereafter for the fisheries within British jurisdiction, and for the navigation of the Mississippi by British subjects, for fair equivalents.

We stated that we could not admit this substitute. As a mere engagement to negotiate hereafter, it amounted to nothing. The parties could always negotiate, if they should both be so inclined; and if either should be averse to it, negotiation would be unavailing, since it would be in its power, by demanding an equivalent which the other would not grant, to make it abortive.

The only effect then of the stipulation would be, the abandonment by us of the ground upon which we claimed the right to the fisheries. We considered the entire Treaty of 1783 not as an ordinary treaty, liable to be abrogated by a subsequent war between the parties, but as a compact containing the terms upon which two parts of one people mutually agreed to constitute two independent nations. By that treaty British subjects were entitled to the right of navigating the Mississippi. Our principle recognized the continuance of that right; Great Britain, however, had asked of us a new stipulation to confirm it. If we agreed to it, a corresponding stipulation became necessary, to confirm our right to that part of the fisheries. We asked no new stipulation in either case. We did not ask of Great Britain to abandon her construction of the treaty. But this demand on her part was a new claim, brought forward after we had been expressly assured that the British note of 21st October contained *all* they had to ask.

Lord Gambier said that they did not consider the fisheries within their jurisdiction as rights, but merely as privileges granted.

Dr. Adams said that it would be very easy to draw a proviso by which it should be agreed to negotiate upon the two subjects, and yet without implying an abandonment on the part of the United States of their claim.

I said, if he thought it so easy, I would thank him to undertake it. I did not believe it possible. We had drawn up, and now proposed, a general article founded on a precedent in the Treaty of 1794, engaging to negotiate upon all the subjects of difference unadjusted, which would include those of the Mississippi navigation, and the fisheries within the British jurisdiction.

They read our article, and immediately rejected it, finding the word *commerce* in it.

Mr. Gallatin proposed to leave that word out.

Adams and Goulburn still rejected the article. Adams still said we might draw a proviso reserving our construction of the Treaty of 1783 and agreeing to negotiate on the two subjects; and added that he mentioned it because he believed that if the other question about the islands could be got rid of, the

British Government would be disposed to some accommodation upon this.

Mr. Bayard drew a proviso for the purpose, and handed it over the table.

They read it, and Lord Gambier immediately said, " I, for one, can never agree to that."

Mr. Bayard asked what the *object* of the article, as proposed by the British Plenipotentiaries, was.

Adams and Goulburn said it was sent to them from England; they were not to account for the *motive* of their Government in proposing that or any other article.

Mr. Bayard said he did not ask them for the *motive* of their Government, but for the *object* of the article. He supposed gentlemen would at least be authorized to explain that.

Dr. Adams said they had sent us the article as they had received it, and we must construe it for ourselves; he had only said (and it was merely his individual opinion; he would not wish to be understood as pledging the opinion of his Government, or even of his colleagues), but he had said he thought we might easily agree to an article with a proviso reserving our claim to the right by the Treaty of 1783.

Mr. Gallatin asked, if we could find any expedient to come to an agreement upon the other article, whether the British Plenipotentiaries were authorized to accede to any modification of this, so that we might sign the treaty, without another reference to England.

Mr. Goulburn said they did not know. We had sent them three alternatives for their last paragraph of the eighth article. One of these alternatives had been adopted in England, and sent back to them, modified into this article. We had offered them the navigation of the Mississippi, clogged with conditions which would render it of no effect, confining their access to a single point, and upon a payment of full duties upon merchandise intended merely to pass through our territories for exportation.

Mr. Gallatin said that had not been our intention. The access would be given sufficient for all the purposes of transporting the merchandise, and by our laws a drawback from the duties was allowed upon the exportation of goods—the benefit of which would be allowed, of course, to the merchandise only passing through for exportation. " But surely," said he, " you could not expect to introduce into the United States your goods and merchandise duty free."

" And," said Mr. Clay, "as you had drawn the first paragraph, you might have gone from Quebec through any part of our territories."

Mr. Goulburn said, " No, that was not their intention."

Mr. Gallatin then took the Mississippi and fisheries article, proposed some alterations to it, and, Mr. Goulburn hesitating upon them, Gallatin said that we labored under great inconvenience and disadvantage in the negotiation. We had no opportunity of communicating with our Government, and were continually obliged to take responsibility upon ourselves, while they referred to their Government for every detail.

Mr. Goulburn said they were so near that the inconvenience was but small, and upon the whole he considered it as a fortunate circumstance, as had it been otherwise we should not now have been here. He did, however, attempt to draw a proviso admitting some of the alterations to the article suggested by Mr. Gallatin; but upon showing it to Lord Gambier he said it amounted to the same thing as Mr. Bayard's. Mr. Goulburn thought there was a great difference between them, but at last found an objection to his own draft, that it admitted a claim of Great Britain to the navigation of the Mississippi by the Treaty of 1783.

I asked him upon what other ground than that of the article in the Treaty of 1783 Great Britain could now demand the navigation of the Mississippi.

He gave no direct answer to this question.

The British Plenipotentiaries consulted together upon the article and Mr. Goulburn's proviso. They at first suggested a wish that the conference might be adjourned to this evening or to-morrow morning, when they would give us a definitive answer whether they could conclude without a new reference to England; but they finally preferred receiving a communication from us in writing, and requested us to give them our ultimatum upon the two points.

We told them with regard to the other two new articles proposed by them we did not think it necessary to discuss them until the other questions should be disposed of; but we thought it proper in candor to say that we should admit in substance that relating to the slave-trade, and that we should object to the other, which we considered as unnecessary, and hoped to convince the British Plenipotentiaries that it is so.

It was agreed that the protocol of this day's conference should be only that the Plenipotentiaries met, and, after much discussion upon the subjects yet unadjusted, adjourned.

At three o'clock we returned home, and were in meeting until our dinner-time, conversing in a desultory manner upon the substance of the note to be sent. The whole tenor of the conference had confirmed me in the opinion that the British Government have insidiously kept these two points open for the sake of finally breaking off the negotiation and making all their other concessions proofs of their extreme moderation, to put upon us the blame of the rupture.

Mr. Clay was so confident that the British Government had resolved upon peace that he said he would give himself as a hostage and a victim to be sacrificed if they broke off on these points.

It was thought by him and by Mr. Gallatin that a note in a single page would be sufficient.

I said it would be enough if we were to yield the points in controversy, but if we were to stand out upon them it would be necessary to send a note of sixteen pages.

Mr. Bayard was for conceding the point respecting the islands in Passamaquoddy Bay, and for standing out to the last extremity upon that of the fisheries, even if we should break upon it. Immediately after dinner, Mr. Gallatin advised the young gentlemen to go and dress for the ball, and we continued to discuss the subject among ourselves until seven o'clock. Mr. Gallatin said that he was, like myself, halting between two opinions, and unable to bring his mind to a conclusion which course would be the best. He must sleep upon it. Mr. Clay was requested to draw up his note in a single page, to be presented for consideration at the meeting at eleven o'clock to-morrow morning.

I did not attend the ball, though "Hail Columbia" was announced to be played, à grand orchestre!! and was actually performed.   But I passed the evening in my chamber, making a draft of a note to be sent to the British Plenipotentiaries.   I gave it to Mr. Gallatin after he returned from the ball, to make such use of it as he should think proper.   It prolonged my evening until near midnight.

13th.   I suspended the journal of yesterday for the sake of writing to my wife, and prepared my letter for her just in time to be prepared for the meeting of the mission in my chamber at eleven.   Mr. Clay produced his draft of a note to the British Plenipotentiaries, and Mr. Gallatin brought mine, with an unfinished one which he had drawn himself.   They were all discussed, and there was a great diversity of opinions as to the course most proper to be pursued.

Mr. Clay was for persisting in the rejection of both the British demands, but with the determination finally to yield both.   He thought that by insisting equally upon both we should most probably obtain a concession upon one.

My draft had insisted upon both, with an intimation that if the case of the islands should be made an ultimatum, we should rather subscribe to it, though without authority, than break off the negotiation, but that we could not concede the point of the fisheries.

Mr. Bayard was for giving up explicitly and without qualification the islands; and he was prepared to be much more flexible upon the fisheries than he had been yesterday.

Mr. Russell declared himself in favor of my draft, but was for yielding eventually, if necessary, upon both the points.

Mr. Gallatin had taken the statement made yesterday by Mr. Goulburn, that the British had exercised jurisdiction over Moose Island since the Peace of 1783, as the motive for our concession upon that point; but his draft intimated too distinctly that we should ultimately yield on the other point if it should be pressed.

Mr. Bayard confined his observations chiefly to the Moose Island question.   He inclined much to the opinion that the British argument was better than ours; that they were right upon the principle. At any rate, we could not break upon it. We should not be supported in it by our own people, nor by the general opinion of Europe. We had at the commencement of the negotiation thrown the blame of the war upon them. Europe and America had pronounced their demands extravagant and absurd. They had raised a powerful opposition against the war among their own people. They might be now playing a similar game against us. They might only want to draw us out to refuse concession upon these trifles, then to break off, retort upon us the blame of continuing the war, and make an ostentatious display of all the concessions they had made only to ensnare us, as proofs of their moderation and of our insincerity. Their own people would support them on this ground of rupture. Ours would not support us. The only chance we could possibly have of a successful continuation of the war was, that our whole people should embark heart and soul in it. They never would do so for a war on the only ground now left us. Our divisions would become infinitely more dangerous and formidable. Our finances were in ruins. Enormous taxes, such as our people have never known, are the only means by which the war can possibly be carried on. A war is nothing to the British Government. They have now no other enemy upon their hands. In a thousand years there could not happen again a concurrence of circumstances under which war would be so unequal between us, so much to their advantage and so disadvantageous to us. He was against hazarding the possibility of a rupture upon the Moose Island question, and was for frankly giving it up at once.

I declared my concurrence in all these sentiments ; I said I had made my draft according to them, and under the full conviction of their weight. I had distinctly shown our intention to yield the point, and had only continued to resist upon it that they might declare it on their part an ultimatum. I wanted that, to convince our country that we had done everything in our power to secure the object, and finally yielded only to prevent the continuance of the war.

Mr. Gallatin thought that if we told them we had no authority to make the concession, while intimating to them

that we should make it, they might insidiously make that the
pretext for breaking off. It was observed that they had already
accepted one article with that understanding, and therefore
could not object to taking another on the same footing.

Mr. Gallatin, however, was unwilling to give them the opportunity.

Mr. Clay was still very urgent for holding out upon both the
points for the sake of obtaining one. I said that the result of
our measure was altogether conjectural. It was possible that
concession upon one point would obtain concession upon
another more easily than resistance upon both. Our experience had been rather in favor of this anticipation, for the
greatest concessions that we had obtained were immediately
after we had agreed to the Indian article. We adjourned from
one to three o'clock, for Mr. Gallatin to finish his draft after
this discussion.

I walked round the city, and part of the Coupure, where I
met Mr. Bayard walking. I returned with him. He said he
had been reflecting upon this Moose Island question until he
had convinced himself that the British were right in their pretension. Their possession was a lawful possession; though
taken in time of war, they did not claim to hold it by the right
of conquest, but by their own title, of which they say we had
wrongfully dispossessed them. On the same principle, they
might have refused to leave the question to reference, and have
insisted upon keeping it as their own.

I admitted that they might. But if they fairly and honestly
waived all claim of conquest, they could not pretend that their
title was unquestionable. They knew, on the contrary, that
our claim was strong; they certainly never would otherwise
have agreed to the reference. But when they did agree to refer,
it was begging the very question in dispute, to retain possession
as upon a valid title. It was also manifestly inconsistent with
the status ante bellum. As to the lawfulness of the possession,
all possession taken in war was lawful. Their possession of
Moose Island was no more or less lawful than ours of Fort
Erie. He had made a distinction, too, which the British Plenipotentiaries had attempted to take, that the war had been

declared by us—as if the rights of either nation could be affected
by the question which party *declared* the war. No such distinction was acknowledged by the law of nations. The rights
of the two parties were precisely the same, and it was one of
the worst features in the practice of the British nation that they
always began war without declaring it.

Mr. Bayard admitted this, but said it did not at all affect the
argument. He said that the war would wean vast numbers of
people in America from their attachment to England, and that
British influence would never again be so powerful in America
as it had been.

At three o'clock we met by adjournment, and Mr. Gallatin
had got his draft ready, with a clause of an article to propose
relative to Moose Island. After some further discussion, it was
agreed that we should successively take and examine Mr. Gallatin's new draft, and meet again to-morrow morning, finally to
decide upon it.

We all dined with the British Plenipotentiaries. There was
no other company present, and the party was more than usually
dull, stiff, and reserved. Mr. Goulburn attempted to be courteous, and told me he hoped I should pay a visit to England
after we have finished here. I said I certainly should, if they
would permit me. Mr. Clay had some conversation with him,
and with Lord Gambier. He expressed a wish that we could
come to a conclusion without a new reference to England,
which I believe to be impossible. Lord Gambier impressed
him with the belief that they would ultimately insist upon our
subscribing to an article abandoning our claim by the Treaty of
1783 to the fisheries within British jurisdiction. Lord Gambier
said to him that we surely could not rely upon that as a right.
Mr. Clay said he did not wish to enter upon that discussion.
Lord Gambier said that if we should not make the stipulation,
our fishermen would continue the practice, and that would produce a new quarrel; that there had been many complaints
against our fishermen, and representations made, to which the
British Government were obliged to pay attention. Mr. Clay
therefore wished us to reconsider our determination, and still to
insist upon both the open points for the sake of obtaining the

concession upon one. It appears to me, by his own account of his conversation with Lord Gambier, and particularly by declining to discuss our claim of right upon the construction of the treaty, he gave our adversaries encouragement to adhere upon the point of the fisheries as well as upon the other.

14th. Began upon the journal of the day before yesterday, and wrote until eleven, the hour of our mission meeting, which was again held in my chamber. I had proposed several alterations, chiefly erasures from Mr. Gallatin's new draft of the note to the British Plenipotentiaries. The most important was one in which he expressed our willingness to agree to an article for negotiating hereafter concerning the Mississippi navigation and the American *liberties* in the fisheries, provided our claim to those liberties by our construction of the Treaty of 1783 should be in no wise considered as impaired thereby. Mr. Bayard had proposed an additional amendment, stating that we were forbidden by our instructions to enter upon a discussion respecting the fisheries. I had intended to propose the same amendment, but omitted it merely from an apprehension that it would not be adopted. I supported that proposed by Mr. Bayard, but he himself did not, and it was not admitted.

The passage which I wished to be stricken out was also retained, and others inserted, expressly and explicitly with the view ultimately to give up the point if necessary. I contended for Mr. Bayard's amendment, and for erasing the passages which I thought objectionable, as long as argument could have any effect.

Mr. Russell at length said that he would insist for the fisheries as long as possible, but he would sooner give them up than continue the war for them. I appealed again to our instructions, and showed them to him. He said he understood them as referring only to the general right, and not to the liberties as within the British jurisdiction. I asked him how they would be construed by our countrymen after we should have given them up. He said he supposed some would construe them as I did, and some as he did. He supposed there would be a great clamor about it, but that must be disregarded. He believed it more for the interest of the country to give up the point rather than continue the war to maintain it.

I finally told my colleagues that I saw the difference between them and me was, that they had determined ultimately to give up the point, and I had not. I believed the ground we had originally taken to be good and solid. I could make no distinction between the different articles of the Treaty of 1783. If I admitted this day that a half of one of its articles was abrogated by the war, I should give the enemy an argument to say to-morrow that the other half is abrogated equally. If we gave up the liberty to-day, we might be called to give up the right to-morrow. Our instructions were in general terms. They authorized no such distinction as that now made, and no new instruction concerning the fisheries has been given us, since our Government knows the pretension of Great Britain.

Mr. Gallatin said he had always thought our ground upon that point untenable, that I had now almost a majority against me, and he did not wish we should commit ourselves to anything precluding us from abandoning our ground at last. Mr. Russell said that he considered everything of a permanent nature and founded on natural right in the Treaty of 1783 as not affected by a subsequent war; but privileges granted by the treaty, and which we should not have enjoyed without it, he thought were abrogated by war.

I said there was no grant of new privileges in the treaty. The liberties, as well as the rights, were merely a continuation of what had always been enjoyed. It was necessary for the fishermen to go to the part of the coast frequented by the fish, and when, by the independence of the United States, it became a foreign jurisdiction, we had a right to reserve the liberty of continuing to fish there, and the circumstance of the jurisdiction alone occasioned the change of the expression.

Mr. Clay said he did not wish to make up his mind upon the subject until it should be absolutely necessary. He said we should make a damned bad treaty, and he did not know whether he would sign it or not; but he could draw, in five minutes, an article agreeing to negotiate concerning the Mississippi and the fisheries without impairing our claim to them by the Treaty of 1783. He drew an article accordingly, which I read, and told him I had no other objection to it than that it would be instantly rejected by the British Plenipotentiaries. I further said that as they were all determined at last to yield the fishery point, I thought they were wrong not to give it up now, and sign the treaty without another reference to England, as well as without my signature. I could not sign it, because I could not consent to give up that point. But if I were of their opinion, I would make sure of the treaty now. They were setting everything afloat by another reference, and it was arrant trifling to be still cavilling about a point upon which they had resolved ultimately to yield.

They said they preferred making one effort more; and the note was adjusted, and given to Mr. Hughes to be copied fair and taken to the British Plenipotentiaries. We adjourned from half-past one to half-past three o'clock, when we met again at my chamber and signed the note. Mr. Russell came in after the rest of us had signed, and when Mr. Hughes had already gone in search of him. I told him again I thought they were wrong in not making sure of the treaty now, if they had resolved to give up the fishery question at last. I said I felt myself under peculiar obligations to defend this interest, besides those incumbent upon the other members of the mission. He said he supposed it was because my father had obtained them before. I said I could not be insensible to that consideration, but that was not all. It was an interest in which the people of Massachusetts were exclusively concerned. As a citizen of Massachusetts, I owed a duty to the State distinct from that which we all owed to it as a member of the Union. I was called upon to make a double sacrifice, both in this and the Moose Island question, and it had placed me in one of the most painful dilemmas I had ever experienced. He said he was now a citizen of Massachusetts also, though he was not born there; that he should yield upon these points with extreme reluctance, and should be sorry to lose my signature to the treaty, but he did not think we could continue the war for them. Mr. Hughes carried the note, and Mr. Baker wrote him a note in the evening, to say that it had been referred to England.

22d. After returning home, I walked round the Coupure, and, as I was coming back, met in the street Mr. Bayard, who told

me that the answer from the British Plenipotentiaries to our
last note had been received; that it accepted our proposal to
say nothing in the treaty about the fisheries or the navigation
of the Mississippi, and, indeed, placed the remaining points of
controversy at our own disposal.   As soon as I came into my
chamber, Mr. Gallatin brought me the note.   It agrees to be
silent upon the navigation of the Mississippi and the fisheries,
and to strike out the whole of the eighth article, marking the
boundary from the Lake of the Woods westward.   They also
refer again to their declaration of the 8th of August, that Great
Britain would not hereafter grant the liberty of fishing, and
drying and curing fish, within the exclusive British jurisdiction,
without an equivalent.   They accepted our proposed paragraph
respecting the islands in Passamaquoddy Bay, with the exception of a clause for their restitution if the contested title to them
should not be settled within a limited time.   Instead of which,
they gave a declaration that no unnecessary delay of the settlement should be interposed by Great Britain.

Mr. Gallatin asked me whether I thought, as they had referred
to their declaration of 8th August concerning the fisheries, it
would be necessary to write a note referring again to our construction of the Treaty of 1783, and to our right to the fisheries
under it.   I said that as we had twice stated it, and in terms
peculiarly strong in our last note, I did not think any further
written declaration upon the subject necessary.   Mr. Gallatin
asked me to write immediately a note to Mr. Boyd, requesting
him to be himself, and to direct the captain of the Transit to
be, ready to start at a moment's notice, which I did.

Mr. Clay soon after came into my chamber, and, on reading
the British note, manifested some chagrin.   He still talked of
breaking off the negotiation, but he did not exactly disclose
the motive of his ill humor, which was, however, easily seen
through.   He would have much preferred the proposed eighth
article, with the proposed British paragraph, formally admitting
that the British right to navigate the Mississippi, and the American right to the fisheries within British jurisdiction, were both
abrogated by the war.   I think his conversation with Lord
Gambier on the subject last week, at their dinner, the day before

we sent our note, had the tendency to induce the British to adhere to their paragraph, and that Clay is disappointed at their having given it up; and he has so entire an ascendency over Mr. Russell, though a New England man and claiming to be a Massachusetts man, that Russell repeatedly told me last week, when I assured him that I would not sign the treaty with an article admitting that our right to any part of the fisheries was forfeited, that he should be sorry to sign a treaty without me, but that he did not think that part of the fisheries an object for which the war should be continued; that he was for insisting upon it as long as possible, but for giving it up at last, if the British would not sign without it. We agreed to meet at half-past seven o'clock this evening.

In the evening we met, and Mr. Clay continued in his discontented humor. He was for taking time to deliberate upon the British note. He was for meeting about it to-morrow morning. He was sounding all round for support in making another stand of resistance at this stage of the business. He evidently thought himself sure of Russell's vote. He said that as to Mr. Gallatin and Mr. Bayard, he knew they were too eager for peace. At last he turned to me, and asked me whether I would not join him now and break off the negotiation. I told him no; it was now too late. I had offered to break off on the Indian article, which he had not chosen to do. There was nothing now to break off upon.

"Well," said he, "will you be of the same opinion to-morrow?" "Perhaps not," said I; "but you can easily ascertain by asking the question again to-morrow."

Gallatin and Bayard, who appeared not to know where it was that Clay's shoe pinched him, were astonished at what they heard, and Gallatin showed some impatience at what he thought mere unseasonable trifling. He said, at last, that he had no objection to Mr. Clay's amusing himself in that way as long as he thought proper, but as soon as he should choose to be serious, he (Gallatin) would propose that Mr. Hughes should be requested to call this evening upon the British Plenipotentiaries and ask a conference with them for to-morrow. Clay was still for taking time, and Mr. Russell called for the vote.

He put the question himself—I suppose to avoid voting himself.
Mr. Bayard, Mr. Gallatin, and myself voted to ask for the conference, and Clay voted against it.

23d. We were to meet this morning at eleven o'clock, previous to the conference. Mr. Hughes sent me a note to say that
the British Plenipotentiaries would meet us at twelve o'clock,
at our own house.

We met before twelve, and agreed upon the manner of opening the conference. The British Plenipotentiaries came at the
appointed time, and when we were seated, I informed them that
we had determined to accept the proposals contained in the
note we had yesterday received from them; that we had asked
for the conference to make the final arrangements for the conclusion of the treaty, and should be ready to sign it whenever
it would be agreeable to them. Lord Gambier expressed his
satisfaction that the negotiation had been brought to this favorable result, and we proceeded to make the definitive amendments for completing the treaty. Mr. Baker read the protocol
of the last conference, which was very short. We have at all
the late meetings taken the protocol as drawn by them. In the
first article they agreed to fix the cessation of hostilities, and
the consequences of that event, from the ratification of the treaty
by both parties, instead of leaving it from the exchange of the
ratifications. They consented to execute triplicate copies of the
treaty, upon either of which the ratification in the United States
might be given. But as the great seal of England could be
affixed only to one ratification, and as the American ratification
could be given in exchange only for that, if any accident should
befall it the hostilities might be continued for several months
on a mere formality. But in agreeing to date the cessation of
hostilities from the ratification, and not from the exchange, the
British Plenipotentiaries insisted upon inserting words import-
ing that it should be a ratification without alterations, because,
they said, the American Government sometimes ratified treaties
with exceptions. Mr. Gallatin said that those were not ratifications at all, that they were merely the advice and consent of
the Senate to the President to ratify with the exception. If the
other contracting party did not consent to the exception, there

was no ratification. They still, however, insisted upon having the words. Mr. Bayard proposed to them the words "in manner and form as herein contained," but they preferred the words "without alteration by either of the contracting parties," and they were inserted. The first article was also definitively settled in regard to the restitution of captured territory and the exception of the islands in Passamaquoddy Bay. After making several successive amendments in the article concerning the restoration of vessels captured at sea after the peace, it was thought best to present it in a new draft, saying the article was altered "so as to read as follows." This proposition was made by Mr. Gallatin. We took the article offered by the British Plenipotentiaries as the basis, and they agreed to the alterations shortening the times and extending the latitudes and longitudes, as proposed by Mr. Gallatin. The article concerning the release of prisoners, proposed on the British side, it was agreed should stand as the third. The *exchange* of ratifications was the date from which the release was to take place, and it was first proposed to let it so stand. I remarked that in case of the accident to the ratification from England, against which it was our object to guard, the operation of the article as it stood would be to prevent for some months the release of the British prisoners in America. Upon which the British Plenipotentiaries desired the alteration in this article, to make it correspond with the others; which was done.

There was a provision for the repayment of the advances made by each Government for the sustenance and maintenance of prisoners taken from the other, and the words *in specie* were interlined. Mr. Gallatin said that all the advances made by the British Government for American prisoners had been in paper. He did not suppose they wished to make ten or twelve per cent. on the repayment. He thought those words should be struck out.

Mr. Goulburn said that their paper was not depreciated; that some of their payments were made in specie; that all their troops in America were paid in specie, and all their advances for prisoners should be in specie at Halifax.

Mr. Bayard proposed that the repayment should be in the

same currency in which it was paid. The British Plenipotentiaries preferred the payment in specie, on account of its simplicity. Dr. Adams said we had ourselves offered an article in
which it was proposed to be made in specie, but that article was
rejected; and had it been accepted, the payment would have
been of sums to be awarded by commissioners for indemnities,
and the awards would have been made with a full consideration
of the mode of payment; but here was to be a repayment in
specie for a payment in paper, under a discount of ten per cent.
or more. The British Plenipotentiaries, however, persisted,
until Mr. Clay said he thought it was not worth while to say
anything more about it. I proposed to Mr. Gallatin to request
that the motion to strike out the words should be inserted in
this day's protocol; but he said, No—that he thought a paper
payment in England must pass for the stipulated payment in
specie.

There is nothing that more distinctly characterizes the temper
and spirit of the British Plenipotentiaries in this negotiation
than this artifice to filch a profit of fifteen or twenty per cent.
upon a sum of perhaps fifty thousand pounds sterling, and their
inflexible adherence to it. The other alterations were of no
material consequence. Mr. Gallatin proposed a slight one, in
the article concerning the abolition of the slave-trade, which
was adopted.

After all the other points were settled, Mr. Goulburn brought
forward again the proposed article, stipulating that the Courts
of each country should be open to the suitors of the other. Mr.
Gallatin said that it would have no operation; that as we had,
in abandoning the article of indemnities, reserved the claims
for those which might be due for damages suffered prior to
the war, we relied upon having access to the British Courts,
although the same object might also be treated of between the
two Governments; that our own Courts would be equally open
to British subjects, and we had thought our declaration to that
effect in our note would be equivalent to an article in the treaty.

Mr. Goulburn said that for the Government and for him it
would be sufficient; but in the office to which he belonged
(the Colonial Department) he was very often troubled with

persons who came with complaints on the subject, and he wanted to have an answer to give them.

Mr. Bayard said that as the Courts of the United States would of course be open to British subjects without any such article, and as it would be known that the British Courts would also, without stipulation, be open to our citizens, it was to be apprehended that our judges, inferring that the article must be intended for something, would apply to it a meaning different from that intended, and a constructive operation which is not meant.

Mr. Goulburn said that if we definitively objected to it they must give it up, but it would be quite a gratification to them to have it.

I observed that I had another objection, which I did not wish to be understood as expressing for any of my colleagues, but for myself alone. It would be known by all the world that such an article would have no sort of operation in England. It would therefore be understood as being unilateral—applying only to the United States—and would thus bring an imputation upon them which they did not deserve, and which I was not willing to expose them to.

Mr. Goulburn at last requested, if we could not admit the article, that it should be entered on the protocol as having been demanded by them and objected to by us; to which we agreed.

The conference was of about three hours, and terminated by an agreement that we should meet at three o'clock to-morrow afternoon, at the house of the British Plenipotentiaries, for the purpose of signing and sealing the six copies of the treaty—three copies to be made by us, to be delivered to them, and three by them, to be delivered to us. They told us that Mr. Baker would go off to-morrow evening for England, with one copy of the treaty, and that he was to go out to America with the English ratification. Mr. Clay proposed to us that we should send out Mr. Carroll, his private secretary, with one of the copies, and he asked the British Plenipotentiaries if there would be any objection to Mr. Carroll's going out in the same vessel with Mr. Baker. They thought there would not, and promised to recommend it to their Government. After the

adjournment of the conference, it was agreed that a dispatch to
the Secretary of State should be written, to go with the treaty.
Mr. Hughes promised to have two copies of the treaty ready by
three o'clock to-morrow afternoon, and Mr. Clay promised to
make one copy for him. We made a short dinner, and I was
engaged until ten at night in making the draft of a dispatch to
the Secretary of State; I took it to Mr. Gallatin's chamber, but
he was gone out.

24th. I wrote letters to the Secretary of State and to my
mother, to be prepared for Mr. Hughes, and took my last letter
to the Secretary of State to Mr. Smith, for a duplicate to be
made. Engaged much of the morning in preparing the copies
of papers to be transmitted by Mr. Hughes. Mr. Clay was not
ready with his copy of the treaty at three o'clock, and Mr.
Hughes called upon the British Plenipotentiaries to postpone
the meeting until four. At that hour we went to their house,
and after settling the protocol of yesterday's conference, Mr.
Baker read one of the British copies of the treaty; Mr. Gallatin
and myself had the two other copies before us, comparing them
as he read. Lord Gambier, Mr. Goulburn, and Dr. Adams had
our three copies, comparing them in like manner. There was
a variation between the copies merely verbal, which arose from
the writing at full length, on both sides, the dates, which in the
drafts were in arithmetical figures. All our copies had the
Treaty of Peace of seventeen hundred and eighty-three. All
the British copies had it one thousand seven hundred and eighty-
three. There was the same difference in the date of the signature of this treaty. It was not thought necessary to alter either
of them. A few mistakes in the copies were rectified, and then
the six copies were signed and sealed by the three British and
the five American Plenipotentiaries. Lord Gambier delivered to
me the three British copies, and I delivered to him the three
American copies, of the treaty, which he said he hoped would
be permanent; and I told him I hoped it would be the last
treaty of peace between Great Britain and the United States.
We left them at half-past six o'clock. Mr. Baker had a carriage
in the yard waiting for him to start for Ostend, where there is
a vessel in readiness to take him over to England. It was

agreed that the signature of the treaty should not be divulged here until to-morrow noon, so that Mr. Baker may have an opportunity to carry the first information of the event to the British Government.

On our return home we found Mr. Bentzon, who had been this morning invited by Mr. Bayard to dine with us. He was during the dinner all eye and all ear—watching to catch some certainty of what he suspected we had been doing. It is but three days since he returned from London. The Danish frigate, The Pearl, which was to have gone to England, there to take him and the other Danish Commissioners to receive the Danish West India Islands, is lost. She sailed at first from Copenhagen, and returned dismasted. She sailed a second time, and was totally lost; the crew saved. Bentzon told me he had this day received the news of this last event, and that he must now go to England, there to find a passage to the West Indies as he could. I asked him when he should go; he said to-morrow, or perhaps this night. He lingered with us some time after dinner, and then went to Mr. Clay's chamber, and afterwards to Mr. Carroll's. About ten at night he wrote a note to Mr. Gallatin to inform him that he was immediately going. He went before midnight. Mr. Baker and Mr. Gambier had started about nine. I went for an hour to Mr. Smith's lodgings.

I cannot close the record of this day without an humble offering of gratitude to God for the conclusion to which it has pleased him to bring the negotiations for peace at this place, and a fervent prayer that its result may be propitious to the welfare, the best interests, and the union of my country.

25th. Christmas-day. The day of all others in the year most congenial to proclaiming peace on earth and good will to men. We had a meeting of the mission at one o'clock. My draft of a dispatch to the Secretary of State had passed through the hands of all my colleagues, and had been altered and amended by them all. I agreed to all the amendments excepting one by Mr. Clay, which, at the first reading, I had not perceived. In mentioning to the Secretary of State the principle on which we had relied respecting the fisheries, I had stated that we *considered* the Treaty of 1783 as a permanent contract, no part of which was liable to be abrogated by the subsequent war. Mr. Clay, with the assent of Mr. Russell, had altered it to read, we *thought* it *might* be considered, and Russell afterwards had written it, we *contended* it *might* be considered. Mr. Russell made out the fair copy of the dispatch to be sent. On reading it over, to compare it with the original draft and amendments, I perceived this alteration, and immediately objected to it. I insisted upon substituting the word *must* for *might*, to read, we contended the Treaty of 1783 *must* be considered, etc. Mr. Russell and Mr. Bayard agreed to this amendment. Mr. Gallatin and Mr. Clay were gone to dine at Mr. Van Caneghem's; Mr. Hughes came to take the dispatches to them there to be signed. I showed him the alteration, and desired him to give notice of it to Mr. Clay before he should sign the dispatch. Hughes took up the dispatch, read it over, and exclaimed, in a great passion, "There, now! my name is not once mentioned in the whole letter!" I looked it over, and said, coolly, it was not; but that it was mentioned in my separate letter to the Secretary of State.

"I assure you," said he, "that it (meaning the omission) takes away great part of my satisfaction in being the bearer of the treaty." Neither Mr. Bayard nor I made him any reply. Bayard asked me, after he was gone, what he could mean. I said I supposed he meant we should have introduced into our dispatch a high-flown commendation of his merits. Bayard said that it would have made both him and ourselves ridiculous. Hughes renewed his complaint at Van Caneghem's to Mr. Clay, who told him that if it was proper to mention him by name it was not too late; but he believed it was not usual in diplomatic dispatches, though customary in military affairs. Hughes wrote me from Mr. Van Caneghem's that, upon his advice, he had concluded, with the approbation of Mr. Gallatin and Mr. Clay, to start at four o'clock to-morrow morning. About eight in the evening we had everything in readiness for him, and delivered to him all his dispatches.

I then went to the Intendant's, where I found assembled a party of about one hundred and twenty persons, almost all at cards. We received the congratulations of the Intendant and his family, and of many others, upon the signature of the peace, and frequently with expressions of pleasure that its conditions were understood to be advantageous to us. The party broke up about ten in the evening. We received shortly after dinner a note from the Intendant, informing us that he had just received an official communication of the conclusion of the peace, and inviting us to dine with him on Wednesday next, to celebrate the event. We had, however, invited the British Plenipotentiaries to dine with us on that day. Mr. Todd had company at his chambers this day, and at twelve o'clock announced to them the conclusion of the peace. Mr. Cornelissen, who was present, afterwards gave notice of it at the Exchange.

27th. We had a meeting of the mission in my chamber at one o'clock. Mr. Gallatin had suggested last Friday, immediately after we had come to the agreement to sign the treaty of peace, that we ought to make to the British Government an official communication of our full power to negotiate a treaty of commerce. The proposition was now renewed, and after some discussion it was agreed that Mr. Gallatin should make a draft of a note for that purpose.

The subject of an answer to the note from the British Plenipotentiaries of the 7th instant, respecting the sale of negroes taken from the Southern States in the West Indies, was further considered. I proposed that, the peace being now made, we should send a copy of the affidavit furnished us by the Secretary of State. This was opposed by Mr. Clay; and he engaged to make a draft of an answer, referring it to the American Government, to give or to withhold the proof requested.

Mr. Gallatin had made a minute of the objects still to be determined upon by the mission, and among them was the disposal of the books, maps, and other effects, and papers. Mr. Gallatin proposed that the books and other articles, except the papers, should be packed up and sent to Mr. Beasley, for the use of the mission to London hereafter.

Mr. Clay thought they ought to be sent by the Neptune to the Department of State. Then came the question about the papers. Mr. Clay was very earnest to have them with him in the Neptune, because he had no copies of them at all, and he thought they ought to be deposited in the Department of State, where he could have access to them hereafter. He said they might hereafter be interesting as historical records, and the Department of State was the proper place for them.

I said that according to the usage in similar cases, and the precedent in the case of the former mission, I considered that the custody of the papers would, at the termination of the mission, devolve upon me, subject to the orders of our Government, and I should take charge of them accordingly.

Mr. Clay immediately kindled into a flame, and said that he should, both physically and morally, revolt at any such pretension, that because I happened accidentally to be in possession of the papers I should assert a right to keep them.

I said it was not because I was in possession of the papers, for I would instantly, or at any other time, put every one of the papers into his possession, if he desired it; but I should still consider myself entitled to the keeping of them. Mr. Gallatin declared himself to be of the same opinion.

It was asked where were the papers of the prior mission. Mr. Gallatin said he had them all, having received them from Mr. Harris, the secretary. I mentioned that Mr. Gallatin had then distributed the papers at his own discretion, and had given to me the full power to treat of commerce with Russia, and to Mr. Bayard the powers to treat of peace and of commerce with Great Britain.

Mr. Clay said he did not pay any regard to the precedent of the former mission, and he knew nothing about the usage. Mr. Russell called for its being put to vote. I said I should not put it to vote, not considering it as a point to be decided by a vote. Mr. Clay seemed to consider this as arrogating a superiority over the other members of the mission, as a claim of prerogative, at which he was excessively indignant. He said it was well known the circumstance of my being first named in the mission was merely accidental. I said I was perfectly sensible of that, and had any other person been first named, I should have considered him as entitled to the custody of the papers after the termination of the mission. I claimed nothing but what I had acquiesced in when I was not the first named of the mission.

Mr. Gallatin proposed to leave the subject for further consideration hereafter, which was done.

28th. We had no meeting, but Mr. Gallatin made his draft of a note to the British Plenipotentiaries, informing them officially that we have a full power to treat of commerce. It was successively amended by the other members of the mission, and I prepared it, and obtained the signatures to it of all the members excepting Mr. Russell.

We had company to dinner—Lord Gambier, Mr. and Mrs. Goulburn, Dr. Adams, Lieutenant-General Alten, Commander-in-Chief of the Hanoverian troops in this city, Major-General Lyon, Commander-in-Chief of the English troops, the Intendant, the Count D'Hane de Steenhuyse and his lady, Major Heise, aid-de-camp and military secretary to General Alten, Mrs. Heise and her friend Miss Halkett, Major Kuntze, quartermaster of the Hanoverian troops, Captain Havelock, an aid-de-camp to General Alten, Mr. W. S. Smith, and Mr. Smith, the private secretary of Mr. Russell. We sat down twenty-two at table.

The Society of St. Cecilia had several times requested to know when they might come and give us a serenade. I sent them word to come this day. They were in the room adjoining our dining-hall, and entertained us with music during the dinner and great part of the evening. The first air they struck was God save the King, and immediately after it, Hail Columbia. Lord Gambier immediately proposed as a toast, "the United States of America." I requested his permission, previously, to give "His Britannic Majesty," to which he assented. Both the toasts were drunk, and afterwards I gave, addressing the Intendant, "The Sovereign Prince of the Netherlands." I wished the band to have played the Dutch national air, but they sent me word they did not know it. The Intendant then desired to give a toast, and gave "the Congress at Ghent," in return for which we gave "the City of Ghent and its prosperity."

We left the table about eight o'clock, and had one card-table for the Intendant's lady. The party broke up between eleven and twelve at night.

Lord Gambier told me that Mr. Baker and Mr. Gambier met with an accident on their way to Ostend; the wheel of their carriage broke down, and they were detained six or seven hours before they could get it repaired. They reached Ostend on Christmas-day, about three in the afternoon, and immediately embarked. Lord Gambier also told me he heard we were to send them a note, proposing the negotiation of a treaty of commerce. Mr. Clay had met this morning Mr. Goulburn and Dr. Adams, and given them the information. Dr. Adams said that their powers were expired, and he doubted whether they could even receive the note. Mr. Goulburn, however, said they could receive and transmit it to their Government. Mr. Clay also told Mr. Goulburn that although we had declined making an official communication of the proof furnished us by the Secretary of State of the sale, by British subjects, of our negroes in the West Indies, yet we could show him, and give him, a copy of it inofficially. This promise Mr. Clay made without consulting any other member of the mission, after having insisted upon refusing the paper, which, since the peace, Mr. Gallatin and myself were for communicating without hesitation.

We had yesterday, and I omitted to mention it then, a formal visit of ceremony from the Mayor, in full dress, with his four adjoints, to congratulate us upon the conclusion of the peace. The Mayor himself was at Brussels when he first heard of it, on Christmas-day, about noon. The Hereditary Prince of Orange, as Commander-in-Chief of the English troops, was informed of it by a courier, and the Sovereign Prince announced it at dinner.

29th. We had a short meeting of the mission, and signed the note concerning the sale of negroes drawn by Mr. Clay. I sent it and the note we had prepared yesterday to the British Plenipotentiaries. We determined to break up our establishment to-morrow, when the fifth month of our residence in this house expires.

30th. We had a meeting of the mission at my chamber. Mr. Clay brought forward again the subject of the books, maps, effects, and papers belonging to the mission, and expressed his opinion that they ought all to be sent to the Department of State by the Neptune. He had, he said, no copies of the papers; he did not like the trouble of copying. He wished, therefore, the papers might be in a place where he could have access to them, if he should have occasion, and they might be hereafter useful as historical archives. It would be convenient to him to have them in the Neptune, and it could be no inconvenience to me, as by my laudable industry I had taken copies of all the papers.

I said I had taken copies of a part of the papers received from the British Plenipotentiaries, but not of any of the papers received from the Department of State, for the very reason that I had considered it unquestionable that they would remain with me.

Mr. Gallatin said he thought it would be ridiculous to send back to the Department of State instructions and papers sent from that Department to us; that when there was only one person in a mission, there could be no question in the case. The Ministers from the United States invariably kept the papers addressed to them; but as in a commission of five persons every member could not have them, he thought that in propriety, and according to general usage, they should be left with the first-named member of the mission.

I referred again to the precedent of the former mission, which Mr. Clay said again he considered as nothing. I replied that I must consider it as something, because it was then unanimous, and the three members of that mission formed a majority of the present one. Mr. Bayard took no part in this debate, but made some observations to Mr. Clay in a separate conversation, which I did not hear. He then asked Mr. Gallatin what was done with the papers of the former mission. Mr. Gallatin said that he had taken all the papers with him, to the time he had withdrawn from the mission, and they were in one of his trunks on board the Neptune; that there was but one dispatch from the Department of State received after they arrived in St. Petersburg—that of 23d June, 1813, of which we all had originals.

I added that the day before they had left St. Petersburg, Mr.

Gallatin had given to Mr. Bayard the full powers to treat of peace and commerce with Great Britain, and to me the full power to treat of commerce with Russia.   Mr. Clay, however, still recurring to his right, I said I supposed he would at least acknowledge that I had an *equal* right with himself.   He said yes, he admitted that.   I then said I would deliver up the papers to any person named to me in writing by a majority of the mission and authorized to give me a receipt for them ; the papers which I should deliver being also specified.   Mr. Clay said he would draw up such a paper, and we passed to another subject.   No vote or resolution was passed.   Mr. Bayard, at least in my hearing, did not give an opinion.   Mr. Russell said to me, " I believe I should be against you upon the principle ;" and added, " but I shall not vote to have the papers taken out of Mr. Adams's hands to be put into those of *any other member of the mission*."   I expected another discussion when Mr. Clay's draft of the requisition to me should be presented for consideration.

31st. Mr. Bayard and myself received the visits of Lord Gambier and Dr. Adams.   Mr. Gallatin was not in his chamber.   Mr. Clay came about one o'clock to my chamber, and delivered to me an open letter, signed by Mr. Bayard, himself, and Mr. Russell, dated yesterday, and requesting me, in conformity with the resolution of the majority of the mission of the same day, to cause to be packed up all the books, maps, and other articles purchased at the public expense for the use of the mission, as also all the original notes, papers, and communications received from the British Government, from the British Plenipotentiaries, and from other persons, and to cause the whole to be transmitted to the Neptune, at the public expense, to be carried to America and deposited with the Department of State.

After reading this paper, I told Mr. Clay that it was very unexpected to me ; that I had not been aware that any vote or resolution of a majority of the mission had been adopted yesterday.

He said that I could not say so with truth ; that after we had finished our business here, he did not wish to part at enmity with any person; that if the leaving of the papers with me had been put on the footing of courtesy, it would have been a different thing; but he could not admit my right to keep the papers, merely because I accidentally had possession of them.

I said that there certainly had been no vote or resolution yesterday on the subject; that my claim to keep the papers was not founded upon my accidental possession of them. I had made him the offer, and would now repeat it, to put every one of the papers into his hands if he desired it, but that the question would remain precisely the same; that as to parting in enmity, I saw no sort of reason for that; it was merely a question with regard to the disposal of the papers. He had one opinion, I had another. I saw no sort of necessity for any further difference between us because we differed upon that. It was not a mere act of courtesy that I required, it was a claim founded upon what I conceived to be the usage, and with which I had acquiesced in the case of the former mission. I asked nothing but what I had granted. It was not a point of law. It was very true, as he had said, that my being first named in the full powers was accidental. But that accident, as I conceived, had assigned to me the custody of the papers, subject to the orders of the Government. There was no *law* which authorized me to sign my name the first, merely because I was first named in the full powers. If in any of the dispatches or papers we had signed he had insisted upon signing his name before mine, I knew of no *law* that would have warranted me in claiming the right of signing first. I considered it as resting upon usage, and that the custody of the papers stood on precisely the same foundation.

This illustration appeared to nettle him, for it conveyed to him my sense of the whole procedure—a piece of chicanery upon a trifle—appeals to law and right upon an object not worth a straw—the pretence that I am arrogating prerogative and superiority, because I claim, as the first-named member of a mission, the custody of its papers, subject to the orders of Government—cavilling upon a bagatelle merely because it would be convenient to himself to have the papers.

As to the precedent of the former mission, he said that Mr. Gallatin and Mr. Bayard did not agree in their account of it. Mr. Bayard did not admit that Mr. Gallatin had the papers, and it appeared to him (Clay) utterly absurd that Mr. Gallatin should have kept them.   After the rejection of his nomination by the Senate, he had not even been a member of the mission. I said that only proved that my claim now was stronger than his could be then; that the fact was so: he had distributed the papers *at his discretion*, and his distribution had been acqui esced in without discussion by Mr. Bayard and myself.

I finally told Mr. Clay that I should take the paper which he had brought me into consideration, and act upon it as I should think proper.

Day. I have risen during the month almost always before six, and without exception before daylight.   Make my fire, read five chapters in the Bible, and write until between nine and ten.   Breakfast in my chamber alone.   Write, read papers, receive visits, and attend mission meetings until three, afternoon.   Walk from one to two hours, dine at half-past four, and sit at table until six.   Go to the theatre, concert, or party at a friend's house, or write in my chamber until eight in the evening.   Spend one or two hours at Mr. Smith's lodgings, and about ten at night return home and retire to bed.   This mode of life will henceforth be varied by a new change in my situation.   The last ten days have been overburdened with business.   Thus ends the most memorable year of my life.   I close the record of it with a fervent tribute of gratitude to Divine Providence for the signal favor granted to my country by the conclusion of a treaty of peace; also for the blessings it has continued to me of a domestic nature, to my parents, wife, and children, for the increased proportion of health I have enjoyed, and for the comforts of a quiet conscience.   And I implore a continuance of the favor of Heaven upon my country, family, friends, and myself; and, above all, the strength and the will to discharge all my duties to my fellow-creatures and my God.

January 2d, 1815. The pressure upon my time is excessive, and accidents continually occurring prevent me from retrieving it. I wrote this morning an answer to the requisition signed by Messrs. Bayard, Clay, and Russell, and presented to me on Saturday by Mr. Clay. I gave it to Mr. Bayard at his chamber. This subject, so insignificant of itself, gives me more trouble than, if it was important, it possibly could. It is one of those occasions upon which, with an extreme anxiety to act with propriety, I feel the hazard of committing an error. The manner in which the paper was drawn up, signed, and presented to me was, I think, irregular; the paper is totally different from that which Mr. Clay promised to draw up, and is drawn in a manner not a little embarrassing to me. It neither specifies the papers to be delivered, nor the persons to whom I am to deliver them. I mentioned these circumstances in my answer to the letter, and added that I had objections to the request itself, which I should state at the meeting of the mission.

Before delivering to Mr. Bayard my answer, I called at Mr. Gallatin's chamber, and showed him the requisition to me. He said he had seen it before; that Mr. Clay had shown it to him, and asked him to sign it. He had answered that he would sign it, with the addition that he was of a different opinion, upon which Mr. Clay had preferred that he should not sign it at all. We all dined with the Hanoverian Lieutenant-General, Baron Charles Alten, excepting Mr. Clay, who was unwell and sent an excuse. The Intendant and Mayor were there, and ten or fifteen English, Hanoverian, and Belgian officers; General Lyons was one of them. About eight we went to the concert and redoute extraordinary on the occasion of the peace. The hall was crowded as full as it could hold. The concert was just over when we went in, but they played Hail Columbia the second time, to greet us. There was an inscription at one end of the hall, "Harmonie entre Albion et Columbia. La Paix conclue, xxiv Décembre."

4th. I finished this morning the copy of the treaty. I had requested a meeting of the mission at one o'clock, but it failed. I paid a visit to Mr. and Mrs. Goulburn, and took to him the newspapers that he had lent us, and the affidavit concerning the sale of negroes taken from the Southern States, which had

been promised him by Mr. Clay. I found them much engaged
in packing up and making preparations for their departure.
Mr. Goulburn consented to stay only from complaisance, to
attend the public entertainment to be given to-morrow in
honor of the peace, and is to leave the city on Saturday. We
all dined and spent the evening at Mr. Meulemeester's, with
his usual family party. While we were at table his daughter
Marianne, a pretty child, about twelve years old, came in, and
played upon the harp, and sang several couplets complimentary
to us, written by Mr. Cornelissen. Her cousin, Madame
Greban's daughter Esther, who is about a year older, played
Hail Columbia. Copies of the verses were given to each of
us, and Mr. Gallatin asked for a copy of the tune, which was
promised.

5th. On rising this morning, instead of diplomatic papers
and letters concerning the loan, of which I have a large file to
copy; instead of the arrears with my correspondents, which I
have to bring up, and the still more urgent arrears of this
journal, which are increasing every day, the fancy struck me
of answering the couplets yesterday sung by Mr. Meulemeester's daughter. So farewell for this day all grave and reverend
occupation. I could think of nothing but my couplets. After
preparing them, four stanzas in number, I went out to a bookseller's shop, purchased three small volumes of Etrennes Géo-
graphiques, with colored plates, packed them up with my song,
addressed them to Miss Meulemeester, and then wrote a note
to her mother, requesting her to present them in my name to
her daughter. The morning was now gone. A meeting of
the mission at Mr. Gallatin's chamber had been appointed for
one o'clock, but he was gone out. It failed again for the
second time. Another important question arose, how we were
to dress for the banquet of this day. To settle it, Mr. Smith,
at my request, called upon Mr. Goulburn, and enquired how he
proposed to go. He answered, in uniform, and we accordingly
all went in uniform. The banquet was at the Hôtel de Ville,
and was given by subscription by the principal gentlemen of the
city. We sat down to table about five o'clock, in the largest
hall of the building, fitted up for the occasion with white

cotton hangings. The American and British flags were inter-
twined together under olive-trees, at the head of the hall.
Mr. Goulburn and myself were seated between the Intendant
and the Mayor, at the centre of the cross-piece of the table.
There were about ninety persons seated at the table. As we
went into the hall, Hail Columbia was performed by the band
of music. It was followed by God save the King, and these
two airs were alternately repeated during the dinner-time, until
Mr. Goulburn thought they became tiresome. I was of the
same opinion. The Intendant and the Mayor alternately
toasted "His Britannic Majesty," and "the United States,"
"the Allied Powers," and "the Sovereign Prince," "the Negotiators," and "the Peace." I then remarked to Mr. Goulburn
that he must give the next toast, which he did. It was, " the
Intendant and the Mayor; the City of Ghent, its prosperity;
and our gratitude for their hospitality and the many acts of
kindness that we had received from them." I gave the next
and last toast, which was, " Ghent, the city of peace; may the
gates of the temple of Janus, here closed, not be opened again
for a century!" There were some French couplets, written
by a Baron Exaerde, which were distributed, and should have
been sung; but they were omitted, and were not worth singing.
We rose from table soon after seven, and went into the hall,
where the ball had commenced. The company was numerous,
and the dancing animated. I met there Madame Meulemeester, who told me she had received my note and had given
my present to her daughter. I came home about ten in the
evening.

6th. We had at length the meeting of the mission, in Mr.
Gallatin's chamber, at two o'clock. It was much hurried, Mr.
Bayard and Mr. Clay being in the midst of the preparations for
their departure to-morrow morning. I now mentioned the
letter I had received from three members of the mission,
Messrs. Bayard, Clay, and Russell, and the answer I had given
to it. I stated that I had not understood that any resolution
had passed at the meeting of 30th December, and that the
paper sent to me was totally different from that which Mr.
Clay had promised to draw up, as it neither specified the

papers I was to deliver up, nor the person to whom I should deliver them; that I had expected Mr. Clay's draft would be submitted to the mission for consideration, and that I should have had an opportunity of making my objections to it. Mr. Clay said that a majority of the mission had expressed their opinions at the meeting; and Mr. Bayard said I had refused to put it to the vote, and said that I knew very well what the vote would be. I immediately denied ever having said so. I admitted that at the previous meeting I had declined putting it to vote, and had said that I considered the custody of the papers as my right, subject to the orders of our Government, and not subject to a vote. But, on further reflection, I had said at the meeting of the 30th of December that I would deliver up any papers specified to me to any person named to me by a majority of the mission, authorized by them to receive them from me and to give me a receipt for them; that so far from having said I knew very well what the vote would be, I had not known what it would be; I did not know what Mr. Bayard's opinion would be. I was not conscious that he had expressed any opinion, and I inclined, from the precedent of the former mission, in which he had acquiesced at least, to the belief that his opinion would now have been for the same course.

Mr. Bayard now said that his recollection was different of the precedent of the former mission; that he himself had all those papers; they were in his trunk on board the Neptune. He was sure at least that he had brought the book with him, and Mr. Hughes had now taken it home.

Mr. Gallatin repeated that, as he recollected, he had received from Mr. Harris all the papers until 31st October, when he (Gallatin) had withdrawn from the mission, and he was confident they were in his trunk on board the Neptune.

Mr. Clay was now set at his ease with regard to the precedent, and said he did not believe there was any such usage as I referred to; that at least there was none such in the British Government; that Lord Gambier had said the papers were all returned to the public office, and all theirs would be so. Mr. Gallatin said Lord Gambier might not know much about it, and Mr. Bayard said he considered his authority as nothing, or next to nothing. But that was what he had said.

It was evident that Bayard himself was the person who had asked of Lord Gambier the question, but that he felt a little awkward at having been to Lord Gambier to ascertain what it would be proper to do with our papers.

Mr. Clay then asked if I had come to a final determination concerning the papers; that if I had, and determined to keep them, it might be proper to transmit to the Secretary of State a copy of the letter from the three members to me, and of my answer.

I said, Certainly; it had always been my expectation and intention that copies of those letters should be transmitted to the Secretary of State; that I had not come to a final determination concerning the papers. I had wished to state at the meeting of the mission that the time was premature for a final disposal of them; that with a written demand from three members of the mission to have the papers packed up and sent away, I should be reluctant at keeping them; but unless the papers were specified, I knew not which to send away nor which to reserve, and unless the person were named to me, I knew not to whom to deliver them. I knew not where nor how to send them to the Neptune. The mission was not terminated. We had just communicated to the British Government that we were empowered to conclude a treaty of commerce. It was probable they would accept the proposal after the ratification of the peace. In that case the effects and papers would be wanted again. I considered myself entitled to the custody of the papers, and if they were to be taken out of my hands, the person must be named to whom I should give them, and must give me a receipt for them.

Mr. Clay said there was the principle and the modus. As to any right of mine to keep the papers, he could not reason about it. He could not think or speak of it with patience. There was nothing in the nature of our Government, nothing in the nature of the mission, that gave any color to it. If it had been asked as a matter of courtesy, he was willing to show all suitable respect to the first-named member of the mission.

But a privilege! a prerogative! he could never acknowledge or submit to it; that as to specifying the papers, that could not have been done by him, because they were in my possession; that there was no necessity for naming the person to whom I should deliver them. I might take them on with me to Paris, and give them to any other member of the mission who would return by the Neptune, or I might send them by Mr. Smith, who would probably go to the Neptune from hence. He was desirous of parting in friendship with everybody; we had here transacted our business together, he hoped to the satisfaction of our country, and he did not wish to go away with any heartburnings between any of us.

All this was said in an acrimonious and menacing tone. I said it was not improbable I should return to the United States in the Neptune myself. I had brought a list of all the books and other effects, except the papers, which was on the table. I should pack them up, and leave them here, to be sent where and how the mission should direct. The copying-press and the papers I intended to take with me to Paris, and would deliver them ultimately to any person named and authorized to receive them, according as I had offered, by a majority of the mission. The paper I had received was not an act of the majority, it was the act of three members.

"And although," said Mr. Clay, "those three members form a majority."

"Certainly," said I; "an act of the greater number without consulting the other members is not an act of the majority."

Clay now lost all the remnant of his temper, and broke out with, "You *dare* not, you *cannot*, you SHALL not insinuate that there has been a cabal of three members against you; no person shall impute anything of the kind to me with impunity. It is not unexampled that a paper should be drawn up and signed without consulting the whole mission. You gave me to sign, the very day when I took this paper to you, the answer to a letter from the Prussian Minister at the Hague. It was already signed by two members of the mission, and I had never seen it—nay, I did not know there was such a letter to answer. The letter I presented to you was shown to Mr. Gallatin; he was consulted upon it, and might have signed it if he had pleased. As it was addressed to you, and known to be against your opinion, it was not necessary to consult you."

I replied, " What I *dare* say, I have dared to say in writing. Gentlemen may draw from it what inferences they please; I am not answerable for them. I am perfectly satisfied that your letter and my answer should be transmitted to our Government, and I assure you that if you do not transmit them, I shall."

I said nothing in reply to Mr. Clay's example that he had given, of a paper drawn up by one member and signed without further consultation of the mission. This has been done several times in cases where there was no diversity of opinion, and where every member, previously to signing the paper, might have stated any objection, or proposed any alteration, upon which the mission would have been immediately consulted. But it has happened in no case where there was any difference of opinion. The case relied upon by Mr. Clay was an unfortunate one. The letter from the Prussian Minister was dated 13th December. Two copies of it had been transmitted to the Secretary of State, with a letter mentioning the substance of its contents, which letter Mr. Clay had signed. The necessity of answering it had been mentioned at several successive meetings of the mission, and Mr. Gallatin had made the first draft of the answer at the meeting of 29th December, while we were in session. I had made a second draft on the 30th, and then, with Mr. Gallatin's approbation, at Mr. Russell's request, wrote it off the morning that Mr. Russell went away, that it might be ready for him to sign. This was the reason why it was definitively prepared without consultation of the whole mission upon its contents. But if Mr. Clay had objected to anything in it, certainly it could not have been sent without a decision of the mission upon it.

On my reply to the dare not and cannot and shall not, Mr. Clay cooled down, and said that, if I had not come to a final determination, he should wish that our letters might not be transmitted to the Government; that if I should go home in the Neptune, there need be no further question upon the subject; that it would cast some dishonor on us all to say anything to the Government about it; that it would look as if we had fallen to a scramble after a few books and papers.

I said that if such was his desire, I was perfectly willing that the Government should not be informed there had been any such question among us, and to say no more about it.

Mr. Gallatin proposed that the books and effects, except the papers, should be sent to Mr. Beasley, at London, to be kept by him subject to further orders. This was agreed to; and I retain the papers also until further orders. The meeting was then indefinitely adjourned.

Mr. Bayard and Mr. Clay, who are going to-morrow morning together, came and took leave of me at my chamber.

7th. I resume the copying of papers respecting the loan, the originals of which I consider as being of right in Mr. Gallatin's hands. He is the person first named in that commission, and I told him I thought he had a right to keep the papers. He said he cared nothing about them, but determined to take them. Mr. Bayard and Mr. Clay went about six o'clock this morning, in the diligence for Lille.

10th. Finished copying the papers relating to the loan, and returned all the originals to Mr. Gallatin. Upon arranging his papers before his departure, he found in his trunk all the papers of the prior mission, which he thought he had sent on board the Neptune, and which Mr. Bayard was so confident were in *his* possession. Mr. Gallatin showed them to me, and said that if it should be finally determined to send the papers of the present mission to be deposited in the Department of State, the same thing should be done with these.

CHAPTER X.

BRUSSELS, *January* 26th, 1815.—I had ordered my horses at ten o'clock this morning, having yet partly to pack my trunks. Antoine came to my chamber just after I had kindled my fire, and we were both busied until eleven in finishing the preparations. I had intended to call yesterday upon Mr. Nuytens to take leave, but had not found a moment for the purpose. It was therefore necessary to write him a note, which I sent by the messenger of the hotel. Nuytens, the son, immediately came to my chamber at the hotel, and took leave of me there. Mr. Cornelissen did the same, and also Mr. Meulemeester, who brought me the music of the couplets sung by his daughter on the 4th instant; they were written by Mr. Cornelissen. At a quarter-past eleven o'clock I entered my carriage and left the Hôtel des Pays-Bas and the city of Ghent, probably never to see them again. My residence in the city has been of seven months and two days, and it has been the most memorable period of my life. I left it with the sentiments suitable to the occasion: of grateful regard for its inhabitants, who have taken a strong interest in our success, and have shown us many civilities and attentions; but, above all, with gratitude to Heaven for the signal favor to my country, in which I have participated at this place. There are three stages between Ghent and Brussels — Quadrecht, Alost, and Assche. The distance is six and a quarter posts. I left my carriage only once, at the first stage, and landed at half-past five in the afternoon at the Hôtel de Flandres, in Brussels. It was the coldest day there had been this winter, and was growing colder the whole day. The ground was covered with one sheet of snow the whole way, though not anywhere three inches deep. The travelling in sledges would have been excellent.

30th. About one o'clock Mr. Renwett called upon me, and went with me to see the collection of pictures of Mr. Burtin. On the way, he pointed out to me the house, or rather the ruins where had been the house, of Count Egmont. I then recollected having seen the house when I was at Brussels before. It has since been demolished. We also went round by the marble fountain erected by the testament of Bruce, Earl of Aylesbury, an English nobleman, who resided forty years in this city, and left to his heir the order to erect this monument, as a token of his gratitude to the inhabitants of the place. He died in 1740, and the work was executed by Bergé, a sculptor of this country, in 1751. It is a costly monument, but gives no explanation how it happened that a British Peer, public-spirited enough to appropriate a part of his fortune to the comfort and embellishment of a foreign city, should have had so little of the sentiment of patriotism as to have lived as a private individual forty years absent from his country, and yet so near it.

We were two hours in surveying Mr. Burtin's collection, which is the choicest private collection that I ever saw. He is himself a thorough connoisseur in painting, and a very proper object for a painter. He is seventy-two years of age, and began by asking me if I was an amateur de tableaux. I told him that I took great pleasure in looking at good pictures, but that I could not assume the pretension of being an amateur. He said he could give me in five minutes the secret which he had been forty years in learning, and which he had fully disclosed in two octavo volumes that he had published, and which he hoped would by my means become known in America. Since the English had got in here, they had taken more than seventy copies of it, so that he had scarcely any left. The French considered his work as the first upon the subject, though he had treated the French school harshly, and Mr. Maltebrun, the critic, had styled him a connoisseur très-éclairé, juge sévère, mais impartial, de l'école Française. His secret was to look at every picture as if the original was behind you and you saw it in a mirror. If it appeared natural to you as an object reflected in a mirror, you might boldly pronounce it a good picture. If not, you might as certainly pronounce it a bad one. As to the French school, it could boast of only one good painter, Eustache Le Sueur. I asked him how he considered Poussin. "As an Italian painter, formed altogether in Italy." "How of Claude?" "Why, his very name," said he, "was 'of Lorraine'; and all his art of painting he learnt at Rome." "But Rubens," said I, "studied likewise in Italy." "Yes; but he was a great painter before he went there. You will find it all explained at large in my book. You see," said he, "this whole side of my library. It consists altogether of books upon the art of painting, and, excepting these four middle shelves, which are catalogues of sales, with their prices, all the rest, now that my book is published, may be thrown into the fire. There is nothing further to be got from them." After this introduction, we went and looked at the pictures, and, as the chambers were cold, Mr. Burtin left us with his housekeeper, a pretty girl, who, he said, could explain to us the subjects of the pictures as well as himself. They are in four small chambers, and all excellent pictures. He prides himself upon not having one indifferent painting in the whole collection. Besides the standards of the Dutch and Flemish schools, Mieris, Rembrandt, Teniers, Ostade, Jan Steen, Van Dyke, and Rubens, there are four capital portraits by Holbein, three pictures of Albert Dürer, one of Michael Angelo, and a small portrait of Titian, painted by himself. The large pictures appeared to me the least remarkable. The water-pieces, flowers, dead game, living animals, and inside views of churches, were like those in all good collections of the Flemish school. A number of sketches, mere daubings, of Rubens, and one admirable portrait by the same master. Several landscapes, like most others, and a singular portrait of Terburg, painted by himself, a bitter satire upon his disciple Caspar Netscher, and upon William III., the Prince of Orange. After having admired these nearly two hours, Mr. Burtin sent his maid with us to see his four finest pictures, in a separate chamber. They were covered with green silk veils. A marriage of St. Catherine, the masterpiece of Van Dyke; a St. Francis, by Rubens; a Christ bearing his Cross, by Leonardo da Vinci; and last, and most exquisitely beautiful of all, a Holy Family, by Guido. If it was mine, I would not give it for all the rest of the collection. The most perfect ideal head of the Virgin that was perhaps ever painted. I took a copy of Mr. Burtin's book, and returned home.

CAMBRAY, *February* 2d.—The horses had been ordered for me at five o'clock this morning, and I was in waiting for them at that time. It was, however, more than half-past five before they came, and I left the Hôtel de Flandres just before six, as the day began to dawn. My principal motive for departing so early was to reach Valenciennes before six in the evening, when the gates of the city are shut; and being now a frontier town, they are not opened for travellers, nor until six in the morning. The distance from Brussels is eleven posts and a quarter, and the allowance to be made is of about an hour for each post, stopping only to change horses. From Brussels to Mons, seven posts, I had only one postilion for the four horses, but from Mons, according to the French ordinances, I had two. On the other hand, there were from two to two and a half francs, at each stage, charged for turnpikes, or barriers, until the French frontier, but which there ceased. I was at Mons between twelve and one o'clock, and there met at the post-house a gentleman belonging to Ghent, who recognized and spoke to me, though I did not recollect having seen him there. I arrived at Valenciennes at five o'clock, just before dark, and then determined to proceed another stage, to Bouchain. There I found the post-house was without the walls of the city, and that there was no house to lodge at; I was obliged, therefore, to proceed another stage of two posts, to Cambray. There I found the gates were shut, but they were opened to let us into the city. I stopped for the night at the Hôtel d'Hollande, opposite the post-office, where I alighted at half-past eight in the evening. I had travelled fifteen and a half posts in fifteen hours, never stopping but to change horses. At Mons I was asked for my passport. At Quiévrain, the Netherland frontier again, and enquiry was made if I had

anything subject to export duties. At Valenciennes the enquiry was, whether I had anything contrary to the King's
ordinances; but no examination of my baggage was anywhere
attempted or required. The roads were as bad as the season
could make them, and at the side of the pavement was a deep
mire. The whole road is paved. The ground was everywhere
bare, excepting here and there a small spot where there was a
remnant of snow. The farmers in some places were ploughing
up the ground. The aspect of the country had all the deadness
and dreariness of the season, excepting the wheat-fields, where
the grain had already shot up enough to cover them with
verdure. The country is generally level, and, in the flourishing
seasons, one of the most fertile regions of the earth. At the
stages from Valenciennes to Bouchain I had to pay four and a
half francs for what the postilions call *le découché*—that is, for
the lodging of the postilions and horses, who, from the shutting
of the gates, are prevented from returning home. From Brussels I had to pay for half a post, and from Mons and Valenciennes a quarter of a post, in addition to the distance—an
allowance granted at most of the principal places where the
postilions and horses are subject to longer detention than at
the ordinary post-houses. I had taken two small rolls of bread
into the carriage, and had neither ate nor drunk anything else
since leaving Brussels. I took a very light supper, and
ordered my horses at half-past five to-morrow morning, the
gates of the city being opened precisely at six.

GOURNAY-SUR-ARONDE, 3d.—I left the Hôtel d'Hollande just
at six of the morning, and the city of Cambray at the opening
of the gates. After travelling five posts, I reached Péronne, at
half-past ten o'clock, and was detained there upwards of an
hour—one of the iron cramps that keep the spring over the
right fore wheel of the carriage (being broken), and employed
a blacksmith an hour to repair it. Two stages further a blacksmith came and examined the carriage, and told me that my
fore right wheel was not solid. I thought he only wanted a
job, and told him so. I proceeded another stage to Roye, and
there, as the carriage stopped at the post, a blacksmith came
up and told me that my left fore wheel was so loose that I

certainly should not get along a quarter of a post further before
it would break down ; that it creaked so loud it could be heard
quite across the street. Though I could not perceive that there
was so immediate a danger of the wheels, this coincidence
between two persons who could not have had any concert
together gave me some alarm, and I stopped three-quarters of
an hour at Roye to have the fellies of the fore wheels bound
with ropes, something to the disappointment of the blacksmith
who had given me the notice, and who had calculated upon a
much longer job of work for himself. I then proceeded three
stages further, to Gournay-sur-Aronde, where I resolved to
stop for the night, though it was only half-past six in the evening and I had travelled only twelve posts this day. With my
precarious wheels, I thought it better to travel before daylight
in the morning rather than after dark in the evening. I lodged
at the Hôtel du Grand Cerf, and ordered the horses to be ready
at four o'clock to-morrow morning.

PARIS, 4th.—At a quarter-past four in the morning I took my
departure from Gournay-sur-Aronde, and reached Pont Sainte
Maxence, the second stage, just after daylight. On starting
from this stage, I found a bridge over the river Oise, which
had been blown up last winter, and which they are now re-
building. This was the first and only trace of injury to the
country from the late war that I perceived on the road. The
bridge is already sufficiently restored for foot-passengers, but
not for carriages. I crossed it myself, and waited on the south
side of it for my carriage, which went over in a ferry-boat,
about two hundred yards below. I met on the Paris side of
the bridge a miller, who told me that the bridge had been
blown up to stop the Cossacks. Eight hundred pounds of
powder, he said, had been employed for the purpose. I heard
the name of the Cossacks mentioned only one other time upon
the road, and that was by a postilion whose horse was restive
and threw him off. He called the horse a "sacré Cosaque" in
revenge. As I approached Paris, the drivers became more alert
in their movements. My carriage was not stopped at all for the
examination of baggage at the entrance of the city, and at one
o'clock in the afternoon I alighted at the Hôtel du Nord, Rue

de Richelieu, a house which had been recommended to me by Mr. Gallatin.   I took the only vacant apartments in the house, which are two small chambers in the second story, upon the street.   There is a restaurateur, or cook, in the house.

6th. Mr. Crawford had mentioned to me yesterday that there would be a Cercle Diplomatique at Court to-morrow, and asked me if I chose to be presented to the King and royal family.   I had answered that I would, and called this morning upon Mr. Crawford, to ascertain the time when it would be necessary to go.   He desired me to call on him at noon.

7th. At half-past eleven o'clock I called at Mr. Crawford's house, where Mr. Russell, Mr. Clay, Mr. Jackson, Colonel Milligan, and Mr. Todd soon after assembled, and we all proceeded together, just at twelve, to the Tuileries.   Most of these gentlemen had already been presented a fortnight ago, and now went again.   Mr. Bayard did not now attend.   We waited only a few minutes in the introductory hall, where I found an old acquaintance of mine, the Chevalier Brito, Chargé d'Affaires from Portugal, whom I had known at the Hague.   I was introduced to General Waltersdorff, the Danish Minister, who told me he had been in America, and had known my father there; and I also was recognized by General Fagel, whom I had known at Berlin, and who is now the Dutch Minister here.   I was introduced to Mr. Dargainaratz, the King's secretary, "à la conduite des Ambassadeurs," and to Mr. Lalive, " introducteur des Ambassadeurs."   We were presented first to the King, and then successively to the Duchess and Duke d'Angoulême, and then to Monsieur, Comte d'Artois, and lastly to the Duke de Berri.   We were presented by Mr. Crawford, as, according to the etiquette of this Court, strangers are presented by the Ministers of their respective countries. The King, Princes, and Princess seldom speak to any person presented to them.   The King, however, asked me if "I was in any way related to the celebrated Mr. Adams."   Mr. Crawford answered for me, that I was son to the former President of the United States.   The Princes also spoke to me, each a few words, all in English, excepting the Duke d'Angoulême, who

spoke in French. The Duchess d'Angoulême did not speak
to any of the persons presented. Lord Fitzroy Somerset had
been previously presented at a private audience, and delivered
his credentials as British Minister Plenipotentiary, since the
departure of the Duke of Wellington, the Ambassador. He
presented several English gentlemen at the circle. Count
Nicholas Pahlen was presented by Mr. Lalive, there being only
a Russian Chargé d'Affaires at this Court, who, according to
the etiquette, does not present. I returned home about two
o'clock, changed my dress, and went to pay visits to Madame
de Staël and to Count Marbois. Madame de Staël was still in
bed, but sent by her son requesting me to come and see her
to-morrow evening, and to dine with her next week, on Wednesday. I was received by Count Marbois, whom I had not seen
since the year 1785, and with whom I had a long and interesting political conversation. Dined at home, and went in the
evening to the Opera Comique. Saw " Les deux Jaloux,"
" Jean de Paris," and " L'Habit de Grammont." The house was
excessively crowded.

9th. I called and spent an hour with Mr. Crawford. He
came at half-past five and took me up, and we went and dined
with Count Marbois. There was a company of about twenty
persons at dinner, and a number more came in afterwards.
The Count's son-in-law, the Duke de Plaisance, the Duke de
Choiseul, and several ladies were of the party; but the Count's
daughter, the Duchess de Plaisance, was not there. A Mr.
Gaussin sat next me at table, and told me he had been Chargé
d'Affaires of France, at Berlin, when Mr. Lee lost his papers.
He mentioned several circumstances relating to that transaction, some of which I had not heard of before. In the evening I went with Mr. Crawford to the Théâtre Français, and saw
" Polyeucte," with a new farce called " Les deux Voisines."
Talma and Mademoiselle Duchesnois performed in the tragedy,
but they were in the third act when we arrived, and we were at
a great distance from the stage, so that I could not distinguish
them. The farce was very bad.

10th. Count Marbois, who is the First President of the
" Chambre des Comptes," had promised to secure seats for Mr.

Crawford, Mr. Clay, and me, at the "Tribunal de première instance," a neighboring Court to that where he presides, and where the trial is pending between the Count and the Duchess de Saint-Leu, the former King and Queen of Holland, upon the question, whether she should be compelled to send to him their eldest son,[1] whom the present King of France has created Duke of St.-Leu.

We were to meet at Count Marbois' cabinet at a quarter before nine this morning, which we did. He requested a gentleman to accompany us with his granddaughter, a girl of eight or nine, to the Tribunal, where we obtained seats. The Court opened at ten. There was a President with eight associate judges. The chamber where the Court sits is very small— I think not thirty feet square—and the crowd of spectators so great that one of the doors of the hall was broken down, and there was danger that some fatal accident would have happened. The cause had already been argued on both sides, and this day had been assigned for Mr. Tripier, the counsel for the father, Louis Bonaparte, to reply to the defence ; and for Mr. Bonnet, the advocate for the Duchess, to make his concluding observations on the reply. It is a cause upon which in the United States no Court could have jurisdiction. There are very few cases in which it would occur here. The basis of Tripier's argument was the paternal authority; that of his opponent, the interest of the child. There was scarcely any recurrence to first principles, no exposition of the laws of France, or of other nations, upon the subject. These had apparently formed the materials of the preceding argument. The opinions of Chancellor d'Aguesseau, of Mr. Joly de Fleury, and of a Procureur-Général at a Court of Cassation, had been cited by Bonnet, and Tripier commented upon them. He spoke about an hour and a half. Bonnet closed in about half an hour.

The Attorney-General, who, in the French Courts, is a sort of mediator between the parties, an Amicus Curiæ, like the judge-advocate of a court-martial, is to sum up the cause on both sides next Friday, to which time the cause was for that purpose adjourned. It appeared, by the admission of the

---

[1] The late Louis Bonaparte, Emperor of France.

counsel on both sides, that in the case of a legalized separation of the parties from bed and board, the Court would have a discretionary power to commit the child either to the father or mother, as they should think its own interest would dictate. The question was, whether such a separation existed. A separation, in point of fact, has existed for seven years. The family statutes had regulated how such separations were to be legalized in the imperial family, and that was to be by the mere authorization of the Emperor, without judicial process or formality. Of this authorization in the present case the evidence was as loose and imperfect as the principle was arbitrary and inconsiderate. It was merely a letter from the Grand Marshal of the Palace, Duroc, to the mother, after the abdication by Louis of the throne of Holland, declaring that by the Emperor's authority he had ordered possession to be taken, in her name, of the hotel belonging to her husband in Paris, and had assigned a million of francs for her, five hundred thousand for the Grand Duke of Berg (the son in question), and two hundred and fifty thousand francs for the youngest son. And this is the proof upon which the Court is called to pronounce the dissolution of the father's rights and his authority over his child. The lawyers were both fluent and eloquent speakers, but both have bad voices, and Tripier speaks thick, with an incapacity of uttering the letters *r* and *s*.

After the adjournment of the Court, I paid a visit to Mr. Le Ray de Chaumont, and upon my return home received a visit from Mr. de Castries, who had come in last evening while we were at Count Marbois'. He is going immediately to Rouen, where his father, the Duke de Castries, has the military command.

12th. The tendency to dissipation at Paris seems to be irresistible. There is a moral incapacity for industry and application, a "mollesse," against which I am as ill guarded as I was at the age of twenty. I received on Friday a letter from Mr. Smith, requesting me to look out for lodgings for him, and Mr. Todd promised me yesterday to call upon me this day at noon and go out with me for the purpose. He came accordingly, and we walked. Among the houses to

which I went was the Hôtel de Valois, the same house where
I lodged with my father in 1778, April, the first time I ever
was at Paris. It was then a magnificent and elegantly furnished hotel. It is now altogether in decay, and scarcely
furnished at all; yet the price of the apartments is as high as
at the best hotels.

I went with Todd, rather by accident than design, into the
Salon d'Exposition and the National Museum, where, intending to spend half an hour, we passed three whole ones, and
finally were obliged to withdraw at four o'clock, when the
doors were to be closed. The multitude of objects was such
as left my mind in a state of confusion—the Apollo, the
Laocöon, the Venus de Medicis, with a great number of other
antique statues. The Transfiguration, of Raphael, the Descent
from the Cross, by Rubens, and all the masterpieces of painting
here collected, contrasted with the glare of coloring and unnatural attitudes of the pictures at this exposition, took from
me all faculty of meditation and almost of discrimination. It
was five o'clock when I came home.

15th. I had received on Monday a note from General La
Fayette, mentioning that he would come to the city this day;
and remained at home expecting him all the morning, until
Mr. de Tracy informed me that he would be at the dinner at
Madame de Staël's. On returning to my lodgings, I waited
until half-past five for Mr. Clay, who was to have called to take
me up. I then took a carriage, and, on arriving at Madame de
Staël's, found Mr. Clay there. He had called for me after I
had left my lodgings. General La Fayette, Mr. Victor de
Tracy, and Mr. Le Ray de Chaumont dined there, with the
Duke de Broglie, who is to marry Madame de Staël's daughter,
several other gentlemen, and one lady. Mr. Benjamin Constant
was of the party. There were seventeen persons at the table.
The conversation was not very interesting—some conversation
between the lady and Mr. Constant, who seemed to consider it as
a principle to contradict her. At one time there were symptoms
of a conversation arising upon a subject of political economy,
upon which she said, " J'interdis tout discours sur l'économie
politique. Ah! je crains l'économie politique, comme le feu."

Immediately after dinner she left us, saying, " Je vous laisse mon fils, qui est très-aimable," and went to the Théâtre Français to see the tragedy of Esther. She invited me to come and see her again, and said she was at home almost every evening. She also apologized for being obliged to leave her company so soon " pour aller au spectacle." I went myself, with Mr. Le Ray de Chaumont, to the Odéon, and saw " Le Nozze de Figaro," with the music of Mozart. They were about the middle of the second act when we went in. The music is charming, but not equal to that of the " Matrimonio Segreto."

16th. After dinner I paid a visit to Count Marbois, at whose house I found some company, ladies and gentlemen, all unknown to me. He introduced me to his daughter, the Duchess of Plaisance, who told me she was born in Philadelphia, but had been taken from it when six months old, and from America at four years and a half. She had forgotten the English language, and afterwards learnt it here. I asked the Count to procure admission for me again at the Tribunal " de première instance" when the St.-Leu cause should again be taken up, which he promised he would, and he introduced me to two gentlemen of the bar, one of whom promised to procure for me tickets for the session of the Cour d'Assise, at a jury trial. I asked him how the trial by jury was found to succeed here. He said, " Not well;" that the jurors were dissatisfied with their functions, and always leaned too strongly in favor of the accused. I went and passed an hour with Mrs. Smith, with whom I found Mr. R. Boyd, and then went to the ball at Count Laval's. The first person I met there was Count Lauriston, who introduced me to his lady. Countess Schuvaloff, General Driessen, the Counts Pahlen, Mr. Swetchkoff, and Mr. Boutiagin, the Russian Chargé d'Affaires, were there, with several other Russians, and a numerous company of French, scarcely any of whom were known to me. The Marquis de Torcy, General Waltersdorff, Madame de Staël, and her son and daughter, were among them. Madame de Laval asked me to come to-morrow at one o'clock and see some pictures which are to be brought to her to look at, and which are for sale. I came home just before two o'clock in the morning.

17th. General La Fayette came and breakfasted with me, and sat with me until noon.   At one I went to Count Laval's, and found Madame La Comtesse examining the pictures which were offered to her for sale.   There was a small picture, damaged, decayed, and repaired, but attributed to Giulio Romano, a sketch painted on copper, of Christ Healing the Sick, and two little paintings on wood, which they pretended were found at Pompeii. Their price for the whole was sixteen thousand francs, for the Giulio Romano alone eight thousand.   A five-franc piece would have been more than the worth of the whole.   Madame de Laval was not the dupe of this imposition ; she dismissed the man and his pictures, though she did not think quite so meanly of them as I did.

19th. At two o'clock I walked out, and spent two hours at the Museum—altogether in the Halls of Ancient Sculpture, and without completing the particular examination of them. The Apollo, the Venus, and the Laocöon absorb the consideration of everything else; the eye of the enquirer begins and ends with them.   The Venus, however, has disappointed me.   It has suffered much damage ; and one of the arms and both the hands are restored.   The modern sculpture of the exhibition is in the same halls with the antique, and offers subjects for comparison to estimate the relative perfection of the art at the present day.   I am still not prepared for committing to paper my remarks.   At four o'clock the doors are closed, and I had just entered the Hall of the Apollo when the company received notice to retire.   I went beyond the river, and took a walk in the Luxembourg Gardens.   Dined at home, and in the evening went to the Théâtre Français, where I saw " L'Orphelin de la Chine," and " Les deux Voisines" again. La Fon performed Gengis Khan, and Mdlle. Georges, Idamé. She has improved since I saw her at St. Petersburg.   The house was crowded.   The air of "Vive Henri Quatre" was performed, and applauded a little.   There were allusions in the tragedy which might have been noticed, but were not.   The play finished soon after ten.

20th. Dined at the Count de Tracy's.   The family were all assembled—the Count and Countess de Tracy, and their son

Victor, General La Fayette, his son George, with his wife, a daughter of Mr. de Tracy, and their three children; the Count and Countess de Laubepin, another daughter of Mr. de Tracy, and their two children, a son and daughter. There were only two strangers besides ourselves, and one of them was the celebrated traveller Alexander Humboldt. After dinner, General La Fayette's daughter, Madame de la Tour Maubourg, came in with her two daughters; the Duke de Noailles, his father-in law, and Mr. Dupont de Nemours. It was an agreeable and social party, and I received the thanks of all the family for the good office I had the opportunity of showing to Victor de Tracy.

21st. Just before eleven o'clock Mr. Clay called upon me, with a ticket to be present at the installation of the Court of Cassation, which had been furnished to Mr. Crawford, with another for Mr. Clay. Mr. Crawford, continuing unwell and confined to his chamber, sent me his own ticket. The hour marked upon it was precisely eleven. We proceeded immediately, but were so late that we found the hall already crowded, and could obtain but very indifferent places. There was a mass performed previously to the installation, in another hall, which was also much crowded, so that those who heard the mass could not be present at the installation. After the mass the procession entered, consisting of the Chancellor of France, Mr. d'Ambray, the newly-appointed First President of the Court of Cassation, the three Presidents and forty counsellors, or members, of the Court, the Procureur-Général and his six deputies, and the clerks.

The Chancellor d'Ambray read a speech, stating the motives upon which the King had seen fit to reconstitute this Court, the Supreme Court of Appeal from all the Courts of the kingdom. The principle assumed was that the Court could not be legitimate unless constituted by the King. Some—a small number—of the former members have been removed. Their appointments had been for life, "but 'peu importe' for that," said the Chancellor, "as nothing but the King's appointment could make them irremovable." The Chancellor paid many compliments to the members of the Court who were retained, and most particularly to the new-made First President, Mr. Desèze.

When the Chancellor finished his speech there was a general clapping of hands, of which some of the judges in their scarlet robes set the example. A plain young man, standing next to me, said, with some emotion, "Il me semble qu'on ne devrait pas applaudir un Chancelier de France."

The First President Desèze followed next, in another written speech, in which he returned with fourfold interest all the Chancellor's compliments, and spoke with eloquence of St. Louis, Henri Quatre, and Louis XVIII. The Procureur-Général made a very short speech, which was not clapped. That of the First President had been applauded, though not quite so much as the Chancellor's. They all speak thick, and all have harsh and inharmonious voices.

After the speeches, the oath was administered to the members of the Court. It was first read by one of the clerks, and then the members of the Court were called over by name, each member rising as his name was called, extending his arm and hand to the elevation of the shoulder, the palm of the hand downwards, and saying, "Je le jure." After which, the Procureur-Général demanded that the ordinance constituting the Court and the proceedings of the day should be registered; and the Chancellor declared "la séance est levée."

22d. I dined at home, and at nine in the evening went to Count Laval's, where there was a small party upon the birthday of his daughter Zénéïde.

Shortly after I went in, a gentleman came up and accosted me, articulating several sentences, but of which I could not comprehend a word. I intimated to him that I did not distinctly understand what he said, and he continued speaking two or three minutes in the same manner, and then left me, and accosted another gentleman in the same manner. We were much surprised, and some of the company said he must be crazy, until a gentleman, smiling, said it was Monsieur Lecomte, a ventriloquist and sleight-of-hand juggler; he was there for the amusement of the company. He soon after returned to me, and asked me if I had understood what he had

said to me before. I said, not one word. He said it was
merely a manner of speaking, by which a person standing on
one side of him could understand him, while a person on the
other could not. He was then continually passing round
among the company, and took away from five gentlemen successively the crosses suspended at their button-holes. The
company then passed into the next chamber, and Mr. Lecomte
entertained us for three hours with sleight-of-hand tricks and
ventriloquism. The last was the most curious. He performed
a sort of extemporaneous play, personating a man, his wife, a
door-keeper, a neighbor, and an infant, with a succession of
dialogues in all those voices. He had an assistant, who, towards the close of the evening, affected to quarrel with him,
and, for some time, part of the company were uneasy, apprehending an unpleasant scene; it terminated, however, in a
reconciliation, upon which his assistant composed, sang, and
recited couplets in honor of the Emperor Alexander, of the
two daughters and son of Count Laval, and finally of Madame
de Laval, whom he concluded by calling "La mère des Graces."
The entertainment finished with verses recited by Mr. Lecomte
himself in honor of the family and the company, finishing with
the declaration, " et l'enchanteur est enchanté."

23d. The Baron Freteau de Pény, to whom Count Marbois
had introduced me at his house last week, and who was then
one of the Procureurs-Généraux at the Court of Assizes, had
promised to procure for me a ticket to attend at the Court of
Assize at a very interesting trial. Yesterday I received from
him a card enclosing a ticket for admittance into the interior
of the hall this day. I went at nine o'clock this morning, and
at three successive doors was stopped by sentinels keeping
guard, with orders to let no person in, not even with tickets.
After waiting nearly half an hour, I finally obtained admission.
The hall was extremely crowded. It was, however, nearly
eleven o'clock when the judges and jurors came in. The President of the Court, Mr. Bastard de l'Etang, having taken his
seat, the Court was opened without any formality, by a crier.
Twelve jurors, and two supplementary jurors, were sworn in
a similar manner to that of the oath taken by the members of

the Court of Cassation.   That is, the jurors' oath was first read
by the clerk, and then every juror as called out by name rose
and said, " Je le jure."   The two prisoners had been previously
brought into Court.   Their names were Charles Dautun and
Girouard.   They were charged with the murder of two persons,
the aunt and the brother of Dautun.   There was but one jury
for the trial of both the prisoners, and for both the murders·
The act of accusation was read to them, and both answered
they were not guilty of the charges.   The Procureur-Général,
a Mr. Giraudet, addressed the jury and opened the cause to
them, repeating the charges, with some additional details and
with occasional comments.   The President then began the
examination or interrogatory of the accused, an incident altogether incompatible with our practice, but which forms a
very essential part of a French trial.   In this case it consumed
three hours of time, during which the President was scrutinizing
every part of the interrogatories to which the accused had been
previously subjected, comparing the answers of the two prisoners with the testimony of the witnesses, and calling upon the
accused to account for every inconsistency of their ówn, and
for every variance between their answers and the other testimony.   Girouard had uniformly denied everything.   Dautun
at four several previous interrogatories had told four different
stories.   At the first, he had denied everything.   At the second,
he had charged Girouard and himself with the murder of the
brother.   At the third, he had charged himself with both the
murders, and exculpated Girouard from both.   At the fourth,
he had again denied everything, but said he had received from
Girouard the key of his brother's chamber.   In this he now
persisted.   The examination being finished, several witnesses
were successively called in, until near six o'clock, when the
Court adjourned to half-past nine to-morrow morning.   The
witnesses in the first instance are kept in a separate chamber,
so that those examined subsequently do not hear the testimony
of those called in before them, but after being once examined
they are suffered thenceforth to remain in Court.

    24th. Before nine this morning I was at the Palais de Justice,
and found still greater difficulty in obtaining admission than

yesterday. My ticket had not been returned to me, and I took this morning the card from the Baron Freteau to me, in which it had been enclosed. With this I finally got in, but this was also now taken from me, and not returned. At half-past nine the Court met, and the examination of witnesses was continued until half-past five. The last person examined was Girouard's wife, at his own demand, with the consent of the Procureur-Général. At half-past five the Court adjourned to seven. I went home and dined, and immediately returned, but then found it utterly impossible to obtain access to the hall.

25th. I learn by the newspapers this morning that the Court of Assize sat almost the whole night through upon the trials of Dautun and Girouard, the first of whom was found guilty of both the murders, and the other acquitted of both by the jury. Sentence of death was immediately pronounced upon Dautun by the Court, and Girouard was immediately liberated. The President pronounced the judgment at three o'clock this morning. I missed, after all, the most important part of the trial, the defence, the argument of the counsel for the prisoners, and that of the Procureur-Général, and the judgment delivered by the President. In the examination of the witnesses, I observed many differences from the practices to which we are accustomed. There was no cross-examination—no objections to any questions by the counsel for the prisoners. In fact, they never appeared or spoke during the whole of the trial, so far as I heard it. This laborious dissipation disqualifies me for all serious occupation at home. Went to the Théâtre des Variétés. I saw "Patron Jean, le ci-devant jeune homme," "Les Anglaises pour rire," and "Les Habitans des Landes." I had been led to expect much humor and wit in the two last pieces, but they appeared to me flat and insipid. The Parisians are delighted with a coarse and vulgar caricature of Englishwomen, but there is nothing ingenious in it. "Le ci-devant jeune homme," of which I had heard nothing, amused me more than all the rest. A rake of sixty, with his doctor, and his mistresses, his drugs, and his debauches, affecting the licentiousness of youth, and tortured with gout and rheumatisms, was inimitably performed by Potier, one of the principal actors at this theatre.

27th. Just after twelve o'clock, at noon, the Chevalier de Brito came, and I went with him to the Palais Royal, where I was presented to the Duke of Orleans.[1]   He asked me whether I was the son of Mr. Adams who had been President of the United States when he was in America, and on my answering in the affirmative he said he saw the resemblance between me and my father, but did not recollect having seen me in America. I told him that I was at that time in Europe.   He said he had a very grateful remembrance of the hospitality with which he had been treated in America, and was very happy to make my acquaintance.   The presentation was over in less than a quarter of an hour.   At a quarter before three I went to the Palais des Arts, where I met the Chevalier de Brito, and attended at a meeting of the first class of the National Institute.   General Andréossi read the conclusion of a memoir upon the aqueducts of Constantinople, which he had commenced last week. Several papers were read, and among the rest one upon a new printing-press invented by Lord Stanhope.   Part of a memoir by a physician of St. Domingo, upon the geological composition of the West India Islands, was read, but it was so tedious that it soon drove away part of the company and shed poppies upon those that remained.   I was not a little amused at observing numbers of the grave academicians slumbering in their chairs, while it was with extreme difficulty that I preserved myself from the infection!   After the memoir had wearied out two successive readers, the President observed that the class had heard enough to form a sound estimate of its merit, and appointed a committee to report upon it.

There were about thirty members of the class present at the meeting; they came and went away as they pleased, and were often engaged in separate conversations, two or three together, requiring the use of the President's bell to restore silence.   The only person among them whom I knew was Mr. Humboldt, a foreign member.   About half-past four the President declared the séance levée.

March 1st. At half-past eight in the evening the Chevalier de Brito called upon me, and I went with him to the Palais

[1] Louis Philippe, afterwards King of the French.

Royal. The crowd of company was very great, and, after waiting nearly two hours, it was not without difficulty that I finally obtained a presentation to the Duchess and to Mademoiselle d'Orléans, the former of whom spoke a few words of civility, the other only bowed. The Duke was also there, and in like manner spoke a few words. As the ladies and gentlemen were all presented successively, and there were at least four hundred persons present, little could be said to any one. There were great numbers of foreigners, and among them many English. The proportion of beautiful women was greater than I ever saw at a Court circle.

2d. Zerah Colburn came this morning with his father and another man, whose name was not mentioned to me. The boy was born 1st September, 1804, and has, it would seem, a faculty for the composition and decomposition of numbers by inspiration. His father says he discovered it in him in August, 1810, when he was not quite six years old and had never learnt the first rules of arithmetic. Even now he cannot do a common sum in the rule of three, but he can by a mental operation of his own extract the roots of any power or number, and name the factors by which any given number is produced. I asked him what it was that had first turned his attention to the combination of numbers. He said he could not tell. His father says that, having arrived here in August last, he already speaks French in perfection, and has acquired great knowledge of the German. His method of compounding numbers and extracting roots is a discovery of which an account is to be published in a quarto volume, with a biography of the boy, which is to be written by a Mr. Barlow, in England. The method, however, the father says, he has not yet revealed to Mr. Barlow. The quarto is to be published by subscription, and I readily subscribed for a copy. By the assistance of Mr. Erving, an opportunity has been given for Zerah to be educated at the Polytechnic School, and the father expressed himself much satisfied with it. I told him I thought he could not obtain a better chance for his education, and strongly recommended him to avail himself of it. The father is a plain New England farmer, and to all appearance a very ordinary man. His language is that of our most uneducated people, and his principal anxiety seemed to be to get a picture of Zerah to send home to America, as a present to Congress. I advised him rather to send it to the President. Zerah is certainly an astonishing and promising boy; but if his promise is ever to realize anything corresponding to it, the sooner his father commits him to the tuition of the Polytechnic School the better.

4th. On returning home last evening, I found a card of admission to be present this morning at the installation of the Court of Accounts, at ten o'clock, which had been sent me by Mr. Todd. I went accordingly at nine, but, even with the ticket, could obtain admission into the hall only as the ceremony was beginning. All the seats in the hall not reserved by the Court were occupied by the ladies. There was a Messe du Saint-Esprit immediately before the installation. The ceremony itself was precisely similar to that at the Court of Cassation. It was singular enough, and characteristic of the time and place, that the mass, a solemn and religious service, was ushered in and concluded by a band of music performing the air of " Vive Henri Quatre," a drinking-song, the words of which are somewhat licentious. The Chancellor d'Ambray, the First President, Count Marbois, and the Procureur-Général all made or read speeches, but they were shorter than those at the Court of Cassation. It was about one o'clock when the ceremony was over.

7th. I called to see Mr. Bayard at the Hôtel de l'Empire, and found him very ill, with a severe cough and some fever; his throat is much ulcerated. While I was there, Mr. Clay, Colonel Milligan, and Mr. Speyer came; also Mr. Gallatin and his son, who had just arrived from Geneva. They had stopped at the Hôtel du Nord, but there was no room there to receive them. Mr. Bayard first mentioned to me that Bonaparte was in France. The proclamation of the King, declaring him a rebel and traitor, is in the Moniteur of this morning. In walking the streets afterwards, I found the hawkers had got it, and cried it as the " Ordonnance du Roi, concernant Napoléon Bonaparte." He landed on the first of this month, near Cannes, in the Department of the Var—they say with twelve hundred

men and four pieces of cannon. In the evening I went to the
opera, where they performed Quinault's "Armide," with the
music of Gluck. The French Grand Opera is to me, as it
always has been, dull and heavy. The dancing and singing
are far inferior to what they formerly were. Before the opera
began, the audience demanded the air of "Henri Quatre," which
was twice performed. They also demanded "Charmante Gabrielle," but it was not performed. At the fifth act, the Duke
de Berri made his appearance, in a box beneath that reserved
for the King; upon which there was a very general cry of
"Vive le Roi!" The air of "Henri Quatre" was again performed with high applause.

8th. In the evening I went to the Théâtre Français, and saw
"Les Templiers," a tragedy, by Mr. Raynouard, with "Les
Fourberies de Scapin," of Molière. The house was crowded.
The versification of the tragedy was excellent; the characters
of the Grand Master of the Templars, and of Marigny,
romantically heroic; that of the King, inconsistent; the
Queen, insignificant and cold. Only one female personage,
and no love, though Marigny talks amorously about a certain
Adelaide. The best of the performers is Talma.

Molière's "Scapin" is truly comical, and it is not the Sac
Ridicule censured by Boileau that I think objectionable. It is
the contempt shed upon old age, and particularly upon the
paternal character, the irreverence of children to their parents,
the complacency with which fraud and swindling is represented,
and the extreme address and ingenuity of valets, which form
the moral and literary defects of this play. I remarked to a
Frenchman who sat near me the contrast in the sentiments of
the tragedy and of the farce performed this evening. He said,
"C'est que l'un montre les hommes comme ils devraient être,
et l'autre, comme ils sont." But I think that is not correct.
Mankind are, in real life, not more like Scapin and his dupes
than like the Grand Master of the Templars and Marigny.

9th. Evening at the French Theatre—"Le Misanthrope" and
"La Gageure imprévue." The house was crowded as if it had
been a new play. The performance of "Célimène" by Mademoiselle Mars has given the "Misanthrope" a new and extra-

ordinary vogue. She is an excellent comic actress, but there is some affectation in her manner, and in that of every performer now at this theatre, excepting Talma. Lafon performed Alceste —not well. Mademoiselle Mars is in such extreme favor with the public that it is dangerous to hazard a criticism upon her. She had an awkward accident in " La Gageure," which excited some laughter in the pit. Her husband gives her a " rouleau de cinquante louis," which she laid on her table, and which rolled off and fell upon the floor. It fell with the sound of wood, and not metal. I was myself in the pit, which, at Paris, is the criticising part of the audience, and it is amusing to observe how sensitive they are to every incident that occurs upon the stage. I was surrounded by persons who, at almost every first line of the " Misanthrope," would repeat in muttering the second—who censured, and approved, the manner of the actors at every passage, and, as I thought, almost always correctly. They were generally dissatisfied with Lafon's performance, and said that he ought to confine himself to tragedy. They called for " Henri Quatre" and " Gabrielle," both of which were twice performed, with many cries of " Vive le Roi!"

11th. Morning visit from the Baron de Bielefeld, who told me there was news in the Moniteur that Bonaparte was within eight leagues of Lyons. My neighbor at the Hôtel du Nord, the Count de Sant Antonio, whose wife is an Englishwoman, left the city this day, having intended to remain here two months longer. At three o'clock I walked out, and went to several booksellers', to complete the collection which I yesterday purchased, of the Bibliothèque des Theatres. I saw in various parts of the city a great number of post-horses, apparently going to take travellers leaving Paris.

After dinner, just as I was going out, I met Mr. Erving, who told me he would call another day. He told me the British had been totally defeated before New Orleans, and forced to re-embark, with the loss of their General, Pakenham, and he says the game is up with these people.

I went for the first time to the theatre of the Porte St. Martin ; saw " Le Boulevard St. Martin," " Le Tanneur de Lesseville," and " Le Berger de la Sierra Morena," a pantomime, with the dancing before a transparent veil, with corresponding dancers on the other side, in imitation of the reflection of a mirror. The illusion is so perfect that, in the box where I was, there was a stubborn dispute between a husband and wife, the woman insisting that it was a real mirror and only one set of dancers, and the man, that it was only a veil and that there were two sets of dancers. The husband was right; but the illusion is so great that when I saw the same sort of exhibition at Ghent, by the same performers, I was completely deceived, and had not even a suspicion that it was any other than the reflection of a mirror. The house was very thin. The Tanneur de Lesseville was one of the tales about Henri Quatre, and there were several couplets with pointed allusions, which were highly applauded, and repeated at the call of the auditory. In the box next to me there was a man, his wife, and their son, a boy of nine or ten years of age. The man was in great agitation and anxiety; he left the box at the end of the second play, and returned after the first act of the third was over. His anxiety was then much increased, and during the remainder of the performance he was telling his wife, in short, interrupted sentences, what he had heard. He spoke in a low voice, and I heard only fragments of what he said. He had been to see some friends, whom he had found " très-abattus." It was said that   (I could not hear the name) was killed. Then some other names. " Ils croyent aller à la Fortune." Then, " Le duc de Berri a dit qu'il resterait à Paris avec le Roi." Then, " On dit que Cambacérès est parti." Then, " On attend avec inquiétude les nouvelles de demain."

On returning home, I found a note from Count Laval, requesting that if Mrs. Adams should arrive here with letters during his absence, I would deliver them to Mr. Boutiaguin, the Russian Chargé d'Affaires.

12th. Evening at the Théâtre Français—" Ariane," by Thomas Corneille, and Molière's " George Dandin." The house very thin. Mademoiselle Duchesnois performed " Ariane" very well. She has a drawling sort of affectation, and habits upon the stage not very pleasing—is, withal, worse than homely, and yet pregnant. Notwithstanding which, she made the tragedy more affecting than I should have thought possible. She was clamorously called out by the parterre, and just appeared for a moment on the stage. This was the first instance of the kind that I have seen at Paris.

"Henri Quatre" and "Gabrielle" were called for and played before the tragedy, and between the two plays. "Où peut-on être mieux" was called for, but not played. The comedy was certainly not so well performed as I had seen it heretofore. On returning home, I found numerous patrols of soldiers, national guards, and sentinels at the corners of the streets; news placarded upon the pillars, and clusters of people collecting and attempting to read them by the light of the lamps. I stopped a moment at one of these clusters, when a patrol came up, and the soldier at their head said, in a low voice, "Dispersez-vous, Messieurs, dispersez-vous." Another patrol, meeting two soldiers in a red uniform, made them stop, and all cried, "Vive le Roi!" A hand-bill of news, "très-satisfaisantes," from Monsieur, was circulating, promising the speedy deliverance of Lyons. The agitation in the city has much increased within these two days.

13th. I called upon Mr. Erving, who was more doubtful of the events of the present moment than he was when he came to see me on Saturday evening. From him I went to the Hôtel de l'Empire, and asked to see Mr. Bayard; but he is yet confined, and I could not see him. I saw Mr. Gallatin, and while I was with him General La Fayette came in. It is ascertained that Napoleon was at Lyons on Friday last, the tenth. The Duke of Orleans, Monsieur, and Marshal Macdonald have returned to Paris. Napoleon had only twelve or thirteen thousand men at Lyons. On leaving Mr. Gallatin I met Mr. Speyer, who said that favorable accounts had been received. Evening at the Odéon. Saw "Oro non compra l'Amore," the music by Porto Gallo, and almost equal to that of Paesiello. The house very thin. "Henri Quatre" was once played without being called for. The pillars of the Palais Royal are plastered with appeals to arms against Bonaparte. On returning home, I found a card from Mr. Storrow, at Havre, enclosed in one from Mr. Jackson, Mr. Crawford's Secretary of

Legation, offering an opportunity to write again to America to-morrow.

14th. Evening at the opera—"Tamerlan" and the ballet of "Télémaque." The opera is the same fable as Voltaire's "Orphelin de la Chine." I met the Baron Bielefeld, who concurred in the opinion prevailing, that the Government will be maintained. A strong spirit to support it has, yesterday and this day, appeared. The moment of consternation has passed away, and that of confidence and energy has succeeded. The number of volunteers who have offered themselves at Paris to march against Bonaparte is greater than the Government could accept. A corps of five hundred men has been formed of the students at law, who offered themselves in a body. I sat next to one of them at the opera, and heard him express all his feelings to his next neighbor on the other side. He would have said the same to me, but, as a stranger, I avoid all conversation upon the topics of the times.with persons unknown to me. He appeared to be in great anxiety. He said he was enrolled in this corps of students at law; that they had been inspected this day, and were to be reviewed to-morrow. They were ordered to appear in uniform; but it was impossible to get a uniform in one day, and he did not think they ought to be required to clothe themselves at their own expense. He did not know what was to happen; he had just finished his studies at the law, and was to have maintained his thesis next week for admission to the bar. Now, God knew what would become of him. He had come to the opera "pour s'etourdir." That the disposition of the nation was very good; an immense number of volunteers had offered their services, but "il n'y a que les militaires." "And not all of them," said the neighbor. "Several officers dined with me on Sunday. They said they had faithfully served Bonaparte when he was Emperor, and would faithfully serve the King now. Many others have the same sentiments, and you may be sure you will have very little to do. It will be all over in a very few days." This same person, speaking to me, said, before the play began, "Perhaps they will announce to us some news from the theatre this evening." The house was very thin.

" Henri Quatre" was called for, and played, with the usual applause.

15th. Evening at the Théâtre Feydeau. Saw L'Opéra Comique " Le Calife de Bagdad" and " Maison à vendre." The house almost empty. The contrast between the crowds at every theatre when I arrived here, and the deserted walls since the middle of last week, is remarkable. Some of my neighbors in the parterre this evening took notice of it, and I heard a discussion between two of them, whether it was occasioned by the state of public affairs or not. The public spirit in Paris now is confident and sanguine. It does not appear that Napoleon has advanced from Lyons. He is undoubtedly there, very weak; and formidable forces are marching from all quarters against him. It is ascertained that a part of the troops, as well as of the highest officers, are faithful to the King, and Napoleon's soldiers will probably desert him in the end. There is but one sentiment to be heard in Paris. After the performance of the Calife this evening, one of the actors came forward and sang some couplets of encouragement and praise to the volunteers. The words and music were indifferent, but there was the "Lys," and the "Bourbons," and "Henri Quatre," and "Ventre saint-gris" in every couplet, and they were received with rapturous applause and loud cries of " Vive le Roi!" On returning home, I found a letter from my wife, dated at Berlin, the 5th instant. She expected to be here in ten or fifteen days from that time.

18th. I went to the Hôtel de l'Empire, and at length succeeded in seeing Mr. Bayard. I found him very much reduced, but evidently much better than when I had last seen him. He had the Morning Chronicle of the 13th and 14th on his table, which Mr. Crawford had sent him. I took up that of the 14th, and the first article that met my eye was one stating that the ratification of the treaty with America had been received the night before.

I then called upon Mr. Gallatin, and found General Turreau with him. I did not immediately recognize the General. He offered us his congratulations upon the ratification of the treaty, and also upon the brilliant defence of New Orleans. He told us that he had been utterly ruined since he left America; that about a year ago he had been starved out of Würzburg; that since then he had been reduced to less than one-third of his pay; that he had lost his eldest son; that his second son was now eighteen years old, and had made already two campaigns; that now it had pleased his Majesty to replace him in full activity of service; that he was expecting his orders to march; that he had been to receive them, and was told they would be transmitted to him.   Mr. Gallatin said he had heard that it was expected Bonaparte would be last night at Auxerres, and he supposed there would be a battle to-morrow.   Turreau smiled, shrugged his shoulders, and said, "Une bataille—allons donc," sufficiently indicating his opinion that there would be no battle.

I called upon Mr. Crawford, and while I was there Mr. Hottinguer and Mr. Dorr came in.   Mr. Hottinguer's visit was to congratulate Mr. Crawford on the ratification of our Treaty of Peace.   He told me he had intended to pay me a visit for the same purpose.   I visited also Mr. and Mrs. Smith.   While I was at dinner, the Chevalier de Brito came and sat an hour with me.   He thinks, like everybody, that Napoleon will be here in a few days.   Mr. Dorr told me that the Chamber of Deputies had addressed the King to remove all his Ministers, excepting the Duke de Feltre, appointed last week Minister of War, in the room of Soult.   Evening at the Théâtre Français, "La Femme jalouse" and "Amphytrion."   Mademoiselle Leverd performed the part of the jealous wife.   The first time I had seen her.   The house was thin, but the calls for "Henri Quatre" and "Gabrielle" were as loud, and the cries of "Vive le Roi!" as ardent, as I have ever heard them.

19th.   Beale is in much anxiety from the fear of events here. He says that Marshal Ney, with all his troops, has gone over to Napoleon, who will be here to-morrow, because it is the King of Rome's birthday.   I went out half an hour before dinner, and walked round by the Tuileries and the Place du Carrousel, where a great concourse of people was assembled. The King was going out to review the troops, who are to march out to-morrow morning to meet Napoleon.   No appearance of anything like defection to the royal cause was discernible, but the countenances of the attendants at the Tuileries marked dejection.   Mr. Crawford told me yesterday that a person of our acquaintance assured him that when the officers of the garrison of Paris attempted to prevail upon the troops to cry, "Vive le Roi!" the soldiers would say, "Oh, yes! 'Vive le Roi!'" and laugh.   They had not a hope that the soldiers would fight for the King.   There was an address from the King posted up on the walls to the army, dated yesterday, stated to be printed from the original in the King's own handwriting. "Telum imbelle, sine ictu."   It begs the soldiers to consider that if the enemy should succeed there would be a civil war, and that three hundred thousand foreigners would immediately rush upon France, and he could no longer restrain them.   He promises pardon, oblivion, and rewards to all those who will return to their duty and desert the standards other than his. The walls of the Palais Royal are covered with the most violent and furious addresses and declamations against Bonaparte, and at the opera this evening the calls for " Henri Quatre" and the shouts of " Vive le Roi!" were as boisterous as ever.

20th. Mr. Beale came in and told me that the King and royal family were gone.   They left the Palace of the Tuileries at one o'clock this morning, and took the road to Beauvais.   It was but last Thursday that the King, at the Séance Royale, talked before the two legislative chambers of dying in defence of the country.

Between one and two o'clock I went out, first to Mr. Smith's. Most of the shops in the streets were shut, it being the Monday of Passion-week.   There was a great crowd of people upon the Boulevards, but the cries of " Vive l'Empereur!" had already been substituted for those of "Vive le Roi!"   I had received a letter from Mr. Beasley, with the account of the arrival in England of the ratification of our Ghent Treaty. The Favorite corvette, in which Mr. Carroll and Mr. Baker went out, has returned.   She arrived on the 11th instant, at Plymouth, after a passage of seventeen days from New York. She had a passage of thirty-seven days from Plymouth to that place, and arrived there the 9th of February.   The treaty was received at Washington the 14th, and was ratified the 17th of

February. The President's proclamation was issued on the 18th. and the Favorite sailed from New York with the ratification the 22d. The ratifications were exchanged at eleven o'clock at night on the 17th. The American ratification was received by Lord Castlereagh in the evening of 13th March, and the event was immediately communicated by him to the Lord Mayor of London, and received after ten at night. Lord Fitzroy Somerset, the British Minister here, wrote a note to Mr. Crawford on Saturday morning, to inform him that he had received an official communication of the event.

Mr. Beasley enclosed to me a slip of an American newspaper, with General Jackson's report of the defence of New Orleans, and the defeat of the British in their attack upon that place, on the 8th of January. I went to the Hôtel de l'Empire to show Beasley's letter, and the enclosure, to Messrs. Bayard and Gallatin. But Mr. Bayard was asleep, and Mr. Gallatin was gone out. I then took the papers to Mr. Crawford, and there met a Mr. Lormery, a Frenchman, who had been a fellow-passenger with him from America. Mr. Crawford had the Moniteur of this day, containing the King's proclamation on leaving Paris. He says that Divine Providence, after restoring him to the throne of his ancestors, now permitted it to be shaken, by the defection of a part of the army who had sworn to defend it; that he had determined to avoid the calamities which might result from an ineffectual attempt to defend the capital, and to retire to a part of the kingdom more favorably situated for defence. The session of the two legislative chambers is declared to be closed, and they are convoked anew, to meet at the time and place to be hereafter notified. The King is satisfied with the attachment and devotion to him of the immense majority of the people of Paris, and promises to return very shortly to them again.

Mr. Crawford told me that he had received an official notice that the Court was to be removed to Lille, whither any of the foreign Ministers who should think fit might repair; but those to whom that would be inconvenient would be at liberty to return to their own respective Governments. Mr. Crawford said he understood the foreign Ministers had for the last week had meetings together every day; that this morning they were to meet at the Turkish Minister's, and General Waltersdorff, the Danish Minister, had promised to communicate to him the result of their meeting. But, he said, he had determined for himself what to do. He should answer the notice he had received by saying that he had already received permission to return to the United States, and had been for some time determined to embark this spring. He should not go to Lille.

I left Mr. Crawford's after four o'clock. It was said that Napoleon was to enter Paris by the Porte St. Antoine at that hour. I walked on the Boulevards until half-past five. The crowd waiting for him there was very great. Two or three troops of horse of his company came in before him. The cries of "Vive l'Empereur!" were repeated wherever they passed, but the general conversation of almost all the persons whom I overheard consisted of remarks upon the inconstancy of the populace, and the facility with which they shouted in favor of whoever was the ruling power of the day. There was a print-seller, who had spread upon the ground the prints of the King and royal family, and was crying, "Allons, Messieurs—à dix sols la pièce." The faces of Napoleon, Marie Louise, and the King of Rome had taken the place at all the print-shops of the family of Bourbon. I heard a man call out to one of the troopers to enquire how long it would be before he (Napoleon) would come in. He said it would be three-quarters of an hour. I then came home and dined, and immediately returned to the Boulevard. The people were all dispersing, and there was no expectation of his entering Paris by that way. I went to the Théâtre Français, first into the parterre, but seeing Mr. Gallatin in the balcon, I went and joined him there. They had announced " Le Cid" and " La fausse Agnès." They performed " L'Ecole des Femmes" and " L'Esprit de Contradiction." The house was almost empty, the performances languid and spiritless. Firmin, one of the actors, appeared with the three-colored cockade in his hat, and was clapped by two or three persons. There was no other manifestation of public sentiment. Mr. Todd, who came into the box for a few minutes, told me that the Emperor was to make his entry at noon to-morrow. As I came home, I found the columns of the Palais Royal covered with Napoleon's proclamations, one to the French people and the other to the army, issued on the first of this month, at the Gulf Juan, the day of his landing at Cannes. And in the garden of the Palais Royal there was a great bonfire burning, of all the addresses, proclamations, appeals to the people, and inflammatory hand-bills which have been loading every column for the last fort-night, many of which had been posted up this morning. The crowd of people in the arches and gardens was considerable, and the cries of "Vive l'Empereur!" frequent, and sometimes accompanied by cries of "À bas les Calotins!" But, although the Palais Royal is not a quarter of a mile distant from the Tuileries, I did not know that Napoleon had actually arrived while I was at the theatre.

21st. About two o'clock I walked out on the Boulevards, and saw some of the troops entering the city. I had found by my newspaper, which was brought me this morning, with the title of Journal de l'Empire, that the Emperor had arrived between eight and nine o'clock last evening at the Palace of the Tuileries, at the head of the same troops which had been sent out in the morning to oppose him. I went around by the Place Vendôme, and through the garden of the Tuileries, to the Place du Car-rousel, where there were several regiments of cavalry passing successively in review before the Emperor. I mixed with the crowd of people, heard their cries of "Vive l'Empereur!" and heard their conversations among themselves. The troops were the same garrison of Paris which had been sent out against Napoleon, and who entered the city with him last evening. The front of their helmets and the clasps of their belts were still glowing with the arms of the Bourbons, the three flower de luces. There appeared to be much satisfaction among the soldiers, but among the people I saw scarcely any manifesta-tion of sentiment, excepting in the cries of "Vive l'Empereur!" in which a very small part of the people present joined their voices. There was a man passing among the throng with a basket of three-colored cockades, and crying, "Voici, Messieurs, les cocardes de la bonne couleur—la couleur qui ne se salit pas." The crowd were laughing and joking, and talking of

the Rhine, the natural boundary of France, and swearing ven-
geance against the Prussians.   Between four and five o'clock
I returned home, without having obtained a sight of the Emperor.   He did not leave the palace.

Evening at the opera—" La Caravane du Caire," with the
ballet of " Venus and Adonis."   The house was very thin, and
the parterre chiefly consisted of persons who came for the purpose of making a cry of " Vive l'Empereur!"   There were several
passages in the opera which this audience chose to understand
as applicable to the present juncture, and which were boisterously
applauded.   One song particularly, sung by Madame Albert, and
then in chorus, beginning, " La victoire est à nous," was most
absurdly applied, and occasioned great shouting.   She was
required to repeat it, and immediately complied.   The royal
arms were removed from the curtain and the royal box, and
the imperial eagle had taken their place.   Even the title-page
of the opera had an eagle over the flower de luces, which the
boys who sell them had not had time to paste over.   All the
theatres have taken the title of imperial instead of royal.   The
Emperor Napoleon has already appointed most of his Ministers,
and all the gazettes of Paris, which were yesterday showering
upon him every execration, this day announce that his Majesty
has arrived at *his* Palace of the Tuileries.

23d. This was the second day of the Promenade de Long-
champs, but it rained almost all day long, as it has done
constantly for these ten days.   Evening at the Théâtre des
Variétés—" Mr. Crédule," " Mr. Crouton," "Le Savetier et le
Financier," and " Je fais mes Farces."   All the performances at
this theatre are samples of low and vulgar humor.   It is the
Dutch school of the drama—low life, vulgar manners, and language in defiance of grammar.   But it is the favorite spectacle
of Paris.   The house, even now, when all the other theatres
were deserted, was full.   At the close of one of the plays, a
paper was dropped from one of the stage-boxes upon the
theatre.   There was immediately a loud call from the pit for
" Le Billet," and after it had been continued for several minutes,
one of the actors came forward with the paper, and sang the
couplets which it contained.   The title was " Le Retour de la

Violette." They were merely allusive to the passing events—
Mars coming forth from his retreat, the return of the violet,
the Spring, and the "beaux jours" which they were to bring
with them. The verses were ingeniously turned, and received
with loud and undisputed applause. When I returned home,
I expected to have found my wife's carriage in the yard, and
was disappointed—but had scarcely got into my chamber when
she arrived.[1]

29th. The day was remarkably fine. The trees are putting
fully forth their leaves. At noon I went to the Hôtel des
Relations Extérieures, and had an interview of half an hour
with Mr. de Caulaincourt, Duc de Vicence. He apologized to
me for my having been delayed, and said he should have called
upon me if he had known I was in Paris. I told him that,
although sensible he could at the present juncture have no
time to spare, I could not resist the temptation of requesting
to see him, to offer him my congratulations on the change
which had just taken place, with which I had been gratified in
general, and more especially as it related personally to him.

He said that a revolution had been rendered unavoidable
by the misconduct of the Bourbons; that with the exception
of a handful of emigrants, who had been twenty years carrying
on a war against their country, the dissatisfaction had been
universal. If the Emperor had not returned there would have
been in less than six months an insurrection of the people,
the operation of which would have been dreadful; that by
the Emperor's return it had been effected without a drop of
blood shed. His government was now established throughout
France, more completely and effectually than it was eighteen
months ago. He (the Duke) had last evening enquired of
Fouché (the new Minister of Police), who received reports
from every part of the country. He had assured him that there
was not one report made to him from any quarter of any act
of violence or resistance. The return to the present order of
things accomplished itself everywhere without an effort. It
was inconceivable. Nothing like it was to be found in history.

---

[1] She had come with her son all the way from St. Petersburg to Paris in a
carriage alone.

But so it was. The Government had not adopted the bad habit which the late Government had fallen into, of disguising or concealing the true state of things; but there was nothing to conceal. France would have a strong Government, and institutions upon liberal principles. The Emperor had renounced all ideas of an extended empire. His earnest wish was peace with all the world. He would execute with the utmost fidelity the Treaty of Paris. The late Government had contracted engagements by which France was bound, and which the Emperor considered as sacred for him.

I said that I was very happy to hear this assurance from him; that the speculative opinions of the public on this subject were various. I myself had expected, first, that he (the Duke) would fill the place where I was now happy to see him, and, secondly, that the Emperor's policy would be precisely such as he now announced it to me. I had believed this would be his course, because it appeared to me the course obviously the best suited to his interest—the wisest course, and that in which he would be the strongest. It remained only to hope that he would meet with the return of the same pacific spirit in the other European Powers. I asked him if he had anything new from abroad. He said he had just received the English newspapers of the 25th, which were now in the process of being translated. He did not know what they contained. As to Vienna, he did not think it would be possible within eight or ten days to ascertain what would definitively be done by the sovereigns there. As to anything done before the information could reach there of the Emperor's entry into Paris, he considered all that as the result of passion. They would not act upon these vague and unsettled impressions. The time for reflection would come, and he still hoped the peace would not be violated. If, however, it should be, the war, on the part of France, would be *national*, and the Emperor would be stronger than he had ever been—stronger in the attachment of his troops, and stronger in the spirit of the people. The Emperor's wish was peace, and he (the Duke) could assure me that if it had been otherwise he would not have been his Minister. He had no doubt that Talleyrand would do everything in his power "pour tout embrouiller, et pour pousser à la guerre," but he hoped it would be without success.

I mentioned to him that while I had been at Ghent, De Cabre had passed through that place, and had spoken to me of him in terms of the highest respect; that in coming to Paris, I had long balanced in my own mind whether I would not take the road by Compiègne, for the sake of calling to see him at his estate, and had concluded at last to go through Péronne, from an uncertainty whether circumstances might not exist which would have made my visit inconvenient to him.

He said that it would have been only two or three leagues from my road, and he should have seen me with great pleasure; that the Emperor had appointed him at a most distressing and disastrous period his Minister of Foreign Relations. The allied sovereigns had been pleased to speak of him to his brother-in-law, at Frankfort, in terms of confidence, and he thought it impossible at that time, and under such circumstances, to refuse the appointment. He had of course been engaged in the negotiations which issued so unfortunately, and the Bourbons had thought proper to send him into exile. He had heard there of the peace we had made, and that it was a "bonne paix." Was his information correct?

I said it was on the basis of the "statu quo ante bellum;" everything was left as it had been, and it might be called a good peace, taking into consideration the situation in which the revolution in Europe has left us. We had to contend against the whole power of Great Britain, without a friend in Europe, with almost all Europe inclining even against us, and with the Government of France in the leading-strings of our enemy, showing us every possible ill will, and, as we had reason to believe, restrained only by the general and strongly pronounced sentiment of the nation in our favor from declaring against us.

He said they would have undoubtedly declared against us if they had dared, and nothing but the national sentiment had restrained them. The Duke of Wellington had been substantially the sovereign of France. The Bourbons had been mere puppets in his hands, and he had dated his dispatches here at Paris, at the head-quarters of his army. The subserviency of the Bourbon Government to him had been unbounded. France had been degraded in her own eyes and in those of the world below the rank of an independent nation. "But henceforth," said he, "we shall neither be English, nor Austrians, nor Russians—nous serons *nous*. We shall not attempt to give the law to any other nation, but we shall be our own masters at home.

"But," said he, "the Emperor of Russia did manifest here at Paris some interest in your favor."

I said that the Emperor of Russia had uniformly manifested an interest in our favor. His disposition had been always friendly to us. He had in the first instance offered his mediation, and had constantly testified his good will. But he had done nothing for us. He had left us to fight our own battles, and we had never asked anything of him.

The Duke said that the attention of the Emperor of Russia had been so entirely absorbed by the great object of the affairs of Europe that he had probably found it impossible to do anything for those of America.

I then observed that I hoped the relations between France and my own country would soon be restored to a friendly and mutually advantageous footing; that I was here waiting for the orders of my Government, and expected to receive in the course of a few days my recall from the mission to Russia, either with permission to return to the United States, or perhaps an order to go to England; that in either case I should probably want a passport from him, and should then apply to him for it.

He said he was entirely at my disposal, and he begged me, when I should see Mr. Crawford, to say the same thing for him to that gentleman. All the other foreign Ministers, he said, were gone. They had all asked for passports, which had accordingly been furnished them.

I observed that I believed Mr. Crawford had been for some time determined to return to the United States, and had already received permission to that effect from our Government. He had mentioned to me that he should probably go in a few weeks.

The Duke said that, under the peculiar circumstances of the times, perhaps it would be better for Mr. Crawford to wait for further orders from his Government, founded on their knowledge of the present events.

I said I should mention to Mr. Crawford the substance of this conversation, and then took leave. I walked home, after taking several turns in the garden of the Tuileries. There was a crowd of people under the windows of the Emperor's apartment, where he was walking with one of his officers, and occasionally appeared at the window, which was open. I saw him, but not distinctly enough to recognize his features.

April 5th. I received this morning a letter from Mr. Beasley, London, dated 31st March, with the account of news from America, and the information that Mr. Gallatin is appointed Minister to France, Mr. Bayard to Russia, and myself to England; Mr. Monroe, Secretary of State, and Captains Rodgers, Hull, and Porter, Commissioners of a Navy Board. I called upon Mr. Crawford to enquire if he had received the English newspapers, but he had not.

Mr. Crawford told me that he had seen the Duke de Vicence, and, finding that there was nothing to be done upon the subject of indemnities, he had determined to return to America immediately. He said the Duke de Vicence told him that before the other foreign Ministers went away he had seen almost all of them, and he had sent to them all a declaration, to take away all pretence of a doubt with regard to the pacific intentions of the Emperor. He said, also, that the correspondence and records in the Department of Foreign Affairs, since the return of the Bourbons, showed that there had been a long deliberation and hesitation in the Royal Council whether France should not declare war against the United States, and make common cause with Great Britain, and when it was finally determined to declare a neutrality, the instructions to the commanding officers in all the ports were to comply with everything to gratify the English.

While I was with Mr. Crawford, General Turreau came in, and complained again of being totally ruined, but he said he was better since the late events, and should perhaps be again employed by the Emperor. He said he had published a book, or rather a pamphlet, concerning the United States; that he censured, not the American nation, but their institutions, and as he expected soon to publish a second edition, referring to the events since he left America, and particularly to those of the late war with England, he should speak with eulogium upon the conduct of the Americans in the war, and particularly by sea. He wished to ask Mr. Crawford for any authentic information he could furnish him with on the subject, especially of the last campaign, and the affair at New Orleans.

Mr. Crawford promised him General Jackson's official reports.

I left them, and called upon Mr. Bayard, whom I found much better than when I saw him last Saturday. He considers himself, and his physicians and surgeons now consider him, out of all danger, but he said he had had a very narrow escape with his life. I showed him Beasley's letter. He said he did not suppose the Government would consider him under an obligation to accept his appointment, and most assuredly he should not go to St. Petersburg; his health would not admit of it. He should, if possible, undertake the journey to Brest in ten or fifteen days, and return to the United States in the Neptune.

On returning from Mr. Crawford's, I went with Mrs. Adams and Charles to the annual public meeting of the Second Class of the Institute, or French Academy. Mr. de Tracy had furnished us with two tickets. The meeting was opened at three o'clock, and was presided over by the Abbé Sicard. A report was read by Count François de Neufchâteau, concerning the prizes which the Academy had granted to two poems, on the last moments of the Chevalier Bayard; one was by Alexandre Soumet, and the other by Madame Dufresnoy—to a poem on the discovery of vaccination, by the same Alexandre Soumet— and to a memoir, upon the question, why the rhythm of the Greek and Latin languages could not be applied to the French. Mr. Soumet and the Abbé Scoppa received the "accolade fraternelle" from the President. Madame Dufresnoy was not present, so that the same compliment was not paid to her. Extracts were also read from two or three of the poems, on the subjects proposed by the class, which had failed of obtaining

the prize.   It was observed that the first prize ever bestowed
by the Academy was obtained by a woman—it was Mademoiselle de Scudéri, in 1671—and that since that time no other
instance of the same kind had occurred until the present.   The
best poem was that of Soumet, upon vaccination.   The meeting
was closed about four o'clock.   We then went and walked in the
garden of the Tuileries.   There was a great crowd assembled
under the Emperor's windows, and he came and threw open
one of the windows and showed himself to them.   We had a
full view of him.

9th.   I paid visits to Mr. Crawford, Mr. Bayard, and Mr.
Erving, but found neither of them at home; then went to the
Place du Carrousel, where the Emperor was reviewing troops.
It was impossible, from the concourse of people, to approach
near enough to the court of the Tuileries to see anything of
the review.   Afterwards I walked in the garden of the Tuileries,
which was throughout crowded with people.   Under the Emperor's windows the throng was very great.   He came and stood
about five minutes at one of the windows, and was hailed with
loud and general acclamations of "Vive l'Empereur!"   I had a
more distant view of his face than when I had last seen him.
On my return home, I purchased in one of the shops at the
Palais Royal a volume just published, entitled "One Year of
the Life of the Emperor Napoleon," with which I amused myself until dinner-time.   Evening at the Theatre Français—"Le
Tartuffe" and "Les fausses Confidences," both performed in
the highest style of excellence.   Fleury, Devigny, Thénard the
younger, Baptiste, Madame Thénard, Mdlle. Demerson, and,
above all, Mdlle. Mars, made it one of the most perfect theatrical
representations I ever witnessed.   The house was overflowing,
and there was some boisterous clamor for the airs "La Victoire," "Le Chant du Départ," and "La Lyonnaise."

21st.   Mr. Crawford told us that he heard the Emperor was
going this evening to the French Theatre.   I went with Mrs.
Adams.   The Emperor was there, but we could get seats only
in a box on the same side of the theatre as he was seated, and
we could not see him.   The house was so crowded that the
musicians of the orchestra were driven from their seats, and the

music was heard only from behind the scenes. The airs of
" La Victoire," "Veillons au Salut de l'Empire," and " La
Marseillaise" were called for, and played repeatedly. A gentleman in one of the balconies was called upon to sing some
couplets now in circulation. He said that he did not know
them, but if they were furnished him he would sing them with
pleasure. They were immediately passed to him, and he sang
them amidst loud and continued shouts of " Vive l'Empereur!"
the parterre joining in the chorus. The couplets were indifferent. The performances were the tragedy of "Hector" and
" Le Legs." Talma and Mademoiselle Duchesnois had just
finished the first scene when the Emperor came in. He was
received with redoubled and long-continued shouts of " Vive
l'Empereur!" after which there was a cry from the parterre,
" Recommencez." Accordingly, they began the play again. In
all the intervals between the acts the shouts of " Vive l'Empereur!" were renewed, and one or two persons in the pit having
put on their hats, as is usual between the acts, there was an
immediate cry of "Chapeaux bas!" At the end of the tragedy
the Emperor went away. In the after-piece, Mademoiselle
Mars and Fleury were excellent, as Talma and Mdlle. Duchesnois had been in the tragedy.

23d. We went to the mass at the chapel of the Tuileries.
The tickets were marked for half-past ten, but we were obliged
to walk in the garden near half an hour before we were admitted, and then waited an hour and a half longer before the
Emperor came in. The mass then began, and lasted less than
half an hour. The music was excellent. The opera-singers
Lays, Nourrit, and Madame Albert assisted in the performance
of the service. The lower part of the chapel, where we were,
was full of company. The ladies only were seated on benches.
I had a full and steady view of the Emperor's countenance.

24th. At five in the afternoon I went to the Restaurateur
Grignon's, in the Rue Neuve des Petits Champs, where the
dinner was given by the Americans at Paris to Mr. Crawford.
We sat down at table about six o'clock, forty-five in number.
Mr. Barnet, the Consul, presided, and under him, Mr. Appleton,
the Consul at Leghorn. The guests invited were, besides Mr.

Crawford, General La Fayette and his son, Mr. Erving, Colonel Milligan, Mr. Todd, Mr Russell's son George, and myself. Two-thirds of the company at least were unknown to me. The dinner was good, and we sat drinking toasts until between ten and eleven at night. I came away, leaving Mr. Crawford and most of the company there. Mr. Erving had left the table immediately after dinner, and before the toasts began.

General La Fayette told me that he had come to Paris at the request of Joseph Bonaparte, who had consulted him on the subject of the proposed supplementary Constitution which was yesterday published in the Moniteur. He says it is very unpopular here, and he thinks the hereditary peerage particularly objectionable. He is also of opinion that they should have begun anew without any reference to the former Constitutions, and that previously to presenting the present project to the acceptance of the people it should have been submitted to the discussion of an assembly of at least two members from each department of the country. He renewed the invitation to me to come with my family and spend some days with him at his country-seat, La Grange. I promised him to go out next Tuesday.

Our young calculator, Zerah Colburn, was at this dinner with his father. He spoke a short address to Mr. Crawford, and gave his toast with the assurance of a man full grown, but without offensive boldness. He endeavored to prevail upon George Russell to do the same; but George, though a lively and intelligent boy, had not so much confidence in himself. Mr. Crawford was toasted in his presence, and the negotiators at Ghent in mine, according to an English custom, which I am sorry to see adopted by Americans. We did not, however, on our part, adopt the custom by answering the toast with a speech.

May 2d. I sent Antoine to the Count de Tracy's to inform him and his family that I was going out to General La Fayette's, and offering to take anything they might have to send. At half-past eight we left the Hôtel du Nord, and came out of the city by the Porte St. Antoine, and through Charenton and Gros-Bois to Brie-Comte Robert, where we dined. We then proceeded through Guignes, Fontenay, and Rozoy to La

Grange, the General's seat, where we arrived between six and seven in the evening. The distance from Paris is fourteen leagues, and Brie is the half-way station. The country, though generally level, is in many places beautiful, and appears in fine verdure, although the fruit-trees have much suffered by the late frosts, and look sickly. The roads are good as far as Fontenay.

The General's seat is an old castle. He is surrounded by a numerous family—his son George, and his lady, who was a daughter of Count de Tracy, and they have three daughters; his two daughters, Madame de la Tour Maubourg and Madame de la Stéyrie, each with three children, among whom there is only one boy; the husband of Madame de la Tour Maubourg is also here, a Commandeur de la Stéyrie, and a Mr. Pillet, an old friend and fellow-soldier in America of General La Fayette, who recognized me as having seen me in the year 1796 at the Hague, where I had the good fortune to do him a good office. We dined a second time, and spent the evening in conversation, chiefly upon the present state of affairs in France. The General appears to be much gratified with the new decree for immediately organizing and convoking a representative assembly. It has probably been adopted in consequence of his advice.

3d. A gentleman of the neighborhood, a Mr. de Meun, was here this morning at breakfast. The General took me out to see his flocks of merinos, of which he has a thousand, his cattle, and his horses. The house is an ancient castle, built of granite, has a centre and two wings, with four turrets, pointed in sugar-loaves. He says there is a tradition that it was built in the time of Louis le Gros. It was heretofore surrounded by a moat with a drawbridge, but he has changed the direction of the water into that of a winding canal. His park was laid out by a painter, in the English style, and is beautifully picturesque. He has surrounded the house with trees—poplars, willows, pines, firs, locusts, and the horse-chestnut and oak at further distance. One side of the wall at the front entrance to the house is covered from the ground to the roof with ivy, which he planted by the advice of Mr. Fox, who came to visit him when he was last in France. Mr. George La Fayette and Mr. Pillet went this day together to Paris. Mr. Meun and Mr. de

la Tour Maubourg also went away before dinner. There was
a very heavy thunder-shower at two or three in the afternoon,
and steady rain all the evening. The General gave me the last
number of the Censeur to read—a periodical work, edited by
two young lawyers, who, after having been in violent opposition
to the Bourbons, are now equally opposed to Napoleon. Quid-
dism is not exclusively the growth of American soil. The Censeur met with every possible obstacle from the Government of
the Bourbons, and the present number was for several days suppressed by the police of Napoleon. It now circulates freely, and
much more extensively for the effort first made to suppress it.

4th. There was a continual rain the whole day, which confined us to the house. The General received the newspapers
from Paris, and we had a variety of topics for political conversation. General Victor de la Tour Maubourg came on a
visit, was here at dinner, and passes the night here. He lost
a leg at the battle of Leipsic. I went into the General's
library, and borrowed two or three volumes of his books.
He recommended to me a volume of Benjamin Constant's
pamphlets, and particularly some observations published last
summer on a speech made by the Abbé de Montesquieu, then
Minister of the Interior to the Legislative Assembly, on the
law then projected relating to the liberty of the press. Constant, who was then one of the most furious adversaries of
Napoleon, and continued to be so until the 19th of last month,
when he published a frantic article against him in the Journal
des Débats, is now one of his Counsellors of State. He is, as
I heard him say at Madame de Staël's dinner, essentially a
pamphleteer. He writes with some ability, and it required
very little to refute the contemptible sophistry of the Abbé de
Montesquieu. But in his pamphlets, as in his conduct, Benjamin Constant shows continual indications of an unsettled
head. He has the merit of having been invariably a friend of
liberty.

5th. We breakfasted at nine o'clock, two hours earlier than
the General's usual time, but it was for the sake of enabling us
to depart in seasonable time to arrive before the night at Paris.
We took leave of the General and his family just at ten, and

returned by the same road that we had gone, excepting that
we joined the high-road without passing through the town of
Rozoy. We reached Brie at half-past two, and dined at " La
Grâce de Dieu." When we went down we had dined at the
sign of " L'Espérance." We changed the house by the recom-
mendations at the General's, but the house which we first went
to was the best. At four we left Brie, and just at eight in the
evening alighted at our lodgings, Hôtel du Nord, Rue de
Richelieu. The weather was all day fair, with the exception
of a light shower in the afternoon. On my arrival h. me, I
found two cards from Mr. Bayard, which he had left this day,
letters from Messieurs Meyer and Brüxner and Harris, and
the newspapers of the last four days, which engaged my attention the remainder of the evening. Our visit to La Grange
has been agreeable, although the weather was bad and confined us to the house almost the whole time we were there.
The General himself is always cheerful, and of pleasant conversation, and the family, though some of them in circumstances at present uneasy, are amiable and attentive to their
guests. The two sons-in-law, La Tour Maubourg and La
Stéyrie, were both officers of the guards of Louis XVIII., and
had both a sort of injunction to reside not within thirty leagues
of Paris. General de la Tour Maubourg is an elder brother
of the son-in-law. He is a man of simple, unpretending manners, but in his conversation now very cautious and reserved.
General La Fayette told me that he should go next Monday
to the meeting of the Electoral College of the department at
Melun.

6th. I sent this morning to enquire if it was Mr. Bayard's
intention to leave Paris this day, and was answered that he
would go at eleven this morning. I called upon him about
that hour, and found him preparing for his departure. The
horses were already there. Mr. Bayard had received a letter
of 28th April from Mr. Clay. Letters of the same date (April
28th) from Mr. Clay and Mr. Gallatin to Mr. Crawford had
been received and opened by Mr. Jackson. Mr. Clay observed
that he had not succeeded in obtaining a passage to the United
States from Liverpool, and should wait for the Neptune.

Mr. Gallatin expresses also the positive intention of returning to America in the Neptune. But they had already had one or two interviews with Lord Castlereagh, relative to the negotiation of a treaty of commerce, and were to have another with him, the President of the Board of Trade, and a third person, to see if they could agree upon the basis of a treaty. Mr. Clay, however, appears not to expect that they would come to any result, and is anxious to return home as soon as possible.

After taking leave of Mr. Bayard, I called upon Mr. Jackson, who showed me the letters from Mr. Gallatin and Mr. Clay to Mr. Crawford. He had also two letters enclosed from Mr. Gallatin to Mr. George La Fayette, which I took and carried with me to the Count de Tracy's. I left the letters with him to be forwarded, as Mr. La Fayette returned yesterday to La Grange.

I had some conversation with Mr. de Tracy on the present state of affairs in France. War appears now to be certain, which the allies will profess to wage only against Napoleon Bonaparte. The first thought and object of the inhabitants of Paris will be to save themselves. They have no attachment either to the Bourbons or to Napoleon. They will submit quietly to the victorious party, and will do nothing in support of either. If the same spirit should prevail throughout France, Napoleon will soon be overthrown. As I walked to the Tuileries, and through the Palais Royal, before dinner, I saw a multitude of pamphlets against the projected supplement to the Constitution. The caricatures, as yet, are all of one side.

7th. Mr. F. Williams called upon me this morning, with Mr. Boott, from Boston. He left London last Wednesday morning, and brought me a letter of the preceding day, the 2d of this month, from Mr. Beasley, enclosing a dispatch from the Secretary of State, dated 13th March, and which, though not marked as such, must be a duplicate. It informs me that I was appointed Minister Plenipotentiary to Great Britain, and mentions the enclosure of a commission and credentials, neither of which, however, was enclosed.

We had a visit from Mr. Todd and Mr. Carter. Mr. Bayard left Paris yesterday, between one and two o'clock in the afternoon. Milligan went with him. Mr. Todd intends to go on Tuesday morning. I wrote to my mother, and took a short walk before dinner. Napoleon was reviewing troops in the yard of the Tuileries. The cries of "Vive l'Empereur!" and "À bas les Royalistes!" were frequent in the streets the whole day. The crowds of people in the public walks unusually great. Evening at the Odéon—"J'ai perdu mon Procès," "Une Journée à Versailles," and "Le Portrait de Michel Cervantes." The "Journée à Versailles" is a good comedy; the rest was trash. On returning home, I found a card of Mr. J. N. d'Arcy, of Baltimore, with two letters from Mr. Beasley, of 3d May, one of them enclosing a passport for me and my family, from Lord Castlereagh.

8th. Mr. D'Arcy paid me this morning a visit, with Mr. Todd. I was mistaken in the expectation that he had dispatches for me from America. He lent me several English newspapers of the 3d instant, and sent me a number of Cobbett's Register, and one of the Edinburgh Review. Mr. Todd told me he should not leave the city until to-morrow evening. I wrote part of a letter to the Secretary of State. On returning from a walk before dinner with Charles, I received by the post a letter from Messrs. Baring Brothers, at London, informing me that they had received from the American Department of State a packet for me, enclosing my commission and credentials to Great Britain, which they are directed to retain until my arrival in England. Their letter is of the 2d instant. I determined to proceed to England with as little delay as possible.

9th. I wrote to the Duke de Vicence, Minister of Foreign Affairs, to ask for a passport, and an interview with him to take leave. Evening at the Théâtre des Variétés—"Le Valet ventriloque," "La Ferme et le Château," "Les deux Magots de la Chine," and "Le petit Enfant prodigue." They are all farces of the lowest kind, but the performers are better of their kind than are to be seen at any other theatre in Paris. Brunet, Potier, Tiercelin, Bosquier, Gavaudan, are all excellent actors—Potier equal, if not superior, to any actor of farces that I ever saw.

11th. All the morning we were engaged in making preparations for our departure. Mr. Petry called upon us with news, which proved to be only a groundless rumor. The Duc de Vicence called immediately afterwards, and told me that the firing of cannon had been for a visit which the Emperor was making to the Hospital of Invalids. He mentioned to me many circumstances relating to the state of public affairs at this time, and said that they were perfectly informed of all the proceedings of the Congress until after the Emperor arrived in Paris; that six dispatches from Talleyrand to the Ministry of Louis XVIII. had been received by him (the Duke de Vicence) since he came to the Department of Foreign Affairs. They had the whole history of the Declaration of 13th March, and knew by whom it was written; that Talleyrand obtained the signatures to it; that it was signed first by Prince Metternich, who was " un homme très-leger," and who scarcely took the trouble of reading it, and never thought of reflecting a moment upon its meaning. The Duke of Wellington signed it in the same manner. The rest signed upon trust. The Duke said it was amusing to be told that Lord Wellington had been highly indignant at learning that he was charged as an instigator of assassination for having signed that declaration. The truth was, he had signed it without knowing what it meant, impelled by a moment of passion. It was a declaration signalizing one individual as a wolf, not entitled to any of the privileges of a human being. They thought that by using high-sounding and bitter words they alone would suffice to destroy him. At the same time, they thought his undertaking so weak and insignificant that they actually wrote here that two brigades of gendarmes would be more than enough to put him down.

I told the Duke that I had seen a remark in the Edinburgh Review, that if the mere facts of the Emperor's landing and resumption of the government of France were put into a romance, they would be rejected as too improbable for a narrative of fiction.

He said it was true, but he could assure me there had been no previous concert between the Emperor and any person here. Not a human being in France knew that he was coming.

The Duke saw by a smile on my countenance that I was not altogether credulous of this fact, and said, "Eh bien! remember what I now say to you. Depend upon it, the fact will ultimately be known, and proved. I repeat, that there was not a human being in France who knew of the Emperor's design before he landed."

I told him what was said in the Edinburgh Review, of a watch-word of "La Violette" and "Elle reviendra au printemps." He said there was nothing in it; that "Le Père la Violette" was a name the soldiers had given the Emperor among themselves, as they had formerly called him "Le petit Caporal." But there was nothing of plot or conspiracy in it. As for himself, when he first heard that the Emperor had landed, he did not believe it. He had been a whole day disbelieving it, until it was ascertained to him by a general, who had received it directly from General Maison. The Emperor knew, however, the universal discontent and disgust at the Government of the Bourbons in France. He received the newspapers; but during the whole time he had been at the island of Elba only two persons had been from France to see him. But the Bourbons were so odious that, if the Emperor had not come, there would nevertheless have been within two months a revolution against them. They knew it very well. All the correspondence from the interior, as well as that to and from Vienna, which had fallen into the hands of the present Government, showed that Louis XVIII. himself saw the impossibility of getting along. The Duke told me that if this change had not taken place, he should himself have gone to America. He had made all his arrangements for going this spring. He could not have lived in France. The Emperor of Russia had kindly given him an invitation to Russia, but he had not chosen to accept it, and had formed the settled determination to go to America. He said also that the Emperor of Russia had spoken to him here at Paris with great disapprobation of the Bourbons and their proceedings, and said they risked everything as they were going on.

He further said that since he had been in the Department they had received three dispatches from the Count de Noailles, the Ambassador of Louis XVIII. at St. Petersburg; that the Count complained that he found himself embarrassed in society, because he heard opinions expressed very freely against the war. When the Duke left me, he said he should send me a dispatch to be forwarded to Mr. Serrurier, the French Minister in the United States, to whom new credentials had been sent, and who was understood to have given general satisfaction in America.

In the evening we paid a visit at the Count de Tracy's to take leave. The Count himself was abroad. We saw Madame de Tracy, and Mr. and Madame de l'Aubépin. They told us that General La Fayette was elected a member of the Representative Assembly, and had been President of the Electoral College at Melun; that the General would be in Paris next Saturday to dine. I had determined to leave Paris at four o'clock, afternoon, on Saturday, but, having a strong wish to see the General before I go, I now concluded to postpone our departure until the next morning. The ladies and Mr. de l'Aubépin made many enquiries as to the manner of living in America. This family, too, has had, and perhaps may have again, the project of removing to America. After our visit, we finished our evening by a walk upon the Boulevards.

12th. We were engaged all the morning again in packing trunks to send away by the diligence to Havre. It was almost four in the afternoon before I could go out of the house. We dispatched nine trunks and boxes by the diligence, which went this afternoon. I called and took leave of the Duke de Vicence, whom I found dressed, ready to go with his portefeuille à l'Elysée. My visit was accordingly very short, in which, however, we had some further interesting conversation. He said that he had asked Mr. Petry to call upon me with my passport, and the dispatch for Mr. Serrurier; that Petry had been long in America, and wished to return there again. He was a very good man, and he (the Duke) should do for him what he could.

I asked him if there was any foundation in the rumor that the King of Naples (Murat) had beaten the Austrians. He said there was no authentic account of it, but many private letters mentioned it with confidence. The Minister of the Police had received one yesterday, and he himself had one this morning.

I observed that the public funds had risen here considerably within these few days; that there must be some foundation for it in circumstances not generally known.

He said there had been some symptoms of hesitation in Austria to join in the latest projected measures of the allies; that there had been since the Treaty of 25th March a further declaration proposed, and actually signed by three persons. He had the declaration itself. Austria had, it seemed, declined signing it. There was also understood to be some discordance in the English Cabinet. Lord Liverpool was understood to be inclined to continue at peace. Lord Castlereagh was ardent for war.

I asked him if he was certain of this.

He said he had reason to believe it. He knew at least that Lord Liverpool had been so earnest for the peace with America that he had tendered his resignation to the Prince Regent if it was not made. Lord Castlereagh was for continuing the war. I said that we knew perfectly well what were Lord Castlereagh's dispositions when he passed through Ghent on his way to Vienna; but we had heard that from Vienna he had written home, advising that they should conclude with us. He said that was true. It was in consequence of the discussions with Russia and with Prussia respecting Poland and Saxony. Lord Castlereagh was then much at variance with the Emperor of Russia, and did write to advise the peace with America. All this was fully disclosed in the correspondence from the French Ambassadors at Vienna with his Department, and was now among the archives.

14th. We walked out this morning on the Boulevards to see the procession of the Confederates of the Faubourgs St. Antoine and St. Marceau, and saw them pass. They were going to the Tuileries to be presented to the Emperor. There were about thirty-five hundred men and boys of the Faubourg St. Antoine, and sixteen hundred of the Faubourg St. Marceau— all laborers of the most indigent class. They marched in ranks of twenty, holding one another arm in arm, and shouting, incessantly, "Vive l'Empereur!" After returning, I went and paid visits to take leave at Mr. Hottinguer's, Mr. Hubbard's, and Messrs. Carette and Minguet's. We then went to the Champ de Mars, and saw the buildings preparing for the assembly of the Champ de Maï; thence to the garden of the Tuileries, through which we walked, and the Place du Carrousel, to the Musée Napoléon, where we entered and took a final view of the antique statues and marbles on the ground-floor. We came home and dined, after which we rode out to the heights of Montmartre, where the entrenchments for the defence of Paris are now carrying on.

As we returned home, we stopped at the Count de Tracy's, where we saw the ladies and General La Fayette. The Count himself was gone out. The General promised he would call at my lodgings and see me to-morrow evening at seven o'clock. He said he was glad of having been elected a member of the Assembly of Representatives, because it gave him a reason for declining to be one of the Peers, as had been proposed to him. I said that if the war should take place, as appeared inevitable, I entreated him to use his influence to prevent the repetition of such outrageous acts as the decrees of Berlin and of Milan; for if such measures should be resorted to, I really believed they would produce a war between the United States and France, He promised me to use his best endeavors to promote a just and liberal policy towards America, and said he would correspond with me through the channel of our Chargé d'Affaires, Mr. Jackson. He said he had seen this morning Mr. Constant, who was quite uneasy under the situation in which he has placed himself, and who has become an admirer of the Emperor Napoleon.

15th. General La Fayette came in the evening, and I renewed the request to him to use his influence, if the war should break out, to maintain a system of moderation towards the United States, even if a different example should be shown by Great Britain.

He said that he had seen Joseph this morning, and he had again urged upon him to consent to be one of the new House

of Peers. He had answered, that having been elected one of
the members of the representative chamber, he was under an
obligation at least to begin by taking his seat there. Afterwards he might with more propriety see what was to be done.
Lucian had also sent him a flattering message by Humboldt.
Joseph had asked him why he had not been to visit the Emperor, and had complained of the conduct of certain Senators
in voting the "déchéance." He had answered, that as a member of the Assembly, there would naturally be relations between
the Emperor and him, which would make a visit suitable. That
as to the "déchéance," he should not disguise that if he had
been a Senator he should have voted for it himself. The Emperor had made of the Senate Conservateur, a Senate Destruc-
teur, and after having, to please him, destroyed everything else,
it was no wonder they should have finished by destroying him.
It was now said that he came with an entirely different system,
and that he was to govern upon liberal and patriotic principles
—which was very well. The General added that he thought it
best to keep upon the reserve, because he thought he saw a
wish to entangle him in connection with them before the meeting of the Assembly. He said that as the most important
object was to prevent the enemy from giving the law to France,
he should be for furnishing the Government (perhaps without
acknowledging Napoleon as Emperor) with the means of carrying on the war successfully, and then to form the Assembly
into a constituent Assembly and make a new Constitution. He
thought Napoleon's great object would be to obtain those
means and then to go immediately and fight a battle. He
said Joseph had told him there were some pacific overtures
from Austria, which amounted only to this, that if he would
sanction not only the Treaty of Paris, but the measures of the
Congress at Vienna, concerning Poland, Saxony, and Italy, his
wife and child should be restored to him. Joseph said this
proposal would not be accepted, for it was itself shameful to
put such an act upon such a condition, and even if it should
be accepted, Austria would probably break the bargain, and
still keep the wife and child.

On the whole, I see that La Fayette is fluctuating in his own

mind. He asked me if I should see the Duke of Orleans in
England. I did not know. He asked me what I thought the
allies would do if anything should happen to Napoleon—for
instance, if he should be killed in battle—whether they would
force the Bourbons upon France. I thought they would leave
France as free as they had last spring.

He wants Napoleon, as a military commander, to defend the
country, and yet fears the consequences of his success. He
thinks much of the Duke of Orleans, much of a republic, and
he would be glad to have a last resort, even if Louis XVIII.
should come back. At bottom, there is an ardent love of his
country, and a sincere desire that it should be governed by a
free and liberal Constitution ; but with regard to the means, he
has nothing settled, and waits for events, especially for the meeting of the Assembly. He asked me to tell them in England
that they were acting against their own views by commencing
this war. Another person said to me, that if Napoleon should
not throw himself into the arms of the people, "J'espère qu'au
mois prochain on le fera sauter." La Fayette has no positive
design of this kind. He is balancing, and I fear that his scale
will not preponderate at the lucky moment. He renewed the
promise of correspondence with me, and asked me to take some
letters from him for America.

CHAPTER XI.

THE MISSION TO GREAT BRITAIN.

May 16th, 1815. Began the day by bringing up the arrears of my journal, at which it is generally inconvenient to write in travelling. The remainder of the morning was occupied with the last preparations for departure. Mr. Erving and General La Fayette came and took leave of us, and Mr. R. Boyd saw us into the carriage. We received a multitude of letters and packages from several persons, to be carried to England. With our large quantity of baggage, they encumber us not a little. We had ordered the horses at three o'clock in the afternoon. They came at half-past three, and at twenty minutes past four we left the Hôtel du Nord, Rue de Richelieu, No. 97, where I have passed upwards of three months of leisure, too unprofitably for any useful purpose, but as agreeably as any part of my life. We travelled three stages, and arrived at Pontoise between seven and eight. We stopped to lodge at the Hôtel du Juste, and ordered horses for three o'clock to-morrow morning. My object in coming thus far this day was to have an easy day's ride to reach Rouen to-morrow, but we find the roads so good, and the days are now so long, that we might easily have gone two stages further this evening, and have reached Havre itself to-morrow night. The country is in its early verdure, and the orchards are all in full blossom. We had green peas this day for the first time at dinner, and within these two days have seen small bunches of cherries for sale in the streets.

LONDON, 25th.—We breakfasted this morning at six, and at seven left Dover with two post-chaises, Mrs. Adams and myself in one, Lucy and Charles in the other.

Itinerary of the Journey from Dover to London.

	Miles.	Post-Houses.	Inn-keepers.	2 Chaises, 4 Horses.	2 Drivers.	Turn-pikes.	Extra.	Total.
				£ s. d.	£ s. d.	£ s. d.	£ s. d.	£ s. d.
From Dover to		York Hotel.	A. Payne.					
Canterbury,	16	King's Head.	Friday.	2 8 0	0 8 0	0 3 4	0 2 0	3 1 4
Sittingbourn,	16	George.	Marshall.	2 8 0	0 6 0	0 3 6	0 1 0	2 18 6
Rochester,	11	King's Head.	Holloway.	1 13 0	0 6 0	0 2 0	0 1 6	2 2 6
Dartford,	15	George & Bull.	Etherington and Micklefield.	2 5 0	0 7 6	0 2 8	0 5 0	3 0 2
London,	18			2 14 0	0 9 0	0 2 8	0 1 6	3 7 2
	76			11 8 0	1 16 6	0 14 2	0 11 0	14 9 8

The expense of travelling in this manner is about the same as in France. There, however, I had the additional charge and trouble of a carriage. In England, the charge is the same whether they furnish you carriages or only horses—one shilling and sixpence a mile for a post-chaise and pair, and the same for the horses alone. From three to four shillings to each driver, a shilling to the hostler, and between two and four shillings for turnpikes are paid at each stage. The expenses of travelling by post have exactly doubled since I first knew them, in 1778, and in England they have also doubled since I first knew them, in 1783. The expenses at inns upon the road, and almost all others in England, are nearly double what they are in France.

The face of the country from Dover to London was quite familiar to me. I had travelled the whole way twice, and the greater part of it many times. Although eighteen years have elapsed since I was last in England, its outward appearance remains much the same, and the ride from Dover to London is one of those which present the country in its most favorable light.

We met on the road a regiment of soldiers, marching to Dover, to embark for Flanders; many beggars, and families of apparent paupers, wandering about the country, without shed or shelter. The cities have all the show of prosperity, but with an extraordinary proportion of cards upon the houses, advertising them for sale. We did not stop to dine on the road, but took, at Dartford, a sandwich and a glass of ale. We stopped at the "Green Man," Blackheath, at the six-mile stone, and found there Mr. Williams, one of Mr. Beasley's clerks, with a letter from him, informing me that he had taken lodgings for me at No. 67 Harley Street, Cavendish Square. It was seven when we received the note, and eight when we arrived at our lodgings in London.

26th. As the dispatches from the Government of the United States, with my commission, were deposited in the hands of Messrs. Baring, I first went to the house of Mr. Alexander Baring, for whom I had a letter from Mr. D. Parker. He resides in Portman Square. I found him at home, but the papers for me were at the counting-house, in Bishopsgate-within, in the City. I paid visits to Mr. Clay and Mr. Gallatin, the latter of whom was not at home. Mr. Clay mentioned to me the state of the negotiation which Mr. Gallatin and he have commenced here in relation to commerce. I then went into the City, to the counting-house of Messrs. Baring, and received from Mr. Alexander Baring the dispatches from America, enclosing my commission as Envoy Extraordinary and Minister Plenipotentiary at the Court of Great Britain, with a letter of recredence to the Emperor of Russia, a letter of credence to the British Prince Regent, and instructions, a copy of which I had already received at Paris. I wrote a note to Lord Castlereagh, informing him of my arrival with a public commission, and requesting him to appoint a time for me to call upon him.

27th. Lord Castlereagh answered my note, and appointed next Monday morning, at eleven o'clock, to receive me.

28th. I received visits from the Duke of Sorentino, Marquis of Salinas, to whom Mr. Erving had given me a letter, and from Mr. Douglas Kinnaird, to whom I had brought a letter from his brother, Lord Kinnaird, at Paris. He invited me to dine with him next Tuesday, at a quarter before seven. The usual dining hour, at this end of the town, is seven. Mr. Gallatin called upon me, and I showed him the dispatch which I have received from the Secretary of the Treasury. He put into my hands the paper he had drawn up as a project for a treaty of commerce.

29th. Lord Castlereagh had appointed eleven o'clock this morning for me to see him at his house in St. James's Square. After waiting nearly an hour beyond that time for my carriage, I took a hackney-coach, and went there. The Duke of Orleans was with him, and I waited about another half-hour before he received me. I gave him a copy of my letter of credence to the Prince Regent, upon which he said that he would take the orders of his Royal Highness as to the time when he would receive it. There was some general conversation upon the subject of the concerns mutually interesting to the two nations. I assured him of the disposition on the part of the American Government to perform with the utmost fidelity all their engagements contracted in the late treaty of peace, and to adopt every other measure calculated to consolidate the friendship and promote the harmony between the two countries. As a token of which, an Act of Congress had passed previous to the close of their late session, tendering on the part of the United States a reciprocal abolition of all discriminating duties of tonnage and upon merchandise imported in our own or in British vessels. I presumed he was in possession of a copy of that act.

He said he believed they were, but he would thank me for a sight of it, and I promised to furnish him with a copy.

I mentioned, also, the message of the President, recommending the exclusion of foreign seamen, not already naturalized, from the naval and merchant service of the United States— a measure which Congress, owing to the shortness of time, had not acted upon, but which would probably be hereafter adopted.

He said that what had been done by the Government of the United States in this respect had given the greater satisfaction here, as an opinion, probably erroneous, had heretofore prevailed that the American Government encouraged and invited foreign seamen. That as to the principle, he was afraid there was little prospect of a probability of coming to an agreement, as we adhered to the right of naturalization, for which we contended, and as no Government here could possibly abandon the right to the allegiance of British subjects.

I said that I saw no better prospect than he did of an agreement upon the principle. But it was not the disposition of the American Government or nation to apply the force of arms to the maintenance of any abstract principle. The number of British seamen naturalized in America was so small that it could be no object of concern to this Government. If British subjects were excluded for the future, there could be no motive for taking men from American vessels. If the practice totally ceased, we should never call upon the British Government for any sacrifice of their principle. When the evil ceased to be felt, we should readily deem it to have ceased to exist.

He said that there would be every disposition to guard against the possibility of abuse, and the Admiralty was now occupied in prescribing regulations for the naval officers, which he hoped would prevent all cause of complaint on the part of the United States. He then mentioned the late unfortunate occurrence at Dartmoor Prison, and the measures which had been taken by agreement between him and Messrs. Clay and Gallatin on that occasion.

I said I had received a copy of the report made by Mr. King and Mr. Larpent after their examination into the transaction, and of the written depositions which had been taken, as well on that examination as previously at the coroner's inquest; that, after what had been done, I considered the procedure as so far terminated that I was not aware of any further step to be taken by me until I should receive the instructions of my Government on the case. The evidence was so voluminous, and I had so lately received it, that I had not yet entirely read it through; but, from the general impression upon my mind made by what I had read, I regretted that a regular trial of Captain Shortland had not been ordered, and I thought it probable that such would be the opinion of my Government.

He said that undoubtedly there were some cases in which a trial was the *best* remedy that could be resorted to, but there were others in which it was the *worst;* that a trial, the result of which should be an acquittal, would place the whole affair in a more unpleasant situation than it would be without it; that the evidence was extremely contradictory; that it had

been found impossible to trace to any individual the most
unjustifiable part of the firing, and that Captain Shortland
denied having given the order to fire.

I admitted that the evidence was contradictory, but said that
from the impression of the whole mass of it upon me, I could
not doubt either that Captain Shortland gave the order to fire,
or that, under the circumstances of the case, it was unnecessary.
It was true the result of a trial might be an acquittal, but, as it
was the regular remedy for a case of this description, the sub-
stitution of any other was susceptible of strong objections, and
left the officer apparently justified, when I could not but think
him altogether unjustifiable. I then mentioned the earnest
desire of the American Government for the full execution of
the stipulations in the Treaty of Ghent, and that my instructions
had expressed the hope of an appointment as soon as possible
of the Commissioners on the part of this country, for proceeding to the settlement of the boundary line.

Lord Castlereagh asked what would be the most convenient
season of the year for transacting the business.

I said I believed it might be done at any season, but, as the
line would be in a high northern latitude, the summer season
would probably be most for the personal convenience of the
Commissioners. He said the appointments would be made
with reference to that consideration.

I then observed that the British Admiral stationed in the
Chesapeake had declined restoring slaves he had taken, under
a construction of the first article of the treaty, which my Government considered erroneous, and which I presumed this
Government would likewise so consider; that a reference to
the original draft of the British projet, and to an alteration
proposed by us and assented to by the British Commissioners,
would immediately show the incorrectness of this construction.

He said it would be best to refer this matter to the gentlemen who were authorized to confer with us on the subject of
a treaty of commerce. He asked if Mr. Gallatin and Mr. Clay
had communicated to me what had passed between them and
this Government on this head. I said they had.

He asked if I was joined to them in that business. I said I

was, but that it was altogether distinct from my mission to this Court.

He said the same persons had been appointed to treat with us who had concluded with us the Treaty of Ghent, and Mr. Robinson, the Vice-President of the Board of Trade, had been added to them. They had already had some conferences with Messrs. Clay and Gallatin, and their powers were now made out and ready for them to proceed in the negotiation.

I asked Lord Castlereagh if he could mention to me the time when the Prince Regent would receive my credential letter. He said if I was desirous of presenting it at an early day, the Prince would receive me at a private audience; otherwise it would be at the first levee day. I said that would suit me perfectly well, and I would not wish to give his Royal Highness the trouble of assigning a particular day for a private audience.

He then asked me if I had not come last from France, and what there was there of news. I told him they were assembling there all the force that they could collect, and it would be a very considerable force. He said that was to be expected. He asked if I had seen any of the fortifications erecting at Paris. I said I had seen what was doing at Montmartre, and thought very little of it. The object, I believed, was rather to employ workmen than to defend the city. He said it was ridiculous to pretend defending the city. It could not be defended. If Montmartre could be defended, there were other avenues equally accessible.

I did not incline to converse much with him upon French affairs, and therefore took leave. His deportment is sufficiently graceful, and his person is handsome. His manner was cold, but not absolutely repulsive.

After returning home, I went and paid a visit to Count Lieven, the Russian Ambassador, who resides in the neighborhood of our lodgings. I told him I had received a letter of recredence from the President of the United States addressed to the Emperor of Russia; that Mr. Bayard had been appointed as my successor at his Court, and if his state of health had been such as to permit him to proceed to Russia or to the place of the

Emperor's abode, I should have made him the bearer of it. But Mr. Bayard was very ill, and intended to return to the United States. I came therefore to consult him (the Count) and ask him what would be my best method of transmitting the letter to the Emperor—whether I should deliver it to him, or address it to the place where the Emperor may be, or transmit it to the Department of Foreign Affairs at St. Petersburg.

The Count said he would write and take the Emperor's orders on the subject. He asked me whether Mr. Bayard was really so ill, or whether it was only a reluctance at going to Russia. I assured him that it was a real, and so severe an illness that it was even doubtful whether he could recover from it.

I had then much conversation with the Count on the present state of France and the prospects of the new war. He thinks that Bonaparte (for so he must be called here) has not, and cannot assemble, more than two hundred thousand men of regular troops; and I am of the same opinion. I gave him such information of the state of France as I think correct, and he said it agreed with all the best information that had been collected from that country. He told me the Emperor Alexander was to leave Vienna the 23d of this month, and was probably now at Munich.

On my return home, I had a visit from Mr. Clay. He said that Mr. Gallatin and he had invitations to dine next Thursday with Earl Grey; that there had also been an invitation to Mr. Crawford, but he was gone, and he (Mr. Clay) had now a note from Sir James Mackintosh, through whom the invitations had been given, mentioning that Lord Grey, having heard of my arrival, wished me also to be of ·the company.

I accepted the invitation. Mr. Clay told me he had also an invitation at Countess Grey's to an evening party to-morrow.

30th. I wrote this morning a note to Lord Castlereagh, enclosing copies of the Act of Congress concerning the discriminating duties, and the message of the President, recommending a law to secure the navigation of American vessels exclusively by American seamen. Wrote also a letter of introduction for Mr. Newcomb to Mr. Jackson, the Chargé des Affaires at Paris.

I had visits from him, from Mr. Murdoch, Mr. Hubbard, and Mr. Snow, who brought me a letter of introduction from Mr. Crawford. I paid visits to Mr. Gallatin and Mr. Clay, and dined with Mr. Douglas Kinnaird, No. 32 Clarges Street. The invitation was for a quarter before seven. The clock had struck seven when I left my lodgings, and I was the first person at the house, and waited about a quarter of an hour before Mr. and Mrs. Kinnaird made their appearance. The Earl of Roseberry, Lord Forbes, General Fergusson, Mr. Fazakerley, Mr. Lamb, and some other gentlemen were there. The conversation was almost entirely about France. Several of the gentlemen were members of the House of Commons, and had paired off until ten o'clock to come and dine. There was a debate in the house upon some Catholic question. Mr. Fazakerley had seen Napoleon at the island of Elba. Mr. Kinnaird related many anecdotes of an Irishman named McNamara, who had also been to Elba, and told foolish stories of his conversations with Napoleon. He also spoke with great indignation against Lord Cathcart, who caused the imprisonment of a Mr. Semple for eleven weeks in the fortress of Silberberg. Mrs. Kinnaird is a violent anti-Bonapartist. We sat a short time at table after Mrs. Kinnaird had withdrawn; it was near eleven when I left the house and went to Countess Grey's. Very few of the company had assembled. The Earl received me with much politeness, and introduced me to his lady. The company shortly afterwards came in crowds. I was introduced to the Duke of Gloucester, Earl Fitzwilliam, Lady Mackintosh, Mr. Rogers, the poet, and a Mr. Sharp, who told me that he had formerly known my father when he was here. There was neither dancing nor card-playing, but there were assembled about three hundred persons, who filled two chambers and passed a couple of hours in looking at one another and occasional conversation among their respective acquaintances. The Duke of Gloucester asked me several questions about America and the American Ministers who had formerly been here. Lord Erskine predicted the immediate downfall of Bonaparte. It was about one in the morning when I came home.

June 1st. I dined at Earl Grey's. The invitation was for

half-past six o'clock. I went at seven, and found Mr. Clay and Mr. Gallatin just there. We were the first of the company. Lord Rosslyn, Sir James and Lady Mackintosh, Sir John Newport, Mr. Horner, Mr. Kinnaird, and a Mr. Clements were of the party. The ladies withdrew after dinner, but the men sat not more than half an hour after they were gone. The conversation was partly about Bonaparte and partly about the business before Parliament. Lord Grey said something to me about America, and strongly expressed his hopes that we should continue on terms of friendship with this country. But with regard to the impressment of seamen, he spoke like other English statesmen. It was between eleven and twelve o'clock when I came home.

3d. In the evening I went with Mrs. Adams to Sir James and Lady Mackintosh's. It was a small party, and, excepting Mr. Gallatin, all persons with whom we were unacquainted. We went between ten and eleven, and came home a little before one in the morning. I received this evening a note from Lord Castlereagh to inform me that His Royal Highness the Prince Regent will receive me next Thursday, the 8th instant, after the levee, to present my credentials.

6th. I received from Messrs. Robinson and Goulburn and Dr. Adams, the Commissioners appointed to negotiate with us for a treaty of commerce, a note requesting me to meet them at the Office for Trade at two o'clock to-morrow, and a note from Mr. Gallatin, asking me to return, with my observations, the sketch of a treaty which he had drawn up and put into my hands. After Mr. Clay and Mr. Gallatin had concluded, in consequence of their interviews with Lord Castlereagh and with Messrs. Robinson and Goulburn and Dr. Adams, that it was expedient for them to enter into a commercial negotiation, Mr. Gallatin made a draft of a treaty in two sets of articles, one relating to objects merely commercial, and the other to the belligerent and neutral collisions, which he gave me some days after my arrival here to examine. I had read them over in a cursory manner, but have not been able to give them the attention which the importance of the subject deserves. Mr. Clay and Mr. Gallatin, at the same time they determined to undertake this negotiation, still adhered to the idea of returning to the United States in the Neptune; and having now received from Mr. Crawford two very pressing letters, urging most especially the earnest desire of Mr. Bayard to sail as speedily as possible, they asked an interview with Lord Castlereagh, which they had yesterday, and declared to him their determination to leave town next Monday, to embark in the Neptune at Plymouth.

Then came this notification to meet the British Commissioners to-morrow. Messrs. Clay and Gallatin had called upon me after receiving theirs this morning, but I was not at home. We dined at four, and immediately after dinner I called at Mr. Clay's lodgings, and found Mr. Gallatin with him. Mr. Clay read the letter from Mr. Crawford, and expressed the full determination to go on Monday. Both he and Mr. Gallatin thought it would be best to confine the negotiation exclusively to the commercial articles, and thought they might be brought to a conclusion before Monday.

I went home, and examined as well as I could Mr. Gallatin's draft of articles, which are principally compiled from the former treaties. I received also a note from Lord Castlereagh, informing me that the Honorable Charles Bagot was appointed by the Prince Regent Envoy Extraordinary and Minister Plenipotentiary to the United States. I answered the note, with thanks to Lord Castlereagh for the communication.

7th. Immediately after breakfast this morning I called upon Count Lieven, the Russian Ambassador, to enquire into the diplomatic forms and usages of the Court, of which he gave me the information that was necessary for me. Before two o'clock, I called upon Mr. Gallatin and Mr. Clay, and we went to the Office for Trade. We found there Mr. Frederic John Robinson, the Vice-President of the Board of Trade, Mr. Goulburn, and Dr. Adams, who produced to us a commission authorizing them to negotiate with us on the subject.

On reading over this commission, there were, in its recital of our authority to treat, two mistakes, one of which was noticed by Mr. Clay, and the other by me. The first was merely in the arrangement of our names, those of Mr. Clay and Mr.

Gallatin being placed before mine. This was immaterial, and Mr. Gallatin remarked that in the British full power for treating with us for peace, in the recital of our power his name had been placed first. The other mistake, I observed, was more material. It recited our powers as having been given by the President of the United States, with the consent of the Senate and House of Representatives. I referred to our Constitution, by which appointments are made by and with the advice and consent of the Senate, without the co-operation of the House of Representatives. Mr. Robinson said that the form had been copied from that of the negotiation with Mr. Monroe and Mr. Pinkney. Dr. Adams said that it was not material: it was the mere recital of our powers, and was no more than if, in our recital of theirs, it was stated that they had been appointed with the approbation and consent of the Lords and Commons in Parliament. Mr. Goulburn said it would, however, be as well to make a minute of it, which he did.

Mr. Gallatin produced our full powers, and copies of them all were made out by clerks in the office, while we were in conference. Mr. Clay then stated the necessity which he and Mr. Gallatin were under, of going to embark in the Neptune, and their engagement to leave town for that purpose next Monday; that they had waited as long as they could, and if it should be found that we could not come to a conclusion before that time, they should go, and leave the business to be finished by me.

Mr. Goulburn said that their commission had not been in readiness before, because the Chancellor (who affixes the great seal) had a fit of the gout. Mr. Robinson said that he hoped Mr. Clay and Mr. Gallatin would find it possible to stay until we should come to some result, but if not, they (the British Commissioners) would not overpower me with numbers.

Mr. Gallatin, referring to the previous conferences which Mr. Clay and he had had with the British Commissioners, reminded them that they had considered the negotiation as naturally dividing itself into two branches, one of arrangements purely commercial, and the other on the belligerent and neutral questions. He observed that as there certainly would not be time at present for the discussion of the second class of articles, he had made a draft of those upon the first, which he had thought might be now arranged, and he put it into their hands.

Mr. Robinson said that the most expeditious method of proceeding would be for them to give us in return a draft of articles proposed by them, or in the form of alterations to the articles as proposed by us, to which we agreed. The only article upon which there was any conversation between us was that relating to the American trade to India. It was the only one for which there has yet been any reason to imagine that we could obtain anything useful by a commercial negotiation at present, and I soon found that the recollections of the two parties were far from being the same with regard to what had passed at the former conferences between them. It had been freely avowed on the British side that, with respect to the American trade with the West Indies, they would do nothing. But Mr. Gallatin and Mr. Clay had understood, and had represented to me, that the trade to the East Indies was to be put upon the footing of the Treaty of 1794, without hesitation or qualification. The British Commissioners now stated that they had distinctly and explicitly expressed their expectation of an *equivalent* in some other commercial point for the admission of American vessels to the indirect trade with India, as allowed in the Treaty of 1794; that they had observed that the state of the question had changed since 1794, when the East India Company exclusively had the British trade to India; that the other British merchants now had a share of the trade, and their interests would thus be differently affected by the same stipulation. They had intimated, therefore, an expectation of some accommodation on our part, and had instanced the *fur trade.* Upon which they had been answered, that we were expressly precluded from any concession in this particular by our instructions, the motive for which had been altogether political, and not commercial.

Mr. Gallatin admitted the substance of all this conversation thus stated, and of which I had heard nothing before, excepting that he had not thought that an equivalent for the indirect East

India trade had been explicitly required. It had indeed been hinted by the British Commissioners that, in return for the India trade, a liberal spirit of accommodation would be shown by the United States on some other commercial ground—the fur trade had been mentioned. He and Mr. Clay had answered that if by that was meant the right to trade with the Indians within our territories, we were precluded by our instructions from granting that; the motive for which must necessarily be merely political, since the trade itself, in a commercial point of view, was entirely to our advantage; that they had told the British Commissioners that we considered our trade to India as carrying its own equivalent with it. We carried there scarcely anything but specie. We had little doubt that it would always find its welcome. It would indeed be convenient for us to have the certainty of admission secured by treaty, but it was not a convenience for which we should think it worth while to give any specific equivalent. Mr. Clay suggested that the claim for an equivalent had been less pointedly brought forward at the former conferences, and in such a manner that he had not expected it would be definitively demanded.

The British Commissioners finally took Mr. Gallatin's draft, and we agreed to meet them again the day after to-morrow, at the same place and hour. As we came out, I told Mr. Gallatin that they had put a checkmate upon the East India trade article. He said he thought they would yet give up the point.

We parted at the door, and I walked home. While I was out, Mr. Bailey, the English Consul at St. Petersburg, had paid us a visit. He arrived a few days since, and is shortly to return. I dined with Mrs. Adams at Mr. and Mrs. Goulburn's—Mr. Gallatin and Mr. Clay, Mr. and Mrs. Hamilton, Miss Stapleton, a relation of Mrs. Goulburn's, Mr. Peel, Mr. Robinson, Mr. Grant, and Mr. Gambier. Mr. Hamilton is Under-Secretary of State in the Department of Foreign Affairs, and was with Lord Elgin at Berlin. He went with us, and, he says, in our carriage, to Potsdam in 1798. The invitation to dinner was for a quarter before seven. It was past seven when we went, and we were the first there. After dinner the ladies withdrew. The men sat about half an hour, and then joined the ladies again in the drawing-room. We came home between ten and eleven.

8th. The Assistant Master of the Ceremonies, Robert Chester, Esquire, called upon me this morning and gave me the information concerning the forms and usages of Court presentations, for which I had yesterday enquired of Count Lieven. Mr. Chester's report was, however, different in some particulars from that of the Count. He asked me, first, whether I had delivered to Lord Castlereagh a copy of my credential letter. I said I had. That, he said, was entirely right. He then asked if I had a letter for the Queen. I said I had not. He said it was usual, though not indispensable; that it was done by the Courts where the Queen had personal connections, and had always been done by the Republic of Holland; that the Queen would nevertheless give me an audience when she comes to town upon business, which would probably be in the course of a week or ten days.

I asked when, and how, it would be proper for Mrs. Adams to be presented to the Queen. He said, by Lady Castlereagh, and at a drawing-room. It was doubtful, however, whether there would be another drawing-room before the winter.

I asked whether it was usual for the foreign Ministers to be presented separately to the Princes of the royal family, and when, and to whom, visits of form were to be paid.

He said that after having an audience of the Queen, and not until then, it would be proper to call at the residences of all the Princes, and write my name in the books kept there for the purpose, and to visit, by cards, the Cabinet Ministers and great officers of the household. I said I had been told that this was to be done immediately after the audience from the Prince Regent. He replied that sometimes the foreign Ministers had done so, but, when referred to, he must say that the other was the regular course. I said I should then observe it. He added that the personal presentation to the Princes was usually made at the Regent's levees, whenever any of them attended; and he or any other person known to them would present me. No particular notice was taken of the Princesses, the Regent's sisters, or of the Princess Charlotte, his daughter.

He promised to come again at a quarter-past one o'clock and accompany me to Carlton House, which he accordingly did. We went in at the private and privileged entrance, and passed through St. James's Park to the palace, Mr. Chester observing to me that I should give directions to my coachman always to go by that way. We arrived there at half-past one, the hour appointed, but were early, finding there only Mr. Freudenreich, the Envoy from Berne, and his Secretary of Legation. Mr. Freudenreich, who has been here about a year, had his audience to take leave. He had also received two notes from Lord Castlereagh, one appointing the audience after the levee, and the other fixing it at half-past one. Mr. Chester was much perplexed to account for this circumstance, which was explained as having arisen from occurrences at the last levee. The private audiences then had delayed the ordinary levee until five or six o'clock, which had detained some of the members of the House of Commons from attendance there in time, which had occasioned complaints, and the first idea had been for the private audiences to be fixed this day, after the levee.

It was almost three when the Prince Regent began to give private audiences. The first was to Lord Grenville, who, as Chancellor of the University of Oxford, presented to him a book containing an account of the visit of the allied sovereigns there last summer. The second was to me. Lord Castlereagh, as the Minister of Foreign Affairs, introduced me into the Prince's closet, where he stood alone, and, as I approached him, speaking first, said, " Mr. Adams, I am happy to see you." I said, " Sir, I am directed by the President of the United States to deliver to your Royal Highness this letter, and in presenting it I fulfil the commands of my Government when I express the hope that it will be received as a token of the earnest desire of that Government not only faithfully and punctually to fulfil all its engagements contracted with that of Great Britain, but for the adoption of every other measure that may tend to consolidate the peace and friendship and to promote the harmony between the two nations."

The Prince took the letter, and, without opening it, delivered it immediately to Lord Castlereagh, and said, in answer to me, that the United States might rely, with the fullest assurance, upon his determination to fulfil on the part of Great Britain all the engagements with the United States.

He then asked me if I was related to Mr. Adams who had formerly been the Minister from the United States here. I said I was his son. He enquired whether I had ever been before in England. I had. With a public mission? Once, with a special mission, during the absence of the Minister then accredited here. He said he had known two of the former Ministers of the United States here, who were Mr. Pinckney and Mr. Rufus King—very gentlemanly men. Mr. King was very much of a gentleman. Where was Mr. Pinckney now? I said there had been two Mr. Pinckneys here as Ministers from the United States. "Ah!" said he, "but I mean the Mr. Pinckney who was here before Mr. King." I said he was now a general in the army. "In the army?" said he. "I did not know that. Had he ever been in the army before?" I said he had. "And where is Mr. King?" I said he was now a member of the Senate of the United States. "And how did you like living there at Brussels?" said the Prince. "Your Royal Highness probably means Ghent," said I. "Ay! Ghent! so it was," said he; "and how did you like Ghent?" I said we liked it very much, for the result of what was done there. "Oh, yes!" said he; "but I mean, did you find any society there?" I said we had found society; that Ghent was a very ancient and venerable city, with proud recollections; that its inhabitants thought and talked much of Charles the Fifth, and that it was now illustrious again, as the residence where a great sovereign holds his Court. "Ay!" said the Prince, "there are a number of those great old cities there."

Lord Castlereagh commented in a few words upon the large cities and the populousness of the Netherlands, and we then withdrew from the Prince's closet. Mr. Freudenreich was introduced immediately afterwards, for his audience to take leave.

After these audiences the levee to the Foreign Ministers was held, which was over in half an hour, and then the doors were opened for what Mr. Chester called the ordinary levee, attended by the persons not privileged with the entrée, and we withdrew. Before the levee, I was introduced by Lord Castlereagh, or Mr. Chester, to the Duke of Clarence, the only one of the Princes of the blood royal that was there, to most of the Foreign Ambassadors and Ministers, and to several of the Ministers and Household Officers of the country. Among them were the Marquis of Hertford, Lords Harrowby and Sidmouth, and some others. Lord Graves, whom I had known at Berlin, recognized and spoke to me. He is now in the household of the Duke of Sussex, who, he told me, was as good, as generous, as noble-hearted, and as imprudent as ever. I told him that of the good part of the Duke's qualities I had often heard with pleasure. He said that he was not a good courtier, but perhaps that would not be a fault to me. I said it might perhaps not be a fault, though I certainly could not consider it as a fault to be one. I enquired after Mr. Brummell, his companion at Berlin. He said that he was here. He had seen him this morning. He was married, and had a family, but was not encumbered with superfluous wealth. In that respect I observed that he had associates enough to keep him in countenance. "Yes," said he, "we are a numerous corps enough." I recognized also Mr. Rayneval, the first secretary to the French (Louis XVIII.) Embassy, and Count Jennison Walworth, secretary to the Bavarian Legation. Lord Castlereagh introduced me also to Mr. Bagot, who kissed hands on his appointment as Envoy Extraordinary and Minister Plenipotentiary to the United States. The Prince, in speaking to him at the levee, remarked that it was on the same day that I had presented my credentials. By which he intended me to understand that the friendly advances of the United States had been met with the utmost promptitude.

The levee itself was not so orderly as those assemblies usually are. The Prince went round and spoke a few words to all the Foreign Ministers, but, excepting what he thus addressed to Mr. Bagot and myself, I heard only what he said to Mr. Freudenreich, which was in a sort of whisper, "Je suis fâché que vous allez partir, mais j'espère que vous reviendrez." As we returned home, I set down Mr. Chester at his house,

68 South Audley Street. Mrs. Adams and I dined at Lord Carysfort's, where we met Earl and Lady Fortescue, Lord and Lady King, Mr. Thomas Grenville, Lord Proby, and Lord Carysfort's three daughters, neither of whom is yet married. Lady Fortescue is Lady Carysfort's sister, and Lady King is a daughter of Lord Fortescue's. I should not have recognized Mr. Thomas Grenville, nor did he recollect me, though we were well acquainted with each other at Berlin.

After dinner, there was a numerous party of both sexes who came, but there were no cards. Sir Humphry Davy, who has very lately returned from Italy, talked much upon his travels there, much upon agriculture and farming, much upon the art of sculpture, and the Laocöon, and the Venus, and much upon his own chemical discoveries. If modesty is an inseparable companion of genius, Sir Humphry is a prodigy.

Lord King and Lord Fortescue went down to the House of Peers, to give their votes upon the Catholic question, which was discussing there. Lord Carysfort had given his proxy to the Marquis of Buckingham. Lord King returned, having found the question decided. I had some conversation with him on the prospects of war in Europe. He told me he believed Napoleon would beat them all, in which opinion I did not concur.

9th. I was scarcely risen this morning, when the marshals, grooms, porters, and attendants at the palaces came to present their humble duty, bringing their books to show what had been paid them by all the foreign Ministers, and other persons presented at Court. Mr. Lawrence and Mr. Moore soon afterwards came for their passports, which I gave them. Mr. Campbell came, and I made a settlement with him for our passage in the Olga, for which I gave him an order upon Mr. Williams. Mr. Brown, the tailor whom I have employed, came, and with great terror and many apologies asked me if I could pay him twenty-five pounds upon his bill. I paid him his whole bill, at which he expressed much surprise. He told me that if he should do the same to any of his customers here, they would never have employed him again.

At one o'clock I called upon Mr. Clay and Mr. Gallatin, and

then paid a visit to Mr. Copley, whom I found broken down by age and infirmities. Mrs. Copley appeared to be in good health. Their youngest daughter is still with them, unmarried. At two o'clock I went to the Foreign Office, and saw Mr. Morier. He said it was contemplated to appoint the Commissioners upon the fourth, fifth, and sixth articles of the Treaty of Ghent. He asked if I thought there would be, on the part of the American Government, any objection to the appointment of the same person as the Commissioner on two of the commissions, those of the fourth and fifth articles.

I first said that I should wish for time to read over the articles, and would give him an answer to-morrow. But afterwards, on recollecting the substance of the two articles, I said I would not give him the trouble of waiting for an answer. I presumed there could be no objection to the appointment of the same person upon the two commissions, particularly as the American Government would not be obliged to appoint the same person on their part, if they should prefer to appoint two. Mr. Morier told me that Colonel Barclay would be appointed Commissioner on the fourth and fifth articles, having been formerly one of the Commissioners for the settlement of the St. Croix River, under the Treaty of 1794, and Mr. who was also employed on that occasion, would go with him. It was intended and expected that he should go out in the July packet.

From the Foreign Office I went immediately to the Office for Trade, where I found that Mr. Clay and Mr. Gallatin had just arrived. Shortly after, we met Mr. Robinson, Mr. Goulburn, and Dr. Adams, who merely told us that they were not ready with the counter-projet for a commercial treaty. They said, however, that they should be very shortly ready.

Mr. Clay manifested some impatience to be gone, referred to his and Mr. Gallatin's promise to go on Monday next, and asked whether the British Commissioners could not before that time send us their answer. Mr. Gallatin seemed disposed to allow them more time. They said they hoped by Sunday, at least, to be able to inform us when they would be prepared with their answer. Dr. Adams said that it was not exactly here as it had been at Ghent, because there, there was nothing else to do.

We left them with the hope of hearing from them again on Sunday. Mr. Clay took a seat with me in my carriage, and I set him down at his lodgings. He told me that he did not expect the negotiation would come to anything, and that if Mr. Gallatin had been of his mind they would have persisted in going away next Monday. He complained that the British Commissioners now held, with respect to the East India trade, a language totally different from that which they had held in the former conferences; that they had said nothing about a specific equivalent for the indirect trade, but had only spoken of expecting, on our part, a liberal spirit of accommodation in some other part of the treaty. He seemed, however, inclined to sign the article for the direct trade, as was proposed by the Treaty of 1806. I told him I did not think it worth the trouble of signing our names for that. The trade was so much more valuable and important to them than to us, that we had in their interest a much more certain pledge for its continuance than any treaty could be, and I thought we might risk more than we could gain by showing an anxious desire for treaty stipulations, to secure what we knew we should have without them. It would encourage them to demand substantial advantages from us in return for nothing from them. He said they had no reason to suppose, from anything that had passed, that we were desirous of a commercial treaty.

11th. At seven in the evening I went and took up Mr. Todd at his lodgings, at the Blenheim Hotel, and we went and dined at Lord Castlereagh's. Mr. Clay and Mr. Gallatin were of the company, as were the Earl of Liverpool, First Lord of the Treasury, Earl of Westmorland, Lord Privy Seal, the Marquis of Camden, Mr. Wellesley Pole, Messrs. Robinson, Goulburn, Adams, Bagot, Planta (Lord Castlereagh's private secretary), Morier, Hamilton, and some others. There were no ladies.

Lord Castlereagh treated us with the politest attention. He seated me at his right hand, and Mr. Clay at his left. Lord Westmorland was at my right, Lord Liverpool between Mr. Clay and Mr. Gallatin. The conversation at table was here, as everywhere else, about Napoleon. Lord Castlereagh had a miniature picture of him on a snuff-box, which he said he had bought of Isabey, at Vienna. It was the general opinion of all the noble lords present that Napoleon would shortly take refuge in America; for as to another island of Elba, that was out of the question. That experiment would not be tried a second time.

Lord Castlereagh spoke of him with studious moderation; said he thought his speech to the Legislative Assembly, this day received, was a very good speech; that it noticed in moderate terms the capture of a French frigate in the Mediterranean, but *pretended* that it was hostility in time of peace. He said that last year, at the time of the Fontainebleau Treaty, Bonaparte had expressed the wish of coming to England, to which he (Lord Castlereagh) had objected, as he could not have been answerable for the safety of his person here; that while he was going from Fontainebleau to embark for Elba, he had been at several places in great personal danger from the honest indignation of the people. But he (Lord Castlereagh) had much rather that he should have come back and be as he now is, than that he should have lost his life while under the protection of the allies. Lord Castlereagh said he had never seen him, though he had felt a curiosity to see him, but the only opportunity that he had ever had for it was at the time of the Treaty of Fontainebleau, and then he had abstained from delicacy.

Mr. Robinson informed Mr. Clay that the counter-projet of a commercial treaty would be sent to us on Wednesday, or about the middle of the week, and Lord Westmorland invited us to dine with him on Monday the 19th. Mr. Clay told me that he and Mr. Gallatin had concluded to stay until that time.

16th. Attended a debate in the House of Lords. I had seen in the newspapers that the Lords were summoned upon a motion of the Marquis of Lansdowne, who was to bring up a report of a committee upon a bill relating to the slave-trade, which had passed the House of Commons. I expected, therefore, to have found a full house and a warm debate. There were, however, not more than twenty Peers present, and the debate turned almost entirely upon the mere drawing up of the bill. The

Marquis of Lansdowne was speaking when we went in, and the Earls of Liverpool and Westmorland, Lords Ellenborough and Stanhope, took part in the debate. It was generally agreed to be the worst-drawn bill that had ever been presented to the House. Lord Ellenborough said it was a monster of legislation, and a disgrace to the British Parliament. He and some other lawyers, and the bishops, were in their official robes. The other Peers were in frocks, and some of them in boots. The debate was of about an hour, and it was agreed to recommit the bill. Lord Castlereagh, Mr. Fazakerley, and some other members from the House of Commons, came in while the debate was going on.

After we came out of the House, Lord Liverpool overtook us in the street, and walked with me as far as Whitehall Place, where we parted. I walked home by the way of Hyde Park, and on reaching home I found a letter from Messrs. Robinson and Goulburn and Dr. Adams, enclosing their counter-projet of a commercial treaty. It is in every respect so different from what Mr. Clay and Mr. Gallatin had expected, and led me to expect, that I think it useless to pursue the negotiation any further. I took it immediately to Mr. Clay's and Mr. Gallatin's lodgings. Neither of them was at home, and I left it with Mr. Gallatin's servant to give to his master.

17th. I found at my lodgings Mr. Clay and Mr. Gallatin, with the letter and the counter-projet of the British Plenipotentiaries.

There were three points upon which Messrs. Clay and Gallatin, upon the result of their conferences with the British Plenipotentiaries before my arrival, had concluded to enter upon a formal negotiation: 1, the intercourse between the United States and Canada; 2, the mutual abolition of discriminating duties, and placing the commercial relations between the two countries on the footing of the most favored nation; and 3, the East India trade.

Mr. Clay said that he had been deceived by the British Plenipotentiaries upon all three. Their counter-projet now offered us a Canadian article, which would give them access to trade with the Indians in our territory. They limited to their

European dominions the offer to treat us as the most favored nation, and they limited the intercourse to be secured to us with India to four places, and to two years from the ratification of the treaty, with high pretensions of liberality in granting so much, and a formal notification that they gave us the two years only for the Government of the United States to be prepared to give an equivalent for the continuation of the privilege. Mr. Clay said that if he had imagined it would come to such a projet as this, he never would have entered into this negotiation, and he was for asking immediately a conference with the British Plenipotentiaries, stating to them that we had entirely misunderstood their intentions, and informing them that we do not think it worth while to proceed any further with them in the business.

Mr. Gallatin was averse to making an acknowledgment that he had been deceived, but for meeting the British Plenipotentiaries, proposing alterations to their counter-projet, and bringing them to a definite answer before breaking off.

We therefore sent a note to the British Plenipotentiaries, proposing to meet them at the Board of Trade this day, at three o'clock, and we accordingly went at that hour. Mr. Gallatin gave me a seat in his carriage. We found only Mr. Robinson at the Office for Trade, who apologized to us, observing that he had come to the office only at half-past two, which was later than he usually came, and that it had been too late to give notice to his colleagues; that Mr. Goulburn lived near at hand, and might perhaps be found, but Dr. Adams was at a distance, and would probably not be at home if sent for. But they would certainly meet us on Monday at the hour most suitable to ourselves. We fixed upon two o'clock, and observed that, for the sake of greater dispatch, we might, before Monday morning, send them a written communication upon their counter-projet. We agreed among ourselves to meet at noon to-morrow, at Mr. Gallatin's chambers, when he promised to have a note in answer to the British counter-projet prepared for consideration.

18th. At noon I went to Mr. Gallatin's chambers, and he sent for Mr. Clay, who immediately afterwards came in. Mr. Gallatin had made the draft of a letter to the British Plenipotentiaries, containing the proposed alterations to their counter-projet, proposing to meet them in conference at the Board of Trade at two o'clock to-morrow, and expressing the hope that they would then be enabled to give us their answer. After the adoption of some alterations suggested by Mr. Clay and myself, a fair copy of the letter was made out, signed by us, and sent by Mr. Gallatin to Mr. Robinson. I dined at the Russian Ambassador, Count Lieven's. Lord and Lady Liverpool, Lord and Lady Mansfield, Lords Westmorland, Mulgrave, and Limerick, Mr. Vansittart, the Chancellor of the Exchequer, the Dutch Ambassador, Baron Fagel, the Würtemberg Minister, Count Beroldingen, and the Bavarian Minister, Mr. de Pfeffel, Admiral Tchitchagoff, and several others, were of the company. I had some conversation with Admiral Tchitchagoff, and told him I had heard he intended publishing an account of the campaign of 1812. He said it was of no use to publish: the truth would not be read, and he was not inclined to publish anything but the truth. A French officer named Vaudoncour had, however, published an account of the passage of the Beresina, of which he (Admiral Tchitchagoff) had procured an English translation to be made and published with some notes of his own.

19th. It was nearly three when I reached the Office for Trade, where I found the British Plenipotentiaries and Messrs. Clay and Gallatin already assembled. We entered immediately upon business, and sat nearly three hours. I took no part in the discussion; the whole business is conducted with so much precipitation, and the reference is so continual to the conferences which had taken place before my arrival, upon the substance of which the ideas of the two parties are so widely different, that I have not felt it safe or prudent to enter into the debates, and have been entirely silent. It became perfectly clear to me this day that upon no one of the three points for which the negotiation was commenced is there any likelihood of our coming to an agreement with the British Plenipotentiaries. Their counter-projet presents the article relating to the intercourse with Canada so drawn that it would indirectly give them the trade with Indians within our territories, and it does not admit us to navigate the river St. Lawrence, even down to Montreal.

They disavowed the intention of obtaining thus indirectly the Indian trade, but they inflexibly resisted the allowance of our navigating the waters under their exclusive jurisdiction, even for rafts, to carry lumber and flour to Montreal.

Mr. Gallatin pressed it upon them that it was merely to carry our own articles to a port of theirs for the purpose of exportation, and that they would have the benefit of that exportation exclusively in their own vessels. Mr. Clay urged to them that it was not a ship, and scarcely even a boat navigation that we asked. It was little more than the mere floating of rafts to be taken down in exchange for gewgaws from Europe.

Dr. Adams was piqued at this term gewgaws, and said that if our people liked those gewgaws, no doubt they would give their lumber and flour in exchange for them. The doctor appeared offended, too, at our proposal to omit the article altogether.

Mr. Gallatin urged, with force, that if the navigation to Montreal was denied us, the article would be of no benefit to us whatever.

Dr. Adams insisted that that was no reason for leaving it out; because if the benefit to us was not in that article, it might be in some other, or in the whole treaty. The proposition of placing the two nations respectively on the footing of the most favored nation was confined by the British projet to the territories in Europe on the British part. The Plenipotentiaries said that by the Treaty of Paris they had granted to the French the privilege of landing and drying fish on the island of Newfoundland, which was given in consideration of the cession by the French of their part of the island. That on the same principle, privileges had been granted to the Dutch, in consideration of the cession by them of the Cape of Good Hope and of certain West India Islands; that in the East Indies special privileges were allowed to nations having themselves colonies there, which were not extended to nations having none.

Mr. Gallatin observed that privileges granted to other nations for specific equivalents, which we could not grant, would not be extended to us by a stipulation to treat us as the most favored nation; that we had on our part granted a privilege of that kind to France for trading to Louisiana during a term of twelve years, which indeed will have expired before any treaty that we can now make could be ratified. But as to the discrimination between nations holding colonies and those holding none in the East Indies, he thought that the benefit to Great Britain arising from the general commerce of the United States, and the consideration that all the advantages which we derive from commerce invariably flow back and centre in Great Britain, would at least entitle them to expect to be placed upon as favorable a footing in their intercourse with India as other nations.

It was replied that the nations having colonies themselves were now allowed the indirect trade with India, and that by placing us on the footing of the most favored nation, it would in point of fact give us for nothing the indirect trade for which we had been informed that an equivalent would be required.

Mr. Clay remarked that the limitation of two years in the counter-projet for allowing us the indirect intercourse with India was in substance a limitation of one year. For, as our ships all go for India in the spring, it was now too late for them to have any benefit from the article this year, and the two years would be expired before the benefit could be enjoyed upon voyages to be commenced the second ensuing spring.

Dr. Adams answered this by saying that he thought two years must of course have two springs.

There remained only one article, that for the equalization of duties, upon which there appears any prospect of our coming to an agreement. There were objections on each side to the draft of the article as prepared by the other. The British draft had omitted the abolition of discriminating duties on merchandise imported in the ships of the two nations, and had confined it to the tonnage duties. It had also omitted the equalization of drawbacks and bounties. Our draft included them all. The British Plenipotentiaries agreed to include them all, but they thought our draft so worded that it would give to American vessels the same drawbacks allowed upon exportations in British vessels upon merchandise not exported in the same vessel that imported them. They objected that this would extend the privilege beyond the intention of the parties, and requested a more precise draft of the article, which Mr. Gallatin promised to give them. Recurring to the East Indian article just before the close of the conference, Mr. Robinson said it was true that if we were placed there on the footing of the most favored nation, it would not be precisely the same thing as granting us the indirect trade without limitation, because, as other nations had the indirect trade only by regulation and not by treaty, it might be revoked by act of Parliament. This, he said, was indeed a new view of the subject, but they were not authorized to accede to the article upon that ground.

We requested them, and they promised, to furnish us as soon as possible the substance of what they had said in the conference in answer to our note of the 17th. As we came out of the office, I enquired of Mr. Gallatin if Mr. Todd was gone. He said no, but the Neptune was gone : she sailed yesterday morning. Mr. Clay and Mr. Gallatin had first fixed the 14th of this month as the time when they would certainly be at Plymouth, and had given notice to Lord Castlereagh of their determination to leave London the 12th. They have, however, been induced to stay until now, and had written to fix again the day of their departure to the Neptune for the 25th. Mr. Bayard and Mr. Crawford, however, did not incline to stay so long, and the vessel has sailed.

Mr. Clay and Mr. Gallatin took seats in my carriage, and alighted at their lodgings. I found both of them inclined to accept an article for the East India trade direct alone, though it is in the face of our instructions. I have not the same inclination. I came home, and at seven went and dined at the Earl of Westmorland's. Messrs. Clay and Gallatin were there. Lords Carysfort and Limerick, Sir William Scott, Mr. Wellesley Pole, Sir Henry Fane, Mr. Bagot, Mr. Goulburn, a younger son of Lord Westmorland's, and some other gentlemen, were of the company. Fifteen at table. I sat between Lord Westmorland and Lord Carysfort. The conversation was cheerful and good-humored. Mr. Gallatin gave to Mr. Goulburn a new draft of the article for equalizing duties. It was there that I heard first of the commencement of hostilities in the Netherlands, Napoleon having attacked the Prussians at Charleroi on the 15th.   There are no particulars.

20th. Just before dinner I received the promised note from the British Plenipotentiaries, containing the substance of what they had said to us yesterday in conference upon our proposed alterations of their contre-projet.   I took it immediately after dinner to Mr. Gallatin's lodgings, where I found Mr. Clay, and it was determined to ask another conference with the British Plenipotentiaries at two o'clock to-morrow.   Mr. Clay and Mr. Gallatin again expressed the inclination to sign an article limiting us to the direct trade with India, notwithstanding our instructions, on the ground that the British Government, having, since the date of our instructions, allowed to their own subjects other than the East India Company a direct trade with China, had no longer the same motive for allowing the trade to us. Mr. Clay repeated what he has said several times, that he believed, if we did not sign an article, that the British would exclude us from the trade with India altogether.   I do not believe that, as it is a trade entirely to their own advantage, and in which we export there scarcely anything but specie.

Mr. Clay said that, from all the enquiries that he had made, and particularly from Mr. Perkins, the indirect trade was of little or no value; but I said that if we should stipulate to be excluded from it, I had no doubt its value would soon be discovered in America, that article in the unratified Treaty of 1806 having been one of those which gave the most dissatisfaction, and having been severely commented on by Mr. G. Morris's pamphlet, published at the time.

Mr. Gallatin said he had never seen or heard of that pamphlet. He added that, if I persisted in my opinion, he and Mr. Clay could not take it upon themselves to sign the treaty with such an article, because it would be unquestionably contrary to our instructions, and the best way was to reserve it for the consideration of our Government.   Mr. Clay was against referring anything to our Government.   He was for concluding or breaking off the negotiation. He has changed his opinion since his interview with Lord Castlereagh and the first conference which I attended.   On the East India article he is flexible

enough, but the Canadian article displeases him, and the intimation from Dr. Adams that it would be insisted on inclines
him to break off entirely. He and Mr. Gallatin, however, would
prefer signing a single article for the equalization of duties,
which they think by far the most important article of the treaty.
Mr. Gallatin thought it would be useless to ask another conference, but Mr. Clay wished for it, and we acquiesced in sending a note to ask for it.

I came home, and then went to a small evening party at
Lady Vincent's. There were about forty persons present,
ladies and gentlemen, none of whom we knew. Some of the
ladies sang a few Italian airs and duets, with accompaniment
of the piano. The conversation was all concerning the battle
in the Netherlands, of which a multitude of rumors, but no
official accounts, have arrived.

21st. Mr. Gallatin sent me a note from Mr. Robinson to him,
promising that the British Plenipotentiaries would meet us this
day at two o'clock. I took it back to Mr. Gallatin, and asked
him for a seat in his carriage. I told him that if the British
Plenipotentiaries should continue inflexible on the East Indian
and Canadian articles, I thought it would be best to sign a
convention in a single article for equalizing the duties without
pretending to make it a treaty of commerce; that our countrymen would think it worse than ridiculous if we should give
them for a treaty of commerce an instrument filled with articles
of mere form, about admitting Consuls and the like, which, with
or without treaty, would stand on precisely the same footing,
and without containing a single article to settle any of the
points, commercial or political, which really belong to treaties
of commerce—that for equalizing the duties being such that it
might safely rest on the legislative acts of the two countries
without a treaty.

He differed from this opinion, and said that as to the political
articles, they did not properly belong to treaties of commerce,
and he did not know why they were ever put into them. He
thought they seldom were.

I said they were in all the modern treaties of commerce, and
instanced that of 1786 between France and England, in which

Great Britain had admitted the principle of free ships making free goods. He said he never knew that, and he believed I was mistaken.

I afterwards appealed to Mr. Clay, who remembered as I did, but Mr. Gallatin persisted in his unbelief. He said he had thought of two proposals to make relative to the East Indian article. One was, to offer a reciprocal admission of British ships from the East Indies into the United States. The other was, to shorten the whole convention to a middle term between the eight years originally proposed and the two years to which the British Plenipotentiaries wish to reduce the East Indian article.

I objected to the first, as going beyond anything contemplated in our instructions, and as an experiment the effect of which we could not foresee, as, since the admission of private British adventurers to the East Indian trade, such a stipulation on our part might enable them to take away a great part of our trade with India from our merchants. I consented that the second should be made.

At two, Mr. Gallatin and Mr. Clay called, and took me with them down to the Board of Trade, where we met the British Plenipotentiaries. Mr. Gallatin had given Mr. Goulburn a new draft of an article concerning the equalization of duties, but Mr. Robinson thought it still not free from ambiguity, and proposed a draft of his own upon the subject. It was, however, understood that we were agreed upon the substance of the article, the final draft of which might be deferred until we should come to a result upon the other points. Mr. Gallatin enquired whether we were to consider the answer of the British Plenipotentiaries as a positive rejection of our proposal for putting the Indian article upon the footing of the most favored nation.

They were not altogether explicit in their answer. Mr. Robinson and Mr. Goulburn intimated that it was, but Dr. Adams was of opinion that writing must speak for itself, and that if we wanted any explanation of anything in their written note we must ask for it in writing.

Mr. Gallatin said that we had asked for the conference to

save time; that if we were to consider our proposal as explicitly rejected, we had another proposal to make, which was to omit the second separate article of their contre-projet, and to shorten the duration of the whole treaty.

They promised to take this into consideration when we should propose it in writing.

As we were returning home, Mr. Clay recurred to his idea of breaking off the negotiation. I mentioned to Mr. Gallatin that in conversation with me before the conference he had spoken of the proposal to shorten the term of the treaty as to be offered for four years, but in stating it in conference he had mentioned no precise period, and they might understand the offer as being to limit the whole treaty to two years. He said that in the written note he should not make the offer at all. Mr. Clay said that if we accepted it with the limitation of four years, it would be saddled with the Canadian article, as drawn by them. Mr. Gallatin and I both thought that Dr. Adams's adherence to the Canadian article was a mere freak of his own, and that they would readily consent to omit the article. We parted at Mr. Gallatin's door, leaving him to make a draft of the note to be sent.

As we were sitting down to dinner, I received a note from Mr. Gallatin, with the draft upon which he and Mr. Clay had agreed, asking me to look it over, and saying they would call upon me immediately after dinner, to prepare and send it. They accordingly came, and we made out the note, which Mr. Clay wrote, and we all signed. Mr. Gallatin took it with him to send to Mr. Robinson, who lives near his lodgings.

22d. Shortly after rising this morning I received a note from Lord Castlereagh's office, announcing the splendid and complete victory of the Duke of Wellington and Marshal Blücher over the French army, commanded by Bonaparte in person, on Sunday last, the 18th. In the course of the day I received from the same office two copies of the Gazette Extraordinary, containing the Duke of Wellington's dispatch of the 19th.

23d. In the evening we all rode round the streets to see the illuminations for the great victory of the 18th. They were not general, nor very magnificent. The whole range of their

variety was, " Wellington and Blücher," " Victory," " G. P. R.,"
and " G. R." The transparencies were very few, and very bad.
We came home about midnight.

24th. Received from the British Plenipotentiaries an answer
to our last note, which I took to Mr. Clay and Mr. Gallatin;
we met again at Mr. Gallatin's, at five o'clock, and wrote and
signed a reply to the British note, to be sent this evening.

26th. Received from the British Plenipotentiaries a note to
inform us that they must refer our last proposals to their
Government.

28th. I went with George to the House of Commons. We
were admitted under the gallery. The debate was upon a
grant of six thousand pounds sterling annually, in addition to
eighteen thousand pounds, the present establishment of the
Duke of Cumberland, on the occasion of his marriage with the
Princess of Solms. The House was unusually full, and the
debate animated, though temperate. The speakers in favor of
the grant were Lord Castlereagh, Mr. Vansittart, the Chancellor of the Exchequer, and Mr. Bathurst; those against it
were Mr. Keene, Sir M. W. Ridley, Mr. Bennett, Sir C. Burrell,
and Mr. Wynne. The characters of both parties to the marriage were treated with very little respect on one side of the
House. The debate was of about an hour, when the committee
of the whole divided, upon which occasions all strangers are
obliged to withdraw. The vote was eighty-seven for and
seventy against the grant. We afterwards returned into the
House, when they were considering the vote of credit of six
millions. Mr. Whitbread said a few words, to express the
hope that no part of it would be given to Spain, and Mr.
Wynne, to say that whatever might ultimately be the government of France, such security would be taken of it as
would prevent her from disturbing the peace of Europe hereafter. Three-fourths of the members who had attended on
the question of the grant to the Duke of Cumberland left the
House immediately after that question was taken.

29th. Wrote a letter to the Secretary of the Treasury, on the
subject of the proposed loan. At half-past eleven o'clock I
went to Lord Castlereagh's, according to appointment. I found

in his antechamber the Russian Ambassador, Count Lieven, the Marquis of Camden, Mr. Planta, and one or two other persons. After waiting a few minutes, I was received in his Lordship's cabinet. I gave him Mr. Maury's commission as Consul at Liverpool, which he had sent me to obtain the "exequatur." Lord Castlereagh said it would be immediately made out. I then spoke to him of the case of Anthony Shaddock, a man taken the last autumn, as master of a coasting vessel between Savannah and Amelia Island, a citizen of the United States—taken as a prisoner of war—paroled at Bermuda for some time as a prisoner of war, and then sent over here in the Vengeur, to be tried by a court-martial as one of the mutineers of the Hermione frigate. I said that it was impossible for me to wish to screen from condign punishment a person who should have been guilty of such a crime as that; but the man was a citizen of the United States; I had reason to believe that the evidence upon which the suspicion against him had been raised was very weak; he declared that he knew nothing of that crime. I hoped and trusted he was innocent. But the principle, to the benefit of which I thought him entitled, was the fulfilment of the treaty stipulation to restore all prisoners of war.

Lord Castlereagh did not at first recollect the affair of the Hermione frigate, but afterwards said he had some remembrance of it, and thought it a very *disgusting* thing. He enquired where the man now was. I did not know, but he had been sent to England, I said, in the Vengeur. He said it seemed to him it brought back again the question of the war; that they did not consider a British subject as a prisoner of war; that every Government in Europe would consider such persons as traitors, and not as prisoners of war.

I said I was not acquainted with any such usage in Europe; that it was true the case of Æneas McDonald, in this country, appeared to sanction the principle in its rigor. He had indeed been sentenced, but not executed. But this man was not triable as a traitor even on that principle. He had not been taken in arms, but in a merchant vessel. While the war had lasted, Great Britain might adhere with what strictness she thought proper to the principle for which she contended in theory, but, having stipulated in the treaty for the restoration of all prisoners of war, I conceived that it was no longer competent for her to make any discrimination, or to enquire where any individual prisoner was born. I said I had preferred asking this interview, and stating the case verbally, to the formality of an official note, with a hope that the man might be released without such public interposition.

Lord Castlereagh expressed himself perfectly satisfied as to the manner of my application, but he gave me no reason to expect that it would be effectual. He said he supposed that the Admiralty Court was that where the trial was to take place.

I said I had supposed so when the case was first represented to me; but I afterwards learnt that the trial was to be by a court-martial. This circumstance had strongly confirmed me in the impression that it was my duty to claim in the man's behalf the benefit of the treaty. The agent for prisoners of war had in the first instance claimed the release of the man, and had been answered that the matter was in a train of legal investigation. But the mode of trial itself was one not congenial to the general feelings either of Englishmen or of Americans, nor such as in their opinions could give the fullest confidence to innocence. First to be sent across the Atlantic Ocean, and then to be tried by a merely military tribunal, were hardships from which I felt it my duty to use every endeavor to redeem any American citizen. The fulfilment of the treaty it was equally my duty to require. This man had some property in America, and had friends who took an interest in his situation here. They had applied to me for my interposition on his behalf, which I could not feel myself justified in denying.

Lord Castlereagh took a minute of the man's name and of the ship in which he was sent to England, as if to make further enquiry into the matter, but without promising anything.

I then spoke of the passports. I told him that until within these five or six days passports to go to France had been delivered at the Alien Office to Americans desirous of going there upon their producing passports given them by me; that several of them had now been told that something further from me would be necessary. Several foreigners had also been to me, stating the wish to go to America, and that they were also referred from the Alien Office to me. It was my desire to conform myself to the regulations of this Government, and at the same time to secure to my fellow-citizens the liberty of going where their concerns may call them.

He said he did not know precisely what the regulations were. The Alien Office was in the Home Department, under Lord Sidmouth. We should see him at the levee, and it would perhaps be best to speak on the subject to him. I mentioned again the misconstruction of an article in the Treaty of Ghent by the British naval commander in Chesapeake Bay, relating to the restoration of captured slaves, and asked him if he had not received some communication upon the subject from America. He said there was a voluminous correspondence concerning it, received yesterday from Mr. Baker. He had apparently not read it, and said that he should be obliged to leave town to-morrow evening for Brussels; but during his absence the business of his department would be transacted by Lord Liverpool and Lord Bathurst. He asked if this matter concerning the slaves was not the same about which Mr. Horner had yesterday made a motion in the House of Commons.

I said I believed not. From what I had seen in the newspapers of Mr. Horner's motion, it referred to slaves said to have been taken in the United States and sold in the West Indies. What I now referred to was the restoration of slaves taken during the war, stipulated to be restored, but still detained by the British naval commanders.

He said it should be attended to, and asked if I had any particular desire that Mr. Bagot's departure should be hastened. I said I could only desire that he might go as soon as would suit his own convenience and that of his Government.

I returned home, and at two o'clock went and attended the Prince Regent's levee. All the foreign ambassadors and Ministers were there, and I was introduced by Mr. Rayneval to the Comte de la Chatre, the Ambassador of Louis XVIII. I also became acquainted with the Spanish Ambassador and the

Sardinian and Turkish Ministers, and renewed old acquaintances with Baron Rehausen, the Swedish Minister, whom I had
known at the Hague, and with Mr. Curtoys, Secretary of the
Spanish Embassy, whom I had known in the like capacity at
Berlin.

The Turkish Chargé d'Affaires, Mr. Ramadani, told me that
he had been formerly acquainted here with Mr. Russell. He
spoke of our war with the Algerines, and expressed a wish that
the United States would send a Minister to Constantinople. He
told me that the Algerine squadron, lately off Lisbon, had
taken a vessel under the Ottoman flag, which had sailed from
this place with his papers, but he had no doubt she would be
restored when she got into port.

The Sardinian Minister said that they were doing infinite
mischief to the navigation of his country, and that our squadron
would meet with every assistance and good office that could be
afforded them in the island of Sardinia.   I spoke to Lord Sidmouth on the subject of the passports at the Alien Office. He
requested me to call on Saturday next at twelve o'clock at his
office, the Home Department, when he said he would introduce me to Mr. Beckett, whom he had placed at the head of
the Alien Office, and who would immediately settle with me
some general rule by which American citizens desirous of going
to France may be accommodated.   He assured me that every
disposition to accommodate American citizens would be shown
that was possible.

The first, or diplomatic levee, was short.   The Duke of Cumberland was the only Prince of the blood royal present.   The
Regent spoke a few words to all the Ambassadors and Ministers, and asked me if I had ever been in England before.   When
the second levee commenced, there was a crowd of persons
thronged into the chamber, among whom I knew only Mr.
Bailey, the Consul at St. Petersburg.   He came up to me, and
asked me if it was over.   He said that he had been presented
and knighted, but that it was done so in an instant that he
hardly knew how it happened, never having been there before.
I congratulated him upon his new dignity.   He said it was
about as good as the order of St. Vladimir.   As we retired,

I spoke to Baron Fagel, the Dutch Ambassador, and enquired after his brother Robert and his brother-in-law, Boreel. He told me that Boreel had escaped unhurt in the late battle, though his regiment had been almost destroyed.

I came home from the levee about four o'clock, and just before dinner received a note from the British Plenipotentiaries agreeing to sign a convention, as we proposed by our note of the 24th, and proposing to meet us at the Board of Trade at two o'clock to-morrow. I took it immediately after dinner to Mr. Clay. He sent over for Mr. Gallatin, who came, and they both read the British note. There was some question whether it required a reply. I thought, and strongly urged, that it did.

30th. Between one and two o'clock Messrs. Clay and Gallatin came to my lodgings, to consult with me upon the note which we received last evening from the British Plenipotentiaries. Mr. Clay thought no reply from us was necessary. I thought one indispensable. Of two alternatives which we offered them in our last note, they accept one, but with pretensions of generosity, as if they were granting a favor, which I thought it essential to repel. I insisted on this, until Mr. Gallatin took from his pocket the draft of a note which he had prepared, and with the substance of which I was satisfied. Mr. Clay ultimately consented to sign it, and immediately transcribed it from the draft. We took it with us, and delivered it ourselves to the British Plenipotentiaries. We were now agreed upon the substance of the convention, which is to be for four years from the signature, and consists of five articles. From the drafts made of the second article on both sides, its ultimate form was agreed upon. Mr. Gallatin had inserted the exception relative to the West Indies in the body of the article. Mr. Robinson had proposed to make a separate article of it. The conclusion was to put it in a paragraph at the close of the article.

There was in the East Indian article a proviso that American vessels might touch for refreshment, but not for commerce, at the Cape of Good Hope, the island of St. Helena, or other British places in the African or Indian Seas, in their voyages to or from the British possessions in India.

Mr. Gallatin observed to the British Plenipotentiaries that

this did not allow the same privileges to American vessels going to or from China. The limitation was a novelty; it had not been in the former treaties; and he mentioned it now, not that we intended to make a point of it, but for the British Plenipotentiaries to consider whether it was worth adhering to—particularly as it would not prevent a single American voyage to China.

It then became proper to consider of the preamble. Mr. Goulburn drew one up from former precedents, which he showed to Mr. Gallatin. He said that in the preamble to the Treaty of Ghent there had been a mistake. Mr. Clay asked him what it was. Goulburn avoided answering the question, but said that one of the clerks in the Foreign Office upon his return here had told him they had made a mistake. It did not, however, affect the validity of the treaty.

I observed then that there had been another error, both in the preamble and in the order of the signatures, at Ghent, which it would be necessary to avoid repeating at present. The first was, that in the copies on both sides the King of Great Britain and the British Plenipotentiaries were first named; and the second was, that the signatures all followed each other in succession, the American Plenipotentiaries signing under those of Great Britain. The usage of all treaties between European sovereigns we understood to be what is called the alternative, each of the parties and his Plenipotentiaries being first named in the copy which he receives; the signatures of the respective Plenipotentiaries being on a line and alternate— those of each party signing first in the copy which he receives. With regard to the order of the signatures, the British Pleni- potentiaries made no positive objection, but Dr. Adams said he did not know there was any such usage, and Mr. Goulburn said the same. I told Goulburn that if he would take the trouble of enquiring at the Foreign Office he would find it a universal usage. As to the alternative in the preamble, and in naming the parties in the treaty, Dr. Adams said that in such a case the copies would not be alike. I said that as it was a practice by common consent generally established and understood, the mere variation of order, in naming the parties, made no change either in the substance or in the words of the treaty; it did not in any manner affect the essential accuracy of the copies.

Mr. Goulburn said that in this case the changes must then run through the whole treaty.

I said if the preamble and ratifying clause were right, it was not so material in the body of the treaty, but if he would have a draft copy made out, as was agreed, and as they intended to execute *their* copy, and send it to me, I would have *our* copy made out corresponding to it, and ready to be executed on Monday morning. They promised to send me such a draft copy.

Mr. Clay and Mr. Gallatin had expressed some wish to finish the business this day or to-morrow. But Mr. Robinson and Mr. Goulburn were under the necessity of attending at four o'clock the House of Commons, where there was to be a close vote upon a question of a grant of six thousand pounds per annum to the Duke of Cumberland upon his marriage, and Mr. Goulburn was obliged to go out of town to-morrow, and will not return till Monday morning. Mr. Gallatin said he did not know how the usage was with regard to the alternatives in the treaty, but he knew the order in which we had signed and sealed at Ghent had been wrong—that it ought to have been in parallel lines. Mr. Robinson finally said he believed we were right. At least he knew it had been so at the Treaty of Chaumont, which was the only treaty that he had ever been before concerned in making. We left the British Plenipotentiaries just at four.

July 1st. At noon I called, according to his appointment, at Lord Sidmouth's office, and was informed that he had gone out of town. I then enquired for Mr. Beckett, and saw him. He apologized to me for Lord Sidmouth, and said that he had no doubt that he could easily arrange with me the subject upon which I had spoken to his Lordship.

I mentioned the difficulty which within these few days had arisen, in obtaining from the Alien Office passports to go to France. Until the commencement of hostilities, they had always obtained those passports at the Alien Office upon producing there passports given by me. Within the last week, those who have applied were told that they must have something more from me than a passport—a letter, or request that they might be permitted to go to France. I said that whatever of this nature was thought necessary by this Government I would readily give, it being understood that all I should pledge myself to by it is, that the person applying is an American citizen, and that he wishes to go to France. I should certainly not give it to any person of whom I should know that he was going with purposes hostile to this country, but I must of course give it to many persons total strangers to me, and of whose purposes I shall have no knowledge. As American citizens, all have an equal right to ask all the facilities that I can give them for travelling, and as belonging to a neutral country, all have an equal right to go to France, as their affairs or inclinations may lead them. It happened that the two persons who had recently found difficulties at the Alien Office, Mr. Bayard and Mr. Ogden, were personally known to me, and I could answer for the respectability of their characters. But many others had applied, and would apply, with whom I had no acquaintance, but who would have a right to the same document from me which I might give to my most intimate friends.

Mr. Beckett took the names of those two gentlemen, and said that he would not put me to the trouble of giving any other paper than my passport. He would see that no further difficulty on that account should be made at the Alien Office.

The other subject upon which I spoke to him was that of foreigners applying to me for passports to go to America—also sent to me from the Alien Office. He said that was because it was intended that no person should go to any country without the consent of the Minister from that country. I told him that everybody of every country had a right to go to America without needing my consent. I had no right to prevent any one from going. It would be certainly troublesome to me if I should be required to furnish a document to every foreigner of every nation going from this country to the United States, but there might be an inconvenience in it to this Government, for as I could not possibly know all such foreigners, and yet must give the same consent for all who should apply, it was possible applications for pretended foreigners might be made to me, when the person really intending to go might be forbidden by the laws from leaving this country. I told him I had put a visa upon two or three passports of foreign Ministers here for persons of their nation going to America, because they had stated they could not get a passport from the Alien Office without it; but I had refused giving passports of my own to several foreigners who had none, and one particularly this morning, to a Jew, who, from his appearance, I suspected of having applied for it in reality for another person.

Mr. Beckett assured me that he would see that this matter should also be duly attended to at the Alien Office. I soon after received a note from the British Plenipotentiaries, with their draft copy of the treaty, from which our fair copy is to be made out. I took it immediately to Mr. Clay's lodgings, and, as he was not at home, to Mr. Gallatin's. We collated it with the several previous drafts which had been agreed upon, and found it correct. But the term Treaty had been used in the preamble drawn up yesterday, and had escaped our attention. It was now in the draft copy, and Mr. Gallatin was desirous of substituting for it the term Convention, because, as the objects of it are limited, and many of the most important objects of a treaty of commerce are not included in it, the general denomination of a treaty of commerce seems improper for it.

We concluded to leave the term in blank in our copy, and to propose to the British Plenipotentiaries to insert the term Convention on Monday. The draft copy names the British Government and Plenipotentiaries first in the preamble and throughout the treaty. I determined to have our counterpart with the alternative, and showed to Mr. Gallatin the passage in the instructions from the Secretary of State to me of 13th of March, on the subject of the precedence and order of signatures in the Ghent Treaty. Mr. Gallatin still thinks it a matter of no importance. He showed me his draft of a dispatch to the Secretary of State, to be sent with the treaty. I suggested to him several considerable alterations, to which he readily agreed, and which will shorten the dispatch by about one-half.

2d. I postponed the usual writing of my journal to prepare the draft for our copy of the treaty. The changes in the order of the parties were, in the preamble, in the first, second, and fifth articles. I made the draft of them myself, and gave them to Mr. Grubb to be copied, with the draft received from the British Plenipotentiaries. He called between ten and eleven, and I requested him to have the fair copy made out, and to bring it to me, at the latest, by eleven o'clock to-morrow morning. I showed Mr. Clay the note received with the draft of the treaty yesterday from the British Plenipotentiaries. In this draft, I told him, they had placed the marks for the seals (L. S.) three and three, in parallel lines, by which it appeared that they meant to accede to our proposal as to the order of the signatures. They had also named the British Government and Plenipotentiaries first in the preamble, and throughout the treaty, which was right for *their* copy. But at the close they had put " done in *duplicate*," which was improper, as the counterparts of a treaty are never called duplicates, and which might be for the sake of insisting that there should be no variation between the two copies. I had, however, directed that our copy should be made out, taking the alternative throughout the whole treaty, always naming the American Government and Plenipotentiaries first, but without any change either of substance or in the words. I had ordered the place of the word Treaty to be left in blank, to be filled with Convention if the British Plenipotentiaries would consent, and I had also directed the word duplicate to be left out, with a blank to insert it if they should insist upon it.

Mr. Clay did not approve of the change I had ordered to be made, and said he thought I myself had agreed yesterday that it should be only in the preamble. I admitted having said that *it was not so material* in the body of the treaty, but I had found, on referring to the French copies of the Treaty of Paris, of 30th May, 1814, that the alternative was also used in the body of the treaty, and, as this was to be a precedent, I thought it best to make it complete. I then showed Mr. Clay the instructions from the Department of State to me, of 13th March.

He said he thought it a matter of no consequence; that Mr. Monroe's argument in the dispatch was a bad one. It was no good reason why we should make a point of such a formality because the European Powers thought it so important; for the most insignificant powers, such as Spain for instance, were those that insisted most upon these punctilios.

I said this was a point to which all the European Powers always adhered; that I had always regretted that the United States had ever admitted a variation from it; that I had mentioned it to Mr. Gallatin at Ghent, and had then forborne to make a point of it only because we had no instruction to warrant us in so doing, and because I thought all the precedents of our treaties were the other way.

This conversation, on both sides, was perfectly temperate and good-humored, and Mr. Clay left me. Within half an hour after, Mr. Gallatin came in. He showed me a note that he had written this morning to Mr. Robinson, requesting that the term Convention might be inserted instead of the term Treaty, so that the American Plenipotentiaries jointly, or I, as one of them, might be at liberty to bring forward the other objects of discussion, which we had agreed for the present to postpone. He also showed me the draft of the dispatch to the Secretary of State, to go with the treaty, and in which he had made all the alterations that I had proposed. It was a sort of argument in favor of the treaty, which I had requested him to omit, for two reasons: one, because if the treaty was a good one, it needed no arguments from us to prove its merits; and the other, that in assigning our motives for admitting objectionable parts, we referred to circumstances which it would be unnecessary to make known here, which they would be if the dispatch should be published.

Mr. Gallatin had made the alterations accordingly, though he said they never published the dispatches when the negotiation succeeded. I then told him that I had given the treaty to be copied, and had taken the alternative throughout the whole instrument. Upon which he said, in a peremptory and somewhat petulant manner, " Oh, that is entirely wrong; it will throw the whole business into confusion. Why, you yourself said yesterday it was not necessary in the body of the treaty." I said I had observed that *it was not so material* in the body of the treaty, but if the British Plenipotentiaries gave up the point in the preamble and ratifying clause, it was im-

possible that they should object to the admission of the same
principle in the body of the treaty. I then showed him the
copy of the Treaty of Paris which I have, printed in France,
and in which the King of France is first named in the first
article, as well as in the preamble. He was yet, however, not
satisfied, and asked me if I had told Mr. Clay of the directions
I had given for making out our fair copy, and what Mr. Clay
said to it. I told him that I had ; that Mr. Clay disapproved
the directions that I had given as he did, and thought the
whole point of no importance.

Mr. Gallatin then said that I must give the transcriber orders
to make out the copy without any alteration in the body of the
treaty ; which I peremptorily refused, and added, in a heated
and angry manner, " Mr. Gallatin, you and Mr. Clay may do
as you please, but I will not sign the treaty without the alternative observed throughout."   " Now, don't fly off in this
manner," said Mr. Gallatin.   " Indeed, sir," said I, " I will not
sign the treaty in any other form. I am so far from thinking
with Mr. Clay that it is of no importance, that I think it by
much the most important thing that we shall obtain by this
treaty. The treaty itself I very much dislike, and it is only
out of deference to you and Mr. Clay that I consent to sign it
at all. I should infinitely prefer to sign no treaty at all, being
perfectly convinced that we obtain nothing by it but what we
should obtain by the regulations of this Government without it."

Mr. Gallatin said that was entirely a different ground, which
I admitted to be true, but said it was a sufficient motive for me
to insist that the principle of the alternative as to precedence
should be settled completely throughout the treaty. There
would not be a particle of change in the substance, nor even
in the words of the two copies. The transpositions were almost
all in the second article. They had all been made by the British
Plenipotentiaries themselves from our projet first delivered to
them, and which he (Mr. Gallatin) had drawn up. If the British
Plenipotentiaries now objected to the transpositions in the
second article, I would propose to them to draw it up without
naming either of the parties first, but using general expressions
applicable to both, as had been done in the corresponding article

of the Treaty of 1806. Mr. Gallatin said that the article of which I spoke was indistinct and obscure, owing to the use of that very phraseology, and he had for that reason purposely varied from it in drafting the present article. I said that if Mr. Gallatin and Mr. Clay chose to have the draft made without any variation in the body of the treaty, I would immediately take it out of the hands of the transcriber and return it to them. They might then have the copy made out as they pleased, but I should decline signing it if it differed from the draft I had ordered to be made. Mr. Gallatin left me, with a request that I would wait (as I was going to dine out of town) until he could see and consult with Mr. Clay, which I promised to do. About half-past four I received a note from Messrs. Clay and Gallatin requesting me to send them my copy of the proposed convention, and also that sent to me by the British Plenipotentiaries whenever my copy shall have been completed.

3d. It was near ten o'clock this morning when Mr. Grubb came with the copies of the convention, and that which he had made to be executed by us was precisely conformable to the directions which I had given him. I collated them together with him, and marked with a pencil on the British draft copy all the transpositions. I immediately sent over both the copies to Mr. Clay and Mr. Gallatin, and gave Mr. Grubb some other papers to be copied, ready for to-morrow morning. Just at eleven Mr. Clay came and introduced to me a Mr. Murray, a relation of one of the families of that name in New York. They left me after a short visit, and about half an hour afterwards Mr. Gallatin came with the copies of the convention. He now spoke coolly on the subject of the transpositions, and I was, of course, equally cool and good-humored.

He said that I had sent the copies so late that it was impossible for Mr. Clay and him to have another copy made out in time for the conference. They were obliged, therefore, to try the experiment of offering mine. But the British Plenipotentiaries would have the best of the argument, on two grounds. One was, that he thought by the European usage the alternative was adopted only when the *Governments* were named, and was not extended to their territories and dominions; and the second was, that in the present instance the alternation in the British copy would not be complete. For there was one clause which they had inserted in their copy precisely as he had drawn it up. In that the United States were named first, and they had it so in their copy. My copy had made no transposition in that clause: so that while our copy would have the United States first named throughout the instrument, the British copy would in one instance name the United States first also. Whereas if the two copies had been made alike, that single clause would have shown that there was no precedence assumed by Britain in the body of the treaty.

I answered him that I had called yesterday, after receiving the note from Mr. Clay and him, upon Mr. Grubb expressly to hasten him in making out the copy. I had urged him, and he had promised, to let me have it by nine o'clock this morning. It was ten, however, before he came with it, and I had sent it over to them immediately after receiving it. That as to the two grounds of the argument, the transpositions in the second article were all made by the British Plenipotentiaries themselves from his draft. He had named the United States first, they had named Great Britain first. The point, therefore, was made by them, and not by us. I consented to the transpositions for their copy, I adhered to the original reading for ours. If the use of the alternatives was confined to the naming of the Governments, why had the British Plenipotentiaries made the transpositions from his draft? If, therefore, they urged the argument, it would recoil upon themselves. It was true that they had inserted one clause, subsequently drawn up by him, without making the transposition, and had inserted it in their copy, naming the United States first. If they should now desire that the transposition should also be made in that clause upon their copy, I should readily agree to it. But there was one other passage in which British were named before American vessels, and which I had left without transposition the same in our copy as in theirs. If they should object to transpositions in the body of the treaty generally, I should propose to make a new draft of the second article, naming the two parties as such, so that neither should be named first. It was so in the corresponding article of 1806, which I had examined since he was with me yesterday, and which, far from thinking confused and obscure, I thought was more clear and distinct than ours, and in much fewer words. He said it was much shorter, but certainly not so precise and intelligible. It was now twelve o'clock, and we had agreed to meet the British Plenipotentiaries at half-past eleven. I went down with Mr. Gallatin in his carriage; Mr. Clay, whom we overtook in Cavendish Square, followed us. At the Board of Trade we found only Mr. Robinson. He told Mr. Gallatin that they agreed to substitute the term Convention instead of that of Treaty. I told him I had also omitted in our copy the term "in duplicate," as the counterparts of the same treaty were not usually called duplicates, and I thought the term improper. We had indeed done in triplicate the Treaty of Ghent, but that was because there were three copies of the treaty on each side. Mr. Gallatin added, that if we should now state this convention to be done in duplicate, it would be understood that there were on both sides two copies.

While we were waiting for Mr. Goulburn and Dr. Adams, I recollected that I had left home without taking my seal. I immediately went in Mr. Gallatin's carriage, and returned with my seal. I found on my return the British Plenipotentiaries assembled. We began by collating the copies. Mr. Robinson took our copy as made out by my direction. I took and read the British copy. Not a word of objection was made by the British Plenipotentiaries to any of the transpositions in our copy. There were in the British copy several errors. Mr. Ellis, the clerk who had made it out, was called in, and made the corrections as the errors were noticed. Our copy was correct, having been previously collated by Mr. Grubb and me this morning. The two copies were then signed and sealed by the Plenipotentiaries on both sides—the three signatures on each side in succession, and those of the two parties on a line, the American signatures and seals being first in our copy, and the British signatures and seals first in the British copy. The alternative was complete, and assented to by the British Plenipotentiaries without objection.

I afterwards observed that it was best to agree upon the

title, which we did. I wrote it on a separate piece of paper, to be inserted at the head of our copy, naming the United States first. Mr. Goulburn copied from mine the title for their copy, transposing the order of the parties. The words " in duplicate" were omitted from the British copy, as I had proposed.

Mr. Robinson said that they had readily agreed to use the term Convention instead of that of Treaty, and they should certainly be ready to receive any further proposals or communications from us, as had been suggested to him in Mr. Gallatin's note of yesterday, upon the subject, the discussion of which had been by mutual consent postponed; but it was very possible that if those subjects were to be discussed, *they* would not be the persons whom the British Government would appoint for such a negotiation.

Mr. Gallatin said we had only desired it that, as we had reserved to ourselves the right of bringing forward those subjects for subsequent discussion, either jointly, or by me, remaining the accredited Minister at this Court, it was to be understood that we did not mean by concluding this convention upon subjects of minor comparative importance to abandon that right.

Mr. Clay said that we should now the more readily leave the vastly more important objects relating to the belligerent and neutral condition for future arrangement, as there was the prospect of an immediate termination to the war, which has newly arisen, so that the questions most likely to occasion collision would again be dormant. But it was still to be understood that we considered all our claims as left entire.

Dr. Adams said that our claims would in no manner be affected by this convention, as, on the other hand, none of them were to be understood as admitted by Great Britain.

I observed that in consequence of what had been said by my colleagues, it might be proper for me to say that it was not my intention to bring forward any further subject for discussion without new instructions to that effect from my Government; and that if I should receive such instructions I should of course address myself in executing them to the Department of Foreign Affairs. With this assurance the British Plenipotentiaries expressed themselves satisfied.

On taking leave of them, Mr. Goulburn said to me, " Well, this is the second good job we have done together." " Yes," said I, " and I only hope we may do a third, going on from better to better."

I returned with Mr. Gallatin to his lodgings, where Mr. Clay soon joined us. As we were coming, Mr. Gallatin said, " Well, they got over the transpositions very easily, but you would not have found it so if Dr. Adams had had the reading of your copy, instead of Robinson." I said that might be. Immediately after we reached Mr. Gallatin's lodgings, Mr. Del Real and another gentleman, two of the Carthagena deputies, came in, upon a visit to take leave. Mr. Hassler soon afterwards followed. Mr. Gallatin dismissed him quite abruptly, telling him that he was very much engaged, and, as soon as he was gone, Gallatin said to me, laughing, " That is a man of very great merit, though I do treat him so roughly. He was sent by the Government to Europe to procure the instruments for the general survey of our coast, but he has outrun his time and his funds, and his instruments cost eight hundred pounds more than was appropriated for them, and he is embarrassed now about getting back to America. I have engaged Messrs. Baring to advance the money for the instruments, and he is to go for his own expenses upon his own credit. He has procured an excellent set of instruments. But he is a great politician, though his politics are of the right sort, and he is so great a talker that, as we have no time to spare, I was obliged to send him away."

We now signed the joint dispatch to the Secretary of State, to be sent with the convention, which Mr. Gallatin had ready prepared. He and Mr. Clay signed their previous joint dispatch, which they gave to me with the accompanying documents to have copied and then transmitted to the United States. Mr. Clay intended to leave town at five o'clock this afternoon, and Mr. Gallatin very early to-morrow morning. Mr. Gallatin told me that he should call upon me this evening, though it would probably be late, and he requested me not to go to bed, but to have all the papers ready for him. We parted about four o'clock, and Mr. Clay took leave. I returned home, and was until dinner-time employed, together with my son George, in making a copy of the joint dispatch, the original of which is to go by Mr. Gallatin with the convention. After dinner I went to Mr. Grubb's house with the convention, to have the title inserted in his handwriting, and to take the copies of all the papers, which he had been making to go with it. He had nearly, but not quite, finished the copies. I took a half an hour's ride, and, on returning to his house, found him ready. I left with him to be copied the dispatch from Mr. Clay and Gallatin, with the documents, and took home with me all the other papers. It was past eleven when I got home. I made up the packet for Mr. Gallatin, and waited for him until one in the morning; he did not come. I then went to bed.

4th. Independence day. Mr. Gallatin called upon me this morning and apologized for not having come last night. He said he had dined with Mr. Baring, and sat so late with him at table that he had concluded I should not wait for him; that he was taken quite ill last night after he got home, and was still so unwell this morning that he should not leave town until to-morrow. He now wanted the packet containing his and Mr. Clay's dispatch, which I gave last night to Mr. Grubb to be copied. He told me Mr. Clay left town early this morning for Liverpool. He afterwards sent his son James, who took the packet containing the dispatches and the convention, together with the letters we had prepared for America.

10th. Mr. Wilberforce paid me a visit, and expressed to me his high satisfaction at the restoration of peace between our two countries. He spoke about an abusive article in the Quarterly Review against America, concerning which he had received from America letters from two gentlemen, one of them enclosing an answer to it, which he had not had time to read. He found the article was ascribed to Mr. Canning, he thought erroneously, and he should write to Canning about it.

I said the *Review* was represented as being under the patronage of Mr. Canning, but the *article*, in two pamphlets answering it which I had received from America, was ascribed to Mr. Southey, who had, however, denied being the author of it, in a letter published in a late Courier. I explained to Mr. Wilberforce the manner in which the friends of Great Britain in

America were affected by such publications as that article in the Quarterly Review. He said that he lamented it, but that those were not the general sentiments of this nation, and that the Quarterly Review itself was a work of limited circulation, much more limited than that of the Edinburgh Review. I had conversation with Mr. Wilberforce upon various other topics, and proposed to call upon him; but he said he was going into the country for the summer.

11th. The forty-eighth year of my life has closed, and I this day enter upon the forty-ninth. It has in relation to public affairs been the most important, and in my private and domestic relations one of the most happy years. May I be duly sensible of the hand from which the blessings have flowed, duly humble in prosperity, duly prepared for adversity, and enabled more fully and faithfully to discharge all my duties than I have been hitherto!

I received from Mr. Chester, the Assistant Master of the Ceremonies, a notification that the Prince Regent would go to-morrow, at two o'clock, to close the session of Parliament, and that if I wished to attend I must go in "habit habillé," and be at the House of Lords about a quarter before two.

I was highly gratified this afternoon by an article in the Courier, headed "Victory of the Americans over the Algerines," and stating that Commodore Decatur's squadron had taken, on the 20th of June, and carried into Carthagena, the Algerine frigate Mazoura, of fifty guns, commanded by the Admiral of Algiers, who was killed.

12th. I went to the House of Lords, and was there at a quarter before two, the time mentioned in Mr. Chester's note. The Dukes of York and Kent were there, in their robes, as Peers, a very small number of the other Peers, most of the Foreign Ambassadors and Ministers, and a houseful of ladies as spectators. The Prince Regent came in with royal state precisely at two. He had the Royal and Regent's crown borne upon cushio ; before him, but was in a military uniform, with a multitude of orders, and over them the robes of a Peer. He wore his hat, and took his seat upon the throne.

The Speaker of the House of Commons, in his wig and

black gown, together with a few members of the House, all
dressed in black, appeared at the bar of the House immediately after the Regent was seated, and made a speech, addressed to him, which he concluded by presenting to him a
bill for raising six millions for the service of his Majesty.
That and several other bills were read by their titles, and when
the Prince by a nod had expressed his assent to them, a clerk
pronounced, in very bad French, the words " Le Roi le veut,"
to some, and " Soit fait comme il est désiré," to others; after
which the Prince Regent read his speech, and then the Lord
Chancellor, who stood behind the Prince and at his right hand,
declared the session of Parliament to be prorogued to the 22d
of August. The Prince then rose and withdrew. Mr. Chester
told me that the Queen had been in town yesterday, only for
an hour, and probably would not come to town again before
the winter. After the Prince was gone, I saw Lord Gambier,
who was there, but not in his robes as a Peer. He was in a
plain frock dress. He introduced me to Lord Bathurst, to
whom I apologized for not having called upon him. I was
also introduced to Count Munster, the Hanoverian Minister,
who has just returned from the Continent.

The Spanish and Dutch Ambassadors, and the Portuguese
and Sardinian Ministers, spoke to me of the reported capture
by our squadron of the Algerine frigate. Lords Bathurst and
Gambier also mentioned it. The Dutch Ambassador told me
that he was informed of it by a letter from the Dutch Minister
at Madrid. The Spanish Ambassador asked if our squadron
had entered the port of Cadiz. I said I believed they had not.
He asked if they had attempted to enter. I did not know.
He seemed to doubt whether it would be admitted, and intimated that there was a state of hostility between Spain and the
United States. I said it seemed by the account received here
that our ships had been admitted to Carthagena. I asked him
what was the state of relations between Spain and Algiers.
He answered that it was also between peace and war. He said
he had not any late communication from his Court respecting
the United States, but the last he had received mentioned that
the Spanish Minister sent to the United States had not been

recognized. I said I believed he had been recognized since the restoration of the King, but that a Minister had been appointed by our Government to Spain whom the King of Spain had refused to receive. He said that was because the Spanish Minister in the United States was not recognized. From the substance of his conversation, I am not without concern that Decatur may meet with some difficulty there.

August 8th. After the morning reading with George and the journal of yesterday, I devoted the remainder of the day to the preparation of a letter to Lord Castlereagh. I have felt for several weeks an obligation of duty to write this letter, and have postponed it from day to day, I believe improperly, for objects of far minor concernment. I finished the draft before dinner. Began before dinner the fair copy of my draft, and continued writing it in the evening until near eleven o'clock. The experience of the last summer has made me distrustful and diffident of my own drafts. My own colleagues were then so dissatisfied with everything that I wrote, and adopted so little either of my reasoning or my style, that it has, or ought to have, taken away all my self-sufficiency, and abated all confidence in my faculty either to convince an antagonist or to satisfy those whose cause I would support. But I am now alone, and must perform my duty in my own way. Whatever error there may be in the performance of it, let there be none of neglect, and no deficiency of earnest zeal. I hope this communication may not have been too long delayed.

16th. I was obliged to attend Lord Liverpool at Fife House at two o'clock. I was immediately introduced into his cabinet, and stated to him the subjects upon which I had been desirous of having this interview with him; observing that Lord Castlereagh, at the time of his departure, had referred me to him and Lord Bathurst upon the subjects belonging to the Foreign Department. My first object was to ascertain what was the understanding of the Government with regard to the fifth article of the commercial convention lately signed. I was informed by merchants that an extra duty of twopence per pound upon cotton imported in American vessels, which had not commenced until a day or two after the signature of the convention, was now levied; and, as the convention was not published, I was asked when its operation was to commence. I had brought a copy of the fifth article with me, and my own opinion was, that although the convention would not be binding upon the parties until the exchange of ratifications, its operation upon that event would be retrospective from the date of the signature.

Lord Liverpool said that was unusual; which I admitted, observing that the article was drawn up in words deviating from the usual form, and that the deviation was the proposal of the British Plenipotentiaries, our projet having proposed that the treaty should take effect as usual from the exchange of the ratifications. He asked me if I had spoken on the subject to Mr. Robinson, the Vice-President of the Board of Trade. I said I had, some weeks since, but he had not formed a decisive opinion upon it. I said that we had understood that an Order of Council would have issued immediately to arrest the levying of the extra duty upon cotton imported in American vessels, and that it would not have been levied at all. This was our impression at the time when the convention was negotiated, and from what was said by the British Plenipotentiaries. At all events, however, it was material to know what the construction of the article by the British Government would be, as the operation in either case must be reciprocal. If it was understood here that the revocation of discriminating duties would commence only from the exchange of ratifications, the same principle must be observed in the United States; but there, when the convention should be ratified, any individual affected by it might claim the benefit of its construction by judicial authority.

He said it was the same here; that the construction must of course be the same on both sides; that they had taken an act of Parliament to enable the King in Council to regulate the trade with America until the meeting of Parliament, as had been done for some years after the Peace of 1783, and an Order of Council was to have been made out conformably to the treaty. It had been for some time accidentally delayed, but perhaps it might be ready to be signed at the Council to-morrow. As it was the disposition here to put all the amicable and conciliatory arrangements in operation as soon as possible, the discriminating duties might be immediately removed, in the confidence that the same measure would be adopted on the part of the United States.

I said that Great Britain had already a pledge of that reciprocity by the act of Congress passed at the last session, of which I had also brought with me a copy. I left both the copies with him.

Before we passed to another subject, he said he thought proper to mention to me that a note would be sent to Mr. Baker, previous to the ratification of the convention, respecting the island of St. Helena; that, by a general agreement of the allies, Bonaparte was to be transferred to custody in that island, and, by a general regulation, the ships of all nations, excepting those of their own East India Company, would be excluded from it. The circumstance which led to the necessity of this measure had not been in contemplation, and the measure itself would not be extended beyond the necessity by which it was occasioned; that it was authorized by the precedent of the treaty which had been signed by himself and Mr. King, and which the American Government had proposed to modify, because a subsequent treaty containing the cession of Louisiana had altered the situation of the parties, though not contemplated by him or Mr. King when they signed the convention; that as the Cape of Good Hope would still be left for American vessels to touch at, he presumed the island of St. Helena would not be necessary for them.

I said I did not know that the stipulation with regard to the island of St. Helena was in itself of very material importance, but the American Government might consider the principle as important. The stipulation was in express and positive terms, and the island of St. Helena was identically named. The case referred to by him did not appear to me to apply as a precedent, for two reasons. One was, that the Louisiana convention had been signed before, and not, as he thought, after, that signed by him and Mr. King; though it was true that neither he nor Mr. King knew that it had been signed. The other was, that

Great Britain had declined ratifying that convention, upon the very ground of the modification to it proposed by the American Government, in consequence of the change produced by the Louisiana convention.

He said that at all events, as such a note would be presented by Mr. Baker previous to the ratification by the American Government, he had thought best to give me notice of it. I then referred to the contents of the letter which I had addressed last week to Lord Castlereagh, and asked him if he had seen it. He intimated that he had. I told him that, having expected Mr. Bagot was on the eve of departure, I had been anxious that he might go provided with instructions, which might give satisfaction to the Government of the United States, with regard to the execution of two very important stipulations in the Treaty of Ghent.

He said that as to the surrender of Michilimakinac there could be no sort of difficulty. The orders for its evacuation had been long since given. It was merely the want of barracks for their troops that had occasioned a momentary delay, and he had no doubt the fort was ere this delivered up. There never had been for a moment the intention on the part of the British Government to retain any place which they had stipulated to restore. But with respect to the slaves they certainly construed very differently from the American Government the stipulation relating to them. They thought that it applied only to the slaves in the forts and places which, having been taken during the war, were to be restored.

I said that, independent of the construction of the sentence which so strongly marked the distinction between artillery and public property and slaves and private property, the process by which the article was drawn up demonstrated beyond all question that a distinction between them was intended and understood by both parties. The first projet of the treaty was presented by *us*. This had been required, and even insisted upon, by the British Plenipotentiaries. The article was therefore drawn up by us, and our intention certainly was to secure the restoration both of the public and private property, including slaves, which had been in any manner captured on shore during the war. The projet was returned to us, with a limitation upon the restoration of property, whether public or private, to such as had been in the places when captured and should remain there at the time of the evacuation. We assented to this so far as related to artillery and public property, which, by the usages of war, is liable to be taken and removed, but not with regard to private property and slaves, which we thought should at all events be restored, because they ought never to have been taken. We therefore proposed the transposition of the words as stated in my letter to Lord Castlereagh. The British Plenipotentiaries certainly knew that, in asking for that transposition, the import of the sentence would be changed; that the limitation applicable to one species of property would no longer be applicable, as they had proposed, to the other, but the construction upon which the British commanders have carried away the slaves would annul the whole effect of the transposition of the words.

He said that perhaps the British Plenipotentiaries had agreed to the transposition of the words there without referring to the Government here, and that although the intentions of the parties might be developed by reference to the course of the negotiations, yet the ultimate construction must be upon the words of the treaty as they stood. He would see Mr. Goulburn and enquire of him how they understood this transposition; but certainly for himself, and he could speak for the whole Government here, if they had understood it to imply that persons who, from whatever motive, had taken refuge under the protection of the British forces should be delivered up to those who, to say the least, must feel unkindly towards them and might treat them harshly, they should have objected to it. Something else, he could not say what, would have been proposed.

I said I had referred to the progress of the negotiation, and the protocol of conferences, only as confirming what I thought the evident purport of the words in the treaty. To speak in perfect candor, I would not undertake to say that the British Plenipotentiaries had taken a view of the subject different from that of their Government. But certainly our intentions were to provide that no slaves should be carried away. We had no thought of concealing or disguising that intention. Had the British Plenipotentiaries asked of us an explanation of our proposal to transpose the words, we should instantly have given it. It was evident that we had an object in making the proposal, and we thought the words themselves disclosed it. Our object was the restoration of all property, including slaves, which, by the usages of war among civilized nations, ought not to have been taken. All private property on shore was of that description. It was entitled by the laws of war to exemption from capture. Slaves were private property.

Lord Liverpool said that he thought they could not be considered precisely under the general denomination of private property. A table or a chair, for instance, might be taken and restored without changing its condition ; but a living and a human being was entitled to other considerations.

I said that the treaty had made no such distinction. The words implicitly recognized slaves as private property. They were in the article alluded to—" slaves or *other* private property." I did, however, readily admit the distinction suggested by him. Most certainly a living, sentient being, and still more a human being, was to be regarded in a different light from the inanimate matter of which other private property might consist, and if on the ground of that difference the British Plenipotentiaries had objected to restore the one, while they agreed to restore the other, we should have readily discussed the subject. We might have accepted, or objected to, the proposal they would have made. But what could that proposal have been? Upon what ground could Great Britain have refused to restore them? Was it because they had been seduced away from their masters by the promises of British officers? It was true, proclamations from her officers to that effect had issued. We considered them as deviations from the usages of war. We believed that the British Government itself would, when the hostile passions of a state of war should subside, consider them in the same light; that she would then be willing to restore the property, or to indemnify the sufferers by its loss. If she felt bound to make good the promises of her officers to the slaves, she might still be willing to do an act of justice, by compensating the owners of the slaves for the property which had been irregularly taken from them. Without entering into a discussion which might have been at once unprofitable and irritating, she might consider this engagement only as a promise to pay for those slaves which should be carried away by paying the worth of them to their owners. Lord Liverpool did not reply to these observations, nor did he appear to take them in ill part, and I added that there was a branch of the same subject upon which I had not written to Lord Castlereagh, because, as it involved considerations of a very delicate nature, I had thought it might be treated more confidentially by verbal conference than by written communications, which would be liable to publication. During the war it had been stated in a letter of instructions from the American Secretary of State to the negotiators of the Ghent Treaty, that some of the slaves enticed from their masters by promises of freedom from British officers had afterwards been sold in the West Indies. This letter of instructions had afterwards been published.

"Yes," said he, "and I believe some explanation of it has been asked."

I said there had; first by the British Plenipotentiaries at Ghent, and afterwards by Admiral Cochrane, of the American Secretary of State. Mr. Monroe had answered this last application by a letter to Mr. Baker, which his Lordship had doubtless seen. But I had been authorized to say that, in making this charge in the midst of the war, the American Government had not expected, and was not desirous, that it should lead to discussions to be protracted to a time and in a state of peace. They believed that evidence to substantiate in some degree the charge was obtainable, but would prefer that if the British Government wished to obtain it they should seek it from other sources, many of which were more accessible to them than to the Government of the United States. The sales, if made, had been in British possessions and from British ships. These were, of course, entirely open to the investigation of enquiries under British authority. The proclamations had

promised employment in the military service of Great Britain
(which could apply only to men), or *free* settlement in the
West Indies.   But, in fact, numbers of women and children
had been received and carried away, as well as of men.   The
numbers of them, and in a very great degree the identical
individuals that had been taken, might be easily proved in the
United States, and I expected to be enabled to furnish accurate
lists of them.   If not sold, some provision must have been
made for them at the charge of the British Government itself.
It could not be at a loss to know those whom it had to maintain; and as the whole subject had a tendency to irritation,
rather than to the conciliatory spirit which it was the wish of
the American Government to cultivate exclusively.[1]

Lord Liverpool is a man of remarkable mildness and
amenity of manner.   I perceived that he was under some
embarrassment how to take what I was saying; that in referring him to the ample and obvious sources of evidence through
which they may ascertain the facts, without recurring to the
medium of the American Government, he thought I was
shrinking from the production of any evidence on our part.
I had anticipated that this would be his impression, and therefore added that with this explanation I was directed to say
that if the British Government still desired evidence from
that of the United States, they would furnish such as they
could collect.

He said that was certainly all that could be asked.   The
British officers had universally and very strenuously denied
the charge, which, if true, deserved the severest animadversion
and punishment.   The British Government certainly had believed, and still believed, the charge to be without foundation,
and, in the deficiency of evidence, could come to no other
conclusion.

A servant had announced Lord Melville, who was waiting,
and I thought it unnecessary to push the subject further.   I
then spoke to him about the tax levied upon my dispatches,
and which Mr. Maury had unwarily paid at Liverpool.   After
the full explanation, he admitted, not however very explicitly,

[1] This sentence appears to be incomplete.

that the tax ought not to have been levied, and said he would speak of it to Mr. Freeling, the secretary of the post-office, of whose fairness and obliging disposition he gave a high and a very unmerited character. I told him that, the law upon which the tax was levied having now expired, it remained important only as respected the principle, as it was my only object to ascertain whether I could send my letters by private hands, or whether I must constitute a special messenger for every dispatch that I should have occasion to send.

20th. We all went to church, and heard a charity sermon preached by a Dr. Crane, before the Duke of Kent, for the benefit of the charity school in the parish of Ealing. The boys were catechised by the junior parson of the parish. Dr. Carr was not there. The text was from Hebrews xiii. 16: " But to do good and to communicate forget not: for with such sacrifices God is well pleased." The sermon was tolerably well written, and very indifferently read. Though a charity sermon, it was not free from the tinge of an uncharitable spirit. For among the excellences of the institution for which the preacher was begging, he did not fail to enumerate its tendency to preserve the boys from the infection of Methodism, or dissent from that most excellent and perfect Church, the Church of England. There is something in the dress, in the gait, in the deportment, in the expression of countenance, and, above all, in the eye, of these clergymen of the most excellent Church, that imports arrogance, intolerance, and all that is the reverse of Christian humility. They will quote the words of the Publican with the tone of the Pharisee, and say " God be merciful to me a sinner" with an air as if they meant to take the kingdom of heaven by violence. In this church are inscribed in gilded characters, on the panels of the gallery pews, all the donations for more than two centuries made to the church or to the parish for charitable purposes. This is an excellent practice, well deserving of imitation. It is at once a testimony of gratitude for benefits received, and an excitement to others to like charitable deeds.

25th. St. Louis's day. At seven I went to the French Ambassador's, to the dinner. The Duke of Orleans, Lords Liverpool,

Bathurst, and Harrowby, Mr. Vansittart and Mr. Wellesley Pole, the Spanish, Russian, and Dutch Ambassadors, the Swedish, Danish, Portuguese, Bavarian, and Würtemberg Ministers, the Austrian and Turkish Chargés d'Affaires, Mr. Morier, Under-Secretary of State, Mr. Croker, Secretary to the Admiralty (between whom I was seated at table), General Dumouriez, Baron Nicolai, Mr. Chester, the Master of the Ceremonies, the Ambassador's aumônier, and several officers, French and English, whom I did not know, constituted the company. There were about thirty-five persons, and two more than there were places at table. Baron Nicolai and Mr. Chester were some time waiting before places could be made for them by crowding the rest of the company together.

I spoke to the Duke of Orleans, who enquired of me how long I had been from Paris. I was introduced to General Dumouriez, and informed him of the papers I have belonging to him, of the manner in which they had come into my hands, and of my intention to call upon him to return them.

I had much conversation with Mr. Croker at table, chiefly about the French and English theatres, Racine, Molière, and Shakespeare, Talma and Kemble, Mademoiselle Mars and Mrs. Siddons, Brunet and Potier. I conversed also with the Turkish Chargé d'Affaires before dinner, who again urged the appointment of an American Ambassador at the Ottoman Porte, and after dinner with Lord Westmorland, who enquired what accounts I received from the American Chargé d'Affaires in Paris. He appears doubtful of what is to be done or what can be done with France. Baron Fagel, the Dutch Ambassador, told me that Mr. Changuion, who lately returned from America, was this day gone for Holland; that he came back delighted with his reception and treatment in the United States. The dinner was over between ten and eleven o'clock. As I came away, the Count de la Chatre very politely told me that he hoped we should see each other again and frequently, as there was an ancient friendship and connection between our countries.

26th. I paid a visit to General Dumouriez, who is almost my next-door neighbor, and returned to him the letters which were left with me about a fortnight since with several letters from the post-office. The letters had given me some insight into the views and present situation of the man, and I had now a long conversation with him, which gave me more. Dumouriez was at one time an important personage in the world. It is now more than twenty years since he was obliged to fly from the army which he had led to victory, and seek refuge among the enemies whom he had vanquished. He is now seventy-five years of age, burning with ambition to return to France and recommence a career in which, by a confession more true than sincere, in one of the letters, he said he had done nothing but " des brillantes sottises." The ineradicable vices of his character are vanity, levity, and insincerity. They are conspicuous in his writings, and were not less remarkable in his conversation with me. Like all vain people, his greatest delight is to talk of himself. He told me that he had been twelve years in the service of this country. That he had first been sent for to assist in a plan of defence for this country against a French invasion. He had made his bargain with the British Government; they had offered him terms which he had accepted, and he lived upon them comfortably, though not in opulence. That while Louis the Eighteenth had been in this country he had often seen and at one time had been much in favor with him. But Louis had a favorite, a Count de Blacas, who had done him infinite mischief; and when he went over to France, in 1814, there was some coldness of the King towards him. After the King was at Paris, settling his government, Macdonald, who had been one of his aides-de-camp, said to the King, " What, sir! come without Dumouriez, without the 'Vainqueur de Gemappe'?" Some proposal had then been made that he should be appointed a Marshal of France and a member of the House of Peers. But this was not obtained, and finally the only thing offered him was the rank of Lieutenant-General, with full pay, but without any command—which he refused. His situation here was better than that. He was here upon good terms with all parties; the Ministers and Opposition were all his friends. He gave his opinions freely, as he thought might be useful, and wrote memoirs when required. He had resided in his present habitation these two years and a half, with the Count

de St.-Martin, his aide-de-camp, and his wife. They had lost
their only son in Portugal. He saw very little society here,
and very seldom went to London, except on occasion of some
solemnity like that of yesterday, which he could not avoid.
He spoke of the present state of affairs in France, but so as
to convince me that he knew nothing more of them than is
contained in the newspapers. He said that he was for the
"Monarchie Constitutionnelle;" for it was impossible at this
time to govern France either "par l'absolutisme" or by a
republic. He had advised that the King should at once make
a Prime Minister, disband the army, and form a new one attached to the royal cause; that the armies of the allies should
all withdraw, and that they should take and keep the fortresses
on the frontiers until the King's government should be settled.
Instead of which, there were now two Prime Ministers, Talleyrand and Fouché, and three armies—the army of the Loire, the
remnant of Bonaparte's troops—an army forming under the
King's authority—and an army collected by the Duke d'Angoulême in the south, violently royalist and which had committed great excesses of reaction. The Duke d'Angoulême
had imprudently said that it would never be well with France
until they were all of the same religion; and at Nismes six
hundred Protestants had been massacred; they were hunted
like wild beasts, and great multitudes of them had been obliged
to fly from their habitations and take refuge in the Cévennes.
These enormous foreign armies were exhausting the country.
The rainy season would soon be setting in, and if they did not
take care they would then have as destructive a war to carry
on as the French had found in Spain.

As to these dangers to the foreign armies, they are so perfectly chimerical that they indicate only the General's old age.
The foreign armies are perfectly safe; but the measure of oppression upon the French people will exceed all bounds. I
asked Dumouriez whether he did not think they would finish
by making a Poland of France. He said, if they did, he should
only regret he was not thirty years younger. He spoke also of
the Duke of Orleans. In one of the letters which I returned to
him he had written, "Espérons toujours, non pas du cote du

faux Télémaque, que je vois ici quelquefois mais sans confiance, mais d'un autre côté." I had observed yesterday that he was very assiduous in paying his court to the "faux Télémaque;" and this day he spoke of him as if with the highest attachment; said he had brought him up; that he was like a child to him; that his sister, Mademoiselle d'Orléans, looked upon him (Dumouriez) almost as a father; that he had advised the Duke to go to France, as he lately did; that he had suffered there every species of mortification; that Court etiquettes had been raised to exclude his wife from the entrées, though she was a King's daughter; that the Duchess d'Angoulême had been mortified because the Duchess d'Orléans's parties had been crowded, while those at the Tuileries had been in a manner deserted. And lately, when they were fugitives here, the Duchess d'Angoulême said to the Duke d'Orléans that her husband was coming from Spain, but not to stay here—he would go immediately to join the King, "parceque c'est sa place." When the Duke went lately to France, they were going to send Princes of the blood to preside at the electoral colleges. Monsieur was at Paris, the Duke d'Angoulême at Bordeaux, the Duke de Berri at Lille. The Duke de Bourbon was to have gone to the Vendée, and the Duke d'Orléans to Lyons; but one obstacle after another had been raised, and the King had told the Duke of Orleans that the Duke of Bourbon could not go into the Vendée, and perhaps he might as well not go to Lyons. The Duke had then asked the King's permission to come to England again, which the King had immediately granted. He told me he was going to dine with the Duke of Orleans to-morrow.

We had a great variety of conversation upon other topics: upon the Emperor Alexander, who received him last summer at London, on the same day that he did Mr. Gallatin and Mr. Harris, and who, he says, has taken such a distaste to Russia that he will not return to St. Petersburg at all, but talks of staying with his army in Germany; of the King of Prussia, who he says is a good man, but entirely under the control of his Generals; that ten or twelve of them, Gneisenau, Kleist, Tauenzein, and others, have formed an association among themselves, a sort of self-created order of knighthood, which they call the order of *Virtue*. Blücher is of it, but has no weight or influence in it, Gneisenau being the effective man. As to their virtue, it means nothing more nor less than ambition and avarice. The spirit of conquest has taken possession of them, and they are for making Prussia now play the part which France played for ten or fifteen years.

28th. General Dumouriez returned my visit, and we had conversation about his former associates, Miranda and Eustace, who, he said, were both madmen, though of different kinds. As I had known them both since their military campaigns under his orders, I had several anecdotes to tell him of them, and he told me several others. Eustace was a mere " miles gloriosus," a sort of Ancient Pistol. After having been a French Major-General, he died, I believe, a volunteer aide-de-camp to General Hamilton. Miranda, after passing through a multitude of adventures, has come to a more tragical end. Dumouriez says he is either in a dungeon in Spain, or has been strangled in it. He says he shall come again to pay a visit to Mrs. Adams, with the Count and Countess of St.-Martin.

Pio[1] went this morning to London, and returned in the evening, with a packet which Mr. Grubb has had for me these three or four days. It contained dispatches from the Secretary of State, of the highest importance, dated 21st July last, with many enclosures, which have given me the heartache. They concur with all the events occurring here to aggravate the difficulties of my situation and of my duty.

September 14th. I went into London, and, as I had anticipated, found a note from Lord Bathurst appointing two o'clock this day to see me at Downing Street. It was then just two, and I went immediately to his office, and had an interview with him of about an hour.

I said that, having lately received dispatches from the American Secretary of State respecting several objects of some importance to the relations between the two countries, my first object in asking to see him had been to enquire whether he had received from Mr. Baker a communication of the cor-

---

[1] Mr. Adams's butler.

respondence between Mr. Monroe and him, relative to the surrender of Michilimakinac, to the proceedings of Colonel Nicolls in the southern part of the United States, and to the warning given by the captain of a British armed vessel to certain American fishing vessels to withdraw from the fishing grounds to the distance of twenty leagues from the coast.

He said that he had received all these papers from Mr. Baker about four days ago; that an answer with regard to the warning of the fishing vessels had immediately been sent; but on the other subjects there had not been time to examine the papers and prepare the answers.

I asked him if he could, without inconvenience, state the substance of the answer that had been sent. He said, certainly. It had been that as, on the one hand, Great Britain could not permit the vessels of the United States to fish within the creeks and close upon the shores of the British Territories, so, on the other hand, it was by no means her intention to interrupt them in fishing anywhere in the open sea or without the territorial jurisdiction—a marine league from the shore; and therefore that the warning given in the place stated in the case referred to was unauthorized.

I said that, the particular act being disavowed, I trusted the British Government, before adopting any final determination upon the subject, would estimate in candor, and in the spirit of amity which my own Government was anxious to have prevailing in our relations with this country, the considerations which I was instructed to present in support of the right of the people of the United States to fish on the whole coast of North America, which they have uniformly enjoyed from the first settlement of the country; that I should in the course of a few days address a letter to him on the subject.

He said that they would give due attention to the letter that I should send him, but that Great Britain had explicitly manifested her intention upon the subject; that there was a great deal of feeling on it in this country, as I doubtless knew, and their own fishermen considered it as an excessive hardship to be supplanted by American fishermen even upon the very shores of the British dominions.

I said that those whose sensibilities had been thus excited had probably not considered the question of right in the point of view in which it had been regarded by us; that the question of right had not been discussed at the negotiation of Ghent; that the British Plenipotentiaries had given a notice that the British Government would not hereafter allow the people of the United States to fish and cure and dry fish within the exclusive British territorial jurisdiction in America without an equivalent; that the American Plenipotentiaries had given notice in return that the American Government considered all the rights to the fisheries on the whole coast of North America as sufficiently secured by their enjoyment of them from the settlement of the country by them, and by the recognition of it in the Treaty of Peace of 1783; that they did not think any new stipulation necessary for a further confirmation of the right, no part of which did they consider as having been forfeited by the war. It was perfectly obvious that the Treaty of Peace of 1783 was not one of those ordinary treaties which by the usages of nations were considered as annulled by a subsequent war between the same parties. It was a treaty of partition between two parts of one nation, agreeing thenceforth to be separated into two distinct sovereignties. The conditions upon which this was done constituted essentially the independence of the United States, and the preservation of all the fishing rights which they had always enjoyed over the whole coast of North America was among the most important of them. This was no concession, no grant, on the part of Great Britain which would be annulled by war. There had been in the same Treaty of 1783 a right recognized in British subjects to navigate the Mississippi. This right the British Plenipotentiaries at Ghent had considered a just claim of Great Britain, notwithstanding the war that had intervened. The American Plenipotentiaries, to remove all future discussion on both points, had offered to agree to an article expressly confirming both the rights. In declining this, an offer had been made on the part of Great Britain stipulating to negotiate in future for the renewal of both rights *for an equivalent.* This was declined by the American Plenipotentiaries, because its only effect would have been an implied admission that both the rights were annulled. There was therefore no article concerning them in the treaty, and the question as to the right was not discussed. I now stated the ground upon which the Government of the United States considered the right as subsisting and unimpaired. It would be for the British Government ultimately to determine how far this reasoning was to be admitted as correct. There were also considerations of policy and expediency, to which I hoped the British Government would give suitable attention before they came to a final decision on this point. I thought it my duty to suggest them, that they might not be overlooked. The subject was viewed by my countrymen as highly important, and I was profoundly anxious to omit nothing which might possibly have an influence to promote friendly sentiments between the two nations or to guard against the excitement of others. These fisheries afforded the means of subsistence to multitudes of people who were destitute of any other. They also afforded the means of remittance to Great Britain in payment for articles of her manufacture exported to America. It was well understood to be the policy of Great Britain that no unnecessary encouragement or stimulus should be given to manufactures in the United States which would diminish the importations from those of Great Britain. But by depriving the fishermen of the United States of this source of subsistence, the result must be to throw them back upon the country and drive them to the resort of manufacturing for themselves, while, on the other hand, it would cut off the means of making remittances in payment for the manufactures of Great Britain. I might add that the people in America whose interests would be immediately and severely affected by this exclusion were in the part of the country which had always manifested of late years the most friendly dispositions towards Great Britain. This might perhaps be less proper for me to suggest than for a British Cabinet to consider. To me the interests of all my countrymen in every part of the United States were the same: I could know no distinction between them. But upon a point where I was contending for what we conceived a strict right, I thought it best to urge every consideration which might influence the other party to avoid a collision upon it. I would even urge considerations of humanity. I would say that fisheries, the nature of which was to multiply the means of subsistence to mankind, were usually considered by civilized nations as under a sort of special sanction. It was a common practice to leave them uninterrupted even in time of war. He knew, for instance, that the Dutch had been for centuries in the practice of fishing upon the coasts of this island, and that they were not interrupted in this occupation even in ordinary times of war. It was to be inferred from this that to interrupt a fishery which had been enjoyed for ages was itself an indication of more than ordinary animosity.

He said that no such disposition was entertained by the British Government; that, to show the liberality which they had determined to exercise in this case, he would assure me that the instructions which he had given to the officers on that station had been not even to interrupt the American fishermen who might have proceeded to those coasts within the British jurisdiction for the present year; to allow them to complete their fares, but to give them notice that this privilege could be no longer allowed by Great Britain, and that they must not return the next year. It was not so much the fishing as the drying and curing on the shores that had been followed with bad consequences. It happened that our fishermen, by their proximity, could get to the fishing stations sooner in the season than the British, who were obliged to go from Europe, and who, upon arriving there, found all the fishing places and drying and curing places preoccupied. This had often given rise to disputes and quarrels between them, which in some instances had proceeded even to blows. It had even disturbed the peace among the inhabitants on the shores, and for several years before the war the complaints to this Government had been so great and so frequent that it had been impossible not to pay regard to them.

I said that I had not heard of any such complaints before; but that as to the disputes arising from the competition of the fishermen, they could surely be easily made a subject of regulation by the Government; and as to the peace of the inhabitants, there could be no difficulty in securing that, as the liberty enjoyed by the American fishermen was in all settled and inhabited places expressly subjected to the consent of the inhabitants and by agreement with them.

I then adverted to other topics—Michilimakinac, Bois Blanc, and Colonel Nicolls. I asked him if he had any account of the delivery of the post.

He said he had no doubt whatever but that it had been long since delivered up. But he had no late dispatches from the Canadian Government. Some delay had occurred by the change of the Governor-General, by Sir George Prevost's leaving Quebec to come to Europe, and consequently by General Drummond's coming from Upper Canada to Quebec. As to the indisposition manifested by the Indians to accept the peace offered by the United States, he regretted it very much. It had been the sincere wish and intention of the British Government that the peace with the Indians should immediately follow that agreed to by this country; the British officers there had been formally instructed to make known to them the peace which had been concluded, and to advise them to take the benefit of it.

As to Colonel Nicolls, I said that the American Government had been peculiarly concerned at the proceedings of that officer, because they appeared marked with unequivocal characters of hostility.

" Why," said Lord Bathurst, " to tell you the truth, Colonel Nicolls is, I believe, a man of activity and spirit, but a very wild fellow. He did make, and send over to me, a treaty offensive and defensive with the Indians, and he is now come over here, and has brought over some of those Indians. I sent for answer that he had no authority whatever to make a treaty offensive and defensive with the Indians, and that the Government would make no such treaty. I have sent him word that I could not see him upon any such project. The Indians are here in great distress, indeed, but we shall only furnish them with the means of returning home, and advise them to make their terms with the United States as well as they can." Perceiving that I had noticed his declaration that he had declined seeing Colonel

Nicolls, he said that perhaps he should see him upon the general subject of his transactions, but that he had declined seeing him in regard to his treaty with the Indians.

I then observed that Mr. Monroe had also sent me his letter to Mr. Baker concerning the island of Bois Blanc. He said it seemed merely a question of fact whether the island had been in the possession of the British at the commencement of the late war or not. He did not know how that was, but he thought it could not be difficult to ascertain, and it was altogether of very little importance.

October 10th. I called and paid a visit to General Dumouriez. He began by asking me if we were quarrelling again with England, and asked what they meant by their proceedings with the Creek Indians. I said that one of their officers had been endeavoring to make mischief, by a pretended treaty, offensive and defensive, with the Creek Indians; but that the Government here had disavowed his conduct to me. He asked if it was not such a disavowal as that of 1755. I said that was what I could not tell. He thought we should not be long without another war with England, and that there would soon be a separation of the United States. As our population increased, he said, with such an immense territory, it would be too large for one Government. I said that, as our Government is federative, I did not see any necessity for a separation, which would be contrary to the interests of us all. He said that mankind seldom pursued the system of their interest, and he thought our Union could not hold together long. He also thought we should soon be encroaching upon the mines of New Mexico, and asked something about our establishment on the Columbia River. He spoke also of Canada, and the danger of the British Possessions in North America, by their vicinity to the United States; of the fur trade, and the diminution of the Indian hunting-grounds. On all these subjects he had some information, but it was all partial, and such as he had apparently imbibed from those with whom he converses concerning them here. In combating his prejudices, I did not expect to alter his opinions, nor would it, that I know, have been of any use if I had.

He passed to the subject of France, where, he said, everything was dark and gloomy. He read me an extract of a letter which he said he had just received, and which was from the Government here. It spoke of the treaty of peace just concluded between the allies and France—mentioned the conditions much as they are stated in the newspapers. But it appeared that he had advised the taking of Calais and Dunkirk by the English. The answer said that they had avoided asking for those places for fear of exciting too much jealousy, but they were to have Ostend, and would fortify it, so as to make it very strong. The General read to me also a letter from the Duke of Wellington, which he received a few days since, dated the 26th of September, and he gave me the copy of his answer to it, dated 4th October, and written on the blank pages of the second sheet of the Duke's letter, that was itself an answer to a previous letter from Dumouriez, in which, as he said, he reproached the Duke for the appointment of Fouché as Minister to the King of France. The Duke says that in prevailing upon the King to take Fouché he had followed the opinions of all the allies, who considered it as indispensably necessary; that when the allied armies advanced into France, the French army, which still existed, and a great part of the nation, were absolutely against the King; that four provinces were in open rebellion, and most of the rest, including the city of Paris, extremely cold; that the allies themselves were more than indifferent about the Bourbons, and Prussia in particular absolutely adverse to their restoration; that the employment of Fouché neutralized a very great party against the King, and gained over great numbers to the royal cause; that if he had not been employed, a great and terrible convulsion would have ensued (Dumouriez said, "Il se trompe beaucoup là"); that Fouché might perhaps have done many bad things, but not one-half so many as his slanderers laid to his charge; that he believed the King was satisfied with Fouché, but the courtiers, that *vile, useless*, and *pernicious* tribe ("Oh! pour cela," said Dumouriez, "il a bien raison"), after the crisis was over, had besieged the King, and finally prevailed upon his too yielding temper; that it was the party of the Princes which had con-

summated the mischief, and particularly the Duchess of An-
goulême, who, having arrived after the danger was over, could
not be persuaded that it had existed. ("That Duchess of
Angoulême!" said Dumouriez—"nothing can beat it out of her
head that France is to be governed 'comme au temps de St.
Louis.'") She (continued Wellington's letter) persuaded the
King to the injudicious step of changing his Ministry, and
I am sorry to add (says the letter), in that transaction the
King treated with "mauvaise foi" not only his own Ministry,
but the allies by whom he had been restored to his throne.

"Eh bien!" said Dumouriez, after reading the letter, "you
see that does not look like quiet times. Vous voyez que les
termes ne sont pas ménagés là. Now read my answer." And
he put it into my hands. The answer was full of flattering
compliments to the Duke upon the wisdom of the course he
had pursued, with great applause upon his invective against the
courtiers, and regrets that they had prevailed upon the "bon
Roi" to change the Ministry which the Duke in his wisdom
had given him. (This is characteristic, for the sentiments were
diametrically opposite to those that the writer had just expressed
to me in conversation.) It proceeded to say that what they were
doing would certainly not finish the affairs of France; that there
was great and very unfounded expectation in public from the
approaching assembly of the Legislative Chambers; that they
would begin with an apparent unanimity, and that very unanimity would be the greatest of deceptions; that upon some
occasion debates would very soon arise, in which the metals
would separate, and they would be then found to be of the
most discordant materials; that a reaction would sooner or
later take place, which would oblige him (the Duke) to put on
the harness again, as well as his venerable companion-in-arms
(Blücher), and which would throw Europe again into a flame;
that he wished the Duke before winter would take care to get
into his hands eight or ten fortresses (which he names), and
among them, and most especially, Calais and Dunkirk; so that,
in case of a new convulsion, forty or fifty thousand English
families now in France might have places of refuge into which
they could retire.

VOL. III.—18

I told Dumouriez I did not think there was any danger like that.

He said that the French nation would need the greatest and most persevering patience. They were now suffering other nations to cut their nails and draw their teeth, and were obliged to see it in quiet. It was necessary to wait until these defences should grow again, and patience was precisely that which the French nation wanted.

I asked him what he thought of the Duke de Richelieu as Prime Minister.

He said the Duke de Richelieu had been these twenty years in Russia; he had been Governor of Odessa, with perhaps sixty thousand souls under him, and two-thirds of them slaves; that it was said he had been a good Governor of a province in a despotism, but to make him Prime Minister of France seemed to him like saying to a man, " Sir, I have seen a very good song of your writing, have the goodness to write me a tragedy." He said that he had many other letters from France, and all painted the state of things in the most gloomy colors. As his dining-hour was come, I took leave of him, and he showed me his library, where he has a good collection of books.

November 24th. I dined at Mr. Vansittart's. The Lords Bathurst, Harrowby, Melville, and Tyrconnel, Baron Fagel, the Dutch Ambassador, and his brother, Baron Jacobi, the Prussian, and Mr. Bourke, the Danish, Minister, Mr. Neumann, the Austrian Chargé des Affaires, Lord Lowther, Mr. Beckett, the Under-Secretary of State for the Home Department, and several other gentlemen, chiefly, or all, foreigners, formed the company. I was seated at table between Lord Melville and Baron Jacobi, with both of whom I had various conversation. Lord Melville asked me several questions about the American squadron which had been at Gibraltar. He is the First Lord of the Admiralty, and has doubtless received particular information concerning it. There was much more general conversation than is usual at such parties, and it very much enlivened the company. The topics were indeed not very important—pedestrianism, boxing, cock-fighting, and a sort of historical commentary upon the house in which Mr.

Vansittart resides, and all the houses in the neighborhood, from Charles the Second, the Duke of Monmouth, and Nell Gwynn, down to Sir Robert Walpole. It was, on the whole, amusing, and there was much social good humor and conviviality. Mr. Vansittart mentioned after dinner that there was now here an American, named Edwards (but Lord Tyrconnel said it was Adams), who had been at Timbuctoo and remained there several months. He said it was a city about as large as Lisbon. He had brought nothing certain respecting Mungo Park, but several particulars tending to confirm the account of his death.

December 9th. I went into town with the view of meeting Mr. J. A. Smith. Mr. Grubb said a gentleman had called about half an hour before I arrived; he had a parcel of American newspapers for me, but had neither mentioned his name nor where he lodged. He had taken the direction of my house at Ealing, and said he would come out to-morrow morning.

10th. Mr. Smith came out about four o'clock. He brought me a bundle of newspapers from the Government, but not one line of dispatches. He had several letters for the family, two for me from my mother, dated 30th September and 23d October, and one from my father, of 22d October. The last from my mother encloses copies of two letters of recommendation of Mr. J. A. Smith for the office of Secretary to this Legation—one from Governor Tompkins, of New York, to President Madison, and the other from Judge W. P. Van Ness to Mr. J. P. Van Ness, of Washington. Smith had written also to me, to ask my recommendation, which I had declined to give, because I had already recommended Mr. A. H. Everett, and because I do not think that an American Secretary of Legation ought to be the nephew of the Minister at the same Court. As, however, the President has thought fit to appoint him, it becomes me to respect his decision.

18th. Dr. Nicholas called for us. He had appointed half-past five o'clock, and rather preceded his time. I found on the table a letter from Count Fernan Nuñez, the Spanish Ambassador, which I had not then time to read, and put in my pocket. Dr. Nicholas immediately took us to Mr. Knox, one

of the masters of the school (Westminster), whose first salutation upon seeing us was, that we could not all have places.
There were only four of us, including the Doctor, and we all
had tickets. After some coaxing, however, Mr. Knox finally
consented to take us all in, and when we were introduced I
was a little surprised to find there was nobody there. It was
about half an hour before the company began to come, and
half-past seven when the play began. The Duke of York was
expected, but he went this morning to Brighton. I saw there
Count Beroldingen, the Minister of Würtemberg, Count Jenison
Walworth, Secretary of the Bavarian Legation, and Mr. Hamilton, the Under-Secretary of State. The place fitted up for a
theatre was the dormitory of the King's scholars, and the names
of great numbers of the former pupils are painted in capitals
round the walls. It seems to be intended as a distinction, but
is done without taste or order, and in most instances, like the
Critics in the Temple of Fame, the new names are painted
over the old ones and efface them. The room was finally
crowded with company. The play performed was Terence's
"Andria." The prologue was very badly spoken, and was a
panegyric upon the discipline of the British schools, with a
due proportion of abuse upon France and Germany, all which
was very highly applauded. The orator had an impediment
in his speech, and could scarcely articulate. His gesture was
as ungracious as his pronunciation, and he made his bows like
a "Magot de la Chine"—all from the neck. Dr. Nicholas told
me that by an established custom the prologue must always be
spoken by the Captain of the school; it was therefore almost
always badly spoken, and was never expected to be otherwise.
The speaker of the prologue had no part in the play, which
was well performed; not better, however, than the "Adelphi"
had been at Ealing. The epilogue was a dialogue between
two of the personages of the play, in which Davus and Crito
make sport with some of the ridiculous things of the present
or recent times—the invisible lady, the Indian jugglers swal-
lowing swords, Joanna Southcote the pregnant old woman,
and, most of all, Dr. Gall and Spurzheim's craniology. It
was not altogether without wit and humor. The prologue and

epilogue were both spoken twice, a strange practice, for the convenience of the semi-Latinists, who can understand better with two hearings than with one. He (Dr. Nicholas) told me that he had attempted, when he began exhibiting these plays, to have these head and tail pieces spoken only once, but the repetition was called for by the spectators, and he had been obliged to conform to the Westminster usage. In our walk into the City this day I was struck with the gas-lights which are introduced in the streets and most of the shops in the neighborhood of the Mansion House. They are remarkably brilliant, and shed a light almost too dazzling for my eyes. They are also attended with an inconvenience of offensive smell, which I thought perceptible even in the streets, and they are thought to be unhealthy. For lighting streets, however, and open places, it is probable they will supersede the use of oil.

January 12th, 1816. I first went to the counting-house of the brothers Baring & Co., and saw Mr. Alexander Baring. We had some conversation upon general topics. I mentioned the approaching session of Parliament. He said it would pass off in perfect quietness. There was no opposition. The Ministers were firm as *rocks*.

I asked him whether something would not be said about the distress of the agricultural interest, of which we occasionally heard; how the revenue would stand, and whether they could give up the property tax.

He said, laughing, that the agricultural interest was, to be sure, in a bad state, but the revenue of the year would exceed that of the last. There had been, however, a falling off in the last quarter—not of the excise, but of the customs. As to the property tax, poor Vansittart was like the man with his wife—"Nec possum tecum vivere, nec sine te;" there was a clamor against the tax, which made it almost impossible for him to renew it, and yet he could not well do without it. He (Baring) had been writing him a letter yesterday, and proposed to him to take it off from the tenants, to leave it on the landlords and on the funds, reducing it to five per cent. This would yield about six millions. He would take six millions more from the sinking fund, and five millions from what

were called the war taxes. This would form an establishment
of about seventeen millions: more could not be necessary.
There never was a period when a small peace establishment
could have been more safe and easy than at this time; never
a period when the country was in such perfect security. The
army was for some years to be maintained by France, there
was no danger to be discerned from any quarter, and (laughing) your navy (said he) is the only one now formidable
to us, and more formidable than all the naval power in the
world beside. Seventeen millions a year, therefore, would be
sufficient for the peace establishment, and the ordinary revenue
of the country would be just sufficient to pay the interest of
the debt. As to the sinking fund, the forms must be observed;
it was to be left untouched in point of form; but loans of about
six millions every year must be made, which would intrench
so much upon it. For the last twenty years this country had
been borrowing, upon an average, twenty-five millions every
year. This, of course, had been collected from the savings of
the people. If now, from a borrower, the country should suddenly become a lender to the amount of eleven millions a year,
it would throw back upon the people a mass of capital without
employment, the effect of which must be to reduce the rate of
interest. It would be as he had known it in Holland, where
he had seen stocks, bearing an interest of two and a half per
cent., above par. He would leave about five millions of the
sinking fund still to operate, which would be as much as it
could without inconvenience. But he supposed we should
hear a great deal in Parliament about economy (laughing), retrenchment, and the like. The Ministry, he said, were very
good sort of people, and quite pacific in their disposition. Lord
Liverpool was a very worthy, amiable man; so was Lord Sidmouth. There was but one very warlike man among them,
and that was Lord Bathurst. It was entirely upon his suggestion that the troops from Spain had been sent over to Canada.
The expedition to New Orleans had been entirely a plan of his.

I said that the disposition upon both sides seemed at present
so pacific that I hoped we should have a long and quiet peace.
I was sorry, however, to hear that they were increasing their

armaments on the Lakes of Canada, because arming on one side would make it of course necessary to arm on the other, and we had been disposed, on the contrary, to disarm there.

He said their arming was the foolishest thing in the world, "for," said he, "we are 'the lamb' in Canada; it is in vain for us to think of growing strong there in the same proportion as America. But surely our Ministers will consent to disarm there on both sides."

I said they had always a sufficient security against a sudden attack upon Canada, by the exposed state of our commerce.

He replied that he wished the British Government would give us Canada at once. It was not worth Sir James Yeo's hundred-gun ship, and was fit for nothing but to breed quarrels.

I mentioned to him the series of articles in the Morning Chronicle against the late commercial convention, and, after speaking of their character and tendency, and of the perverse ability with which they were written, said I was a little surprised at the quarter from which they came. He had not seen the papers, but from the description that I gave of them he thought he knew whence they came; that Perry (editor of the Morning Chronicle) had formerly been under control, but now he was under none, and his main object doubtless was to worry the Ministers. He said he would collect the papers and read them.

15th. I was employed in making out from the first draft a note to Lord Castlereagh on the fisheries. How much to alter! how much to strike out! how much to add! My progress is slower with the fair copy than it was with the first draft.

16th. The journal for yesterday was so barren that I neglected writing it this morning, and resumed the Fishery note. But the further I advance in it the more dissatisfied I am with what I have done. There is in the note to which I reply much groundless assertion and much erroneous principle not bearing directly upon the point in controversy. I have in my first draft wasted argument in reply to these untenable positions. "Effacez souvent," is the advice of Boileau to the poets. It is very good advice for me, but I am not sure of my own judgment in acting upon it. I advanced only one page in my new copy.

25th. I gave up this morning to the business of the day, and, having a variety of subjects upon which I wished to confer with Lord Castlereagh, I made a minute of the principal points to be borne in mind, classing them under the different heads, and, to preserve the order of them, arranged them alphabetically—fixing upon a word which would immediately remind me of the whole subject—the initials of the word proceeding successively from A to J. This was an application of the principles of a technical memory which I had never made before, and which, for a first attempt, succeeded, not completely, but beyond my expectation. I have often experienced inconvenience in conferences of this kind, by forgetting, while engaged in the conversation upon some of the topics for which I had proposed the interview, others perhaps of equal importance, or, at least, observations that before the meeting I had intended to make, and which after the meeting I regretted to have omitted. I did not entirely escape the second of these "maladresses," but had less of it than I have often experienced, and none of the principal topics were omitted. In one instance the order of my arrangement was discomposed, much to my own satisfaction; for, as it was a subject upon which my instructions were to feel the pulse of this Government without committing my own, I was under some embarrassment how to introduce it. But it had an incidental connection with another subject which I had classed in order before it, and, as I was to disclose explicitly my instructions on the first point (Florida) and to speak entirely from myself on the other (South America), I had separated them, with an interval of two others between them. But in the midst of our discussion of the former, Lord Castlereagh himself introduced the latter, and more than compensated for the inroad upon my arrangements by relieving me from the awkwardness of entering upon the most delicate and difficult matter upon which I was to treat. I did not lose by this incident the clue of my alphabetical arrangement, which, though in appearance whimsical, I found decidedly useful.

I went into town immediately after breakfast, and was at Lord Castlereagh's door at half-past eleven, the hour that he had appointed for the meeting.   I sent away the carriage, with orders to come for me to Craven Street at four.   I was detained not five minutes in the antechamber, where I saw a young man, I suppose a private secretary, but not Planta.

Lord Castlereagh immediately received me in his library. He began upon the dampness and foulness of the weather; then enquired whether I resided in town; said Lady Castlereagh had made enquiries for Mrs. Adams, but was informed we were still in the country.

I enquired if he had any accounts this morning from the Prince Regent, who is laid up at Brighton with the gout.

He said the Prince was now free from pain, and recovering, but it had become at last, after shifting about for several days, a regular attack, and, as it had left him weak, his medical attendants had advised that Parliament, which is to sit on the 1st of February, should be opened by Commission, and that the Prince should remain ten days or a fortnight longer at Brighton before coming to town.   He said the Prince had exposed himself to the damp weather in going round with him to show him the place (the new Pavilion at Brighton), and afterwards to the Queen when she came.   The gout had been some days unsettled, but had finally fixed, and the attack, while it lasted, had been sharp.

We now entered upon the subjects for which I had requested the interview; and I shall give the dialogue to the best of my recollection as it passed, distinguishing the speakers respectively by the initials of their names.

A. I have observed by the public papers that your Lordship has received the ratification by the President of the United States of the commercial convention concluded in July last.

C. Yes; and the ratifications may be exchanged in a few days—or—I believe they were exchanged there—at Washington.

A. That was what I wished to enquire of your Lordship, having myself no advices from my Government since the ratification.

C. Yes, the ratifications were exchanged there.

A. At the time when that convention was concluded, the

full powers of the American Plenipotentiaries were much more extensive than the objects upon which it was found the parties could then come to an agreement, and, as my two colleagues were shortened for time and anxious to return to America, it was thought best to conclude what we could then adjust, and notice was given by us that further proposals might afterwards be brought forward by me for negotiation. The British Plenipotentiaries told us that their powers would be terminated by the convention then signed, and in case of a further negotiation they did not know whether it would be committed to them. I then informed them that I should not propose anything further without new instructions from my Government, and in that case should address myself through the regular channel of the Foreign Department. Since then I have received instructions directing me to make proposals for arrangements which I presumed could be settled only in the form of a treaty. Other proposals of negotiation had been made in the course of my correspondence here, during your Lordship's absence in France, by Lord Bathurst. I wished, therefore, now to enquire what are the views of his Majesty's Government in this respect—whether they are disposed to enter upon a new negotiation; and, if they are, whether they will consider the full power heretofore produced by my colleagues and me as competent for concluding an additional treaty, or will they expect me to produce a new power; and whether I shall treat with the same British Plenipotentiaries with whom we treated before, or with your Lordship.

C. Yes, I remember we thought it best then, for restoring harmony and good understanding between the parties, to get along as far as we could at that time agree, and to postpone everything upon which the different views of the two sides precluded an agreement. Our dispositions are now the same. We have with the utmost sincerity the desire to preserve and cultivate peace and harmony with you. But what are the subjects upon which you would propose a further negotiation?

A. Several. The first and most important is that relating to seamen—impressment—a subject which has heretofore been the greatest cause of the unfortunate differences between the two countries; about which there is much anxiety in America, and to which the attention of the Government of the United States is yet strongly riveted, as appears by the President's last message to Congress, in which he again recommends a law for confining the navigation of American vessels to American seamen.

C. Why, your Government is taking the right measures for removing the grounds of those differences—and I am glad to see it—by encouraging your own seamen, which is certainly a wise and proper policy. But it is a question to be considered, whether such measures as these, tending to take away the cause of dissension, will not be more effectual as a practical remedy for the evil than any arrangement which could be made by treaty. The British Government are, and always have been, ready and willing to discuss any proposal that can be offered for an arrangement by treaty, but the views as to the right of the two Governments are so opposite, the popular feeling is so strong and so irritable, on your side in one direction, and on ours in the other, that, while there is no practical operation of the inconvenience, perhaps it is not the best time for any formal stipulation concerning it.

A. There is another point of view, in which the present may be considered as the best time for an arrangement, as being a time when the passions on neither side will be interested to take part against it—a time of peace, when the whole subject may be considered coolly, and no irritable feelings would mingle with the discussion.

C. The public feeling on this subject is yet very keen. It will be better to wait for the effect of the full disclosure of the policy of your Government. It is a change from its policy heretofore, when foreign seamen were rather invited and encouraged into your service, and undoubtedly you had a very large body of British seamen in your ships. If the law passes, and is carried into effect, of confining your navigation to your own seamen, we shall have no occasion for taking our men from your ships, because there will be none to take. We shall always be ready to make such regulations as may guard the exercise of our rights from abuses.

A. The policy of the Government of the United States cannot be said to be changed. They have not indeed heretofore *excluded* foreign seamen from our service, but they never were encouraged or invited into it. Whatever number of British seamen there may have been in it were led to it by their own inclinations.

C. At least your former colleague, Mr. Gallatin, told me that your Government had *latterly* determined to pursue the policy of encouraging your own seamen.

A. But, my Lord, even this may be counteracted by the British Government. Since the discharge of the British navy, it has been alleged that great numbers of your seamen have gone into foreign services—many to the Russian, many to the American. I know not what foundation there may be for this, but it is notorious that you have vast numbers of seamen out of employ, and I have received two official requisitions from you to send home from London and Liverpool destitute American seamen most of whom came from your naval service, and many of whom have no proofs of being Americans. The second requisition came to me without any reply to the answer I had given to the first. I concluded that your Lordship had not seen my answer. I stated in it that many of the distressed American seamen who were, according to the Lord Mayor's representation, wandering about the streets of London, had just been discharged from the British naval service, and had stronger claims for relief from the British than from the American Government; that others had claims for small pensions upon this Government, and, if they went to America, were compelled to sell their annuities for two years' purchase. I had represented that I thought if those persons were to be sent to America, Great Britain ought to furnish them the means of receiving their pensions there. I had also alleged that the Lord Mayor's representation was in general terms—*numbers* of American seamen—and that when I was required to send Americans home they must be named, and some proof given that they are really Americans.

C. I have not seen your note on this subject, for it was received while I was in the country; but certainly these are very fair and proper subjects for consideration. I will attend to them.   It was impossible that so large a body of men as was discharged from the British navy, amounting to sixty or seventy thousand, should be thrown at once out of employment without some inconveniences.   London and Liverpool being our two principal seaports, an extraordinary proportion of them naturally resorted there, and for a time there were multitudes who could not find employment; many became burdens upon the public.   But commerce is now very flourishing, those people are gradually finding employment, and the incumbrance which they have occasioned was very temporary, and has nearly passed over.   The note founded upon the Lord Mayor's representation was a circular to the foreign Ministers, and the statement from the Mayor of Liverpool was of a number of Americans who had become burdensome to the parish.

A. Yes, my Lord; the number mentioned was twenty-six. I immediately wrote to the American Consul, requesting him to take measures for ascertaining who they were, and what their claims were as Americans.   I have his answer.   Of the twenty-six sent by the Mayor to his office, only nineteen presented themselves, and he had no means of compelling the attendance of the others.   Of the nineteen, only five had any document of any sort to show that they were Americans.   It is obvious, therefore, that if I am required to send to the United States every man who calls himself an American seaman in distress, the chances would be that numbers of British seamen might find their way there, contrary to the intentions of both Governments.

C. I will attend to the subject, and take the sense of the Government upon it.   As to the question respecting your power, if you declare that your Government considers that heretofore produced by you as yet in force, and you treat under instructions from them, I should not suppose there would be any necessity for you to produce a new power.

A. The next subject upon which I am directed to consult with his Majesty's Government relates to Canada, another source of disagreement heretofore, and which may be one of great and frequent animosities hereafter, unless guarded against by the vigilance, firmness, and decidedly pacific dispositions of the two Governments.   There are tendencies to continual dissensions, and even acts of hostility, in that quarter, proceeding from three causes—the Indians, the temper of the British local authorities, and the British armaments on the Lakes.   The post of Michilimakinac was surrendered not immediately after the peace, nor until late in the summer, and some of the British officers in Upper Canada were so far from entering into the spirit of their Government, which had in substance made a peace for the Indians, that they took no small pains to instigate the Indians to a continuance of hostilities against the United States.   The consequence was, that it remained long doubtful whether the Indians in that quarter would accept the peace that had been secured for them.   Mr. Monroe represented these circumstances in a letter to Mr. Baker.   I was instructed to repeat the representation here, and had interviews with Lord Liverpool and Lord Bathurst for that purpose.   They both gave me the strongest assurances that the intentions of this Government were sincerely pacific, and its earnest wish had been that the Indians should agree to the peace; that no detention of Michilimakinac had been authorized by its orders, and no instigation of the Indians against the United States had been warranted by it.   The fort was surrendered in July, and as soon as the Indians found they would not be supported by Great Britain in war, they manifested a readiness for peace, and I believe it has been with the tribes in that direction generally accomplished.   Other and more recent instances, however, of an unpleasant nature have occurred.   A British officer pursued, took, and carried away from the territory of the United States a deserter from his corps.   The officer himself was afterwards arrested within the American jurisdiction, tried, and, owing to the absence of a principal witness, was convicted only of a riot, and moderately fined.   An Indian with a party trespassing on the property of an American citizen at Gros Isle was killed in a boat, in the act of levelling his own musket at the American. And although this happened on the American territory, the British commandant at Malden offered a reward of four hundred dollars to any person for apprehending the man who had killed the Indian.   An American merchant vessel upon Lake

Erie had also been fired upon by a British armed vessel. But
a circumstance of still more importance is the increase of the
British armaments, since the peace, on the Canadian Lakes.
Such armaments on one side render similar and counter-arma-
ments indispensable on the other. Both Governments must
thus be subjected to a heavy and, in time of peace, a useless
expense, and every additional armament creates new and very
dangerous incitements to irritation and acts of hostility. The
American Government, anxious above all for the preservation
of peace, have authorized me to propose a reduction of the
armaments upon the Lakes on both sides. The extent of the
réduction the President leaves at the pleasure of Great Britain,
observing that the greater it is the more it will conform to his
preference, and that it would best of all suit the United States
if the armaments should be confined to what is necessary for
the protection of the revenue.

C. Does your Government mean to include in this proposition the destruction of the ships already existing there? As
to keeping a number of armed vessels parading about the
Lakes in time of peace, it would be absurd. There can be no
motive for it, and everything beyond what is necessary to guard
against smuggling is calculated only to produce mischief. The
proposition you make is very fair, and, so far as it manifests
pacific dispositions, I assure you, will meet with the sincerest
reciprocal dispositions of this Government. I will submit the
proposal to their consideration. But you know we are the
weaker party there. Therefore it was that we proposed at
Ghent that the whole Lakes should belong to one party—all
the shores; for then armaments would not have been necessary. Then there would have been a large and wide natural
separation between the two territories; and those, I think, are
the best and most effectual to preserve peace.

A. But the proposition at Ghent to which we objected was,
that the disarming should be all on one side. There was
indeed afterwards intimated to us by the British Plenipotentiaries an intention to make us a proposal so fair and reasonable
that it was thought no objection could be made against it. We
did suppose that it was this identical proposition which I am

now authorized to make. It was not, however, brought forward, nor was any explanation given by the British Plenipotentiaries of what they had intended by their offer. My instructions now do not explicitly authorize me to include in the agreement to keep up no armament the destruction of the vessels already there; but if this Government assents to the principle, there will be ample time to concert mutually all the details. What I could now agree to would be, to have no armed force actually out upon the Lakes, and to build no new vessels.

C. It so happened that just at the close of the war we were obliged to make extraordinary exertions there, and to build a number of new vessels to maintain our footing there.

A. But it is the new armaments *since the peace* which have necessarily drawn the attention of my Government.

C. You have so much the advantage of us by being there, immediately on the spot, that you can always, even in a shorter time than we can, be prepared for defence.

A. The stipulation to keep or build no new armed force during the peace would therefore be in favor of Great Britain, because the very act of arming would then be an act of hostility.

C. That is, there could be no arming until the war actually commenced, and then you would have such an advance of time upon us by your position that we should not stand upon an equal footing for defence.

A. Still, the operation of the engagement would be in favor of Great Britain. We should have our hands tied until the moment of actual war, a state which it is impossible should suddenly arise on our part. It is impossible that war should be commenced by us without a previous state of things which would give ample notice to this country to be prepared. She might then have everything in readiness to commence her armaments upon the Lakes at the same moment with us, and we should be deprived of the advantage arising from our local position.

C. Well, I will propose it to the Government for consideration.

A. At the other extremity of the United States the Indians occur again in an unpleasant manner. A certain Colonel Nicolls undertook after the peace to form a treaty offensive and defensive, and a treaty of navigation and commerce, with some runaway Indians, whom he chose to style the Creek Nation, and he formally notified these treaties to the agent of the United States with the Creeks, adding that he should hear more of them when they should be ratified here. Mr. Monroe complained of this conduct of Colonel Nicolls in a letter to Mr. Baker. I was instructed to make the same complaint here. I mentioned it to Lord Bathurst, who in the most candid and explicit manner *verbally* disavowed to me the proceedings of Nicolls. He said that Nicolls had made a pretended treaty, offensive and defensive, with the Indians, and had even brought some of the Indians; but that he (Lord Bathurst) had answered that assuredly no such treaty would be ratified or sanctioned by the Government. I had given my own Government information of the assurance, which I knew would give them the highest satisfaction. I mentioned the same affair in a letter to Lord Bathurst, of which no written notice has been taken. Whether any more formal disavowal of Colonel Nicolls's proceedings has been given in answer to the complaint through Mr. Baker, I do not know; but I speak of it now, because by the President's message I perceive that the conduct of the Indians in that part of the United States still threatens hostilities, and because there, as in the more northern parts, the Indians will certainly be disposed to tranquillity and peace, unless they have encouragement to rely upon the support of Great Britain.

C. I have no such treaties as those you mention among those that I am to carry down to Parliament.

A. This affair has given the more concern to the Government of the United States, because they have received strong and confident intimations from various quarters that there had been a cession of Florida by Spain to Great Britain.

C. As to that, I can set you at ease at once. There is not and never has been the slightest foundation for it whatsoever. It never has been even mentioned.

A. Your Lordship knows that such rumors have been long

in circulation, and that the fact has been positively and very circumstantially asserted in your own public journals.

C. Yes, but our public journals are *so* addicted to *lying*. No; if it is supposed that we have any little trickish policy of thrusting ourselves in there between you and Spain, we are very much misunderstood indeed. You shall find nothing little or shabby in our policy. We have no desire to add an inch of ground to our territories in any part of the world. We have as much as we know how to manage. There is not a spot of ground upon the globe that I would annex to our territories if it were offered to us to-morrow.

A. What your views in that respect may be generally, we do not think it our province to enquire; but we did think that, with dominions so extensive and various as those of Great Britain, she could not wish for such an acquisition as that of Florida, unless for purposes unfriendly to the United States, and hence it was that these rumors have given concern to the American Government. I am sure they will receive with much pleasure the assurance given me by your Lordship that no such cession has been made.

C. None whatever. It has never been mentioned, and, if it had, it would have been decisively declined by us. Military positions may have been taken by us during the war, of places which you had taken from Spain, but we never intended to keep them. Do you only observe the same moderation. If we should find you hereafter pursuing a system of encroachment upon your neighbors, what we might do defensively is another consideration.

A. I do not precisely understand what your Lordship intends by this advice of moderation. The United States have no design of encroachment upon their neighbors, or of exercising any injustice towards Spain.

C. You may be sure that Great Britain has no design of acquiring any addition to her possessions there. Great Britain has done everything for Spain. We have saved, we have delivered her. We have restored her Government to her, and we had hoped that the result would have proved more advantageous to herself as well as more useful to the world than it has been. We are sorry that the event has not altogether answered our expectations. We lament the unfortunate situation of her internal circumstances, owing to which we are afraid that she can neither exercise her own powers for the comfort and happiness of the nation, nor avail herself of her resources for the effectual exertion of her power. We regret this, but we have no disposition or desire to take advantage of this state of things to obtain from it any exclusive privilege for ourselves. In the unfortunate troubles of her colonies in South America, we have not only avoided to seek, but we have declined, every exclusive indulgence or privilege to ourselves. We went even so far as to offer to take upon us that most unpleasant and thankless of all offices, that of mediating between the parties to those differences. We appointed a formal mission for that purpose, who proceeded to Madrid; but there the Court of Spain declined accepting our offer, and we have had the fortune of displeasing both the parties by refusing to interfere in support of either.

A. The policy of the American Government towards Spain has been hitherto precisely the same. They have not, indeed, made any offer of their mediation, because the state of the relations between them and the Spanish Government neither warranted nor admitted of such an offer. But they have observed the same system of impartial neutrality between the parties. They have sought no peculiar or exclusive advantage for the United States, and I am happy to hear from your Lordship that such is the policy of Great Britain; as that of the United States may, and probably will, be influenced by it and co-operate with it.

C. I have always avowed it to be our policy in Parliament. We have never acknowledged the Governments of the South Americans, because that would not have comported with *our* views of neutrality. But we have never prohibited the commerce of our people with them, because that was what Spain had no right to require of us. Our plan in offering the mediation which Spain rejected was, that the South Americans should submit themselves to the Government of Spain as colonies, because we thought she had the right to authority over them as the mother country; but that she should allow them commerce with other nations. Nothing exclusive to us: we neither asked nor would have accepted any exclusive privileges for ourselves. We have no little or contracted policy, but we proposed that Spain should allow a *liberal* commercial intercourse between her colonies and other nations, similar to that which we allow to our possessions in India.

A. And what does your Lordship think will be the ultimate issue of this struggle in South America? that Spain will subdue them, or that they will maintain their independence?

C. Everything is so fluctuating in the councils of Spain, and generally everything so dependent upon events not to be calculated, that it is not possible to say what the result may be. Our policy must be founded upon the actual state of things, and be shaped according to events as they may happen.

A. There is another subject, not indeed for discussion upon a new treaty, but relating to the execution of that of Ghent, upon which my instructions are very urgent.

C. Stay. Let me take a minute of what we have been speaking about. There were, the seamen, impressment, and the notes on the distressed seamen now at London and Liverpool; Canada, and the proposal to disarm; Colonel Nicolls. There was something else, was there not?

A. Only my question as to the full power.

C. Ah, yes (and after making the minute on the paper); as to what I have said to you with regard to Spain and the situation of her internal affairs and the conduct of her Government, I have spoken with the most perfect freedom and openness. I wish you, therefore, to understand it as confidential, and, if you report it to your Government, to give it as such.

A. Certainly, my Lord; and I wish what I have said to you on the subject to be also received as confidential. The subject on which I wish now to urge the further consideration of this Government relates to the slaves. There are three branches of it, which have formed points of discussion between the two Governments.

First, the slaves carried away from the United States by the British commanders, contrary, as the American Government holds, to the express stipulation of the Treaty of Ghent. It was complained of by Mr. Monroe to Mr. Baker. I spoke of it to your Lordship before you went to France. I afterwards addressed a letter to you concerning it, to which I have received an answer from Lord Bathurst. It came to me at a time when I was confined by illness and for several weeks could not write. I have not yet replied to it, but shall shortly. It seems, indeed, to intimate that this Government has taken its final determination on the matter, but I hope it is not so. I hope they will give it further consideration. It has given so much anxiety to my Government . . . it is urged so constantly and so earnestly in my instructions . . . the language of the treaty appears to us so clear and unequivocal, the violation of it in the carrying away of the slaves so manifest, and the loss of property occasioned by it to our citizens is so considerable and so serious, that I cannot abandon the hope that you will give it further consideration, and ultimately, to the United States, satisfaction.

C. I have not seen the correspondence that has passed relating to it. I will have it looked up, and examine it. (He made a minute of it on his paper.)

A. There is a special representation concerning eleven slaves taken away from a Mr. Downman by the violation of a flag of truce sent ashore by Captain Barrie. I have also received from Lord Bathurst an answer to this complaint, to which I shall reply. The answer states that the complaint was referred to Captain Barrie to report upon it, and gives the substance of Captain Barrie's report. It does not disprove any of the facts alleged by Mr. Downman, but Captain Barrie was himself the person who sent the flag of truce and responsible for the violation of it. As a general principle, it can scarcely be expected that satisfaction for an injury can ever be obtained if the report of the person upon whom it is charged is received as a conclusive answer to the complaint.

C. I suppose the complaint itself was only the allegation of an individual, and naturally reference must be made to the officer complained of for his answer to the charge.

A. The documents that I furnished in Downman's case did not consist of his allegations only. There are affidavits of several other persons, taken indeed ex parte, because they could not be taken otherwise. But they are full, and strong to the points both of the violation of the flag and of the carrying away of the slaves.

C. I do not know how we could proceed otherwise, unless, if the matter were of sufficient importance, a commissioner from each of the two Governments might be authorized to examine —but I have not seen the papers. I will look into them.

A. The other point concerning slaves relates to the charge contained in the instructions from the American Secretary of State to the Plenipotentiaries at Ghent, that sales had been made in the West Indies of slaves taken in the United States.

C. I do not think it was possible; the law prohibits it expressly.

A. I am not now speaking with regard to the fact, but respecting the allegation of it. On the publication of the instructions, the British Plenipotentiaries applied to those of the United States for the evidence in support of the charge. Admiral Cochrane addressed a letter to Mr. Monroe containing the same requisition. There was a correspondence on the subject between Mr. Monroe and Mr. Baker, and it was noticed here in Parliament. As the charge itself had been made in the midst of the war, the American Government had not expected that it would be a subject of discussion after the peace. And as it involved many circumstances of an unpleasant nature and irritating tendency, they would have preferred that, as between the two Governments, it should be by mutual consent laid aside and nothing further said about it. At the same time, they were ready to communicate such evidence as they could collect of the fact, if that course should be preferred by this Government. I made the proposal of both alternatives last summer to the Earl of Liverpool, who appeared to prefer that the evidence should be produced. I have now received a considerable mass of it, and if your Lordship also thinks it the best course I will furnish copies of it; but I would rather repeat the proposal of dropping the subject altogether.

C. So far as there may be anything of an irritating nature in it, we have no wish or intention to pursue the enquiry any further. If the American Government in the heat of war and under the feelings of that state have advanced a charge upon our officers beyond what the proof of facts will bear them out, we have no thought or wish to carry the discussion of it into the state of peace; and in that point of view would willingly dismiss it. As between the Governments, therefore, we set it altogether aside, and assure you that it shall have no effect whatever on our friendly dispositions. But with regard to the fact, we are obliged to ask for the evidence of it; because, if established, it affects the character of our officers and the observance of our laws. Perhaps it may be well if you and Mr. Hamilton would go over the evidence together. If the fact is ascertained, the officers who have been guilty of it should be punished; if otherwise, it should be known, for the vindication of their individual characters.

A. In the charge as made by the American Secretary of State, no individual officer was named. In the documents which I have received, several officers are named. The papers are voluminous, but I will have the copies of them made out as soon as possible. From one of the papers, it appears that slaves taken as prize are actually sold.

C. They are not sold as *slaves*. By the Act of Parliament, all those that are taken in the vessels that carry on the slave-trade by contraband are committed to the care of certain conservators; but they are not slaves.

A. The documents that I possess may perhaps induce his Majesty's Government to pursue the investigation further. That which the American Government *can* obtain in the places where the sales were alleged to have been made must be imperfect. It has no control over the local authorities, but for a full and satisfactory investigation the co-operation of both Governments is necessary. The mode suggested to me, and already proposed by Mr. Monroe to Mr. Baker, was, that the American Government would furnish lists of the slaves taken during the war, and in most instances the names of the vessels into which they were taken, and then——

C. We can show what disposal was made of them. Yes, I see no objection to that course.

A. Another subject, which I barely mention now, is that concerning the fisheries. I left here a day or two since a note in reply to one from Lord Bathurst, received while I was confined and unable to write.

C. I have received your note, and read it last evening.

A. I speak of it because there was in Lord Bathurst's note a proposal to negotiate on this subject.

C. Yes; we adhere to our construction and understanding in regard to the treaty, because it involves our rights of territorial jurisdiction; but we do not wish you to be prevented from fishing, and shall readily enter into arrangements on this point.

A. I wrote your Lordship a note respecting a discrimination made in the ports of Ireland between British and American vessels in respect to the number of passengers they are allowed to take. I received a note from you in answer, to which I replied.

C. Probably the regulation to which you refer may have been adopted before the commercial convention was concluded. We might, however, question the application of it to the case, as the convention was not intended to interfere with any restrictions under which we may think proper to prevent emigration from Ireland.

A. I hope I have not been, and shall not be, understood as objecting to the regulation at all as a restriction upon emigration. That must be entirely discretionary with the British Government. We have nothing to say about it. But it is the discrimination between the shipping of the two countries of which I complained—the allowance to British vessels to take five passengers for the same tonnage which in American vessels is limited to two. I presume that an order to the port officers would remove the distinction.

C. I don't know that. It may be made by Act of Parliament, and we might question your right to consider passengers as articles of merchandise. We may regard the discrimination itself as a mode of restriction upon emigration. You do not want our people.

A. Not at all. We increase fast enough by the progress of our own native population.

C. No! Our seamen and our people, . . . you really do not want them, and when they *do* go, you get only the worst part of them.

A. Why, in that case, my Lord, you ought to be much obliged to us for relieving you from them.

C. I don't know. However, we shall see what there is to be done.

A. I have been requested to obtain authenticated copies of certain papers in the Colonial Office—the commission and instructions issued to Arthur Dobbs, as Governor of North Carolina, some time before the American Revolution.

C. Write me a private note, mentioning what the papers are, and I will speak to Lord Bathurst about it.

A. Mr. Smith has lately arrived here, and will be desirous of being presented at Court when the Prince Regent returns to town. Will it be necessary to make a written application for that purpose?

C. No; bring him on the first levee day with you to Carlton House.

A. There may perhaps be other American gentlemen desirous of being presented. Will any application be necessary for them?

C. None at all; bring them with you to the levee, and you may be always sure that any person presented by you will be well received.

To this I made my acknowledgments, and took my leave, after a conference of nearly two hours.

30th. The weather was clear and cold, and I took the occasion for a longer walk than I have taken for several days, and also to pay a visit to my neighbor, General Dumouriez. We had much conversation upon various topics.

He appears to have abandoned his expectations of being recalled to take upon him the administration of affairs in France, and he disapproves of what has been done and is doing there. His opinions with regard to the future I think erroneous. He says there will be a great and concerted insurrection there within two or three months, "et tout sera perdu, et là et dans le reste de l'Europe." There is, however, no positive confidence to be given that this is his real opinion. He spoke in the highest terms of the Duke of Orleans, who, he said, was a "parfaitement honnête homme," of whom he boasted as of his "élève," and whom, he said, he now saw every week. The Duke, he said, sometimes came to see him, and sometimes sent his carriage for him. The Duke had given him the fullest account of his own proceedings, of the motive upon which he had come over to England last, and of his still remaining here, all which he repeated over to me. The causes of it were—1, the general jealousy of all the reigning part of the Bourbon family against him; 2, the special jealousy of the Duchess of Angoulême against him and his wife for having children while she herself is barren; 3, the disposition of all the discontented people in France to make him a rallying-point, and the danger to which he must be exposed in that situation; and 4, his disapprobation of the system now pursued by the Government, which brought him in opposition from the first moment when he took his seat in the House of Peers. The Princes his cousins, who were stupid, insignificant men, and excessively disliked, had been in point of form civil enough with him, and told him that although they disagreed in opinions they might yet remain very good friends. But he very wisely had not trusted to their assurances, but had gone candidly to the King, told him explicitly the dilemma of his situation, and informed him of his wish to return to England, of which the King had fully approved.

Dumouriez said that Monsieur had given himself up entirely to devotion, but was universally disliked; that the Duke d'Angoulême was a good sort of a man, totally insignificant; that the Duke de Berri was a "mauvais sujet," addicted to the lowest and vilest debauchery, and had assumed a tone with the army which had given universal disgust; and that the Duchess d'Angoulême, bigoted and vindictive as she was, had all the sense and all the spirit of the family. He said that the two Houses had got along badly enough, but it was now very soon "que les grandes douleurs vont venir"—now that money was to be raised not only for all the other exigencies of the country, but forty millions of francs, every three months, to be paid to foreigners.   He spoke with strong disapprobation of the vindictive measures now pursued against the revolutionary characters, and censured the conduct of the Duke of Wellington.   He also gave me many particulars of the history of the new French Ambassador, the Marquis d'Osmond, and his daughter, Madame de Boigne.   He says the Duke de la Châtre is "au désespoir" at being recalled, and thinks he will remain in this country upon his pension or half-pay as Colonel of a regiment in the British service.   Dumouriez said he had not been into London these three months, and that he scarcely ever went from home.

February 18th.   I was obliged to go to London this morning, and Mr. J. A. Smith went with me.   He left me at Hyde Park corner, and I went first to the Austrian Ambassador, Prince Esterhazy, in Stratford Place.   The Archdukes were then at mass at his house, but it finished soon after.   I saw the Prince for a few minutes, and he went with me to the house where the Archdukes reside.   I there found Count St. Julien, our old acquaintance, and Baron Jacobi, the Prussian Minister, was in the drawing-room.   The Dutch Ambassador, Baron Fagel, came in shortly afterwards.   The Austrian Consul and another gentleman were likewise there.   We were all introduced to the Archdukes John and Louis, brothers of the present Emperor of Austria.   They were in plain undress frock-coats, as were all the visitors excepting Baron Fagel, who was full dressed.   The Archdukes are young men apparently between twenty-five and thirty.   They have been travelling in England and Scotland since the month of October, and are to leave this country about the end of the month.

Count St. Julien told me where all the Secretaries of his old Legation at St. Petersburg now are—Lebzeltern at Rome, Maréchal in the army, Berks at Copenhagen, and Sturmer in France, where he is just married, and is coming to England to embark for St. Helena, to be the Austrian Commissioner, or, as St. Julien said, laughing, to be one of Bonaparte's jailers and fellow-prisoners.   I spoke to St. Julien about our old colleague Bussche, and asked him, if he should have an opportunity, to say a good word for him to Count Munster, the Hanoverian Minister.   I told him what Bussche had written

to me, and the difficulties in which he is now involved. He
promised to speak to Count Munster, and to give testimony in
his favor. From the Archdukes' I went and called at Mr.
Alexander Baring's house, in Portman Square; but he was
not at home, and I left a card. Thence to the Portuguese
Minister's, where I left the two letters for Rio Janeiro, received
the other day from Mr. Jackson at Paris. I then called at
Fenton's Hotel, St. James Street, and saw Lord Kinnaird,
with whom I found Mr. Benjamin Constant. He went away
immediately afterwards. Lord Kinnaird gave me one of his
pamphlets which he is publishing, concerning his having been
ordered to quit France. It is a letter to the Earl of Liverpool.
While I was with him, his publisher, Ridgway, came in. He
corrected some typographical errors, and said he had promised
to review Mr. Hobhouse's letters from Paris.

19th. I had barely time to dress and go to the Mansion
House, to the party given by the Lord Mayor and the Lady
Mayoress to the Archdukes John and Louis of Austria. All
the Princes of the blood royal, the Ministers of the country,
and the Foreign Ambassadors had been invited; but there
were present only the Duke of Kent, none of the Ministers
of State, the Austrian Ambassador, the Ministers of Bavaria,
Portugal, Würtemberg, and myself. The rest of the company
consisted of Lord and Lady Torrington, and the aldermen and
other City officers, their wives and daughters. About sixty
sat down to table. Mr. Braham was there to sing, and Mr.
Perry, the editor of the Morning Chronicle—I suppose, to
publish an account of the entertainment. The dinner was
good, the wines generally indifferent.

Several singular City usages were observed. The preliminary to the drinking of the toasts was by two large gold or
gilt cups being brought, and the Lord Mayor and Lady
Mayoress drank from them to the health of all their company,
a clerk or steward behind the Lord Mayor addressing by
name all the principal guests and announcing that the Lord
Mayor and Lady Mayoress drank to them all in "loving cups."
The same cups were then passed round to all the company,
and every guest in turn drank from them. Two basins and

ewers were afterwards brought and passed round in the same way to all the company. Rose-water was poured into the basin from the ewer, and every guest in turn, after the Lord Mayor and Lady Mayoress, dipped a corner of his napkin into the basin and wiped his lips. Then came the toasts, the paper of which was given to the Duke of Kent, who arranged their order. The King. The Prince Regent. The Queen and Royal Family. The Emperor of Austria. The Arch-dukes John and Louis, successively. The Duke of Kent. The Emperor of Russia and King of Prussia, whose Ministers were not present. (This toast was given by Prince Esterhazy, the Austrian Ambassador.) The King of Bavaria. The King of Würtemberg. The Prince Regent of Portugal; and The United States of America.

At these toasts, all except the first, there were cheers of three times three. After the first, Braham sang "God save the King," and after "The Queen and Royal Family," another song. For this time "Rule Britannia" was omitted. At the four or five first toasts, the steward behind the Lord Mayor repeated the call of names of the guests, and announced the toast. The ladies then retired; after which the Lord Mayor announced some of the toasts, and the Duke of Kent the others. When "The Archduke John" was given, he gave in return, "The Lord Mayor and the City of London;" "The Archduke Louis" (by Prince Esterhazy), "The Duke of York, and the British army." The Duke of Kent gave, "The Lady Mayoress." The Bavarian Minister, in return for his King's health, "The British nation, which assists all nations." The Würtemberg Minister, "Perma-nency to the general peace." The Portuguese Minister, "The Duke of Wellington and the British army in Portugal."

The Duke of Kent gave, "The United States of America, and perpetuity to the friendship between Great Britain and them." On which, addressing the Lord Mayor, I said that, sensibly affected as I was by the honor done by his Royal Highness to my country by the toast he had given, it was impossible for me to do more than to echo the sentiment he had expressed. I would ask leave therefore to offer, in a twofold manner, the earnest wish I entertained that between the ancient and the new hemisphere there may henceforth be no division other than that of the ocean, and that the harmony between Great Britain and the United States may be as lasting as the language and the principles common to both.

This was very well received, and the company immediately afterwards rose in good humor from table. The company passed then into the Egyptian Hall, where there was a ball of four or five hundred persons. I met a Mr. Sharp, whom I had seen last summer at Earl Grey's, and who now told me that he had just obtained a seat in Parliament. I had some conversation with him, and with Mr. Perry. It was about two in the morning when I left the Mansion House.

There was an important debate in both Houses of Parliament this evening, upon the treaties, which was the cause why all the Ministers of State, and almost all the members of both Houses, were absent.

27th. At the Mansion House I found a large company assembled—ladies and gentlemen. It was a dinner to the Company of Fishmongers, of which the Lord Mayor himself is a member. As soon as I went in, I was accosted by the Duke of Sussex, who recollected the old acquaintance we had at Berlin. The Lord Mayor introduced me to the Duke of Kent, the Marquis of Lansdowne, Lord Holland and Lord Erskine, Sir Edward Hamilton, a naval officer, the Prime Warden of the Company, and other gentlemen. Mr. Sharp was likewise there. The company consisted of about fifty persons, nearly half of whom were ladies. I was the only foreign Minister, and, I believe, the only foreigner, present. Lord Holland apologized for not having returned my visit, but I told him I resided out of town. He recollected having seen me in 1800, at Dresden, which he said he supposed I had forgotten; though I certainly had not.[1] The Prime Warden told me that the Company of Fishmongers would themselves give a dinner before long at their hall, to which they should invite me.

The dinner this day was much like that to the Archdukes, though not quite so formal. The loving cups and the rose-water passed round after dinner, and the toasts were announced

[1] See vol. i. pp. 240–241.

in the same manner. "The American Minister" was given next after the Dukes of Kent and Sussex, and my own toast at the former dinner was repeated verbatim by the Duke of Kent. In thanking the Lord Mayor for the honor done me by the toast, as well as by his friendly invitation to this social meeting, I reminded him of the observation made by a distinguished and ingenious traveller in the United States, a foreigner. He had remarked that from the moment when an Englishman landed in the United States he still found himself at home, while a foreigner of every other nation, whatever length of time he resided in America, still felt himself a stranger. It was my earnest wish that the first part of this observation might ever prove to be true, and I would add the hope that it might also prove reciprocal. I would say, therefore, May every Briton who sets his foot in America, and every American who visits England, still find himself at home!

This was very well received, though not so remarkably well as my former toast, perhaps because, according to the regular etiquette of these symposia, my toast should have been, "The Lord Mayor and the City of London." The Duke of Kent, when toasted, gave, "The Lady Mayoress." The Duke of Sussex, "Miss Wood." The Marquis of Lansdowne, "Lord Holland and Lord Erskine." Sir Edward Hamilton, the Prime Warden, and the Company of Fishmongers were all toasted, and the Lords and gentlemen all returned thanks with short speeches.

Mr. Sharp told me that he had not yet taken his seat in Parliament, because the writ was not returned. He also told me that my father had sent him a copy of my lectures. The Duke of Sussex was in fine spirits, and recollected many circumstances which had occurred while we were at Berlin. He frequently mingled the political topics of the day in his conversation, and pronounced his decided opposition to the continuance of the property tax, and to the proposed large military establishment. He offered himself to present any petition against the property tax to the House of Peers, and almost canvassed to be made a member of the Fishmongers' Company. All the noblemen present are members (honorary) of the

Company, and so are the Duke of Gloucester and Earl St. Vincent, both of whom had been invited to the dinner, but sent excuses, the Duke having lost a near relation, and Lord St. Vincent had met with some accident.

The Duke of Kent was more reserved than his brother, and talked no politics at all. He told, however, some humorous anecdotes about the Duke of Sussex, and said that he had been intended for the navy, and afterwards for the Church. He was to have been Bishop of Durham, but they set him to write a sermon, to see what his disposition for the Church was, and instead of a sermon he produced a composition of a very different kind. The Duke of Kent appealed to him to say himself if it was not so.

He answered that he had certainly no vocation for the Church. He said to me that he prided himself especially upon the stability of his sentiments, and asked me if I did not find him precisely the same man that I had known him at Berlin sixteen years ago.

I assured him that I was very confident his name would never appear in the "Dictionnaire des Girouettes."

The Duke holds forth a little too much of his opposition, and he appears too much occupied with himself. He said he heard they had been caricaturing him; he had not seen the caricature, but he was told they had represented him standing on the tomb of Charles the First, singing psalms. The last part he had no particular predilection for, but he broadly hinted that he did not disapprove the execution of Charles the First. One of his toasts was, " May our family never forget the principles which placed us in the situation which we hold in this country!" which, of course, was received with great applause.

Lord Holland was toasted as " the nephew of Charles Fox," and Lord Erskine, with "trial by jury." Lord Holland is yet a popular champion, but Erskine has become a pliable courtier; he answered feebly the toast to him, and his answer was received with faint applause. Lord Holland said that, as the nephew of Mr. Fox, there was no merit in him for adhering to his principles, but it would make him doubly contemptible if he should abandon them; which was received with high approbation. As soon as the Duke of Sussex withdrew, I left the Mansion House, and reached home about half-past one in the morning.

March 1st. After breakfast we went into London. I stopped at Lord Castlereagh's, and he received me. He apologized for not having yet answered my late notes, as having been unwell, and much pressed with business in Parliament. I told him there was but one of them which required immediate attention, and that was the one relating to the discrimination between British and American vessels in Ireland. Since my last note to him on that subject I had received a new statement from Ireland, upon a representation from several masters of American vessels now at Londonderry, waiting for a decision of this Government, and who, if that should be against them, would be obliged to go away in ballast, or to come to this country for freight. He enquired how it was in America with regard to the execution of the convention of 3d July last, and mentioned the account he had seen in the newspapers, that the bill for carrying it into effect, passed by the House of Representatives, had been rejected by the Senate.

I told him that I had received no communication from the Government on the subject, but the convention having been ratified was, by the Constitution of the United States, the supreme law of the land, and the introduction and the failure of the bill in question could only proceed, as indeed it was stated in the newspapers, from a difference of opinion between the two Houses as to the mode of giving effect to the convention.

He asked if, in the mean time, the convention was actually carried into effect; and if so, from what time the execution had commenced.

I said I had no doubt it was in full execution, for, as it was the law of the land, the extra duties upon British vessels could not be levied in contravention to it. As to the time when it had commenced, I could not say. The purport of the convention was, that when ratified it should be binding upon the parties for four years from the time of the signature. This variation from the usual term of commencement, the exchange

of ratifications, had been introduced at the desire of the British
Plenipotentiaries, and I had some conversation concerning it
soon after the conclusion of the convention—first, transiently,
with Mr. Robinson, who had been one of the British Plenipotentiaries, and afterwards with the Earl of Liverpool. For
some time after the signature an extra duty upon cotton
imported in American vessels had been levied. An Order of
Council had then issued, placing the vessels of the two nations
on the same footing. My own opinion had been that the convention was binding on both parties from the day of the signature, and that whatever duties contrary to it had been levied
must be refunded. I had communicated all these circumstances to the American Government, and had received for
answer, that the President had not issued a proclamation corresponding to the Order in Council, because the Order had
never been communicated, and because it did not extend to
tonnage duties; that the convention would be ratified, and
after that, if there was any diversity of opinion as to the time
of its commencement, it might be arranged by a mutual understanding between the two Governments.

"But, then," said Lord Castlereagh, "there is yet something
to be done to carry the convention into effect, and I will ask
Mr. Robinson to appoint some time when I will ask you to
see him and come to some arrangement about it, particularly
as there would be a great inconvenience in refunding duties
already collected. In the mean time we will endeavor to settle
this matter in Ireland without touching upon the question as
to the right—either by enlarging the privilege of American
vessels to take a number of passengers in equal proportion
with British vessels, or by reducing the numbers that British
vessels may take to the same proportion to which American
vessels are restricted."

I said that in either case we should be satisfied; but it was
necessary the vessels of the two countries should be placed on
the same footing, particularly as I was now given to understand
that the discrimination extended to the amount of the cargo as
well as to the number of the passengers. It was by an Act of
Parliament described to me as being known by the name of the

" Passengers Act," but I had not seen it, and knew not when it had passed or what were more particularly its provisions.

With regard to the extra duties levied at the Trinity House, Lord Castlereagh said it was not in the power of the Government to remove them. They had been laid for the maintenance of light-houses. The Trinity House was specially privileged to collect them, and they were not considered as among the duties and charges contemplated by the convention.

I told him that as we had similar charges for the maintenance of light-houses, the principal object must be to have a decision, as the principle must of course be reciprocal. I then observed that it was announced in the newspapers that the Queen would hold a drawing-room next Thursday, and I had thought it probable her Majesty might fix that time to grant me an audience. She had appointed a time for that purpose at the last drawing-room which she held in the autumn, upon the arrival of the Austrian Archdukes. I was then confined to my house by illness, and could not avail myself of her Majesty's condescension. I wished also to know whether Mrs. Adams would be received by the Queen at the same time, and, as she must ask the favor of Lady Castlereagh to present her, she wished to know when it would be convenient to her Ladyship to see her.

He said he believed the paragraph in the newspaper was a mistake; that the Queen would hold no drawing-room next week, nor until after the Prince Regent's return to town; that he hoped the Prince would return next week; he was entirely recovered from the gout, but still had a weakness in the joints, which made it difficult for him to stand. But whenever the Queen should hold her drawing-room, I should have notice. Lady Castlereagh was usually at home every morning until two o'clock, and would be glad to see Mrs. Adams whenever it should suit her convenience.

11th. I dined with Baron Fagel, the Dutch Ambassador, with a diplomatic company of about thirty persons—the Duke de la Châtre, Count Fernan Nuñez, Chevalier de Freire, Mr. Bourke, Baron Rehausen, Count St. Martin d'Aglie, Count Beroldingen, Mr. Pfeffel, and Count Jenison, Earls Bathurst,

Mulgrave, Harrowby, and Cassilis, Lord Binning, Messrs.
Croker, Beckett, Hamilton, and Planta, and five or six others
whom I did not know. The invitation was for a quarter before
seven. I went at seven, and was the first there. We sat down
to table at eight, and rose about ten. I sat between Fernan
Nuñez and Freire—Spain and Portugal. The Spanish Ambassador spoke to me of the accounts in the newspapers of this
day that Don Onis had left finally Washington, and that an
immediate war between the United States and Spain was expected, and he expressed great surprise at them. I regretted
the circumstance very much, and deprecated a war. He said
he thought the American Government should not suffer any
assistance to be given to the South American insurgents, nor
admit the vessels bearing their flag into our ports. For since
the insurgent chief Morales had been taken, and since Carthagena had surrendered, they had no Government; they were
mere robbers and pirates—they could have no flag.

I told him that was a thing of which the American Government could not make themselves the judges. They had issued
a proclamation forbidding the citizens of the United States from
giving aid to the South American insurgents, but they could
not prevent individuals from going out of the United States.
They had no walled frontier towns, and scarcely any army. As
to prohibiting all commerce with the South Americans and
excluding their flag, it was not to be expected of any Government. He knew, and I knew, that it had been refused by the
British Government, the close ally of Spain (he nodded assent),
and the American Government had done everything for Spain
on this occasion that Great Britain had done. And if the
Chevalier Onis had left Washington for that cause, I did not
see but that he (Fernan Nuñez) must go away from London
for the same reason.

He laughed, and said it was not his affair, but he added that
lately he had reason to be satisfied with what he had obtained
here against the South Americans. It is an Order in Council
prohibiting the exportation to them of arms and ammunition.
He asked me if I had been acquainted with the Chevalier Bardaxi at St. Petersburg. I had, and enquired where he now was.

He said, at Madrid, not in public office, but holding still that of Minister in Russia.   He said Bardaxi had been a very ardent patriot, and apparently a warm admirer of the Constitution made by the Cortes, but that had not been his real sentiment. It was only because the Constitution had been drawn up by his intimate friend, who had prevailed upon him to support it with his influence.

I asked him if there was any truth in the report that King Charles the Fourth was about returning to Spain.   He said, no; that the report had arisen because four frigates had sailed from Cadiz upon some expedition, and it was thought they were gone to take him and his wife, who were at Rome.

Mr. Freire told me that he had been acquainted with my father, and very intimate in the family when they were here from 1785 to 1788 and lived in Grosvenor Square, and he spoke with much gratitude of the treatment he had met with in America while he was Minister there, which was during the Presidency of my father.

Lord Mulgrave introduced me to the Earl of Cassilis, who told me that his brother owned a valuable estate in the city of New York.   His mother, it appears, was a native of New York.

I spoke to Mr. Hamilton, the Under-Secretary of State, about the copies of Governor Dobbs's commission and instructions, and asked him what fees were to be paid for them.   He said, none.   The demands for fees in their public offices, he said, were not very systematic; there were certain specified papers for which fees were prescribed, such as, for instance, the "exequatur" upon Consuls' commissions, but none were allowed for copies of public papers of any kind.   He asked me if I had received the answer with respect to the discrimination upon American and British shipping in the Irish ports.   I said I had not.

He said it was then owing altogether to the indisposition of Mr. Cooke (the other Under-Secretary of State in the Foreign Department); that the vessels of the two nations would undoubtedly be put upon the same footing, perhaps by increasing the restrictions on British vessels with regard to passengers, as a check upon emigration.

I spoke to Mr. Hamilton of the petition from Colonel Drayton to the Lords of the Treasury, of which I told him the substance, and asked him if I could send it to him. He said he would take charge of it, and if it went from the Foreign Department to the Treasury it would be immediately referred to the proper officer, and perhaps obtain a speedier answer. While I was in conversation with Mr. Hamilton, the carriage came, and I was obliged to leave him. It was about half-past twelve at night when we reached home.

13th. We went to the Oratorio, at Drury Lane, and heard " Israel in Egypt." The principal singers were Braham, Bellamy, Pine, Wulfingh, Mrs. Salmon, Mrs. Dickons, Miss Burrell, and Barnett, a boy about twelve years old. Braham, Mrs. Salmon, and Barnett were the best. " Israel in Egypt" was in two parts, to which was added a third part, consisting of several foolish ballads, and a grand battle symphony, composed by Beethoven, to show the triumph of " Rule Britannia" and " God save the King" over " Malbrook." Bad music, but patriotic. The house was full; the entertainment, like that of all English oratorios, dull. It was past eleven when it finished. I left Mrs. Adams and George at Craven Street, and went to the very small party at the Marchioness Dowager of Lansdowne's. It was a ball, and the two drawing-rooms were so crowded with company that there was scarcely room for dancing, or even for moving in them. I made my bow to her Ladyship, whom I found out as well as I could, for I saw nobody whom I knew to introduce me; but she said, " How do you do?" and I passed on. When I went in, the Duke of Cumberland was conversing with her. The only dancing was the valse. There were three times more ladies than gentlemen present, and one of the young ladies said to a gentleman that there were all sorts of extraordinary people there. The only persons whom I knew were the Earl of Westmorland, Mr. Bourke, the Danish Minister, and his lady, Count Fernan Nuñez, the Spanish Ambassador, who introduced to me Mr. Onis, a son of the Spanish Minister in America, who is attached to the Embassy here, the Bavarian and Würtemberg Ministers, and the Austrian Secretary of Embassy, Neumann. I expected to have met there the Marquis of Lansdowne, but I learnt there that he and the Marchioness Dowager were not upon good terms together.   Among the ladies were two daughters of the Marchioness by her first husband, a Mr. Gifford.

I had some conversation with Lord Westmorland about th large military establishment and the property tax, which now form the principal subjects of the discussions in Parliament. He said the military establishment was very large, but not greater than, upon considering the details, was found indispensably necessary.   And yet, among other things, they were charged with the intention of going to war with America because, with a frontier, he supposed, of twelve hundred miles there, they had two or three thousand men more than formerly.

I said, laughingly, that I hoped the charge was not true— that they did not intend going to war with us.   He protested to me with the utmost solemnity that they had not the most distant intention of going to war with any nation, and most especially not with us.   He said that before, when the war with us had been only one more enemy added to those with whom they were already engaged, they had not felt it so much.   But after they had made peace with France, then it was that they found the American war excessively burdensome; and now what could they possibly get by a war with America?

I told him, certainly nothing which could compensate for the cost of obtaining it, and I was happy to find that he thought so.   I asked him how he thought the property tax would go.

He spoke of it doubtfully, and rather unfavorably of the tax. I told him I had thought the Ministers intended to lose it in the House of Commons.

He did not deny it, and expressed his expectation that they would not have to debate upon it in the House of Peers.

He asked me about the state of our affairs with Spain, and whether we were likely to have a war with that country.

I said I hoped not, but I had no official account of the Spanish Minister's having left Washington, as was stated in the newspapers.   He asked if I knew whether the Foreign Department here had received any official intelligence of it. I did not know.

15th. The message to the two Houses of Parliament, announcing the intended marriage of the Princess Charlotte of Wales with Prince Leopold of Saxe-Coburg, was sent yesterday, and received with unanimous approbation.

18th. I began the draft of a note to Lord Castlereagh, to send with copies of the correspondence between Governor Cass and Colonel James. It engaged me until breakfast, and the journal was of course neglected. Mrs. Adams went with me into London. We called at Lady Castlereagh's at a quarter-past one. It was too soon, though Lord Castlereagh had told me until two. The servants asked us to call again in about an hour. Mrs. Adams went and called upon Mrs. King, but did not find her. She then came to me at Craven Street, and we went again to Lady Castlereagh's, when she received us. She promised to present Mrs. Adams to the Queen at the drawing-room on Thursday, and asked her to be at the Queen's house, where she would meet her, at half-past two o'clock. I mentioned that I had enquired of Lord Castlereagh whether Mrs. Adams was to be presented at the drawing-room and I was to have my audience on the same day, and he had promised to let me know. Lady Castlereagh said she would ascertain, and write to Mrs. Adams to inform her to-morrow.

We returned to Craven Street, where I left Mrs. Adams and went down to the Foreign Office. I enquired for Mr. Cooke, but he was not there. I saw Mr. Hamilton, and asked him whether the discrimination between British and American vessels in Ireland was yet removed. He said, not yet, but Lord Castlereagh had spoken to him about it again this morning. It would certainly be done; but the business in Parliament, and especially the pressure about the property tax, had so absorbed all the time lately that they could do nothing else.

I mentioned that I had seen by the newspapers that Mr. Robinson was introducing a bill into the House of Commons for carrying into execution the convention of 3d July, 1815, and I had wished to ascertain if this Irish affair had been provided for in that bill.

He said he did not know, but advised me to see Mr. Robinson, whom he thought I should find at the Board of Trade. I enquired if he had received the tin cylinder box for me from Hamburg, containing Bode's astronomical charts; but he had not.

I asked him if he thought the property tax would be carried in the House of Commons. He said it would be hard run, and spoke doubtingly. I hinted that I thought the Ministers intended to lose it; but he said, " Oh, no! it was a measure of too much importance for that." I saw at the Foreign Office Baron Jacobi and Mr. Bourke, the Prussian and Danish Ministers.

I called at the Board of Trade, saw Mr. Robinson, and enquired of him whether the Irish discrimination was abolished by his bill. He said, no, and entered upon an argument to show that it was not within the objects and purview of the convention. I told him there had been some discussion upon the question in writing between Lord Castlereagh and myself, and that although his Lordship maintained, as he did, that it was not strictly within the purpose of the convention, yet I had understood him as promising that the question as to the right would be waived, and the discrimination in fact done away ; that the ships of the two nations should be placed at all events on the same footing.

He said, if so, he would see, and consult with the Irish Government whether it could be introduced into his bill or must be done by a separate act. Indeed, when the convention was signed, he had not been aware that this discrimination existed, and he thought its policy rested upon another motive. It restricted the number of passengers, perhaps with a view to the comfort of the passengers themselves, and from a supposition that they might suffer in health from being too much crowded.

I said I could scarcely think that was the motive, because the difference between the restrictions upon British and Americans was too great. That upon the British vessels was amply sufficient to ensure the health and comfort of the passengers, and it was, besides, the interest of the captains who took passengers to make their accommodations healthy and comfortable; that Lord Castlereagh had supposed a different motive for the restriction, namely, as an indirect check upon emigration. He had therefore told me that perhaps the equalization would be effected not by diminishing the restriction upon American vessels, but by increasing that upon the British. I had told him that this Government must exclusively judge of that. We could not interfere with any regulations of theirs, the sole object of which might be to control emigration, but we asked that they should be the same upon the shipping of both nations. In this case, the difference operated upon the cargoes of the ships which carried passengers, and thus, I thought, brought the point within the very letter of the convention. Provisions were among the principal articles of exportation from Ireland, and they must necessarily form a considerable part of the cargo of a vessel carrying two or three hundred passengers. A limitation of the number of passengers would also be a limitation upon the quantity of provisions to be taken for their consumption upon the passage, and the whole together would produce the same effect as a prohibitory duty.

He thought it could hardly be considered in that light, but said, however, that if Lord Castlereagh had engaged that the difference should be done away, he would see that it should be accomplished in one way or the other. I asked him if his bill provided for the equalization of the tonnage duties. He said no; that the only discrimination of tonnage duties between British and foreign shipping was made in favor of certain chartered corporations—for instance, the Trinity House—for light-money and some other charges of that kind; Parliament could not take these away; but the mode of carrying the convention, in this respect, into execution, would be by observing in favor of American vessels a regulation already established and practised for Portuguese vessels, which are entitled by treaty to the same privileges; that is, to levy the extra duties, but to have them returned by allowance at the Custom House. He recollected that at one of the meetings for the negotiation of the treaty he had mentioned this to the American Plenipotentiaries. He said it had been expected when we signed the treaty that a proclamation of the President of the United States, founded upon the Act of Congress of the preceding session, would have removed the discriminating duties independently of the ratification of the convention.

I told him that the reasons assigned to me by the American Secretary of State why such a proclamation had not been issued were, that the Orders in Council of August had not been officially communicated either to me, or, through Mr. Baker, to the American Government, and that it had made no mention of tonnage duties. It had therefore been thought best to wait till the ratification of the convention, and afterwards to come to an understanding about the time when it should begin to operate. My own opinion was, and I had expressed it to my own Government, as well as to Lords Liverpool and Castlereagh, that the convention took effect from the day of the signature, and that all extra duties contrary to it, levied after that time, must be refunded by both Governments.

Mr. Robinson questioned this, but, on reflection, said he thought its effect would be in favor of Great Britain; which I admitted. He said the omission to communicate officially the Order in Council had certainly been wrong, but the neglect was not in his department. Nor was that even relating to the tonnage duties; for an official notice that the allowance for them was to be made had been sent to the Treasury, and he had been surprised to find, upon being informed of my late application upon the subject, that the Treasury had not acted upon it. He had lately been there and showed them this notice, sent to them at the time, but they could give no account why it had not been acted upon, though they admitted that it had not. He would see, however, that it should be properly attended to in future.

19th. The question upon the property tax was taken last night in the House of Commons, and lost by a majority of 37 against the ministers. The votes were 238 to 201—an issue generally unexpected by the public.

21st. Soon after nine this morning left home with Mrs. Adams, and went into London. We stopped at Craven Street.

We had expected there would have been a letter of notice from
Lady Castlereagh to Mrs. Adams, or from Mr. Chester to me;
but there was none. Mrs. Adams went to Mrs. King's lodgings, 60 Conduit Street, to dress. Mr. Hartshorn, an American, called for a passport, which was given him. While he was
at the office I received a note from Mr. Chester, the Assistant
Master of the Ceremonies, by his servant, enquiring whether
I had received a note which he had written me yesterday, and
whether he might expect me at half past three o'clock, to go to
my audience of the Queen. I knew not what he could mean.
The drawing-room was appointed for two o'clock, and I saw
my audience was to be after it; but knew not whether it was
understood that Mrs. Adams was to be presented at the drawing-room or to wait for another. I apologized to Mr. Hartshorn for leaving him, and walked to Mr. Chester's house, 68
South Audley Street. I had not received his note written
yesterday, but found that although I was to have my audience
after the drawing-room, and could of course not appear at it,
Mrs. Adams was still to be presented at it. Mr. Chester had
proposed to me to call upon him, and go at half-past three, to
spare me the trouble of waiting there until the drawing-room
should be over; but as in that case Mrs. Adams would have
been obliged to go alone, would be a stranger there, and might
miss meeting Lady Castlereagh, I concluded to go with her
and wait. Mr. Chester agreed to go with us. I went to Mr.
King's,[1] at Conduit Street, and informed her of this arrangement. Mrs. Von Harten, Mrs. Morison, and Miss Carnell
were there to see her dressed. I then took a hackney-coach,
to go to Craven Street, but met my own carriage on the way.
Went in it, dressed at Craven Street, returned to Mr. King's
and took up Mrs. Adams, called and took up Mr. Chester at
his house, and at a few minutes after two were at Buckingham
House. Earl and Countess Bathurst arrived just at the same

[1] Mr. Charles King, a son of Rufus King, of whom much will be found in a later
volume of this work, and his first wife, Miss Gracie, were at this time making a
journey in Europe. They stopped some time in London, where an intimacy was
formed with Mr. and Mrs. Adams, which lasted for the rest of their lives. Mr.
King was afterwards, for many years, the honored President of Columbia College,
in New York.

time that we did.   There is a special entrance into the Park, reserved for certain privileged persons, among whom are the foreign Ministers, and for which Mr. Chester gave us a ticket. The convenience of it is to avoid the crowd and waiting.   It is the entrance by Constitution Hill, at Hyde Park Corner. There is also a hall adjoining that where the drawing-room is held, where only the privileged persons are admitted, and their presentations are before those of the crowd of nobility and gentry of the country.   These are kept in a hall below. Lady Castlereagh did not arrive until after the first part of the presentations was over, so that, to avoid the crowd, Countess Bathurst presented Mrs. Adams.   When the crowd from below were shown up into the hall, Mr. Chester showed me into that which they had left, and I waited there until the drawing-room was over.   Mrs. Adams, after having been presented, met Lord and Lady Castlereagh, as they were just going in.   Mr. Chester told us that Lady Castlereagh was noted for always coming too late.   Mrs. Adams returned then to Mrs. King's, and sent back the carriage for me.   I waited in the hall below until past four o'clock.   While I was there, the Duke and Duchess of York passed through it, going by a private passage to the drawing-room, and the Duke of Sussex, and the Duke and Princess Sophia of Gloucester, in coming from it.   The Duke of Sussex stopped and spoke to me.   He talked of the victory gained by the fall of the property tax, and remarked to me that he was in a Court dress, not a military uniform, because in time of peace it was proper to lay that aside.   After changing his dress in a next room, he said, " You are going to have your audience, and must wait some time ; I am going to dine with about five hundred Jews."

I laughed, and said, " I see your Royal Highness is of all religions."   " Yes," said he ; " at least for tolerating them all, and for supporting the Ministers of the Established religion in such a manner as should not alienate from them the affection of their flocks."   He said he was also going to a ball at the Lord Mayor's.

Part of the time while I was waiting, Count Beroldingen, the Minister from the King of Würtemberg, was also there.

He had a letter from the King to the Prince Regent, and another to the Queen, announcing the marriage of the Crown Prince of Würtemberg, his son, with the Grand Duchess Catherine of Russia, Dowager of the Prince of Oldenburg. These letters were to be delivered in private audiences, but the question of etiquette was whether the Queen could receive the one addressed to her before that to the Prince Regent had been delivered to him. The Count had asked the question, and was kept waiting for the answer until I returned from my audience. He was then told that the Queen could not receive the letter in private audience until after the Prince Regent should have received his; but that if he (the Count) preferred it, he might send the letter for the Queen to the Lord Chamberlain. He chose to deliver it in private audience, but was somewhat mortified at the manner in which he was treated, and told me that they did not understand here their own rules of etiquette.

Mr. Chester accompanied and conducted me to the Queen's cabinet. The Earl of Morton, her Majesty's Lord Chamberlain, introduced me. The Queen[1] was standing about the middle of the chamber. Just behind her, at her right hand, stood the Princess Augusta; at her left, the Princess Mary; further back, several ladies in waiting, and the Duke of Kent in military uniform. I had been repeatedly told, and particularly by Mr. Chester this morning, that the Queen always expected on these occasions to be addressed in a set speech.

I said thus: " Madam, the President of the United States having accredited me to his Royal Highness the Prince Regent, I have been ambitious of the honor of being admitted to your Majesty's presence, to assure you of the respect entertained by the Government of the United States for your Majesty's person. When upon a former occasion your Majesty was pleased to appoint a time for that purpose, I was confined by illness, a circumstance with which I hope your Majesty was made acquainted. I am now happy to be able to avail myself of your Majesty's permission, and pray you to accept the assurance of the venera-

[1] It is hardly necessary to explain that this was Charlotte, wife of George III., at this time in seclusion on account of his alienation of mind.

tion uniformly felt by the American Government for your Majesty's character. The political relations between the two countries have been subject to the versatility which attends all human affairs. Causes of dissension, and even of enmity, have sometimes unfortunately risen between them. These are now removed. It is hoped, and most earnestly desired by my country, that they may be permanently removed. But the reverence commanded by your Majesty's virtues is subject to no such change. It has been invariably entertained by my Government under every variety of circumstances, and I can express no wish more propitious to the happiness of both countries than that the friendship and harmony between them may hereafter be equally lasting and unalterable."

The Queen answered that she was much obliged to the American Government for the sentiments I had expressed in their name, and, with respect to myself, she had much regretted the illness I had mentioned.

She asked me several questions concerning it: what it had been? how long I had been confined with it? whether I was perfectly recovered? whether it had been the effect of the climate? All which I answered as briefly as possible. She enquired also concerning the climate of my own country, and I told her how much milder and more pleasant I found that of England than the one from which I had last come, which was Russia. She asked me whether I was related to the Mr. Adams who had been formerly the Minister to this country, and appeared surprised when I answered that I was his son. She forgot that I had given her the same answer to the same question twenty years ago, and had apparently no recollection that I had ever been presented to her before. She now dismissed me, and I withdrew with Mr. Chester.[1]

25th. While at dinner, we received a mourning card, with Miss Bond's compliments to Mr. and Mrs. Adams, and returning thanks for their obliging enquiries. Mr. and Miss Bond visited us once upon our arrival here last summer, but we were not at home, and they left cards. We returned the visit, but

---

[1] Mr. Adams had been in England nearly eleven months. Such a delay would scarcely happen to a Minister of the United States in these days.

Mr. Bond was gone to Brighton, and Miss Bond was unwell and could not receive us. We only saw Miss Travis. We had no personal acquaintance with Mr. or Miss Bond, and I never saw either of them. Mr. Bond died two or three months ago, but neither Mrs. Adams nor I sent or thought of sending to make enquiries of any kind concerning Miss Bond, so that we were at some loss to understand the meaning of this card of thanks for enquiries that were never made. We had received lately a similar card from Dr. Nicholas and his family, after the decease of his father. I understand it to be a custom among people of genteel society to send round such cards, as a sort of visiting-cards, shortly after the decease of near relations, and that they are sent to all acquaintances, whether they have made enquiries or not.

29th. Went with Mrs. Adams and George to the Oratorio at Covent Garden. The principal performers were Braham and a Mr. Tinney, Miss Stevens, Madame Fodor, Madame Marconi, and Miss Smith. The first act was a selection from Handel's "Messiah," the second from his "Acis and Galatea," with an Italian air from Mozart, sung by Madame Fodor. The third act was a selection from various modern composers. After the first act, Mr. Drouet, first flute player of the King of France's Chapel, performed a concerto upon the flute, and surpassed everything that I had ever heard upon that instrument. Braham and Miss Stevens were the best singers. The house was very much crowded. After the second act was finished, Mrs. Adams was unwell, and we came away. I left her and George at the office, and went to spend the evening (passer la soirée) at the Duke de la Châtre's. It was half-past eleven o'clock, and the company was just assembling. It consisted of about a hundred persons—most of the foreign Ambassadors and Ministers, Lady Castlereagh, Lords Bathurst, Westmorland, Melville, Stafford, Harrington, Mrs. Wellesley Pole, the Countess of Jersey, Lady Harrowby and her daughter Lady Susan Ryder, Mr. Chester, Mr. Hamilton, the Under-Secretary of State, Mr. Planta, and many others whom I did not know. Prince Esterhazy, the Austrian Ambassador, was there, with his father, Prince Paul Esterhazy, who has very lately arrived in England, and to whom he introduced me. Naldi, a performer at the opera, was there with his daughter and a French young lady, and they sang several French and Italian airs and duets, with accompaniment of the piano. Drouet, the performer on the flute, was likewise there, and played some of the pieces I had already heard at the theatre, and several others.

The Duke de la Châtre told me that he was appointed " Premier Gentilhomme de la Chambre" of the King, and was only waiting to have his audience of leave of the Prince Regent. He had been to Brighton to obtain it there, but he had been told he should have it at the first levee. Lord Melville, the First Lord of the Admiralty, told me he had heard from the Niger frigate, in which Mr. Bagot and his family took passage from Madeira. The ship met with some damage from the shock of an earthquake, which they felt at sea. It was at the same time felt at Madeira and at Lisbon. Mrs. Wellesley Pole had no letters from her daughter,[1] and was very anxious to hear from her. Lord Westmorland told me that my prophecy about the property tax had come to pass, and I told him I was more than ever convinced that I had given him the true reason for the event. The Spanish Ambassador told me that he had letters from Mr. Onis, at Philadelphia, of 9th February. He writes that some ill-intentioned persons had spread the report that the intercourse between the American Government and him was broken off, but it was not so. He had only gone to Philadelphia to see his wife, who was sick there. Fernan Nuñez also told me that he had ordered the appeal of jurisdiction to be entered in the case of the Sabine, perceiving that it came within the same principle as that of the William and Mary. I came away a little after one o'clock.

April 4th. We went to the Queen's drawing-room, at Buckingham House. It was announced for two o'clock, and precisely at that hour the drawing-room commenced. The forms of this presentation are different from those of the circles on the Continent, and of those held by the Prince Regent at the levees. The Queen does not go round the circle. She takes

[1] Mrs. Bagot.

a stand before a sofa. The persons attending the drawing-room go in from the adjoining hall, go up to her, and are spoken to in succession, after which they pass on to the Princesses and Princes, who stand at her right hand, each of whom speaks a few words, and then the person files off by another door and goes down-stairs to go away. Privileged persons, however, among whom are the foreign Ministers, may remain in the drawing-room after having been presented. All the foreign Ambassadors and Ministers were there, excepting Baron Jacobi. I spoke to Count Munster, the Hanoverian Minister, about my old friend Bussche, and bore testimony to the sentiments he had always avowed to me.

He said he had already taken some steps in Bussche's favor, but there were reports in circulation much to his disadvantage, especially of his having been too intimate with Mr. Caulaincourt, and even to have served him as a spy.

I told him I was convinced Bussche never did act, and never would have acted, as a spy; that he was by his situation placed in a state of necessary intimacy with Mr. Caulaincourt, but that he always spoke to me of it as a situation which he had been forced to accept, and that it had been invariably repugnant to his own feelings and inclinations. I mentioned that I had spoken upon the subject to Count St. Julien while he was here with the Archdukes, and had entreated him, if he should see Count Munster, to bear his testimony concerning Baron Bussche, and he had assured me that he would testify to the same facts as myself. The Count proposed to call upon me to converse further with me on this matter, but I observed to him that I resided out of town, and that I would call again upon him to give him any more particular statement that he might desire.

I spoke to Count Lieven concerning my letter of recall from the Court of Russia. He said that at the time when I had given him notice last summer that I had it, he had immediately written to take the Emperor's orders concerning it; that Count Nesselrode had replied it would be best to wait until the Emperor's return to St. Petersburg, to make the official arrangements suitable to the occasion, and for transmitting to him the customary present to be given me on his receiving from me the letter, which he expected now to be very shortly authorized to do. I told him I was sorry there had been any delay on that account; that by the Constitution of the United States their Ministers abroad were not permitted to accept presents from foreign sovereigns, and that I had made this fully known to Count Romanzoff while I was in Russia, and when he was Chancellor. I regretted not having thought of it when I informed him last summer that I had the letter of recall, but it was only because the idea had not at all occurred to me that any offer of a present would be made.

The Count asked me whether my distance from town was such that he could, without indiscretion, invite me to his house; to which I could only answer how much I was obliged to him. For one of my strongest reasons for remaining out of town is to escape from the frequency of invitations at late hours, which consume so much precious time, and with the perpetually mortifying consciousness of inability to return the civility in the same manner.

When the drawing-room opened, the Corps Diplomatique first entered it, and went up and paid their respects to the Queen. Mrs. Adams went with Princess Castel-Cicala and Mrs. Bourke. The Ambassadors and Ministers afterwards succeeded, and Prince Esterhazy presented his father.

Mr. Chester accompanied me, as it was my first presentation at the drawing-room, and after the Queen had spoken to me he presented me to the Princesses Elizabeth and Mary, to the Duke of Gloucester and his sister the Princess Sophia. The Queen, and Princesses Elizabeth and Mary, have a topic to speak to me about—my health, the climate, and my residence in Russia. The Princess Sophia of Gloucester told me she was glad to see an American Minister here again, and she hoped we should long continue friends. I thanked her for the wish, and said it was the first duty of my station, and the first inclination of my heart, to promote the friendship between the nations. The Duke of Gloucester said he was happy to renew the acquaintance he had made with me last summer at Earl Grey's. The Dukes of Kent and Sussex also spoke to me; the latter came late, because, he said, he thought proper to take his time.

The Duke of Clarence was there, but I had not the opportunity of speaking to him. After passing through all the presentations, we stood and saw the succession of others pass through theirs, for about an hour. The Duke of Sussex and Lord Graves came up and conversed with my wife, with whom they remembered their ancient acquaintance at Berlin.

We left the drawing-room between three and four o'clock. Dined with the Earl of Westmorland in Grosvenor Square. The company was small, only thirteen persons, all men, and of whom I was acquainted only with Mr. Bourke, Count Beroldingen, and the Under-Secretary of State, Mr. Hamilton. There was a Sir Charles Flower, who has been Lord Mayor of London, a Mr. Lowther and his son, and others whose names I could not catch. One gentleman came from the House of Commons, where he had left them debating upon an insult suffered by Lord Milton and Lord Essex this morning as they were riding in an open carriage in Pall Mall. They were stopped by a soldier, and not suffered to proceed. The soldier struck the horses with his sabre, and threatened to cut down Lord Milton himself if he attempted to proceed. The member had come away, preferring the dinner to the debate. Lord Westmorland showed Mr. Bourke and Mr. Hamilton, as connoisseurs, three old pictures which were offered to him to purchase, and which those gentlemen assured him were not worth half a crown apiece. Yet one of them was professedly a sketch by Rubens— the meeting of Jacob and Esau.

The dinner-party was pleasant. They spoke of a company of French players now performing here, to which some of them were going this evening, and of certain subscription balls, at seven shillings a head, under the direction of Lady Castlereagh and other persons of rank, select to the last degree, and to which I was told we could be admitted by applying to Lady Castlereagh.

8th. Called upon Count Munster, the Hanoverian Minister, at his house, and he received me. I showed him the letter I had received from Baron Bussche Hunnefeldt, and repeated the information I had given him at the drawing-room concerning Bussche's conduct and sentiments, so far as they were known

to me, while we were at St. Petersburg together.   I also told
him I had requested Count St. Julien to speak to him when he
was here, and to bear his testimony to the same points, trusting
that he knew still more of Mr. Bussche's conduct there than I
did, as having been more intimate with him.

Munster said that St. Julien had in fact spoken to him, and
given the same account that I did; that he (Munster) had
spoken to the Prince Regent in Bussche's favor; that the
Prince had increased the pension which Bussche enjoyed, and
he would certainly not be molested.   But as for his being employed again, that must be out of the question.   He was glad
that my testimony and Count St. Julien's went so strongly to
exculpate Bussche, because he had been charged by some Russian gentlemen with having not only been very intimate with
Caulaincourt, but with having even served him as a spy; that
he (Munster) had asked Bussche himself whether he had not
been excluded from Count Orloff's house, and that Bussche
had not been able to deny it.   I said that Bussche's situation
at St. Petersburg, which he had invariably stated to me to have
been involuntary and forced upon him, had, however, necessarily
placed him in great intimacy with the French Ambassador; but
I did not believe he had ever served him as a spy, or that he
was capable of serving any man in such a capacity.   I had
always considered him as a man of strict and delicate honor.
As to the Russian nobility at the Emperor Alexander's Court,
for two years after I went there they were to a man at least as
subservient to Mr. Caulaincourt as ever Bussche was.   As to
Count Orloff, I had never heard, and did not believe, that he
had any particular reason to complain of Bussche.   But Orloff
had at one time fallen into disgrace with the Emperor, and
been sent into a sort of exile.   After his return, he gave, as I
had heard, notice generally that he would receive none of the
foreign Ministers, and no persons belonging to their legations,
at his house, because he attributed the Emperor's displeasure
to something which had been reported by some persons belonging to the foreign missions who frequented his house.
But I had never heard that he had attributed it to Bussche,
and I knew that his exclusion had not been confined to him.

I had been myself for a year and a half in strong opposition to the French Ambassador, and had witnessed the singular fact of three Ministers almost under his direction, yet by their personal inclinations most decidedly against the French system. They were Count Schenk, from Würtemberg, General Pardo, Minister from Joseph, as King of Spain, and Bussche, who was the Minister from Westphalia. De Bray, the Bavarian Minister, though a Frenchman born, had come off the best, and even now retained his place. The Count said that as to De Bray, he had always considered him as belonging to the French system, and so considered him now. But with regard to Bussche, it was not what he had done in Russia that had most injured him, but his conduct since his return. The acceptance of office under the French, while they had been in possession of Hanover, had not been considered by the King or the Prince Regent as an offence. On the contrary, it had been recommended that well-disposed persons should take any of the subordinate offices, in order that they might not fall into worse hands. An exception had been made only to those who had taken oaths contrary to their duties of allegiance. Bussche's mission to Russia, therefore, would not have been objected against him ; but it had been thought extraordinary that afterwards, when all Germany rose in the struggle to recover their independence, and every German was showing his devotion to the cause, Bussche alone, or with only one other person, should have taken the time to go off and follow the ragged Court of that Jerome into France. He had done another foolish thing. He had married a Frenchwoman, a reader (lectrice) to Jerome's Queen of Westphalia, a woman of very indifferent character, of whom Bussche was now, he believed, heartily tired, and who made him very miserable.

I told the Count that with regard to Mr. Bussche's conduct since he left St. Petersburg I could bear no testimony. I knew nothing of it, and had never before heard that he was married. I could speak for him only as to the time when he was in Russia. I was sorry if he had made a bad marriage, and could not judge how far his obligations may have justified his going away with Jerome, which had also been unknown to me. The Count

concluded by saying he was obliged to me for the kindness I
had in this instance shown to one of his countrymen, who was
also one of his relations.

9th. I alighted at the top of St. James's Street in Piccadilly,
and walked to Lord Castlereagh's house, where I came at precisely half-past eleven.   The servants told me he had not yet
come down (from bed), and showed me into the parlor, where I
found Mr. Planta writing.   He sent for a couple of the morning
newspapers, and after I had waited about half an hour, Lord
Castlereagh came down, and I was shown into his cabinet.
He apologized for being so late, saying he had never known a
session of Parliament when there had been so much of a spirit
for detailed debate ; that from the commencement of the session
until this day the House of Commons had been sitting at an
average of eight hours every day, and that last night again they
had not adjourned until about two o'clock in the morning.   He
then proceeded to say that the first subject upon which he
wished to speak to me related to a note that I had sent him
concerning a memorial to the Lords of the Treasury from a
man named George Cook, an American, and he wished to know
precisely what the object of the note was.   I said I had never
seen Mr. Cook, and knew nothing of his case but what was set
forth in his memorial to the Lords of the Treasury, a copy of
which had been communicated to me by a Mr. Page, his agent,
and likewise agent to several Spanish subjects, who had made
complaints similar to that of Mr. Cook.   The only ground
upon which I had interfered in behalf of Mr. Cook was that
he was a citizen of the United States, and as such entitled to
all the assistance that in my official capacity I could give him.
The only thing that I had been requested by Mr. Page to ask
for him, and which I had asked by my note, was a *speedy* decision, and, presuming that I might speak in perfect confidence
to him (Lord Castlereagh) on the subject, I would state to him
the reason why the necessity that this decision should be speedy
had been alleged to me by Mr. Page.

Lord Castlereagh said that he wished me to speak in perfect
confidence, and that whatever was said between us on the
subject should be private.   I then said that Mr. Cook's memo-

rial alleged a claim to be indemnified for great wrongs suffered by him in the form of judicial and executive proceedings by the Judge and Governor of a British settlement in Africa; that the Governor of that settlement was now here, but he had received another appointment to some foreign colonial establishment, and might be expected from day to day to embark for his new destination. It was the intention of Mr. Page, as Mr. Cook's agent, in case the decision of the Lords of the Treasury upon the memorial should not be satisfactory to him, to prosecute the Governor (Maxwell) in the proper Court of law, and he was anxious not to lose the opportunity of arresting his person. This was the motive upon which I had addressed to his Lordship the note concerning Cook. It was altogether distinct from the merits of the case, of which of course I could not judge. I had only asked for a decision.

Lord Castlereagh said the fact was that this Mr. Cook had been one of the greatest and most notorious offenders against the laws of the United States relative to the slave-trade, as well as against those of Great Britain. But the proceedings against him had been illegal, because his establishment had been upon the Rio Pongas, not within the territorial jurisdiction of Great Britain. If he had been taken at sea, his trial and condemnation would have been perfectly legal and regular; but he had been taken out of the British jurisdiction. The sentence of the Court that condemned him could not, therefore, be maintained, and that was the reason why it had been remitted here by a pardon. He then read me a letter from Mr. Goulburn to Mr. Cook, the Under-Secretary of State, in which he gives him the same account of his *namesake*.

I repeated to Lord Castlereagh that I could not judge of the merits of the case. Cook's memorial stated a case of great hardship and very severe treatment; he denied altogether having had any concern in the slave-trade, and averred that his establishment was of a commerce altogether different. He complained also of great partiality and oppression upon his trial—of not having been allowed to make his defence or to produce the evidence in his favor. But I was not competent to re-try the cause.   He must find his remedy in the Government, or in the laws of England.

Lord Castlereagh said they would then determine whether the Government itself would make him indemnity, or whether they would leave him to his remedy, by suit in the Courts of law, against the individuals.

He next referred to the notes I had sent him concerning the fisheries, and the armaments on the Lakes.   He said the British Government was ready to make a proposition to avoid all collisions in the fisheries, and they were willing to meet the proposal of the American Government that there might be no unnecessary naval force upon the Lakes in active service or in commission, so that there should be nothing like an appearance of a dispute which side should have the strongest force there.   The armed vessels might be laid up, as they called it here, in ordinary.   It was, in short, the disposition of the British Government fully to meet the proposition made to them, and the only armed force which they should want to have in service might be vessels for conveying troops occasionally from one station to another.   He asked if I had instructions from the American Government, or a power upon which I could conclude anything upon the subject.   I told him that I had not; I had transmitted the papers that had passed here concerning the fisheries—my first note to Lord Bathurst, and his answer—the last autumn.   I was expecting instructions in reply to them every day and every hour.   As to the armaments on the Lakes, it being mutually understood that no new armaments are to take place on either side, and that orders shall accordingly be given, there will be ample time to concert between the two Governments the details of a specific article for the future, which might be signed either here or at Washington.   As, however, the instructions which I am expecting may, very possibly, give me no new power, but consist only of observations upon the papers that I had forwarded, it would save time, and perhaps be most advisable, to have the proposal made immediately to the Government of the United States, and through the British Minister there.   He said, as the fishing season was now approaching, it would, he

believed, be best to send the instructions and power to Mr.
Bagot, and then the instructions to the naval officers on the
American coast might be given accordingly.

I then asked him if anything had been done upon my last
note to him, enclosing copies of the correspondence between
Governor Cass, of the Michigan Territory, and Colonel James.
Lord Castlereagh appeared not to understand me, and had
evidently not read, or retained no sort of recollection of, the
correspondence, or of my remarks upon it. Whether this
ignorance was real or assumed I could not positively determine; but I believe he had never even read my note. I
recapitulated to him all the material facts, and urged to him
the great danger that such transactions should lead to actual
hostilities between the bordering authorities. He assured me
that very strong instructions should be sent out to secure due
respect to the American jurisdiction, and at the same time an
opportunity might be given to the officers complained of to
offer an explanation of their proceedings.

I then enquired if anything had been done with regard to
the discrimination in the Irish ports. He said that orders had
been sent to Ireland which would remove the discrimination.
Without admitting the right, they would put away the cause
of complaint. But he could not tell whether it would be by
increasing the restriction on one side, or by diminishing it on
the other.

I repeated that as to the ground of our claim, we must leave
that choice to their option; but I believed if they should subject the ships of both nations to the restriction of one passenger
to every five tons, the effect would be equivalent to a prohibition of trade between the United States and Ireland. He
asked, how?

I said that it would be equivalent to a prohibition of exports
from Ireland to America. Passengers, and the cargo required
to carry them, constituted the only exports. Provisions were
among the principal exports of Ireland. Forty passengers for
a vessel of two hundred tons could not be equivalent to a
freight. There were now nearly a hundred American vessels
in the ports of Ireland, waiting for this decision, and I supposed

if it should be to allow only one passenger for every five tons they would all be obliged to come away in ballast. The servant had been in and announced Sir Henry Holford. I took my leave, and went to Craven street.

15th. Easter Monday. Mrs. Adams came with Mr. and Mrs. King just at six o'clock. I had been doubtful whether to go in full Court dress, or in frock: an accident determined me to go in full dress, which I found was right. We reached the Mansion House at a quarter-past six, but it was too late. Six was the hour appointed, and the company were actually sitting down to table when we arrived. The seats at the Lord Mayor's table were therefore all occupied; and it was with the utmost difficulty that we obtained seats at the side-table, at the head of which sat the Sheriff, Mr. Bell. Mr. King could not get a seat, and was obliged to go into another hall. There were about four hundred persons at the dinner. The Dukes of Kent and Sussex, the Bishops of London and Chester, Sir George Warrender and Sir Joseph Yorke, Lords of the Admiralty, Lords Erskine and Kinnaird, and Mr. Douglas Kinnaird, Sir Gilbert Heathcote, Sir Thomas Acland, Mr. Lyttleton, Alderman Sir William Curtis, and Mr. Sharp, members of the House of Commons, were of the company. The only foreign Minister present besides myself was the Chevalier de Freire, the Portuguese Minister. The dinner was managed much like those on the two former occasions at which I have attended in the same place. The men of official character were all in full Court dresses, and the Lady Mayoress wore the Court hoop. The same toasts, and the same order of them, were given, but the golden loving cups, and the basins of rose-water, were not passed round. The King, the Prince Regent, the Queen and family, the Princess Charlotte and a happy Union were successively toasted—the first in silence, and each of the rest with the cheers of three times three huzzas. Then came the Dukes of Kent and Sussex, then the Prince Regent of Portugal, and then the President of the United States. The healths of the Dukes of Kent and Sussex were drunk, after an introductory speech to each of them, by the Lord Mayor. He complimented the Duke of Kent upon his great regard and attention to all the benevolent and charitable institutions in the City. The Duke answered by a very short and handsomely-delivered speech, declaring that in his regard for benevolent institutions he only followed the liberal example which was invariably set by the citizens of London, whose welfare, and the prosperity of which institutions, whether present or absent, he should always have at heart. In introducing the Duke of Sussex's health, the Lord Mayor said that, owing to this Royal Duke's infirm state of health, he had not so much patronized the City institutions, and particularly had not so much frequented the churches, but he would propose his Royal Highness's health, with thanks for his great and patriotic exertions in support of the liberties of the people.

The Duke, with much good humor, and with a laughing air of high indignation at the charge of not sufficiently frequenting the churches, said it was a challenge from the Lord Mayor, which he accepted, and he begged to be understood that, while he was an invariable friend to religious liberty and an enemy to all persecution, he was deeply convinced of the superior excellence of the Church of England, and unalterably attached to its establishment. But, he added, if his friend's toast had done him wrong on one side, it had more than made him amends on the other, by complimenting him on his exertions in the cause of those principles which had seated his family in the station which they hold in this country. He had gratified the wish which would always inspire his conduct, and which uniformly actuated him in that branch of the legislature in which he was honored with a seat. He had lately had the satisfaction of presenting to that House a petition drawn up and agreed upon in this hall, and was happy that the measure against which it remonstrated had been abandoned. He regretted that he saw so few of his Majesty's Ministers here present, as he should have been desirous of offering them his thanks for the attention which they had shown to the wishes and remonstrances of the people.

The Duke's speech was longer than that of his brother, but he is not quite so fluent. The next toast was, " The Prince Regent of Portugal," for which the Chevalier de Freire returned thanks in a very few words, spoken in so low a tone that I could not hear him.

The Lord Mayor next gave, " The President of the United States," upon which I arose from my seat and said, " My Lord, I pray your Lordship to accept my hearty thanks for the honor which you have done my country in drinking the health of its Chief Magistrate. I receive it as an earnest of peace, harmony, and friendship between the two countries. To promote peace, harmony, and friendship between Great Britain and the United States is the first duty of my station. It is the first wish of my heart. It is my first prayer to God. I hope it will not be deemed unsuitable on this occasion to recur to considerations of a religious nature. In ordinary cases, and at ordinary times, it may be proper and sufficient for Britons and for Americans to say to themselves, It is our interest on both sides to live in peace, harmony, and friendship together. But, my Lord, the event which was yesterday commemorated by religious solemnities, and which is this day commemorated at this table in the convivial and loving cups of your Lord and Ladyship, is the most important event that ever occurred upon this globe. It is an event in which we are all interested—a pledge to us all of immortality. It is the warrant to us all of another state of existence, where all is peace, harmony, and friendship. May it ever have the proper influence on the minds of your Lordship's countrymen and of mine ! May it ever remind them of a higher motive than any possible temporal interest to peace, harmony, and friendship ! In return for your Lordship's obliging toast, I beg leave to drink, ' All religious blessings and all temporal prosperity to the Metropolis of the British Empire and its Chief Magistrate.' "

Immediately after this toast, the Lady Mayoress, and all the other ladies, left the hall, and the Duke of Sussex, after an introductory speech, proposed the health of the Lord Mayor. In returning thanks, the Lord Mayor[1] adverted to his situation and to the earnestness of his endeavors to give satisfaction to all his fellow citizens during the year of his Mayoralty. He

---

[1] Better remembered as Alderman Wood, the father of the present Lord Hatherley.

said that he had particularly felt it his duty to discard the
influence of all political opinions in the faithful and impartial
discharge of his official functions. He had his political opinions, they were earnest and decided, they had grown up with
him, and he should abide by them to the last hour of his life.
But he had never suffered them in the slightest degree to in-
trude upon his execution of the office of Chief Magistrate, and
his highest ambition was to go through that career doing equal
justice to all, without distinction of party or profession. The
speech was received with much approbation and applause.

After this the healths of the Bishops of London and Chester
were drunk, and to the latter, with thanks for the excellent
sermon he had given this morning at Christ's Hospital. The
Bishops severally returned thanks, adding a few words expressing their attachment to the City and its charitable institutions.

Lord Erskine was next toasted with " Trial by Jury," and he
made a very animated speech in returning thanks. He declared
how much he felt himself gratified and honored by the connection of his name with that popular institution. He said that
in looking round the table there was scarcely a face but was
familiar to him, from the recollection of his having at some time
or other addressed almost every one of them, in the character
of a juror. It was his highest glory to reflect upon his exertions in support of that popular branch of the constitution, as
he was fully convinced that in proportion to the respect and
veneration in which it was held would be the security and
durability of all the other branches. It might be supposed,
and he doubted not that many persons had thought, it was presumption in him to have adopted the words " Trial by Jury" as
the motto to his arms, as if he had meant to boast of having
any peculiar merit in his zeal for that institution. But it was
no such thing. When by the gracious favor of his Majesty he
had been introduced into that branch of the legislature where
he now held a seat, he had determined to give a lesson to the
young men who should come after him, and, by incorporating
those words in the heraldic distinction connected with his new
station, he resolved that whenever they should see his carriage

drive up to the House of Lords they might also see that that was the way to get there.

This speech was received with acclamations of applause. Lord Kinnaird's turn came next, and he returned thanks in a few words, very handsomely delivered, and which were much applauded. His brother, Douglas Kinnaird, next to whom I was then sitting, said to me it was a thousand pities that he was not at this time in Parliament. His observations were of the popular cast, and he said that there was nothing more suitable to the dignity of a British nobleman than a liberal intercourse with the citizens of London.

The Lord Mayor next gave, " The Members in Parliament from the City." Alderman Sir William Curtis was the only one of them present, and he returned thanks for the whole. He apologized for his insufficiency, and regretted that none of his colleagues, more able than himself to address the company, were present to assume the task. He complimented the Lord Mayor upon his faithful, able, and impartial discharge of the duties of his office as Chief Magistrate, and this testimony he the more cordially gave because upon general politics it was well known, and God knew, that they did most materially differ, and had long and often differed, from each other. Yet, however great those differences had been, and however earnestly he had always maintained, and should maintain, the opinions which in his conscience he thought right, he was thoroughly convinced that in the ultimate results they were agreed. Their motives and intentions were the same. The last time he had been in that hall, it was a meeting which, by its numbers, the weight of character, the ability and virtues of the characters composing it, was not to be paralleled in the world. A petition had then been drawn up, and agreed to by them, which he had the honor to present to the House of Commons. The effect of it had been seen by the event, and he thanked God that Madam Property Tax had been put to rest. The Alderman sat down with a mixture of applause and of a low, murmuring disapprobation. One voice from a crowd of persons between and around the tables spoke just as he was closing, and said, " Ay ! very well *for that!* good *for that !*"

The Lord Mayor immediately proceeded to the next toast, which was, "The House of Commons—thanks to them for all their exertions in the cause of the people, and particularly for their recent decision." Two members of the House successively rose and returned thanks for this toast. First, Sir Gilbert Heathcote, who fully concurred in the sentiments of the toast, and expressed his hopes that the House would always show itself equally careful of the interests of the people and equally ready to yield to their wishes; and, secondly, Sir Thomas Acland, who said he felt himself called upon to express his feelings with regard to both parts of the toast. He was grateful to the generous and magnificent hospitality of which he was now partaking. It was the first occasion of the kind at which he had ever been present, and, from what he had seen and shared of it, he readily believed that upon no other occasion of the same kind had it been more worthy of this great and noble city. The commendation bestowed on the House of Commons in the toast was twofold—for their general attention to the interests of the people, and for their particular decision upon a late occasion. To the latter part of this tribute of thanks he must avow that he had for his personal share no claim whatever. He had voted for the property tax, from a conscientious conviction that it was a measure calculated to support the best interests of the country. Of that act he was not ashamed, nor would it become him in any manner to disown it. But for the more general compliment of thanks to the House for their regard to the interests of the people, he could cheerfully accept his part, and, so far as an earnest and ardent devotion to their interests and their welfare could go, he would not yield his claim to zeal and good intentions equal to those of any other person whomsoever. This speech was also very well received.

The last toast given was, "The wooden walls of Old England," with the air of "Rule Britannia" by the band, and for which Sir Joseph Yorke returned thanks in a few words, regretting that the task had not fallen to a person more accustomed to speaking before a public assembly. The company then rose from table. There had been during the dinner an allegorical silk flag, wove by the Spitalfields weavers, as a specimen of their skill, exhibited and displayed in the centre of the hall, by permission of the Lord Mayor. The object appeared to be to excite the patriotic spirit in favor of the drooping national manufacture, but it was not much admired, and the work was said to be very indifferent.

As we rose from table, Mr. Lyttleton, whom I had seen at St. Petersburg, recognized and spoke to me. Lord Erskine asked me if I had ever seen his speech in the House of Lords upon the Orders in Council. I told him I had seen it only as it had appeared in the newspapers. He said it had been taken in short-hand by his friend Mr. Perry, and published in a pamphlet. He would give me one of them, and would come out and see me at my house. I asked him after his son, who had been Minister in America; he said he resided at Brighton, and his wife had just brought him her eleventh child. He said what a pity and a shame it was that they had refused to ratify his arrangement and recalled him. I said he had been one of the best friends to both countries that had ever been concerned in their affairs, and I was very sure if his bargain had been confirmed, and he not recalled, the war between the two countries would never have taken place.

" Damn them !" said he. " And now that Canning is coming back again—and coming into office again !"

I said he had a little too much wit for a Minister of State.

"Oh," said he, "he is utterly and totally unfit for the office."

Here I parted from his Lordship, and made my way as well as I could to the dancing-hall up-stairs, to which the Lady Mayoress had repaired, and where the ball was to be opened. The crowd was so excessive that it was with the most extreme difficulty that I reached the hall, and the end of it where the Lady Mayoress was seated in state, under a canopy. The ball was to have been opened according to the usual form, by a minuet, which Lord Kinnaird was to dance with the Lord Mayor's daughter, Miss Wood. But Lord Kinnaird had got lost in the crowd, and had not found his way to the hall. The crowd was increasing and encroaching constantly upon the small space left for dancing the minuet. The Duke of Sussex offered himself as a volunteer to dance the minuet, and actually danced it with great elegance, though he said he had not danced before since he was at Berlin, and remarked to me that he had forgotten to put on his hat. He introduced me to his son by the name of Captain D'Este. The Duke said he believed I had seen him at Berlin, but in that he was mistaken. The Captain laughed, and said that I had certainly not seen him then, bearing the same name. He was then a boy only seven or eight years old. He is now a young man of four- or five-and-twenty, certainly more than six feet high, and rather stout in his proportions.

After the minuet there was an attempt to dance a country-dance; but it was impossible for more than four or five couple to stand up, and the crowd soon pressed upon them so that they could not proceed. The heat was scarcely less oppressive: several ladies fainted, and the Lady Mayoress sat in state with her smelling-bottle constantly at her nostrils to keep herself from fainting. The Lord Mayor, one of the Aldermen, and the Recorder successively addressed the crowd, entreating them not to press forward, but to withdraw into the other halls. The Lord Mayor threatened even to call in constables to clear the hall. It was all in vain. The Lady Mayoress was obliged finally to leave the hall, of which the Recorder gave notice to the company, saying she would be glad to meet them in the Egyptian Hall. It was with the utmost difficulty that room was made for her to go out, and she was followed by so many of the ladies that in the course of a quarter of an hour the crowd thinned off, leaving space enough to pass to and fro. On getting out of the hall, I found Mrs. Adams and Mrs. King seated on a window-bench in the entry. There I stood some time with them, when the Lord Mayor and Lady Mayoress passed by and invited us to walk round with them. We followed them down-stairs and round through the Egyptian Hall, where we lost them again in the crowd. The dinner-tables were yet standing, and covered with people standing on them. We were obliged to pass over them to get out of the hall.

20th. I received a letter from Count Lieven, informing me

that he had been authorized by his Court to receive my letter of recredence, as he calls it; that is, the letter from the President of the United States to the Emperor of Russia, notifying him of my removal from the legation of the United States at his Court. The Count, to save me all unnecessary trouble, proposes to me to send the letter to his house. There was also an invitation from Countess Lieven to Mrs. Adams and me to spend the evening to-morrow.

21st. I wrote the draft of a note to Count Lieven, to enclose with the letter of recall, or, as he calls it, of recredence, and I made a fair copy of it to take with me. We left home about nine in the evening, and, after stopping at the office in Craven Street, proceeded immediately to Count Lieven's. The party there was not numerous—I think not exceeding seventy persons. The Duke de la Châtre, late French Ambassador, and the Marquis d'Osmond, his successor, Prince Esterhazy and his father, Fernan Nuñez, with Curtoys and Onis, Count and Countess Munster, Mr. and Madame Bourke, Baron Rehausen, Chevalier de Freire, Count Beroldingen, and Mr. Pfeffel, were there, of the Corps Diplomatique; Earl and Lady Bathurst, Lord Melville, Marquis and Marchioness of Lansdowne, Earl and Countess Grey, Earl of Harrington and two daughters, Countess of Aberdeen, Lady Heathcote, Miss Barings, Sir Gore Ouseley, Mr. Chester, Mr. Planta, and some others. The Duke de la Châtre, and the other Ambassadors, had been dining with the Prince Regent. The Duke told me he had his audience to take leave, and must go immediately, to be present at the marriage of the Duke de Berri, which is to be on the 16th of next month, and he must attend, being the " Premier Gentilhomme de la Chambre," and then "de Service." The other Ambassadors had all been this evening verbally invited to attend at the nuptials of the Princess Charlotte of Wales, which are to be on the 2d of May.

Fernan Nuñez told me that the Chevalier Onis was at Philadelphia, "très-content;" that he had indeed asked a leave of absence for some time personally for himself and on account of his private affairs, but that it would not be granted him. Curtoys told me that he was weary of living in this country;

he found the climate did not agree with his nerves, and he thought of returning to Spain. I had some conversation with Mrs. Wellesley Pole, with the Marquis of Lansdowne, Earl Grey, and Mr. Freire, who told me that the Prince Regent of Portugal had appointed a new Minister Plenipotentiary to the United States, a Mr. Correa de Serra, a man of science, who is already, and has been some time, at Philadelphia, and he asked me to forward a packet of dispatches to him, and one for the Portuguese Chargé d'Affaires and Consul-General in the United States, which I readily promised to do. The Danish Minister's lady, Mrs. Bourke, engaged Mrs. Adams and me to go to a concert next Friday evening—a subscription one, for a French young lady patronized by Countess Lieven and her. She promised to send us tickets. I gave Count Lieven the packet containing the letter from the President to the Emperor of Russia, and my own to the Count. Just as the supper was about to be announced, about half-past twelve, we came away, and reached home between two and three in the morning.

23d. I went to the Prince of Wales Hotel, Leicester Place, General Mina's[1] lodgings, but he was already out, and on proceeding to the office in Craven Street I found him there. He wished for a passport to go to the United States. He has a permission from the Alien Office to reside here as a foreigner, and I offered to endorse that, as good to go to the United States. But he said he was proscribed in his own country; the Spanish Ambassador here would not dare to give him a passport, even if he were disposed so to do; and he was afraid if I should endorse the Alien Office permission, they would not only refuse to give him a passport to go to America upon it, but that it might deprive him of the means of obtaining a passport in another way. He asked me if I could not give him a passport of my own, and make it out in the name of his mother, which it was very customary in Spain

---

[1] Xavier Mina, nephew of the celebrated guerilla chief in the wars in Spain of the early part of this century. Driven out of Spain, he was now preparing to try his fortune in raising an insurrection in Mexico. He embarked on his expedition soon after this date, and, having passed through a series of adventures in that country, was finally taken, with his followers, and shot in the city of Mexico in November of the next year.

for persons to assume. I told him that as a general rule I gave my own passports only to citizens of the United States, and I endorsed the passports of foreigners from their own Ministers when they were going to America. When they could not obtain passports from their own Ministers, if they had permissions from the Alien Office to reside here, I would endorse them as good to go to America, and had done so in several cases. I considered every person as having a right to go from this country to the United States whom the laws of this country did not restrain, and if my passport for this effect was required, I would give it in any form that would be accepted. I would leave it, therefore, at his own option whether to take my endorsement upon his license from the Alien Office, or an original passport from me. He said he would in the first instance try the endorsement, and if that should not succeed he would ask me for an original passport. And he had the same request to make for several of his officers, who are with him. I promised him the same for his officers as for himself.

27th. The card of invitation that I had received for the dinner at Somerset House mentioned that the doors would be opened at two o'clock, and dinner on table at six. I went between two and three o'clock, but, finding, upon enquiry, that there was nobody there, returned to the office.

About five o'clock I went again, and found the company assembling. I went through the apartments where the paintings were exhibited. Many of them are very good, but the proportion of portraits is much greater than at any exhibition that I had ever seen here before. It was precisely twenty years since the last exhibition I had witnessed at this place, and now, as then, the finest portraits are those painted by Beechey and Lawrence. The historical paintings now are fewer, and do not appear to me to be better executed.

The company at the dinner amounted to upwards of two hundred persons, among whom were the Dukes of Kent, Cumberland, and Sussex, of Bedford and Somerset, almost all the Cabinet Ministers, many of the nobility, the Lord Mayor, the Archbishop of York, and several Bishops, the Russian, Spanish,

and Dutch Ambassadors, the Swedish, Danish, Portuguese, Ba-
varian, and Würtemberg Ministers. The diplomatic party were
seated almost all together, at a table opposite to the President,
Mr. West. The dinner was tolerable. The toasts after dinner,
The King, as the founder of the Academy ; The Prince Regent,
its patron ; The Queen and Royal Family. Then, The Duke of
Sussex and the Society of Arts, Manufactures, and Commerce ;
The Marquis of Stafford and the Royal Institution ; The Royal
Society (Sir Joseph Banks, the President, was not present, and
not toasted); The Earl of Aberdeen and the Society of Antiquaries; The Lord Mayor and the City of London ; and the foreign Ambassadors and Ministers present. The Duke of Sussex
and the Earl of Aberdeen made short speeches in returning
thanks for the toasts in which they were mentioned. The Marquis of Stafford simply rose and returned thanks. The Lord
Mayor and the Ambassadors said nothing. The Duke of Kent,
after a speech of eulogium upon Mr. West, the President, proposed his health, for which he returned thanks with a speech.

There was a band of music, which performed various airs
and marches, and after dinner a sort of prayer was chanted to
the words of " Non nobis, Domine ;" " God save the King" was
likewise sung. The company broke up between eight and
nine o'clock. We returned first to Craven Street, where I
found two invitations, which I took home with me without
reading, as it was late and we did not alight from the carriage.

When we got home, I found the invitations were, a card
from the Lord Steward (Marquis of Cholmondeley), inviting
the American Minister to dine with his Serene Highness the
Prince of Saxe-Coburg at St. James's, on Wednesday next, at
a quarter before seven o'clock. Full dress. Dated, Board of
Green Cloth, 25th April, 1816; and an answer on Sunday is
most particularly requested. The other was, The Master of the
Ceremonies is commanded by his Royal Highness the Prince
Regent to invite the American Minister and Mrs. Adams to
Carlton House, on Thursday next, the second of May, at
eight, or between eight and nine, of the evening, to be present
at the ceremony of the marriage of her Royal Highness the
Princess Charlotte Augusta of Wales with his Serene High-

ness Leopold George Frederick, Duke of Saxe, Margrave of Meissen, Landgrave of Thuringen, Prince of Coburg of Saalfeld. Dated this day, and with a note. The company will be in full dress, but the ladies without hoops. To this invitation no answer is necessary, and the direction upon the other, to answer on a particular day, seems intended to balance the courtesy of inviting by an assumption of authority in demanding the answer.

29th. Went into London with Mrs. Adams, and called at eleven o'clock at Lord Castlereagh's house, in St. James's Square. The Chevalier de Freire, the Portuguese Minister, was there before me, and had a short interview with his Lordship. Baron Fagel, the Dutch Ambassador, came in while I was waiting in the antechamber. I was only a few minutes, and mentioned to him the letter that I had received from Messrs. George and James Abel, and which I read to him, with the copies of the answers they had received from the India House and the Board of Control. Lord Castlereagh asked me to send him copies of these papers, and said the matter should be arranged as soon as possible. He also desired me, if I could conveniently, to call upon Mr. Robinson, the Vice-President of the Board of Trade, and to converse with him on the subject. I went to the Board of Trade, and obtained an interview with Mr. Robinson. He at first sent me word that he was engaged with a person by an appointment, and would be glad if I could call again to-morrow morning. But being informed that I would not detain him more than five minutes, and that I had called upon him at the request of Lord Castlereagh, he received me. I read to him the letter from the Abels, and its enclosures; from which it appeared that a clearance cannot be obtained for an American vessel, from London, to any of the British ports in India. Mr. Robinson at first said that the convention of 3d July last could not be understood to authorize that.

I said that if such a construction should be given to it as would exclude our vessels from that advantage, it would certainly be altogether different from what I and my colleagues expected at the negotiation and conclusion of the convention.

He said there was not in the terms of the convention any explicit allowance of an indirect trade from the United States to the British possessions in India. It was not, however, his intention to deny that it was understood when the convention was concluded that American vessels might go, indirectly through other countries, to British ports in India; but surely that could not mean to give them the privilege of clearing from the ports of England itself to go there. He remembered we had urged the indirect voyages through South America, and that we ought to be placed on as favorable a footing as other nations, none of which could clear out for British India from this country.

I admitted in reply that the indirect trade to India was *not* given in express words by the convention, but a general trade was given, without restriction upon the outward voyage. The homeward trade was restricted to the direct voyage to the United States. The restriction being expressed in the one case, its omission in the other obviously implied that it was not to operate. I was confident there had been a judicial decision in this country upon the corresponding article in the Treaty of 1794 to that effect. But he perfectly well knew, and now candidly admitted, that it was on all sides understood, at the negotiation of the convention, that it contained the indirect trade to India for American vessels; it was even explicitly recognized in the notes of the British Plenipotentiaries during the discussion, and I had observed in a private account of the debates in Parliament on the passage of the bill, which he had introduced, for carrying the convention into effect, that a question had been put to him by some member upon the very point; to which he was stated to have answered that the convention did allow an indirect American trade to India, but restricted the return voyage to the United States.

He neither explicitly admitted nor denied that such a question had been put to him, and that he had given this answer. It seemed as if he had been since told that he had conceded too much by that acknowledgment; that the express words of the convention did not give the indirect trade, and that an effort has been making to narrow the construction of the article so as to exclude us at least from trading to India through England.

I told him that if the clearance from British ports should continue to be denied it would produce one of two effects. It would either, in a very great degree, defeat the indirect trade which the convention was intended to contain, or it would merely operate to put American vessels to some additional trouble and expense, and some change of custom-house forms. All the important commerce of the world centred so much in Great Britain, that we could not have any indirect trade to India of any importance which would not bring our vessels going thither to England on the way. If clearances from England for India should be effectually prevented, the trade itself would be good for nothing. But, as it was admitted American vessels might clear out from any other country for India, what other effect would the denial to clear them from British ports have than to compel them to clear out for intermediate ports, there to take fresh clearances for their ultimate destination? Indeed, I could not see how the clearances from England could be denied while the indirect trade through other countries was admitted to be granted. It was not given in express terms, I admitted. It was given by obvious and just inference, he admitted. But if the inference was just as it respected a trade through other countries, it was just for a trade through England. Granting that a question might be made, whether the indirect trade was stipulated at all, it would apply to all other countries as well as to England. There was no special exception of England, nor was there any argument which would warrant the refusal of clearances from English ports but that which would annihilate the indirect trade altogether. I had seen Lord Castlereagh, and shown him these papers, this morning, and had understood from him that the matter would be satisfactorily arranged, and it was at his Lordship's request that I had called to have this conversation with him on the subject.

He said I might rely upon his disposition to give the fullest effect and most faithful execution to the convention. He would see and converse with Lord Castlereagh concerning it this day, as he should meet him in the House of Commons, and he would do everything in his power for our accommodation.

At four o'clock I left the office to walk part of the way home. Opposite Carlton House there was a great crowd of people collected in Pall Mall. It was to see the Prince of Coburg, who this day came in state into London. We had met the royal carriages going out to Sir Joseph Banks's seat at Hounslow to take him up. He came this morning from Windsor, and, after visiting the Prince Regent at Carlton House, he took his residence, until the marriage, at the Duke of Clarence's apartments in St. James's Palace. There had also just been presented an address from the City of London to the Prince Regent, of congratulation upon the peace. I had met the procession of the Sheriff's carriages on their return, in Charing Cross.

At the corner of the new street opening from Pall Mall, opposite to Carlton House, I met the Earl of Carysfort, and stood with him nearly half an hour in conversation. I had seen his name in the newspapers as having been present at the dinner on Saturday at Somerset House, but did not see him there. He told me that he had been to look at the pictures, but did not stay to the dinner, being quite an invalid with his asthma. He said Lady Carysfort was also unwell, confined to her chamber; that they had been only a few days in town, and should not stay long, as he had let his house in Berkeley Square. We had some loose political conversation, in which he said he was now of the opposition, but he was disposed to be very candid towards the Ministers. He disapproved their large military establishment, but he knew they must gradually reduce it, and the reduction must require considerable time to be effected with convenience. I said I thought it must end by a partition of France; and he expressed a wish that it might.

In the conversation this morning with Lord Castlereagh, I began by showing him the letter of instructions from the Secretary of State to me of 27th February, directing me to consider it as an authority and instruction to negotiate a convention respecting the fisheries. After perusing it, he asked me if a new power had been sent to me. I told him there had not;

but I was authorized to show him that letter, which my Government had undoubtedly considered as containing a power sufficient for the purpose. He said that, conformably to the agreement at our interview on the 9th instant, he had already sent out authority and instructions to Mr. Bagot for this negotiation, which it would be more convenient to have conducted at Washington, because he was authorized also to give instructions to the British commanders on the coast according to the result of the discussions. I replied that it would be personally more agreeable to me, and I presumed more convenient to my own Government, to have the arrangement made at Washington. As, however, this authority had been transmitted to me, it was my duty to lay it before him, and to act upon it, if this Government should be so disposed. He said he thought it would only make the subject more complicated, without bringing it nearer to any result; and I readily acquiesced in this opinion. He said nothing of the nature of the proposition which Mr. Bagot is authorized to make.

May 1st. A letter from Henry Nodin & Co., requesting a passport from me for a Mr. Richard Baxter, a British subject, to go to the United States. I desired Mr. Smith to inform the person applying in this case that no passport was necessary or proper for me to give to a British subject. From the frequency of such applications to me, I incline strongly to the belief that they do at the Alien Office make use of their powers over aliens to obstruct the departure of British subjects, by suffering them at least to believe that they must have passports to go to America. A letter from Mr. G. M. Woolsey, at Liverpool, complaining that an entry had been refused by the Collector of the Customs there to certain tobacco, because the collector at Richmond had certified that the master of the vessel in which it was shipped had been *qualified* to the manifest instead of saying that he had been sworn to it. The Act of Parliament requiring that the manifest should be sworn to at the place of shipment, the master had taken an oath before a magistrate at Liverpool that he had sworn to his manifest at Richmond; notwithstanding which the collector at Liverpool refused to allow the entry of the tobacco. I immediately addressed a note to Lord Castlereagh on the subject, and answered Mr. Woolsey's letter. It was only a quarter before seven when the carriage arrived, and I was afraid of being belated at the dinner. Just then came in a Frenchman, named Thibert, who is about publishing a new French grammar, and has made repeated applications to obtain my subscription or patronage, which I have as often declined, having been surfeited with new systems of French grammar. He enquired for Mr. Smith, who had gone out to dinner. I left him to wait for Mr. Smith, and went immediately to St. James's Palace, to the Duke of Clarence's apartments, and dined with the Prince of Saxe-Coburg. All the foreign Ambassadors and Ministers were there; the Archbishop of York, Bishop of London, Marquis of Cholmondeley, the Lord Steward, Lord George Beresford, Mr. Chester, and Colonel Hardenbroek, the Prince's cavalier or gentleman.

The Prince is a tall, well-formed, handsome man, modest and reserved in his deportment, wearing as easily as could be expected the new and extraordinary fortune that has befallen him. The transition from the condition of a third son to a petty German Prince, whose whole dominions scarcely surpass the extent of an English manor, and from the rank of a captain of cavalry in the Russian service, to the office of husband to the presumptive heiress of the British realms, is one of those vicissitudes in human life which every head would not be of strength to bear. The Prince has nothing of arrogance in his manner. He shows nothing of an elated spirit. But there is a point of view from which a proud spirit with a delicate sense of honor must perceive something to discolor, at least in part, the flattering complexion of his present state. There is an apparent consciousness of this nature in his manners, which, though different from the perfect ease of greatness familiar with itself, is neither unnatural nor absolutely unbecoming. He was polite and attentive to all his company, and especially to the German Ministers, of whom there were six present. He spoke a few words to me in English, enquired how long I had been in this country, and observed that he spoke English very imperfectly himself, but hoped to acquire it soon. There was a crowd of people collected in the stable-yard before the windows of the chamber in which the company were received before dinner. They shouted occasionally to make him show himself, and he went out once or twice on the balcony to be seen, stood two or three minutes, and then came in again. I was, luckily, not the latest person that arrived; Count Beroldingen, the Minister of Würtemberg, came a few minutes after me.

The dinner was then immediately announced. There was turtle-soup, venison, and strawberries, with other dishes more in season. The wines were merely good. I sat between the Danish Minister, Mr. Bourke, and the Archbishop of York, whom I found very ready in conversation and very agreeable. He mentioned several particulars of the present situation of the King, being one of the Queen's council for the guardianship of his person. He has been for nearly five years confined to two or three chambers in Windsor Castle. His bodily health is good, his appetite regular, and the Archbishop says he considers him as the best life of his age in the kingdom. He is blind, but immediately recognizes by the voice every person whom he has known. His principal amusement is music— playing upon a bad piano which he has in one of his chambers. He is attentive to the neatness of his person to great excess. He had for some time a long white beard, but is now regularly shaved. The Archbishop spoke slightingly of the form of prayer now used in the churches for the King's recovery, which, he said, you must read almost through before you could discover what it was about; but, he said, when it had been drawn up and prescribed by the Archbishop of Canterbury, it had been expected that the King's illness would last only a few weeks.

The prayer is indeed neither sense nor grammar, nor can any one discover from it what it is about. It implores that God would restore the King to his family and his people, and then puts the case whether this great calamity with which we are afflicted shall be removed or still suspended over us.

The Archbishop spoke of the Society for the Propagation of the Gospel, and the Bible Society, of his office as Archbishop, and his office as Lord High Almoner, in which capacity, and not in the other, he is to be present at the marriage to-morrow. He told us that the sum which he has to distribute as Lord

High Almoner is about two thousand four hundred pounds a year, two-thirds of which was distributed in small pensions to poor widows, which he had limited to the widows of officers in the army or navy or of clergymen. The rest was given out in silver pieces of one, two, three, and four-penny silver pieces, which were coined at the mint for that single purpose. He showed us several of the four-penny pieces, which he had in his pocket. The dinner was of about two hours' duration, and the company returned to the drawing-room to coffee for about a quarter of an hour, and all retired at once, before ten o'clock.

2d. Marriage of the Princess Charlotte of Wales. The dissipation of yesterday and that of this day disqualified me for any serious occupation, and I could write nothing but an answer to the invitation from the Fishmongers' Company to dine with them at their Hall on the 23d of this month. At three in the afternoon I left home, and walked until the carriage, with Mrs. Adams, overtook me, a mile beyond Acton. Just at eight o'clock we went to Carlton House, which we reached without difficulty, although the streets from Piccadilly, and particularly Pall Mall, were thronged with immense crowds of people. The company to be present at the nuptial ceremony were collecting until about nine o'clock, in an apartment called "the crimson room." There were perhaps two hundred persons present—the Royal family, the Cabinet Ministers, the foreign Ambassadors and Ministers, the household officers and all their ladies, the Archbishops of Canterbury and York, and the Bishops of London and Salisbury. About nine the Queen and Princess came in, followed by the Prince Regent, and soon afterwards by the parties to be married. The service was read remarkably well by the Archbishop of Canterbury, and the responses were very distinctly and audibly made by the Prince and Princess. After the ceremony, they both kneeled to the Prince Regent and to the Queen.

They immediately afterwards went away in a travelling chariot to the Duke of York's country-seat, at Oatlands, about twenty miles from London, where they are to pass a week or ten days. The Queen and the rest of the company remained, and about an hour after the ceremony was over, the Queen

and the Prince Regent walked round the circle, after which
the Queen retired to a party at cards in another apartment.
There were refreshments served at a sideboard—cold sand-
wiches, wedding-cake, lemonade, orange-water, wines, and
ardent spirits. Prince Esterhazy, the father, took, with some
effort of complacency, a glass of cherry brandy. The Dukes
of York, Clarence, and Kent were there, the Duchess of York,
the Princesses Augusta, Elizabeth, and Mary, and Princess
Sophia of Gloucester; but neither the Duke nor Duchess of
Cumberland, the Duke of Sussex, nor the Duke of Gloucester.
The heat of the rooms was almost insupportable. The Queen
went away about midnight, after which it was allowable for the
rest of the company to depart.

3d. I walked down to the office in Craven Street, and soon
after came in a Mr.   , who arrived yesterday from New
York. He brought me three dispatches from the Secretary of
State. I enquired of him whether Mr. Bagot and his family
had arrived in the United States before he sailed. He said he
had, and had been presented to the President. I had met at
Carlton House last evening Mrs. Wellesley Pole, Mrs. Bagot's
mother, who was extremely anxious at not having heard of her
arrival. She had earnestly desired me, if I should hear of their
arrival, to give her notice of it, which I had promised, and
assured her it should be within ten days, and I hoped within
three. Mrs. Adams came with the carriage at two o'clock.
We went immediately to Mrs. Wellesley Pole's house. She
was just gone out to see her daughter, Lady Fitzroy Somerset.
We left cards, and I directed her servant, who came to the
door, to inform her that I had called to tell her of the safe
arrival of Mr. Bagot and his family at Washington. We then
went and had our names written at Camelford House, for the
Prince and Princess of Saxe-Coburg; at Buckingham House,
for the Queen; and at Carlton House, for the Prince Regent.
It was for this formality that we had remained in town over-
night. Mr. Chester had told me that it would be a proper
mark of attention. As I went into the antechamber at Carlton
House to write our names, I found Lord Walpole there upon
the same business. I had not seen him since I left St. Peters-

burg. I spoke to him, and, as he appeared not to recognize
me, mentioned my name. He said, without moving a muscle
of his face, " You've grown fatter ;" and, having written his
name, went out without making me any salutation. As he
had been introduced to me at St. Petersburg, at his own
request, while our two countries were at war, and as he had
always been very civil and sociable when we met there, I was
surprised at his conduct now, and know not how to account
for it, unless from a remnant of ill-humor from certain mortifi-
cations which he experienced at St. Petersburg after I came
away, before the close of our war. Harris often wrote me
that Lord Walpole was extremely discourteous to him ; and
this sulky insolence may be a sequel of the same pettish
temper.

7th. Mr. Del Real informed me that he had written several
letters and memorials to Lord Castlereagh, to which he had
received no answer; that he was desirous of obtaining an
interview with him, to request an answer, that he might know
upon what to rely in relation to his official situation. He
rather intimated, than positively expressed, the wish that I
would introduce him to Lord Castlereagh, and asked if I could
indicate any means by which he could obtain access to him.
I told him that I was fully disposed to render him any service
in my power, but he would recollect the conversation which
had lately passed between us, in which we had agreed in
opinion, that any extraordinary interest shown on the part
of the United States towards the South Americans would
unavoidably indispose in the same degree the British Government against them. The policy of the British Government
hitherto, decisively, is not to acknowledge the independence
of the South Americans. Knowing this, I had neither officially
nor individually such a state of personal relations with Lord
Castlereagh as would warrant me in assuming the liberty of
introducing Del Real to him, nor was it in my power to point
out to him any other channel through which he might obtain
such an introduction. I knew of no more favorable prospect
of success than by a note to Lord Castlereagh, explicitly asking for an audience as an answer.

He said that he was unwilling to push on to extremities at once; that soon after his arrival here he had seen Mr. Vansittart, the Chancellor of the Exchequer, who had then made no difficulty to receive him. He had told him that the British Government had ordered their naval commanders to respect the flag of the South Americans; their vessels would be admitted into the British ports, and the commerce of British subjects with them would be allowed; but that their Government could not be acknowledged.

I told him that he must expect to find the British Government just at this time colder and more averse to an acknowledgment than they were. The fall of Carthagena, and the late successes of the Royal party in Mexico and Peru, had very much shaken the opinions of people in Europe generally as to the final success of the insurgents. Perhaps the impression of those events had been much greater than was warranted by their importance. I knew that such had been the effect of similar events during the war of our Revolution. I believed he would find it better to wait until some more favorable turn to the independent cause should take place, than to press for an answer now. He acquiesced in this opinion, and left me.

9th. Went with Mrs. Adams into town, and dined with Mrs. Porter, a Scotch widow lady. The company were Lord St. Helens, Mr. Liston, the British Ambassador at Constantinople, now here on a leave of absence, and his lady, Mr. Aust, formerly an Under-Secretary of State in the Foreign Department, and his lady, a third wife, many years younger than himself, Mr. and Mrs. King, Mr. Gracie, and a Mr. Boswell, a brother of Dr. Johnson's friend and biographer. Mr. and Mrs. Liston were several years in America while my father was President, and well acquainted with my father and mother. Lord St. Helens had also been acquainted with my father at Paris, in the year 1782. He was then Mr. Alleyne Fitzherbert, and, as the British Plenipotentiary, negotiated the treaties of peace with France and Spain. He also signed the article regulating the cessation of hostilities, with the American Plenipotentiaries.

12th. At eleven o'clock was at Lord Castlereagh's door. I was shown in o the anteroom, and within five minutes Lord

Melville, the First Lord of the Admiralty, came in. He told me that they had not yet received any dispatches from Mr. Bagot, not even of his arrival at Washington. But they had letters from the captain of the Niger from Bermuda, to which island she proceeded, after having landed Mr. Bagot and his family at Annapolis.

I said to Lord Melville, in the tone between jest and earnest, that I heard Lord Exmouth had been making peace for Naples and Sardinia, and a quarrel for us with the Dey of Algiers. He said that was the subject upon which Lord Castlereagh had requested to see me this morning. They had no intention to make a quarrel between us and Algiers, and hoped no such consequence would follow.

I replied that if it should, the quarrel would, I hoped, be rather useful to us than otherwise; "and, my Lord," said I, "if we had only for three years one-third of your naval force, I assure you that the Christian world should never more hear of tribute, ransom, or slavery to the African barbarians."

Just then the servant came, and ushered us into Lord Castlereagh's cabinet. He began immediately upon the subject, and told me that he had asked this interview for the purpose of communicating to me *confidentially* their instructions to Lord Exmouth, and his proceedings under them, with a view to satisfy the Government of the United States that the conduct of the British Government in these transactions had been fair and honorable, and that although there was one article of the treaty between the United States and Algiers which Great Britain considered as objectionable, it had not been at all noticed or referred to in Lord Exmouth's negotiation.

He then read to me two papers, and gave me to peruse three others, serving to elucidate all the proceedings of this Government in this affair.

They were—1. A letter from himself to Earl Bathurst, directing, by an order of the Cabinet Council, that instructions from the Lords of the Admiralty should be sent to Lord Exmouth to go and notify to the Barbary powers the dispositions by which the allied European sovereigns have placed the Ionian Islands under the protection of Great Britain, to obtain the

acknowledgment of those dispositions, and at the same time to
negotiate a peace between the Barbary powers and the king-
doms of the Two Sicilies and of Sardinia. The motives alleged
for this measure are the obligations of Great Britain to extend
to the Ionian Islands, since they have been made a part of the
British dominions, the same privileges enjoyed in the Mediterranean seas by other British subjects; the general indignation
arising throughout Europe against the mode of warfare practised by the Barbary States against Christians; and the urgent
applications of the King's two intimate allies, the Kings of
Naples and Sardinia, more particularly a very recent one from
the latter of these sovereigns, through his Minister at this
Court, for the interposition of Great Britain to effect this peace
in respect to his dominions. It is observed that by the annexation of Genoa to the Sardinian dominions the importance to
them of a peace with the Barbary States had increased; that
the object of that annexation having been to strengthen the
barrier on the side of Italy against France, it would be more
consonant with that policy that all the resources of Sardinia
should be applied to its military power by land, than that any
part of them should be diverted to the purpose of making it a
naval power; that while the island of Malta had been possessed
by the knights of that order, they had been at perpetual war
with the Barbary powers, and had thereby afforded considerable protection to the commerce of the Mediterranean States
against their cruisers. And as Great Britain now possessed
Malta, although she was not obliged to take upon her the duty
of protecting all the Christian flags, the revenues of the order
not having been transferred to her, yet it was proper she should
exercise her influence of protection to a certain extent. Lord
Exmouth was therefore to be instructed to go to Algiers, Tunis,
and Tripoli, and to persuade their Governments to make a
peace with Naples and Sardinia upon the footing of that with
Portugal. He was to agree that the same rate of ransom as
had heretofore been paid for prisoners, subjects of those powers,
should be paid for those he should find there in captivity, and
that the usual presents in money should hereafter be paid for
them. He was to resist and reject all demands for contribution

of naval or military stores, and to require the release without ransom of all prisoners natives of the Ionian Islands. But although he was to refuse any stipulated compensation for their deliverance, he was authorized to give it to be understood that a suitable present would be made for them. He was also to admonish the regencies of the rising indignation of Europe against their mode of warfare, and to advise them to abandon it and to resort to more creditable resources for the support of their Government. At the same time he was to assure them of the friendly disposition of Great Britain towards them, and that she would not support any Christian state in any unjust claim or pretension against them. He was in the first instance to urge all this in an amicable manner, but was explicitly authorized to use force if necessary.

2. A second letter from Lord Castlereagh to Earl Bathurst, dated 13th March, stating that the treaty between the United States of America and Algiers concluded on the 30th June, 1815, and ratified at Washington on the 26th of December last, had engaged the attention of his Majesty's Government; that the eighteenth article in particular would, in the case of a future war between Great Britain and the United States, be incompatible with the ninth and tenth articles of the Treaty of 1698, between Great Britain and Algiers, which had been recognized and renewed in all the subsequent treaties between them; that it might not for this reason be necessary to require the abrogation of the treaty between the United States and Algiers, but that Lord Exmouth should be instructed formally to protest against the application of that article of the treaty to Great Britain in the case of any future hostilities between this country and the United States.

3. A report from Lord Exmouth, dated 17th April, at Tunis, to the Lords of the Admiralty, of his execution of the first instructions at Algiers and Tunis. He states that he had not received the second instructions (those relative to the treaty between the United States and Algiers) until after he had left Algiers, and that he should therefore execute them upon his return.

4. A summary statement of the terms upon which the peace

was concluded, both at Algiers and at Tunis, for Sardinia and for Naples. The ransom for the Sardinian prisoners was five hundred dollars for each man, and for the Neapolitans one thousand. The consular and other presents to be as *usual* heretofore, but only in money. The Ionian Islanders to be restored without ransom.

5. A declaration by Mahmoud Bashaw, Bey of Tunis, addressed to Lord Exmouth, and promising, in consideration of the anxious desire manifested by his Royal Highness the Prince Regent of England to put an end to the slavery of Christians, and to prove his esteem for the *European* powers and his pacific disposition, that in case of war with any of *the said* powers the prisoners shall not be reduced to slavery, but treated as prisoners of war, and at the end of the war exchanged and sent home.

After thanking Lord Castlereagh for the communication of these documents, the purport of which I assured him I should immediately report to the Government of the United States, I told him that as the instructions to Lord Exmouth had positively forbidden him to stipulate for any future contributions to the barbarians in naval or military stores, I hoped that in the next arrangement which Great Britain should make with them, for her friends, she would proceed one step further, and prohibit the payment to them of money, which was equivalent to and would procure them all. And as the Prince Regent's anxiety to put an end to Christian slavery had obtained a declaration from the Bey of Tunis that he would no longer reduce Christian prisoners to slavery, the same influence would hereafter be exerted effectually to abolish that practice on the part of all the Barbary powers, and especially Algiers; that it was worthy of Great Britain to take the lead in the abolition of this species of slavery, as she had done with regard to that of the Africans; that she was perfectly able to accomplish it alone, and in that case would enjoy all the credit and glory of having effected it, but if she preferred to have the co-operation of others, I was confident she might rely upon that of the United States to the full proportion of their power; and that I thought her having succeeded to the possession of the island of Malta really did impose upon her the obligation of affording to the Christian commerce at least all the protection that it could derive from the perpetual war between that order and the infidels.

Lord Castlereagh declared that it was the earnest wish of the British Government that all the Barbary powers should abandon altogether this mode of warfare; but he thought that mild and moderate measures and persuasion would be better calculated to produce this effect than force. He seemed even to consider that this payment of money to them would have the tendency of relaxing them into good humor, and incline them to compliance with the wish that they would make no more slaves to be ransomed. He said that although Great Britain possessed the island of Malta, she had none of the revenues which had been assigned by all the principal states of Europe to the order; that Great Britain, with all her exertions, had not been able to obtain the abolition of the African slave-trade by Spain and Portugal; and as she would not have felt justified in resorting to war to compel them to it, so she could not make war upon the Barbary States to force them to renounce the practice of making slaves of Christians, so long as they never applied it to her subjects or had given her any cause of offence. It was for other powers to vindicate and maintain the liberties of their own people; and, besides, the northern maritime states, France, Spain, and all those who had possessions on the Mediterranean, had as strong an obligation to put down the scandal of Christian slavery as Great Britain. She had for herself no complaint against the Barbary States to make. She had often found them useful friends, and especially during the late war in the Peninsula, which it would have been impossible for her to have carried through successfully without the supplies which her troops had received from the coast of Barbary, from which they had almost all their fresh provisions. Great Britain, however, had no interest or desire to countenance or encourage the wars of the Barbary States against the other navigating European powers. She had no unworthy policy of securing by such means an exclusive privilege to her own flag of securely navigating in the Mediterranean seas. But she did not think that the obligation of putting an end to the depredations of the Barbary States was incumbent upon her alone; and if it was to be effected, she thought the best mode of accomplishing it would be by convincing them that it would be better for their own interest to resort to other and more honest sources of prosperity.

I observed that as to the manner of accomplishing the object, if Great Britain would undertake it, that must be at her own option. There could not be supposed any necessity for her resorting to the use of force. The intimation of her will, and the exhibition of her means of enforcement, would infallibly be as efficacious upon the Dey of Algiers as the Prince Regent's wish had been upon the Bey of Tunis. As to the assistance which had been derived from supplies of provisions to the British troops in Spain, the interest of the seller was doubtless the motive for that, and it could lay no claim to the merit of an obligation. If, however, Great Britain should not incline to assume the task of putting an end to Barbary piracy, if she would leave them in our hands I believed we should be able to give a good account of them. The experience of the last year had proved that they were not very formidable antagonists upon the ocean, and if we had to deal with them alone, I had no doubt but that our navy would be competent to the protection of our commerce against them. I was not informed what the precise point of difference between Algiers and us now was, but as to the conflicting articles of the two treaties, there could be no difficulty in an arrangement between the two Governments concerning it.

He replied that we might depend upon meeting no molestation in our operations against Algiers on the part of Great Britain. He thought that the place itself could not be attacked with any prospect of success. There had been of late years a change in the system of Algerine warfare, which had been to their own disadvantage. Formerly they had been accustomed to send out small galleys, and xebecs, and gunboats for shallow waters, which cost nothing, and against which it was scarcely possible to protect commercial vessels, especially during certain seasons of the year. Of late they had undertaken to maintain a sort of navy, large, expensive frigates, with which they had effected their descents on the coasts of Italy and Sardinia, and carried off whole villages. But such vessels were not so well adapted to the annoyance of commerce as those which they had formerly employed. The large ships could be out only part of the year, and then they could neither fight nor navigate them well. Defence against them would not be difficult; but it was Lord Exmouth's opinion that if they should resort again to their old system there could be no effectual protection for merchant vessels against them through all seasons.

This was the substance of the conversation, in which Lord Melville took no, or scarcely any, part—appearing merely to assent to the observations of Lord Castlereagh. Before leaving them, I mentioned to Lord Castlereagh the note that I addressed to him the first of this month concerning the American vessel refused entry at Liverpool because the collector at Richmond certified that the master had been *qualified*, instead of saying sworn, to the manifest of tobacco. I told him that in some parts of the United States I knew the term qualified was used, and received, as equivalent to sworn. Lord Melville said that sometimes it was so used in this country. Lord Castlereagh had not seen, or had forgotten, my note, but he promised to enquire after it. I also told Lord Castlereagh that I had received instructions to ask for a permission to export rollers for the use of the Mint of the United States. He said there could be no difficulty in that; but Lord Melville remarked that the prohibition was by Act of Parliament. Lord Castlereagh asked me to write him a note about it.

13th. Attended the meeting of the British and Foreign School Society, at the London Tavern, Bishopsgate Street. The meeting was appointed for twelve o'clock, the chair to be taken precisely at one. It was near one when we arrived. They were waiting for the Duke of Kent, who was to preside. The Lord Mayor was there, but he was engaged to go with an address from the Common Council to the Prince of Saxe-Coburg and the Princess Charlotte. It was agreed, therefore, that the Lord Mayor should take the chair to open the meeting, and immediately resign it to Lord Darnley, who should

preside until the Duke should come. All this was arranged
in the committee-room, into which I was introduced, and where
I knew not a soul excepting the Lord Mayor.

I followed the company into the hall, which was crowded
with a numerous auditory, and took my seat upon the plat-
form. The Lord Mayor opened the meeting, apologized that
he was obliged to go to change his dress and go in the old
State wagon to Camelford House, but said he would leave the
Lady Mayoress to supply his place, and Lord Darnley would
take the chair until the Duke of Kent should come.

Lord Darnley accordingly took the chair for a few minutes,
until the Duke arrived. He apologized for being late, and said
that his carriage had been detained twenty-five minutes at a
place in the City, where the street had been so obstructed by
other carriages and wagons that he could not get along.

The report of the Treasurer of the Society was then read,
and immediately afterwards a written motion was put into my
hand, with a request that I would move it. It was marked
" No. 1. His Excellency the American Ambassador will move,
That the Report which has now been read be received and
adopted, and that it be printed under the direction of the Committee. To be seconded by   ." I had suspected that
they would call upon me for some address, motion, or speech,
but not that I should have been summoned out the very first ;
and I was not a little embarrassed what to say. The Duke of
Kent, however, in calling upon me to make the motion, relieved me from much of my awkwardness by observing that
the Report just read had been very long, but that the time
remaining to transact the business to be done was short, and
that he requested all those who proposed to address the
company to be as brief in their remarks as possible. I said,
" Mindful of that admonition which has just been so properly
given by his Royal Highness, the illustrious Chairman of this
meeting, I shall not waste a moment of your time in commenting upon the Report which you have just heard. I am
sensible that no encomium of mine can add grace or dignity
to that spirit of benevolence which walks abroad, communicating wisdom and virtue (for education is wisdom and virtue)

wherever it goes. To enlarge upon it would in me be presumption, for I am well assured that I could utter nothing in
its praise which has not already been anticipated in every
bosom of those whom I have now the honor to address. One
remark only I may be permitted to make, in reference to that
passage of the Report in which honorable notice is taken of
my native country for the ardor and zeal with which it pro-
motes and encourages institutions devoted to the purposes of
education. It would certainly not become me to question the
accuracy of this compliment, or to detract from the merit
which may be ascribed to my country for it. I shall only say
that it would be utterly impossible for a nation descended from
British ancestry to be neglectful of the education of their
children." I then made the motion, which was seconded and
adopted.

A number of other motions were successively made and
passed, and the meeting was addressed in speeches by Lord
Darnley, the Rev. Rowland Hill, a Methodist clergyman, the
Rev. Mr. Lindsay, a Dissenting minister, Mr. Schwabe, the
foreign secretary of the Society, and some others. From
their speeches, I collected that this institution is viewed with
jealousy by the Established Church, and that their favor is
confined to a rival institution, where the benefits of education
are bestowed only upon children bred upon the principles of
the Establishment. Count Lieven, the Russian Ambassador,
was to have been present, but sent an excuse; but there was
present a Mr. Bolk-Oleff, who is going out as Minister from
the Emperor of Russia to Brazil, who was requested to make
one of the motions, and who made it by proxy. A gentleman
spoke for him, and expressed for him his regret that his acquaintance with the English language was not sufficient to
enable him to speak in public himself. The last vote, being
No. 9, was to have been moved by some other person, but,
from what cause I know not, they brought it to me. It was
thus: " No. 9.   will move, That the thanks of this
meeting be presented to his Royal Highness the Duke of
Kent for his unremitting exertions in the cause of this institution, and for his able conduct in presiding at this meeting.

To be seconded by   ." But I did not wait for a second; I said, " Ladies and gentlemen, the motion which I have now to present to you is one which I have as high and sincere pride and gratification in being permitted to make as I am sure you will unanimously take in adopting it." I then read the motion and put the question, upon which the whole auditory rose and held up their hands.

The Duke answered the vote by an address, in which he declared his warm attachment to the institution and his good wishes for its success, his satisfaction at the crowded and respectable appearance of the meeting, which he had appointed to be held there, in the *east* part of the town, from a conviction that a most liberal collection for the benevolent purposes of the Society would be made there. He felt the greater satisfaction, too, at the respectability of the meeting, as this was the last time he should have the opportunity of giving his attendance on a like occasion for several, he could not say how many, years. He was shortly to leave the country, to reside some years upon the Continent, and when the objects for which he should thus absent himself should be accomplished, he now pledged himself to give one thousand guineas to this institution. If he had not given them before, it was not because the will, but because the means had been wanting. It gave him peculiar satisfaction that the motion of thanks to him had been made by the Minister of the United States, a country in the neighborhood of which he had several years resided, which had his best wishes for its prosperity, and the unfortunate differences with which had always given him great pain and concern. He concluded by appealing to the liberality of the meeting to contribute to the funds of the Society, and observed that the Lady Mayoress and Lady Darnley would hold the plates at the door. The meeting then dissolved.

14th. I went into London and attended the Prince Regent's levee at Carlton House. I presented to him Mr. J. A. Smith, as the Secretary of Legation, and Mr. Charles King. The usage is to give cards, with the names of the persons to be presented, to the Lord-in-waiting; but Mr. King had forgotten to take his card with him, and I was obliged to write his name on the back of Mr. Smith's card, which I gave to the Lord-in-waiting. But the presentations were so numerous that the Lord-in-waiting, after presenting Mr. Smith, forgot to turn the card, and the Prince was passing on, when I presented Mr. King to him myself. The Prince spoke to him in handsome terms of his father.

The crowd at the levee was very great. The Dukes of York, Clarence, Kent, and Gloucester, and the Prince of Coburg, were there. I also met Mr. Thornton, now the British Minister in Sweden, and whom I had seen in 1803 as the Chargé d'Affaires at Washington. I did not recognize him until I heard him named, nor he me until I spoke to him. Mr. Liston was also there, and told me that he should leave town the day after to-morrow for Bath and Scotland. When the entrée levee was over, and the door for the great levee was opened, the stream began, and we stood, observing the persons as they passed, an hour and a half, and we withdrew before it was exhausted.

16th. We attended the Queen's drawing-room. We reached the palace at Buckingham House in very good season, at half past one o'clock. Precisely at two the doors of the chamber where the Queen was were thrown open for the foreign Ambassadors and Ministers, and we were among the first that passed. The Queen was sitting in a chair. The Princesses Augusta, Elizabeth, Mary, the Princess Charlotte of Wales, and the Princess Sophia of Gloucester were standing at her right hand in a sort of semicircle, at sufficient distances from each other to leave space for their hoops. The Prince of Coburg stood at the window, behind the Princess Sophia. The Duke of Sussex was there, but went away before the Prince Regent came. The Dukes of York, Clarence, Kent, and Gloucester were also there, and from two o'clock until five the stream of persons passing before the Queen never ceased to flow. The antechambers, the staircase, all the rooms on the lower floor, were so excessively crowded that many of the gentlemen in their full dresses, and of the ladies in their hoops, were obliged to stand for hours on the green in front of the palace before they could get admission within the doors. There were, it was said, three thousand persons there. I presented to the Queen Mr. J. A. Smith, as the Secretary of the American Legation, and Mr. Charles King, whom she remembered to have seen at Harrow School. I gave their cards, before presenting them, to the Earl of Morton, the Queen's Chamberlain, who stood at her left hand. The Prince Regent came about four o'clock. The crowd and the heat were so great that several of the ladies fainted. I introduced Mr. Smith to Lady Castlereagh, who invited him to her evening parties on Saturdays after the opera. She told me she had mentioned them to Mrs. Adams, but supposed it might be inconvenient to us to come in so far from the country.

I spoke to Lord Castlereagh about the Algerine affairs; mentioned the motion said to have been lately made in the French House of Peers by the Vicomte de Chateaubriand, which was, that the King of France should be requested to instruct his Ambassadors at the different Courts of Europe to propose that they should all unite in the endeavor to prevail upon the Barbary powers to abolish their practice of making slaves of Christians. I enquired if any proposal of that sort had been made by the French Ambassador here. He said there had not, and, with a sneering smile, added that he thought it was only a project of Sir Sidney Smith's, which would not meet with much encouragement. We came away just before the drawing-room closed. It was with the utmost difficulty that we made our way down the staircase, and at the door we were stopped to make way for the Princess Charlotte and her husband, and after them for the Duchess of York, to go.

20th. Mrs. Adams, among her other visits, had called on Mrs. Bourke, the Danish Minister's lady, who enquired if we had received an invitation to the Prince Regent's dress-party for to-morrow evening, and was much surprised on hearing that we had not. She herself had received her invitation yesterday morning, and her husband, Mr. Bourke, late last evening.

21st. Mr. J. A. Smith arrived with a card of invitation from the Lord Chamberlain to the Prince Regent's dress-party this evening at nine o'clock, to have the honor of meeting the Queen. The card was to me only (not to Mrs. Adams), and had been left at the office in Craven Street about seven o'clock this evening. Mr. Smith immediately brought it out himself on horseback. He stopped only a few minutes, and returned to town. I dressed with all possible expedition, but on my way to town recollected the absolute necessity of going to complete my toilet at Craven Street. I reached Carlton House about half-past eleven, and found some of the company going away. The Queen, with the Prince Regent and the Princesses, had been round the circle about ten o'clock. I did not see the Queen at all. The Prince Regent came into the hall again. I was seen by him, and he bowed, but did not speak to me. The Portuguese Minister had received his card at two o'clock this afternoon; the Bavarian and Würtemberg Ministers at seven this evening. The Prussian, Swedish, and Saxon Ministers were not there.

Among the company I met there was Mr. F. Robinson, the Vice-President of the Board of Trade. I spoke to him of the several objects relative to the execution of the convention of commerce of 3d July, 1815. He asked me to send him a written minute of them, and promised to do everything in his power for the arrangement of them all to my satisfaction.

I spoke also to Mrs. Wellesley Pole, who told me that she had received budgets of letters from Mrs. Bagot. She was very much gratified with her reception, and there was not a word of truth in the story told in some of the newspapers about the salute having been refused to the frigate. On the contrary, the frigate's salute of thirteen guns had been returned with eighteen. Mrs. Bagot had seen Mrs. Madison, and was much pleased with Washington. I left Carlton House about one in the morning, and reached home about three.

23d. I dined at Fishmongers' Hall, at the anniversary dinner of that Company. Before dinner we witnessed the swearing in of the Dukes of Kent and Sussex as members of the Company. The Duke of Gloucester was already a member, and was present, as were the Marquis of Lansdowne, the Earl of Darnley and his son, Lord Clifton, Lords Holland and Erskine. The Prime Warden of the Company, Nathanael Brickwood, Esq., presided at the table. The Lady Mayoress and two Miss

Woods, her daughters, Mrs. and Miss Brickwood, and a large number of ladies were there. I was the only foreign Minister, and, I believe, the only foreigner, present. The Lord Mayor and Lady Mayoress sat at the right and left hand of the Prime Warden; at the right of the Lord Mayor, Mrs. Brickwood, the Duke of Kent, the Duke of Gloucester, Miss Wood, myself, Miss Brickwood, Lord Erskine, &c.; at the left of the Lady Mayoress, the Duke of Sussex, the younger Miss Wood, the Marquis of Lansdowne, Lord Holland, &c. The process after dinner was the same as at all these great entertainments. "Non nobis, Domine," was sung instead of saying grace. Then came the toasts. "The King," in respectful silence; the other toasts, with three times three: "The Prince Regent;" "The Queen and Royal Family;" "The Princess Charlotte and the Prince of Saxe-Coburg." Then, "The Lord Mayor;" "The Dukes of Kent, Sussex, and Gloucester," successively. Then, "The American Minister, and perpetual peace and friendship between Great Britain and the United States." Then, "The Marquis of Lansdowne;" "Lord Erskine and trial by jury;" "Lord Holland and the Earl of Darnley;" "The Prime Warden;" "The Wardens of the Company," &c.

As usual, every person present who was toasted returned thanks by a speech. This part of the ceremony, always excessively irksome to me, was peculiarly so this day. I said, " Mr. Prime Warden, Gentlemen Wardens of the Fishmongers' Company, Ladies and Gentlemen: I beg leave to return my thanks, as well for the distinguished honor that is done me by this notice, as for that of having been permitted to participate in the festivities of this entertainment on this auspicious occasion. From my earliest infancy I have always been accustomed to hear the city of London celebrated for the liberality of its principles, nor is this the first day upon which I have heard the praises of the Company before which I stand, as being among the liberal distinguished for its liberality. Since my residence in this country, I have had ample opportunities to experience in my own person the truth of that which I have before heard, and to say, with one of our ingenious poets, ' I thought so once, but now I know it.' Sir, I have been very recently informed of the arrival in the United States of a Minister from the British Government accredited to that of my country. It will be his duty to support the interests of his countrymen and the rights of his sovereign in the United States, as it is my duty to support the interests of my fellow-citizens and the rights of my sovereign here. But there is one duty common to us both. It is, in my estimation, by far the most important of those with which I am charged, and I am persuaded that he will consider it as among the most important of those incumbent upon him. It is the duty of contributing the utmost in our power to make these two great nations better known and better friends to each other—the duty of softening the asperities, of cultivating and multiplying all the harmonies, between them. I will only add the wish that he may have equal reason to be gratified with the reception and treatment which he will meet in that country, as I have to feel myself honored and gratified by that which I have experienced in this." This speech was well received, and something complimentary to the United States was said in the speeches of the royal Dukes, and of almost all the noblemen who were toasted. The ladies left the table about ten o'clock. It was near twelve when the rest of the company rose, and there was still to be a concert in the hall above. The band of instrumental performers was numerous, and there were several fine voices among the singers. They performed and sang at intervals, while the company were at table. Lord Erskine told me that he was determined to pay a visit to the United States, and he promised again to send me his speech upon the Orders in Council. Lord Holland told me that the Fishmongers were the only Whig Company in the city, and had uniformly been so. The Prime Warden in his speech observed that the King's father, Prince Frederick of Wales, had been a member of the Company. Lord Holland invited me to dine with him at Holland House next Sunday week, and said he would send me a card.

25th. Mr. Planta told me that he had been directed by Lord Castlereagh to apologize to me for not having sooner answered my note of the 18th, which had only been owing to the extreme pressure of business, particularly in Parliament; to inform me that it was not consistent with their official rules to give copies of the papers, as I had requested, but he had brought copies of them all, which he was authorized to put into my hands to read, and he would wait until I could read them through. I might also take any short minutes from them, whilst reading them over, which I desired. He gave me the papers accordingly, and waited until I had read them through. I took minutes to correct the error of dates and numbers which had occurred in my dispatch to the Secretary of State, detailing the conference of the 12th instant.

The letters from Viscount Castlereagh to Earl Bathurst, relative to the instructions to be given to Lord Exmouth; the three Treaties with Algiers, and the three with Tunis, and Lord Exmouth's letter to the Admiralty, from Tunis Bay, with the declaration of the Bey of Tunis that he would make no more slaves of Christian captives, were the papers. The Treaties were at full length, instead of abstracts which were shown me by Lord Castlereagh. They were without preambles announcing the negotiators, but Lord Exmouth was the general undertaker on the European side in them all. The papers were all in a file, and all endorsed " copies, to be sent to Lord Cathcart, the British Ambassador at St. Petersburg;" an odd circumstance, taken in connection with Planta's assurance that it was incompatible with their official rules to let me have copies of the papers. After perusing them, I returned them to Planta, with my thanks, and he left me, saying Lord Castlereagh had directed him to express his hope that I would consider this communication of the papers " in extenso" as a strong mark of confidence.

27th. I dined at the Freemasons' Hall, Great Queen Street, with the Society for the Encouragement of Arts, Manufactures, and Commerce. The Duke of Sussex, President of the Society, was in the chair. The Duke of Athol, Lord Dundas, the Marquis of Stafford, Mr. J. C. Curwen, a member of Parliament and a distinguished agriculturist, were of the company. The only other foreign Minister was the Chevalier de Freire. The Duke of Sussex introduced me to Mr. John Penn, who told me that he was in correspondence with my father. Mr. Sanders[1] was also there. There were about two hundred persons at the dinner, principally artists. Part of the entertainment was some very fine roast beef, fatted upon an experimental plan by Mr. Curwen. A printed account of the experiment was also circulated round the table. After dinner, and " Non Nobis" sung, the usual toasts were drunk, with the usual cheering of three times three. Among them, the Duke of Sussex gave, " The Ministers of Portugal and of the United States of America," which he accompanied with a speech complimentary to our countries, and personally to us, particularly dwelling upon the pleasure with which he recollected his former acquaintance with me, upon what he termed neutral ground, at Berlin.

Mr. Freire simply returned thanks. I added, that on this, as upon all other occasions, I naturally must cast a reflective look to my own country. Though not yet competent to equal the perfection in the arts for which Great Britain was so eminently distinguished, she was competent to admire, and might, at a future day, be competent to emulate them. In the mean time she must be content to follow her parent, " non passibus æquis," and if hereafter she could rivalize her in the works of art, I prayed that that, and the emulation of good offices, might be the only rivalry between the two countries. Then, apologizing to the Duke for addressing the company instead of him, I said that it had been my good fortune, little less than twenty years ago, to meet his Royal Highness on what he was pleased to term neutral ground. I needed not to say that I considered it as one of the happiest circumstances of my life; but I could not forbear or deny myself the gratification of remarking that from that moment I had entertained for his Royal Highness the same sentiments which the company I had now the honor of addressing had so signally manifested by placing him in that chair. The Duke of Athol, Marquis of Stafford, Lord Dundas, Mr. Curwen, and Dr. Taylor, the Secretary of the

---

[1] This was Prince Sanders, a negro from the United States, who came out as an agent of the authorities in St. Domingo. It was said that some persons in good society in England mistook the Christian name for a title, which helped him to a fleeting notoriety.

Society, were all successively toasted, and returned thanks by speeches. There were songs, serious and jocund, and between nine and ten o'clock the company broke up.

29th. I attended with Mr. Smith the Prince Regent's levee at Carlton House. It was very thin. Prince Esterhazy, the Austrian Ambassador, was there, having returned last evening from Paris and brought his Princess with him. The Duke of Gloucester was also at the levee, a reconciliation having taken place since the difficulty occasioned by the Princess Charlotte's marriage. Mr. Chester, the Assistant Master of the Ceremonies, spoke to me of the manner in which I had received the invitation to the Prince Regent's dress-party on the 21st instant, and the omission of an invitation to Mrs. Adams. He said that it was owing entirely to mismanagement, but it was impossible to fix where the blame was. Baron Just, the Saxon Minister, and who had signed the marriage contract of the Princess Charlotte, had received no card for this party. Chester himself, though he had been specially appointed to attend upon the Prince of Coburg before the marriage, had no card. Baron Just made a formal complaint about it to Lord Castlereagh, who made an apology to him, assuring him that it was not intentional.[1]

June 2d. I dined with Lord Holland, at Holland House, his country-seat. It is about midway between the Brentford and Acton Roads, and the entrance-gate is at the side of the Kensington Turnpike. A very large brick house, built in the Gothic style, and four or five hundred years old. The library is in a central hall, which extends through the whole breadth of the house, nearly two hundred feet long, not more than thirty wide. The company were Count and Countess Lieven, with whom came a young English lady, Count Beroldingen, the Minister from the King of Würtemberg, the Earl and Countess of Jersey, the Earl of March, eldest son of the Duke

---

[1] It is obvious, from these various reports of the Court circles, that there must have then prevailed a singular negligence in the official courtesies towards the representatives of foreign powers. This was doubtless owing in part to the peculiar situation of the members of the royal family at that time. Such has not been the characteristic of the British Court in the present reign.

of Richmond, Lord and Lady Grenville, Sir James Mackintosh, and some other gentlemen. Eighteen sat down to table. The dinner was elegant, the wines choice, the dessert excellent, and might have seemed to me better but that Madame Bourke, an accomplished epicure, had forewarned me that Lord Holland had the best confectioner in London. The tone of society was easy and agreeable. Lady Holland was perfectly well-bred, and by several unaffected marks of maternal attachment to her son Henry, a boy about twelve years of age, who was present, bespoke a favorable opinion of her domestic character. Lord Holland introduced the Earl of Jersey to me at his request. I sat between Count Lieven and Sir James Mackintosh at dinner, and had much conversation with the latter. I had much also with Lord Holland after dinner, and was pleased with every part of the conversation except my own. I offended Count and Countess Lieven by bluntly saying that I had never known such a thing as hot weather in Russia. I said two or three silly things to Sir James Mackintosh, and was altogether stiff and dull beyond my usual measure.

I asked Sir James if he was engaged upon a history of England. He told me he was, from the revolution of 1688. He asked me if I thought Dr. Franklin had been sincere in the professions which he made here, that he lamented the Revolution which was to separate the colonies from Great Britain; which he said he did the day before he last left London, even to tears.

I told him I did not believe Dr. Franklin wished for the Revolution—nor Washington. He asked me if any of the leading men had. I said, perhaps my father, Samuel Adams, and James Otis. He asked me if we had any popular writers in America. I said, none. Any good history of the Revolution? I mentioned Gordon, Ramsay, and Marshall's Life of Washington. He said he had met in India several masters of American merchant vessels, particularly from Salem, and found from them that America had two strong characters of English descent—a multitude of newspapers, and stage-coaches. He also told me that he had last year introduced Walter Scott to Mr. Clay, the first of his admirers that he had ever seen from

Kentucky. He spoke of Scott's three novels as admirable
delineations of Scottish manners, and of characters. The construction of the stories, to which I objected, he said was good
for nothing. I thought there was in the last of the three no
new picture of manners peculiarly Scottish; that is, nothing
which had not already been painted in " Waverley" and " Guy
Mannering." He mentioned " The Antiquary" himself. I
said the character was well drawn, but I did not perceive it to
be peculiarly national. He said there was its pedantry, altogether Scotch; he was himself a Scotchman, and he understood that whatever contest there might be about other
qualities, the palm of pedantry was universally awarded to
his country.

I observed that there must be something very powerful in
the principle of legitimacy, which made the Scotch nobility and
gentry now proud of their rebellions in favor of the Stuarts,
and instanced the late addresses to Louis XVIII., in presenting
him the Gaelic Ossian, and to the Prince Regent, also in Gaelic.
He said there was a sort of concession " even in their *errors.*"
I told him that I had great admiration for the principle of legitimacy, but I hoped he would give it the finishing-stroke in his
History : it was to me like Octavius to Cicero—ornaṅdus and
tollendus.

He said he should certainly not think it laudandus. It was
merely the fashion of the day. Hume himself, in speaking of
this principle, said it was admirable, inferior only to the more
exalted principle of the rights of the people. Hoadley was
made a Bishop in the reign of George the Second, and Horsley,
who somewhere called Hoadley the republican Bishop, was
made a Bishop in the reign of George the Third—the first for
preaching against the principles of legitimacy, and the second
for preaching in favor of them.

My conversation after dinner with Lord Holland turned
much on a comparison between the political institutions of this
country and of the United States. He enquired about our
forms of representation, of which I gave him an account, and
told him that the result of them was, that the very great proportion of our public men were lawyers. He said it was

precisely the same here. The theory of their representation in the House of Commons was bad, but perhaps no theory could produce a more perfect practical representation of all classes and interests of the community. Even the close boroughs often served to bring in able and useful men, who, by a more correct theory, would find themselves excluded. Men of property could always make their way into Parliament by their wealth. Men of family, such a man as the Earl of March, might go into the House of Commons for a few years in youth, to get experience of public business and employ time to useful purpose, and there was no man of real talents who, in one way or another, could fail of obtaining, sooner or later, admission into Parliament. But a great proportion of the House of Commons were lawyers, and most of the business of the House was done by them. In the House of Lords all that was of any use was done by lawyers. The great practical use of the House of Lords was to be a check upon mischief that might be done by the Commons. Many bills pass through that House without sufficient consideration. The Chancellor is under a sort of personal responsibility to examine and stop them. His character depends upon it. He is at the head of the nobility of the country, and all that *fudge;* and his consideration depends upon his keeping this vigilant eye over the proceedings of the Commons. All the ordinary business of the House, therefore, rests upon a lawyer. Lord Holland observed that, from what he had heard, the most defective part of our institutions in America was the judiciary; which I admitted.

Count and Countess Lieven went away immediately after dinner. The Countess had an evening party at her own house, to which we were invited. Mrs. Adams was to come with the carriage for me about eleven, and I had specially directed the servants to send me in word when the carriage came. But this was neglected until I had stood waiting until past midnight. There still remained there the Earl and Countess of Jersey, Lord and Lady Grenville, and Sir James Mackintosh, who sat round the fire in the library, conversing upon the Methodists, Foster's Essays, the Church, the Athanasian

Creed, and other miscellaneous subjects. Sir James Mackintosh and Lady Grenville had been this morning to church,
where, Sir James said, they had heard a mild and moderate
sermon. But, said I, by way of atonement for his moderation,
he gave you the Athanasian Creed. Sir James said, yes, to be
sure, they had that. Lord Holland said there were many
Church clergymen who, at their peril, took it upon them to
omit reading it; and that the Duke of Grafton always got up
and went out of church when it was begun to be read. Lady
Jersey said she wished she could go to a Methodist chapel
without being known.

5th. Mr. J. A. Smith went with me to the City of London
Tavern, in Bishopsgate Street, where we dined with the Society
of " Friends of Foreigners in Distress." The Duke of York
was to have been in the chair, but sent an apology of being
engaged in business and with the Prince Regent. The Duke
of Kent brought his excuse, and presided in his stead. The
Duke of Sussex was prevented from attending by illness ; the
Duke of Gloucester, by particular engagement. Prince Paul
Esterhazy, Count Lieven, Mr. Pfeffel, Baron Rehausen, Count
Munster, and Baron Just and Count Jenison Walworth, were
there, with a company of about five hundred persons. Lord
de Dunstanville and Mr. J. C. Villiers, brother of the Earl of
Clarendon, were the principal personages of this country
present. Lord Castlereagh, Mr. Vansittart, and some others,
sent excuses. Mr. Dubachefsky and the Chevalier Seguier,
the Russian and French Consuls, were also there. I sat at
table between Lord de Dunstanville and Mr. Dubachefsky,
whom I met at Countess Colombi's at dinner in the summer
of 1813, and had not since seen. Mr. S. G. Perkins, of Boston,
was likewise of the company.

Mr. Villiers recognized and spoke to me, having been
present when I had my first audience of the Queen. I had
seen him before that, when we were presented to the King of
France, at the Tuileries, in February, 1815. I did not then
know him, nor his name, until this day. He told me that Mrs.
Bagot, the wife of the British Minister in the United States,
was his niece, and I find that he married Mrs. Wellesley Pole's

sister. He spoke highly both of Mr. and Mrs. Bagot, and told
me that they were much pleased with their reception in
America. Count Lieven and Prince Esterhazy, before dinner,
hinted to the Duke of Kent that if their sovereigns should be
toasted, or themselves, they could not make speeches. He
said, laughing, that if they would tell him in three words what
to say he would speak for them, but that I could speak English
very fluently, and I must speak for them all.

The hour appointed for the dinner was precisely half-past
five o'clock, and the company actually sat down about six.
The dinner was good, and the toasting began early. "The
King," in respectful silence; "The Prince Regent, Protector,"
and "The Queen, Protectress, of the Society;" each, as well as
the following toasts, with three times three. "The Emperor of
Russia and the King of Prussia" were drunk successively, as
Protectors, the Duke of Kent introducing their healths with an
appropriate eulogium in each case, and especially reminding
the company of the urbanity and affability displayed by those
sovereigns when they dined with the Society at their anniversary two years ago. The Duke also returned the thanks
of Count Lieven for the toast, and also for the Prussian
Minister, when the King was toasted. Baron Jacobi was not
present. The next toast was, "The Emperor of Austria," upon
which the Duke, for Prince Esterhazy, addressed the company,
assuring them that although the Emperor was not yet one
of the Protectors of the Society, it was only because he had
been prevented from executing his intention of coming to this
country with the other sovereigns two years ago; but that he
(the Prince) should write an account of this meeting, and had
no doubt he should receive authority to subscribe for the
Emperor as one of the Protectors.

The Duke next toasted his royal sisters the Princesses,
patronesses of the Society, with an apology for his egotism,
and an affectionate panegyric upon the benevolence of their
dispositions. "The Princess Charlotte and the Prince of Coburg"
were drunk with the same marks of enthusiasm in her favor
which I have witnessed on many late occasions. The Duke of
Kent's own health was then proposed by Lord de Dunstanville,

one of the Vice-Presidents and Stewards of the day, who introduced it with some complimentary remarks. The Duke returned thanks, with assurance of his attachment to the Society and its objects, and with allusions to his intention of shortly leaving the country for some years. "The Duke of York and the army;" "The Duke of Clarence and the navy;" and "The Duke of Gloucester, the first patron of the Society," were toasted successively, after which the Duke of Kent gave, "The foreign Ambassadors and Ministers present," prefacing it with remarks upon his personal satisfaction at seeing so large a number of them, ministers of peace, from countries with whom this nation but a few years since had unfortunate differences. The hall, he said, in this respect, exhibited a contrast most auspicious to this country to the aspect which it would have had only four years since. The Duke then, with the assent and request of all the Ambassadors present, called upon me to answer the toast, which I did nearly to this effect: "Gentlemen: Deeply sensible as I am to the honor done me by my illustrious and excellent colleagues in calling upon me to make our common acknowledgments for that which you have done us in the toast just given by his Royal Highness from the chair, I feel myself no less at a loss for words than they can be suitably to make this return for your goodness to them and to me. For although I am indebted for this distinguished charge to the accidental advantage of speaking the same language as most of you, yet I must entreat your indulgence when I say that expressions suitable to convey the sense of their gratitude and mine are at this moment as little at my command as at theirs. If, gentlemen, it were the highest honor of this institution that it has for its Protectress her Majesty the Queen Consort of this realm, a Princess who throughout life has been by her private and domestic virtues a model for her sex, as by her civic virtues she is an ornament to her exalted station; that it has for its Protector his Royal Highness the Prince Regent, the acting sovereign of this great empire, and joined with him a second Alexander, more glorious than the first—glorious not by the conquest of the earth, but by saving the earth from conquest—and a Frederick William, glorious by having redeemed his kingdom and his country as by fire entire and unimpaired from the furnace of adversity; that to these you have had this day the promised expectation of shortly adding the name of their brother in arms and in virtue, his Majesty the Emperor of Austria; that among the names of your patrons and patronesses you reckon those of many Princes and Princesses of the most resplendent lines in Europe; that you have the happiness of seeing in that chair a Prince of the illustrious House of Brunswick, to whose personal character beneficence is so congenial that wherever it forms the basis of association there he seems naturally called to preside;—if, I say, gentlemen, these were your highest honors, well might my honorable colleagues, well at least might I, find my powers of language exhausted in attempting to convey to you the sentiments which would animate us in hearing our names thus associated with such great and glorious names. But, gentlemen, these are not your highest honors. Proud as you have reason to be of these high distinctions, your highest honor, in my estimation, and, I will presume to say, in that of those noble persons who have permitted me to address you in their names, is the principle of your association—that principle which has connected all those great and glorious names with your Society and with your exertions. Gentlemen, the sublime language of your immortal poet, who asked a kingdom for a stage, princes to act, and monarchs to behold the swelling scene, is not large enough for the purposes of your institution. Your theatre is not a single kingdom, but the whole habitable globe. Your actors are princes and monarchs, and the beholders are the blessed spirits that encircle the throne of Omnipotence. They look down on labors like these with complacency, they behold the swelling scene with delight. For the action, the object of your labors, is the first and noblest of moral and Christian virtues—charity; charity in its most extensive sense; charity not confined to one language, one religion, or one country, but expansive as the globe and universal as the blessings of Providence. Gentlemen, to give utterance to the feelings which fill the bosoms of my noble colleagues and my own, in return for the notice bestowed upon us by such an association, is beyond the powers of language possessed by us all. We can only say, in the honesty and simplicity of our hearts, we thank you."

This address was very well received. Lord de Dunstanville, Mr. Villiers, and the Russian and French Consuls, complimented me civilly upon it. Mr. Villiers asked me if I had been prepared for it. I told him I had not had a conception, until the moment when we sat down to dinner, that I should be called upon to answer for the whole Corps Diplomatique; but the truth is, I was not gifted by nature with the talent of extemporaneous speaking, and on this and all the other similar occasions I have felt myself in much embarrassment, and have got through without discredit only by revolving during dinner-time what to say; a process not remarkably favorable to the enjoyment of the conviviality of the table.

My awkwardness was this day aggravated by an observation of a gentleman who sat opposite to me at the table, that he had heard at one of these same dinners, some years ago, a speech from Mr. Pinkney, which he should never forget, and of which he spoke in an ecstasy of admiration. I confess the eulogy might have come at a more acceptable moment; but this table-cloth oratory is one of the duties of an American Minister in this country which I had not anticipated.

18th. At ten, Mrs. Adams and I went into London to an evening party at the Dutch Ambassador's, Baron Fagel's. It was rather late. There had been a party at dinner, and it was a sort of celebration of the battle of Waterloo, of which this is the anniversary. Some of the company were gone, but others were coming. The Duchess of Wellington, and the Duke's mother, Lady Mornington, were there; Lord and Lady Castlereagh, Mr. Wellesley Pole, Mrs. Villiers, Lord Fitzroy Somerset and his Lady, Mr. and Mrs. Hamilton; the Spanish Ambassador, and the Sardinian and Saxon Ministers. Count Beroldingen took leave of me, and told me he should leave London the day after to-morrow.

Lord Castlereagh told me that Brougham had been asking this day in the House of Commons for the papers of Lord Exmouth's proceedings with the Barbary powers, but he had answered that he was not yet quite ready to give them. He also said there had been this day a sort of confirmation of the story which has been for some days in circulation, that there had been some subsequent hostilities by the Algerines against the British at Oran. I told him that I hoped it would tend to recommend the advice which I had taken the liberty to give him, and to persuade the British Government to put down the crying scandal of those Barbary piracies.

He intimated that the new quarrel was owing to an attempt of Lord Exmouth's to obtain from the Dey of Algiers a declaration that he would in future make no more Christian slaves, similar to the declarations which had been given by the Bey of Tunis and the Bashaw of Tripoli; and added that it could not be on account of the mere protest which Lord Exmouth was to make on his return to Algiers against one article of the Algerine Treaty with the United States, because he was not even to ask that the treaty should be annulled, but only that the prior engagements with Great Britain should not be broken.

But Mr. Hamilton, the Under-Secretary of State, told me that they had this day received advices that the late quarrel between Lord Exmouth and the Algerines had been arranged, and that the vessels and the Vice-Consul seized at Oran had been restored. I spoke to the Sardinian Minister about the peace made for Sardinia by Lord Exmouth, and found that he was content to consider it as a very advantageous one. He said to be sure they had some money to pay, but that was a trifle, and they had got all their prisoners ransomed, besides a stipulation by the Bey of Tunis not to make any more Christian slaves.

We came away at half-past twelve, and, as we were descending the stairs, met the Marquis of Camden, the Earl of Lonsdale, Viscount Sidmouth, and the two Miss Addingtons, his daughters, going up. The Earl of Westmorland immediately followed them. It was about two when we got home.

July 2d. I went into London immediately after breakfast, and first called at Mr. Chester's house, in South Audley Street, to enquire whether the session of Parliament was to be closed

this day, and whether the foreign Ministers were to attend. I
met Mr. Chester in his carriage, just starting from his door,
dressed, and going to the House of Lords. He told me that
he had written me a note yesterday to give me notice of the
ceremony this day, and requested me to be at the House of
Lords about a quarter before two, as the Prince would be punctually there at the hour. It was then a quarter past one.
Went to the House of Lords, which I just reached in seasonable time. The House was very much crowded, principally
with ladies. There were less than thirty Peers in their robes,
among whom were the Dukes of York and Kent. The House
was understood to be in session.

As I passed before the throne to go to the place assigned for
the foreign Ministers, I met the Earl of Limerick, who said to
me, smiling, "You see us here in our robes. But robes, you
know, and furred gowns hide all." "Your Lordship at least,"
said I, "has nothing to hide." Earl Bathurst told me that he
had received a letter from Mr. Lawrence Bathurst, asking to see
him, and claiming to be his relation, and that he had referred
him to me for testimony of his being the person that he professed. I told the Earl that I had received a letter introducing
this Mr. Bathurst to me from a person of the most respectable
character, with whom I had served some years as a Senator of
the United States. Mr. Bathurst had been to me to enquire
how he could obtain access to his Lordship. I had advised
him to write a note to him, stating who he was and his wish to
see his Lordship, and told him I had no doubt the Earl would
see him, adding that he might refer his Lordship to me for my
knowledge of him. He had told me he was descended from a
brother of his Lordship's grandfather, who had been one of the
original settlers of Georgia. He had shown me some of his
papers, and I had supposed his Lordship would have known
something of the family which might have served to ascertain
the correctness of his story.

The Earl said there had been, not a brother of his grandfather's, but a distant relation of the family, who went many
years ago to America, and about seven or eight years since Mr.
Phineas Bond had made some application to him in behalf of

an old man who was descended from that person, but he had understood that this old man had no children, and that he was since dead.

I told him that Mr. Bathurst had shown me a letter to him from Mr. Bond, and some other papers. The Earl asked me if I should have any objection to let him see the letter that I had received, and to which I referred. I said, none, and promised to send it to him.

Before the Regent came in, the Earl of Donoughmore referred to some papers received from the Lord Lieutenant of Ireland, and gave notice of his intention, early at the next session of Parliament, to move the taking into consideration the state of Ireland, particularly with reference to the Catholics, unless the subject should be brought forward by better hands, —he meant his Majesty's Ministers.

The Prince Regent entered the hall two or three minutes before two. His escort was similar to that of last year, but the sword of state was borne by the Duke of Wellington, who arrived yesterday from Paris. The summons was sent to the House of Commons, and the Speaker immediately came to the bar, with a number of the members. He addressed a speech to the Regent, the topics of which were, the glorious establishment of general peace and tranquillity by the restoration of legitimate government, and by its being placed under the proper custody of the Duke of Wellington; the new coinage; the consolidation of the English and Irish treasuries; the new regulation of the civil list; and the happy marriage of the Princess Charlotte with the Prince of Coburg; with a very slight notice of the distresses of the agricultural interest, to which he said they had given what immediate relief they could, but which was to be expected after a long war, and for the remedy for which they trusted much to the healing influence of time. He concluded by presenting the bill for the appropriations of the year. The titles of that, and of several other bills, public and private, were then read by a clerk, and another, upon a nod from the Prince, pronounced the royal assent to them in old law French, in the three several forms mentioned by Blackstone.

The Prince then read his speech, seated, and covered with an enormous three-cornered military hat. He began by lamenting the continuance of his Majesty's indisposition; touched upon most of the topics to which the Speaker had referred; promised a continuance of peace; announced that he had given the royal consent to a marriage betweeen his Majesty's daughter the Princess Mary, and the Duke of Gloucester; and in bewailing the distresses of some classes of the people, trusted that they would bear them with fortitude and energy, as they had their former difficulties; and that they would prove to be only temporary, and soon remedied by the increase of public credit, and the relief from burdens already granted.

When he had finished, the Lord Chancellor, standing behind the throne, prorogued the Parliament to the 24th of August, and the Prince withdrew. A cannonade announced his arrival and his departure. As I left the hall to go to my carriage, I heard a loud shouting among the people, and was told it was for the Duke of Wellington. The crowds of spectators in the streets were not so great as they had been upon the same occasion last year.

3d. After employing the morning upon this journal and part of a letter, which I could not finish, I complied with a petition from my sons. We dined at three o'clock, and immediately afterwards all went to Covent Garden Theatre, and saw "The Jealous Wife," a comedy by the elder George Colman, with a farce called "Love, Law, and Physic," a translation from the French play "Le Collatéral, ou la Diligence de Joigny." We arrived at the theatre in good season, and had, after the first act, very good seats. The rule at the theatres here is, that seats may be engaged for any particular day at any time before. The name of the person taking the seats is entered on the box-keeper's book, but the tickets are not paid for. A shilling is given for a man to keep the seats until the first act of the play is over; but if the persons engaging the seats are not then arrived, they lose their right to the seats engaged, and must take their chance for others. The first row of boxes are called dress-boxes, and those immediately over them are called the first row. We could get no seats in the dress-boxes, and only the fifth bench in a box of the first row. But the first act was over before the company who had engaged the first and second benches appeared. The instant the curtain dropped, the occupiers of the third and fourth benches advanced to the first and second, and we stepped forward to the third. We were scarcely seated when the party who had engaged the first seats came in; but it was too late—they were obliged to put up with the seats behind us which we had left.

The comedy was, on the whole, very well performed, but in comparing it with the French comedy of Desforges, which I saw when I was last in Paris (18th March, 1815), " La Femme jalouse," I think the French play the best of the two, and the performance of Mademoiselle de Verd superior to that of Miss O'Neill. The general plot of the two plays, and the principal characters, are the same; but the excitement of the wife's suspicions in the French comedy is more natural and less absurd than in the English. The French jealous wife is pathetic, the English one is only ridiculous and contemptible. In the English play the young gentleman, the successful lover, is degraded by a scene of beastly drunkenness—of that drunkenness which Count Almaviva calls " ivresse du peuple," and in the " Barbier de Seville" refuses even to simulate. There is no drunken scene in " La Femme jalouse." Great part of this English play is evidently borrowed from " Tom Jones." Lady Freelove, Lord Trinket, Squire Russet and his daughter, and Charles Oakley are little more than copies of Lady Bellaston and Lord Fellamar, Squire Western, his daughter Sophia, and Tom Jones. Miss O'Neill's performance was very good, but not so strikingly excellent as I expected. Young, Terry, Charles Kemble, Fawcett, Jones, and Emery, Mrs. Gibbs, and Miss Foote all performed well, but some of them might have done better.

Mathews and Liston provoked much laughter in the farce. Mathews sang a song describing the bustle at the theatres on coming to them for a crowded night, the incidents within, disputes for seats in the boxes and pit, and the tumult at going out; mimicking the confused voices of men, women, children, box-keepers, link-boys, footmen, hackney-coachmen,

&c., with much humor. He was encored, and sang the song a second time with a total variation of the mimicking dialogue. The play finished about eleven o'clock. House crowded.

5th. The levee was more numerously attended than the last, but less crowded than the preceding one. The Duke of Wellington was there, and his brother, Mr. Wellesley Pole, introduced me to him. Mr. Pole and Lord Westmorland told me that they had seen last evening Mrs. Patterson and the Miss Catons. They brought letters from Mr. and Mrs. Bagot, who, Mr. Pole told me he was happy to hear, were very popular in America. Count Lieven asked me what was the explanation that had taken place between Lord Castlereagh and me relative to the late transactions of Lord Exmouth at Algiers and with the Barbary States. I told him the substance of what had passed between us. Baron Nicolai told me that in the course of eight or ten days he should embark for St. Petersburg, and that the Emperor had appointed him Minister at Copenhagen. The levee was soon over. The Prince Regent passed me, simply saying, " How do you do, Mr. Adams?" which is the same thing he always says on these occasions. He seldom says anything more to others ; but he was peculiarly gracious to the Duke of Wellington, and complimented him upon the cheerings of the people with as much apparent satisfaction as if they had been bestowed upon himself. The Dukes of Kent and Gloucester, and the Earls of Liverpool and Westmorland, spoke to me, the two former about the weather, and the latter about the distresses of the commercial interest in this country and in America. It appears they are as great in the United States as here.

At nine in the evening went with young Chambré to Mr. Sanders's ; there was there an assembly of sixty or seventy persons strangely collected together. Among them were Mrs. Opie the novelist, a General Burgoyne, Mr. Marcet, a Genevan, Mr. Beresford, a son of Dr. Beresford, now at Berlin, Mr. Amory, Captain Magee, Mr. Prescott,[1] the young man who brought me letters of recommendation, Mr. Bryden, John Clerkson, and others. Mr. Sanders made me an apology

---

[1] Since distinguished as the author, W. H. Prescott.

for having by mistake omitted to send me a card for his dinner. There was a band of music, and an intended ball, which partly failed. About eleven we left the party, and went to Mr. Penn's, where we found another ball, and a company perhaps of three hundred persons, scarcely a soul of whom we knew. After some time, however, we met Mr. West the painter, and had much conversation with him. His original picture of the foundation of Pennsylvania by William Penn was also there.

6th. W. Cook, the man whose boy has the smallpox at Brentford, came again with his girl, and told me the child was getting better every day. Two other men came from different parts of the country to enquire after work—ragged, penniless, and almost famished. At the shop where we stopped in Brentford, there was a woman who came from Basingstoke, in the same condition. The distress of the country, about which so much has been saying these nine months, is just beginning to show itself here in this shape. The colliers who were on their way to London have been stopped by magistrates sent out for that purpose, who purchased their coals, persuaded them to return home, and gave them money for their journey back. The effect of this example remains to be seen. The ministerial newspapers praise it as an act of great wisdom in the Home Department.

8th. Went to the Countess of Jersey's rout. It was excessively crowded with company, few of whom I knew. I spoke again to Count Lieven about the British new naval expedition to Algiers, which he said was fitting out, but that Lord Exmouth had received no instructions, the official accounts of the massacre at Bona not having been received. I asked Count Lieven and Mr. Pfeffel if they had received cards expressive of the Prince Regent's desire that the company at the ball on Friday should appear in British manufactures. They said they had; that the cards must have been sent by some mistake of the servants to the foreign Ministers, for whom Pfeffel said they could not be intended, as they were neither nobility nor gentry.

Lord Castlereagh told me that they had passed the Act of Parliament for allowing American vessels to take as many

passengers from Ireland as British vessels. I mentioned to
him also the clearance of American vessels direct for British
ports in India. He said the Act had followed the example
of our Act. Mr. Rogers, the poet and banker, asked me to
call and see him at his house. Mr. and Mrs. Patterson were
there, and Miss Caton. Mrs. Wellesley Pole and Lady Fitzroy
Somerset were with them, and taking the greatest notice of
them. Miss Louisa Caton was so much indisposed that she
could not come. Mr. Patterson told me they now talked of
going to Cheltenham on Friday, but they were putting it off
from one day to another. He hoped to go about that time.
The Earl of Jersey was not at the party, being out of town.

9th. I received by this evening's post a letter from James
Marsh, who says it has fallen to his lot to be one of those
unfortunate men afflicted with an inventive genius in mechanics. He has seen a paragraph in the newspapers about
fortifying the coast of the United States, and among his own
inventions that of a gun-carriage which supersedes the great
expense of batteries and prevents the loss of men working the
gun in time of action is what he now offers to my notice ; but
he has many others, and requests an interview to convince me
that, without any vanity on his part, the United States would
find in him a valuable subject not only in a military point of
view, but also in manufactures. His grammar and spelling are
not so inventive as those of some other great geniuses who
have offered themselves to my notice, but from the outside
of his letter I took it at first for an epistle from a petitioning
sailor, and the handwriting within had every appearance of
the same character. It is evidently self-taught.

12th. Evening. At seven o'clock I went and dined at
Lord Castlereagh's, with a company somewhat curiously composed—part of the Diplomatic Corps, in full Court dress, and
the rest English nobility and gentry, most of them in frocks
and undress. The Marquis d'Osmond was the only Ambassador, and the Ministers of Portugal, Denmark, Bavaria,
Saxony, Würtemberg, and Hanover were there, and Baron
Nicolai ; the Dukes of Beaufort and Rutland, Lords Paulett
and Clanwilliam, Messrs. Arbuthnot, Hamilton, Planta, and

nearly an equal number of persons whom I did not know; in all, a company of thirty persons. No ladies. The company were received before dinner in Lord Castlereagh's cabinet. They were more than half assembled when he appeared. The varieties of dress made a motley appearance, and before dinner was announced, Mr. Planta went round among the diplomatic guests and requested that they would not all sit together, but would scatter among the others, to avoid the appearance of two distinct companies.

Lord Castlereagh told me that they had just received dispatches from Mr. Bagot by the packet from New York, but he had not yet read them. I mentioned to him that I had received instructions from the Government of the United States to propose an additional commercial treaty or convention: I should soon address a note to him on the subject, and should be glad to have some previous conversation with him when it might suit his convenience. He said he should go out of town to-morrow for some days, and appointed next Thursday at one o'clock to see me at the Foreign Office. He enquired what were the objects upon which the American Government were desirous of treating. I said, in the first place, the old subject— seamen. The President had at two successive sessions of Congress recommended the passing an act for excluding foreign seamen from our naval service. An act to that effect would probably have passed at the last session, but it was thought best to make the proposal to establish the principle with this country by treaty, which would make the arrangement reciprocal. It was thought by the American Government that the present time was peculiarly favorable for such an arrangement, as by a mutual exclusion of each other's sailors, at present during peace, the questions upon which there was a difference of principle between the two Governments would be altogether avoided, and a system might be concerted which, in the event of a future maritime war, would prevent the collisions which were so strongly to be deprecated by both nations.

He said they would be ready to receive our proposals, and to agree to anything which might tend to *diminish* the inconveniences heretofore experienced.

Another subject of the proposed negotiation, I said, was the commerce between the United States and the British colonies in the West Indies and in North America. By the operation of the commercial convention of 3d July, 1815, connected with the regulations subsequently adopted by the British Government, the whole of that trade was exclusively carried on by British vessels; the operation of which was so injurious to the United States that it could not continue long in its present state. The American Government were desirous that it should be regulated by an amicable arrangement, and had therefore instructed me to propose this negotiation in preference to adopting, in the first instance, legislative measures to counteract the exclusive British measures.

He said that those exclusive measures arose from the long-established colonial system. It was the essential character of that system to confine the trade of the colonies to the mother country. To admit foreigners, therefore, to trade with them was an indulgence for which it would be necessary to expect some equivalent, and, as the United States had no colonies, it did not appear how any arrangement of that nature could be made reciprocal. He enquired, as with an air of doubt, whether there was any considerable commerce between the United States and the British colonies in the West Indies.

I told him there was a great deal, and that its present condition was such as left the United States no alternative but either the regulation of it by concert with Great Britain or by internal measures of legislation.

I enquired of Mr. Planta whether any press warrants had recently been issued. He said, no; at least not to his knowledge. Colonel Aspinwall had written me that there were rumors to that effect in circulation, and requested me to make the enquiry, as, if it should prove true, some measures of precaution would be necessary for the protection of the American seamen.

The dinner at Lord Castlereagh's was very light, served upon plate and porcelain of many different kinds, looking as if they had been collected from a pawnbroker's shop. The servants were all out of livery. I sat at table between the Chevalier de Freire, the Portuguese Minister, and Lord   , the latter of whom spoke French to me half the dinner-time, for which he apologized when he finally discovered that I could speak English. The hour appointed for the Prince Regent's ball was ten o'clock, at which time I went to Carlton House by the entrance of the Horse Guards. Happening to arrive just at the time when the Queen was passing, the carriage was stopped some time before it could obtain admission. I was shown immediately into the building where the ball was given, a rotunda, adjoining Carlton House, and connected with it by a covered staircase—a large rotunda in the form of a marquee, with a roof in the umbrella-form. It was erected two years ago for the purpose of entertaining the Emperor of Russia, the King of Prussia, and the other imperial and royal guests of that time. It is upwards of a hundred feet in diameter, and would easily contain one thousand persons. There were not more than seven hundred present this night. Mrs. Bourke and Mrs. Adams were there already when I arrived. The company in general were not so punctual to the hour, and it was past eleven when the Queen went round the circle, arm in arm with the Prince Regent. The Princess Charlotte of Wales was not there, having been confined the whole week to her chamber by indisposition. The dancing, waltzes, and cotillions began about twelve o'clock, and at half-past one the party went to supper. There were special tickets for the Queen's table to about one hundred and fifty persons, including the Ambassadors, but not the foreign Ministers of the second order. They were generally dissatisfied with this, and agreed to go away without waiting for the supper. We assented the more readily to this, not being in the habit of supping. Mr. and Mrs. Bourke, the Chevalier de Freire, Mr. Pfeffel, Mrs. Adams, and I came away together, but were obliged to wait a full half-hour before our carriages could be brought up. While there, we walked to and fro about the hall, occasionally meeting and having scraps of conversation with almost all our courtly acquaintance. The most extraordinary attentions were shown to Countess Lieven, who was seated at the Queen's right hand, and with whom Lord Castlereagh danced a waltz. He introduced Colonel Gordon to me; and Mr. Bourke, in the antechamber, as we were going away, introduced Lord Morley to us. After some difficulty and delay, we obtained our carriage.

18th. I went to town, to Downing Street, and was there precisely at one. Lord Castlereagh was not there, and the servants attending there told me that he had sent a note to me last evening to Craven Street. I went there, and found the note, which stated that the Prince Regent had directed Lord Castlereagh to attend him this day between twelve and one o'clock, and, as he might be detained, requested me to call at the Foreign Office at half-past one o'clock instead of one. When I returned to Downing Street it was forty minutes past one, but Lord Castlereagh had not come in. I waited until two, when he arrived and received me.

I told him I had mentioned at his house last week in general terms the subject upon which I had requested this conference. I showed him the letter from Mr. Monroe, Secretary of State, to me of 21st May last, containing the authority and instruction from the President to negotiate a new commercial convention, if the British Government should be disposed to such a negotiation. I said that the first and most urgent subject to be treated of in the view of my Government was that of the trade between the United States and the British Colonies in North America and the West Indies. He enquired, and said he did not recollect, how that had been left by the convention of 3d July, 1815. I said that the British Government had at that time declined to include it in the negotiation. " But," said Lord Castlereagh, " was there not some discussion concerning it ?"

A. There was; but it was before I arrived in England. The conferences, your Lordship will recollect, had been commenced by Messrs. Clay and Gallatin, and they had proposed that there should be an article in the convention to regulate this part of the trade, but it had been declined by the British Plenipotentiaries, so that after my arrival nothing was said about it. The state of things, however, in relation to the trade between the United States and the colonies was very different then from its state now. The commerce then was allowed in the vessels of both nations. The convention equalized the duties upon British and American vessels in the intercourse between Europe and the United States, and thereby admitted British vessels into the ports of the United States upon terms of equal competition with American vessels. But since that time the exclusive system of colonial regulations had been resumed in the West Indies with extraordinary rigor. American vessels had been excluded from all the ports, and some seizures have been made, with such severity that they are cases upon which I shall be under the necessity of addressing this Government in behalf of individuals who have suffered, and who consider themselves entitled to the restitution of their property. The consequence of these new regulations, as combined with the operation of the commercial convention, is that British vessels, being admitted into our ports upon equal terms with our own, and then being exclusively received in the British West Indian ports, not only thus monopolized the trade between the United States and the West Indies, but acquired an advantage in the direct trade from Europe to the United States, which defeated the main object of the convention itself, of placing the shipping of the two countries upon equal terms of fair competition. In North America the same system is pursued by the Colonial Governments, and I was specially directed to notice the measures of the Government of Upper Canada. An Act of the Colonial Legislature was passed at their last session vesting in the Lieutenant-Governor and Council of the province the power of regulating their trade with the United States, and immediately afterwards a new tariff of duties was issued by an order of the Provincial Council, dated the 18th April, laying excessively heavy duties upon all articles imported into the province from the United States, with the exception of certain articles of provisions of the first necessity, and a tonnage duty of twelve and sixpence a ton upon American vessels, which is equivalent to a total prohibition.

C. I have not been in the way of following the measures adopted in that quarter, and was not aware that there had been any new regulations either in the West Indies or in North

America. In time of war, I know, it has been usual to open
the ports of the West India Islands to foreigners merely as a
measure of necessity, and it was not until your attempt to
starve them by your embargo acts that they were driven to
the resort of finding out resources from elsewhere. But in
time of peace it has been usual to exclude foreigners from
them. What is the nature of your trade with them ? and is it
very considerable ?

A. It is, my Lord; and even in time of peace highly necessary to the Colonies—in respect to some of the imports, indispensable to their subsistence, and by the exports, extremely
advantageous to the interests of Great Britain, by furnishing a
market for articles which she does not take herself, and which
could not be disposed of elsewhere. At the very time of which
your Lordship speaks, during our embargo, the Governors of
the islands, so far from adhering to the principle of excluding
our vessels, issued proclamations inviting them, with promises
even that the regular papers should not be required for their
admission, and encouraging them to violate the laws of their
own country to carry them supplies. I mention this now
only to show how necessary to the Colonies this trade was felt
to be then. In time of peace it is undoubtedly not so necessary. Still, however, it is so in a high degree. The mother
country can supply them in part, but she does not produce some
of the most important articles of their importation—rice, for
example, and Indian corn, which are the best and cheapest
articles for the subsistence of the negroes. Even wheat and
flour, and provisions generally, were much more advan-
tageously imported from the United States than from Europe,
being so much less liable to take damage in these hot climates
by the comparative shortness of the voyage. Their other
importations from us are of lumber, which is necessary for
buildings upon the plantations, and which, after the hurricanes
to which the islands are frequently exposed, must be had in
large quantities. But it is not now on the usual ground of
your necessities that the American Government propose that
those ports should be opened to American vessels. Neither
do they ask for a participation of the British trade with them;

Great Britain may still prohibit the importation from the United States of such articles as she chooses to supply herself; but they ask that American vessels from the United States may be admitted equally with British vessels to carry the articles which can be supplied only from the United States, or which are supplied only to them. The effect of the new regulations that I have mentioned has been so injurious upon the shipping interest in America, and was so immediately felt, that the first impression upon the minds of many was, that they should be immediately met by counteracting legislative measures of prohibition. A proposal to that effect was made in Congress, but it was thought best to endeavor in the first instance to come to an amicable arrangement of the matter with the British Government if possible. Immediate prohibitions would affect injuriously the British Colonies. They would excite irritation in the commercial part of the British community. The consideration, therefore, of enacting legislative regulations was postponed, and I was instructed by the Government to make this proposal of a new convention.

C. The subject shall be taken as soon as possible into consideration, and you may be sure it shall be with the most earnest disposition in this Government to concur in the general purpose of promoting the harmony between the two countries; but I cannot be now prepared to enter upon the particular points of the question, owing to the absence of Mr. Robinson.

A. There is no immediate urgency to enter upon the details of the negotiation, and my object now is merely to give your Lordship a general outline of the objects which the American Government is desirous of embracing in the negotiation; that the determination may be taken whether the British Government is disposed to the discussion of those objects or not. This subject of the trade with the British Colonies is the most pressing of any, but the great anxiety of the American Government to guard against the recurrence of those causes of dissension which heretofore, unfortunately, terminated in hostility, makes them extremely desirous of settling if possible by treaty all the points of collision between neutral and belligerent rights which in the event of a new maritime war in Europe might again arise:

—blockade; contraband; visits and searches at sea; colonial trade, and that between the ports of enemies; but most of all the case of the seamen. The proposal is that each party should stipulate not to employ in its merchant or naval service the seamen of the other.

C. But how shall we avoid falling into the old difficulty of the disagreement between us, who we are to understand by the seamen of the other? Do you propose to include in the stipulation only native citizens and subjects? and if not, how is the question to be escaped whether any act of naturalization can avail to discharge a man from the duties of his original allegiance?

A. It is proposed to include in the arrangement only natives and those who are on either side naturalized already, so that it would not extend to any person hereafter naturalized. The number of naturalized persons included in it would of course be very small, for our laws respecting naturalization are of such a nature that there are excessively few British sailors who have taken or could take the benefit of them, so few that it could be no object to Great Britain to except them.

C. But by what regulation would you propose to carry the stipulation into effect?

A. If the principle be agreed to, there can be no difficulty in concerting regulations which would carry it into execution; I can now only say that I shall be ready to agree to any regulations which Great Britain may think necessary to secure the bonâ fide fulfilment of the engagement and consistent with individual rights.

C. Is it expected by the American Government that by agreeing to this stipulation we should abandon the right of search which we have heretofore used? or is the stipulation to stand by itself, leaving the rights of the parties as they were before?

A. It is undoubtedly the object of the American Government that the result of the stipulation should ultimately be the abandonment of the practice of taking men from American vessels.

C. But how shall we escape the old difficulty? The people of this country consider the remedy which we have always used

hitherto as the best and only effectual one. I am not sure that
it is so. With all its advantages and all its inconveniences, I
am not myself certain that it would not be better to substitute
something else. But such is the general opinion of the nation,
and there is a good deal of feeling connected with the sentiment. If we give up that, how will it be possible to devise any
regulation depending upon the performance of another State
which will be thought as efficacious as that which we have in
our own hands? I am for myself convinced that in this respect
the policy of the American Government has changed—that its
policy formerly was to invite and encourage our seamen to
enter your service, but that at present their policy is rather
to give every encouragement to your own seamen; and I was
in hopes that the effect of their internal legislative measures
would be to diminish the necessity of our resorting to the right
of search.

A. Your Lordship has made a similar observation to me on
a former occasion, and, as it is now repeated, it is my duty to
take particular notice of it. I do not know that anything I
can say will have the effect of removing the impression from
your mind. I am nevertheless under the most perfect conviction that it is erroneous. The American Government never
did in any manner invite or encourage foreign seamen generally
or British seamen in particular to enter our service.

C. I meant only to say that their policy arose naturally
from the circumstances. From the extraordinary, sudden, and
almost unbounded increase of your commerce and navigation
during the late European wars, you had not native seamen
enough to man your ships, and the encouragements to foreign
seamen of which I spoke followed from that state of things.

A. I understand your Lordship perfectly; but what I assert
is, my profound conviction that you are mistaken on the point
of fact. That without knowing whether anything I can say
will change your opinion, I must in the most earnest manner
assure you that it never was the policy of the American Government to encourage British seamen to enter our service. I
know not how the policy of any Government can be manifested otherwise than by its acts. Now, there never was any

one act, either of the Legislature or of the Executive, which could have even a tendency to invite British seamen into the American service.

C. At least, then, there was nothing done to prevent them.

A. That may be, my Lord; but there is a very material distinction between giving encouragement and doing nothing to prevent them. Our naturalization laws certainly hold out to them nothing like encouragement. You naturalize every foreign seaman by the mere fact of two years' service on board of your public ships, ipso facto, without cost or form of process. We require five years of residence in the United States, two years of notice in a Court of Record before the act of naturalization is granted, and a certificate of character. Thus far only may be admitted, that the great and extraordinary increase of our commerce to which you have alluded had the effect of raising the wages of seamen excessively high. Our Government certainly gave no encourgement to this. Neither did our merchants, who would surely have engaged their seamen at lower wages if possible. These wages no doubt operated as a strong temptation to your seamen to go into the American service. Your merchant service could not afford to pay them so high. The wages in the King's ships were much lower, and numbers of British seamen accordingly found their way to America and into American vessels; but encouragement from the American Government they never had in any manner. They were merely not excluded; and even now, in making the proposal to exclude them, it is not from any change of policy, but solely for the purpose of giving satisfaction to Great Britain and of stopping the most abundant source of dissension with her. It proves only the earnestness of our desire to be upon good terms with you.

C. In that general disposition it is impossible for the American Government to be more desirous to promote the harmony between the countries than we are.

A. With regard to the proposal for excluding each other's seamen, I am not prepared to say that an article could not be framed by which the parties may stipulate the principle of mutual exclusion without at all affecting or referring to the rights or claims of either party. Perhaps it may be accomplished if the British Government will assume it as one of the objects to be arranged by the convention.

C. In that case there will not be so much difficulty, if it is a mere agreement of mutual exclusion, tending to diminish the occasion for exercising the right of search; and undoubtedly if it should prove effectual, it would, in the end, operate as an inducement to the forbearance to exercise the right entirely.

A. There is one point upon which there has been much discussion between the two Governments, and upon which notes have been passed between me and Lord Bathurst, as well as between your Lordship and me. It relates to slaves carried away from the United States by British commanders after the peace.

C. After the peace? You mean between the signature of the treaty of peace and the ratification of it, do you not?

A. No, my Lord; I mean slaves which had been taken during the war, and which, after the ratification of the peace, were carried away by the British commanders, contrary, as the American Government conceive, to the first article of the treaty. But, as the British Government appear to be decidedly of a contrary opinion, I am directed to propose that the question be referred to the determination of a third party—to a sovereign the common friend of both—a mode of arrangement already agreed upon by the Treaty of Ghent in the event of a final difference between the parties upon other questions.

C. By an arbitration? I was not aware that there had been any slaves carried away from the United States after the peace; and as to the supposed sales by our officers of those that were taken, there are several answers of officers who have been referred to, of which I have requested Mr. Hamilton to send you copies. They are, indeed, expressed in very strong terms, but you will consider them as having been addressed to their own Government only—to the Admiralty—in answer to letters sent them for their reports upon the complaints. They all deny the charges in the most positive manner.

A. My Lord, the charges were of a nature to be denied; but, in the papers which I transmitted you, several officers were signalized by name, the statements implicating them were attested upon oath, and, so long as they are not brought to trial, their denials, however positive, are no more than the denial of any other men.

C. I cannot help thinking that, by our laws, it was impracticable that they could have effected such sales as were alleged.

A. I lately addressed to your Lordship a note, I am sorry to say a very long one, which perhaps you have not had time to read, but in which I think it is proved that the law for the abolition of the slave-trade was neither applicable, nor applied, to the slaves taken in America. And the copy of the decree of the Vice-Admiralty Court in Jamaica, which I likewise sent you, proved not only an actual sale, but a mode by which real sales of any numbers might be effected.

C. I do not recollect any such decree of the Vice-Admiralty Court. What decree was it?

A. It related to several American slaves taken at sea. They were libelled in the Admiralty Court, with the vessel in which they were captured. They were delivered upon a bail-bond to certain persons, who presented themselves as claimants, and when afterwards condemned as a prize, the sentence of the Court directed that the penalty of the bail-bond should be paid, and the slaves were of course left in the possession of the claimants; that is, they were substantially sold to them.

C. I have no recollection of this case, and I think it cannot be so; for if it were, our philanthropists would have seized and sounded it forth, so that we should have no end of it.

A. Perhaps not. Your philanthropists might not choose to notice transactions connected with the operations of Government in a war with America. They might not wish to appear to take part against officers of the navy.

C. Oh, that would not have restrained them: war or peace, navy or no navy, the moment the slave-trade became concerned they would have had neither scruples nor respect for persons.

A. But as it was, my Lord, the philanthropists, at the late session of Parliament, did press you very hard to account for the increase of the black population in the island of Jamaica, and this evidence, to which I now refer you, was not in their possession; it has never been published. But this is not the subject which the American Government proposes to refer to a friendly sovereign. The whole correspondence since the peace on this subject has been very reluctantly entertained by them, nor do I see that it can lead to any useful result. The impression in the United States, with respect to some individual officers, is indelible, and all the evidence hitherto collected tends to confirm the allegation originally made. It is not, therefore, the disposal of the slaves after they were carried away, but the carrying them away after the peace, which it is proposed to refer; and these are all the subjects comprised in my instructions relative to a new convention. There are other topics which I was desirous of noticing at this interview. Your Lordship was good enough to communicate to me for the information of my Government the proceedings of Lord Exmouth upon his first visit to Algiers, and until his arrival at Tunis. You also informed me that he was to return to Algiers and make a protest there against one article of the Algerine treaty with us. Since that time, the public newspapers have announced the return of Lord Exmouth to England; that he had made his second visit to Algiers; that circumstances of a hostile nature had subsequently occurred; and that a new expedition under Lord Exmouth is now fitting out, and soon to sail for the Mediterranean.

C. I have not the least hesitation in telling you everything that has occurred since our last communication to you. Lord Exmouth returned, after having been to Tunis and Tripoli, to Algiers. He made then the protest against that article of your treaty. The Dey fully admitted the validity of the prior treaty with us, and said that he could easily settle that matter with you. He said that treaty with you was suspended on account of some ship that had not been sent to him. But what is the state of your relations there now?

A. The treaty, as he said, is suspended. The ship of which he spoke was an Algerine brig, taken by an American squadron off Carthagena last summer. There were a frigate and a brig

taken, and both were sent into Carthagena. At the peace it
was agreed that they should be restored precisely in the state
in which they were at Carthagena. They were restored, but
the Spaniards for some time detained the brig, on the allegation that she had been taken within the Spanish jurisdiction.
They did, however, afterwards give her up.

C. Well, but if he has now got the vessel, what difficulty
can remain ?

A. I suppose the pretence of delay. But after the first visit
of Lord Exmouth to Algiers, the Dey, thinking his treaties
had settled him in peace with Great Britain, Naples, and Sardinia, concluded that it was time to put an end to his treaty
with the United States, and it was accordingly the very next
day that he first refused to acknowledge it.

C. Well, he acknowledged the validity of the articles in our
treaty, and said that he would settle it accordingly with you.
That transaction, therefore, was all finished. But afterwards
Lord Exmouth, having obtained from the Beys of Tunis and of
Tripoli those declarations that they would not in future make
slaves of Christian prisoners, demanded a similar declaration of
the Dey of Algiers. This was entirely a new and unexpected
thing, and the Dey said that he could not make such an engagement without the consent of the Grand Signor, whose interests,
as well as those of the Dey's Government, would be deeply
affected by it. After this the Dey appears to have had the
impression that Lord Exmouth intended to enforce his demand
by measures of hostility, perhaps because the English Consul
had gone on board the fleet. Some English officers were in-
sulted and exposed to ill treatment at Algiers. Orders of
hostility were sent to Oran and to Bona. But Lord Exmouth
thought he had gone as far as his instructions would warrant ;
that he could not commence hostilities without further authority
from his Government. He therefore renewed the negotiation,
at which it was agreed that the Dey should have time to consult the Sultan at Constantinople upon the proposal for abolishing Christian slavery. He made many apologies for the orders
sent to Oran and Bona. Counter-orders were immediately
sent. The vessels taken at Oran were immediately restored;

but, Bona being more to the eastward, the counter-order unfortunately arrived too late. The first order had been to secure the persons of the Christians, and it is said their resistance to it produced the unfortunate event of which you have seen the account. Since that, Lord Exmouth has returned to England. We are now fitting out an expedition to the Mediterranean under his command. We expect he will soon sail. It is not in my power to communicate at present the precise tenor of his instructions, but from all these circumstances that have occurred our regard for the general interest and the cause of the other European States has been manifested in the clearest manner.

A. I have mentioned this subject, my Lord, because the former proceedings of Lord Exmouth had an immediate and powerful effect upon the state of our relations with Algiers, and, supposing that his future operations there may again have an effect upon them no less powerful, I thought it proper to suggest to you that the Government of the United States would take it as a mark of good neighborhood if you would communicate to me from time to time so much of his movements, and of the measures of this Government directing them, as there may be no particular motive for withholding.

N.B.—To this Lord Castlereagh made no reply, but drew up his feet as if he was about to rise from his chair. The servants had told me that he was to attend a Cabinet Council ordered at two o'clock, and it was now near three. One of the red morocco dispatch-boxes had been brought to him by a servant a few minutes before, which he had opened, and taken a paper from it, at which he had frequently cast his eyes while we were talking. I saw his impatience, and, rising from my chair, said, "I have received a letter from Liverpool, complaining that there is still levied upon merchandise sold at auction, when imported in American vessels, a duty of five per cent., which is not levied when the goods are imported in British vessels."

C. I agreed with Mr. Robinson before he left town, that is, six days ago, that this should be remitted, and he was to write to the Treasury accordingly. If not, send me a memorandum of it, and I will attend to it. We consider that and the matter of iron as standing much on the same foundation, and we are

determined to do everything on our part to give the convention
its full effect on the most liberal principles, trusting that the
same disposition exists on the part of the American Government.

A. What does your Lordship particularly refer to concerning
iron?

C. A discrimination of duties in the United States between
hammered iron and rolled iron. The preparation of the iron
in Sweden, it seems, is usually by hammering; in this country
it is performed by rolling. The duty upon rolled iron, being
heavier than upon hammered iron, falls therefore upon the
locality more than upon the article, and operates to the disadvantage of the British manufacture and to favor that of
Sweden.

A. I had one thing more to mention. Your Lordship recol-
lects the case of an American named George Cook (C. A very
bad fellow, I believe), whose establishment in Africa was
broken up by an English military party from Sierra Leone,
and concerning whom, at the instance of his agent, a Mr. Page,
I addressed you a note?

C. Yes.

A. I received an answer from your Lordship that this Government had determined to leave him to his remedy at law
against the Governor of Sierra Leone.

C. You did.

A. A process was accordingly served upon Governor Maxwell in the month of April, and Mr. Page now applies again
for my offices. He says there is a British officer named Appleton, now at the island of Guernsey, whose evidence is material
to Mr. Cook's cause, and who he apprehends is going away.
Page therefore has written a letter to Lord Bathurst to ask that
Appleton may not be permitted to go until Cook can have had
an opportunity to obtain his testimony, and he requests me to
support him in this demand.

C. I shall see Lord Bathurst immediately, and will speak to
him on the subject.

A. And with regard to the proposal for negotiating a new
commercial convention, I shall take it as a favor if your Lord-

ship will let me know the determination of his Majesty's Government as soon as it may be convenient.

C. You may rely upon having it without one moment of unnecessary delay.

I took my leave, and on passing through the entry of the office saw by the clock that it was just upon the stroke of three. I went and paid a visit to Dr. Bollmann, at No. 16 Buckingham Street, intending to walk from thence, and expecting the carriage would overtake me in Hyde Park. I found Dr. Bollmann with one of his daughters, whom he introduced to me. By his conversation, I found that he was mortified and soured by the disappointment of the projects with which he went to the United States last autumn. He spoke of the dreadful state of affairs in the United States in relation to the finances, the circulating medium, and the overwhelming floods of depreciated bank paper, in which he concurs too well with all the other accounts that I have heard of late, but he considers the evil as irretrievable, which I hope it is not. He says that Mr. Dallas, the Secretary of the Treasury, was foiled in the principal object of his bank, which was a secret design to introduce Treasury notes as the circulating medium of the country. But Congress took the alarm, and struck out that part of the plan by which he would have accomplished that; the consequence of which will be that the bank when organized will be able to do no business, and then will come with a petition to Congress to have their powers enlarged. But a redemption from the depreciated paper he holds to be utterly impracticable. He said the Government had declined the offer from Austria about the ships at Trieste, preferring to build seventy-four-gun ships at an expense of five hundred thousand dollars each, to purchasing them at one hundred thousand. He told me he had now come here upon some new project of a manufacture, and that he should stay at least two years in Europe. I doubt whether he intends ever to return to the United States again.

19th. The weather throughout the day was cold and showery, and the season has been so unusually and constantly cold that fires have been kept without intermission in almost every house. I have not yet ventured to throw aside my flannel

waistcoat, nor as yet for one night to discard the blanket from
the bed. The weather has been equally extraordinary over
the greater part of Europe, and by our late accounts also in
the United States. About six weeks since, the French and
English newspapers mentioned that an astronomer in Italy,
in the Papal dominions, had published a prediction that the
spots on the disc of the sun, of which several then were, and
still are, visible, were the beginning of the total extinction of
that luminary, which would be so speedily consummated that
on the 18th day of July of this present year the world would
come to an end. It was added that this prophecy had alarmed
so many weak people that the police of the Pope's Government had found it necessary to interpose, and the prophet had
been imprisoned. The effect and agitation of this story have
been very considerable, both in France and England. The
churches and chapels have been unusually crowded; at Paris,
public prayers have been ordered for favorable weather, and
not ten days since, in the City of London, a coroner's inquest found a verdict of insanity, occasioned by this prediction,
upon an old woman aged sixty-two—a cook-maid, who hung
herself in a fit of melancholy at the prospect of the world's
coming to an end. Such is human credulity!

21st. At nine o'clock we left home and went to the party
of the Duke and Duchess of Cumberland. It was an entertainment given to the Duke of Cambridge upon his arrival in
England. He has come over from Hanover to be present at
the marriage of his sister, the Princess Mary. He and the
Prince Regent, with the Cabinet Ministers and Ambassadors,
and their ladies, had dined there. The Duchess and the ladies
were in the drawing-room when we arrived. The Duke, with
his male guests, came up from table about half an hour afterwards. The Lord Chancellor was among them. At the
evening party there were about one hundred persons. The
singers of the Opera—Naldi, Madame Fodor, Mainvielle, &c.—
were there, and sang with accompaniment of the piano. I
had conversation with Messrs. Bourke, Pfeffel, and Jenison,
with the Earls of Westmorland and Limerick, and with Captain McDonald, who had been one of Lord Cathcart's aides-

de-camp at St. Petersburg, and who recognized me.   He introduced to me, as his cousin, a Mr. Ward, a member of Parliament of some distinction, who, Lord Limerick told me, was
self-educated.   For he said that although in the theory the
sons of Peers ought to be better educated than others, the
fact was quite the reverse.   Mr. Ward was the son of Lord
Dudley and Ward, and at the age of seventeen, discovering
that he was perfectly ignorant of everything worth knowing,
had commenced his application with great assiduity, and had
educated himself.   The Duke of Cumberland spoke to me,
and asked me to introduce him to Mrs. Adams.   The Duke
and Duchess both spoke to her, and treated her with much
politeness.   On first going into the hall, Lady Castlereagh
was sitting at the side of the Duchess, on a sofa.   Count
Jenison, at my request, asked Lady Castlereagh to present
Mrs. Adams to the Duchess, but she said it was not necessary.[1]   I was not presented to the Duchess.   The Prince Regent
remained about half an hour in the drawing-room, and then
went away.   Mrs. Bourke, the Danish Minister's lady, was not
there—confined at home by indisposition.

.22d. I was obliged to leave most of the papers at the office
and to hasten to Buckingham House, that we might not be
too late.   We entered the Park by the Horse Guards, and consequently arrived at the palace by the side-entrance door.
We were just in season.   The company and the ceremonies
were as nearly as possible the same as they had been at the
marriage of the Princess Charlotte.   The Archbishop of Canterbury read the Church service.   The Princess was very much
affected, and made the responses with far less intrepidity than
the Princess Charlotte.   The Prince Regent gave away his
sister,[2] and supported her through the whole service.   The
Queen, the Duke and Duchess of York, the Dukes of Clarence, Kent, and Cambridge, the Princesses Augusta, Elizabeth,

---

[1] This lady, the sister of Queen Louisa of Prussia, had been married to the Duke
of Cumberland the year before.   Queen Charlotte had refused to receive her at
Court, on account of her damaged reputation.   Possibly this may account for the
reluctance of Lady Castlereagh to act on this occasion.

[2] The Princess Mary, who married the Duke of Gloucester, her cousin.

and Sophia of Gloucester, the Duke and Duchess of Orleans, and Mademoiselle d'Orléans, the Duke de Bourbon, the Cabinet Ministers, and foreign Ambassadors and Ministers, with their ladies, were all present. The Duke and Duchess of Cumberland were absent, the Duchess not having been received at the Queen's Court; the Duke of Sussex, owing to his misunderstanding with the Prince Regent, and the Princess Charlotte, on account of an indisposition, which keeps her confined to her chamber. The Prussian Minister was likewise absent, as he does not attend the Queen's drawing-rooms since her determination not to receive the Duchess of Cumberland. The King of Prussia has thus far interested himself in favor of the Duchess, who was sister to his late Queen, and first married to his brother, Prince Louis of Prussia. She was his widow when we went to Berlin — November, 1797 — and while we resided there was married to the Prince de Solms, her second husband. The Danish Minister's wife, Mrs. Bourke, was also absent from indisposition. The ceremony began a few minutes before nine o'clock, and finished in less than half an hour. After the salutations, the royal family retired with the new-married couple for about half an hour. The Duke and Duchess then went off in a travelling chariot for his seat at Bagshot, and the Queen returned with the Regent, the Princes and Princesses, and walked round the circle in the hall, receiving the congratulations of the company. After this, the company passed into an adjoining room, called the Japan Chamber, where refreshments were served. At half-past ten we came away, with the company generally, and as we descended the great staircase, a large slice of wedding-cake, rolled up in paper, was given to every person to take home. We reached our house just at midnight.

26th. In November, 1779, in the thirteenth year of my age, I first began to keep a journal. It was upon embarking on board the French frigate La Sensible, at Boston, for Brest, though we landed at Ferrol, in Spain. But, easy as this practice of journalizing appears to be, it requires one quality not very common among men, and yet scarcer among boys—perseverance. I had it not. My journal soon became irksome, and I dropped it—not, however, for any length of time. I resumed it again in 1780, in July, on leaving Paris with my father to go to Holland, but soon dropped and resumed it again. At various periods of my life I did the same; and from my first effort, in 1779, until 1795, I believe there was never at any one time six months of intermission, and seldom six months of unintermitted journal. It was kept sometimes on loose sheets of paper, sometimes in paper-covered books, and sometimes in bound volumes of various dimensions. Several years I followed the practice, which I now expect will be my last resort, of giving one line to every day, and one page for each month. At other times I attempted to note only the days upon which something remarkable occurred, once or twice a week, for example. This I soon found the most impracticable of all; that is, it soon glided into total neglect. My last attempt was on the first of January, 1795; since which I have kept my journal, I think, without intermission of a day. I began it, however, in a small duodecimo leather-covered book, which I ran through in two months. I then concluded to use volumes of the small quarto form—small enough to be portable, and large and thick enough to contain a considerable portion of time—several years in each volume. The first and second of these volumes, containing the diary from 1st March, 1795, to 4th August, 1809, I left in a trunk in the charge of my brother, at Boston, when I sailed for Russia. The preceding loose sheets, sibyl leaves, interleaved almanacs, and motley volumes of all sizes, are many of them lost, and the rest in that same trunk. On the first of this month I began in a separate volume, at page 301, the index to my diary for the future. And this day, after closing my late arrears, I commenced the retrospective index, beginning with the immediately preceding month, and proposing to allow five days to make out the index for each previous month.[1]

29th. In the evening we went into London and attended Mrs. Wellesley Pole's rout. The Prince Regent was there, but none of the foreign Ministers, and very few persons whom

---

[1] This work, far more difficult than the other, was carried on some time; but it finally gave way under the stress of public occupation.

we knew. There was much melancholy music on the harp and piano, and some singing. We were there nearly two hours, during which the Prince sat lolling on a sofa, between two old ladies dressed in black (a Court mourning for the Queen of Portugal), dropping now a word at the right hand, now a word at the left, and unapproachable to all the rest of the company. There was a Lady Caroline Lamb[1] there, a very notorious character, authoress of a scandalous novel lately published, called " Glenarvon."

30th. I received letters from Mr. Grubb, and from Mr. Smith, who scruples to give a passport to William Temple Franklin as a citizen of the United States. His case is a very peculiar one. He was born in London, before the American Revolution. His father, Governor Franklin, was a refugee, and of course never ceased to be a British subject. But he was adopted when a child by his grandfather, Dr. Benjamin Franklin, was educated by him, and resided with him the whole time of his mission in France, from 1777 to 1785. He was the Doctor's secretary, and was also the Secretary to the American Commissioners who negotiated the preliminaries of 1782 and the definitive Treaty of 1783. I consider him, therefore, as having been then constituted a citizen of the United States. In 1785 he accompanied his grandfather to America, resided there five or six years, and the Doctor left him a principal part of his estate. Shortly after the old gentleman's death, Temple came to Europe, and has never since been in America. I wrote to Mr. Smith to give him a passport.

August 8th. Dined at the Mansion House, with the Lord Mayor. It was a dinner to the Duke of Wellington, and for the purpose of presenting to him a resolution of thanks from the Common Council of London, voted shortly after the battle of Waterloo, and upon that occasion. The party was small— a single table of about thirty-six persons. The Duke of Cambridge and Prince Leopold had been invited, but sent excuses.

---

[1] The wife of William Lamb, afterwards Lord Melbourne, notorious for her relations with Lord Byron, who, in revenge for her allusions to him in this novel, put into " Don Juan" the line,—

"Some play the devil and then write a novel."

The Duke of Sussex had engaged to attend, but the Queen sent for him to dine with her—a summons that he was of course obliged to obey. He came before the company left the table after dinner. The Lord Mayor received an excuse from Prince Esterhazy, the Austrian Ambassador, just before going to table. He said he had not expected him. I had called upon Mr. Bourke, partly to enquire if he had been invited to the dinner. He had not. I was the only foreign Minister present, a favor for which I have more than once been indebted to the present Lord Mayor, without precisely knowing why—probably because he is a Whig, and friendly to liberal principles with regard to America. I had been doubtful whether to go in full Court dress to this party, or in frock dress. On consulting Mr. Bourke, he advised me to go in frock. I accordingly went so, but found the Lord Mayor, and most of the company, in full dress. The Duke of Kent, however, the only person of the royal family who attended, came in frock, as did the Earl of Darnley, and his son, Lord Clifton. The Duke of Wellington himself, and his aides-de-camp, Lord Arthur Hill, and Colonels Percy, Harvey, and Freemantle, were in military uniform. Lord Erskine and the Aldermen were in Court dresses. I apologized for being in undress.

Before dinner, the Lord Mayor introduced me to the Duke of Wellington. I observed that I had already been introduced to him. "Oh, yes," said he; "at Paris." "No: at the Prince Regent's last levee at Carlton House, by your Grace's brother Mr. Wellesley Pole." "Oh! ay! yes!" said the Duke, who had obviously forgotten me and my introduction. This is one of the many incidents from which I can perceive how very small a space my person, or my station, occupies in the notice of these persons, and at these places. The Lord Mayor intimated to me that I was to take my place at table after Lord Darnley and Lord Erskine, and before Lord Clifton, who, he observed, was not a Peer. But as, in handing the ladies down, I took the Lord Mayor's eldest daughter, Miss Wood, it happened that I found myself at table next above Lord Darnley, with Miss Wood between us. There were no cards, as on former occasions, in the plates. Before we were seated, the Lord Mayor repeatedly told Lord Darnley that he was not high enough; but there was no higher place that he could have taken except mine, and I did not take the hint of offering it to him. We kept our seats, therefore, as we had taken them.

The Lord Mayor and Lady Mayoress sat, as usual, at the head of the table, side by side; the Duke of Kent at the right hand of the Lord Mayor, and the Duke of Wellington at the left hand of the Lady Mayoress. The dinner was of turtle and venison, and otherwise luxurious as usual. At the dessert the loving cups of champagne punch and the basins of rose-water went round. The steward, at the passing of the cups, and at the first toast, "The King," went through the nomenclature of the company, according to custom, naming the American Minister immediately after Lord Erskine. The Lord Mayor gave us the toast immediately after the King, "The Queen and female branches of the Royal Family," forgetting the Prince Regent, of which he was immediately reminded by the Duke of Kent. He corrected his mistake; but this forgetfulness led me to inferences similar in principle to those I had drawn from the Duke of Wellington's oblivious faculties at the introduction to him by his brother of an American Minister.

The routine of standing toasts followed—"The Duke of York and the Army;" "The wooden walls of Old England, and better health to the Duke of Clarence." He was, it seems, yesterday seized suddenly with an illness so violent that he was last night in the most imminent danger, but had been relieved, and the danger entirely removed. Next came the personal attacks. The Lord Mayor gave every toast with a speech. First, "The Duke of Kent," who only bowed, without returning thanks. Just as the Lord Mayor was about proposing "The Duke of Wellington," the Duke of Sussex came in. He would not permit the Lord Mayor to postpone on his account the toast proposed, and accordingly "The Duke of Wellington" was given. He also answered only by a bow. The Duke of Sussex was toasted next, and his brother said to him, laughing, "Now you must make a speech; I made a speech of about a quarter of an hour." But Sussex saw he was joking, and only bowed.

The Lord Mayor introduced the Earl of Darnley's health with a high eulogium upon his hospitality last week to the whole City party, who went with the Lord Mayor on the septennial tour to claim the City jurisdiction upon the rivers Thames and Medway. Lord Darnley returned thanks with a short speech, expressing his pleasure at having had the opportunity of showing attentions to the City party, and his wish that a similar opportunity would occur annually instead of once in seven years.

Then Lord Erskine was given, with Trial by Jury. He said that if that addition had not been made he should have remained silent, though thankful, but when trial by jury was given, he could not suppress his feelings. He then made a short speech, in which he said that he had not changed his principles, made a very flattering compliment to the Duke of Wellington, and declared himself inexpressibly happy to have entered Paris with him last summer, all which was owing to trial by jury.

Now came the turn of the American Minister, whose health the Lord Mayor introduced with thanks for having had several times the pleasure of his company on these occasions. I returned my thanks in a few words, with a reference to the popular and conciliatory conduct of the British Minister in the United States, and expressing my pleasure in remarking that he was a near relation to the illustrious commander whom Britain claimed as her own, but who in a more enlarged point of view belonged to the whole human race, as every individual whose virtues and achievements do honor to our common nature is the pride and glory not merely of one nation, but of all human kind.

The City members of Parliament were toasted next, for whom Alderman Atkins, the only one of them present, returned thanks in a speech. Then the Aldermen, for whom Mr. Scholey answered. Then the Duke of Wellington's aides-de-camp, whose thanks were laconically returned by Lord Arthur Hill. General Witherell was succeeded by the Sheriffs, Sir Thomas Bell and Mr. Thorpe, both of whom answered. The Lord Mayor then proposed giving the Sheriff-elect, Mr. Kirby, but the Duke of Sussex insisted upon giving, "The long pull, the

strong pull, and the pull altogether." This was meant as a
compliment to the Duke of Wellington, pledging and asking
for harmonious co-operation, though Sussex is in high opposition to the Ministry and at personal variance with the Regent.
Wellington received the compliment as it was meant. His
countenance lightened up, and he made a speech of thanks to
the Lord Mayor and the City of London for their resolutions
and the dinner. He was not fluent, but he expressed his
earnest hope for a long and general peace, and most especially
with America, upon which occasion he spoke in terms of great
civility of the American Minister.

The company had already risen from table, but the Lord
Mayor renewed the proposition for drinking the Sheriff-elect,
and Mr. Kirby returned thanks and promised to devote himself
and all his efforts to the service of the City. The gentlemen
then returned to join the ladies in the drawing-room above-
stairs. The ladies had withdrawn soon after the Duke of Sussex came in, and the Duke of Kent immediately afterwards
went away. "The Lord Mayor and the City of London" was
then given by the Duke of Wellington, after which the Duke
of Sussex gave, "The Lady Mayoress," for whom the Lord
Mayor returned thanks. Every toast, excepting the first
("The King"), was drunk standing, with what they call three
times three—hip! hip! hip! and nine huzzas—for the Lord
Mayor observed that it was impossible to do anything in the
City without noise.

With all this, the dinner was inexpressibly dull. The company was obviously not well assorted. The Duke of Wellington yawned like L'Eveille in the "Barbier de Seville," and his
aids occasionally laughed in the sardonic manner, as if it was
at themselves for being in company with the City. Wellington
has no lively flow of conversation, but he bore the daubing of
flattery spread over him at every toast with moderate composure.
The general aspect of his countenance is grave and stern, but
sometimes it opens to a very pleasing smile. The City Resolutions, elegantly written and illuminated upon parchment,
were read by a City officer and delivered to him in the drawing-
room before dinner. After dinner, a drawing of the silver

column with a shield covering its base, which is to be presented to the Duke by a subscription raised in the City, was
exhibited and freely criticised by the Duke's aids.

I had conversation with Lord Erskine before, and with the
Earl of Darnley after, dinner. Lord Erskine said it was very
well for us to come and dine there upon turtle and venison, but
the country was ruined. He told me again of his determination
to go and travel in the United States. Lord Darnley seemed
to be under apprehensions of a new war with the United States,
which he deprecated. He thought also that the British Government ought to furnish assistance to the South Americans
to accomplish their emancipation. One of the Aldermen disclosed to me his consternation that the stocks had fallen this
morning full one per cent., which he attributed to the man-
œuvring of certain Jew stock brokers and to Lord Cochrane's
assertion at the late meeting in the City to relieve the poor, that
the interest upon the national debt must be reduced. Mr. Sheriff
Thorpe made enquiries of the health of Mrs. Adams. I told
him that she had been long intending to go and pay his father
a visit. The Duke of Sussex told me that he intended in the
course of three or four weeks to make me a visit at Ealing and
to ask me for a joint of mutton. He said he would give me
notice beforehand; and I asked him to bring his son, Captain
D'Este, with him, which he promised. I spoke to the Captain
himself about his expedition to New Orleans, where he was
aid-de-camp to General Pakenham; but he said it was a shocking affair, and did not incline to talk much about it. He said
it was a foolish thing ever to attempt an invasion in America.

It was half-past eleven when I left the Mansion House, and
there was still such a crowd of people at the door that it was
with difficulty the carriage could come up. When I went, there
had been a similar crowd. The Lord Mayor said they had
been there from nine o'clock in the morning. They shouted
on the arrival of the Royal Dukes and of the Duke of Wellington. I stopped a moment at Craven Street, and got home
at half-past one in the morning.

12th. We dined at half-past five, and at half-past seven left
home, and were at the Queen's Palace, Buckingham House,

precisely at nine. An accident had happened to the Duke of
Orleans's carriage at the front iron grate, so that the gate was
shut, and we were obliged to go in at the side-entry. Within
half an hour the Queen appeared, arm-in-arm with the Prince
Regent. She went round the circle and spoke a few words to
each person. The Dukes of Kent and Cambridge were the
only brothers of the Regent there. The Duke of York was
absent—I know not why; the Duchess was there. He had
been at the dinner. The Duke of Clarence is yet confined by
illness, Cumberland is at variance with the Queen because she
will not see his wife, and Sussex at variance with the Regent
for politics, and perhaps other causes. The Princesses Augusta
and Elizabeth were there; Prince Leopold, but not the Princess Charlotte; the Duke and Duchess, and Princess Sophia
of Gloucester; the Duke and Duchess of Orleans; the Duke
of Bourbon; the foreign Ambassadors and Ministers; and
about two hundred of the nobility and gentry of the country,
of both sexes.

Mr. Neumann, the Austrian Secretary of Embassy, asked me
if I had any answer to the proposal concerning the ships at
Trieste and Venice. I had none. He said he had an answer
to my enquiries about muskets—that they could be obtained
without difficulty, but it was thought best that it should be
by the way of commerce. I asked if he could mention the
price. He said he would let me know it near-abouts in a few
days.

I enquired of Count Lieven, the Russian Ambassador, whether
it was true, as was intimated in some of the newspapers, that
the new British armament under Lord Exmouth, fitted out
against the Barbary powers, had been sent in consequence of
the interest taken in the affair by the Emperor Alexander, and
by his influence. The Count asked me to call at his house at
eleven o'clock to-morrow morning, which I promised. I mentioned to the Marquis d'Osmond, the French Ambassador, that
I had received an answer from the United States to an application made at the request of his predecessor, the Duke de la
Châtre, to stop the transfer of certain stocks purchased here
by a Frenchman, a fraudulent cashier of a commercial house,

who had absconded with its funds.   The Marquis asked me
to write him a line about it.   I enquired of Mr. Chester, the
Assistant Master of the Ceremonies, and of the Chevalier de
Freire, the Portuguese Minister, whether there was any settled
principle of precedence at this Court between foreign Ministers
of the second order and persons of distinction natives of this
country.   Chester equivocated, and evaded answering.   He said
that on occasions of etiquette the Ambassadors and foreign
Ministers were always considered as a corps by themselves ; a
special place was assigned for them all together, and that was
always as near as possible to the King.   Mr. Freire had no
more settled notion upon the subject.   Chester ultimately admitted that there was no settled etiquette in the case.   The
practice, as I have found it, is this.   They give precedence to
Ambassadors next after the blood royal.   When there are
several Ambassadors and Ministers of the second order, they
put them together as a corps ; the Envoys then immediately
succeed the Ambassadors, and thus precede the nobility.   But
when there are only Ministers of the second order, all the
Ministers of State, all the household Lords, and all the Peers
of the realm take precedence of them, and have it assigned to
them.   The Lord Mayor marked this at his dinner last week by
assigning to me the place next to Lord Darnley, and before
his son, Lord Clifton, who is not a Peer.   That is the principle;
though, by particular occasions and incidents, they sometimes
place the foreign Ministers before the Peers.   They placed me
so at the Fishmongers' dinner—probably because the Peers
present were considered as members of the Company and at
home.   The general practice here is conformable to that in the
other European Governments that I have known.[1]   In Russia,
where all rank is graduated upon the military scale, an Ambassador ranks with a Field-Marshal, and an Envoy, or Minister
Plenipotentiary, with a Lieutenant-General.   Mrs. Wellesley
Pole told me she had received my note, but did not know where

[1] The Congress of Vienna and the protocols of Aix-la-Chapelle, in 1818, settled
anew the grades of the Diplomatic service and the right of precedence, in a manner to avoid the confusion which seems to have prevailed at this period.   There
are no such difficulties now in Great Britain as are described here.

Madame Fusil lived. The Duke of Wellington took leave of Mr. and Mrs. Pole just as I was speaking to them; he told me he should go to-morrow morning for Paris. Count Munster, at my request, introduced me to the Duke of Cambridge, who recollected that he had formerly known me at Berlin, in 1801. He told me that he was happy that peace between this country and America was restored, and hoped the good understanding would continue. Viscount Sidmouth earnestly recommended to me to see their dock-yard at Portsmouth, which he said he had visited with much satisfaction last week; but when I hinted a doubt whether I could obtain admission, he told me, not very confidently, that he thought there would be no difficulty.

The Earl of Limerick, as usual, conversed freely with me. This is an Irish nobleman, who, last summer, was created a Peer of the United Kingdom, by the title of Lord Foxford. He has strong Irish and republican propensities, which are overpowered by his honors and preferments and other courtly shackles. He told me that his uncle had been Speaker of the Irish House of Commons in 1783, when they made the great stand for the independence of Ireland; that he himself had been a very turbulent fellow formerly, but that now they treated him so well that he was quiet and well satisfied. He said that if America had been treated so she might have been kept forever, but there never was a country so foolishly thrown away as she had been. Mr. Greville spoke to me of the new packet that sails between Milford Haven and Waterford; and his wife, the Countess of Mansfield, told me about her brother, Lord Cathcart, the Ambassador in Russia—what an extraordinary favorite he was of the Emperor's, who had dined with him at his house, an honor which he had never done to any other Ambassador, and who occasionally paid him evening visits, as Lord Cathcart lives in a very domestic manner, with his family. These scraps of conversation, and others more insignificant, consumed the evening. The Queen, after going round the circle, retired to her card-party, and most of the company to the Japan chamber, where refreshments were served. About twelve we came away, and, after waiting full half an hour

at the side-entry, found the carriage at the front door.   Home
at two in the morning.

13th. Breakfasted at nine, and immediately afterwards went
into London, to Count Lieven's.   Count Lieven, referring to
the questions that I had put to him last evening, told me that
since the general peace the Emperor had been desirous of promoting and protecting the commerce of his subjects.   That,
finding it was much annoyed by the Barbary States, particularly
the commerce of the Black Sea, which was of the utmost importance to Russia, he had found it necessary to consider of
measures to be taken.   The commerce of several other nations
was annoyed in like manner.   Not only the Italian States, but
Spain and the Netherlands were in a state of hostility with
them.   Various propositions had been made by these powers.
The Netherlands were desirous of concerted operations.   Spain
had gone so far as to propose that a joint naval armament
should be fitted out to act against the Barbary States, the command of which should devolve upon the power which should
furnish the greatest contingent of force.   Without acceding
exactly to this, the Emperor Alexander had been sensible of
the inconvenience of partial operations and negotiations, which,
by making peace for one or two nations, would immediately
have the effect of producing hostilities against others.   Before
he took any decisive measures, the Emperor had thought it
expedient to consult with Great Britain, and to enquire what
were the views, the " manière de voir," of this Government on
the subject.

In the first instance, and before the late outrages which have
occurred in the Mediterranean, they answered, that as to the
general sentiment of dissatisfaction at the Barbarian mode of
warfare, their practice of making slaves of their prisoners, and
their cruelties to them, the British Government perfectly concurred in the sentiments of the other European States, and of
the Emperor in particular ; that they were disposed to assist
their allies in the endeavors to restore peace to them, but that,
having themselves no cause of complaint against the Barbary
Powers, they did not think it would be justifiable to join in any
general confederacy against them, such as was proposed ; but

considered that it would be best for each European nation to negotiate for itself, and provide for its own security.

This was the substance of the first answer. The Count said he had yet received no reply from his own Court to that communication, and did not know how it had been received. Since then, however, the new hostilities of the Algerines and Tunisians had been committed, upon which the new expedition, under Lord Exmouth, has been fitted out, and in which he trusted that the general interests and objects of the European nations, in relation to the Barbarians, would be duly pursued, as he was assured they should be.

I told the Count I was happy to find that this was his impression, and sincerely hoped his anticipation would be realized, but I must say, in the utmost confidence, to him, that I had strong misgivings that the result would be quite different. I referred to the proceedings under Lord Exmouth's former expedition; to his instructions to protest against the Algerine treaty with America; to the heavy ransom paid and promised for the Sardinian and Neapolitan prisoners; to the future contributions stipulated; to the moral lecture which the Admiral was to give the Barbarians against making slaves and exacting ransom on the one hand, while with the other he was paying the ransoms as high as ever; and finally to the result, which was, that, the next morning after signing his treaties with Lord Exmouth, the Dey had annulled his treaty with the United States; and from all the proceedings of that time, from the manner in which Lord Castlereagh had talked to me, from the language he had held in Parliament upon Brougham's motion relating to this affair, and particularly from an article concerning the Barbary States, in the Quarterly Review, just published, I inferred that Lord Exmouth's expedition might lead to a heavy atonement from the Barbarians for the late particular outrages and insults to the British, but would do nothing for the general European cause, or for that of humanity. I told the Count I supposed he knew that the Quarterly Review was a mere ministerial pamphlet.

He said, Certainly. He had not yet looked into the number just published; but he had got it, and was going to take it with him into the country to read. As to the general policy and inclination of this Government, he perfectly agreed in sentiment with me; that so far from being friendly to the navigation of other nations in the Mediterranean, they would prefer to have it continue subject to the depredations of those pirates; but the prospect of a concerted armament by the other powers, which might proceed to act without them, had also its inconveniences. They had been very far from giving satisfaction to their allies of Naples and Sardinia for the bargains they had lately made for them. They had received heavy reproaches instead of thanks for them. He thought, therefore, that they had now taken the quarrel into their own hands, to prevent a confederacy of the other powers, which might have accomplished the object without their assistance, and he expected they would do something of importance for the general interest.

This was the substance of an hour's conversation with the Count, after which I left him, and called at Mr. West the painter's, but he was not at home. Received at the office a card of invitation from the Lord Mayor and Lady Mayoress, to Mrs. Adams and myself, on board the Lord Mayor's barge, on Thursday, the 22d instant, at Westminster Bridge, at eleven o'clock precisely, to proceed to Richmond, and dine on board the Navigation Barge, at four precisely. Carriages to be ordered in the evening, at Kew Bridge, at eight o'clock. An immediate answer was requested, and written, and sent by Mr. Smith. The objects of attention this day have been so multitudinous that the recollection of all of them loses much of its distinctness. Important business, dissipation, visits, variety of conversation, letters, dispatches, newspapers, pamphlets, books, and invitation cards are all so blended together in the memory that the impressions wear out one another, and all are faded and confused. Such days frequently occur to me, particularly when I go to London, and they give me a strong sympathy with what appears to be the ordinary state of Lord Castlereagh's mind. He appears to me scarcely ever to have a distinct remembrance of anything.

14th. The Spanish Ambassador, Count Fernan Nuñez, had

told me the evening before last, at the Queen's House, that he had received an answer from Lord Castlereagh to the note which, at my request, he had sent in, relative to the case of the William and Mary, now depending in the Admiralty Court, and that Curtoys was making out a copy of it to send me. This morning I received a note from Fernan Nuñez, enclosing the copy. Castlereagh, in very courteous terms, recommends that if there are any circumstances which make an immediate decision of the cause necessary, the parties should be advised to suggest them to the Court, and if not, that the cause will be taken up in its turn. I expected some such answer as this, and remark in it, principally, the politeness and complacency of the manner, which is in a style very different, when addressed to the Spanish Ambassador, from what it is in similar cases when addressed to me.

16th. I went to the Foreign Office, in Downing Street, and the only person whom I found there was Mr. Planta. Lord Castlereagh, Hamilton, and Cook were all out of town. I told Planta that I had addressed, lately, several notes to Lord Castlereagh, and was pressed by the individuals whose interests some of them concerned for answers. He said that as to that relative to the machinery for the Mint, he knew the order had already been sent to the Treasury. I mentioned the case of the ship at Glasgow. He said he knew that immediately after the receipt of my note concerning it, Lord Castlereagh had written to the Lords of the Treasury, recommending that the vessel might be allowed a clearance under the order from the Treasury issued before the new Passengers Act. I spoke of the extra auction duties. He sent to enquire of Mr. Bidwell what had been done relative to that note; but Bidwell was not at the office.

21st. My proposed occupation for the day was disconcerted by a note from Lord Castlereagh, brought me by the second post, requesting me to call upon him this day, at the Foreign Office, at four o'clock. I went immediately into London, left the curricle at Hyde Park corner, with orders to the coachman to come for me to the Foreign Office at a quarter-past four o'clock, and walked first to my office, where I stopped a few minutes, and then went to Downing Street, where I was soon admitted to Lord Castlereagh.

The preliminaries to his conversations usually turn upon the weather. He said that he hoped we should now have a month or six weeks of fine weather, and if so, from the accounts he had from the different parts of the country, there would be a fine harvest. The observation struck me the more remarkable, as all the appearances of the harvest in our neighborhood are unfavorable; as there have been now for a full month public prayers in the churches for a change of weather; and as the average price of flour and wheat throughout England and Wales has been gradually rising at the moment when the harvest season is arrived.

Lord Castlereagh proceeded to tell me that he had requested to see me relative to the subjects of our conversation of the 18th of July. The proposal on the part of the United States to enter upon the negotiation of a new treaty of commerce had been considered by this Government. As to a general treaty of commerce, they did not think it advisable, particularly as there was a commercial convention already existing. With regard to the intercourse between the United States and the British Colonies in the West Indies, Great Britain declined entering into any stipulation. She thought herself competent to furnish them all the supplies that they needed, and concluded to adhere to the ancient colonial system. He did not know whether it was a wise system; much had been said for and against it; but, as it had been so long established, it was thought best not to depart from it. Besides other considerations, an objection against any new stipulation would be to affect the treaties with other powers entitled to claim the privileges of the most favored nation. It had been mentioned by me as an argument in favor of a new article, that by the exclusion of American vessels from the British West India Islands, the object of the existing convention, of placing the ships of the two nations upon an equal footing in the direct intercourse between the British dominions in Europe and the United States, was defeated; as the British vessels, by circuitous voyages, first from Europe to the United States, thence to the West Indies,

and thence back to Europe, had a great advantage even for the
first part of the voyage over American vessels, confined as
they were to the freights obtainable for the direct voyages to
and from Europe.   This disadvantage it would, however, be
in the power of the United States to remove by regulations of
their own, either by prohibiting the intercourse between the
United States and the British West India Islands in British
vessels, or by charging it with additional duties.   This Government were aware that the United States had the whole subject
at their discretion, and would feel no dissatisfaction at any
measure they might adopt, trusting that the measures would
be adapted only to the object of counteraction and without
resentment.

I said the natural reciprocal and corresponding measure
would be a prohibition ; probably that would be adopted.   Lord
Castlereagh intimated that additional duties would be more
acceptable, but again acknowledged that the whole ground
would be at our disposal.   As to the intercourse by land between the United States and the British Colonies in North
America, he said there had been proposals made and discussed
at the negotiation of the commercial convention.   It had not
then been found practicable to agree upon that article, but the
British Government was willing to receive any proposition upon
the subject, and to make an arrangement concerning it.   He
said the same in relation to seamen, but as it seemed to be
agreed that the policy of both Governments should be to
encourage its own native seamen, Great Britain would be willing to wait the favorable effects of that policy.   Concerning
the points of collision between neutral and belligerent pretensions and maritime rights in time of war, Great Britain was
desirous of not touching upon them at present, and particularly
of not undertaking a negotiation without a prospect of bringing
it to a successful result.   It was better to leave things as they
were, and give time for prepossessions and prejudices on both
parts to subside, than to encourage expectations by a formal
negotiation of a treaty which might terminate in disappointment.

I said then that I understood him as giving me the determination of the British Government as declining any negotia-

tion relative to the intercourse between the United States and the British West India Islands, or relative to the objects of blockade, contraband of war, and the other points connected with maritime neutrality which are usually included in the adjustment of commercial treaties; but as being willing to receive proposals in relation to seamen and to the intercourse by land between the United States and the British Colonies in North America. He assented to this.

I told him that I knew the measures which the American Government would find itself compelled to adopt would be taken with great reluctance; that the renewal of the colonial exclusions in all their rigor since the conclusion of the convention, and the effect of those measures upon the operation of the convention itself, had already occasioned much uneasiness among the merchants in our cities, and occasioned a loud call for counteracting restrictions. The Government had preferred to make the attempt to settle the business by an amicable arrangement, knowing that restrictive measures have always the tendency to excite irritation, and anxious in the highest degree to avert by every possible effort everything that can even tend to impair the harmony or add to those prepossessions and prejudices to which he had alluded. The same principle had prompted the renewed proposals to treat upon the most interesting points of maritime neutral commerce. The experience of the evils produced by the want of stipulations on these points, and the earnest desire to guard against their recurrence, were the motives which induced them again and again to urge these subjects to the attention of the British Cabinet. My instructions to this effect were so earnest, that my Government would expect me to receive the ultimate decision of this Government in writing. I should, therefore, shortly address a note to him, with a formal restatement of the proposals, and to which I should solicit at his convenience an answer.

He said there would be no objection to that so far as related to the seamen and the West India trade, but he wished me to consider whether it would be advisable to say anything relative to the neutral and belligerent questions, by proposing a negotiation without a prospect of bringing it to a successful termination.

I told him I should seriously consider of this observation before sending in the note. I then mentioned the instruction that I had received respecting the improper conduct of a British naval officer in boarding several American merchant vessels upon Lake Erie, and told him I should send him copies of the papers.

He said he wished me in the note to express the fullest conviction that this Government will disapprove of every such proceeding on the part of their officers, and take every proper measure to suppress them.

I replied that this was the light in which the affair was viewed in my instructions. The American Government was fully persuaded that the conduct of this officer would be disavowed. But Lord Castlereagh professed not to have heard of this transaction before, which I can scarcely believe, for it has been in the newspapers here, and an advertisement from the Admiralty for transports, to carry five thousand two hundred tons of ordnance stores to Canada, happening to be published about the same time, gave an alarm of war, and occasioned a depression of the funds of at least one per cent.

I also spoke to him of the several notes that I have lately sent him.

He said he had just received that relating to the American seamen whom the Consul wishes to send home; that there would be no difficulty in giving the order authorizing the vessel to take more than the limited number of one person to every five tons—because this case stood upon a foundation altogether different from that of vessels taking ordinary passengers. Concerning the extra duty of five per cent. on merchandise sold at auction, he sent for Mr. Planta, who came, and said that the order from the Treasury to remove the duty had been dispatched this day.

Upon the case of the ship Independence, at Glasgow, I observed that some of the parties interested were apprehensive that, notwithstanding Lord Castlereagh's recommendation, there would be some difficulty in obtaining the order at the Treasury.

He said it might perhaps depend upon the state of preparation of the vessel before the new Act of Parliament was known. If the preparations had been all made, and the expense incurred, he thought the order would be granted; but if it was merely a speculation of the shippers, that might raise a difficulty. It might all depend upon the strength of the case that the shippers should make out.

I said that from their representation to me, a stronger case could not be made out; for the shippers had no knowledge of the new restriction until they applied to clear out the vessel; and the Act of Parliament had been received at the Custom House only the day before.

He said then perhaps the Lords of the Treasury had referred it to some of their own officers for a report of the facts, and that had occasioned the delay. My note respecting the damaged provisions said to have been furnished to the American prisoners of war at Dartmoor had been referred to the Lords of the Admiralty. Lord Castlereagh then adverted to the expedition against the Algerines, and gave me to read a copy of the last instructions to Lord Exmouth. They were dated the 18th of July, the very day that I had a long interview with Lord Castlereagh, and in which much was said upon this same subject. These instructions recite that the Dey of Algiers, by his insults and outrages since the treaties concluded by Lord Exmouth with him, had placed himself in a state of war with Great Britain. Lord Exmouth is therefore directed to go with his squadron to Algiers. On his arrival there, he is to offer peace to the Dey upon three conditions. 1. That he shall sign a declaration like those already obtained from the Bey of Tunis and the Bashaw of Tripoli—namely, to renounce forever the practice of reducing prisoners of war taken from Christian nations to slavery, and promising to exchange prisoners according to the practice of Christian nations. 2. To liberate without ransom all the Christian slaves now in the Dey's possession, and to place them in the first instance at Lord Exmouth's disposal, by sending them on board his fleet. 3. To repay the whole sum of money paid by Lord Exmouth for the ransom of Sardinians and Neapolitans last April. No modification of either of these conditions is to be admitted. If either of them is refused by the Dey, Lord Exmouth is to commence immediate hostilities against the Algerine fleet, and to use all the means in his power to effect its destruction. If the Dey complies with the three conditions, Lord Exmouth is to conclude a peace with him, but is to admit no stipulation for the payment hereafter of any consular present whatever.

I observed that the instructions did not contemplate, in case the Dey should refuse the conditions, an attack upon Algiers itself.

Lord Castlereagh said if the state of war should ensue, hostilities would then be directed against any point where they might be found vulnerable. He said he had been particularly desirous, and had quite made a point of it, to avoid making a demand that the fleet should be delivered up, because other nations were already sufficiently jealous of the British naval power, and ready to suspect this Government of the wish to annihilate the naval force of others; and if they had insisted upon having the Algerine fleet, it would have given countenance to such surmises. They had in the first instance declined entering into any combination of European powers against the Barbary States, because they had no particular cause of complaint against them. But as the Dey of Algiers, by his subsequent conduct, had chosen to place himself in a state of hostility to Great Britain, she was now released from the obligation of her treaties with him, and free to espouse the general cause of Europe against him. She had therefore determined to prescribe those conditions that I had read as the terms upon which alone she would listen to the renewal of peace, and when those were settled she would willingly co-operate with the other nations interested in maintaining the observance of the principles of civilized nations by the Barbary Powers in future, by supplying her proportion of a force commensurate with that object. But it was her intention to combine this purpose with that of completing the abolition of the African slave-trade, and to obtain the assent of the nations which will contribute to the joint armament to put down forever the Barbary piracies, to allow the same joint application of power to arrest every ship pursuing the traffic in black slaves.

I told him this appeared to me perfectly fair. The instructions to Lord Exmouth were such as must give satisfaction to every power annoyed by the Barbarian piracies, and if Spain and Portugal were so anxious for the abolition of one slavery, it could not consistently be refused by them to lend a hand for the abandonment of another. As to the United States, they, as well as Great Britain, had totally prohibited the slave-trade by their own citizens, and could have no objection to measures which may serve to put down these odious practices, the one by the other.

While I was in town this day, I went into St. James's Park, and took a view of what is called " The Regent's Bomb," a huge mortar, used by the French at the siege of Cadiz, abandoned by them when the siege was raised—presented by the Cortes to the Prince Regent, now mounted upon an allegorical carriage, a three-headed monster, with a Latin inscription on one side, translated on the other, and a second English inscription in the rear, immortalizing the Duke of Wellington, the Prince Regent, and the Earl of Mulgrave, Master-General of the Ordnance. It was uncovered to public view first on the Prince's birthday, and immediately caricatured under the title of " The Regent's Bomb uncovered." The people are constantly crowding to see it, but it is surrounded by a palisade to keep them off, and two soldiers are stationed there as sentinels, to guard it from being defaced. They are surly as bull-dogs, and allow no person to touch even the palisade.

22d. At eleven o'clock this morning I was, with my wife, at Westminster Bridge, where we embarked in the Lord Mayor's barge, but it was near twelve when he came himself, with the Lady Mayoress and his family. There was a company of about one hundred persons, among whom were Lord Erskine, her Highness the Margravine of Anspach, Lady Elizabeth Forbes, the Sheriffs, Sir Thomas Bell and Mr. Thorpe, several of the Aldermen and their families, with other City officers and strangers, and a musical party—Sir George Smart, Mr. Lacy, Mrs. Bianca Lacy, Mrs. Billington, Mrs. Salmon, Miss Goodall, and some others. The barge was elegantly ornamented with streamers, and the Duke of Kent's band of music was on board.

We started from Westminster Bridge just at noon, and were rowed down the Thames to Richmond, passing through the Vauxhall, Battersea, Putney, Kew, and Richmond Bridges. The weather was fine, and the barge was surrounded all the way down by a number of boats, perhaps twenty, filled with company, ladies and gentlemen, as witnesses of the scene. We passed by Chelsea Hospital, Craven House, which is the Margravine's villa, and some other country-seats, as well as several villages on both sides of the river. But the prospects are not, on the whole, equal to my expectations. The country on both sides is very low, and not remarkably picturesque. The Duke of Sussex and Lord Arthur Hill came on board at Kew Bridge. At Richmond we found the new, or Navigation Barge, called the Maria Wood, in honor of the present Lady Mayoress. It is much larger than that in which we had come from Westminster Bridge, and the whole company passed from the one to the other. Just then the Duke of Cambridge was seen walking with Sir Carnaby and Lady Haggerston, and the Lord Mayor, accompanied by the Duke of Sussex, went on shore and invited them to come on board. They came accordingly, but could not stay for the dinner. The Navigation Barge was towed up the river to Twickenham, as far as the Lord Mayor's villa, passing by Pope's House and Grotto, which now belong to Lord Mendip, and several other country-seats. We returned and anchored, about five o'clock, near Richmond Bridge, when the whole company sat down to an elegant cold dinner. The carriages were ordered to be at Kew Bridge at eight o'clock, but it was nine before we left the table, and ten by the time we got back to Kew Bridge.

The usual toasts were drunk and the usual speeches made after dinner by the Lord Mayor, the Duke of Sussex, Lord Erskine, the Sheriffs, the Aldermen, and Lord Arthur Hill, and myself. The Duke of Sussex, as he always does, put politics into his speeches. Lord Erskine was more shy, although the Lord Mayor, in toasting him, alluded to his inactivity of late years, and hoped he would soon come forward again. The Duke of Sussex is ambitious enough to come forward, and told us that he was to move for the repeal of the Alien Act at the next session of Parliament. He also declared himself against the new political doctrine of legitimacy; but Lord Erskine took care to declare himself in its favor. This party consisted for the most part of Whigs, and they were very much perplexed at the result of a meeting of the City of London yesterday in Common Hall. It was a meeting called to deliberate upon the distressed state of the country. A number of violent resolutions were passed unanimously, at a very numerous meeting, and a petition to the Prince Regent was voted, to be presented to him seated on the throne, which it is known he will refuse. At this meeting there were only three speakers, all on one side, that of the Reformers, and equally inveterate against the Ministers and the leading Whigs. Neither a Whig nor a Tory ventured to open his lips at this meeting, yet the resolutions, and the petition, were voted unanimously at a meeting of two thousand persons. The Lord Mayor mentioned it with surprise to Alderman Christopher Smith, who, it seems, is to be Lord Mayor the next year, and who is a staunch ministerial man. "All the resolutions unanimous!" said the Lord Mayor, "and some of them very strong!" "Ay," said Smith, "and if they had put it to vote to hang the Lord Mayor, they would have passed that unanimously too!" "No, not this year; perhaps they might the next," replied the Lord Mayor, much to the diversion of the company, who enjoyed a hearty laugh at the expense of Alderman Smith.

Perry, the editor of the Morning Chronicle, was of the party this day, and invited me to dine with him next Saturday, in company with the Duke of Sussex and Sir Robert Wilson. Perry is a Whig, and not satisfied at all with the proceedings of the City meeting yesterday. There was an article in the Morning Chronicle asserting that, notwithstanding the lateness of the season, there would be this year an uncommon fine harvest. Mr. Hunt, one of the speakers in the City yesterday, contradicted this statement, upon his honor as a gentleman, and censured the Morning Chronicle as attempting to impose upon the people by it. Perry still insists that according to his information from all parts of the country the harvest will be excellent, if they have yet good weather. Lord Castlereagh told me the same thing yesterday. Cobbett proclaimed three weeks ago that the harvest would be bad. Hunt yesterday pledged his honor that it would be. It is strange that such a thing should be made a party question; but so it is.

Lord Erskine told me this day that he still intended to pay a visit to the United States. I observed to him that it would be best to fix a time to carry his project into execution. He said he thought he should go the summer after next. He was much gratified with receiving from Dr. Romayne, at New York, by Dr. Mason, a copy of his speeches reprinted at New York from an edition published here by Ridgway.

The Margravine of Anspach was once a Lady Elizabeth Berkeley, sister to the late Earl of Berkeley and the Admiral. She married first a Lord Craven; and, as Lady Craven, published her travels in the Crimea. Her second marriage was with the Margrave of Anspach, of whom she is now the widow. She is nearly seventy, and very tenacious of her title of Highness. She has been heretofore a very distinguished person in fashionable life, but is now so forgotten that she puts up with a Lord Mayor's and City party. Lady Elizabeth Forbes, who accompanied her, is her niece. The Margravine was toasted after dinner, but made no speech. There were some country-dances, before and after dinner, but the most delightful part of the entertainment was the songs and glees sung by the musical guests, which were without accompaniment of instruments, but in the very highest style of excellence. The Duke of Sussex sang a glee, "Rosy Bacchus, God of Wine," tolerably well. When his health was given, the singing-party gave the cheer of three times three hurras in musical intonation, which was called for again and repeated. As the night came on, the surrounding boats drew up closer to the barge, which was thus surrounded by genteel people looking in upon the company and participating in the pleasures of the music. A Mr. Henry Newman, holding some office in the City, introduced himself to me as having been invariably a friend to America. It was very dark when we landed in a boat from the barge at Kew Bridge. We found our carriage there, and were at home shortly after ten.

I forgot to mention that among the company at the Lord Mayor's party this day was Mr. John Reeves, formerly of the Alien Office. This person, from having been one of the most inflexible supporters of the doctrine of inalienable allegiance, and being a lawyer, was led to pursue the principle into its consequences, and brought himself to the conclusion that all Americans born before the Declaration of Independence, and at least their children, were entitled inalienably to the privileges of British subjects. So that while he was at the head of the Alien Office, where he had been placed in consequence of the fiery zeal of his loyalty, he used to tell every American who came to him for a passport that he was no more an alien than himself, and that he needed no passport. The Government, who could not answer his argument, but whom his inferences did not suit, removed him from the Alien Office; upon which he published a book in support of his theory. He has now all the stubbornness of a religious or political bigot upon the subject of his doctrine. It was but just as we were going down to dinner that he discovered who I was, and he was quite anxious to have a long conversation with me. He told me that he had read Mr. Hay's pamphlet on expatriation, and asked my opinion of his book.

I told him I thought his conclusions were correctly drawn from the British premises, but that in America our principles were different, and of course they led to different conclusions.

He said that some people here did not like his doctrine. What was that to him? He knew it to be the law, and no lawyer in England would dare to say it was not. Let anybody try it in the Court of King's Bench. No Judge would dare to decide the question against him.

I told him I thought if the question was brought before them they would devise some means to get rid of it; they were subtle persons, and I should be sorry to have a stake depending upon that question before them.

Mr. Reeves was very sanguine that they must decide it according to his theory; but he had not time to explain it to me at large.

24th. I went to see Mr. West, and at last found him at home;

it being the fourth time I had called at his house. I was with him an hour and a half, and he showed me all the collection of his pictures that he now has at home. They are principally scriptural subjects. He told me that he had been these many years painting a series of these pictures for the King. The whole number of them was to be thirty-six—twenty-five of which are finished. He classes them into what he calls the four dispensations—the Patriarchal, the Mosaic, the Christian or Gospel, and the Revelation or Apocalyptic dispensation. He is now engaged upon a picture of Death upon the Pale Horse, from the sixth chapter of the book of Revelation, verse eighth, which he says must be in the terribly sublime style. The picture is to be twenty-eight feet long and twenty-two feet high. The sketch was before him, and the head of the figure of Death is completed, or, as he calls it, settled. The head of the horse is nearly finished. He expects to have it finished by next spring. He is also painting a large transparent piece, to be copied upon glass for a church-window. It is the Angels proclaiming Peace on Earth at the Nativity of Christ. He has one large picture from the Scottish history, an incident which he says founded the family of McGregors, and one copy of his Death of Wolfe, of which he told me he had painted four, with some varieties in the backgrounds. He says he has been offered a hundred guineas for his proof-copy of Woollett's print of that picture, and that there is no engraver now living equal to Woollett. He showed me two pictures which had been sent to him by British officers to judge of them. They were bought in Spain, one for a Titian, the other for a Raphael. West says they are not only copies, but very bad copies; and he adds that many of the British officers have been greatly imposed upon in the same manner.

Soon after six I left Mr. West, and went and dined with Mr. Perry[1] at Tavistock House, north of Tavistock Square. The Duke of Sussex, Sir Robert Wilson, General Long, Mr. Dupin, a French engineer, brother of the Dupin who was Sir Robert Wilson's counsel on the late trial at Paris, Mr. Richard

---

[1] James Perry, then the proprietor of the Morning Chronicle, the organ of the opposition to the ruling party. He died in 1821.

Wilson, and another gentleman, whose name escaped me, constituted the company.   Mr. Bruce, Sir Robert's associate in
effecting the escape of Lavalette, had been invited, but was
prevented by some accident from coming.   The conversation
at table was very free on political subjects, and sentiments were
expressed without reserve.   The company were Whigs, evidently
not satisfied with the issue of the City meeting last Wednesday,
yet railing at sinecures, and complaining that many of their
friends will not come out; and something was said about trim-
mers.   Sir Robert Wilson asserted, as a fact which came from
Fouché himself, that the royal French proscription list of the
Ordonnance of 24th July, 1815, was submitted to Lord Castlereagh, and had his sanction, before the proclamation was issued.
It was remarked that he ought to be impeached for this, and
that it deserved a capital punishment.   There was much talk
about sinecures, the Marquis of Camden, Lord Arden, &c.
But this is a point upon which the Whigs ought to be tongue-
tied, for many of their leaders are upon the list.   It was said
that the Lord Chancellor Eldon, and his brother, Sir William
Scott, had made by the public a property of at least a million
sterling; and some very ludicrous stories were told about "Old
Bags."

The Prince Regent has been very dangerously ill.   He went
to Windsor the 16th, to keep the Duke of York's birthday
with the Queen.   He was unwell there, but returned after the
party to the Stud-house, at Hampton Court, where he was
seized with extreme violence.   It was inflammation of the
bowels.   He had a girdle of thirty-six leeches round his waist,
and, when they dropped off, was put into a warm bath to continue the bleeding.   In the whole, he had eighty ounces of
blood taken from him.   It was not until yesterday that his
signature could be obtained to the prorogation of Parliament,
which was from this day to the 4th of November.   The public
knew nothing of the Prince's illness until he was recovering.
The Queen left Windsor to go and see him, but was met on
the road by the Duke of Cambridge, and persuaded to return.
Perry had a letter from a gentleman of respectability, giving
it as an undoubted fact that the Prince was raving mad; the

only foundation for which was the delirium occasioned by the violence of the fever.

There was something said of Lord Erskine's having had a long conference with the Lord Chancellor, and of high words having passed between the Regent and the Chancellor. They related to the projected divorce from his wife, which the Regent is very desirous of obtaining, but which is vehemently opposed by the Chancellor. The Princess Charlotte and Prince Leopold are so disgusted with Camelford House, their town residence, which they have now left and removed into the country, that they will not return to it. They are to have apartments in Kensington Palace; but the Duke of Sussex said he would not give up his there. They were granted to him, he said, by the King, and he insisted that they could not be taken from him during the King's life. There was question to whom the Regency would be assigned in case of the Prince of Wales's demise, and it seems it would be a great question between the Princess Charlotte and the Duke of York. The Duke of Sussex was earnest in the wish for the dissolution of the political connection between this country and Hanover, by the separation of the crowns. After dinner, I reminded the Duke of the promise he had made me, of naming a day when he would come and dine with me. He named next Friday. I also invited Sir Robert Wilson, who promised to come, and Mr. Perry, who excused himself, being obliged to go on Thursday to Brighton. It was near twelve when the Duke left the company; and I came away immediately afterwards.

25th. I stopped and paid a visit to my neighbor, General Dumouriez. I found he was not going to the dinner this day at the French Ambassador's. Dumouriez has lost all hopes of being recalled to France under the present order of things, and is not so much in the secret of affairs as he was last year. I asked him if it was true, as the newspapers had announced, that a person had been arrested in Paris for corresponding with him. He said it was—a General Morgan, who had been one of his aides-de-camp. The letters had been so far from containing anything exceptionable that he had shown them, when he received them, to the Duke de la Châtre, then French

Ambassador here. But Monsieur Cazes, the Minister of Police, had taken it into his head that he (Dumouriez), with his seventy-eight years upon his head, was the chief of a party in favor of the Duke of Orleans. And although Morgan's letters were sent through the British Minister, Stuart, and enclosed to Mr. Vansittart, the Chancellor of the Exchequer, Monsieur Cazes had broken them open, and sent Morgan to prison. But that is not surprising, when it is considered that there are now fifty-eight thousand State prisoners in France. He (Dumouriez) immediately applied to Vansittart that Stuart might be instructed to remonstrate against this procedure; but it was without effect, and Morgan was not released until the Duke de la Châtre went home, when he made such a noise about it that they let the man go. But Monsieur Cazes had also broken open letters addressed to Mr. Hamilton, the Under-Secretary of State, and found treason lurking in one of them, because the writer stated that he had paid for something eighteen shillings.

I asked Dumouriez what had been the object of the Duke of Wellington's last visit to England.

He did not know; he had not seen the Duke, though he had called at his house for that purpose. Perhaps it was on account of his health, as he went for some time to Cheltenham. Sir Robert Wilson and Mr. Bruce, since their return from France, have been to visit Dumouriez, who has a much higher opinion of Bruce than of his associate. He thinks that Bruce will shortly be brought into Parliament, and will make a figure there.

I went into London, and dined at the Marquis d'Osmond's, the French Ambassador. It was St. Louis's day, and a great diplomatic dinner; but, as "full dress" had not been marked upon the invitation cards, as is usual on such occasions, and as was done upon the Count de la Châtre's cards on the same occasion last year, I went in frock undress, but found all the rest of the company in full dress, excepting the Marquis de Grimaldi, the Sardinian Chargé d'Affaires, who had made the same mistake, and two French Bishops, who could not appear in their full dress conveniently. The company consisted of the Cabinet Ministers, the Earls of Liverpool and Bathurst, and Mr. Canning, the new President of the Board of Control, most of the foreign Ambassadors and Ministers, the two French Bishops above mentioned, and a number of French officers, with the Consul Seguier. One of the officers next to whom I was seated at table told me that he had married a sister of De Cabre's, and spoke in handsome terms of the Duke de Vicence.

Mr. Canning came late, after the company had sat down to table. He made acquaintance with me by asking me to help him to a dish that was before me, and to take a glass of wine with him. After dinner, at his request, the Earl of Liverpool formally introduced him to me. This gentleman, whose celebrity is great, and whose talents are perhaps greater than those of any other member of the Cabinet, has been invariably noted for the bitterness of his inveteracy against the United States, and I suppose considers it as a rule of personal courtesy to make up by an excess of civility for the rancor which he has so constantly manifested against us. Mr. Russell more than once mentioned to me that such had been his conduct towards him. He and Lord Liverpool both talked about the great and rapid increase of the population of the United States. They enquired when the next Presidential election would take place, and who would probably be elected. I told them Mr. Monroe. Lord Liverpool said he had heard Mr. Monroe's election might be opposed on account of his being a Virginian. I said that had been made a ground of objection to him, but would not avail.

I asked Mr. Pfeffel and the Chevalier de Freire to come and dine with us next Friday. Freire promised to come; Pfeffel had a previous engagement. The weather was so cold that there was a fire in the drawing-room; so there was yesterday at Mr. Perry's. The Ambassador's Lady, Madame d'Osmond, was much out of humor at being obliged to live at this season of the year in town. Their daughter, Madame de Boignes, is a handsome and agreeable woman. They all speak English well—they lived many years in this country as emigrants. I left the Ambassador's about ten o'clock, and was at home before twelve.

28th. The day was warm and fine; yet last night there was a frost. There has not been this whole summer one day of steady sunshine, not one day of heat, nor one night when a coverlet and blanket could have been thrown off with comfort. I left off my flannel waistcoat one night, but was obliged to resume it the next day. There was not one of the forty days from St. Swithin's, to a certainty, without rain: so that the old prediction seems to have been this year made good. The harvests of hay and grain are precarious, but the last week has been what they here call fine weather—cool, generally cloudy, and almost without rain. This day was most like summer.

29th. Baron de Just, the Saxon, and Mr. Pfeffel, the Bavarian, Minister, paid us a morning visit. Pfeffel recollected now that his engagement on Friday was to the Margravine of Anspach. These gentlemen spoke much of the Prince Regent's project of obtaining a divorce from his wife, which is understood to be with the design of marrying again. Pfeffel spoke in very contemptuous terms of the Princess of Wales, who, he said, had left a very bad reputation behind her at Brunswick, and who had always been accustomed "à tenir des propos au moins très-indiscrets." He said that she made such advances to a gentleman in Italy that he answered her, " Il faudroit pour cela que Votre Altesse perdit deux fois la tête." Pfeffel added that he himself had had occasion to know the extreme reserve of the Duke of Brunswick, the Princess of Wales's father, in his communications with England. He (Pfeffel) had resided at several German Courts, and had then corresponded with the Duke of Brunswick. The Duke had always encouraged the correspondence, and never failed to answer his letters. When Pfeffel was first appointed Chargé d'Affaires here at London, he wrote again to the Duke, mentioning the circumstance, and offering him his services here. But to this letter he had never received an answer. He attributed this to the Duke's caution to avoid even the appearance of having correspondents here. Pfeffel is a widower: his children have lately arrived, and he thinks of taking on their account a house in the country. The gentlemen walked with me round our garden, and went from hence to visit Sir Joseph Banks.

30th. The Duke of Sussex, Lord Erskine, the Lord Mayor, the Chevalier de Freire, Portuguese Minister, Sir Robert Wilson, Doctor Nicholas and his two eldest daughters, dined with us. The Duke was unwell, but in good spirits. Sir Robert Wilson told us many very interesting particulars of the escape of Lavalette, most of which, however, were already known. There was some allusion to the moral and political question as to the propriety of the conduct of the three Englishmen concerned in that affair. There is much diversity of opinion upon the subject, and the political bias generally decides the question in the mind of each individual. It is my opinion that when the municipal laws of a State, or the laws of military discipline, come in too violent collision with the laws of humanity, it is just and proper that they should snap asunder rather than that the ties of nature should be dissolved. I think, therefore, that the action of Bruce, Wilson, and Hutchinson, in assisting Lavalette to escape, was laudable and proper. It would have been perhaps more prudent, and possibly not unjustifiable, to have declined. There are other particulars in the life of Sir Robert Wilson of far more doubtful character in my estimation, and his conversation this day and last Saturday gave me no very high opinion of his judgment. The letter by which he and his associates were detected after their success was a great indiscretion. He appears to me to be in desperate circumstances, and told me he had thoughts of going to South America to offer his services to the South American insurgents; which I advised him not to do. He conversed much upon the state of affairs here, and said he thought Lord Grey would come out with effect at the next session of Parliament. But Lord Grey and all the parliamentary opposition, with the single exception of Sir Francis Burdett, are as much out of favor with the people as any of the Ministers. Wilson says some incident will occur to make them popular —which I very much doubt. They are pledged to opinions with which they and the Ministers will sink or swim all together. Wilson told me that Mina was at Baltimore, and that he knew the whole story how he had gone away from this country.

Lord Erskine was quite entertaining, and amused the company with many of his puns. He is much addicted to this practice. He repeated to us an epigram which he had sent to the Morning Chronicle, and which was published in that paper. It was in four lines, and the idea was, that of all the people slain on Waterloo's immortal field there was not one who fell half so flat as Walter Scott. He insists positively that Scott is not the author of Waverley, Guy Mannering or the Astrologer, and The Antiquary. Lord Erskine says the country is ruined; but as, after opposing the original wars against the French Revolution for many years, he finished by supporting the wars against Napoleon, he is a little puzzled and a little over-anxious to maintain his own consistency. He never once attended in Parliament the whole of the last session, and it will probably be wise for him not to attend the next. He is, however, upon good terms with the Prince Regent, and may possibly come in again as Chancellor, if Lord Eldon should go out. This both he and Lord Liverpool are said to have threatened upon the divorce question.

I asked the Lord Mayor how those resolutions at the late City meeting could be passed, as they were, without opposition. He said the friends of the Government had not dared to make any opposition. I asked him how many Whigs there were among the Aldermen. He said, scarcely any. Birch was no Whig. He had had a little difference with the Ministers at the time of the Corn bill, but Curtis had afterwards made it up with them for him. As for himself, he had never invited any of the Ministers to any one of his parties, excepting those public entertainments to which they were officially invited, and of course they had not chosen to attend at them, and he did not, and would not, invite them to any others. He said it would be Smith's turn to be Lord Mayor next year, and he would doubtless be elected, as they scarcely ever went out of the regular course. Smith is highly ministerial. The Duke of Sussex was more moderate and reserved in his conversation than he sometimes is.

September 2d. The gale has abated, and the weather this day was, part of the day, fair, but with the decided character of autumn, and so cold that we had a fire again in the evening. The newspapers announce that there was on Friday last snow at Barnet, within forty miles of London. For ten days preceding the middle of last week the weather had been so fine that the prospects of a good, though a very late, harvest were generally thought favorable. They are now desperate.

7th. In the Grecian mythology Orpheus is said to have charmed lions and tigers, the most ferocious wild beasts, and to have drawn after him the very trees of the forest and the rocks of the desert, by the harmony of his lyre. Its power was said to have triumphed even over the tremendous deities of the infernal regions, over the monster Cerberus, the Furies, and Pluto himself. The meaning of this allegory is explained by Horace, De Arte Poeticâ, v. 390. Orpheus was a legislator, whose eloquence charmed the rude and savage men of his age to associate together in the state of civil society, to submit to the salutary restraints of law, and to unite together in the worship of their Creator. It was the lyre of Orpheus that civilized savage man. It was only in harmony that the first human political institutions could be founded. After the death of Orpheus, his lyre was placed among the constellations, and there, according to the Astronomics of Manilius, still possesses its original charm, constituting by its concords the music of the spheres, and drawing by its attraction the whole orb of heaven around with its own revolution. It is the application of this fable, and of this passage of Manilius, to the United States, the American political constellation, that forms the device of the seal. The following is the passage in Manilius, with a translation :

> " At Lyra diductis per cœlum cornibus inter
> Sidera conspicitur, qua quondam ceperat Orpheus
> Omne quod attigerat cantu, manesque per ipsos
> Fecit iter, domuitque infernas carmine leges.
> Hinc, cœlestis honos, similisque potentia causæ;
> *Tunc*, silvas et saxa trahens, *Nunc sidera ducit*,
> Et rapit immensum mundi revolubilis orbem."
>
> *Manilius, Astronomicon*, i. 322, &c.

The Lyre of Orpheus, with erected horns,
Next in the sky the starry world adorns;

> That Lyre, which once with fascinating spell
> Tamed the dread Lord and tyrant laws of Hell;
> With soft compulsion won the Master's way
> From Death's dire regions to the realms of day;
> Nor yet, transferr'd in glory to the skies,
> Has lost the power to draw by kindred ties.
> *Then*, rocks and groves obey'd its magic force,
> *Now*, of the starry orbs it leads the course,
> Extends its charms to Heaven's remotest bound,
> And, rolling, whirls the Universe around.

The modern astronomers have connected a vulture with the constellation of the Lyre, and it is marked upon the charts of Bode's Uranographie by the name of "Vultur et Lyra." In-

stead of that bird, by a slight poetical license, I have assumed the American eagle as the bearer of the lyre. The thirteen original stars form a border round the seal. The stars marked upon the lyre, and upon the wings of the eagle, are placed in the relative positions as they may be seen by the naked eye in the constellation of Lyra. The motto from Manilius is upon the lyre itself. The moral application of the emblem is, that the same power of harmony which originally produced the institutions of civil government to regulate the association of individual men, now presides in the federal association of the American States; that harmony is the soul of their combination; that their force consists in their union, and that while thus united it will be their destiny to revolve in harmony with the whole world, by the attractive influence of their union. It is the lyre of Orpheus that now leads the stars, as it originally drew after it rocks and trees. It is harmony that now binds in its influence the American States, as it originally drew individual men from the solitude of nature to the assemblages which formed states and nations. The lesson of the emblem is UNION.

16th. The newspapers of this morning contain the official dispatches from Lord Exmouth, announcing the complete success of his expedition against Algiers. The attack was on the 27th of August, and the whole Algerine fleet was destroyed, with the arsenal, storehouses, and part of the batteries on the shore. He gives the loss of the Turks as between six and seven thousand men. The returns of his own loss, including that of the Dutch squadron co-operating with him, are one hundred and forty-one killed, and seven hundred and forty-two wounded. The next morning the Dey submitted to all the terms prescribed, delivered up all the Christian slaves in and near Algiers, repaid all the money which had been paid for the ransom of the Neapolitans and Sardinians under Lord Exmouth's former treaties in April, and stipulated the formal abolition of slavery in Algiers forever. This is a deed of real glory.

October 1st. Went first to the Foreign Office. Met in the antechamber the Chevalier de Freire, with Count Palmella, and a Secretary of the Russian Embassy. After waiting a full half-hour, I saw the Under-Secretary of State, Hamilton. I spoke to him about the warrant for the exportation of machinery for the Mint of the United States. Hamilton has just returned after an absence of two or three months, and knew nothing of the state of the business of the office. Planta is gone with Lord Castlereagh to Ireland. I mentioned my first note to Lord Castlereagh about the Mint machinery, the Act of Parliament passed in consequence of that application, a printed copy of which I had with me, and showed him my second note to Lord Castlereagh, after the Act, and the verbal answer of Lord Castlereagh and Planta that the order had been given. But I had no written answer. The intended exporters had now written to me to ask for the warrant for exportation, and I came to enquire whether the order was now in the possession of the officers of the customs at Liverpool, and if not, that it might be immediately dispatched, as the machinery would be there in a day or two, and the vessel in which it was to be exported would be ready to sail by the 6th or 7th of this month.

Hamilton told me that, according to their forms of business, the warrant for the exportation must be issued from the Home Department and signed by Lord Sidmouth. I observed that the Act of Parliament authorized any one of the Secretaries of State to issue the warrant. He said that although the authority was general it was exercised only by the Secretary for the Home Department. In this, however, Hamilton was mistaken. He sent to several of the clerks to know what had been done upon my application. At last Bidwell, the son, came, and he sent him to the Treasury to ascertain whether the order to the customs had been issued there. My note to Lord Castlereagh could not be found, nor any record in the office relating to it.

While Bidwell was gone, I spoke to Hamilton about the notes which I had lately sent to Lord Castlereagh, and to which I had not received answers. He said he had just been reading my note proposing the negotiation of a commercial treaty. I told him I had received a letter from Lord Castlereagh postponing the answer to that; but the notes to which I referred were one respecting the refusal of the officers of the customs to return the extra tonnage duties levied upon American vessels unless they came directly from or were bound directly to ports of the United States, and one to request that the destitute American seamen shipped by order of the Consul on board of American vessels for conveyance to America may not be counted as part of the number of passengers, limited to one person for every five tons of the vessel's burden.

He said this case was so clear that he wondered there should have been a necessity for any application about it. I told him there was another practice of the officers of the customs, on the subject of which I had not yet addressed or written a note, because I thought it best to mention it in the first instance verbally. I thought they were not warranted in the practice by the law. I had been inclined to advise the parties interested to contest it at law, by a process, I supposed, in the Court of Exchequer. But before giving this advice I had preferred stating the case to the Government, so that if they thought proper they might issue an order to the customs to alter their practice and make it conform to the law, which would save the trouble and expense of a suit. The practice was of allowing only one passenger for every five tons of a vessel, of what they call the unoccupied tonnage—that is, of the part in which there is no cargo. I showed him the two Acts of Parliament, and pointed out to him how the officers of the customs had unwarrantably applied the restriction in one section of the first Act to another section where it was not included. It was some time before he understood me. He thought at first I meant to contend that by the new Act American vessels were placed on a more advantageous footing than British vessels, and said that if the Custom House should be now obliged to alter their practice, it would only make it necessary to pass a new Act of Parliament at the next session. When I had fully explained to him the real question, and he had attentively read over the provisions of both the Acts, he took minutes of them, and requested me to send him a memorandum, not in the form of an official note, but exhibiting my view of the proper construction of the Acts, and said he would attend to it. I enquired also about the "Exequatur" for H. Visger's commission as American Consul at Bristol, and after much research was told it was ready, and would be delivered if I would send for it to-morrow.

Bidwell at length returned, and said the order from the Treasury to the Custom House for the exportation of the Mint machinery had been sent on the 16th August; but it was still doubtful to me whether it had been received by the Collector at Liverpool: so, at the recommendation of Mr. Hamilton, I went myself with Bidwell to the Treasury Office, where a clerk showed me the record of the order from the Treasury to the Commissioners of Customs issued the 16th of August, upon a letter from Mr. Planta. So it seems no signature of Lord Sidmouth, nor even of Lord Castlereagh, was necessary in this case; the proxy of Planta's name was sufficient. Still, I had no certainty that the order had been sent to the Collector at Liverpool. Bidwell said it must have gone, of course; but the Treasury clerk referred me to the Secretary of the Commissioners of the Customs, at the Custom House in the City. It was now close upon four o'clock, and too late to go down there this day.

3d. Mr. Rotch came out with his son, whom he introduced to me, and who, he said, had something to communicate to me of so secret a nature that he himself could not be present at its disclosure. He therefore went out and walked in the garden while the young man was unfolding to me his mystery. It was a proposal from a person now an officer in the British artillery, but not born a British subject, and in principle an ardent republican. He has a great mechanical genius, and has invented an improvement in fire-arms, which has been approved by the Board of Ordnance, and adopted, but for which, by the report of a committee of officers appointed to examine it, but every one of them utterly ignorant of the first principles of mechanics, he had received a compensation of only five hundred pounds, a sum in his own opinion so inadequate to the merit of the invention that it has given him extreme disgust. But he had another and a far more important invention in reserve. Its principal use would be in the Naval Department, but it might also be made useful for war by land. He had written a private letter to the Duke of York, proposing it in general terms, to which the Duke had answered by requesting of him a communication in his official capacity. That having been made, the Duke, finding that the chief use of the invention was to be for the navy, had referred him to the Lords of the Admiralty, and there Mr. Croker had referred him back to the Board of Ordnance, where he would be sure to fall again into the hands of the committee of ignorant officers who had so much undervalued his former invention. He had therefore determined to offer his invention to the Russian Government; but young Rotch, having met him, and conversing with him upon the subject, had prevailed upon him to make the proposal to me, of offering it to the Government of the United States. He came, therefore, to enquire if I should be willing to transmit the offer to the American Government. The invention is a projectile upon a new principle, but of such simplicity that an idea of it could not be given without disclosing the secret, yet of such prodigious effects impossible to avoid, that with it any sloop of war would be more than a match for any line-of-battle-ship.

I told young Rotch that the very magnitude of promise in such an invention was a motive for distrusting it. After seeing what had been accomplished by the steam-engine, it was scarcely possibly to say what could not be effected by an application of mechanical powers; but great projects were so common, and great discoveries so rare, that I should not incline to make even a proposal of this kind known to the American Government without some further knowledge of the person proposing it, and something specific as to the nature and extent of the compensation which he would require or expect.

He said that the inventor had been a Major in the British service, but having been twice unfortunately involved in duels, and consequently twice compelled to quit his regiment and rise again from the lowest rank, he was now only a Lieutenant. He could not leave the British service without having a certainty of employment elsewhere, and he had told him that if his invention should be approved and adopted by the American Government he thought he might fairly expect for it the rank of a Lieutenant-Colonel in their army.

I said that would be very difficult, as he must be aware how ungracious it would be to the officers of our army to have a foreigner thus promoted over their heads. However, I said, if the character of the invention could be specified, so that its probable usefulness could be fairly judged of, and the inventor would state specifically what he would demand for his compensation, I would mention it to the Government, particularly with the consideration that the inventor, though now an officer in the British service, is not a native British subject. For had he been such, I should not consider it as a fair procedure from one Government to another to hold out any encouragement to him in the design of withdrawing him from one service to enter the other. Rotch is to report to him my answer, and I shall hear from him again. But it is another of the projects from the Limbo of Vanity.

November 8th. The day was fine, and I walked to Ealing, Acton, Gunnersbury, and Brentford. In the lane from Gunnersbury down to the Brentford Road I saw a man, decently dressed, lying stretched upon the ground by the side of the road, his face downward, and apparently asleep, or dead. There was in the adjoining field a man trimming the hedge, of whom I enquired whether he knew anything of this person. He said he found him lying there, had attempted to raise him up, but could not get him to speak. I asked him if the man was in liquor. He did not know. I requested him to come and repeat the attempt to raise him up. I then spoke to him, and he answered; said he was not in liquor, but had a bad leg; had walked from near Windsor, going to Lambeth, to try and get into the hospital, for which he had a certificate from a physician. He had found himself faint, and laid down there. I asked him if he was in want. He said he had eaten nothing for two days. By this time two other persons had come up. I gave him a shilling, and advised him to stop at the public house at Turnham Green and take some nourishment. The number of these wretched objects that I meet in my daily walks is distressing. Many of them beg. They are often insolent, and sometimes exhibit figures that seem prepared for anything. It is not a month since a man was found dead, lying in a field by the side of the road, between Dumouriez's house and Dr. Goodenough's. Not a day passes but we have beggars come to the house, each with a different hideous tale of misery. The extremes of opulence and of want are more remarkable, and more constantly obvious, in this country than in any other that I ever saw.

9th. This was Lord Mayor's day. According to the annual custom, he came in procession by water from Blackfriars Bridge to Westminster Hall, where he was formally presented to the Barons of the Exchequer. He returned to Westminster Hall by land, through the streets—a measure which annoyed and alarmed the Ministers so much that Lord Sidmouth, the Secretary of State for the Home Department, wrote him a letter to dissuade him from it, but without success. I waited in Craven Street until the procession passed by it in the Strand, and then joined in it. The crowd of people throughout the way was as great as the streets could hold. The horses had been taken out of the Lord Mayor's and the Lady Mayoress's coaches opposite the Horse Guards, and they were drawn from thence to Guildhall by the people. The invitation for the dinner had been for four o'clock, and the procession arrived there just at that hour, but the company were

assembling until six. None of the Cabinet Ministers were
there, nor any of the chief Judges of the King's Courts, but
the Puisné Judges of the King's Bench, Common Pleas, and
Exchequer were almost all there. Sir William Scott, the
Judge of the Admiralty Court, was peculiarly polite and attentive to me. No other foreign Minister was there; which
made my situation somewhat awkward. At first the company
were received in the Council Chamber, but soon after passed
into the Court of King's Bench, where the Lady Mayoress sat
in state, full dressed, and hooped, to receive them. About six,
they all repaired to the great hall, where tables were laid for
upwards of one thousand persons, and all except the company
of the Lord Mayor's own table were already seated. My card
was on a plate at the right hand of the Lord Mayor, but after
the members of both Houses of Parliament. This is the rule
at the City feasts, and is the reason why the foreign Ministers
scarcely ever attend them. Sir William Scott several times
hinted to me before dinner that I should have higher precedence; but I was not disposed to dispute about the place assigned to me. I sat next to Mr. Bennett (Henry Grey), a
member of Parliament for Shrewsbury, and second son of the
Earl of Tankerville. His elder brother, Lord Ossulston, was
also present. Also the Earl of Essex, Lord Montfort, Sir
Samuel Romilly, the Attorney-General, Garrow, the Master of
the Rolls, Mr. William Smith, member from Norwich, Sir Robert
Wilson, Mr. Curran, Major Cartwright, and Mr. Reeves. The
Duke of Sussex would have attended, but the Queen sent him
yesterday a message positively enjoining him not to go, on
account of the death of the King of Würtemberg, who married
the Princess Royal of England. The Lord Mayor and Lady
Mayoress sat, as usual, side by side; the Earl of Essex at
the Lord Mayor's right hand, and Sir Robert Wilson at the
Lady Mayoress's left. A part of the procession on Lord
Mayor's day consists of three persons clad in complete ancient
armor, one of which is the armor of Edward the Black Prince,
from the Tower. These persons are called ancient knights.
After all the company were seated, they took their places in
three niches in the wall, behind the Lord Mayor's table, one at

each corner, and one in the centre, where they stood and sat during the whole dinner.   They were soldiers of the Life Guards, and some of the most athletic men that could be selected, but the armor was so oppressive to them that two of them were obliged to have their helmets taken off, and they were saved from fainting only by a succession of glasses of port wine which were administered to them.   After dinner, the usual loving cup was passed round, and then the ordinary toasts.   After the range of the royal family was gone through, the Lord Mayor gave, " The Earl of Essex, and the House of Peers," in return for which the Earl gave, " The Lord Mayor and the Lady Mayoress."   The Lord Mayor, after making some question who was the oldest member of the House of Commons (who was said to be Mr. W. Smith), said he must settle himself the question, and gave, " Mr. Grey Bennett and the House of Commons," at the same time observing that the City of London was grateful to Mr. Bennett for the very great and important service he had rendered, by the report to the House of Commons, at the last session of Parliament, of the committee of which he was Chairman, upon the police of the metropolis.

There was a flourish of trumpets from the head of the hall, answered by one from the bottom (as there had been at the giving of every toast), for Mr. Bennett to answer; but he declined, pleading the example of the Earl of Essex, who had answered only by toasting the Lord Mayor and Lady Mayoress. But the Lord Mayor himself in returning thanks had made a speech, expressing his gratitude to his fellow-citizens for his re-election.   He said he felt a double weight of responsibility arising from this second election, and a double anxiety, not merely that of discharging the duties of his office, but that of justifying by extraordinary exertions the extraordinary confider :e which had been manifested to him. .   He promised that nothing on his part should be wanting to fulfil the expectations of the public.   He retained all his political opinions, but should continue to set politics entirely aside in the performance of his duty, without connecting himself with any political party, or turning to the right hand or the left.   None of his Majesty's

Ministers had thought fit to honor him with their company,
either at this entertainment or on the same occasion last year.
He knew not what the motives of their absence were, but he
found a consolation for it in the high respectability of the company present.

Immediately after Mr. Bennett had declined answering, the
Lord Mayor gave, " The American Minister," upon which I
returned thanks in a very few words, observing that having
frequently received the same honor from him before, I could
only repeat the same acknowledgments. I would add only
one remark: that gratitude was a sentiment addicted to repetition, as had been most strikingly illustrated by nis fellow-
citizens of London in the repetition of his name at the late
election. In return for the honor of his toast I begged leave
to propose that of " Prosperity to the City of London," which
was drunk with three times three. The company was, however,
so large, and the noise in the hall so great, that very few could
hear a word of what was said. The Attorney-General, Sir
William Scott, the Judges, Lord Erskine, the City members
of Parliament (for whom Alderman Atkins answered), the
Sheriffs, and the Board of Aldermen were toasted. Lord
Erskine answered, but, though near him, I could hear nothing
that he said.

About nine o'clock the Lady Mayoress, and the other ladies,
retired into the Court of King's Bench, and half an hour afterwards the Lord Mayor and his party followed them. There
had been for upwards of an hour an unceasing stream of ladies
and gentlemen passing round the tables and looking at the
company. The hall was lighted with gas. Its principal orna-
ments are monuments to the Earl of Chatham, to his son,
William Pitt, opposite to each other, and one to Lord Nelson,
at the bottom of the hall. Bennett told me that they came
very near throwing down the monument of Pitt a few days
ago, and he should not be at all surprised if within a year from
this time it should be removed. He said he heartily wished
it was thrown down. He also told me that the inscription
upon the monument to Chatham was written by Burke, and
was admirable. That of Pitt was by Canning, in very bad

taste, and that of Nelson by Sheridan, and the worst of all. I followed the Lord Mayor into the Court of King's Bench, where there was a very large collection of ladies. The ball was opened by a minuet, danced by Colonel Camac and Miss Wood, immediately after which I came away. Sir Robert Wilson passed by as I was standing there (in the hall), and was greeted by a universal shout of applause.

23d. Dined with Mr. William Frend. The company consisted of Mr. Maseres, Cursitor Baron of the Exchequer, an old gentleman in his eighty-fifth year, Mr. Jonas Burdett, a brother of Sir Francis, Mr. Frend's brother, Dr. Cook, the Chaplain in the United States Navy, Mr. Aspland, the Unitarian Minister of Hackney, and Dr. Cook, with whom I was first acquainted at Leyden in the year 1781, and whom I have since seen once or twice, in the spring of the year 1796. He remembered me from Leyden, but did not appear to recollect our having met at the latter period. This company was remarkable as composed of learned men, but dissenters both in religion and politics from the Establishments of the country. Their conversation was freer than any that I have heard since I have been in England. While we were at dinner there came in a Mr. Solomon Bennett, a Jew, and a native of Poland—an engraver and a literary man—author of a pamphlet entitled " The Constancy of Israel," of which he gave me a copy. Baron Maseres, Mr. Frend, and Mr. Aspland are likewise all authors as well as reformers. Frend was a Fellow of a College, and a Tutor at Cambridge University, and expelled in 1793 for publishing an heretical pamphlet. He is now Actuary to the Rock Life Insurance Company, and publishes books upon Mathematics and Astronomy. Dr. Cook, the navy Chaplain, belonged also to Cambridge University, and left it on the same account of heretical infection.

December 23d. By the second post, after twelve at noon, I received a note from Lord Castlereagh, dated on Saturday, and requesting me to call on him at eleven o'clock this morning. I immediately went into London, and at three o'clock, when I reached his house, found him still at home. He told me that, as he was going out of town for two or three days, he had sent for me to tell me that he had not forgotten the promise that he had made me before he went to Ireland; that the subject of my note of 27th September, proposing the negotiation of a commercial treaty, should be taken up by this Government immediately after his return; that it had been taken up—two Cabinet Councils had already been held upon it; and as it embraced a variety of important objects, as soon as they could be sufficiently matured for instructions to be given him under which he could discuss them with me, I should hear from him again.   I said if the general determination had been taken to enter upon the negotiation, there could be no objection to taking time for arranging particulars.   He replied that his present purpose was merely to assure me that he was mindful of his promise, and that the Government were earnestly engaged in the consideration of the proposal.   He then enquired if I had any late accounts from the other side of the water, and what had been the state of our harvest.   I told him I was informed that the Indian corn had almost universally failed, and in a very great degree.   The other grains had suffered little; but, as in all the Eastern and even in some of the Southern States that article formed the principal ingredient in the bread of the most numerous class of our population, a scanty harvest of it would necessarily affect the consumption, and the price of the other materials for bread. He said their harvest here had been partially bad; there would turn out to be enough for the consumption of the people; but he was very much afraid that would not be the case in the interior of Germany, where he heard the distress was very great.   I said I heard the harvest in France was also very bad.

He said it was so in some parts of France, and good in others, but the vines had universally and entirely failed.   In Ireland the harvest was worse than here, and at one moment they had been much alarmed for the crop of potatoes, the article which formed the whole subsistence of the great majority of their population.   There had been a severe frost, which it had been apprehended had cut them off to an alarming degree; but fortunately the frost had been preceded by a deep fall of snow, which had prevented it from penetrating deep into the ground, and had saved the potatoes.

From this topic he passed immediately to that of the slave-trade, which he said was now carrying on to a very great extent, and in a shocking manner; that a great number of vessels for it had been fitted out in our Southern States, and that the barbarities of the trade were even more atrocious than they had been before the abolition of it had been attempted. The vessels sailed under the flags of the nations which still allowed the trade, Spain and Portugal; they were very small, and sailed like lightning. One vessel of one hundred and twenty tons, taken by Sir James Yeo, had six hundred slaves on board. She had been out three days, and there were thirty of them already dead. These vessels escape capture by the rapidity of their operations. They have agents on the slave coast, who purchase and collect the slaves together on the shore. The vessels occasionally approach until they see on the shore the flag flying, which is the signal that the agents are ready with the slaves. Then they go and take them on board, and disappear again in the course of a very few hours. If on approaching the land they do not see the flag, they immediately go off again, and remain some time out of sight of land. The slaves, when taken, are carried to Brazil, the coast of South America, and the Havannah. Neither Spain nor Portugal, even if they favored the total abolition of the traffic, has a force adequate to the suppression of it as thus practised. For the extent of a thousand miles on the coast of Africa, Portugal has not more than two armed vessels, and for another thousand miles on the coast of South America, perhaps two more. It is impossible they should be adequate to put down a traffic thus carried on. What he (Lord Castlereagh) had thought of, and believed would be ultimately necessary, was, that the nations which were agreed upon the abolition should authorize the capture of the slave-trading vessels by the armed force of other nations, but that the trial should be by Commissioners not exclusively of the capturing nation; that each of the powers, for instance, should appoint one "Commissaire Juge," and that whenever a capture was made it should be tried by

the Commissary Judge of the capturing nation, and the one of
the nation under whose flag the slave-trading vessel should be
taken, and, if they could not agree, then to call in the Commissaire Juge of a third and indifferent party to decide. This
had been the course adopted with regard to the claims of the
subjects of the several powers upon France under the Treaties
of Paris. There was a French Commissaire Juge, one of the
claimant's nation, and if they could not agree, the Commissaire Juge of a third party was added to come to the decision.
It was found that the business was thus done without difficulty
or inconvenience.

Lord Castlereagh did not say it was his intention to propose
that the United States should take part in this system and have
their Commissaire Juge among the rest; so that I heard all
his observations on the subject without thinking it necessary
to make any reply. What led to his speaking about the slave-
trade was my congratulating him on the result of Lord Exmouth's expedition against Algiers. I said that the United
States had still an arrangement to make of their relations with
Algiers; that Mr. Shaler and Commodore Chauncey were the
Commissioners appointed for the purpose, and that I had been
informed by the Secretary of State that their instructions
authorized them, in the renewal of the treaty, to consent to a
modification of the articles which had been objected to by this
country, so that they should not be taken as applicable, contrary
to the engagements of previous treaties between Great Britain
and Algiers. I had been highly gratified that the success of
Lord Exmouth's attack had been such as I had anticipated; and,
as the system of Barbary warfare appeared to be now broken
down, I hoped it would never again be suffered to revive.

He said that the success had been equal to their most sanguine expectations; that when Lord Exmouth was first sent
there, measures of hostility had not been authorized, owing to
the considerations which he had mentioned to me at the time.
Afterwards, when they had ceased to operate, the expedition
had been undertaken, with a full knowledge of its difficulties
and hazards. Lord Exmouth himself had been asked whether
it could be attempted with a prospect of success, and had

answered that it might be done. He had told them how it
could be done, and precisely as he had effected it—by running
his ship close in to the shore, directly opposite to the battery,
and see which would hold out the longest, the stone or the wood.
It had happily proved a successful experiment, and it might be
hoped would lead to the breaking up of Christian slavery in
Africa.   He wished there were a prospect equally fair of breaking up the African slave-trade; and then he proceeded to the
remarks just noted.

I asked him if he had any late dispatches from Mr. Bagot.
He said, to some time in October, when he was about returning
to Washington. There had been some discussion between him
and Mr. Monroe about the fisheries, but nothing definitively
adjusted.

I observed to him that there were several objects relating to
individual interests upon which I had representations to make
to him, and should shortly address him in writing.   In one of
them the United States themselves had an interest.   I spoke
of a number of Custom House revenue bonds, executed by
citizens of the United States, which had been taken by the
British at Moose Island in July, 1814.   These bonds had been
carried to Halifax, and not only condemned as prize, but some
or all of them had been put in suit.   One of the obligors had
been arrested and held to bail before the Judge of the Admiralty
Court at Halifax, who had pronounced a decree against him.
There was an appeal in his behalf now pending in the High
Court of Appeals here.   The other obligors being in the United
States, the process of the Admiralty Court at Halifax could
not reach them; but, living on the borders of the British province, if their affairs occasionally called them there, they could
not step over the boundary so long as this sentence should be
hanging over them.   The United States had proceeded and
recovered the moneys due upon these bonds from the obligors.
I understood it was the opinion of the most respectable lawyers
here that the sentence of the Admiralty Court at Halifax could
not be supported, and it was desirable, if possible, to have the
case taken out and settled without waiting for a formal decision
of the High Court of Appeals.   Another case was that of the

William and Mary, a vessel taken at Cadiz, within the Spanish jurisdiction, and condemned by the Vice-Admiralty Court at Gibraltar; it was also pending in the High Court of Appeals. The Spanish Ambassador had already presented to him (Lord Castlereagh) two notes, claiming the restitution of this property on the ground of the jurisdiction. There was no doubt that the claim of Spanish jurisdiction was valid; the evidence in support of it was clear and complete, and the persons interested in the property wished the case to be taken out of Court and settled. A third case was that of a vessel called The Hope, fitted out at New York and dispatched on a voyage of discovery in the year 1812, just before the commencement of the late war. She had a special passport from the Government of the United States, and particular letters of recommendation from the foreign Ministers then residing in the United States, among which was one from Mr. Foster, the British Minister. She was taken by boats from a British armed vessel in the harbor of Buenos Ayres, within neutral jurisdiction. In this case, however, the Spanish Ambassador declined interfering in behalf of the jurisdiction, on the ground that Buenos Ayres was then in a state of revolt against the authority of Spain, and that by the laws of Spain neither the capturing nor the captured vessel had any right or business to be there.

Lord Castlereagh said that if all the British ships that had been there were to be made answerable for it, Spain would have work enough upon her hands. I replied that this was the reason alleged by the Spanish Ambassador for refusing to interpose on account of the jurisdiction, but the capture had certainly been made within the neutral boundary, and the voyage was one of that description which, by the usages of civilized nations, is allowed to be unmolested in time of war. The parties interested in this vessel were also desirous that the case should be taken out of the Admiralty Court and settled ministerially.

"We are very much in the habit," said Lord Castlereagh, " of referring such cases to the King's Advocate for a report; and if you will write a line to me about them, I will see that they shall be attended to."

Hereupon I took my leave.

24th. In September, 1815, I received a letter from H. G. Spofford, of the State of New York, dated 8th August, 1815, in which he says he had been the preceding winter at Washington, where the President had told him they were intending to re- serve for me the best office in the gift of the administration, as long as possible without injury to the public service. As this referred to a period previous to my appointment for the mission to England, I did not understand what was meant by it, but supposed it was an intention contingent upon my return home immediately after the Peace of Ghent. After this, the first intimation that I had on this subject was from G. Boyd, who, when last here, told me there was a talk about the offices at Washington—that the place of Secretary of State would be offered to me by Mr. Monroe. The next was from Mr. John Winthrop, on the 5th of this month. Since then it has been announced in all the newspapers, as extracted from American newspapers, that it is settled I am to be recalled and to be Secretary of State. Lastly, my mother, in her letter of 26th November last, mentions a message from the President, by the Secretary of the Navy, that if Mr. A. returned, that office would be offered to him. Spofford's letter had entirely escaped my recollection until within these few days. I had no expectation, or belief, that the office would be offered to me, until the receipt of my mother's letter, and now I consider it still a matter of great uncertainty. The question whether I ought to accept the place, if it should be offered, is not with- out difficulties in my mind. A doubt of my competency for it is very sincerely entertained, and ought perhaps to be de- cisive. At all events, if I could be rationally justified in accepting it, if offered, I perceive no propriety in taking any step whatever to seek it. The person who is to nominate for the office will be Mr. Monroe, and from him I have received no such intimation; nor any from the present President, with an express authority to ask me for an answer. If Mr. Monroe's real intention be to propose to me the acceptance of the office, I think it but consistent with what is due to my own char- acter, as well as conformable to my own doubts whether I am fitted to discharge the heavy and laborious duties of the office, to wait for a direct communication from him, signifying his intention, before I take any step on the presumption that it will be carried into effect.

31st. Mr. Walker, of the house of Grey, Lindsay & Co., came to speak of the case of the Nanina, and brought a letter from James B. Murray, of New York, to J. A. Smith concerning it. The Nanina was taken during the late war by a British armed vessel, while her captain and crew were in the act of saving the people of a British vessel shipwrecked on a desert island upon the eastern coast of South America. The captain and people of the Nanina, in return for their humanity and kindness to British subjects, endured much harsh treatment and ill usage after their capture. The vessel was carried to Rio Janeiro, where, after a long detention, the British Admiral commanding there offered to deliver her up to the captain, which offer was accepted. But the Admiral afterwards annexed a condition that the captain should give a written renunciation of all further claim upon the captors. This he declined; in consequence of which the Nanina was condemned as prize of war by a Vice-Admiralty Court, and sold for a song. An appeal from the sentence of condemnation was prosecuted, and is now pending before the High Court of Appeals. Having been instructed by the Secretary of State to support the claims of the proprietors of the Nanina ministerially, I addressed, on the 10th of June last, a note to Lord Castlereagh in their behalf, which he answered on the 27th of that month, by a refusal to interfere in the case, referring to the rigorous right of war, and to the refusal of the captain to take back his vessel without reserving a further claim for costs and damage.

A copy of my note, and of Lord Castlereagh's answer, were sent last summer to Mr. Murray, but, from his letter to Smith, it is very doubtful whether he has received it, for he still urges most earnestly that I should apply to the British Government, and supposes it impossible that they should shut their eyes to the justice of his claim. Mr. Walker now comes to ask my advice upon a proposal made by the captors, to relinquish to the owners of the Nanina the net proceeds of the sale, and have the cause dismissed from the Court. He said if it was pushed on to trial the condemnation must be confirmed. He supposed the proposal made by the captors was to save themselves the expenses of the appeal, which would absorb all the proceeds, or leave a mere trifle not worth being distributed among them. Mr. Walker and his house thought nothing better for the owners could be done than to accept the proposal; but the amount of the proceeds will not exceed four hundred pounds sterling, and, Mr. Murray's claim being upwards of six thousand pounds, they had thought it necessary to ask my advice before they concluded what to do. I told him I thought it best to save from the wreck what they could; that by the positive refusal of this Government to interfere for the owners they were left at the mercy of the captors, and I believed nothing better could be done or expected than to accept their proposal. He said the house thought so too, and Colonel Palmer, a member of Parliament, had offered to present the case to the attention of the House of Commons, which might still be done, though he did not expect to any good purpose.

General Boyd with Mr. Storer, and Mr. Rotch with Mr. Maurice Birkbeck, successively followed. Mr. Birkbeck is a very intelligent English farmer, and has published a "Tour in France," which he made in the summer of 1814. But he has the project of removing with his family to settle in the United States. The account that he gives of the state of the country is as dark and gloomy as those which come in all other directions. He says that notwithstanding the great increase in the price of grain and flour since last winter, the agricultural state of the kingdom is worse than it was then. But he admits that the appreciation of bank-notes, to be of equal value with gold and silver, is unaccountable to him, and contrary to all his prognostications. And his explanations how, in the midst of all the cries of distress, the revenue continues to be nearly as productive as ever, are not quite satisfactory.

January 4th, 1817. I called upon General von Neuffer, the Würtemberg Minister, with three notes which I have received from him, containing enquiries concerning Würtembergers deceased at New York and Philadelphia. The first was of 16th July last, concerning Anton Henry Bach, who died at

New York in 1798.   I had requested J. A. Smith to write to
some friend at New York to make the enquiries. He wrote to
James Smith, and a few days since received his answer, which
I took with me to General Neuffer.   He desired me to leave
it with him, as he was desirous of sending it to his Government,
and said he would retain a copy of it here.   The second was
of 4th December, a certificate of the Minister of the German
Lutheran Church at Philadelphia, authenticated by the Mayor
of Philadelphia, but of which further authentication was requested.   I asked the General if mine would answer.   I knew
that R. Wharton was Mayor of Philadelphia, and had no doubt
it was his signature, and the seal of the city, that were upon
the paper. He said my certificate to that effect, to which he
would then add his own, would suffice.   I retained the paper,
to make out my certificate upon it.   The third was of the 23d
December, asking me to obtain a certificate of the decease of
a man named Schwarz, at New York, and information concerning the estate left by him.   I observed that this could be
obtained only in the same manner as I had got that relative to
Bach, and enquired whether that would be satisfactory.

He said it would, and that he would pay every expense that
might be occasioned by it.   He apologized to me for giving me
so much trouble about these concerns of individuals.   He said
that the Governments in Germany were so organized that all
such business was transacted through the medium of ministerial
departments.   A note to the Minister of Foreign Affairs produced a reference to the Minister of the Interior, and there all
information upon such subjects was to be obtained.   But it
was not so in this country, nor, he supposed, in America, and
here, when he had enquiries of this kind to make, he was
obliged to make them not in his official character, but in his
private capacity. He had written so to his Government, but
they continued to send him instructions of that sort, and he
was obliged to execute them.   He thanked me for the attention
I had paid to the cases concerning which he had written to me,
and offered any services that might be in his power in return.

I asked him if there was any agent or Minister of the Grand
Duke of Baden anywhere. He said, none.   I said I had a

letter from the President of the United States to the Grand
Duke, which had been sent to me on the supposition that he
had a Minister here, and with instructions to deliver it to him.
I asked him if he could put me in the way of having it transmitted. He said Baden was their next-door neighbor, not
fifteen miles German from Stuttgard: if I would send him the
letter he would forward it to his Government, and thence it
would be safely transmitted to the Grand Duke. The General
then, after noticing the newspaper paragraphs about my being
recalled, launched out into general politics, and said he thought
the Government here were very much embarrassed, and that
they would have a stormy session of Parliament. I was not of
that opinion. Warm debates there probably will be, but a
heavy majority of Parliament are pledged body and soul to the
Ministers upon every object they may choose to carry, and all
Parliament are so pledged upon every public subject now at
issue that it is not at all from Parliament that the Ministers
have any serious difficulty to expect.

He then spoke of Spain, and said he strongly suspected
Cevallos would be taken again by the King, for the seventh
time, to be his Prime Minister; that he personally knew Pizarro,
who, upon this last dismission of Cevallos, had taken his place.
He was certainly a man of talents, but a very violent man. As
to the Spanish affairs in South America, he could make nothing
of them; but he believed Spain would never recover her
authority over the Colonies. As for us in Germany, said he,
"je crois que nous nous tirerons d'affaire." On the 16th of
this month we shall have in Würtemberg a new Constitution,
"et une très-belle Constitution," proclaimed, and when we have
once begun, Baden must follow the example. Bavaria perhaps
will be reluctant, but must at last "prendre son parti," and
that will give an irresistible impulse to the South of Germany,
and when that is accomplished the North of Germany cannot
linger long to come into the change.

So, according to the General, everything is to be done by the
example of Würtemberg. I observed that there seemed to be
much difficulty to the introduction of a Constitution in Prussia.
He said there was, but Prussia would get along. The great

misfortune was that the Emperor of Austria, who was one of the best and worthiest and most honorable men in the world, could not, however, endure to hear the very word—Constitution—mentioned. He had a horror even of the word. I said I supposed that was the result of the French Revolution, and, besides that, no absolute Prince, such as all the sovereigns of Germany were, could be expected to relish a word the only meaning of which must operate as a limitation of their own authority.

He said that his country (Würtemberg) was an exception to my remark; that all the German Governments were absolute (I had myself excepted the imperial free cities), but Würtemberg had had a Constitution, under which the people had lived free and contented, more than two centuries.

I spoke of the contests which I had heard mentioned as prevailing between the late King and the States, both at the beginning and the close of his reign. He said he might now say it without hesitation, and it was too notorious to be denied, that the late King was a violent despot; but that he had never been able to overcome the resistance of the States until he made his league with Napoleon, who said to him in no other than these words, "chassez ces bougres"—and who supported him in it.

But I observed that in the last days of the late King, and even since the accession of his son, I had heard the States were insisting on the ancient Constitution of the country. It was impossible, he said, that that should be allowed. The great point for which they contended was not only that all public moneys should be levied by them, which was perfectly proper, but that they should also have the management of its expenditure by a secret committee of their own, which was incompatible with any rational theory, and had been found excessively pernicious by experience. I asked him if there had not been some controversy on the part of certain mediatized Princes. He said, Yes; they would be very glad to resume the exercise of their sovereign authorities, but it was obviously impossible to indulge them in that humor. I asked him if he thought the new Constitution would give general satisfaction. He had no doubt it would, and the States would have the power of levying all imposts and taxes, and all the accounts of the expenditures of public moneys would be laid before them.

28th. Mr. Chester's note informed me that the Prince Regent would open the session of Parliament at two o'clock, and there was a notice from the Lord Chamberlain's office that the Queen's birthday drawing-room, which had been fixed for the 6th of February, was postponed to the 20th. I ordered the carriage at half-past one. Mr. Boyle called, and Mr. A. H. Everett, who had been promised admission for himself and Mrs. Everett by an order from Sir Benjamin Bloomfield, but was disappointed. It was about twenty minutes before two when the carriage came. Mr. Smith and myself were dressed to be present at the ceremony. Mrs. Adams and John went with us to stay in the carriage and see the show. But the crowd of people and of carriages was so excessive, and the passage was so much obstructed, that the clock at the Horse Guards, as we passed it, was within three minutes of two, and it was near half an hour later before we reached the door of the Parliament House. The Prince had nearly finished his speech, and the doors of the House of Lords were closed, so that it was impossible to obtain admission. My error had been in not ordering my carriage at one, instead of half-past one. We turned round, and moved slowly up Parliament Street, till the Prince passed by us on his return. As we turned round, we saw Viscount Hampden in his robes as a Peer, in his carriage next behind ours, and in like manner belated. The Prince passed us within ten minutes after we returned. A mixture of low but very audible hissing, of faint groaning, and still fainter attempts to raise a shout among the populace, contrasted with the heavy magnificence of the gilded but tasteless and clumsy State coach, the gorgeous splendor of the golden harness, and the sky-blue silk ribbons with which the eight cream-colored royal horses were bedizened. The populace manifested no symptoms of riot, but a troop of horsemen preceded the carriage with drawn swords, pressing back the crowd, preventing their approach to the carriage, and urged by a leader constantly repeating in a tone of extreme earnestness, " Keep them back! keep them back!" There were among the crowd great numbers of very wretched and ill-looking persons. They talked with more or less freedom. We heard one man say, "He is gone into a strong hysteric." Another said, "Throw mud at him." He has been so long accustomed to this sort of treatment from the populace, that he may perhaps have grown callous to it; but I did not envy him his feelings.

29th. The humors of the populace yesterday were, it seems, not confined to the hissing, groaning, mocking, and evil speaking which we heard. The Prince Regent's carriage entered St. James's Park at the Horse Guards. He returned to St. James's Palace, and on his way thither, after passing by Carlton House, the window at the left side was broken by bullets shot from an air-gun, or stones thrown by the rabble. The Duke of Montrose, Master of the Horse, and Lord James Murray, a Lord of the Bedchamber, were in the carriage with the Prince. Lord James Murray was examined before both Houses of Parliament, and declared that he had not the least doubt that the first fractures were made by two bullets shot from above—it might be from a tree—but no report was heard, no bullets found in the carriage, and the opposite window, though up, was not broken, and immediately after, a large stone was thrown, which shattered the glass to pieces. The two Houses voted a dutiful address to the Prince, expressing their horror at this outrage, and requesting him to take measures to discover the perpetrator. The debate in the House of Commons upon the address, in answer to the speech, was interrupted by this episode, and adjourned to this day. We came through St. James's Park on our return home last evening about five. The crowd was then entirely dispersed.

February 3d. I took with me (to London) the dispatches to be forwarded to-morrow, and a letter to the Proctors, Cresswell and Addams, with their bills, which I send back to them, to have regularly taxed. I had written to them last Saturday morning that I thought this would be necessary, and Mr. Addams called that day at the office, and spoke with me about it. He was somewhat reluctant at suffering the bills to go through this scrutiny, and said he was very sure the taxer of the bills, who must of course be the Register of the Court, would reduce none of the charges, unless here and there one, where thirteen shillings and fourpence was charged, and where he might think the charge should have been six shillings and eightpence, and the whole reduction would not exceed, and perhaps not equal, the addition for the taxing fees. He also said it was not usual for bills like these, of the Proctors with their own parties, to be taxed, but only the bills of costs, which are to be paid by an adverse party; and that they had sent me the printed statements of the cases, showing that General Lyman had defended the causes in his official capacity, and that the counsel and advocates had been employed, for whose fees there were charges in the bills. I preferred having the bills taxed, and was rather confirmed in that opinion by the unwillingness which Mr. Addams manifested to go through the operation. He said, however, it should be done by one of the Deputy Registers of the Court, and suggested a wish that, in sending back the bills, I would write a note stating that it was to make merely the voucher regular. It struck Smith more than it did me that the object of asking for this note was to show it to the taxing officer, as a hint that he might relax from legal rigor in taxing the bill, as the object of it was merely to comply with a formality. I took care, in writing the letter this day, to show that it was a real and responsible taxing that I required. Addams admitted that when they had been formerly employed by S. Bayard for the United States he had always required that the bills should be taxed. But he said General Lyman did not. I left my letter and the bills with J. A. Smith, to be sent to the Proctor's to-morrow.

I found at the office in Craven Street letters from J. Maury, which I immediately answered; from Count Caraman, Secretary to the French Embassy, enclosing two letters from the Pattersons, at Paris, to be forwarded to the United States; and from James Monroe, a letter of introduction to young Astor, which he has just left at the office, but which is dated November, 1815. We went to Drury Lane, and saw "Richard the Third," with the pantomime of "Harlequin Horner," with a clown issuing from the Christmas pie. Kean performed Richard. The play is not exactly Shakspeare's. Colley

Cibber brought it out improved and amended, and John Kemble has improved upon it again. More than half the original tragedy, including many of the finest scenes, is discarded. Two or three scenes from the third part of Henry the Sixth are transferred to this play. There are modern additions, not well adapted to Shakspeare's style, and his language itself is often altered, and seldom for the better. As it is, however, it has constantly been from Cibber's time one of the standing favorites of the public on the English stage, and the character of Richard is one of the trying tests of their greatest tragic actors. I never saw it performed but once before, and that was at Boston in 1794. It is by many of Kean's admirers considered as his greatest part; but his performance this night in some degree disappointed me. There is too much of rant in his violence, and not smoothness enough in his hypocrisy. He has a uniform fashion of traversing the stage from one side to the other when he has said a good thing, and then looks as if he was walking for a wager. At other times, he runs off from the stage with the gait of a running footman. In the passages of high passion he loses all distinct articulation and it is impossible to understand what he says. But he has much very good subsidiary pantomime, which is perhaps the first talent of a first-rate actor. He has a most keen and piercing eye, a great command and expression of countenance, and some transitions of voice of very striking effect. All the other male performers were indifferent, and the women below mediocrity. The two children (girls) were very good. The house was crowded, and the applause of Kean incessant during the tragedy. The fight between Richard and Richmond was skilful and vigorous. Kean always contrives to make a claptrap of his dying scenes. The clapping at his death continued five minutes long. The Duke and Duchess and Princess Sophia of Gloucester were present, and received with great applause. At their entrance, "God save the King" was performed by the orchestra, and sung by part of the players, the audience all standing.

6th. Precisely at two o'clock I went with Smith and attended the Prince Regent's levee. We were not out of time, but quite late enough. The levee was well attended, but not crowded like the first levee last year. The Prince Regent came in before half-past two, and was dressed in a blue Prussian General's uniform. The special levee was over in less than ten minutes; the Prince spoke to very few persons, and a very few words to each. He passed on immediately, and took his stand at the door, for the general levee, which was also over in the course of an hour. The foreign Ambassadors and Ministers were all there, as was the Russian Grand Duke Nicholas. I mentioned to Count Lieven that I had not been presented to the Grand Duke since his arrival in this country. The Count said the notification of his arrival had not been sent to me, owing to my residence in the country, but that if I would give him notice at any time, a day or two beforehand, he was very sure the Grand Duke would readily receive me. I asked the Bavarian Minister, Pfeffel, whether notice had been sent to the other Ministers of the Grand Duke's arrival and of the time when he would see them, or whether they had sent to ask to be presented to him. He said they had been notified. I do not feel myself, therefore, under any obligation to ask to be presented to him, and shall not put myself, or him, to inconvenience about it. General Koutousoff, the sometime Police Master of St. Petersburg, and Baron Nicolai are in attendance upon the Grand Duke, and were present.

The Spanish Ambassador, Fernan Nuñez, asked me if I had received the card of invitation to his ball. I had, and told him we purposed attending it. The Dutch Ambassador, Fagel, said if I did not return this evening to the country he should invite me to an evening party at his house. He gives a dinner to the Prince Regent and the Grand Duke Nicholas, and the evening party afterwards. I asked the Portuguese Ambassador, Count Palmella, if the late newspaper reports, that the King of Portugal intended to return next summer to Lisbon, were true. He said he believed there was no foundation for them whatever; that the King was to be crowned next April in Brazil; that the Austrian Duchess Leopoldine was going there, and that it would not even be prudent for the King to return to Europe while the Spanish provinces all around him were in a

state of revolt against Spain.   The Count spoke to me in very
respectful terms of Mr. Correa de Serra, now the Portuguese
Minister in the United States.   Jouffroy, the Prussian Chargé
d'Affaires, told me that he had lately heard from St. Petersburg
that Clementina Bode was married to young Livio.   Jouffroy
has been in ill health, and has much fallen away since I left
him in Russia.   Count Caraman thanked me for the note which
I had sent him this morning, and which he had received.

The Duke of Gloucester asked me if I had heard from the
Pattersons at Paris.   The Earl of Westmorland enquired also
about them, and told me they had spent considerable time with
him at Althorp, his country-seat; that they had made themselves universally beloved by every one who had become
acquainted with them; that, while they were with him, Mr.
Patterson had gone for a few days into Leicestershire, to a fox-
hunting party, which was quite a new and extraordinary scene
to Patterson, and he gave me a ludicrous account of his having
supplied Patterson an old broken-down hunter to mount, and
of Patterson's inability to manage him.   He asked whether
they intended to return soon from Paris, and how they were
pleased there.   I told him I heard they were to return very
soon, but they were very well pleased with Paris, as the Duke
of Wellington, who was king of kings there, had taken much
notice of them, and thus introduced them to all the good
company.

The Earl then commenced upon politics, and asked me about
the harvest in America.   I told him that it had been indifferent,
and that my letters complained that the great exportations of
flour from the United States to this country were increasing the
prices there to an alarming degree.   He said it was so much
the better for America; that the first and greatest policy for a
country should be to encourage the cultivation of grain, so as
to raise a sufficiency for their own consumption; that he was
thoroughly convinced almost the whole distress of which the
people in this country were complaining had arisen from the
importation of corn.

As I expressed some little surprise at this opinion, he repeated it, adding that he did not mean to deny that there were

other causes contributing to the effect, particularly the sudden transition from war to peace, and the great numbers of people thereby thrown out of employment (not a word about the debt and taxes); but the great and effectual cause was the importation of foreign corn, which, by reducing the price below what the farmer could afford to sell for, disabled him from employing workmen, and from applying his capital to the improvement of cultivation. I observed to him that the price of corn had now risen again, sufficiently to encourage cultivation and the employment of workmen. He replied that it was too late; the mischief was done. The farmer had lost his capital, which had been wholly sunk. He possessed no longer the means of paying laborers. The rise in the prices, therefore, had increased instead of diminishing the evil. The prices now were too high, and the poor were suffering in both ways; on one side by the want of employment, and on the other by the dearness of the necessaries of life. The commerce of the country had suffered, comparatively speaking, nothing. Their commerce of exportation had actually suffered very little. Just as he was upon these remarks, some person came and called him away. I soon after left the levee-room and retired. Sir Robert Liston was waiting to receive, immediately after the levee, the investiture of Grand Cross of the Order of the Bath, together with Sir Gordon Drummond. As I passed through the first anteroom, I spoke to the Lord Mayor, who had presented an address from the Common Council of London to the Prince Regent, on his providential escape from the bullets, stones, and potatoes discharged by the mob at the state carriage on his return from the House of Lords after opening the session of Parliament.

17th. I left home at nine o'clock this evening, and went to Count Fernan Nuñez, Duke of Mortellano, the Spanish Ambassador's ball. I made up a packet of newspapers for the Secretary of State, and a packet to my father. I took them with me in the carriage, and, on alighting at the Ambassador's, told my footman, William Hegg, to carry them to Mr. Smith, at Craven Street. I also left in the carriage my round hat and my surtout. When I came out to return home, on entering the carriage and driving off, my hat was missing. On enquiring for it, William told me that it had been stolen from the carriage, together with the packet of papers, while he was riding with the coachman on the box from the Ambassador's house to Cavendish Square. The surtout luckily escaped.

At the ball there were between three and four hundred persons, among whom were the Dukes of York and Gloucester, the Grand Duke Nicholas, several of the Cabinet Ministers, all the foreign Ambassadors and Ministers, Earl Grey, Lords Erskine and Holland, Sir Robert Liston, Sir Gore Ouseley, &c.— more gentlemen than ladies. The Prince Regent was to have been there, but sent an excuse this morning. It was said he had the gout. I had scraps of conversation with most of the foreign Ambassadors and Ministers, and particularly with Mr. Poletica, who is now a counsellor of the Russian Embassy here. He told me he did not think Mr. Daschkoff had been recalled from the United States, though he supposed he ultimately would be. I spoke also to Lords Westmorland, Grey, Erskine, and Holland, to Lady Castlereagh, and Mr. Planta, and to Mr. Chester. The only dancing was of quadrilles. I came away at half-past twelve, and got home a quarter after two. It seems that the glass windows were stolen from several carriages. There was a crowd of people before the house, and no strange servants admitted into it.

18th. Two or three hours were absorbed in reading the debates of last evening in the House of Commons—discussions about Brougham's declarations heretofore in favor of annual Parliaments and universal suffrage, and about Croker, the Secretary of the Admiralty, obtaining a war salary during the time of Lord Exmouth's last expedition against Algiers. Both these gentlemen are distinguished personages on the political theatre at this time. They were both vigorously attacked last night upon points affecting their personal reputation, and both made most lame and impotent defences. Croker is one of the scavengers of the Ministry, a Quarterly Reviewer, a Courier scribbler, and, above all, an inveterate and rancorous enemy to America. He is Secretary to the Admiralty, and obtained from the Lords an increase of his salary for a whole quarter, on the pretext of the two days of Algerine war. Lord Milton's motion in the House of Commons last night was for a vote of censure upon the Lords of the Admiralty for having allowed this increase. The motion was lost by one hundred and sixty-nine to one hundred and fourteen votes; which is considered as a very small ministerial majority, and a very large minority. Lord Grey, Lord Holland, and Planta all spoke to me of it last night. Grey considered it as a proof of the weakness of the Ministry. Planta said it was a very large minority, and that there ought never to have been any occasion for the motion. Holland said that it was a bad minority, and a worse majority, because it showed there were many of the ministerial members who would not vote on this question. Brougham is a violent opposition member, who has gone out of his way this session to attack the Reformers who petition for annual Parliaments and universal suffrage. He said, last week, that they might be divided into two classes—the deceivers and the deceived. The Reformers have retorted upon him by publishing a speech made by him in 1814 at a London tavern dinner, in which he declared himself in favor of annual Parliaments and representation co-extensive with taxation. Lord Cochrane read last night, in the House of Commons, an extract from this speech. Brougham's only defence was, that he had meant *direct* taxation. The whole opposition in Parliament are running themselves down to nothing in the popular opinion.

20th. Three dispatches from W. Shaler, Consul-General at Algiers, and from Commodore Isaac Chauncey, were brought in, which I was obliged to leave then unread to be in seasonable time for the Queen's drawing-room. We were there at half-past one, and among the first. Before the drawing-room Count Lieven presented me to the Grand Duke Nicholas, who recognized me as an "ancienne connoissance," and said that when he had known me at St. Petersburg he little expected to have met me here. He said he was very shortly going away, and was highly gratified with his tour in England, where he had been treated with the kindest possible attentions.

The drawing-room commenced precisely at two o'clock, and continued until half-past four. It was far less numerously attended than either of those of the last year. The dresses of the ladies were principally of British manufacture, heavy and inelegant. The Prince Regent, the Dukes of York, Sussex, and Gloucester, and Prince Leopold were present; the Princesses Augusta, Elizabeth, Duchess of Gloucester, Sophia of Gloucester, and Charlotte of Wales. She has grown very thin since her marriage, and had the appearance of being out of health and out of humor. The Duke of Sussex appeared in a magnificently gold-embroidered Court dress, and in stockings with gold clocks. The Marquis d'Osmond, French Ambassador, told him, as if intending to pay him a compliment, that that was the fashion at least a century ago. The Duke said that when he assumed the gala Court dress, which he hated, he was, however, determined to have it complete; his dress was made here, and was a proof that good embroidery could be worked in this country. The officers of the household appeared in new Court uniforms of splendid embroidery, said to be from designs of the Prince Regent himself. The principal conversation at the drawing-room was about these dresses. The Duke of Sussex told me that he had of late been very busy, and that these were busy times. Lord and Lady Castlereagh were not there, being in deep mourning for the death of her mother. After the drawing-room had closed, we were nearly an hour waiting for the carriage to drive up to the door.

25th. Received a note and a letter from Mrs. Agnes Porter, enclosing for my perusal a letter from Sir Robert Liston to Joseph Ewart, who was Mrs. Porter's brother. It is dated Turin, 26th October, 1782. Ewart was then at Berlin, private secretary, as appears from the letter, to Sir John Stepney, then British Minister at the Court of Prussia. He had written to Liston, who was Secretary to the British Legation at Turin, for advice and instructions for his conduct, Liston having been previously Secretary of Legation at Berlin, while Mr. Hugh Elliot was the Minister. The letter is full of the most excellent advice, given in an easy, familiar style, and with a sportiveness of manner to disguise the gravity of instruction, and it contains notices of many persons at the Court of Berlin whom I afterwards knew there, with observations, not unimportant to the history of the time, upon the state of the political relations between Great Britain and Prussia. He says they were upon a very bad footing, and that it was altogether the fault of the British Ministry. There are several good remarks upon the British diplomatic characters of that day, and upon the manner of doing business in the Foreign Department. The advice to Ewart is all prudential and wise, though by no means profound. It is a summary of the "art de parvenir," and appears to have been successfully practised both by the writer of the letter and by his correspondent. Ewart afterwards became Chargé d'Affaires and then Minister Plenipotentiary at Berlin, where, Mrs. Porter says, he resided twelve years. He married there a Countess Wartensleben, and has now been some years dead. Liston began life as private tutor to Mr. H. Elliot on his travels, then became his private secretary, when Elliot, barely after coming of age, was appointed British Minister at Munich, to the Elector of Bavaria. When Elliot was transferred to Berlin, Liston went with him, and soon after became his Secretary of Legation. Since then he has constantly been in the diplomatic career—was some time Minister in the United States, and is now Ambassador at Constantinople, whither, at the age of seventy-six, he is to return next May.

His letter to Ewart gave me occasion for reflection. He blames the British Ministry for the bad footing upon which they were with Prussia. It is well known that one of the causes of that misunderstanding was the outrage by which Mr. Elliot became possessed of Mr. Arthur Lee's papers. Elliot himself told me that it had not been done by his orders; that the papers were brought to him, and he read them, but had no agency in obtaining them. Richards, the Swiss, who had been a sort of appendage to the British missions at Berlin for many years, told me that Liston was the man who had contrived to get the papers, and if so, he was one great cause of the disgust that Frederic had taken against the British; all which, though not absolutely incompatible with the contents of this letter, does not exactly tally with them.

March 1st. The boys came home from school at eleven o'clock, and I took them with me to London to see the Mint. We stopped at Craven Street and took up Mr. Smith. The

Mint is upon Tower Hill. They made some difficulty at
letting us in. They said Mr. Wellesley Pole gave cards only
for Thursdays. I mentioned that Mr. Lawson had advised me
to come that day. They said Mr. Lawson had nothing to
do with it. At last, however, a man was called, and directed
to show us the works. He hurried us along through the
different apartments, without absolute incivility, and with very
little civility. There is only one steam-engine, with a thirty
horse power. We saw the various operations of rolling the
bars, of cutting, heating, weighing, washing, cleaning, and coining the blanks of half-crowns and shillings. I had twice seen
all the same works at the Mint of St. Petersburg. The workmen here were more numerous. The washing of the blanks in
vitriolic acid I had not seen in Russia. Our conductor told me
that they struck four hundred thousand pieces in a day. I
dined with Count Palmella, the Portuguese Ambassador, 74
South Audley Street. Lord Castlereagh was to have dined
there, but is confined to his house with a cold and sore throat.
The Earl of Harrowby, Lord Palmerston, and Admiral Berkeley were there; Count Lieven, and Poletica, Baron Fagel and
his brother, Baron Rehausen, Count Caraman, Mr. Planta, and
some other persons attached to the Portuguese Embassy. At
table I sat next to Lord Harrowby, and had much conversation with him, chiefly on the subject of Government—Whigs
and Tories; the rights of the people and the rights of kings.
He appeared disposed to appreciate highly the free and liberal
parts of the British Constitution, but he spoke with the contempt of derision about radical reform, annual Parliaments, and
universal suffrage; sneered at Tom Paine; spoke slightingly
of Locke, and censured the phraseology of the Act of Parliament by which James the Second was declared to have broken
the compact between the King and the people. He attempted
an argument about the duty and obligation of obedience binding upon the people. I asked him if he admitted Government
to be an affair of compact, and told him I would not ask any
other concession. He was not willing to admit it nor prepared
to deny it, and I forbore to press him. He finally said the
people had a right to be well governed, and when they were

not, it was not of much consequence what the right of Government to their obedience might be.

4th. Went to the Foreign Office in Downing Street, and enquired of Mr. Hamilton if he could inform me what was the object of a bill now pending in Parliament respecting the number of passengers in foreign vessels. He did not know. I told him there had been so many obstacles thrown in the way of American vessels about their passengers, and I had been so unsuccessful in my applications to remove them, that, seeing in the newspapers a notice of this bill, I was apprehensive it would raise new embarrassments, and wished to know its purport, and to enquire if some clause could not be introduced into it at least to facilitate the means for the American Consul to send home destitute American seamen. He sent to Mr. Robinson, to enquire what the intention of the bill now before the House of Commons was; but Robinson was gone to the House, and Hamilton promised to write me the purport of the bill. I pressed upon him the singularity of my position, receiving from the Government one day the most urgent requisitions to send home to the United States the Americans found here in distress, and the next day refusals of every accommodation to enable the American Consul to send them home.

He said the requisitions to send them away were mere circular letters sent to all the foreign Ministers in the same words, adopted no doubt from a letter from Lord Sidmouth's office, and founded altogether upon representations from the Lord Mayor. It was merely an invitation of which the foreign Ministers were not obliged to take any notice at all, or they might say, if they pleased, that their Governments would not charge themselves with providing for their countrymen who came here. I told him I had viewed the application in a very different and more serious light, and had taken every possible means of complying with the requisition. I mentioned the delays which had interposed before the Consul could obtain the permission for the last transport to be dispatched, and the restrictions which limited the number of her passengers, so that finally ten men who were sent on board and ready to go with her were turned back upon the Consul's hands; the refusal to allow the masters of American vessels to take each five or six of these destitute seamen, without reckoning five tons of the ship's burden, and abridging proportionally the number of profitable passengers they may take. I complained of the inequality which this occasioned between British and American vessels—the British not being bound to take any destitute American seamen. He said British vessels were obliged, in like manner, to take destitute British seamen in our ports. But, I observed, they were not subject to any limitation of the number of their passengers. He said our masters of vessels were required to take our seamen by our own laws, which the British Government could not control; that we were not obliged to send our seamen to America, we might send them anywhere else where we pleased; that returns had been made to Lord Bathurst's office of all the passengers that had gone from England in American vessels in the course of the last year, and the number was very small. I said that was a proof how unnecessary all these restrictions were. He thought it was a proof that the regulations could not affect any considerable American interest, and therefore there could be no cogent motive for altering the law. It is curious to observe to what shifts of argument these people resort rather than candidly to come out with their real reasons and motives.

Hamilton asked me if British seamen did not apply to be sent to the United States upon pretence of being Americans. I told him there were such cases, but the Consul always rejected them when he could ascertain the attempt at fraud; that I had suggested this difficulty in a note to Lord Castlereagh when he sent me the first requisition to send home all the destitute American seamen, and had desired that this Government should take upon itself the scrutiny and specifically point out who were the Americans; but to this proposal I had received no answer. It was evident from the tenor of Hamilton's conversation that the restrictions upon the carrying of passengers will be increased, and in no respect relaxed.

6th. Attended the Prince Regent's levee, and presented General Boyd. Mr. Storer had concluded not to be presented, and Mr. Coles not this time. The Prince spoke very graciously to General Boyd, and much to his satisfaction. The general levee was very numerously attended, and many addresses were presented, some for retrenchment and reform, and the others to congratulate the Prince upon his escape from the barbarous and traitorous bullet and potato plot and outrage. The presenters of many of the addresses of this last description were knighted.

I had short conversations with many of the persons attending the levee. The Spanish Ambassador, Fernan Nuñez, asked me if Congress had passed the bill to prohibit the sale of armed vessels by the citizens of the United States to the South American insurgents. I had not heard. He said it was of great importance that it should pass. Lord Holland told me they considered their division in the House of Lords for suspending the Habeas Corpus Act a remarkably strong one. They mustered with their proxies thirty-five votes against about one hundred and fifty-six—not one to four. Lord Erskine asked me if I had seen his late publication, a sort of political romance, entitled "Armata," in form an imitation of Gulliver's Voyage to Liliput, but in fact a review of the history of England during the last half-century. I had bespoken the book, but had not yet received it. He said he had given very freely his opinion there both of the American Revolutionary War and of the French War. He was determined that his opinion on both those subjects should go recorded to posterity. People might say it was damned nonsense, but when, by whatever course of events it happened, a man had sat upon the woolsack, his opinions would have some weight with posterity. I told him it needed not his seat upon the woolsack to give weight to his opinions. He said Sidmouth had told him he had read his "Armata," and, although there were many things in which they had differed, he admired many things in this book. It was a curious observation to me to see a man of Erskine's powers taking pride in the admiration of Lord Sidmouth. Erskine said he had given *them* a trimming for the American and French Wars. *Now*, there was not much diversity of opinion about the first, but he had not the least doubt that if this country had not gone to war with France, Louis the Sixteenth would have been at this day living and King. He said that he himself had drawn up the French judicial code. He had been five months a member of the Committee for the Administration of Justice, and had worked for them the whole time, almost night and day. He had drawn up the whole system in English, and the simple translation from his work had been adopted. I took it that he spoke of the period under what was called the Constituent Assembly.

I spoke to Lord Melville, and mentioned to him the terms of our new arrangement with Algiers, with which he expressed himself to be very well satisfied. The Earl of Harrowby, in a good-humored manner, told me that he thought our conversation at Count Palmella's the other day would make a figure in print as a political dialogue, though his part of it would show to very little advantage. I told him I was afraid if it should be printed it would be thought to have an inflammatory tendency. He said, no; and that, if due allowance was made for the situations of the respective speakers, very little difference of principle would be found between us. He then recurred to France again, and said that Monsieur Gallatin (he begged his pardon—Mr. Gallatin) had spoken to him last summer with great contempt of the French notions of liberty. I said it seemed to me that the French were unable to combine all the simple ideas that were essential to constitute the complex idea of liberty. They had, for instance, never been able to realize the principle of the Habeas Corpus Act. I considered this principle, as completely carried into effect by practice, to be the only distinguishing feature of liberty possessed by the British over the other nations of Europe, because in it was included the liberty of the press, which could not co-exist with a power of arbitrary imprisonment. He said he thought it not the *only* distinct feature of British liberty, because there was the immense, the overbearing power of public opinion, which was such that a British Government, even possessing the power of arresting individuals, must exercise it with such extreme caution and reserve that it was scarcely any power at all. I admitted the force of public opinion, but said it was not peculiar to this country. It was as great in France, and indeed all over Europe, and, indeed, on the Continent was the only control

against the abuse of power by the Governments. He said it
was true; within the last forty years public opinion had risen
up and become the queen of the world; it was the dominion
of the newspapers. He agreed with me as to the great value
of the principle of the Habeas Corpus Act; but he also believed that its efficacy and its value depended entirely upon its
being occasionally, and upon particular emergencies, suspended.
He did not know whether this would apply to America; but
here he was convinced it would, unless occasionally suspended,
operate not to the preservation but to the destruction of public
liberty. I told him I had once, as a Senator of the United
States, voted for the suspension there, in the case of Burr's
conspiracy. The Senate had unanimously passed the bill, but
it was thrown out by the House of Representatives, and we
had got along without it.

He asked me what had been the object of Burr's conspiracy.
I said it had been twofold—one a military project against
Mexico; the other, a plan to break up the union of the States,
and set up a government of his own at New Orleans, drawing
as many of the Western States into it as he could.

He enquired what had become of Burr, and whether he was
not a man of considerable talents. I said he certainly possessed
talents, and was now living in New York in obscurity.

Recurring again to France, he said he had been at Paris at
the time of the first restoration of Louis XVIII., and again
last year, in the midst of the party struggles between the ultra
Royalists and the Ministerialists; and it was strange to observe
the ultras, at the last period, contending against a mere remnant,
proposed by the Ministers, of a restrictive law which but the
year before had been enacted by the ultras themselves. The
King had granted him a private audience, and the first question
he had asked him was, whether he had read Chateaubriand's
new pamphlet. It was only two days after it had been suppressed by the King's authority. He therefore had answered
the King that he had paid too much respect to his Majesty's
laws to have read the book yet, but that he had it, and should
soon read it. The King told him that Chateaubriand might
have attacked his Ministers and their measures if he thought

proper—they were fair subjects of discussion; but when he insinuated the personal duplicity of the King himself, it was impossible for him to overlook it, or to avoid manifesting his displeasure. Lord Harrowby added, that the conduct of the ultra Royalists was indeed very extraordinary, but it was an exact counterpart of the latter portion of Sir Robert Walpole's administration in this country, when all the motions in Parliament in favor of liberty were made by the Jacobites and the Tories.

I spoke to Lord Bathurst of the state of things in South America, and of a petition presented a few days since by Mr. Sharp to the House of Commons, from an Englishman named Davison, complaining of having suffered torture by the thumb-screw under the tyranny of the Haytian black King, Henry. I said it gave a very different impression of that person's government from that which I had received from Mr. Prince Sanders.

Lord Bathurst said Davison had been to him and shown him his thumbs. They were, indeed, somewhat flattened, but did not appear to have suffered essential injury. The charge against him was that he had written politics in a professedly commercial letter; and he certainly had mentioned the failure of an expedition of Christophe's, without any comment, indeed, but in such a manner as to show that he was pleased with the failure. As to the South American affairs, he said, the wars there appeared interminable. Neither party could obtain any permanent advantage over the other. It was very clear that Morillo would not even be able to maintain his own advantages without further reinforcements.

While the Prince Regent was going round the levee-room, Lord Castlereagh came up to me and told me that he should soon wish to have some conversation with me. I said I should be at his service at any hour that he would appoint. He replied that he would give me notice, he hoped, in a few days, and that he should be authorized to discuss with me at least the commercial parts of the subjects I had proposed; but now he was incessantly harassed with business, more than at any other period of his life. As to the afternoon and evening, he had been accustomed to be then occupied; but now the mornings were also absorbed, and he could only step from one committee-room to another. I introduced General Boyd to him.

The Earl of Westmorland also spoke to me, and, as he usually does, was entering into the most prominent topics of the day, but some person came and called him away. He was making enquiries of me about our methods of conducting elections in America, and asked me if we allowed universal suffrage. I told him, not altogether. In some of the States the right of voting was confined to freeholders, but in most of them it was universal, or extended to all who paid direct taxes —which was nearly the same thing. But, even where the right of suffrage was universal, the elections were in general orderly. Riots seldom happened, and those only in the large cities, such as New York. We found nothing impracticable in universal suffrage; though I had observed it was considered here that it would be so in this country.

He said he did not know that it would be impracticable; but it would be a revolution. England would be no longer England with it; for with a House of Commons so constituted no other branch of the Government could subsist. I said I believed with him that it would be a revolution, but how far it would extend I was not intimately enough acquainted with the practical construction of the Government to foresee. He said the revolution would be total; "and as it is," said he, "it is doubtful whether we shall be able to save it. The popular power in this country has increased, and the power of the Crown has diminished, within the last forty years, enormously."

This is the ministerial doctrine of the day. I intimated a doubt of its correctness; remarked the power of the Crown over the House of Peers, three-fourths of which have been created in the present reign ; the influence of official patronage in the House of Commons, and in the army and navy.

He said the army and navy were nothing, or next to nothing, to the Crown. The patronage was that of the Ministries as they came in succession. The influence of offices in the House of Commons was much less than it had formerly been; in the

House of Lords it was scarcely anything, for the few offices held by Peers were so small, either in power or emolument, as to be no object at all of pursuit or desire to a Peer. The House of Peers had now become so numerous that they were much less under the influence of the Crown than formerly. They were created, in fact, not by the Crown, but by the Ministers, and when once created were altogether independent of the Crown, which could not take the Peerage away. I thought still there was a sense of personal obligation to the King, weighing more or less upon all the Peers created by him; but he said, No, nothing at all. I said there was at least a sense of the common interest—a conviction that the dignity of the Peerage could not exist without that of the Crown. That, he said, was something; and then I noticed the great influence of the Peers in the House of Commons.

Oh, yes; that, very fortunately, was great, and that was the only thing that could maintain the Constitution; for if once the House of Lords should take a wrong turn there would be no remedy. The partisans of revolution had changed their point of attack: formerly it was against the Crown, but now they had turned against the House of Commons; but their object remained the same.

Here, much to my regret, our conversation was interrupted. Between four and five o'clock we left the levee-room, before the general levee was over. On returning to Craven Street, I found Captain Upton, of the British Navy, who wished to have a deed proved before me of an estate in the State of New York. I appointed next Tuesday, between two and four o'clock, for that purpose. I sent several packages to Colonel Aspinwall's office, to go by the Galen, Captain Tracy, to Boston, with a note to the Consul. Returning home, a gentleman riding on horseback knocked at the glass of my carriage-door, and, on my stopping, complained that my coachman had startled his horse and exposed him to danger, and then laughed at him. I assured him it must have been unintentional, as my coachman was a quiet, sober man, incapable of insulting or willingly injuring any one. He strenuously insisted it was so. I said I would then make enquiry, as soon as I should get home, into the circumstances. He said there was no occasion for enquiry, as he assured me it was so. I asked the favor of his name. He said, Ponsonby, and he hoped I would at least reprimand the man. I promised him I certainly should if he deserved it. As soon as I got home I made enquiry how the accident had happened. It was at the short turning of a street. The gentleman's horse had started on suddenly meeting those of my carriage, but he suffered no injury, and the insult was imaginary. Robert says it was Mr. Ponsonby, the opposition leader in the House of Commons, and ex-Chancellor of Ireland. As I was coming home, I read Southey's poem of Wat Tyler.

11th. Dined with the Lord Mayor at the Mansion House. I was ·punctual at the appointed hour, half-past five, and was the first there. It was a dinner to the Aldermen and their ladies, and the Duke of Sussex. The Earl and Countess of Darnley, Lord Erskine, Lord Arthur Hill, Captain D'Este, Sir Charles and Lady Flint, and some others, were there. Lord Darnley came only at the dessert, having been engaged at a debate in the House of Lords upon a question moved by the Earl of Grosvenor for abolishing sinecures. The Lord Mayor had proposed to omit giving the usual Easter Monday dinner the present year, in consideration of the distresses of the country, and to distribute among the charitable institutions of the City the sum of one thousand pounds usually expended upon this entertainment. He wrote a note to each of the Aldermen, requesting his opinion upon this proposal, and then submitted it to them at a Court of Aldermen. But they unanimously declined giving any opinion upon the question, as involving the ancient usage and the dignity of the City—which, as Miss Wood observed to me, was giving an opinion in the very act of declining to give one. She said it was a subject upon which they were very sore.

The Lord Mayor told the Duke of Sussex that he had had a list made out of all the members of both Houses of Parliament who had voted against the suspension of the Habeas Corpus Act, and had sent them all cards for the dinner, and to no others : so that if they would come, it would serve as a memento to the Ministers. The Duke said they would come—

he would take care they should come. I led Miss Wood down
to dinner, and sat next to her at table, by which means I was
seated lower down than my place should have been, but for my
own satisfaction I could not have been more agreeably seated.
After the ladies retired, the Lord Mayor called me up next to
him. The party was less numerous than any that I had met
before at that place—not more than forty persons, and with less
of formality than usual. It was, however, impossible to escape
the tax of toasting the healths of persons present, and the
speeches to return thanks, but they were short and unpretending, in the mere style of conviviality. I went through this
ceremony like the rest. The Lord Mayor in naming me alluded
to the expectation of my early departure, and the Dúke of
Sussex spoke of me in a very flattering and complimentary
manner, which I answered with as little confusion and as few
words as I could. There was an evening party after dinner,
and dancing. There I met Sir William Beechey and Mr.
Reeves. I told Reeves I would show him some papers concerning Crosby's case. Captain D'Este told me he was going
to Canada with Mr. McGillivray, a gentleman at the head of
the Northwest Company. He also gave some hint as if he
thought of settling himself in America, being here, he said, in
a very different rank of life from that in which he might be
expected to move, and having all his prospects in life already
blasted. I encouraged him to hope for better times.

12th. There was a curious meeting at my office of Mr. John
Reeves and of Dr. Cook, the Chaplain in our navy. Reeves
came to look at the papers in Crosby's case, of which I had
here only a general statement. Cook came to tell me that he
had engaged his passage and should sail in a few days for New
York. About the year 1793, Cook had been prosecuted at
Cambridge and convicted of seditious words, and Reeves about
the same time was the founder of the loyal associations all over
the kingdom against the Republicans and Levellers. He was
shortly after employed, and very active, in the prosecutions of
persons charged with seditious practices. Cook began by
saying (not knowing Reeves) that since the suspension of the
Habeas Corpus Act, and the revival of all the measures of rigor

and restriction of the period when he had suffered, he was extremely anxious to get away from this country and safely landed in America, for there were so many rascally spies about, there was no knowing what they would swear against a man, and he could not feel himself secure of not being from one hour to another thrown into prison. This immediately roused Reeves's curiosity, who asked Cook if he was an American born. "No, sir," said Cook, "I am an Englishman born, but have resided upwards of twenty years in America. I came over here some months since, to see once more the friends yet surviving of those I had left behind, and am now returning to America, for 'a burnt child dreads the fire.'" "Then you have been a burnt child?" said Reeves. "That I have," replied Cook. "Two rascally spies swore that I had said I meant to keep the 30th of January, not by going to church, but by dining upon a calf's head; that I thought the English nation had done right in cutting off Charles the First's head, because he was a tyrant; that if other Kings and Emperors of our own times acted as tyrants, I thought their heads should be cut off, and if George the Third should ever become such a tyrant as Charles the First had been, he would deserve to lose his head in the same manner." "But you were acquitted?" said Reeves. "No, sir; I went to jail, and lay there three months, and but for the intervention of a friend I should have lain there two years. At the end of three months, however, I was discharged; and, that score being settled, I came and took a house in London." "Why," said Reeves, "I must have you upon my black-book." Cook looked up, and I said to him, "This is Mr. Reeves." "I dare say you have, sir," said Cook, "and I am pretty sure it was you who drew up the indictment against me." Reeves asked him if he had been tried at the Assizes or at the Quarter Sessions. He answered, at the Assizes, and asked Reeves if he did not remember a man by the name of Portlock. He said he did not. Cook then said he was by no means ashamed of having undergone that trial, and related an occurrence which had happened a few months afterwards, at a trial before Lord Kenyon at the Old Bailey. It was a civil action between two parties, in which he (Cook) was subpœnaed as a witness, and his evidence was so material that it decided the cause. When he had given his testimony, Mr. Mingay, who was counsel for the party against whom it operated, began to cross-question him, and, with a view to discredit his evidence, asked him if he had not lately been in trouble. Cook answered that his troubles or his pleasures were nothing to him, but he was perfectly ready to give the Court an exact account of the troubles to which he knew that Mingay alluded, and he then told Lord Kenyon of the prosecution that he had suffered at Cambridge on the report of the rascally spies. Mr. Mingay called upon him to say what the words were for which he had been prosecuted. Cook said to him, " It was something very much like what you have got under your wig. It was about a calf's head." Upon which Lord Kenyon and the whole Court burst into a laugh at Mingay's expense. Some time afterwards, Mingay met him walking in the Strand, stopped and spoke to him, and told him he had never in his life been put to such confusion as by his joke about the calf's head. Reeves seemed to be afraid that if he stayed longer Cook would begin to crack his jokes upon him, and went away. Cook soon followed him, after taking a passport.

I went into St. Paul's Church, where they were performing the service of the day. The last time I had been in the Cathedral, which was in 1797, there was only one monument there, which was that of Dr. Johnson. There are now more than twenty, executed chiefly by Flaxman, Bacon, and Banks. They are for the greatest part in honor of officers who have fallen in battle, and there is neither genius nor variety in the designs. The inscriptions are all in English, and all marvellously insipid; generally a bare recital that they were erected at the public expense, by a resolution of Parliament. The monument to Howard has an inscription upon the pedestal, not in front, but at the left side of the statue. It begins, " This extraordinary man," &c., but does not give his name. It appears like the last part of an inscription, of which the first part should be on the other side. Johnson's inscription is in Latin—well enough, excepting the notice that it was erected by a subscription of his friends, " pecunia conlata" —they might as well have inscribed the sculptor's bill.

13th. There was a meeting of the inhabitants of Westminster held this morning in Palace Yard, to petition the Prince Regent for the removal of his present Ministers. Having occasion to walk that way, I had the curiosity to attend the meeting for about half an hour—long enough to have my pocket picked of my handkerchief, and to hear detached parts of a speech of Lord Cochrane's, who repeated a joke already many times given out at the public meetings—a calculation of the number of farthings given by subscription in charity, by the principal sinecurists and placemen, upon the amount of the sums which they receive of the public money. There was a general laugh from the meeting at most of the names, when he announced one with twelve farthings and fifty-six-hundredths, and so down to two farthings and a half; but the moment he named Lord Castlereagh, and before he mentioned his quota of farthings, there was an almost unanimous groan uttered, such as I never before heard, and when he had got through the whole list there was an exclamation of " Knaves! knaves! knaves!" from thousands of voices at once.

After Lord Cochrane, a Mr. Walker spoke, but in so low a tone of voice that I could not hear a word he said. Some of the people around me said he was mad. A vote of thanks to the High Bailiff, Arthur Morris, was passed, for which he returned thanks, and the meeting was dissolved. The meeting was very numerous, but they dispersed in perfect order. A petition to the Prince Regent was voted.

15th. I dined with Mr. Boddington, No. 31 Upper Brook Street, by the invitation of his partner, R. Sharp, who was there. Lord and Lady Holland, a Mr. Allen,[1] who came with them, Mr. Brougham, Mrs. Alexander Baring, and a Mr. Jekyl, who, Mr. Sharp told me, was reputed the wittiest man in England, constituted the company, with Mr. Boddington, his son, and daughter. Mrs. Siddons was invited, but sent an excuse, as being indisposed. Mrs. Baring brought the same apology for her husband. Lord Erskine had a previous engagement.

---

[1] Better known now by the publications lately made of Reminiscences of Holland House.

The party was one of the most agreeable and entertaining that I ever attended. The conversation at table turned upon a great variety of topics, upon which Lord Holland and Mr. Jekyl were extremely humorous and amusing—literature, the fine arts, very little politics, but personalities in great abundance, ludicrous anecdotes, ridiculous sayings, and burlesque characteristics of many distinguished personages known to most of the company, with no small intermixture of satirical observation, but all in the most perfect good humor. Lord Holland's wit principally consisted in " taking off" ridiculous persons, and Mr. Jekyl's in telling jocular stories and repeating puns. Mr. Brougham is not a man of wit, but has taste and learning, great information, indefatigable industry, and a moderate portion of eloquence. Much of the wit, and especially of the mimicry, was lost to me for want of acquaintance with the persons. The late Lords Thurlow and Kenyon, Judge Buller, Lord Ellenborough, and Justice Parke, the poets Southey, Coleridge, and Wordsworth, Dennis O'Brien, Michael Angelo Taylor, T. Tyrwhitt, and General Bloomfield, the Duke of Montrose, and others, names unknown to me, were introduced, and afforded large scope for merriment. Mr. Jekyl told me that he was born in Boston, and that his father had resided there many years.

18th. At half-past eleven I went to Lord Castlereagh's. After repeating apologies for having delayed so long an official communication in answer to my note of the   September last, which he attributed to the excessive pressure of business upon himself, and upon the whole Government, arising from the state of their internal affairs, he said he was at length authorized to make certain propositions to me relative to the commercial part of my proposals; the other, or political part, involving so many and so extensive and complicated considerations that the Government had not been able to come to any conclusion upon it.

With regard to the intercourse between the United States and the British West India Islands, this Government still adhered to the policy which had been long established, and were not prepared for any departure from their ancient colonial policy, nor had they any complaint to make with respect to the Act of Congress lately passed, prohibiting British vessels from clearing out from the ports of the United States for those islands. They considered it merely as the exercise of a fair reciprocal right on the part of the United States, to which they could have no objection, and at which they entertained no dissatisfaction.

I told him I had no information that the Act had passed, but he said they had received the information. But he added that they were willing to extend the privileges of the Free Port Act, which I had stated to be, and which really were, now confined to the vessels of European nations, to those of the United States, and also to admit them to the island of Bermuda. And with respect to the intercourse between the United States and the British Provinces in North America, they were willing to agree to an article like one formerly proposed, which he read from a paper in his hand, and which seemed to me a transcript from the Treaty of 1794. He said he was not yet quite prepared, but he hoped to send me to-morrow, or perhaps in the course of this day, a note containing all these propositions, which they would agree to upon conditions of reciprocity, and with a view to manifest their disposition to promote the harmony between the two countries.

I said that immediately upon receiving his note I should recur to my instructions from my Government, and would submit to him the result of my observations upon his proposals.

He said that if I should find it came within the extent of the powers from my Government, so that it would not be necessary for me to refer the subject to them, he should propose to conclude the articles as supplementary to the convention of 3d July, 1815, and to be of the same duration.

I said that so far as related to the principle of reciprocity there would be nothing incompatible with it in the prohibitory Act of Congress, which applied only to ports from which the vessels of the United States are excluded, and of course would immediately cease to apply to any port that should be opened. I mentioned to him the accidents that had happened to some of the letters and dispatches addressed to me from America, by the operation of the Act of Parliament which requires that letters brought in merchant vessels should be delivered up to be sent by the post-office. Lord Castlereagh did not know how the law was in this respect, nor did he suggest any means of removing the inconvenience. I also spoke to him concerning the case of W. B. Crosby, all the particulars of which I stated to him. I mentioned the laws of the State of New York confirming the claims of British subjects to estates liable to escheat, and told him I understood Mr. Bagot had promised Crosby any assistance that he could give him to obtain restitution of the property. Lord Castlereagh said he did not know that Mr. Bagot had written anything upon the subject; that the laws of the State of New York were, he supposed, founded on the policy of the United States to encourage foreigners to speculate in our lands, but, very naturally, the policy of this country was to give no such encouragement. I spoke to him of Reeves's pamphlet, and of his doctrine that the disabilities of alienage could not apply to citizens of the United States; and observed that Mr. Crosby might perhaps want nothing more than the power to prosecute his appeal before the King in Council, which the late war only had prevented him from prosecuting. He said nothing to encourage the expectation that anything in favor of Crosby would be done. My interview with him was of not more than half an hour, and he repeated that heretofore he had been used to devoting his evenings to the House of Commons and the mornings to foreign affairs, but now he was obliged to employ his mornings also in the internal affairs of the country, being in constant and daily attendance upon two committees—one of Finance, embracing the whole system of public expenditure of the country, and the other upon the Poor Laws.

19th. I received this evening a short note from the Under-Secretary of State in the Foreign Department to Hamilton, with the note promised yesterday by Lord Castlereagh, that is, a draft of four articles, without preliminary, conclusion, or comment. The first is for admitting American vessels under thirty tons' burden, and having only one deck, to the free ports in the

West Indies, with certain specified articles of importation and exportation. The second admits American vessels to the island of Bermuda; and the third, to Turk's Island for salt, with liberty to export certain specified articles. The fourth stipulates a free intercourse between the United States and those ports of the adjoining British Provinces in North America where the division-line is the middle of rivers or lakes, but ex-cluding from the right of navigation wherever both sides of the lake or river belong to the same party.

25th. I wrote a note to Mr. Bourke, the Danish Minister, enquiring whether he proposed going to the Duchess of Cumberland's party this evening in full dress or in frock. This is one of those affairs insignificant elsewhere, but of great importance at Courts. There are occasions upon which full dress is indispensable, and others where it is disused. The line of distinction is not clear in this country, and there is always an awkwardness in finding oneself differently garbed from the rest of the company. My doubt in this case arose from the card of invitation's expressing that the party was to meet the Prince Regent. Mr. Bourke answered me that he should go in frock, and that all the company, he believed, would do the same. Dined with Mr. Smith, at Mrs. A. Porter's; my wife declined going. Sir Robert and Lady Liston, Lady Lowrie, Mr. Lockhart, Mr. and Mrs. King, Mr. Boswell, and one other gentleman, were the company. After dinner there were several other persons came in, among whom Mr. Basil Cochrane was introduced to me, and a Mr. Marsh, one of the very few persons whom I have met here who knew my father at the time of his mission in this country. Marsh was then one of the Commissioners upon the claims of the refugees. They sent out a Mr. Anstey to America to ascertain many of the facts relative to those claims. Marsh says that upon his application my father furnished Anstey with letters to the Governors of the States, and to his own friends, which enabled Anstey to transact his business entirely to the satisfaction of the Commissioners, and for which they were entirely indebted to my father.

We came home about ten o'clock, and shortly afterwards I went with my wife to the Duchess of Cumberland's evening party. The Duke and almost all the men were in frocks, but the Prince Regent himself, and several others, were in full-dress uniforms. Captain D'Este, the Duke of Sussex's son, told me he thought the Prince had done it by way of example, and as a hint for imitation. The party was numerous—perhaps three hundred persons; the rooms crowded, and very warm. There was music—the piano, and the opera-singers Naldi, his daughter, and Madame Camporesi. The Duke and Duchess were very attentive in going round and speaking to their company—the Duke to the men, and the Duchess to the ladies. Count Fernan Nuñez, the Spanish Ambassador, told us he was recalled, and appointed Ambassador to Paris. He also told us that Curtoys went off yesterday.

April 1st. Jouffroy, the Prussian Chargé d'Affaires, came and told me he had made an excuse to Fernan Nuñez for to-morrow, and would come out and dine with us at Ealing. I had asked him on Sunday evening, but he then pleaded an engagement to Fernan Nuñez. I asked also Mr. Pfeffel, the Bavarian Minister, and Mr. Poletica, both of whom had engagements. Jouffroy told me that his Government had appointed Mr. Greuhm, who was some time here as Chargé d'Affaires, to go as Prussian Minister to the United States, and that he expected him here, on his way to America, by the end of the month. I spoke to Jouffroy about the misunderstanding between this and the Prussian Courts relative to the Duchess of Cumberland. He gave me some particulars concerning it, but let them out with reserve and reluctance. He said that the Queen's refusal to receive the Duchess had been much instigated by tittle-tattle scandal from the Queen of Würtemberg; that the Prince Regent, though he had not taken part against the Duchess, might, however, have prevented the extremities to which things have been pushed, and have reconciled all the parties, if he had chosen; that the Duke himself by his violence had contributed to make the breach as it now is, utterly and forever irreparable; that Baron Jacobi had very injudiciously taken up the affair, without instructions, in a very high tone, and most absurdly, by attacking Lord Castlereagh about it, who could have had no concern in the Queen's animosities, and could have no influence in removing them.; that the King of Prussia had indeed approved of Jacobi's proceedings after the fact, because he had been unwilling formally to disapprove the acts of an old and faithful servant, but the approbation had been merely formal. Jacobi was now living in retirement, in the neighborhood of Dresden, and without any public employment. He had made the situation of Prussian Minister here extremely awkward, for he could not appear at the Queen's drawing-rooms, and that excluded him from a very extensive circle of society. But that was not all. The Minister was exposed to meet the Queen at the Prince Regent's, and to have the Queen turn her back upon him, as she had turned her back upon Baron Jacobi; "et c'est que quand la Reine tourne le dos, tout le monde tourne le dos." The matter had now become involved in such inextricable confusion, and the Queen had become so inveterate, that it never could be reconciled during her life; and she might live these ten years. The Duke and Duchess would ultimately be obliged to go and live in Germany, for the manner of interdict under which they were living here would in the end prove insupportable. Indeed, they ought not to have come here after they knew how the Queen was indisposed towards the Duchess. Jouffroy cautiously avoided mentioning if he knew the particular causes of the Queen's displeasure—and they are not publicly known.

I dined at the Earl of Harrowby's, 29 Grosvenor Square. Count and Countess Lieven, Mr. and Mrs. Bourke, Counts Fernan Nuñez, Palmella, and Caraman, Mr. Neumann, Earl and Countess Bathurst and their eldest daughter, formed the company, with the family, Earl and Countess of Harrowby, and their eldest daughter, Lady Susan Ryder. There was one other daughter, a child of four or five years, in the drawing-room before dinner, and two daughters, of perhaps twelve and fourteen, after dinner. There was altogether a general and a very pleasing appearance of domestic life about the house and family. I was seated at table between the Countess of Bathurst and Lady Susan Ryder, whom I found very agreeable and sensible. She is one of the most beautiful and fashionable young ladies of the Court. Lady Bathurst told me that Colonel Harvey, who is to marry Miss Louisa Caton, was a relation of Lord Bathurst's.

Fernan Nuñez, before dinner, asked me if I had any late accounts from the United States. There was an article in this morning's newspapers, of 11th February, from New Orleans, stating that Spain had ceded the two Floridas to the United States. He asked me if I knew anything of it. I said I knew it could not be true, because there were authentic accounts from Washington to the last days in February, when a voluminous correspondence with the Spanish Government was communicated by the President to Congress, from which it appeared that no arrangement with Spain had been then made. He then said, "Etes-vous maintenant content de Monsieur Onis?" I answered, laughing, that I certainly could not be otherwise than content with him, not having the honor of any personal acquaintance, and never having been in any direct relation with him.

But, he said, he meant to ask whether the Government were satisfied with him. I said that when Mr. Onis had been first received, it was not without reluctance on the part of the Government, because his previous conduct had given offence, and about a year ago it had been mentioned to me in a dispatch that there was some personal dissatisfaction; but since then I had not heard of any further cause of complaint. I added that I most earnestly hoped that Spain and the United States would not quarrel with each other. He said that he very cordially concurred in the same hope, and that the policy of his Government was entirely pacific, a very decided proof of which they had just given by asking for the mediation of the allies in their dispute with Portugal. I told him I had seen it intimated, and thought it probable, that the invasion of Buenos Ayres had been by some understanding between the Governments of Spain and Brazil. He said, Oh, no, none in the world; but Spain, instead of invading Portugal, as she might have done upon such provocation, had preferred to ask the mediation of the allies, and, he could tell me confidentially, that was the business upon which he was going to Paris. He asked me who was our Minister at Paris, and, when I told him, said he thought he had seen Mr. Gallatin here.

Earl Bathurst asked me whether I was acquainted with Mr. Cobbett, and whether I thought the American Government would give him any encouragement. I said I had never seen him, and did not suppose there would be any intercourse between him and the American Government. I knew not what his projects or intentions were in going to America, but if he should interest himself much in the politics of that country, I should, from the character of his mind, expect very soon to see him writing against that Government.

Lord Bathurst agreed in that opinion, and said Cobbett was a very vain man, though he certainly had the talent of writing with great effect to a certain class of readers. He said Cobbett's change of politics had proceeded from two causes. First, Mr. Windham had invited him to dine at his house with Mr. Pitt. He had there introduced him to Mr. Pitt, who had taken little or no notice of him beyond that of common civility. This gave him an immediate and decided turn against Mr. Pitt; and he had afterwards quarrelled with Windham, because, being in power, Windham had declined appointing him Under-Secretary of State. I think, however, there were other causes.

7th. I called at the Portuguese Minister's to enquire whether it would be necessary to appear at the Te Deum in Court dresses, and found it would not. We went to Craven Street, and I returned at half-past eleven to the Portuguese chapel, next door to the Minister's house, in South Audley Street. Count Palmella himself, and the members of his Legation, were in full Court uniforms. The tribune is a small apartment partitioned off from the body of the chapel, and at the right hand of the altar. The Corps Diplomatique were alone admitted to it by cards. I was the first there, excepting Palmella and his Legation. The mass began immediately afterwards. The other foreign Ministers dropped in successively. There were present the Austrian Ambassador, Prince Esterhazy, with one of his Secretaries; Count Lieven, the Russian Ambassador, with the Counsellor of Embassy, Poletica; the Marquis d'Osmond, French Ambassador, with the Secretary of Embassy, Count Caraman; the Spanish Ambassador, Count Fernan Nuñez, Duke of Montellano; the Prince of Castel-Cicala,

Neapolitan Minister; Baron Rehausen, Swedish, Mr. Bourke, Danish, and Mr. Pfeffel, Bavarian, Minister; and Mr. Jouffroy, the Prussian Chargé d'Affaires. The members of the Corps not present were Baron Fagel, Ambassador to the Netherlands, and his brother, Secretary to the Embassy; Baron Just, the Saxon, and General Neuffer, the Würtemberg, and Count Munster, the Hanoverian, Minister; and the Marquis de Grimaldi, Sardinian Chargé d'Affaires. These, with the Turkish Chargé d'Affaires, Ramadani, constitute all the foreign missions now in England. The mass took up at least two hours, and the Te Deum that succeeded, about three-quarters of an hour more. The organ was good, and the singing all excellent. Most of the vocal performers at the Opera are attached to this, or some other of the Roman Catholic chapels belonging to the foreign Legations. It gives them the privileges allowed to the suite of public Ministers, which is ample compensation to them for the occasional calls to sing at the religious solemnities.

The principal singularity that I remarked this day was the English pronunciation of the Latin, as chaunted by two of the priests, who were Englishmen. The third, who was a Frenchman, made an attempt to pronounce like them, but could not support it, and soon relapsed into his French pronunciation. I remarked that Mr. Bourke, the Danish Minister, joined in the devotional parts of the ceremony, and found, upon enquiry, that he was a Roman Catholic. His father, he said, was an Irishman, who emigrated from Ireland on account of religion. He was himself the first Roman Catholic that the King of Denmark had ever employed in missions abroad; but since him there had been several others. He remarked as a curious circumstance, indicating the increased religious liberality of the age, that the Danish Lutheran Church in London was under his protection as Danish Minister, though a Roman Catholic, while the Bavarian Roman Catholic chapel was under the protection of Mr. Pfeffel, a Protestant, and the Russian Greek chapel was under that of Count Lieven, who was a Lutheran. He explained to me several of the particularities of the ceremony, and the several occasions at which they kneel, as the Gloria Patri; and he pointed out to me a

lamp at the right of the altar, with five knobs, significant of
Christ's five wounds at the Crucifixion—two in the feet, two in
the hands, and one in the side.   This lamp is always hung up
at Easter, and remains suspended forty days, the time from the
Resurrection during which Christ continued to be seen upon
earth, and on Ascension-day is taken away.   Towards the close
of the ceremony on this day, there was a lady introduced into
the tribune, I believe at the desire of the Marquis d'Osmond.

After it was over we were invited into the house, where a
very elegant cold collation was provided, and to which all the
Portuguese subjects now in London were invited.   There were
about one hundred and fifty persons.   Among them was the
Count de Lima, with whom I some time since dined at Mr.
Bourke's—the same of whom the Abbé de Pradt tells the story
of his having pronounced a superb No! to the Emperor
Napoleon at Bayonne.   It was about three o'clock when we
came away.   I asked Fernan Nuñez when he expected to go
to Paris.   He said, immediately after the celebration of the
Prince Regent's birthday, which is to be the 23d of this month.
His Court, he said, were very urgent for him to hasten his
departure, but it would not be decent for him to go before
then.

12th. In the evening I read two of Bishop Horsley's ser-
mons upon the Forty-fifth Psalm.   There are four, but I had
already read the two previous ones.   They have a very high
reputation in this country, and are undoubtedly discourses of
great learning and ingenuity.   But they are dogmatical and
bigoted; and their object is to inculcate doctrines so odious
that I could not believe them if I would.   Here are four ser-
mons to explain one psalm, and, if the Bishop's exposition is
correct, the psalm has been waiting three thousand years to be
made at last intelligible by him.   Calvin, and other expositors,
and even the English translators of the Bible in Elizabeth's
reign, supposed this was a nuptial song on the marriage of
Solomon, with mystical allusions to the Messiah.   But the
Bishop charges Calvin with want of taste and poverty of
imagination, and insists that Solomon had nothing to do with
the psalm, which was all about the Messiah.   The exposition

of Calvin appears to me much better supported by the tenor of the psalm than the Bishop's. How far it was applicable to the Messiah may be a subject of doubt and controversy. The Hebrew seems to have been a language never completely formed, very indefinite in the force of its terms, and remarkably destitute of precision. The psalm is poetical, and Oriental poetry; that is, figurative to excess. It purports to be a marriage song for a king, a conqueror, and his bride. It could not apply to Solomon, says Bishop Horsley, because he was not a warrior. But how can it apply to Jesus, who not only was no warrior, but never was married? By the mystical exposition, which out of anything will make everything, the Messiah is a conqueror, and Christ is the husband of the Church. All this may, or may not, be true. I should be sorry to stake my faith in Christianity upon the mystical meaning of the Forty-fifth Psalm, or on the question of Calvin's taste or Bishop Horsley's richness of imagination. But when the Bishop tells me that "it is the mere cant of puritanism to allege the precept of mutual forgiveness, the prohibitions of returning evil for evil, and of resisting persecution, as reprobating religious wars," and at the same time contends that "the peaceable submission of the subject to the very worst of kings is one of the most peremptory precepts of Christianity," I hold him to be preaching doctrines false, pernicious, and damnable, for which, if eternal punishment could be compatible with a merciful and benevolent dispenser of it, the Bishop would be a promising candidate for it. For if there be one species of perverseness more detestable than any other, it is that which inculcates vicious principle under the sanctified garb of religious instruction. But so it is, and so it always will be, with priests who are at the same time Lords. Horsley was not worse than Massillon. In merely human enmities there is nothing so remorseless as in the rancors of a Bishop.

13th. Read Horsley's Ninth Sermon of the first volume, the object of which is to establish by an argument drawn from the context the authenticity of 1 John, v. 7 and 8—a text of main reliance to the supporters of the Trinity, but which is stoutly

disputed by the unitarians as spurious. The Bishop admits
that the text has lately been given up by many sound Trini-
tarians. He declines defending it directly, but he is unwilling
to part with it, and endeavors to support it by an elaborate
misconstruction of the verse immediately preceding. He considers the doctrines of the incarnation and atonement of Christ
as indissolubly connected together, and marks it as the great
distinction between this Christian dogma and the incarnations
(avatars) of Veeshnu, in the Hindoo Mythology. It is an idle
waste of subtlety to urge the incarnation, or the atonement,
upon principles of human reason. The stumbling-block is at
the threshold—atonement and incarnation both transcend
human reason. If the potter makes a vessel with a flaw in it,
either it is because he could not make it perfect, or he is himself responsible for the flaw. The vessel cannot be answerable
for the frailty of its nature—it did not make itself. Had the
Creator made man perfect, he would not have fallen. The
Creator is responsible for the consequences of the infirmity of
his creature. So says human reason. Existence was not the
choice of Adam or Eve. But it was the will of the Creator to
make them. He made them not for misery, but for enjoyment,
and if he chose to make that enjoyment conditional, being
omnipotent, he could have made them with firmness to resist
temptation, and to fulfil the conditions imposed upon them.
According to the Scriptures, the woman was beguiled by a
superior, but fallen, spirit, and the man was led to ruin by the
woman. They were punished in themselves, and in all their
posterity. They became beings degraded in the scale of creation. Christ died to redeem them and their posterity. But
how, or why, Christ's death could redeem them, and how, or
why, Almighty God should himself become man, to suffer and
die for their redemption, is utterly inconceivable to human
reason, and by human reason can never be explained. That
the Omnipotent God should have no better expedient for
appeasing his own wrath at the transgression of a creature
made by himself, but by becoming that creature and perishing
upon the cross, is so little consonant to human reason that it is
hardly within the compass of pardonable human absurdities.

Yet Bishop Horsley says that the incarnation of Christ was for a purpose which God only could accomplish, and God himself could accomplish in no other way—and that the same God who in one person exacts the punishment, in another himself sustains it, and thus makes his own mercy pay the satisfaction to his own justice. This is not reason; it is mystery.

16th. Soon after rising this morning, I received four letters. One from James Monroe, President of the United States, dated the 6th March last, informing me that he had, with the sanction of the Senate, committed to me the Department of State. He requests me in case of my acceptance of the office to return to the United States with the least possible delay to assume its duties, and mentions that he sends a special messenger with the letter, and copies by various conveyances. That which I received is a quadruplicate, and came by a vessel from Boston to Liverpool. There was also a letter from Dr. B. Waterhouse, of Cambridge, dated 14th March, which came by the same vessel, and the two other letters were from James Maury, of Liverpool, mentioning that he had forwarded to me a packet of dispatches and one of letters by the mail-coach. Afterwards, in the course of the day, I received these two packets, one of which was a dispatch from Mr. Monroe while yet Secretary of State, dated 5th February, with various documents relative to his negotiation with Mr. Bagot on the subject of the fisheries, which has not succeeded, and a copy of a letter from Jos. Hopkinson to Mr. Daschkoff upon Kosloff's affair, and a printed copy of President Madison's message to Congress, with the correspondence of the negotiation with Spain.

These are hard knots, with which I am to enter upon the discharge of the duties of the Department of State—a trust of weight and magnitude which I cannot contemplate without deep concern. For the faithful and acceptable discharge of it I rely upon the support of that Being whose signal favor has hitherto carried me through all the trials of my life, and upon whom alone safe dependence can be placed. My wife had procured tickets for the assembly and ball at Almack's this evening, for herself, Smith, and me, from Countess Lieven. This is a subscription assembly, attended only by persons of the highest distinction in this country and most of the foreign Ambassadors and Ministers. Our residence in the country prevented us from subscribing, but my wife had the curiosity to see it once, and we went between eleven and twelve at night. The company were just beginning to assemble, and it was about one in the morning when the hall was well filled. There are about four hundred subscribers, and there were at least that number of persons present. There was a small proportion of the company with whom I was acquainted, but I had occasional conversation with the Duke of Cumberland, Earls Darnley, Grey, and Cassilis, Count Lieven, Mr. Pfeffel, Mr. Poletica, Douglas Kinnaird, Mr. and Mrs. Patterson, and Miss Caton, Mr. Gambier, Mr. Mansfield, Captain Forbes, and some others. Captain D'Este again talked of going to America. We came home about three in the morning, leaving most of the company still there. The dancing was altogether quadrilles and waltzing. Many of the young women beautiful, and a few elegant.

17th. I answered the letter from the President of the United States, and accepted the appointment of Secretary of State. Mr. Monroe's injunction to me to return home as soon as possible brings a pressure of business upon me to be done in a short time.

It may not be deemed out of place here to introduce a more extended expression of the writer's inmost feelings than appears in the diary on this occasion. In writing to his mother, a few days later, he says:

The manner in which the President has thought proper to nominate me was certainly honorable to himself, as it was without any intimation from me, or, as far as I knew, from any of my friends, which could operate as an inducement to him. His motives were altogether of a public nature; and I trust I shall be duly sensible of the personal as well as of the political duties which this unsolicited and spontaneous confidence imposes upon me.

As to the popular favor with which you observe the appointment has been attended, I well know how to appreciate its stability as inherent in its own nature; but that is the smallest of my concern.   I have no fear of injustice from my countrymen, for throughout the whole course of my life I have experienced from them favor far beyond my deserts.   They have always overestimated, not the goodness of my intentions, but the extent of my talents.   And now, when *their* anticipations go so far beyond what I have the consciousness of being able to realize, mine have too much reason to apprehend that they will terminate in disappointment.   I have no anxious forecast but of my inability to justify the President's choice by active, efficient, and acceptable assistance to his administration, and the expectations of the public by solid and useful service to my country.

You observe that among the various public speculations there have been some expressing apprehensions that my public opinion and feelings would not harmonize with those of the President. It is certain that our sentiments upon subjects of great public interest have at particular periods of our public life been much at variance.   That they may be so again is as certainly not impossible.   If I had any present reason for expecting it, I should deem it my duty to decline the office which he has tendered to me; but I have none.   Ever since his appointment to the Department of State has brought me into official relations with him, I have known few of his opinions with which I did not cordially concur, and where there might be shades of difference, have had ample reason to be satisfied with the consideration which he had given to the candid expression of mine. I am aware, however, how much more delicate and difficult a task it will be to conciliate the duties of self-respect and the spirit of personal independence, with the deference of personal obligation and the fidelity of official subordination, under the new station assigned to me, than it has hitherto been in those which I have held.   I am aware that by the experience of our history under the present Constitution, Mr. Jefferson alone of our four Presidents has had the good fortune of a cabinet harmonizing with each other and with him throughout the whole period of his administration.   I know something of the difficulty of moving smoothly along with associates equal in trust, justly

confident of their abilities, disdainful of influence, yet eager to
exercise it, impatient of control, and opposing real stubborn
resistance to surmises and phantoms of encroachment; and I
see that in the nature of the thing an American President's
cabinet must be composed of such materials. For myself, I
shall enter upon the functions of my office with a deep sense
of the necessity of union with my colleagues, and with a suitable impression that my place is subordinate; that my duty
will be to support, and not to counteract or oppose, the President's administration, and that if from any cause I should find
my efforts to that end ineffectual, it will be my duty seasonably
to withdraw from the public service and leave to more competent persons the performance of the duties to which I should
find myself inadequate. The President, I am sure, will neither
require nor expect from me any sacrifice of principles inconsistent with my own sense of right, and I hope I shall never
be unmindful of the respect for his character, the deference for
his sentiments, and the attachment to his person due from me
to him, not only by the relative situation in which he has placed
me to himself, but by the gratitude with which his kindness
ought to be requited.

18th. I paid visits to the Portuguese and Saxon Ministers,
and left cards withal at Mr. Boddington's and the Spanish
Ambassador's. General Neuffer, the Würtemberg Minister,
who has been several weeks ill and confined to his house, came
in while I was with Palmella. I had received from him two
days ago a note with a copy of the Constitution proposed by
the King to the States of Würtemberg, and three memoranda
of enquiries concerning individuals in the United States. I
thanked him for the copy of the Constitution, and made some
remarks upon the enquiries, which, at his request, I promised
to send him in writing. I had various desultory conversation
with Count Palmella and Baron Just, both of whom complained
of the despotism exercised by the five great European powers
over all the minor States. In speaking of their present mediation between Spain and Portugal, the count said Spain "a fait la
sottise" of asking for it, and thereby countenanced them in their

dictatorial measures. And those gentlemen who were always ready enough "à se mêler des affaires des autres" had accepted the proposal of Spain, had agreed that the negotiation should be conducted by the Ministers of the several powers at Paris, and had addressed two notes, one to the Spanish Government, altogether complimentary, and the other to the Portuguese, also in very civil terms, but asking for explanations of the late movements of Brazilian troops into the Buenos Ayres territories, and intimating that unless these explanations should be given, Spain would find, " dans l'appui de ses hauts alliés," a substitute for measures which would rekindle the flame of war in Europe. But, he said, there was not much meaning in that, for it did not appear that Spain had either the inclination or the power to commence a war against Portugal in Europe, nor could she be very formidable while her revenues should continue to fall short, as they now do, of one-quarter part of her expenses. As to the invasion from Brazil of the Buenos Ayres territory, he said, the justification of it was complicated, and arose from a multitude of circumstances in the peculiar situation of these countries. He gave me some explanation of it, but was interrupted before he had finished by the coming in of General Neuffer.

I left them, and called upon Baron Just, who, with many enquiries about affairs in the United States, also complained of the Great Powers. He said that Russia, after having taken away from the King of Saxony one-half of his territory, was not content with that, but was chicaning for twenty villages more. Austria had finally offered her mediation, and, as it was accepted, Prussia would doubtless be obliged in the end to abide by the treaty; and surely where the stipulation had the effect of taking away from a State its indisputable possessions, if there was any ambiguity in the expressions, the construction must be in favor of the party which is already injured by the loss of its territories. But it was impossible to say what was to become of Germany. There was a mass of discontent among the people in all parts of it. The middle ranks of society were in Germany more enlightened than in any other part of Europe, not excepting England; but they had not their due share of influence in the Governments, and were dissatisfied with their condition. They felt as if they had escaped from one tyranny only to fall upon another. The situation of Germany was therefore far more perilous than that of England. He was fully satisfied, and had been so from a very short time after he arrived in this country, that there was not the least danger of a revolution here. One Ministry and another might be overthrown; there might be " des crises," but no material change of the Government. When the debt comes to press too heavily, which it will before long, they will tax the stockholders somehow or other, no matter how, and they must put up with it as well as they can. It will produce no commotion in the State.

I told him that was my own opinion, but I thought the obstinacy with which the Government now persisted in refusing to tax the stockholders would increase their difficulties, and ultimately weaken the nation. He also thought that Great Britain had been at the zenith of her power, and must henceforth decline.

I wished to have seen Count Fernan Nuñez, but he was not at home. Palmella asked me if the United States had been invited to accede to the Holy Alliance. I believed not, and supposed there might be two reasons for the omission. One, that by the policy both of Europe and of the United States, they were totally disconnected with the general politics and alliances of the European powers. The other was, that the Holy Alliance had been a personal league between the sovereigns, signed by themselves. He said that, by the general purport of the Holy League, the United States had as much interest in its professed object as any European power. The other reason could not apply, because it went to exclude all republics from the League. Yet the Swiss Cantons had been invited to join, and had acceded to it. He added that the real object and effect of the Holy League was not fully disclosed. It would be good or bad, according to its application. The Emperor Alexander was ambitious, and if it should be made an instrument of his ambition it might effect bad purposes. He said Portugal had been invited to accede to it, but the answer from Rio Janeiro had not yet been received.

21st. I attended the Prince Regent's levee, and presented Mr. R. Patterson and Mr. E. Coles. The Duke of Wellington was there, having arrived this morning with Colonel Harvey, who is to be married next Thursday to Miss Louisa Caton. Count St. Martin d'Aglie, the Sardinian Minister, who has just returned after an absence upon leave, had an audience of the Prince upon that occasion. Count Palmella, the Portuguese Minister, had also an audience, to announce the marriage of the Hereditary Prince of Brazil with the Austrian Archduchess Leopoldine; and Baron Rehausen, the Swedish Minister, to compliment the Prince Regent upon the " dernier événement," as he called it—the sneaking potato-bullet atrocious outrage. Rehausen shrugged his shoulders, and said it was " un peu tard" for this compliment, but better late than never. The Prince of Castel-Cicala, who is in the singular predicament of being Ambassador of the King of the Two Sicilies at Paris and at the same time his Minister Plenipotentiary here, presented a Duke of Spinelli, and a Count Romano as Neapolitan Chargé d'Affaires. Fernan Nuñez presented his Secretary of Embassy, Campo Sano, who has lately arrived, and taken the place of Curtoys. The Marquis d'Osmond also presented several Frenchmen. It was past three when the general levee commenced. Sir Robert Liston was there, and told me Lord Cochrane and Sir Francis Burdett were to present the Westminster petition for the removal of the Ministers. I waited till near half-past four to see them, but they did not make their appearance. Sir Robert Liston told me he should go about next Monday for Constantinople.

24th. The Duke of Wellington called in person, and invited me and Mrs. Adams to the wedding at his house this evening. The Duchess afterwards called and left her card. Mrs. Adams also went and left cards for herself and me at the Duke's house. We were obliged to make a short dinner, and left the table at nine o'clock to go to Apsley House, at Hyde Park Corner, which is now the Duke of Wellington's. We were, however, very early. The family had dined, partly at Mr. Wellesley Pole's, and partly at Mr. Freemantle's, a relation of Colonel Harvey's. It was near eleven before the company were all

assembled, about thirty persons—the Marquis of Cholmonde-
ley, Lord Steward of the Household, and his family, the Earls
of Liverpool, Bathurst, and Westmorland, the latter with his
youngest daughter, Mr. Coke, of Norfolk, and his niece, Mr.
Wellesley Pole, Mr. and Mrs. Villiers, Count Fernan Nuñez,
Mr. and Mrs. Mansfield, Mr. and Mrs. Patterson, and Miss
Caton, Lord Arthur Hill, and several other young men of the
Duke's family. The service was read by Dr. Goodall, Provost
of Eton School, who had been formerly the Colonel's tutor.
The special license from the Archbishop of Canterbury for the
marriage was on the table, and described the parties as Felton
Bathurst Harvey, a Colonel in the army, and Louisa Caton,
of Annapolis, in the province of Baltimore, spinster. I signed
my name on the parish Register Book as one of the witnesses.

After the ceremony was over, the bride distributed her favors,
roses of silver ribbon, to all the company. Mr. Wellesley Pole
invited us all to go to his house. The servants had all white
cockades distributed to them, which they put into their hats.
We went to Mr. Pole's, and passed another hour there. We
came home before supper, and between one and two in the
morning. The bridegroom and bride went from the Duke of
Wellington's immediately to Englefield Hill, near Windsor, a
country-seat belonging to Mrs. Freemantle, Colonel Harvey's
mother. The bride is a Roman Catholic, and they had been
married in the morning at the Bavarian Chapel. They had
first applied to the priest of the Spanish Chapel, who refused
to perform the ceremony, because the parties declined taking
the oath that the daughters that might be born of the marriage
should be brought up Roman Catholics. Fernan Nuñez said
he had attempted to persuade his priest, who had only answered
him, "Vous ne savez pas votre Catéchisme." The Bavarian
priest was, however, not so scrupulous; but his indulgence was
propitiated by a hint that it would be politic not to indispose
the Duke of Wellington against the Catholics.

27th. I had some conversation with Dumouriez, who is more
cautious in talking about French affairs than heretofore. He
lamented the absence of his friend the Duke of Kent, who, he
said, would reside abroad at least two years longer. And now

his other friend, the Duke of Orleans, was also gone; and he told me all the particulars of the Duke's return. He was not to reside at the Palais Royal, because it would have too much the appearance of a rival Court to that of the Tuileries, and because it was in the very centre of the " mauvaises mœurs"— a sort of prison, where he had no garden, and could not step out of the house without being overlooked and surrounded with spies. He had therefore determined to purchase the estate of Rosny, which had belonged to the famous Duke of Sully, about fifteen leagues from Paris, and to reside there. But the King himself had given him Neuilly, in exchange for his stables in Paris, which he (the King) had taken, and the Duke is to live there. It is only one league out of Paris, but it parries the objection of the rival Court, and will enable the Duke to go to Paris every week, and to transact all his business at his convenience. As to general affairs, Dumouriez says it is very desirable that the King should live two years longer, or until the foreign troops shall have been withdrawn from France, and in that time everything will settle into quiet. He trusts treacherous appearances.

He spoke of the St. Helena manuscript, a copy of which he showed me, with his own marginal notes upon every page. He thinks it was written by the Abbé de Pradt. I objected that it was in that case an imposture, which I was willing to believe the Abbé, who was an Archbishop, too honest a man to practise, and too prudent a man to hazard. "As to the prudence," said Dumouriez, "il ne s'en vantera pas, that is, of the imposture, and as to the honesty, est-ce que Talleyrand n'a pas aussi été évêque?" He added, that Benjamin Constant had also been suspected to be the author of the manuscript, but it was not his manner, and, besides, Benjamin Constant was an honest man. Another conjecture was, that it had been written by Las Cases, upon materials furnished by Bonaparte, in which case, he said, it would be genuine. Las Cases, he said, was, he believed, no longer with him, but was now at the Cape of Good Hope, and if he wrote it, his object was to prepare the way for obtaining leave to return to France himself. There was, he added, some truth in the book, and " de l'esprit;" it was characteristic of the man, of the age, and of the French nation. It was a sort of imitation of Rousseau's Confessions, but there was a style of "mauvaise plaisanterie" and of "persiflage" in it which was not natural to Bonaparte, and there were things in it which he would not have said of himself. It did not represent him favorably to the world.

I thought it curious to hear this observation from Dumouriez, who has published three volumes of Memoirs of his own life, of which the general opinion has been that they by no means give a favorable representation of him. He admitted that the manuscript was in sentiment and character very much like the account in Warden's Letters from St. Helena.

Changing the subject, he said he had read with much pleasure the speech of Mr. Monroe at his inauguration, and that he had been slightly acquainted with Mr. Monroe when he was here as Minister from the United States, having dined in company with him twice. He spoke likewise of the contest between Spain and Portugal concerning the invasion of the Buenos Ayres territory. He said that it was on the part of the Government at Rio Janeiro the greatest folly that ever was committed. For they had three provinces adjoining those they had invaded, which were in a state of the most perfect preparation for insurrection themselves. The insurgents of the Spanish Colonies had hitherto avoided giving them encouragement, because they did not wish to quarrel with the Government of Brazil, but now they will let loose their missionaries, and the insurrection will spread like wild-fire through those provinces. There was a Capitainerie de Saint Paul, in which all the good-for-nothing outcasts of all the world, the very refuse of mankind, were congregated together; another, of St. Vincent, which was no better; and a third, which would join them for anything mischievous and pernicious.

I said I thought the allied powers by their mediation would very easily settle the question as between Spain and Portugal, but I believed they would not find it so easy to arrange matters between the insurgents and Spain. It would be no trifling task for the allies to mediate the South Americans into submission. He said it would be impossible. "But your Government," he added, "will have great trouble to avoid getting embroiled in that affair—vous aurez quelques pages à écrire sur ce sujet là." I said that was very likely, but the course of the American Government in relation to it was very plain— absolute neutrality. I mentioned the Marquis d'Osmond, the French Ambassador, to him; but he had very evidently no acquaintance with him, and spoke of him with great reserve. He said Prince Esterhazy was going to take the Duke of Orleans's place at Richmond, and that, like all the Austrian Ambassadors he had ever known, his hope of Paradise was to go as Ambassador to Paris. The Princess wanted to go still more—"c'est un enfant;" and here she cries her eyes out with ennui. The old General came out with me to his gate, and bade me farewell, with a compliment in the French style.

29th. Visit this morning from Jeremy Bentham, on occasion of some correspondence he has had with Mr. Madison, the late President of the United States, to whom Bentham, in the year 1811, made a proposal to prepare for the use of the United States, or any one of them, a Digest of the Common Law, to embrace in a very small compass the whole system of legislation. Mr. Madison answered the letter last summer—of course, though with very obliging expressions of acknowledgment and regret, declining the proposal. Last evening I found on the table a note from Mr. Koe to Smith, mentioning that Mr. Bentham would call here this morning, and there were copies of Mr. Madison's letter to him, and of a message from Governor Snyder to the Legislature of Pennsylvania, respecting Mr. Bentham's proposal. Mr. Bentham came this morning, but told me his only object now was to arrange a time for seeing me again. He engaged me to dine with him next Tuesday. He said he wished to have much conversation with me, and particularly concerning family relations of my own. I did not understand what he meant by this. He left me the pamphlet containing his letter of 1811 to President Madison, and promised me the second part of his Chrestomathia, which I have not been able to procure at the bookseller's. Mr. Bentham is a man of seventy, somewhat eccentric in his deportment, but of great ingenuity and benevolence. He told me that he was a radical reformist, and should in a few days publish a book on the subject. Sir Francis Burdett's motion for reform, he said, would not be brought forward until some days after the publication of his book, which was written for Sir Francis and at his request. He said, also, that Mayor Cartwright wished to call upon me, and asked if I should be willing to see him. I said I should receive him with much pleasure.

30th. W. T. Franklin is now preparing for publication an octavo edition of Dr. Franklin's correspondence, the quarto edition of the volume published last December being already exhausted. The first volume, containing the Memoirs of the Doctor's Life, written by himself, lingers. The connected Memoirs, written by the Doctor himself, come only to the year 1757; but there are two subsequent tracts, one of which contains a full account of the publication of Governor Hutchinson's letters. Franklin mentioned to me the publication, in four volumes, by Duane, who, he said, had offered him five hundred copies of it in exchange for a certain portion of the work published here. But by Duane's having five hundred copies of his book to dispose of, it probably did not meet with a ready sale. He had published a number of public letters, to which it did not appear how he obtained access, and some which ought not to have been published at all. He (Franklin) had not thought himself authorized to publish any of the joint letters of the Plenipotentiaries of the Peace of 1783.

I observed that there were several letters in his volume, and particularly one containing expressions concerning the King, which I should have thought it dangerous to publish in this country even now.

He said he had been accused of having sold the Doctor's papers to the British Government. If he had suppressed any of the passages like that to which I alluded, it would have been attributed to the like unworthy motives. He had, therefore, resolved to publish the whole, be the consequences what they might. He did not suppose the Government would take notice of those passages, but he expected to be violently attacked for them in the Quarterly Review. He had first offered the work to Murray, the publisher of the Quarterly Review; but he, after having the manuscript several days, had returned it, and declined having anything to do with the publication. He said the octavo edition now publishing would contain considerable new matter, and, among the rest, showed me the proof-sheet, upon which there were three letters from the Doctor to my father, dated in October, 1781. I asked Franklin if he knew anything now of the Hartley family, or of Caleb Whitefoord. They are all dead; and of the Hartleys he knew nothing more. Whitefoord, he says, married and left two children. Franklin himself, whom I had not seen for more than twenty years, has grown fat, and his resemblance to his grandfather has greatly increased.

I had received last evening a note from W. Hamilton, the Under-Secretary of State, asking me to call and give him some explanations about the request for the free exportation of Hughes's baggage. I went to the Foreign Office this day at four o'clock, and waited, after sending in my name, about an hour in the antechamber. Three gentlemen were successively shown into the same room, and waited with me. One of them, who appeared to have been often in the room before, said he called it the School of Patience. I became at last weary of the school, and spoke to one of the messengers, who told me that Mr. Hamilton was very much engaged with Lord Castlereagh. I desired him then to go and tell Mr. Hamilton that, having called there at his request, and waited an hour, I would thank him to send me word when he could see me. This message immediately procured me an audience from Hamilton, which was, however, short. I explained to him the circumstances relating to Hughes's baggage, and he immediately wrote a note to the Treasury, requesting the order for its exportation duty free. I then mentioned to him the two notes I had lately sent to Lord Castlereagh. He said the answer to that upon the fisheries would be sent to me in two or three days. The other, relating to Crosby, was referred to the law officers of the Crown. I told him I had some other papers of the case, which might perhaps be properly referred to the same officers, particularly a legal argument. He said there was a great difficulty in admitting a whole nation, eight millions of foreigners, to all the privileges of British subjects without having any claim upon their allegiance.

I said that so far as it might be prospective, and an affair of compact, the difficulty would be reciprocal, and not more arduous to be got over on one side than on the other. The practical inconvenience, I believed, would be very trifling on either side. The mere privilege of holding lands would never, in the present condition of the world, have consequences important to either Government, and there was something very harsh in stripping individuals of their estates on the mere ground of alienage.

He said he thought the best principle would be, that the two nations should be placed on the same footing in relation to each other as any other nations. But in Crosby's case, I said, the question was not how the law ought to be, but how the law is. Mr. Reeves in his pamphlets, and Mr. Emmett in his argument, consider the law as decidedly on Crosby's side. The highest Court of Judicature in the island of Jamaica had decided otherwise. The late war had prevented Crosby from prosecuting his appeal before the King in Council, and perhaps all that was necessary for him would be to restore him to his law. Hamilton said he wished to have further conversation with me on the subject, but he heard Lord Castlereagh's bell. He would come back to me in a minute. I told him I would not detain him longer now, but postpone the further conversation to a future day. I followed him out of the office, and found Lord Castlereagh had just stepped into his carriage to go home. He apologized for not alighting, on account of his lameness, and asked me to call upon him at half-past eleven on Saturday morning, which I promised.

May 2d. My brother had remitted to me a bill of exchange, drawn by Jonathan Ogden, at New York, upon Bolton and Ogden, at Liverpool, payable in London. The bill was accepted 28th February, payable by Joseph Denison & Co., No. 106 Fenchurch Street. The bill was at sixty days' sight, and payable this day. I took it to Denison's, and there was again referred to Hoare & Barnett, bankers, No. 162 Lombard Street. Of all the insolence I ever experienced, there is nothing equal to the insolence of counting-house clerks. One of these fellows treated me with so much impertinence, refusing to pay me in the description of bills that I wanted, and telling me, in a tone of superciliousness, that I must go to the bank, that I lost my temper. In his pursy pomposity he had paid me two pounds ten short of my bill. I threw his papers back in his face, and told him to give me my bill again. He refused, and was attempting to force back upon me the bills I had refused, when a person, apparently a partner of the house, or a superior clerk, took them back and gave me the bills I had asked for. I obtained my object, but left the place mortified and vexed with myself at having been irritated to intemperance by a banker's clerk.

To get rid of my own reflections, I walked my rounds, and purchased Todd's Milton and other books. I came home, and found Mr. Joy at the office; a small packet for Mr. Harris from the Marquis d'Osmond, and a note from Sir John Coxe Hippisley, Bart., a member of Parliament, with a folio printed volume, a report of a committee of the House of Commons, of which he was chairman, upon the regulation of Roman Catholic subjects in foreign States. I took the packet for Mr. Harris to his lodgings, and went and dined and spent the evening at Mr. J. C. Villiers's. The company were the Duke and Duchess of Wellington, the Earl of Westmorland, the Marquis and Marchioness of Worcester, Mr. Wellesley Pole, Sir Sidney and Lady Beckwith, General Alava, the Spanish Minister to the Netherlands, Lady Burghersh, Sir Colin Campbell, Mr. and Mrs. Patterson, and Miss Caton. After dinner Sir William Scott came in, and in the evening there was a numerous party. I had much conversation with Lord Westmorland, Sir William Scott, Mr. Villiers, Mr. Charles Arbuthnot, and Miss Caton, between whom and Lady Worcester I was seated at table. Mr. Villiers appears to be a man of literary taste and scientific acquisitions, of liberal principles and honorable sentiments. Sir William Scott, the celebrated Judge of the Admiralty and Ecclesiastical Court, is a person of great urbanity of manners and playful wit. I asked him what was the news from his Castle of Indolence, which he had

told me his Court had become since the peace. He said the
ladies now gave him some occupation. He had still enough
to do with the weaker vessels. He has now a question before
him to decide, upon the competency of Lord Cochrane to give
testimony as a witness. He said it was a new question, and
promised to send me word when he gives the judgment.

3d. In Hyde Park, I met Count Fernan Nuñez, who stopped
his curricle and spoke to me. He told me he had had his
audience to take leave of the Prince Regent yesterday, and
was no longer Ambassador here. He should proceed for Paris
to-morrow morning. He assured me that I should be "très-
content" with Onis, and that our affairs with Spain should be
settled entirely to our satisfaction ; that we should have what
we wanted, and secured to us in the most effectual manner.
" Seulement—de l'autre côté—les voisins." He himself had
lately received instructions upon the subject, and was glad to
let me know it before my return to America. Spain was
resolved to give us full and entire satisfaction. It might not
suit at all the views of some others, but I might depend upon
it, Spain was firmly resolved to settle all affairs amicably with
us. There was much nodding of the head, much significance
of look, and much show of mysterious meaning in all this, but
nothing specific or precise. What he meant me to understand
him as saying was, that Spain would cede to us the Floridas,
although England was taking all possible pains to prevent it,
but that we must satisfy Spain about the South American
insurgents. Neither the time nor place would admit of my
asking further explanations, and it was evident he meant to
raise expectations in me without saying anything explicit. I
answered him in general terms, with strong assurances of our
earnest desire to settle everything amicably with Spain, with
my thanks for his communication, the great pleasure which I
took in learning from him that the policy of Spain towards the
United States was thus decidedly pacific and friendly, and my
best wishes that he might have a prosperous negotiation at
Paris.

I attended the dinner at the Royal Academy, Somerset
House, on the opening of the annual exhibition. It was much

like the same party last year. The only person of the royal
family present was the Duke of Cumberland. The Marquis
d'Osmond, Count Palmella, Mr. Bourke, Jouffroy, and myself
were the only persons of the Diplomatic Corps there. As
usual, there was a large assemblage of noblemen, gentlemen,
and distinguished artists. The toasts and songs after dinner
were like those of last year, but no speech-making. The foreign Ambassadors and Ministers were not separately toasted.
The Earl of Aberdeen, President of the Society of Antiquaries,
in returning thanks, added a very few words in praise of the
appearance of the exhibition. Altogether, the dinner was dull,
and there was an air of "tristesse" about everything. About
nine o'clock the company rose from table, and I walked home.

5th. At half-past eleven this morning I called upon Lord
Castlereagh, according to appointment. I gave him a copy of
the letter from the President to the Prince Regent, announcing
my recall from this mission. Lord Castlereagh was upon this
occasion as civil and obliging as I could expect or desire. He
congratulated me upon my appointment to the office of Secretary
of State at home, and at the same time expressed his regret
that it would necessarily remove me from this mission. The
compliments, of course, from a European Minister of State, are
but so far significant that they show there is no cause of personal complaint against the person to whom they are addressed.
I explained to Lord Castlereagh the reason why an immediate
appointment had not been made of a person to take my place
at this Court, the President not having known whether I
should accept the new office assigned to me at home; but I
assured him that a new Minister to this Court would be
appointed as soon as circumstances would admit, and told him
I was instructed in the strongest manner to declare the new
President, Mr. Monroe's, earnest and anxious desire to cultivate
the most friendly and harmonious intercourse with Great Britain.

He said that the same and an equally earnest disposition and
desire existed in this country to cultivate and improve the
friendly relations with the United States, as an earnest of which
he should in the course of two or three days send me a note in
answer to that which I had addressed to him a few days since

in relation to the fisheries. He asked me if I was informed of
the state of the negotiation upon the subject in America. I told
him I had received copies of the correspondence concerning it
which had passed between Mr. Monroe and Mr. Bagot. He
then recapitulated the substance of it, and said that Mr. Bagot
had been authorized in July last to offer a certain extent of
coast, being part of the British territories in North America,
for the accommodation of the American fishermen, and if that
should be declined, to offer another portion, and eventually both
of them. Neither of the propositions had, however, been found
acceptable; but in February Mr. Monroe had suggested that
the President would be prepared to make a proposition on his
part, which he hoped would conciliate the views and interests
of both parties. Mr. Bagot was not then authorized to receive
this proposition, but the authority to that effect had now been
sent to him. He had been empowered at the commencement
of the negotiation to suspend the orders to the British naval
commander on the station to prevent the American fishermen
from frequenting the British coast, and had accordingly written
to him to suspend it. After the failure of his propositions, he
had notified the naval commander that the suspension of the
order was to cease, and the order was accordingly now in force.
But as the President, having now a full knowledge of the views
of this Government, had intimated the disposition to make a
proposal which would conciliate the interests of both parties,
and as a signal proof of the desire of the British Government
to cultivate the most friendly relations with the administration
of the new President, they had determined to renew the suspension of the order to the Admiral during the present season,
and it would be immediately sent out. He read me the note
to that effect, which he said he should be authorized to send
me in the course of two or three days. He said he would take
the commands of the Prince Regent as to the time for the
delivery of my letter of recall.

I then mentioned my note to him upon Crosby's case, and
told him I had some other papers besides those I had sent
him concerning it, among the rest a written opinion of Mr.
Emmett, a person known to him perhaps under unfortunate

circumstances, but now one of the most eminent lawyers at the bar in the United States.

He said, Yes, he had known him, and he was one of the most eloquent men he ever had known.

I told him that the argument in the opinion was in perfect coincidence with that in Mr. Reeves's pamphlets, although written before they were published, and this agreement between two lawyers so entirely different from each other in all their political opinions formed of itself a strong presumption in favor of the soundness of their conclusions. I observed that I thought the principle would be of great importance by its influence upon the intercourse between the two nations, and mentioned again the hardship of Crosby's case, who, after having been prevented by the war from entering his appeal to the King in Council from the decision of the Court in Jamaica within the limited term of one year, had also been disappointed in the hope that the principle would have been arranged at the negotiation for the peace. Perhaps all that would be necessary for his case would be to restore to him the right of entering his appeal.

Lord Castlereagh said that could not be done without an Act of Parliament. I said I thought there was a discretionary power in the Court of Appeal to extend the time within which appeals are admitted. He replied that in Admiralty cases they had, because, being governed by the rules of the Law of Nations, they were brought within the reach of the King's prerogative. But in cases depending upon the Municipal Laws there was no such power. He said he had not seen my note upon the subject, and supposed Mr. Hamilton upon receiving it, seeing that it must be referred to the law officers of the Crown, had sent it immediately to them. He likewise told me that there would be sent to Mr. Bagot, to be communicated to the American Government, a full statement of all the disorders and inconveniences which had been experienced in consequence of the fishing rights of Americans in the British jurisdiction in North America, to show that it was not any commercial jealousy, or any wish to disturb our people in the enjoyment of their fisheries, that induced the British Government to adhere to this object, but the absolute necessity of protecting their own territorial authority.

6th. I was obliged to leave him (G. Joy) at St. Paul's Church-yard, to go and dine with Mr. Jeremy Bentham, in Queen Square Place, Westminster, St. James's Park, at the back of which his house stands; and I walked with him an hour, till dinner-time. The company were, Mr. and Mrs. Koe, who live with him, Mr. George Ensor, a Scotchman, and Mr. William Mill, an Irishman, both authors, and a boy of twelve or thirteen, whom Mr. Bentham is educating. Bentham had engaged to come for me at five o'clock, to my lodgings, which he did. Just before dinner he took me into his library, and there asked me if I would dine with him there and have a tête-à-tête conversation after dinner with him next Sunday, to which I readily agreed. He had told me that he had something to say to me about my own family, and now explained his meaning by showing me a letter from* Robert Bentham, of Charleston, South Carolina, to Samuel Bentham, Civil Architect, Navy Office, London, Jeremy's brother, containing a number of family enquiries. In this letter Robert Bentham asserts that his father, who had emigrated from England to South Carolina in 1760, had there married a young lady by the name of Mary Hardy, a cousin of his Excellency John Adams, former President of the United States. I think this must be a mistake, never having heard that my father had any relations by the name of Hardy. Mr. Bentham allows me to take a copy of the letter. There was much conversation at dinner, and many things were said of which I should have been desirous of taking note, but such is now the pressure of my occupation that the time necessary for a daily record of them absolutely fails. I abandon the attempt in despair.

7th. In the evening I attended the debate in the House of Commons, and heard a great variety of speakers on several subjects in succession. First on some motion of Mr. Grenfell's concerning the Bank. The speakers, beside him, were Mr. Vansittart, Chancellor of the Exchequer, Mr. Ponsonby, Sir John Newport, and Mr. Manning. Then a motion for a bill to shorten the duration of elections, upon which Mr. C. Wynn and Mr. W. Smith spoke. Next a desultory conversation upon the Army estimates, by Lord Palmerston, Mr. J. P. Grant,

Messrs. Goulburn, Brougham, Robinson, Vansittart, and Ponsonby; and lastly, a motion by Sir James Mackintosh, upon a horrible incident which occurred last week.

An Irishman by the name of Ryan was executed for a highway robbery. A few days before his execution, his wife, Mary Ryan, had been taken in an attempt to effect his escape from prison. For this offence she was put to the bar, tried, convicted, and sentenced to two months' imprisonment, on the very day of, and within two hours after, the execution of her husband. Sir James Mackintosh's motion was only for a return to the House, from the Home Department, of the dates of the man's execution and of the woman's trial; but his object was to pass a vehement censure upon the City Magistrates for having tried the woman at all. The motion was feebly resisted by Mr. H. Addington, by Alderman Atkins, who was one of the trying Magistrates, and by Mr. B. Bathurst. Some explanations were given, and some apologetic defence of the Magistrates was offered. It appeared that the Prince Regent, upon being made acquainted with the circumstances, had granted to the woman a pardon. Sir Samuel Romilly and Mr. Martin supported the motion. Lord Castlereagh expressed his hopes that, after the explanations which had been given, it would be withdrawn. Sir James Mackintosh replied with great feeling and eloquence, insisting upon the motion, with which he said the House should dispose as they pleased, but upon which he felt it to be his duty to take their sense. Lord Castlereagh then said that upon so serious a subject he could not divide the House, and should therefore support the motion, which then passed without a dissenting voice.

There was something curious in this case, inasmuch as it presented the identical conflict of Law and Morality which had happened in the case of Lavalette and his wife, so that in disapproving the trial of Mary Ryan there was a sort of oblique stigma cast upon the severity with which Madame Lavalette was treated in France. There was also a discussion upon the second reading of Mr. D. Gilbert's bill for abolishing the offices of the Chief Justices in Eyre, upon which the speakers were Sir John Newport, Messrs. Ponsonby, Grant, Brougham, Lord

Milton, and Mr. Huskisson, and Tierney. Between the two last there was some sharp debating, which became at last strongly personal. Tierney was very severe upon the pompous promises and paltry performance of the Finance Committee, and Huskisson retorted that Tierney, with all his professions of ardent passion for reform and the abolition of sinecures, had no sooner found that they were to be really effected than he had shown his dissatisfaction at the event. Tierney, with much warmth, called upon Huskisson for his proofs of this charge, and Huskisson alleged his having attended only once at the meetings of the Finance Committee. Tierney said he left the House to judge what credit was due to Huskisson's assertion. Mr. Sharp and Mr. W. Lyttleton came under the gallery and sat some time with me.

9th. After dinner I attended the debate in the House of Commons upon what they call the Catholic Question, one of the subjects which are discussed once every two or three years in Parliament. This time it was upon a motion of Mr. Grattan's, and great expectations were entertained of the eloquence which would be displayed on both sides. It is a question upon which the members of the administration itself are divided in opinion, Lord Castlereagh and Mr. Canning being in favor of the Catholic claims, while other members of the Government are decidedly against them. Mr. Grattan had opened the debate with a short speech, reserving himself for the reply. When I entered the House, Mr. Leslie Foster was speaking against the motion. The other speakers on the same side were Mr. Yorke, Sir John Cox Hippisley, Mr. Webber, member for Dublin, Mr. Bragge Bathurst, and Mr. Peel. On the other side were Sir Henry Parnell, Mr. William Elliot, Lord Castlereagh, Mr. Canning, and Mr. Grattan. The motion was, nevertheless, so weakly defended that its supporters appeared almost as earnest to lose the question as their opponents were to defeat it. Castlereagh's speech was, in substance, much the best that was made on the Catholic side. He speaks with tolerable fluency, but is greatly deficient in precision. His sentences are never grammatical or congruent. They begin with a fire and end with a waterfall. If his speeches were taken down word for word as they are delivered, they would make nonsense; and this is the reason why the opposition have, or affect, so much contempt for his understanding. But although his sentences are ill constructed, so that, like Gonzales's Commonwealth, their latter end forgets their beginning, yet they generally do make out to convey an idea to the mind of the hearers, and that idea is often strong enough to make an impression. The cause of the Catholics, in this case, was so evidently right, the arguments in their favor so obvious and so clear, and the subject, from the frequent discussions which it has undergone, was so familiar to all present, that it was difficult to suppose any one could be at a loss what to say. Lord Castlereagh was at no loss, but he spoke like a man not seriously earnest in his own argument— like a man pleading for his own consistency rather than for his cause. The same remark applies to Canning, whose language is good, and who is sometimes the most eloquent man in the House. It was but two nights since he had been called to defend himself for what they call here a job—a useless and extravagant Embassy to Lisbon, where there was no Court; the Queen and Regent being in Brazil—a case in itself utterly indefensible, but in the debate upon which, he spoke so powerfully that he was universally admitted to have obtained a triumph over his adversaries. But his wits were then sharpened by his personal interest and feeling. This evening he was cold and tame—spoke very shortly, and with very little apparent impression or effect. Mr. William Elliot came off still more haltingly. This gentleman is a Right Honorable, and a sort of half Ministerialist, with pretensions to independence. He is a man of fortune, and one of the Borough-mongers. He appeared to enjoy great consideration in the House, and was much cheered when he rose to speak. He began boldly and freely enough, and seemed so much in earnest, that I was in hopes of hearing at last a real champion for the Catholics. But in the course of five minutes he lost the thread of his argument, became confused and bewildered, stood several minutes silent to recover his thoughts, then resumed an incoherent discourse, of which it was impossible to make sense or reason. The more he failed, the louder and the more generally the House cheered

him, and whenever he could get out a few words they listened
to him with the utmost politeness and attention. He hobbled
along about a quarter of an hour—uttering three or four sentences, and stopping alternately two or three minutes at a time,
to rally his reflections. At last he gave it up, and said he would
not trouble the House any longer.

The most eloquent speech of the evening, and one of the
most eloquent that I ever heard, was that of Mr. Peel,[1] Chief
Secretary to the Lord Lieutenant of Ireland, a subordinate
office in the Ministry, of which Peel is the ablest member. He
is quite a young man, but already in high repute, and likely to
become the most distinguished personage in the kingdom. His
speech was against the Catholics, and had the effect to make
the worse appear the better reason. It far more than outweighed
all the speeches in their favor. It was heard with the most
undivided attention, and at its close was long and loudly cheered
from every part of the House. Its style and manner were
altogether temperate, but persuasive; energetic, but without
vehemence; the language elegant and plain, but moderately
ornamented; the sentiments so liberal that they almost dis-
guised the illiberality of the cause. Its effect upon the House
was evident, and I perceived it no less by the anguish of two
or three Roman Catholic clergymen who were sitting beside
me under the gallery.

Mr. Webber, the member from Dublin, also made a long and
passionate speech against the motion, but scarcely a word of it
was to be heard, and his voice was finally drowned by the calls
for the question from every part of the House. Mr. Grattan,
in his reply, was greeted by the House much in the same manner. Little of what he said was heard, and less still was worth
hearing. His manner was disgustingly fantastical and affected,
and his argument weak and inefficient. He, too, was at last
put down by the coughing and impatient calls for the question.
Mr. Canning came over and sat by me in conversation about
half an hour. The question was taken at two in the morning,
when we came away. The decision was against the motion
—two hundred and forty-six and two hundred and twenty-two.

[1] Afterwards Sir Robert Peel.

In the year 1812 they lost the question by a majority of only four.

13th. We breakfasted early, and I went with Smith to the Admiralty Court at Doctors' Commons, to hear the judgment of Sir William Scott with regard to the admissibility of Lord Cochrane's affidavit. Sir William had promised me at Mr. Villiers's to give me notice when the decision should be delivered, and last Saturday, Mr. Slade, a Proctor of the Court, called while I was out, and left a note informing me that it would be this morning at ten o'clock. We went first to Mr. Slade's office, and he accompanied us to the Court. The Judge read his decision, which was in favor of the admission of Lord Cochrane's affidavit. It was upon a question of prize money, arising from the affair of the Basque Roads. An affidavit of Lord Cochrane's was material to the issue, and, having been tendered, its admission was opposed by the King's Advocate-General, Sir Christopher Robinson, who was engaged on the other side. The objection was, that Lord Cochrane, having been judicially convicted of a fraud upon the Stock Exchange, was incompetent to give testimony in any Court of Justice whatsoever. The Judge, after observing that this question came only incidentally before his Court, that it was a question strictly of the law of England, that it ought properly to be settled by the Courts of Common Law, that his Court was scarcely bound to know anything of the peculiar law of England, and that his decision would be of no authority in the Common Law Courts, proceeded to lay down the rule of his judgment, that he was bound to adhere to prior decisions, and could not go a hair's-breadth beyond them. He then took a historical review of the doctrine of incapacitation to give testimony, resulting from a judicial conviction of ignominious offences. The principle of the elementary books was, that persons convicted of the "crimen falsi" were incompetent to give testimony; but what was the "crimen falsi"? He then cited the definitions given by Lord Coke, Hale, Hawkins, and Blackstone, all of which he found were loose and unsatisfactory. He inclined to think it always implied falsehood accompanied by the sanction of an oath. He next traced the series of decisions from the time when the incapacity was held to be derived from the nature of the punishment, the pillory, until it was finally determined to proceed from the nature not of the punishment, but of the crime. He finally stated that he had found no case which would warrant him in rejecting the affidavit of Lord Cochrane, which he should therefore admit, and if his judgment was erroneous it might be corrected elsewhere.

Mr. Slade had told me that it was expected the decision would have been the other way. Sir William's extreme caution, almost to disqualify his own decree, gave him very much the appearance of pronouncing it with reluctance. Nor did he forbear to cast out some insinuations that Lord Cochrane ought not to have offered his affidavit, but to have proceeded in a form which would not have required it. Even after the affidavit was admitted, a subsequent question was made, by which it was rendered entirely nugatory. The object of Lord Cochrane's affidavit was to enable him to amend his libel, in which a material fact had been misstated by the Advocate's clerk who drew it up. The motion upon the affidavit was for leave to amend the libel. This was again objected to, and the question was argued for Lord Gambier, Lord Cochrane's adverse party, by Sir Christopher Robinson and Dr. William Adams, our old associate at Ghent, and for Lord Cochrane by Dr. Lushington, whom Mr. Slade mentioned to me as the most eloquent advocate at the bar, and by another.

The Judge decided that the libel should not be amended, because the other party had already answered it as first drawn, and could not be put to answer again, and because Lord Cochrane was bound to know before the answer was given what his own libel contained. The affidavit has been admitted, said the Judge, "valeat quantum valere potest;" but without the amendment of the libel I did not see how it could be at all available. We left the Court sitting about noon, and returned home.

After dinner I went and heard the debates in the House of Commons. The Saxon Minister, Baron Just, came in while I was there. They were upon the Army estimates, a dull subject for an auditory. Lord Castlereagh came under the gallery and sat with me. He asked me to name a day when Mrs.

Adams and I would dine with him and Lady Castlereagh. I mentioned Friday, the 23d. Mr. Croker, the Secretary of the Admiralty, likewise came and spoke to me. He was courteous in his compliments, and hoped our countries would continue long in cordial friendship with each other, as they ought never to have any differences other than as brothers. Croker's real sentiments with regard to America are so well known, and he knows they are so well known, that I set down his kind words to me neither to the account of politeness nor of hypocrisy, but simply to that of impudence, for which he is highly renowned.

14th. The time appointed for my attendance at Carlton House was half-past two o'clock, at which time I was there. I found there Mr. Chester, the Assistant Master of the Ceremonies, and the Swedish Minister, Baron Rehausen. Half an hour later, Lord Castlereagh came, and we waited then an hour longer before it was announced to us that the Prince Regent was ready. Lord Castlereagh first went in with Baron Rehausen, who took leave upon a permission of absence. He is going to Sweden upon that profession, but does not expect to come back again. While he was with the Prince, Chester remarked, with a smile, that it was a singular kind of life that the Regent led—that we had waited so long because he had not risen when we came, and that he was scarcely ever out of his bed till three in the afternoon. Chester also enquired of me in what manner I should choose to receive the usual present given to foreign Ministers on the termination of their missions, which, he said, was for Ambassadors one thousand pounds, and for Ministers of the second order, five hundred. I told him that by the Constitution of the United States no person in their service was permitted to accept a present from any foreign sovereign, and I must therefore decline any one that might be offered me here. He said that, having had some idea of the existence of such a regulation in America, he had made enquiries at the office how the fact had been in the cases of former American Ministers, and had found the present had been in some instances accepted, and in others declined. I told him I supposed the cases of acceptance were prior to the

Constitutional prohibition; that I must for my part decline it, and would explain to Lord Castlereagh my motives for so doing. He acquiesced in this with apparent cheerfulness, though probably not without reluctance.

The prohibition of the Constitution of the United States in this case has my hearty approbation, and I wish it may be inflexibly adhered to hereafter. The usage itself, as practised by all European Governments, is, in my judgment, absurd, indelicate, with at least very strong tendencies to corruption. On the part of the United States there is a peculiar reason for prohibiting their servants from taking such gifts, because, as they never make presents to the Ministers of foreign powers who have been accredited to them, there is not even the plea of reciprocity to allege for allowing it. For American Ministers to be receiving gifts from foreign powers whose diplomatic agents in America never receive anything in return, would exhibit them rather as beggars receiving alms from opulent princes, than as the independent representatives of a high-minded and virtuous republic. The governments of Europe are themselves becoming ashamed of this despicable custom. Count Romanzoff, since his resignation as Chancellor of the Russian Empire, has made up a fund from the value of all the presents of this kind that he had ever received, and made an appropriation of the whole, together with an additional sum from his own property, to the public service of the State, in aid of the pensions granted to invalid and wounded soldiers. I have a strong impression that the peculiar propriety of this patriotic sacrifice was suggested to him by the example of the principle established by this regulation in the Constitution of the United States. Lord Castlereagh, in the course of his negotiations at the Vienna Congress, and at Paris, received twenty-four snuff-boxes, each worth one thousand pounds sterling, besides other articles equally costly; but even there they at least found it necessary to put a check upon this market of snuff-boxes, and dispensed with the presents in concluding some of the treaties. The practice here is to give money—which has not even the palliation of sentimentality to plead in its favor; but as by the standing usage ten per cent.

from the Minister's present is deducted as a douceur to the Master of the Ceremonies, Mr. Chester was probably not so fully convinced of the propriety of the American principles as I was.

Immediately after Rehausen came out from the Prince's cabinet, I went in, accompanied by Lord Castlereagh, and delivered the letter of recall. At the same time I told him I was especially instructed by the President of the United States to assure his Royal Highness of the earnestness of his desire that the relations between the two countries, and the intercourse between the Governments, should continue upon the most friendly terms. I was further ordered to say that an uncertainty in the President's mind whether I should immediately return to the United States was the only cause which had deferred the appointment of a Minister to succeed me at this Court, and that such an appointment would be made with as little delay as possible.

The Prince returned the assurances of his disposition to continue and promote the harmony between the two nations, which, he said, was required by the true interests of both. There was no formality in the discourse on either side, and the generalities of friendly assurances were much alike, and estimated at their real value, on both sides. The Prince immediately passed to conversation upon other topics, and enquired who were the persons that would compose Mr. Monroe's Cabinet. I mentioned the names of the Secretaries of the Treasury, of War, and of the Navy. He did not know either of them, but spoke in handsome terms, as he had done at my first presentation to him, of Mr. Thomas Pinckney and of Mr. King. He said Mrs. Patterson had told him that Mr. Pinckney was now a General in the army. He asked also various questions respecting the organization of the American Government, and made his remarks upon it, which were neither profound, ingenious, nor complacent.

The character of this person is a composition of obtundity and of frivolity. He is a Falstaff without the wit, and a Prince Henry without the compunctions. His only talent is that of mimicry, which he exercises without regard to dignity or decorum, to the fitness of his own character, or to the feelings of others. His supreme delight is to expose persons dependent upon him to ridicule, and to enjoy their mortification. He seemed not to comprehend how it was possible to manage a Government where the members of the executive Government could not sit as members of the Legislature, and he thought the mode of communication between the Legislative and Executive Departments, by the means of Committees, was a sucking of brains on both sides, which must encumber all public business and increase all its difficulties. He spoke, however, in perfect good humor, and dismissed me as graciously as he had received me.

It was almost five o'clock when I returned home. There was yet the Queen, of whom, according to the etiquette, I was to ask a private audience to take leave; but, as she is much out of health, I desired Mr. Chester to take measures for having it communicated to her Majesty that I should be earnestly desirous of the honor of a private audience, to pay my respects in person to her upon my departure; but that if it should put her to any trouble or inconvenience I should much rather make the sacrifice of my own gratification, and would pray her to dispense with the formality of an audience, which I might be entitled to claim.

15th. At nine o'clock this morning I called upon Mr. Bentham, and took a walk of three hours with him before breakfast. We walked in a part of the town where I had not before been. We went and viewed the spot where Ranelagh had formerly stood. It was once a place of highly fashionable resort in the summer season, but was gradually deserted, and at last totally broken up. I was there in the zenith of its fashion, a few days after I was married, in 1797. I have not seen the place since then till this day. " Quantum mutatus ab illo." Instead of the splendid company, the song, the dance, the festive banquet, the walls are down and removed, the spot is covered with grass, and the cattle are feeding upon it. There is not even a window for the fox to look out at—nothing but furrows on the ground, to show the rotunda upon which the building stood. It might serve as an illustration of Spenser's

Canto of Mutability. We also went and viewed the outside of the hospital at Woolwich, with the garden, the inscriptions, and the statue. It was Ascension-day, and we met one or two charity schools walking in procession with the parish officers.

16th. Called upon Sir James Mackintosh, from whom I had received yesterday a note requesting information concerning the restoration by the American Government of the British vessels seized in the ports of the United States at the commencement of the late war. He wrote the note before he had seen the answer I had written to that of Mr. Sharp. I now told him how the facts were: that the American Government had allowed British subjects six months from the declaration of war to remove their vessels and other effects, considering this an indulgence usually allowed between nations in modern times; that in some instances, where the removal had not been effected in the six months, the liberal spirit of the Government had permitted the removal even after the expiration of the time; that under peculiar circumstances one instance of a seizure had occurred, and in that case, by the formal decision of a judicial tribunal, the vessel was restored. I added that upon this state of facts the American Plenipotentiaries at the negotiation of the Peace at Ghent had been instructed to call upon the British Government to make restitution of the American vessels which, at the breaking out of the war, had been seized in their ports; but this demand had not been successful. The reasons assigned on the British part for rejecting it were—first, that all property afloat was, at the breaking out of a war, lawful prize; and the second, that the United States, by the declaration of war, were the aggressors, and thus had liberated Great Britain from any obligations to restore such property.

Sir James observed that the first of these arguments might perhaps be urged, but the second was ridiculous. It was not the declaration of war that constituted the aggressor; and in all modern negotiations for peace both parties were universally considered as standing upon equal terms.

I said we had not thought either of the arguments well urged, but I had mentioned them to him as those which in point of fact had been urged. The American Plenipotentiaries had pressed the subject as far as it would bear, until they had no alternative but to abandon the demand or break off the negotiation upon it. Then it was of necessity given up. I would show him the notes that had passed between the Plenipotentiaries of both parties relating to this claim, but they were packed up with my other books and papers, to take with me to the United States, and I had no access to them. He thanked me for the information I had given him, and said he should certainly make use of it upon the discussion of his motion.

18th. Morning walk with Mr. Bentham, upon which we had agreed when we parted last Thursday, and we now agreed to walk again next Thursday morning. He takes these walks before breakfasting, and says that his faculties are at that time benumbed into a state of torpidity, from which they are aroused only by a tea breakfast. We walked this morning through his garden into St. James's Park, out at Buckingham gate, by a street behind the Queen's house, to Hyde Park Corner, through Hyde Park to the Kensington Garden gate adjoining the Tyburn Road, through the gardens, out at the opposite gate, then returning through Hyde Park Corner gate, and the entrance of St. James's Park at Constitution Hill. He went with me to Major John Cartwright's, and there left me to go home and breakfast.

Major Cartwright is the great patriotic reformer. I saw his sister, wife, and niece, the two last of whom came in from church while I was with him. Our discourse, being upon political topics, soon drove the ladies away. Major Cartwright is a grave old gentleman of seventy, who has spent forty years of his life in pursuing the shadow of Parliamentary Reform. He appears to be no nearer his object now than he was when he began; but he still adheres to his purpose. Like all such steadfast characters that I have ever known, the Major's perseverance is accompanied by an equal portion of dulness, and therein differs from Mr. Bentham, who, though of nearly the same years, is not so old a reformer, but is much more lively as a social companion. Major Cartwright, however, is a very sensible man, with a high reputation of integrity. He has published a book called "England's Ægis," containing a plan for a national militia, of which he promised to send me a copy.

19th. I went with J. A. Smith and looked at the Courts in Westminster Hall. The Exchequer and Chancery were shut. The Common Pleas were sitting, but just about to adjourn for the day, not engaged upon business of any importance. The Court of King's Bench was so much crowded that no convenient place either for seeing or hearing was to be found. They were arguing upon motions, it being the last day of the term. The hall where the Court sits is so very small that there is scarcely room for the judges, jurors, lawyers, and officers of the Court. It is the same with the other Courts. The gowns and wigs of the judges and lawyers give them a grotesque appearance. The only remarkable incident that occurred while I was there was an indication of the absolute and domineering discipline of the Court, and the servile submission of the Bar.

Mr. Chitty, one of the most eminent counsel at the Bar, and author of several legal treatises in high esteem, was arguing with great temper and moderation a question before the Court, when Lord Ellenborough said, "You have practised a deception upon the Court." Chitty sat down immediately, without uttering a syllable in reply.

From the King's Bench we went into the House of Lords, below the Bar. The Lord Chancellor Eldon was sitting upon the woolsack, and there were six or eight Peers present, coming and going, but the House was in session. We heard the oaths of allegiance and abjuration administered to a number of foreigners, who were to be naturalized, and saw the form of the delivery of several messages from the House of Commons. The same ceremony was repeated for every message. The folding-doors of the House were thrown open, and the Sergeant-at-Arms announced a message from the House of Commons. Four or five members of that House then entered, one of them bearing rolls of parchment. They advanced up to the Bar, while at the same time the Lord Chancellor, quitting the woolsack, and taking his bag in his hand, came down to it.

There he received the parchment rolls from the member of the
Commons who brought them, and who then, with his companions, withdrew, while the Chancellor returned to the woolsack. The folding-doors were then closed, and immediately
afterwards opened again for another message in the same form.
From the Lords I went into the House of Commons, and sat
half an hour under the gallery. They appeared to be expecting
an important debate, and there were an unusual number of
members present for so early an hour, between five and six
o'clock. I soon left the House, to go home to dinner.

20th. I went to the House of Commons, and heard the debate
upon Sir Francis Burdett's motion for the appointment of a committee to consider and report a plan for a reform in the mode
of election for the Commons House of Parliament. It was
with some difficulty that I obtained admission for my son
George. Mr. Patterson came under the gallery. We went in
about eight o'clock, and found Sir Francis drawing towards the
conclusion of his speech, which was temperate and much less
animated than I had expected. He appeared as if overwhelmed
by the majority which he knew there would be against his
motion in that House, and as if the suspension of the Habeas
Corpus Act had been passed purposely for him. The motion
was seconded by Mr. Brand, who made a short speech in support of it, in no wise remarkable. Sir John Nicoll, the King's
Advocate, made a long, dull, and heavy speech against it. This
person has a high reputation for eloquence as an Admiralty
lawyer, but I was much disappointed in him as a Parliamentary
orator. There was no novelty, and very little ingenuity, in the
argument with which he exhausted in an hour and a half the
patience of the House. The calls for the question finally
brought him down upon his seat again. Mr. Curwen, Lord
Cochrane, Sir Samuel Romilly, and Mr. Tierney spoke also in
favor of the motion, and Mr. John William Ward, Mr. Lamb,
and Lord Milton against it. The most vehement and bitterest
speech was made by Lord Cochrane in favor of reform, and
the most splendid and eloquent one against it by Mr. Ward.
Cochrane's consisted of little more than sarcasm and invective. Ward's was in its principal parts prepared, and doubtless

composed beforehand. He was two hours in delivering it, and has certainly no natural fluency. He speaks slow, repeats the greater part of almost every sentence, utters the whole with much hesitation, makes wry faces, and sucks oranges. His speech, however, was as powerful an argument as the cause which he supports could produce. He gave a just and very severe character of the Whigs, or, as they style themselves, the Moderate Reformers in Parliament, who, he observed, were utterly disavowed and contemned by the Radical Reformers without-doors. The real object of the Radical Reformer, he said, was a revolution, the very idea of which was his abhorrence. To prove that revolution was the object of the Radical Reformers, he pulled from his pocket the book published last Saturday by Mr. Jeremy Bentham, called the Catechism of Reform, and read several passages from it, which excited great laughter in the House. He observed that the book having been put into his hands only this morning, he had not had time to read it, and the quotations which he had read were adduced only to show the tendency of the doctrines in the book. He spoke in very respectful terms of Mr. Bentham, both in regard to his abilities and his integrity. But this very book is the boldest and most vehement argument for radical reform that has yet appeared in print. Bentham told me that he had found some difficulty in getting it printed, and was finally obliged to put his name to it, which he had not intended. Mr. Ward could not have chosen his proof better than by quoting this book to show that revolution is the real object of the Radical Reformers. He read particularly one passage, where the author insists that the Reformers ought to be satisfied with nothing less than the *ascendency* of the democratic part of the Constitution. Ward declared himself satisfied with the Constitution as it is. He deprecates all experimental innovation. He is willing to judge of the tree by its fruits. He finds that this Constitution has raised England to greatness and glory; that it has led to the triumphs of her navy and the victories of her armies; that it has raised her to high consideration and influence among the nations of the earth; and so riveted is he to all her institutions that in the system of her elections he

considers Old Sarum as essential as Yorkshire. Sir Samuel
Romilly and Mr. Tierney answered Ward, principally by personal reflections. Ward is what they call a rat. He was formerly a Whig, and has turned Tory. Romilly said no other
answer was necessary to his speech than a reference to his
own speeches in former sessions of Parliament. Romilly complained that it was unfair in Ward to read quotations from
Bentham's book, but he did not show why. I thought them
very much to the purpose. With a high panegyric of Bentham,
Romilly said he regretted exceedingly his having published
that book. Tierney was also sarcastic upon Ward's premedi-
tated speech, and its inconsistency with his speeches in former
times; but he did not answer it. He declared himself in favor
of moderate reform, and of the present motion, though he had
no hopes it would succeed, and he greatly lamented the excesses
of the deluded Radical Reformers, because their effect was to
render all reform impracticable. Sir Francis Burdett made no
reply. The House was cleared for taking the question about
two in the morning, when I came home. The motion was
rejected by a majority of four or five to one.

22d. I took a walk this morning with J. Bentham through
Hyde Park and Kensington Garden, in the course of which I
had much conversation with him upon his political opinions and
views, and upon the situation and prospects of this country. I
mentioned to him the notice taken in the House of Commons
of his Catechism of Reform the evening before last, the quotations and comments of Mr. Ward, and the remark upon it of
Sir Samuel Romilly. Bentham writes in a very peculiar style,
and uses a multitude of words of his own coining. Ward said
it was a sort of lingua franca—no language of itself, but a
compound from various tongues, in which, however, an ap-
proximation of meaning was to be obtained.

Bentham said that was a fair joke, with which he was very
well pleased, but he always took the privilege of coining words
when they were necessary to express his ideas. He was much
obliged to Mr. Ward, both for the respectful manner in which
he had spoken of his personal character, which from him he
had no right to have expected, and for the quotations which he

had read from his book, because that would bring it more immediately into public notice. It was singular that the reference
to the book should have been made from that quarter, which
was totally unexpected to him, while it had not been even mentioned by Sir Francis Burdett, from whom he had expected that
something of it would have been said. But Sir Francis himself was not an efficient Reformer. He was rich. His education had been bad. He was, above all, indolent. There was no
steady reliance to be placed upon him. As to Sir Samuel
Romilly, who was his intimate friend, he (Bentham) knew that
he would not be pleased with the book. Romilly was a Whig,
and the Whigs, as a party, were just as corrupt and just as
averse to reform as their adversaries. I told him with how
much keenness and severity they had been characterized by
Mr. Ward, and he said they deserved it all.

I then remarked to him upon the force with which Mr. Ward
argued that the real object of the Radical Reformers was revolution, and intimated to him my impression that it was so.
And, recurring particularly to the passage of the book where
the Reformers are exhorted to be satisfied with nothing short
of democratic ascendency, I asked him how he could reconcile that even with the sound theory of the British Constitution, which I conceived to be a balance between the monarchical,
aristocratical, and democratical branches, forbidding the ascendency of either of them. I was aware that he had ridiculed the
idea of the balance, by referring his reader for it to " Mother
Goose" or " Mother Blackstone ;" still, it was the theory of
the English Constitution, and how could the ascendency of the
popular part of it be established without subverting the whole ?
He said the ascendency of one part did not necessarily imply
the destruction of the others ; that in regard to religious
affairs, Protestant ascendency was established by law, yet the
Roman Catholic religion was tolerated. As to the ascendency
of one branch of the Government over the others, that existed
in the present state of things, or rather the combination of the
Crown and the aristocracy overpowered the democracy to
such a degree that the popular check upon them was a mere
name. The liberties of the country were utterly gone—gone

forever, unless the ascendency of the democracy could be substituted for that which now predominated.

I told him I thought this neither demonstrated nor necessary to the cause of reform; that the only principle upon which reform could be pursued distinctly from revolution appeared to me to be that of restoring democracy to its equal share of power, of removing the existing ascendency, but without substituting the other in its stead. I asked him whether he thought it possible for the monarchy and aristocracy to subsist at all with his democratic ascendency.

He said he had provided for them in his book. The principle of the "uti possidetis" was a common basis for negotiation in international law; he was willing to assume it as a principle of municipal government. He would touch none of the privileges of the Peerage, and none of the prerogatives of the Crown, excepting that of creating new Peers at its pleasure. He would leave every one in possession of his own.

I said that was very well so far as his own opinion and conduct were concerned; but, whatever might be the advantages of reform, it must, in the most favorable of all contingencies, be introduced by intrenching upon the ˙principle of "uti possidetis." It must take franchises or property from somebody. The disfranchisement of Old Sarum itself could not be effected without violating the principle of "uti possidetis." He, to be sure, would stop at the point where democratic ascendency should be established, and then would let in the principle of "uti possidetis" to guard the remnant of power left to the Crown and the Peers. But let him suppose a Parliament assembled, with a reformed House of Commons, possessing the ascendency which his book recommends. Did he think that House of Commons would feel themselves restrained from encroachments upon their co-ordinate, but not coequal, authorities by his international principle of the "uti possidetis"?

He did not maintain that they would. And what if they should put down the Crown and the Peerage? said he. Is your Government in America the worse for having neither King nor Lords? Or are you exclusively entitled to the enjoyment of good government, and must you begrudge it to others? I said he was joking to escape from the consequences of his own argument. The question was not between the comparative merits of the British and American Governments, but whether a radical reform in England does not involve an inevitable revolution. I considered him now as having conceded that reform, with his democratic ascendency, would lead to the abolition of the Crown and Peerage. But these institutions were too powerful and too deeply rooted to perish without a struggle; and what would be the consequences of that?

He said, probably a civil war. Upon the whole, it was likely that no great and real reform could be effected in England without a civil war. Corruption had so pervaded the whole mass of the Government, and had so vitiated the character of the people, that he was afraid they could be purified only by fire. But anything was better than the present state of things, and that in which it must terminate, unless a vigorous effort on the part of the people should rescue them from that absolute despotism under which they are sinking.

From this conversation the inference is tolerably clear that Mr. Ward was not mistaken in the views of the Radical Reformers.

23d. I dined with my wife and Smith at Lord Castlereagh's. The Earl and Countess of Harrowby, Lord and Lady Ellenborough, the Earls of Liverpool, Westmorland, and Aberdeen, Messrs. W. Pole, Robinson, and Goulburn, were there. I spoke to Lord Castlereagh on the subject of the present, and expressed my regret that, by the necessity that I was under of declining it, Mr. Chester would lose his usual portion of it.

He said that if I was inclined to take it I was entitled to it—not as a matter of favor, but of right.

I observed that the Constitution of my own country was imperative in its prohibition, and left me no alternative.

He said the East India Company allowed their servants to take such presents, but required that they should give credit for them in their accounts.

I then mentioned to him General Boyd, and his claim upon the East India Company, with his desire to see and confer with his Lordship on the subject. He said he would be glad to see him next Thursday, at half-past eleven. At table we were entertained with Lady Castlereagh's female bull-dog " Vernon," and with the rejoicings and mutual gratulations of the company at the issue of an election for a member of the House of Commons for the County of Norfolk, where a Ministerial candidate has succeeded in opposition to·the interest and influence of Mr. Coke. Lady Castlereagh most especially enjoyed the triumph, and Lord Ellenborough said there had been an hereditary opposition between the Cokes and the Hobarts, in the County of Norfolk, from the time of the two Chief Justices. I sat at table between Lady Castlereagh and Lord Ellenborough, to whom I spoke of his brother, Mr. Law, at Washington. He had not heard from him for a long time, and appeared not to take peculiar satisfaction in being reminded of him.

Went to the French play and ballet, at the Argyll Rooms. This is one of the places of most highly fashionable amusement, where, under the cover of a subscription ball every week, the people of the highest rank in the country enjoy the luxury of seeing French plays surreptitiously, illegally, and very wretchedly performed—the Lord Chamberlain not daring to grant them a license. They were introduced under the patronage of Countess Lieven and the Countess of Jersey, and it was through Countess Lieven that Mrs. Adams obtained our tickets this evening—for while residing in the country we declined subscribing for the season, both to this establishment and to the balls at Almack's. The tickets are at half a guinea each. We found the play, " Brueys et Palaprat," just begun; it was followed by " La Jeune Femme Colère," and all the performers in both rather below mediocrity.

24th. VIII. Rose barely in time to take the morning walk with J. Bentham. Since the second of our long walks, we have fallen into one and the same track through Hyde Park and Kensington Garden. It makes for me a walk of about seven miles, and takes about three hours of my time. I now generally breakfast before going out. He says his mind is all the morning in a state of torpidity until he has taken his exercise and his tea. He gave me this morning an account of the dinner yesterday to celebrate Sir Francis Burdett's first election for Westminster, of which it was the tenth anniversary. It was attended by several of the Whig members of Parliament, and among the rest by Mr. Brougham, and they made speeches about reform and the purity of elections. Bentham thinks very little of the Whigs, but very highly of a man named Francis Place, a tailor, who, he says, is the most effective man to influence elections in all Westminster. He is a fashionable tailor, keeps a shop in Charing Cross, and is in very thriving circumstances, but his political is so distinct from his professional character that he will not make a suit of clothes for those who are his political associates. Bentham brought him one morning to my door in Craven Street, and introduced him to me there; but neither of them would come in. On returning from this day's walk, I called to return Place's visit, but he was not at home. I met Count Lieven almost at my door; he went back and sat half an hour with me. I had also a succession of visits, from Mr. Charles Murray, Mr. Bourke, the Danish Minister, General Boyd, to whom I mentioned that Lord Castlereagh had promised to receive him next Thursday morning; and from a Mr. Robertson, a miniature-painter, who brought me a letter of recommendation from Sir John Sinclair.

This Mr. Robertson has two brothers who have long resided at New York; one of them has lately written to him that the corporation of the city had determined to erect a monument to the late Mr. Fulton, and his brother wrote to consult him with regard to a design. But he said he had bethought himself to enquire what America had done towards erecting a monument to that character who was her greatest glory and an ornament to human nature, General Washington. He was preparing a letter to the President and Congress of the United States upon this subject, recommending it to their attention, and proposing a general subscription throughout the United States, to which every individual might contribute at his option to defray the expense of a magnificent monument to General Washington. He should then propose to erect a building, copied from the Parthenon of Athens, one of the noblest structures that had ever been raised by the hands of man, and of which he possessed a perfect model. He had proposed it to the Committee for the Waterloo Monument, but they had thought proper to prefer a column. The next nation to which he was desirous of offering his model, after his own country, was the United States, for it would redound to the highest glory of any modern nation to show their liberality of spirit and their taste in the arts by erecting an exact imitation of the Parthenon.

I scarcely knew whether this gentleman was in earnest or jesting, but the solemnity of his manner, and the pride of taste with which he extolled his Parthenon, could not have been greater if the design had been an original invention of his own. I told him that neither subscriptions nor resolutions for monuments to Washington had been wanting, and promised to call at his house and see his model of the Parthenon. Mr. Page also called upon me, and Mr. Ogilvie, the Scotchman who has been delivering orations and lectures upon eloquence all over the United States. He has now come to England with a view to deliver them in London.

The following entries appear to have been made after leaving Great Britain, and while at sea in the merchant ship Washington:

I propose during the remainder of this voyage, which I still hope may be terminated by the close of the present month (July), to add from day to day some notice of incidents which occurred during the last fortnight of my residence in London, and which the narrowness of the space that I had left to fill up the record prevented me from mentioning. Thus, I should have noticed on the 24th of May, that as I was going out for one of the morning walks with J. Bentham, I met in Craven Street Mr. Chester, the Assistant Master of the Ceremonies, who told me that the Queen was much pleased with the footing upon which I had placed the subject of the private audience to take leave of her, and that she would not wish me to take any further trouble; she wished me a prosperous voyage home, and all health and happiness to myself and family. I desired Mr. Chester to reply to her Majesty by the assurance how much I regretted the cause which had deprived me of the honor of taking leave of her in person, and of my earnest wishes for the speedy and entire restoration of her health. It was the last time I saw Mr. Chester, and closed my relations with the ministerial branches of the royal family. Of the Dukes of Kent and Sussex I was to see and hear something more. Mr. Rae Wilson, the gentleman who introduced me to the Lancaster School in the borough of Southwark, is in close and frequent correspondence with the Duke of Kent, who is now residing at Brussels. The Duke, in one of his letters, had mentioned me, which I believe was the occasion of his first calling upon me. He sent me a copy of the passage in the Duke's letter which spoke of me, to which I requested him to return in his answer to the Duke's letter something from me in a like complimentary style. The Duke replied much in the same manner, but more at large, and Mr. Wilson sent me also the extract of this second letter.

The Duke of Sussex's polite attentions to me were still more unreserved. It was by his own proposal that he went with me and showed me the new Bedlam Hospital, and by an odd co-incidence it was on the King's birthday. He promised then to call upon me and Mrs. Adams the next day, but he was accidentally prevented, and came the day after. Mrs. Adams and I were both out, but Smith received him. He left a copy of his printed speech, in 1812, upon the Catholic question, as presented to me by himself. His kindness and civility to me have been signal and uniform from the time of our first acquaintance at Berlin; but he is now in so strong opposition that his friendship itself was the reverse of a recommendation at Court.

25th. Sir William Scott came and paid me a morning visit. He is a man of the most lively wit and playful imagination under the form of a grave and almost solemn deportment. I left cards at Lord Castlereagh's and Count Lieven's, and called at the lodgings of Mr. Leslie, the painter, to see him; but he was not at home. Mr. Allston was there, and showed me a new picture that he is painting, the subject of which is Jacob's Dream. Instead of a ladder, upon which, according to the passage in the Scripture, he saw the angels ascending and descending, Allston has painted the staircase of a palace. The departure from the story is too great, the imitation has no resemblance to the original, and there is no idea of an interesting nature connected with a number of human figures going up and down the stairs at the same time.

26th. I dined with Smith at Mrs. Copley's and her son Mr. Sergeant Copley's.[1] My wife was too ill to go out. The company were Dr. Bollmann and his two daughters, Mr. Wetherall, a lawyer, and member of the House of Commons, and Messrs. Fox and Bowen, persons whom I had never before seen. Copley and Wetherall are employed as counsel to some of the prisoners now in the Tower and shortly to be tried for high treason; but Copley has little left of that republican spirit which was ardent twenty years ago in his father. We were looking before dinner at the picture of Charles the First demanding the five members of the House of Commons, by far the best of his father's works.[2] The Sergeant smiled, and said, "A fine republican picture." But he spoke it as if he was thinking that his father might have employed his time and talents much better. I was in England while Copley was employed upon that picture, and witnessed his enthusiastic attachment to it. But before his death he found that was not the subject for a popular painting in England. It has never been engraved.

27th. Mr. Bentham has a strong desire to obtain books and documents published in the United States and relating to America. I have mentioned to him the obstructions thrown in the way of this species of literary communication by the English laws, and particularly by the post-office regulations. He then proposed that this intercourse should be established by means of some bookseller or publisher of a literary journal, and asked me if I would see Sir Richard Phillips, the editor of the Monthly Magazine, if he should call upon me. I willingly consented to see him, and he called upon me this morning. Sir Richard Phillips is a Whig and a Reformer, and a sort of Republican, but most of all editor of the Monthly Magazine. He said he had a correspondence already established in the

[1] Afterwards Lord Lynd'iurst. He died, at a very a lvanced age, in 1864.
[2] Now in the public library in the City of Boston.

United States for procuring American books, but complained that they often sent nothing but trash, which they could not dispose of there. He said the editor of the Port Folio had proposed an exchange with him of a certain number of copies of that publication in return for copies of the Monthly Magazine, which he would gladly agree to do if he could have a prospect of disposing of the copies of the Port Folio that he should receive. And in order to recommend it to English readers, he was preparing an extract from it to be republished in the next number of the Monthly Magazine. He gave me a proof-sheet of this extract, which I had, however, not time to read.

Sir Richard then proceeded to tell me what exceedingly erroneous opinions the English people entertained of the Americans, and how desirable it would be to spread more correct notions on the subject among them. This might be done by a daily newspaper, which should be published, and the expense of supporting which should be defrayed, by the American Government. Ten pounds a day, together with what would be collected by the daily sale of the paper and for advertisements, would be sufficient for that purpose. Less it could not, and more it need not, cost. This was the only way in which it was possible to have such statements of facts and opinions generally circulated as might be favorable to America. The Times was a paper employed in that manner by the King of France and the Bourbon family; but it cost them much more. He verily believed that the downfall of Bonaparte had been occasioned altogether by his having despised to employ such means. He himself had heard editors of some of the papers say, "Damn him, why should not he be put down?—he pays us nothing." I could have no conception of the extent to which they carried this principle. There was not an individual who had a lawsuit or a case before a magistrate to be reported but must pay for it, on the penalty of having the statement made in the manner the most disadvantageous to him.

I told Sir Richard I was aware how little correct and just representation of American affairs could obtain circulation through the English press, but there could be no motive to the American Government for spending money merely to make impression upon the minds of the British public in relation to the United States.   Even if there could, the sum that he spoke of would in the course of one year amount to more than I believed the American Government had expended for secret service in time of peace from the establishment of the Constitution of the United States to this day.   The money could not be expended without its being at least known that so much had been expended in secret service.   It could not long escape discovery how and for what it would be expended; and, once known, it would do more injury to the American Government than a hired daily newspaper in London could do them good in a century.

Sir Richard said it was much to the credit of the United States to have spent so little money for secret service, for it was one of the modes of extravagance in which the British Government had run to the worst excess.   He had merely meant to suggest a mode of enlightening the public opinion here concerning America, if it should be thought advisable.   He then asked me if I had ever taken an interest in the question so much and so often agitated in England, Who was the author of Junius?   I said I had shared the public curiosity so much as to have read many of the speculations imputing those letters to various persons, but I had not read the book lately published to prove that Sir Philip Francis was the author of them.   I had heard that the evidence adduced in support of this opinion was very strong; but I had not examined it.

He said that he had started another candidate in the last Monthly Magazine, a person named Lachlan McLean.   There would be more about him in the next number; and perhaps some information upon the subject might be obtainable from America.   There was said to be a gentleman in Virginia who possessed Junius's own copy of his printed letters.   He did not recollect his name, but would write it to me, and if I could hereafter give him any further information concerning this fact it would greatly oblige him.   I promised him I would if it should be in my power.   It was past two when Sir Richard left me, and a moment before he went away I recollected an appointment I had made with Sir John Sinclair at half-past one, a time that he had named in order that I might be present at a meeting of the Board of Agriculture. I went immediately to the house, but it was too late—the meeting was over. Sir John told me, however, that it had been very thinly attended, and little or no business done. Two of the members, Arthur Young and Sir Robert Vaughan, a Welshman, were still there. Mr. Young is a very old man, upwards of eighty, and now blind, but he yet appears cheerful, enjoying lively spirits, and expressing his sentiments with energy. I congratulated him upon the improvement of the agricultural condition and prospects of this country; but he shook his head, and said they were bad enough. America, he added, was the only country in the world enjoying happiness and with prospects of greatness. "Of too much greatness," said he, "if you should remain long united; but you will not. You will soon break up into several Governments: so extensive a country cannot long remain under one Government." I told him I hoped we should prove to the world that it could, and that its greatness would be a benefit, and not an injury, to the rest of mankind. Sir John Sinclair gave me several letters to correspondents in the United States, and showed me some of their new-invented implements of agriculture. I spoke of the hay-making machine of which Mr. Coke had spoken to me. Sir John told me that Sir Robert Vaughan, to whom he introduced me, was going immediately to several shops where they had them for sale, and advised me to go with him. I went accordingly, and Sir Robert Vaughan, a man of portly stomach, after stopping to take an ice-cream at a pastry-cook's in Oxford Street, took me successively to four or five shops, where I saw all the knick-knack machinery of English agriculture. I saw several of the hay-making machines, but could not well judge of their usefulness. Their construction is of great simplicity. There were ploughs and churns in great number and variety; iron fences for farms; wagons, water-pots, and much costly trumpery of which the usefulness is altogether questionable; also samples of iron pavements and iron railways.

I was finally obliged by the shortness of time to leave Sir Robert Vaughan in the midst of his machinery, and to call at

Mr. A. Robertson's, in Gerard Street, where I found again Sir John Sinclair, of whom Robertson is painting a miniature. I stopped merely to look at the model of the Parthenon, and told Robertson I would call upon him again to-morrow.

30th. Mr. West came at eleven, and told me that he was engaged to meet the Committee for the Waterloo Monument at the Marquis of Stafford's this morning. They were to fix their choice upon one of the designs presented to them. But he would not be detained there more than a couple of hours, and if I would call at his house at three o'clock he would then accompany me to Rossi's. When we reached Mr. West's he was not returned from the Marquis of Stafford's. We had about half an hour to look over his pictures. His " Death on the Pale Horse" is nearly finished, and much improved since I saw it last August. He came home about four, and went with us to Rossi's, who showed us many of his models and designs, and the manufacture of the composition which they use for statuary. Rossi's greatest work is the monument of Marquis Cornwallis, erected by the East India Company in Saint Paul's Church. Rossi gave a curious account of his having been employed to take a bust of the Prince Regent. He was in attendance upon him about six months. The first time that he sat, it was for about twenty minutes. After that, he was time after time kept waiting several hours, but succeeded in seeing the Prince only once, and then he took out his watch and told him he could give him just ten minutes. During these precious minutes some of his social companions were present, and the conversation, in which the Prince took the most earnest and lively interest, was all about dogs and horses.

June 1st. *Sunday.* At half-past eleven this morning I called upon Lord Castlereagh, and had an hour's conversation with him upon a variety of general topics. He said he had desired to see me previous to my departure, to enquire if there remained anything upon which further arrangements would be necessary, and to give me such a view of the sentiments of this Government as might be useful upon my return to the United States. I said I would make out a minute of the notes which I had addressed to him and to which answers had not yet been de-

finitively given. I should request to see him once more before
I should sail. He named next Thursday morning for that purpose. He then enlarged upon the general and earnest desire
of the British Government not only to remain themselves at
peace with all the world, but for the preservation of peace and
tranquillity among the other nations. In these views I told
him they might be sure of the hearty and earnest concurrence
of the United States, so far as it would depend upon them.

He then said that, without wishing to penetrate into the
political intentions of the American Government in regard to
anything upon which they were desirous of keeping them
secret, he would ask me what was the present state of our
relations with Spain.

I said there was nothing in them upon which the American
Government were desirous of observing secrecy; that very
serious misunderstandings existed between the United States
and Spain. There were questions of territorial boundary, and
questions of indemnity for commercial depredations. Spain was
so utterly intractable upon both points that there was no prospect of an early accommodation upon them. Whether they
would ultimately terminate in hostilities would depend upon
Spain herself. I thought there was much less prospect of
that result now than there had been some months since. The
United States would not seek hostility, and, as Congress would
not meet until December, there could be no declaration of war
on their part, at least for the present year.

He said an idea had occurred to him, upon which he had not
consulted his colleagues in office, and therefore could not offer
it as having the sanction of the British Government, but merely
as his own individual sentiment. How did I think it would be
received by the President if Great Britain were to offer her good
offices to effect an amicable arrangement between the United
States and Spain?

I answered, that, with every disposition to tell him in perfect
candor, it was not in my power. The affairs of my Government
with Spain had formed but a very incidental part of their
correspondence with me. I knew not how the President might
be affected by such a proposal, but I had no reason to doubt it

would be taken as a kind and friendly measure, and it might, if he thought proper, be immediately adopted, through the medium of Mr. Bagot. There was, so far as I could anticipate, only one ground upon which any hesitation could arise against the acceptance of the proposal. It would be within his recollection that in the course of the negotiations at Ghent there was some reference to the controversies between the United States and Spain. It then appeared that Great Britain had formed an opinion upon those questions unfavorable to the United States, and, as I conceived, quite erroneous. But, as that opinion might naturally be supposed to have been biassed by the state of war in which it was urged, I should suppose it would not operate as an objection against the acceptance of a proffered mediation, if it should appear that the sentiments of Great Britain had undergone such a change as would give the United States the assurance of that impartiality on her part which is essential to the character of a mediator.

Lord Castlereagh made no very significant reply to these remarks, but asked if the United States were not very desirous of obtaining a cession of the Floridas. I told him that we contended the cession of West Florida was included in that of Louisiana, because it had formed a part of the original French colony, the whole of which had been retroceded by Spain to France, and then by France to the United States.

He asked whether there was not also some question of boundary to the west of the river Mississippi. I said there was, but I did not know precisely where Spain pretended the line was to be drawn in that quarter. He hinted that Spain might perhaps consent to an accommodation upon the Florida side, if the United States would concede on the side of the Mississippi. Fernan Nuñez had told me as much.

I spoke to Lord Castlereagh of the mediation of the allies between Spain and Portugal, and of the affairs of the insurgents in South America. The insurrection at Pernambuco, he said, had not extended to Bahia, and he thought would be subdued without much difficulty by the Brazilian Government. He intimated that there would be a necessity for taking measures to protect commerce against the depredations of the privateers under the insurgent colors, which, he said, were becoming as bold and as terrible as the buccaneers of the former century. I asked him if there was any prospect that the allies, or Great Britain alone, would ultimately take a hostile part against the South Americans. He said nothing of that sort was at present contemplated: it was impossible to say what system of policy the general course of events might bring about, but no intention of a hostile interference between Spain and her colonies was now intended.

On leaving Lord Castlereagh I returned home to receive Prince Esterhazy, who came about three o'clock. I had also an hour's conversation with him on the general state of political affairs in Europe. He says that the Cabinets were never so universally and sincerely pacific as at the present time; that all the Governments want a period of long repose after the excessive exertions of the last twenty-five years; that all have ravages to repair and finances to redeem; that all have inquietudes with regard to the dispositions of their people, and a fear of the recurrence of the dangers that are past. There is a community of interest among them which will cement the alliance formed in the first instance for defence against the overwhelming power of France, and now perhaps equally necessary to secure the general tranquillity.

Esterhazy is quite a young man, of the highest rank of the Hungarian nobility. His wife is daughter to the Princess of La Tour et Taxis, niece to the late Queen of Prussia, and grand-niece to the Queen of England. The Prince is an Ambassador for the show, and is a courteous and accomplished gentleman. Neumann and the Marquis of Bombelles are the men of business belonging to the Embassy. I dined with J. Bentham and Mr. and Mrs. Koe. After dinner, I walked an hour with Mr. Bentham in St. James's Park. He gave me a paper of written questions, which he desired me to answer without enquiring of him what use he proposed to make of the answers. They related to the state of religious opinions in the United States, and particularly to the effects which an avowal of infidelity may have upon a person's reputation or his condition in life.

2d. Mr. Owen, of Lanark, called upon me, and gave me a

pamphlet and several newspapers, containing an exposition of
what he calls a new view of society; some project like that of
the Moravian fraternity of Herrnhut—a community of goods
and of industry—projects which can never succeed but with very
small societies and to a very contracted extent.   Mr. Owen,
however, seems to think that it is of universal application, and
destined to give a new character to the history of the world.   I
went with my wife and all the children to Mr. West's, where
we met the French tragedians Talma, with his wife, and Miss
George, Mr. East, Mr. Winthrop, and Dr. Reynolds, besides a
company of ladies and gentlemen, visitors at the house merely
to see Mr. West's pictures.   Talma and Miss George are occasional visitors in this country, probably with a view of ascertaining whether they can succeed to introduce a regular French
theatre for a season in London; but they decline performing at
the Argyll Rooms.   Mr. West introduced them to us.   We
had already known Miss George at St. Petersburg.   We all
went with Mr. West to the British Museum, where we saw the
whole collection of its curiosities, as well those that have been
there in former years as the more recently acquired treasures
of the Townley and Elgin marbles.   It is rather to be regretted
that they have been all assembled together.   The old collection
of the British Museum was amply sufficient to exhaust the time
of one visit, and even more.   The Townley and Elgin marbles
are curiosities of a different description, and are each deserving
of more than one day's examination.   We were obliged to hurry
over them all in one visit of two or three hours.   We had therefore no time for inspecting any of the remarkable manuscripts,
and could give but a cursory glance to the fine antique statues
of the Townley collection.   Mr. West's enthusiasm is all con-
centrated upon the Elgin marbles, and he was impatient until
we were among them.   Since they were brought into England
he has persuaded himself that the Laocöon, the Apollo, and
the Venus are works of inferior merit, and he quotes a passage
from Pliny's Natural History, purporting that in the age of
Alexander painting was in its most flourishing state, but that
sculpture had then already begun to decline, the statuaries after
Phidias having substituted system instead of simplicity in the

imitation of the forms of nature. It is this perfect simplicity which constitutes, in Mr. West's opinion, the supreme excellence of the Elgin marbles, all of which are mutilated, and some of them crumbling away by the mere effect of time. There are two colossal statues, supposed to be of Theseus, which are the least injured, that is to say, having lost only their feet and hands. They are in sitting and reclining attitudes, entirely naked. There is also a horse's head, Mr. West says the most perfect sample of art that he ever saw, but the under lip of which was broken off by the carelessness of the carmen who brought it to the Museum, and who tumbled it from the wagon as if it had been a pavement-stone. The hour for closing the hall where these statues are yet being put up was four, when all visitors were warned to withdraw; but an exception was made for Mr. West and his company, and we stayed an hour longer. Talma and Miss George left us there. We took Mr. West to his house, and returned home.

3d. I called at two o'clock upon Count Palmella, the Portuguese Minister, according to our appointment. He read to me copies of two notes which he has lately sent in to Lord Castlereagh—one concerning the occupation of Montevideo by troops from Brazil, and the other relating to the case of the American privateer General Armstrong, destroyed in the harbor of Fayal by a British ship of the line during the late war. The first of these notes gives, by order of the Court of Rio Janeiro, explanations of the motives of the military movement by which Montevideo was taken—explanations directed to be given before the Portuguese Government knew of the offer of mediation between them and Spain, made by the allies, and which of course, as Count Palmella remarked, could not be ascribed to intimidation resulting from that event. The reason assigned is, the necessity of securing their own territories against the incursions or influence of the insurgents, and there is a formal disclaimer of any intention to keep the possession of the places which they have occupied. The note respecting the case of the privateer was a demand of satisfaction for the violation of the neutral territorial jurisdiction, couched in language very courteous and complimentary, which, he told me, was owing to the very conciliatory manner in which Lord Castlereagh had received and answered a former note of his upon the subject. The Count spoke again about the late insurrection at Pernambuco, which he still considers as neither formidable nor extensive, and he said he was informed that there was a naval armament now fitting out in this country of at least twelve sail of the line. He said he had mentioned it yesterday to Prince Esterhazy, who appeared to be acquainted with the fact. I, nevertheless, think it not well founded, or at least much exaggerated.

After dinner I attended a debate in the House of Lords. It was upon a motion of Earl Grey's for a copy of a letter of Lord Sidmouth's, directing that county magistrates should not be admitted without special orders of the Council to visit State prisoners in the county gaols. Lord Grey insisted that these directions from the Secretary of State were not warranted by law. The Chancellor and Lord Eldon and the Earl of Liverpool supported Lord Sidmouth in defence of the order, while Lord Grey's motion was supported by the Earls of Rosslyn and Spencer, and by Lord Holland. There was a person who sat beside me, apparently a tipstaff of the Chancellor's, who was constantly commenting, in soliloquy, upon the Peers as they were speaking. His opinions coincided with those of the Chancellor, and by no means with those of the opposition Peers.

I came away about ten, before the debate was concluded, and went with my wife to see the pictures of the gallery of the British Institution. The crowd of company there was so great that we were obliged to go almost to the top of St. James's Street to fall into the file of carriages that were drawing up to the door. We met at the gallery Mr. West and his son with his wife, Mr. Sharp, and Mr. and Miss Boddington. The collection of pictures now exhibited here is entirely different from that of the last summer. It is quite miscellaneous, consisting partly of pictures of the old Italian and Flemish schools, and partly of English pictures by Reynolds, Hogarth, Opie, Wilson, Copley, and others; none, I believe, of living painters. A considerable number by Reynolds, of various merit, and most of them portraits ; among the rest, one of himself between Johnson and Goldsmith. Also a very good portrait of Burke. It was one in the morning when we came home. Mr. Bentham sent me this morning a large package, containing twenty-five copies of almost all his works, to be distributed, one copy to the Governor of every State in the Union, and the rest to some other persons. Madame de Berg paid a visit to take leave of my wife. I had also a visit from Mr. Columbus O'Donnell ; and Lord Erskine called while I was out. He left word that he had fully determined to pay a visit to the United States, and should probably go next spring.

4th. Mr. J. R. Wilson called upon me at ten this morning, and Smith and I went with him to the Lancaster school in the borough of Southwark. I saw the whole process of instruction, both to the boys and girls, and satisfied myself of the great excellency of the method. We also saw the procession of the pupils and of their teachers, and witnessed their taking possession of the new school-house. The Duke of Sussex was there, and the late Sheriff, Sir Thomas Bell. Mr. and Mrs. Lamb came just as the ceremony was concluding. The Lord Mayor was to have been present, but was detained by the necessity of canvassing for his election as a member of the House of Commons in the room of Alderman Combe, who, by a resolution of the Common Hall, moved and carried by Mr. Hunt, has been invited, and prevailed upon, to resign his seat. When the affair of the school was over, the Duke of Sussex took me and Smith with him in his carriage to the newly-erected Bedlam Hospital, which is in the borough, and quite in the neighborhood of the school. The Duke, as one of the governors of the hospital, was immediately admitted, and accompanied by Dr. Monroe, the regular attending physician of the hospital, and by a lady, the superintendent of the female patients, both of whom accompanied us over the respective apartments in which the women and the men are confined. The order and discipline of the house are very good—the cells all perfectly clean, the house throughout well aired, and among all the patients not one in that state of frenzy which I have never failed of seeing at such establishments. There is a class of those unhappy persons whom they call *criminal* patients; that is, persons who have been tried for capital offences and acquitted upon verdicts of insanity, which by law subjects them to be confined during the King's pleasure, that is, for life. Among these was Margaret Nicholson; a man who shot an air-gun at the King in the playhouse; and one of my quondam correspondents, A. McKenroth. After going over the house we took leave of the Duke of Sussex, who told me he would call and see me at Craven Street to-morrow.

6th. Mr. Wilberforce had called at Craven Street the day before yesterday while I was out, and left a note requesting to see me. I answered him yesterday morning, that I would call at two this day at his lodgings, 8 Downing Street. I went at the time, but he had missed of receiving my note, and was not at home. Lord Castlereagh had also, by a note, requested me, instead of calling at his house yesterday morning, as we had agreed, to come this afternoon at four o'clock to the Foreign Office; but when I went at the time, he was not there. I went twice to the House of Commons to see if I could find either of them there. Lord Castlereagh came at last, and, with an apology for missing his appointment, asked me to call at his house to-morrow morning. Mr. Goulburn and Mr. Sharp came under the gallery, and took leave of me. Sir John Cox Hippisley, whom I met in the lobby, did the same, and charged me with a message of his kind remembrance to his old friend H. Cruger at New York.

I finally found Mr. Wilberforce at his lodgings, with his friend Mr. Babbington, also a member of the House of Commons. The suppression of the slave-trade was the subject of Mr. Wilberforce's wish to see me, and we had an hour's conversation relating to it. His object is to obtain the consent of the United States, and of all other maritime powers, that ships under their flags may be searched and captured by the British cruisers against the slave-trade—a concession which I thought would be liable to objections. There had been published in the London papers of 4th June a resolution of the Congress of the United States, passed at their last session, requesting the President to enter into negotiation with Great

Britain and other European powers for completing, if possible, the suppression of the slave-trade, and for sending certain free people of color from the United States to Sierra Leone, or some such settlement on the coast of Africa. Wilberforce intimated to me, but did not expressly assert, that he had not seen this resolution till after he had written me the note in Craven Street requesting to see me, and he said he had been gratified at the coincidence. But the great object of his wish to see me was evidently to start the proposition that the British cruisers against the slave-trade should be authorized to overhaul and search, and even capture, American vessels suspected to be engaged in that trade.

Probably this project originated in the brain of Master Stephen, the author of "War in Disguise," and brother-in-law to Wilberforce, one of the party called in derision the Saints, and who under sanctified visors pursue worldly objects with the ardor and perseverance of saints. Wilberforce is at the head of these Saints in Parliament, and is said to possess more personal influence in the House of Commons than any other individual. Lord Castlereagh has more than once thrown out this idea of a mutual stipulation that the cruisers of every nation which has passed laws for abolishing the slave-trade should be authorized to search and capture the slave-trading vessels of the other nations by whose laws the trade is prohibited. In substance, it is a barefaced and impudent attempt of the British to obtain in time of peace that right of searching and seizing the ships of other nations which they have so outrageously abused during war. I never discussed the subject with Castlereagh, because he never brought the point to an explicit proposal, and it was not necessary to sift the proposition to the bottom; but Wilberforce, after much lamentation at the inefficacy of the existing laws and measures for suppressing the trade, and asserting that it was now carried on with as much activity and inhumanity as ever, professed to be unable to devise anything that should effectually suppress it. And yet, he said, there was one thing that would accomplish the end if the nations would agree to it, and then came out with the proposal, and enquired whether the United States would agree to it: that all vessels, whatever nation's flag they should bear, but which might be suspected of being engaged in the slave-trade, should be liable to search and capture by the cruisers of any other nation.

I told him I thought there would be some objection to this. In the first place, no American vessel engaged in the slave-trade could use the American flag, for the trade was prohibited by law, and a vessel which should be captured while engaged in it could not obtain any interference of the American Government to rescue her. The flag could be no protection to her. The commander of the capturing vessel would only act *at his peril*, and if he seized a vessel not really concerned in the trade he must be responsible to indemnify the sufferer. Again, a stipulation of this nature, though nominally reciprocal, would be really one-sided. Cruisers against the slave-trade are in fact kept only by Great Britain. British vessels, therefore, would be liable to no search or capture but by officers under the authority of their own Government, while the vessels of other nations would be subject to seizure by foreigners not amenable or accountable to their own sovereigns. Some degree of prejudice must also be supposed to exist against the naval power of Great Britain, and particularly some jealousy of the exercise of an arbitrary power by her naval officers.

Mr. Babbington appeared to admit there was more foundation in these objections than Wilberforce was ready to allow. He suggested that in each cruiser there should be an officer of each power agreeing to the principle, and that he should be present at every search, and no capture be made without his consent. I objected to this, that it would lead to conflicts of opinion, and perhaps even of authority, between the officers of the different Governments; and Wilberforce did not like this expedient any better than I did. I also alluded to the misconduct of many naval British officers, to the manner in which they had taken slaves from the United States and had probably sold many of them, and I explained the manner in which the Judge of the Vice-Admiralty Court had evaded the British Statute and Order in Council by which captured slaves were to be liberated, or rather made the King's slaves for life.

Wilberforce was much struck by this information, of which I authorized him to make such use as he thought proper. He somewhat equivocally expressed his disapprobation of Admiral Cochrane's proclamation inviting the slaves to run away from their masters and join him, and said he knew too much of what had been the lot of those slaves. He added that there were very few of them in Halifax. I believe that Wilberforce was, on the whole, disappointed in the result of this interview; though we parted in perfect good humor and civility.

Mr. West, with Zerah Colburn and his father, spent the evening with us. Mr. West then told me that he had in the year 1783 made a sketch for a picture of the peace which terminated the war of the American Revolution, which he would send me to look at the next morning, as he accordingly did. I then recollected having seen it before, at the time when my father was sitting to him for his likeness in it. The most striking likeness in the picture is that of Mr. Jay. Those of Dr. Franklin, and his grandson, W. T., who was Secretary to the American Commission, are also excellent. Mr. Laurens and my father, though less perfect resemblances, are yet very good. Mr. Oswald, the British Plenipotentiary, was an ugly-looking man, blind of one eye, and he died without leaving any picture of him extant. This Mr. West alleged as the cause which prevented him from finishing the picture many years ago. Caleb Whitefoord, the Secretary of the British Commission, is also dead, but his portrait exists, from which a likeness may be taken. As I very strongly expressed my regret that this picture should be left unfinished, Mr. West said he thought he could finish it, and I must not be surprised if some day or other it should be received at Washington.[1] I understand his intention to be to make a present of it to Congress.

Zerah Colburn's father urged me to let him communicate to me the secret of his instinctive arithmetic. I consented, and he made the attempt, but without success. I might perhaps have understood him but for the continual interposition of the father himself, who, without understanding it, by his frequent

---

[1] This picture is now in the possession of Lord Belper, at whose residence the writer saw it some years ago.

explanatory interruptions disconcerted both Zerah and me.   I
was, however, satisfied that the secret is only a rapidity of intellect with which the boy performs the processes of multiplica-
tion and division, and that it is communicable only to minds
equally quick in their operations.

7th. Mr. Bentham came to ask if I could walk with him this
morning; but I was obliged to call upon Lord Castlereagh, with
whom I had a last interview, which was short.   I left with him
a minute of the notes which I have addressed to him and to
which answers are yet desirable.   We had some further conversation upon the state of relations between the United States
and Spain, and examined the ground upon a map.   He asked,
if the Floridas were ceded to the United States, what objection
they would have to the Mississippi for a boundary.   I showed
him the whole range of territory marked upon his own map
" Louisiana," and said that would be the objection; but that if
Spain would but for one moment be rational with us, we could
easily come to an accommodation with her.   He said, smiling,
that he must admit Spain was not the easiest of parties to
concede, and he might say the same of the United States.   I
answered, in the same tone, that there could be no better judge
of stubbornness and compliance than a party so very easy and
accommodating as Great Britain.   As I left Lord Castlereagh,
Count Lieven was calling upon him.   I saw a man standing in
the pillory at Charing Cross.[1]   J. Bentham walked with me to
the corner of St. James's Square, where Lord Castlereagh's
house stands, and, when I went in, agreed to wait for me, walking up and down the street, ten minutes.   If I should be detained longer than that, he was to go home, and if, on coming
out from Lord Castlereagh's, I had still time for a walk, I was
to call for him at his house.   I was with Lord Castlereagh
about half an hour.   His project of offering the mediation of
Great Britain to settle the differences between the United
States and Spain surprised me much, after what had passed
at Ghent.   But his plan of bounding us by the Mississippi was
exactly what I should have expected from a British mediator.

[1] The record from this point seems to have been written at some time after
leaving England.

Castlereagh had in the first instance very cautiously spoken of the scheme of mediation as being merely an extra-official idea of his own, and now he did not seem to expect much from it. As to the mediation of the allies between Spain and Portugal, he told me the substance of the latest communication from the Court of Rio Janeiro, which had already been told me by Count Palmella. The only difference that I perceive between the two statements is, that Palmella told me the explanations given by his Government of the occupation of Montevideo were communicated before they had received the offer of mediation, and therefore were altogether uninfluenced by any impressions from Europe. Castlereagh said the explanations were given before the offer of mediation was received, but after the Court of Brazil was informed of the first impressions in Europe (meaning England) by the movement against Montevideo, intimating that England had taken some step to call for explanation before that general one of the allies.

With respect to the Spanish South American insurgents he was not altogether explicit, but rather evasive, in regard to the probable future policy of England. All that could with certainty be collected was, that she will intermeddle as much as possible; that she will side to the utmost extent she dares against the insurgents, but without proceeding to direct hostilities against them, and serving herself by urging Spain to allow them a free trade, at least with the English. In all her mediations, or offers of mediation, her justice and policy will be merely to serve herself.

Count Lieven was waiting in the antechamber to speak with Castlereagh while I was with him, and when we went into the antechamber to look at the map, Castlereagh asked Lieven to go into the room from which we had come. Lieven *looked* curious to know what we were about. He afterwards called at Craven Street, but I had not returned home, and did not see him. Both he and Poletica several times hinted to me a desire to know how we stood with Great Britain, and a suspicion that there was a prospect of early hostilities between us. They have some indistinct idea of the question and discussion concerning the fisheries, and have the expectation that it will terminate in a war.

When I left Castlereagh it was too late for the walk with Mr. Bentham, and instead of going to his house I called upon his friend Place, the tailor and Republican. He keeps a shop in Charing Cross, and is quite prosperous in his trade, notwithstanding his dabbling with politics. Place, who was unwell, received me in his library, two pair of stairs up from his shop. He had a very considerable library, all the shelves of which, that I noticed, were full of books of history and political economy. He told me he was very glad I had rejected that ridiculous proposal of Sir Richard Phillips's to set up and pay for an American newspaper in London. Place asked me where he could procure a volume of the Constitution of the United States, and I promised to send him one. I had given mine to Bentham. Place was much interested about a man named Wooler, a printer, who had just been tried for a libel upon Lord Castlereagh and Mr. Canning in a weekly periodical publication called The Black Dwarf. Wooler was tried at the Old Bailey, before Judge Abbott, of the King's Bench. He pleaded his own cause, and astonished a crowded auditory by his eloquence. He was tried upon two informations, upon both of which the Judge strongly charged the jury against him. One of the jurymen of the first jury asked the Judge what they must do if they found the matter charged as libellous true. He said that by the law truth was no justification of a libel. The jury were out several hours without being able to agree. There were three talesmen who stood out for the defendant against nine special jurors still more stiff for the crown. At last the talesmen agreed to a verdict in this form, "As truth has been declared to us to be by law a libel, we of the jury are compelled to find the defendant guilty," but they stipulated that if the Court refused to receive the verdict in that form, the jury should go out again. Instead of this verdict, Abbott, the Judge, ordered a general verdict of guilty to be recorded, and refused to receive the affidavit of the talesmen as to the agreement about the terms in which the verdict was to be delivered. The next day, upon a statement of the facts by Abbott himself in the Court of King's Bench, Lord Ellenborough, in a manner, compelled Chitty, whom Wooler had in the mean time employed as his counsel, to say that he asked for a new trial, and immediately granted it. Subsequently, however, Chitty moved that the defendant should be discharged, which motion still remained to be argued when we left London. Bentham told me that it was a general opinion among the lawyers that Abbott had lost his reputation by his conduct on this occasion. He also told me that if a vacancy should occur in the election for Westminster it was intended to set up Wooler as a candidate. Place told me that if Wooler had not argued his own cause he would certainly have been convicted; that no lawyer would have dared or been suffered to put the cause upon its real and strong point of defence; that Lord Ellenborough, by his overbearing and browbeating control over the Bar, had annihilated the spirit of all the lawyers; that if any lawyer had a pretension to independence, Ellenborough would harass and persecute him till the suitors found out he was not well with the Court, and then no soul would give him a brief. He had in this manner ruined the practice of Brougham and many others. Place said he had often served as a juryman in Courts where Ellenborough presided, and seen much of him, but never without having his most vehement indignation excited by his despotic and insolent control over the lawyers. In all causes of mere property between man and man, he was an able and upright Judge, but in every case where the Court had an interest he was an unprincipled and unblushing despot and oppressor; and they had rewarded him for it by making him a Privy Councillor. It was somewhat curious that, after receiving this character of Ellenborough, Smith and I were on the same day received by him when we went our round of official visits.

8th. Walk with J. Bentham, and had a glimpse at his sentiments on religion. He says Place is an atheist. I fear he is one himself. Visits from R. Patterson, McLeary, Tabb, Da Costa with Brazilian papers, Poletica, and Dr. Bollman. Visited with Smith at Holland House; the Duke and Duchess of Bedford, Sir James Mackintosh, and Mr. Allen, Lord Holland's librarian, there. Last ride in Hyde Park. Left a card for Mr. Howard at Brunet's Hotel. Dismissed our carriage and horses. It was the last morning walk that I took with J. Bentham, and we went as usual through Hyde Park and Kensington Gardens. The written questions upon the state of religious opinions in America, and particularly upon the effect of avowed deism or atheism upon a man's reputation and influence in society, with the answers I had given to them, formed the principal subject of our conversation. I perceived that my answers were not exactly such as he would have desired. He spoke with more reserve than usual, as if unwilling to shock prejudices which he had found rooted in my mind. The general tenor of his observations, however, was to discredit all religion, and he intimated doubts of the existence of a God. His position was, that all human knowledge was either positive or inferential; that all inferential knowledge was imperfect and uncertain, depending upon a process of the human mind which could not, in its nature, be conclusive; that our knowledge of the physical world was positive, while that of a Creator of it was inferential; that God was neither seen nor felt, nor in any manner manifested to our senses, but was the deduction from a syllogism, a mere probability from the combinations of human reason; that of the present existence of matter we have positive knowledge; that there was a time when it did not exist we assume without proof, for the purpose of assuming, equally without proof, an eternal Creator of it.

I observed in answer to it that inferential knowledge was in numberless cases more to be relied upon than what he called positive knowledge, meaning the mere testimony of the senses; that our knowledge of physical nature, such as it is, consists entirely of inferential corrections of the testimony of the senses. While we trust the positive knowledge of the senses, we must believe that the sun and the whole firmament of heaven move daily round the earth, and so stubborn are these cheating senses, that after they have been convicted of imposture, and when we know it is the revolution of the earth round its axis that produces all these phenomena, we persist in saying that the sun, moon, and stars daily rise and set, and it is only when we sit down to astronomical calculations that we discover the truth, the triumph of inference over the senses. I said that the proofs of intellect in the operations of the material world were as decisive to my mind as those of the existence of matter itself; intellect not residing in matter, but moulding and controlling it. What is that intellect, and where is it? Everywhere in its effects; nowhere perceptible to the sense. That this intellect is competent to the creation of matter I know, not from reason, but from revelation; but that it modifies and governs the physical world is apparent both to my senses and my reason.

He replied little to this argument, apparently because he saw that my opinions were decided, and he did not wish for controversy. He said, however, that Place was a professed atheist. From the general tenor of his part in this conversation, and from several inconsistent remarks of his upon other occasions, I consider him as entertaining inveterate prejudices against all religions, and that he is probably preparing a book against religious establishments. If he had found my sentiments congenial with his own, I have no doubt he would have disclosed his sentiments more fully.

N.B.—I have now completely brought up the arrears of this journal, which, during my last residence in Europe, and most especially from the time when I left St. Petersburg to attend at the negotiation of the Peace of Ghent, has occupied so large a portion of my time that I can henceforth no longer continue it with the same minuteness. On my return to my native country, a new and, for some time at least, a busy and laborious scene threatens to open before me—a scene so laborious and so full of perils and perplexities that a stouter heart than mine would be appalled at the prospect of it. From the time of my arrival in the United States my journal must be a mere abstract of loose memoranda. My whole time must be devoted to the performance of duties; and may the mercy of Heaven assist me duly to discharge them!

10th. VI. *Tuesday.* London, farewell! Dr. Bollman called upon me this morning, and requested me to look in at his lodgings before leaving town, and see his two inventions. I went accordingly, and saw his yellow color formed from the chromate of iron, the most beautiful and durable yellow that exists, and making also, when compounded with Prussian blue, a green color equally beautiful. It is now used for painting carriages, and gives them a more brilliant yellow color than was ever before known.   The chromate of iron is produced in the neighborhood of Baltimore, and also in Norway, but is there very dear.   Bollman has about three tons of it with him, and from five pounds of the ore produces, by mixing it with lead, two pounds of the yellow pigment.   He has a laboratory, in which he keeps only one man employed, and makes about sixteen pounds in a week.   It sells at twelve shillings a pound. His other discovery is a vinegar distilled from burnt wood, which he calls the pyroligneous acid.

At a quarter before one we left London in a post-chaise. For my own part, I bade adieu to London in all probability forever.   We came over Westminster Bridge, and our first stage was to Kingston; we proceeded thence to Cobham, Guildford, Farnham, where we dined, and Alton, where we arrived a quarter before nine in the evening, and stopped for the night.

11th. At eleven we proceeded upon our journey to Alresford, Winchester, where I stopped to visit the cathedral but had not time to visit the college, and to Southampton, where we arrived at half-past four in the afternoon.

15th. *Sunday.* Cowes, Isle of Wight.—At eleven o'clock in the morning I embarked with all my family on board the ship Washington, which was lying in the roads.   The anchor was immediately weighed, and we proceeded upon our voyage.

END OF VOL. III.